Latin American Economic Outlook 2017

YOUTH, SKILLS AND ENTREPRENEURSHIP

Please cite this publication as:
OECD/ECLAC/CAF (2016), *Latin American Economic Outlook 2017: Youth, Skills and Entrepreneurship*, OECD Publishing, Paris.
http://dx.doi.org/10.1787/leo-2017-en

ISBN 978-92-64-26254-6 (print)
ISBN 978-92-64-26500-4 (PDF)

ECLAC Reference Number: LC/G.2689
CAF Reference Number: CAF-513i-2017

Photo credits: © Cover design by the OECD Development Centre based on images © sattva78, katarinka, phipatbig, justone, Zilu8, Bokica, maverick_infanta, 007NATALIIA, ashva, Ellegant, phipatbig, Aha-Soft, TCmakephoto, PODIS, Yafeto, mariakraynova, BestGirl, PictureStudio, okart, JKI14/Shutterstock.com

Corrigenda to OECD publications may be found on line at: *www.oecd.org/about/publishing/corrigenda.htm.*

Foreword

The *Latin American Economic Outlook* analyses issues related to Latin America's economic and social development. Ever since the launch of the first edition in November 2007, the report has offered a comparison of Latin American performance with that of other countries and regions around the world sharing experiences and good practices.

Since 2011, the report has been published in conjunction with the United Nations Economic Commission for Latin America and the Caribbean (ECLAC) incorporating the economic theme of the annual Ibero-American Summit organised by the Ibero-American governments and the Ibero-American General Secretariat (SEGIB). In 2013, CAF – Development Bank of Latin America – joined the team of authors. This tenth edition was released at the XXV Ibero-American Summit of Heads of State and Government held in Cartagena, Colombia in October 2016.

This edition focuses on youth, skills and entrepreneurship for more inclusive and sustainable growth in the region. It provides in-depth analysis of Latin America's youth participation in society as well as in productive activities by examining the role of youth in the labour market, their acquired skills and entrepreneurial activities. It includes a macroeconomic analysis and explores how the global context influences the region's economy. The different chapters analyse the social, political and economic integration of young people in Latin America, as well as the education, skills and entrepreneurship opportunities and barriers they face. Finally, the report portrays how the future of jobs, politics and cities will present new challenges and opportunities to youth in the region and offers recommendations for improving public policies.

Acknowledgements

This report was jointly produced by the Economic Commission for Latin America and the Caribbean (ECLAC), CAF – Development Bank of Latin America, and the Development Centre of the Organisation for Economic Co-operation and Development (OECD).

For this edition, the contribution of the Development Centre to this report was led by Ángel Melguizo, Head of the Latin America and Caribbean Unit, with support from Juan Vazquez Zamora, and Paula Cerutti and Elena Crivellaro, under the guidance of Mario Pezzini, Director of the OECD Development Centre. ECLAC's contribution was led by Economic Affairs Officer, Sebastián Rovira, and Daniela Trucco, and that of CAF – Development Bank of Latin America by Adriana Arreaza, Director of Macroeconomic Studies. Production of this report was co-ordinated by Paula Cerutti, Elena Crivellaro and Juan Vazquez Zamora.

This report benefited from the research, drafting and fruitful collaboration between various authors across these organisations, including: Adriana Arreaza (CAF), Rolando Avendaño (OECD), Juan Carlos Benitez Molina (OECD), Paula Cerutti (OECD), Elena Crivellaro (OECD), Santiago Guerrero Archila (OECD), Rebecca Lavinson (OECD), Ricardo Martner (ECLAC), Ángel Melguizo (OECD), Sebastián Nieto-Parra (OECD), Alejandro Nuñez (OECD), José René Orozco (OECD), Daniel Titelman (ECLAC), Daniela Trucco (ECLAC), Heidi Ulhmann (ECLAC), and Juan Vazquez Zamora (OECD). Romina Boarini (OECD) and Katherine Scrivens (OECD) authored the well-being section. A special thanks go to experts for providing boxes on a range of interesting topics including Ian Brand-Weiner (OECD), Carolina Camacho (CAF), Marta Encinas-Martin (OECD), Alejandro Franco (Ruta N Medellín), Andrés Mariño (Universidad del Rosario), Claudio Alberto Moreno (iNNpulsa Colombia), Noel Müller (World Bank), Pauline Musset (OECD), Daniel Riera-Crichton (Bates College), Emilie Romon (OECD), María Ruiz (Ruta N Medellín), Manuel Toledo (CAF), Fernando Vargas (ILO-CINTERFOR), Carlos Vegh (Johns Hopkins University), Luisa Vergel (iNNpulsa Colombia), Elkin Velasquez (UN Habitat) and Guillermo Vuletin (Inter-American Development Bank). The team would also like to thank Francis Carmona (Global Entrepreneurship Monitor), Lucía Perez Villar (OECD), Annalisa Primi (OECD), Mike Herrignton (Global Entrepreneurship Monitor), Pascal Marianna (OECD) and Sebastian Martin (OECD) for sharing data and insights.

The OECD Development Centre is especially thankful to Oscar Calvo-Gonzalez, Gabriel Facchini, German Jeremias Reyes and Liliana Sousa from the World Bank Poverty Global Practice for their generosity in sharing their databases and insights, and their close collaboration in the preparation of this report.

The content of the report was enriched by constructive feedback received during the Experts' Meeting which took place in Paris on 30 May 2016. We are particularly grateful to the experts who joined us for this rich discussion; Roberto Angulo (Oxford Poverty & Human Development Initiative), Lucila Berniell (CAF), Matias Bianchi (Asuntos del Sur), Lucia Cusmano (OECD), Carl Dahlman (OECD), Marcelo Díaz (InverSur Capital), Ariel Fiszbein (Inter-American Dialogue), Robert Ford (OECD), Ulrich Frei (FUNDES), Ignacio Hernando (Bank of Spain), Martin Hopenhayn (Consejo Iberoamericano de Investigación en Juventud), Miriam Koreen (OECD), Ramón Moreno (BIS), Hugo Ñopo Aguilar (GRADE), Markus Pilgrim (ILO), Juan Rebolledo (Secretary of Economy and Public Credit, Mexico), Javier Roca (Ministry of Economy and Finance, Peru), Stefano Scarpetta (OECD), Andreas Schleicher (OECD), and Juan Yermo (OECD). Adriana Suarez (Endeavor), Guillermo Dema (ILO) and Susana García-Robles (IDB) also sent us very useful comments.

We are also thankful to all our colleagues within the OECD that provided comments including Aimee Aguilar, Nadim Ahmad, Aziza Akhmouch, Jose-Luis Alvarez-Galvan, Sonia Araujo, José Antonio Ardavin, Jens Arnold, Bert Brys, Thomas Dannequin, Christian Daude, Martine Durand, Balázs Egert, Marta Encinas, Montserrat Gomendio, David Halabisky, David Khoudour, Humberto Lopez, Adrien Lorenceau, Maria Rosa Lunati, Carlo Menon, Eduardo Olaberría, Mauro Pisu, Anne-Lise Prigent, Jonathan Potter, Julien Reynaud, Lynn Robertson, Oriana Romano, Ji-Yeun Rim, Angelica Salvi, Alain de Serres, Pablo Suárez Robles, Monika Sztajerowska and Anna Wiersma.

The country notes also benefited from constructive scrutiny and verification by delegations to the OECD from Chile and Mexico, as well as the Embassies in France of Argentina, Brazil, Colombia, Costa Rica, the Dominican Republic, Panama, Paraguay, Peru and Uruguay.

The launch of the report at the XXV Ibero-American Summit of Heads of State and Government at Cartagena de Indias (Colombia) on 28 October 2016 was co-ordinated and organised by Rita Da Costa and Agustina Vierheller. They also provided, with Ana Gonzalez, administrative support throughout the elaboration of the report. Particular thanks go to Adriana Mendoza, Director of Coordination and Integration Mechanisms at the Ministry of External Relations of Colombia and to her team for their support throughout the process.

The OECD Development Centre would also like to express its sincere gratitude to the Agencia Española de Cooperacion Internacional para el Desarrollo (AECID) of the Spanish Ministry of Foreign Affairs and Cooperation, the Agencia Presidencial de Cooperacion Internacional de Colombia (APC), the Swiss Development Agency, the LAC Regional Office of the International Labour Organization, CAF – Development Bank of Latin America, Universidad del Rosario (Colombia), and Santander Group for their financial backing of the *Latin American Economic Outlook*.

Finally, many thanks go to the Publications and Communications Division of the OECD Development Centre, in particular Aida Buendía, Delphine Grandrieux and Vanda Legrandgérard, for their steadfast patience and expedient work on the production of this report and associated materials. We also appreciate the support received from the OECD Public Affairs and Communication Directorate, including that of Anne-Lise Prigent and Laurence Gerrer-Thomas. The authors also sincerely appreciate the editing activities undertaken by Mark Foss and Jane Marshall, and the translation services provided by Yolanda Bravo Vergel, Lidia García de Vicuña and Gerardo Noriega.

Table of contents

Acronyms and abbreviations 13

Editorial 15

Executive summary 17

Chapter 1. **Overview: Improving youth inclusion through better skills and entrepreneurship opportunities** 19

References 38

Chapter 2. **Macroeconomic prospects for Latin America and the Caribbean** 41

Introduction 42
Sluggish global context in the short term 42
Macroeconomic trends in Latin America: Still looking for potential 49
Policy options to restore inclusive growth in Latin America 67
Conclusion 77
References 78
Annex 2.A1. Beyond growth: Measuring well-being in the LAC region 82
Annex notes 86
Annex references 86

Chapter 3. **Youth inclusion in Latin America and their main challenges** 87

Introduction 88
Why a focus on youth? 88
Youth labour market outcomes in Latin America 91
Youth social inclusion beyond jobs 111
Conclusions and policy recommendations 132
Annex 3.A1: Further results 136
Notes 139
References 141

Chapter 4. **Education, skills and youth in Latin America and the Caribbean** 145

Introduction 146
Latin American youth education at a glance 147
Latin American youth skills at a glance 159
Educational attainment and labour markets 166
Skills-enhancing interventions for low-educated youth in LAC 175
Conclusions and policy recommendations 188
Notes 191
References 192

Chapter 5. **Youth entrepreneurship in Latin America and the Caribbean** 199

Introduction 200
The face of young entrepreneurs in Latin America and OECD 200
Similar attitudes in Latin America and the OECD towards entrepreneurship 204
Better targeting needed for youth entrepreneurship policies 206
Public policies for enhancing youth entrepreneurship 208
Financing and targeting of youth entrepreneurship programmes in Latin America 214
An evaluation of youth entrepreneurship programmes in Latin America 220

Conclusions and policy recommendations 224
Notes 228
References 229
Annex 5.A1. Business ownership and job creation among young and adults in Latin America 232
Annex 5.A2. Global Entrepreneurship Monitor Database 233

Chapter 6. **The future of work, politics and cities** 237
Introduction 238
The *future of work*: Implications for skills, jobs and the nature of work 238
The *future of politics*: Reconnecting emerging social demands and the political system 242
The *future of cities*: The urban dimension of policies for youth 245
Concluding remarks 252
Notes 254
References 255

Country notes

Argentina 258
Brazil 262
Chile 267
Colombia 272
Costa Rica 276
Dominican Republic 281
Mexico 286
Panama 291
Paraguay 295
Peru 300
Uruguay 304
Methodological note 309

Figures

1.1. GDP per capita in selected Latin American economies, OECD and People's Republic of China 21
1.2. Youth population in Latin America and the Caribbean 23
1.3. Activity status of youth by gender in Latin America and the Caribbean, 2014 24
1.4. Activity status of youth by single year of age and socio-economic status in Latin America and the Caribbean, 2014 25
1.5. School to labour market transitions of youth in selected Latin American countries, 2005-15 26
1.6. Youth population by maximum educational level achieved in Latin America and the Caribbean, 2014 27
1.7. Firms reporting difficulties to hire in Latin America and the Caribbean, China and OECD countries 2014 28
1.8. Entrepreneurial motivation in Latin American and Caribbean countries and OECD, 2015 31
1.9. Barriers to entrepreneurship in Latin American countries and OECD 32
1.10. Youth and adults who express confidence in elections in Latin American countries and the Caribbean and OECD, 2014 35

2.1. Economic growth outlook by groups of economies 43
2.2. Contribution to global GDP growth, by areas 45
2.3. Capital flows to emerging markets and risk aversion 46
2.4. Volatility index and risk aversion to Latin America 2015-16 47
2.5. Financial volatility in selected Latin American economies, 2015-16 48
2.6. Commodity prices outlook 49
2.7. GDP growth in Latin American economies with different scenarios for China 50
2.8. An illustration of the cyclical position of selected Latin American and Caribbean economies 51
2.9. Exchange rates of selected Latin American currencies against the US dollar 52
2.10. Current account balances and foreign direct investment for selected Latin American economies 53
2.11. Overall fiscal and primary fiscal balances in Latin America 54
2.12. Gross public debt in Latin America 55
2.13. Fiscal balance and debt levels in Latin American countries 55
2.14. Inflation rates in selected Latin America and the Caribbean economies under different inflation regimes 56
2.15. Diffusion index for monetary policy in Latin America 57
2.16. Labour productivity in Latin American countries, Australia, China and South Korea 59
2.17. RBC GDP trend and GDP trend growth in selected Latin American economies (in logs) 61
2.18. Production-based function GDP trend in selected Latin American economies 62
2.19. GDP per capita in selected Latin American economies, Asia and OECD countries 64
2.20. GDP growth and poverty rates in Latin America and the Caribbean 65
2.21. Latin American population by socio-economic groups 66
2.22. Change in public primary expenditure in Latin American and Caribbean economies 68
2.23. Public expenditure multiplier for Latin America 69
2.24. Public expenditure multiplier for Latin America, and the business cycle 70
2.25. Tax multipliers in Latin America 71
2.26. Fiscal multipliers for government consumption expenditure and investment expenditures in Latin America 71
2.27. Tax and debt in selected Latin American countries, 2014 74
2.28. Public debt at 2025, by different primary-balance scenarios 76
2.A1.1. The OECD well-being measurement framework for developing countries 82
2.A1.2. Comparison of actual and expected well-being outcomes for the LAC region, given its level of economic development 84
3.1. Latin America and the Caribbean: Population by age groups over time (in millions) 89
3.2. Latin America and the Caribbean: Duration of the demographic dividend (in years) 90
3.3. Youth and socio-economic status in Latin America 91
3.4. Labour market situation of youth (aged 15-29) 93
3.5. Unemployment rates among youth and adult population in LAC and the OECD 94
3.6. Activity rates of youth aged 15-29 in LAC and OECD 96
3.7. NEET rates for men and women in LAC, 2014 98
3.8. Activity status by single year of age, LAC average, 2014 102
3.9. Youth (aged 15-29) school-to-labour market transitions, 2005-15 102
3.10. Flows into and out of NEET status in selected Latin America countries – Youth (aged 15-29), 2005-15 103
3.11. Job quality and quantity outcomes by socio-demographic groups in Latin America 105
3.12. Informality rates in Latin America by age and socio-economic characteristics 106

3.13. Flows into and out of informality – Youth (aged 15-29), 2005-15 ... 108
3.14. Latin America average monthly labour income of the employed population, around 2013 ... 109
3.15. Informality and formalisation costs in Latin America ... 110
3.16. Latin America and the Caribbean: Specific mortality rates, by age and sex, 2010 ... 112
3.17. Cause-specific mortality, by age group and sex, in Latin America and the Caribbean, 2010 ... 112
3.18. Latin America (seven countries): Women aged 15 to 19 who are mothers, according to socio-economic quintile and area of residence ... 114
3.19. Latin America and the Caribbean (15 countries): Students who smoked cigarettes at least once in the past 30 days ... 115
3.20. Latin America and the Caribbean (18 countries): Students who consumed at least one alcoholic drink in the past 30 days ... 115
3.21. Students in Latin America and the Caribbean who have used drugs at least once ... 116
3.22. Latin America (17 countries): Young people and adults who report voting in the latest presidential elections, 2000-13 ... 118
3.23. Latin America (17 countries): Young persons and adults who report having participated in demonstrations at least once during the past year, 2000-13 ... 118
3.24. Latin America (17 countries): Young persons and adults who report having voted in the most recent elections and having taken part in a demonstration at least once in the past year, 2000-13 ... 119
3.25. Latin America (17 countries): Support for democracy as the best form of government by persons between 16-29 years of age and by persons aged 30 and over, 2013 ... 120
3.26. Latin America (18 countries): Persons aged 16-29 and persons aged 30 and over who believe that powerful groups, rather than the people, are running the government of their country, 2013 ... 121
3.27. Mistrust of young people (aged 18-29) in national institutions in El Salvador, Peru and Latin America ... 122
3.28. Population declaring satisfaction with their lives in Latin America, 2013 ... 124
3.29. Belief that the personal and household economic situation will be better or slightly better in the coming 12 months in Latin America, by country and age group, 2013 ... 124
3.30. Latin America (simple average of 17 countries): Assessment of the economic situation of the country, 2000-13 ... 125
3.31. Population claiming to have been the victim of crime in the last 12 months in Latin America and the Caribbean, by age group, 2012 ... 126
3.32. El Salvador, Guatemala and Honduras: Rate of mortality from interpersonal violence, by age group, 1990-2010 ... 128
3.A1.1. Youth and socio-economic status in Latin America, 2014 ... 136
3.A1.2. Labour market situation of youth in Latin America, 2004 and 2014 ... 138
4.1. Youth population by maximum educational level achieved, Latin America and the Caribbean, 2014 ... 147
4.2. Population by maximum educational level achieved, Latin America and the Caribbean, 2004-14 ... 148
4.3. Youth by highest level of education achieved, LAC, 2004, 2009, 2014 ... 149
4.4. Change in the average years of education for 17 LAC countries, 2004-14 ... 150
4.5. Change in the average years of education by socio-economic group and age group, LAC, 2004-14 ... 150
4.6. Gross enrolment ratio, tertiary education, 16 LAC countries, circa 2013 ... 151

4.7. Youth with complete tertiary education by year, LAC 152
4.8. Students in secondary education enrolled in vocational programmes, LAC, circa 2013 154
4.9. Students at each level of proficiency in reading, mathematics and science, LAC, 2012 159
4.10. Young student performance in mathematics and equity 160
4.11. Annualised change in performance throughout participation in PISA 161
4.12. Mean numeracy proficiency in PISA (2000 and 2003) and in the Survey of Adult Skills, 2012 162
4.13. Conditional correlations between labour earnings and measures of skills in Bolivia, Colombia and Peru 167
4.14. Size effects of conditional correlations between measures of skills and labour outcomes in Colombia 168
4.15. Relative earnings of workers by educational attainment, LAC, 2013 169
4.16. Tertiary education wage premium and relative supply over time, LAC 170
4.17. Firms identifying difficulty filling jobs, 2015 172
4.18. Average time to fill job vacancy, regions of the world, circa 2012 (weeks) 173
4.19. Average time to fill job vacancy, selected LAC countries, circa 2012 173
4.20. Public spending on training programmes, LAC 176
5.1. Distribution of employed population by occupational category in Latin America and the OECD (aged 15-29 years) 202
5.2. Distribution of entrepreneurs by educational and socio-economic background 203
5.3. Percentage of the population who agree with the statement that, in their country, successful entrepreneurs receive high status 205
5.4. Entrepreneurial motivation in Latin American and Caribbean countries and OECD, 2015 205
5.5. Relative productivity and firm size of small and medium-sized enterprises 206
5.6. Net employment growth rates by surviving young and old firms, 2001-11 207
5.7. Percentage of entrepreneurs with at least 25% of revenues from international customers 210
5.8. Barriers to entrepreneurship index 213
5.9. Estimated spending of entrepreneurship programmes in Latin America (percentage of GDP, 2010-14) 214
5.10. Taxonomy of instruments for start-ups support, 2016 216
5.11. INNpulsa financing instruments and external leveraged capital (2011-15) 218
5.A1.1. Share of population who currently own a business by age group 232
5.A1.2. Job creation among young and adult entrepreneurs in Latin America and the OECD 232
6.1. Projections of job creation and destruction by sectors by 2030 in Latin America 239
6.2. Perceptions of youth towards democracy and government in LAC 243
6.3. Urbanisation in Latin America and other regions of the world 246
6.4. Distribution of population in cities by 2030 by size 247
6.5. Cities in Motion Index 2015 252

Tables

1.1. Components and outcomes in youth training programmes in Latin America and the Caribbean 30
1.2. Components and outcomes of youth entrepreneurship programmes in Latin America and the Caribbean 33
2.1. 4G Road infrastructure programme 73
2.2. Initial variables used for public debt scenarios 76

3.1. Relative probabilities of not being in education or employed, LAC 2014 ... 97
3.2. Youth (aged 15-29) neither in education nor employment by type of activity in Latin America ... 99
3.3. Contributions of NEET youth to the Argentinean economy ... 100
3.4. Latin America and the Caribbean (33 countries): Main diseases and disorders contributing to the disease burden, by sex and age, 2010 ... 113
3.5. Residents' perception of the incidence of gangs or maras in their local area in Latin America and the Caribbean, by country and age group, 2012 ... 129
3.A1.1. Type of jobs held by youth, LAC average 2014 ... 138
4.1. Young people with less than secondary education and out of school (aged 15-29), LAC, 2014 ... 148
4.2. Students enrolled in tertiary education by type of programme in LAC, circa 2013 ... 153
4.3. Share of apprenticeships' participants among total participants in VTI programmes, LAC, 2015 ... 156
4.4. Returns to STEM education in Uruguay and Peru, 2014 ... 171
4.5. "Jovenes" type of youth training programmes, LAC ... 177
4.6. Characteristics of selected youth training programmes in LAC ... 178
4.7. Evidence available on the impact of youth training programmes, LAC ... 180
4.8. Evidence available on the impact of youth training programmes, LAC, selected programmes ... 182
4.9. Components and outcomes in youth training programmes in Latin America and the Caribbean ... 184
5.1. Areas of intervention (components) in entrepreneurship programmes ... 222
5.2. Components and final outcomes in youth entrepreneurship programmes ... 224
5.A2.1. Youth entrepreneurship programmes and evaluations ... 233
5.A2.2. Youth entrepreneurship programmes and outcomes ... 234
5.A2.3. Unevaluated youth entrepreneurship programmes ... 235

Acronyms and abbreviations

4G	Fourth generation
ALMPs	Active Labour Market Policies
ASELA	Latin American Association of Entrepreneurs
BoJ	Bank of Japan
BDE	Bank of Spain
BIS	Bank for International Settlements
Brexit	British exit
CAF	Banco de Desarrollo de América Latina
CCT	Conditional cash transfer
CEDLAS	Centre for Distributive, Labour and Social Studies
CIAT	Inter-American Centre of Tax Administrations
CPI	City Prosperity Initiative
ECB	European Central Bank
ECLAC	Economic Commission for Latin America and the Caribbean
EMBI	Emerging Markets Bond Index
EU	European Union
FDI	Foreign direct investment
FED	Federal Reserve System
GDP	Gross domestic product
GEM	Global Entrepreneurship Monitor
GHG	Greenhouse gas
GNI	Gross national income
ICTs	Information and Communications Technologies
IDB	Inter-American Development Bank
IEA	International Energy Agency
IIF	Institute of International Finance
ILO	International Labour Organization
IMF	International Monetary Fund
IoT	Internet of Things
ITF	International Transport Forum
KBC	Knowledge-based capital
KILM	Key Indicators of the Labour Market
LABLAC	Labour Database for Latin America and the Caribbean
LAC	Latin America and the Caribbean
LAPOP	Latin American Public Opinion Project
MIT	Middle income trap
NEET	Not in education, employment or training
OIJ	Iberoamerican Organization for Youth
OECD	Organisation for Economic Co-operation and Development
OPEC	Organization of Petroleum Exporting Countries

PIAAC	Programme for the International Assessment of Adult Competencies
PISA	Programme for International Student Assessment
PMR	Indicators of Product Market Regulation
PPP	Purchasing power parity
PPP	Public-private partnership
SDGs	Sustainable Development Goals
SEDLAC	Socio-Economic Database for Latin America and the Caribbean
SMEs	Small medium enterprises
STEM	Science, technology, engineering and mathematics
STEP	Skills Towards Employability and Productivity Programme
TEA	Total Entrepreneurial Activity
TFP	Total Factor Productivity
TVET	Technical and vocational education and training
UIS	UNESCO Institute for Statistics
UNDP	United Nations Development Programme
UNESCO	United Nations Educational, Scientific and Organization
UNICEF	United Nations International Children's Emergency Fund
UNODC	United Nations Office on Drugs and Crime
WB	World Bank
WEF	World Economic Forum
WHO	World Health Organization
USD	United States Dollar
VAT	Value added tax
VTI	Vocational Training Institutions

Editorial

GDP growth in Latin America will be negative for the second consecutive year in 2016 (between -0.5% and -1.0%), a contraction the region has not seen since the early 1980s. This evolution is testing Latin America's socio-economic progress – notably the reduction of poverty and inequality and the expansion of the middle class. Around 7 million Latin Americans became poor in 2015, increasing the region's total poverty rate to 29.2% or 175 million people. Moreover, between 25 and 30 million vulnerable middle-class Latin Americans, one of out of three whom exited poverty during the recent period of economic growth, face the risk of falling back into poverty in the near future.

Economic projections continue to depict uneven short-term growth throughout the region. The picture is more favourable for Mexico, Central America and the Caribbean, given their stronger links with the U.S., than for net commodity exporters in South America, particularly affected by global economic conditions and relatively low international commodity prices. In general, the challenge will be larger for countries with weaker policy frameworks.

Starting in 2017, the region should resume economic growth and per capita income convergence with OECD countries. But this catch-up will take place at too modest growth rates (in the range of 2% to 3% annually), confirming weak long-term growth in Latin America, with significant differences across countries. This highlights the importance of expanding the growth potential in the region.

Still, Latin America has plenty of untapped potential. The region is young, facing a unique demographic opportunity. One quarter of the Latin American population – 163 million citizens –- are aged between 15 and 29. This demographic bonus opens a window of opportunity for inclusive growth in the region, and represents a potential driver of domestic growth to support future progress. This is the case if such a strong domestic supply of youth eager to work can match labour market demands and is accompanied by productive development policies towards more diversified and upgraded productive structures, and more integration. All this should be accompanied by better quality education for all.

Indeed, the social and economic progress of the last decades, notably with an increase in access to education, raised expectations, especially among the youth. However, 64% of young Latin Americans – more than 100 million – still live in poor or vulnerable households. That means that most youth have access only to poor quality public services, low and informal savings, and little social mobility. One fifth of the 163 million youth living in Latin America work in informal jobs, and an equal share is not engaged in employment, education or training, a situation that is even worse for young women. This sharp disconnection between society's expectations and demands on the one hand and actual outcomes on the other hand has fueled social dissatisfaction and weakened trust in democratic institutions. Only 36% of Latin American youth expressed having confidence in the transparency of election results, much lower than the OECD average (62%). For the first generation born and raised in democracy, the gap between expectations, with new and emerging demands, and actual socio-economic outcomes widened the distance between societies and their governments, explaining recent protests and social movements in the region.

This year's *Latin American Economic Outlook* focuses on Latin American youth by analysing their social, economic and political behaviour, challenges and opportunities. Fostering youth inclusion requires recognising what excludes them in the first place. Limited access to decent employment, education, health services and civic participation are all factors that prevent young people from playing a full role in their societies. Overall, better jobs and skills for youth in Latin America, notably for the poor and vulnerable middle-class, are necessary. Two pathways can help steer youth on this course to meaningful economic activity.

First, skills have become the global currency of 21st century economies, and even more so in Latin America, the region with the widest gap in the world between the pool of available skills and those skills that economies and businesses require, as highlighted in the 2015 and 2016 editions of this outlook. Progress requires strengthening the education system and promoting lifelong learning. Educational curricula and skills-enhancing programmes should provide Latin American youth with more technical and foundational training, which is critical for their mobility and ability to adapt to changing external conditions.Combining classroom with workplace learning of both technical and soft skills (such as creativity, working in teams, commitment, leadership, or communication), and coupling that with job search services, can improve the quality of youth job prospects.

Second, youth entrepreneurship is another key vehicle for improving employability and social mobility in Latin America. Just like young entrepreneurs in OECD countries, those in Latin America exhibit the same creative thinking, management skills, goal-oriented objectives and risk-taking. Multi-dimensional policy support is required, such as complementing micro-credits with lower regulatory barriers, tailoring financing instruments, linking young entrepreneurs with commercial networks and expanding business training.

Backed by such evidence, Latin American skills and entrepreneurship policies for the youth also need the flexibility to embrace future change. Technological and demographic changes, alongside globalisation, are driving major economic, political and social transformations that impact the world of work, the cities youth will live in and the way young Latin Americans participate in politics. Policy makers need to systematically collect information and evaluate youth programmes to identify better ways to improve youth skills and entrepreneurship opportunities as well as to anticipate future demands in a constantly changing environment. At the same time, these investments should be programmed within a credible and sustainable fiscal framework.

We hope this joint effort by CAF – Development Bank of Latin America, the Economic Commission for Latin America and the Caribbean (ECLAC), and the Development Centre of the Organisation for Economic Co-operation and Development (OECD) will contribute to policy discussions on skills and entrepreneurship for youth in Latin America to optimise the region's opportunities. Finding ways to boost the economic, social and political inclusion of youth will be key to passing the economic, social and political tests ahead.

Alicia Bárcena Executive Secretary ECLAC	L. Enrique García Executive Chairman CAF – Development Bank of Latin America	Angel Gurría Secretary-General OECD

Executive summary

The *Latin American Economic Outlook 2017* analyses the attitudes, challenges and opportunities of Latin America's youth. Youth in Latin America and the Caribbean (LAC) aged 15 to 29 number more than 163 million – around a quarter of the region's total population. The region's once promising economy is now slowing down, challenging the social, political and economic progress of the last decade. As such, young people stand at a crossroads, embodying the region's promise and perils.

Social and economic progress of the last decades raised expectations, which have not been fulfilled. In recent decades, public policies became more inclusive and long-time neglected sectors began participating in society. The middle class reached 35% of Latin America's population, growing by 14 percentage points in the last decade. Yet inclusion of youth in the region remains unfinished. As many as 64% of young Latin Americans live in poor or vulnerable households and have been unable to enter the consolidated middle class. Ideally, access to quality education and health services, as well as civic engagement, all set the stage for youth to take part in labour markets and productive activities. In practice, however, many young people in Latin America are cut off from these opportunities. The sharp disconnection between expectations and demands and actual outcomes is fuelling social dissatisfaction and weakening trust in democratic institutions. As a result, only one out of three young people express confidence in elections.

Most youth leave school for inactivity or informal jobs. One-fifth of the 163 million youth living in Latin America work in informal jobs, and another fifth are neither working nor engaged in education or training (NEET). This situation is prevalent among the most disadvantaged. Youth from poor and vulnerable households leave school earlier than their peers in better-off households, and when employed they mainly work in informal jobs. At age 15, almost 70% of youth living in poor households are in school, but at age 29, almost three out of ten young people are NEETs, another four work in the informal sector, only two work in the formal sector and the remainder are either working students or students.

The recent expansion of education coverage has to be coupled with stronger links with the labour market. Despite remarkable progress in education during the last decade, less than one-third of young Latin Americans aged 25 to 29 have received some education at college, university or a higher level technical school. Many young Latin Americans leave school too early: as a result, a third – 43 million – have not completed secondary education and are not enrolled in school. Moreover, technical and vocational education rarely train youth in pertinent, high-level trade, technical, professional and management skills. In fact, the LAC region exhibits the widest gap in the world between the available pool of skills and those demanded by firms. This creates a challenge for the region in transitioning into a knowledge-based economy, where citizens need to innovate, adapt and leverage advanced human capital.

Investing in youth's skills is key to igniting endogenous engines of growth and building a solid basis for future progress. Improving the skills of Latin American youth involves strengthening the education system and promoting lifelong and comprehensive skills policies. Education curricula and skills-enhancing programmes should provide youth with technical training for productive inclusion, as well as foundational skills. These are critical throughout people's lives, making them better able to switch jobs and adapt to changing external conditions. Evaluations of skills-enhancing programmes for youth in LAC show that combining classroom with workplace learning of both soft and technical skills and job search services improves the prospects of youth for quality jobs.

Moreover, countries need an efficient way to collect information on the skills individuals possess and those skills businesses need. This would help identify skills shortages and gaps allowing countries to plan for future skills needs. In this way, countries could become more productive and competitive. Creating a healthy supply of youth ready to work and create competitive businesses must be matched by more demand for their skills and entrepreneurial activities.

Entrepreneurship ecosystems for high-growth entrepreneurs are developing quickly, but offer employability and social mobility only to a few. LAC has few high-growth youth entrepreneurs and many subsistence entrepreneurs. The prevalence of own-account workers among youth (16%) is almost three times the prevalence in OECD countries (6%). Only 13% of young entrepreneurs in the region possess tertiary education, compared to 33% in OECD countries. Support for start-ups in Latin America is moving from experimentation to consolidation of their institutional support. Private sector participation has increased, not only from the perspective of financing and investment, but also through new actors supporting the seeding of innovative entrepreneurship activities. Nevertheless, young entrepreneurs face challenges in accessing financing instruments, improving capacity building, developing business networks and an entrepreneurial culture, accessing new markets and overcoming regulatory barriers, even more so than their adult counterparts.

Fostering entrepreneurship can improve and facilitate youth transition from school to work and adult life. An inclusive entrepreneurship approach with different instruments will increase productivity and equity. Broader, multi-dimensional support, beyond micro-credit, is required for subsistence entrepreneurs to address vulnerabilities outside the labour market. This includes tailored financing instruments adapted to the needs of young entrepreneurs, with more flexible requirements on credit history, collateral and risk. Public financial institutions can play a role in making financing instruments for the young more flexible, both through credit and new instruments. Angel investment and risk capital are still embryonic, and public policy can provide investors with more incentives to participate in the later stages of firm development.

Strengthening Latin American youth skills and improving their entrepreneurial opportunities should be done embracing the future. Technological and demographic changes, alongside globalisation, are driving major economic, political and social transformations that affect the world of work, the cities in which youth will live and the way young Latin Americans participate in politics. New jobs will emerge leading to a shift in skills demanded. Automation will replace semi-skilled jobs, while complex tasks will require genuine human skills; hence, skills and training policies should anticipate and adapt to new demands. Young people have the potential and technological possibilities to be key drivers of smarter, more sustainable cities in the region. And they are also using new technological instruments to voice and organise their demands and shape emerging political developments.

Empowering youth is a smart investment towards inclusive growth in these challenging economic and political times. Skills and entrepreneurship can empower youth to develop knowledge-intensive economic activities to transition successfully from schools to jobs. This will create the future they seek and promote gains in productivity for the region. The unfolding youth demographic opportunity and 18 presidential elections in LAC over the next two years set the stage to fuel changes and place youth inclusion, skills and entrepreneurship at the top of the policy agenda.

Chapter 1

Overview: Improving youth inclusion through better skills and entrepreneurship opportunities

This chapter sets the scene for the entire publication by offering an overview of the recent economic trends as well as of the main opportunities and challenges faced by youth in Latin America. It also explores how better skills and entrepreneurship opportunities can provide better prospects for youth inclusion today and for the future. Finally, the chapter summarises a set of policy goals and recommendations emerging from the analysis conducted in the following chapters.

The statistical data for Israel are supplied by and under the responsibility of the relevant Israeli authorities. The use of such data by the OECD is without prejudice to the status of the Golan Heights, East Jerusalem and Israeli settlements in the West Bank under the terms of international law.

The *Latin American Economic Outlook* 2017 (LEO 2017) shines a spotlight on youth by analysing their behaviour, challenges and opportunities. Youth in Latin America and the Caribbean (LAC) aged 15 to 29 number more than 163 million – around a quarter of the region's total population. LAC's once promising economy is now slowing down, challenging the social, political and economic progress of the last decade. As such, young people stand at the crossroads, embodying the region's promise and perils.

This overview sets the scene for the entire publication by summarising key findings:

- Macroeconomic conditions are testing Latin America's recent socio-economic progress. Investing in youth is one way to overcome these conditions and fuel endogenous engines of growth to chart a future of greater social and economic inclusion.
- Latin America's youth lack good employment prospects today. Changing this reality requires investing in skills and entrepreneurship to improve and facilitate youth transition from school to work and adult life.
- Investing in skills and entrepreneurship also means embracing trends in these areas and mobilising youth to steer – and not be derailed by – social, political and economic changes.

Based on these findings, the report makes a series of recommendations for skills and entrepreneurship policies to empower youth as economic actors:

- strengthen the education system and promote lifelong skills-enhancing programmes;
- combine classroom teaching with practical on-the-job training to better prepare youth for the world of work;
- develop skills programmes that are more responsive to the needs of the marketplace;
- collect information on the skills of the population and those demanded by businesses to build better national skills-enhancing strategies;
- connect young entrepreneurs with business networks through mentoring and supply-chain development programmes;
- support entrepreneurial training among youth to develop management and financial skills;
- introduce staged financing instruments adapted to the needs of young entrepreneurs, including early-stage grants, seed capital, asset-based finance, angel investors and venture capital networks;
- reduce regulatory barriers for young entrepreneurs, simplifying legislation for firm creation and licence permits, and consider incentives (e.g. temporary exemptions of taxes and social security contributions) to support young entrepreneurs;
- apply systematic evaluations of youth training and entrepreneurship programmes to identify what works and what needs to be redesigned;
- support access to broadband services, improving infrastructure and affordability to help youth make the most of opportunities brought about by the digital economy.

Creating a healthy supply of youth ready to work and create competitive businesses must be matched by generating demand for their skills and entrepreneurial activities. Latin American economies have to diversify and upgrade their productive structure to take full advantage of skilled and entrepreneurial youth, and respond to their aspirations. Economies in the region depend too much on natural resources and on activities with relatively low value-added. The region has to explore innovative productive development policies to better participate in global value chains and boost economic diversification to become more competitive (OECD/CAF/ECLAC, 2015). This will create more quality jobs to address the opportunities posed by the demographic change, and employ skilled and entrepreneurial youth.

Better-skilled youth with improved entrepreneurial opportunities will propel inclusive economic growth. In times of economic hardship, the region should look for internal sources of sustainable progress. Skills and entrepreneurship can empower youth to develop knowledge-intensive economic activities to transition successfully from schools to jobs, creating the future they seek and promoting gains in productivity for the region. Investing in the most disadvantaged will help close the skills and entrepreneurship opportunity gap, offering better job market conditions and ultimately reducing income inequality (OECD, 2016a). The region now faces a unique moment. The unfolding youth demographic opportunity and 18 presidential elections coming up in the next two years set the stage to fuel changes and place youth inclusion, skills and entrepreneurship at the top of the policy agenda.

Challenging macroeconomic conditions and stagnant productivity growth in Latin America will test socio-economic progress and the ability to fulfil people's expectations...

The tailwinds that propelled economic growth in LAC in the past decade are gone. The region is undergoing a prolonged economic slowdown, with contrasts among countries. After five years of economic slowdown, the growth rate was negative in 2015. Gross domestic product (GDP) in the region is expected to fall between -0.5 and -1.0 percentage points in 2016, before slightly recovering in 2017. Weak global growth prospects, low commodity prices and tight financing conditions have undermined potential for the region's growth (OECD, 2016b). Short-term economic projections depict a more challenging picture for net commodity exporters in South America, particularly for those with weaker policy frameworks, than for Mexico, Central America and the Caribbean. However, mounting evidence points to the deterioration of productivity and potential output growth in most LAC countries (Pagés, 2010; OECD/CAF/ECLAC, 2015; Cavallo and Serebrisky, 2016; IMF, 2016; Powell, 2016).

Potential growth is weaker than previously expected, confirming the region's challenge to overcome the middle-income trap. The middle-income trap refers to the long-lasting slowdown in growth that many countries experience when they approach middle levels of per capita income. This is tied to the inability of countries to restructure towards innovation and more knowledge-intensive production. So far, only Chile and Uruguay have managed to escape the middle-income trap in Latin America (Figure 1.1). The trap is especially prevalent in the rest of Latin American economies due to shortcomings related to the rule of law, rent-seeking behaviours and productive structures less concentrated in knowledge-intensive activities (OECD/CAF/ECLAC, 2015).

Figure 1.1. **GDP per capita in selected Latin American economies, OECD and People's Republic of China**

(USD PPP 1990)

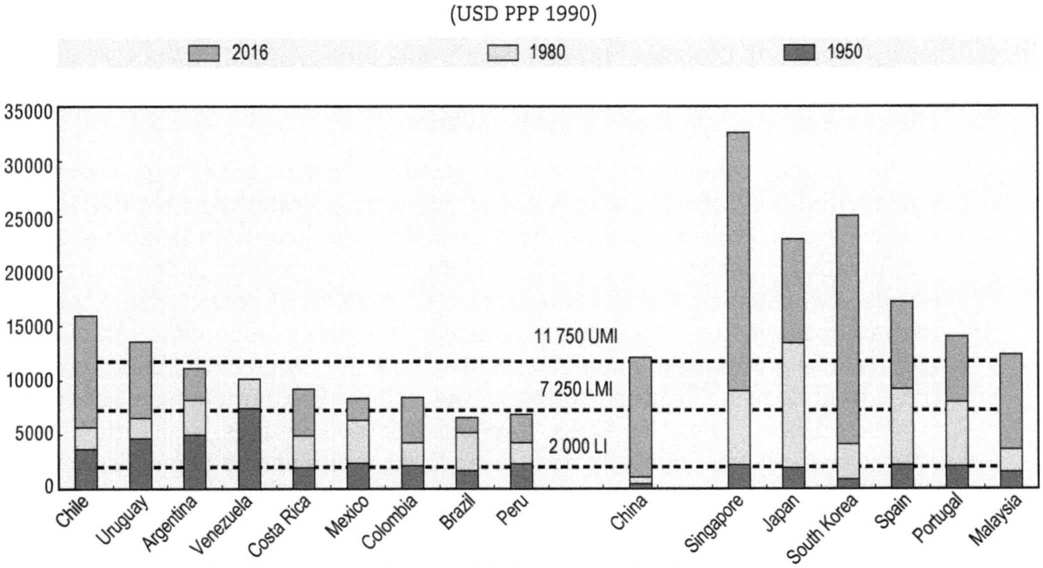

Note: UMI = upper-middle income; LMI = lower-middle income; LI = low income.

Source: OECD/CAF/ECLAC calculations.

StatLink http://dx.doi.org/10.1787/888933413924

The current slowdown is reducing available resources to finance crucial long-term investments, particularly in physical and human capital. Lower economic growth and a setback in commodity-related revenues have deteriorated fiscal balances and increased debt levels in LAC economies. Fiscal authorities must tread carefully to avoid large spending cuts, particularly on infrastructures and skills. Nonetheless, the scope for fiscal action varies across countries. Some economies in the region have accumulated public savings and moderate debt levels that allow some room to manoeuvre, although in some cases they remain bound by structural fiscal rules (Alberola et al., 2016). Other countries are already undergoing some form of fiscal consolidation, including spending cuts and tax reforms. Finally, given their low fiscal pressure and moderate debt levels, some economies have space to strengthen taxation. Overall, all countries need more efficient and focused allocation of available resources based on improving state capacity to deliver goods and services.

The weaker macroeconomic context in Latin America is testing socio-economic progress, notably the reduction of poverty and inequality, and the emergence of the middle class. Over the last decade, LAC has achieved important progress, boosting income growth and reducing poverty from 42.8% to 23.3% between 2000-14 (CEDLAS and World Bank, 2016). Most of the decline in poverty can be attributed to higher labour income, due to both higher employment rates and higher earnings per worker, as well as the spread of cash transfers (World Bank, 2013). Still, around 7 million Latin Americans became poor in 2015, increasing the total regional poverty rate to 29.2% and totalling more than 175 million Latin Americans (ECLAC, 2016). Likewise, income inequality has declined at a slower pace since the 2010s in Latin American economies with the exception of Colombia, Ecuador and Uruguay (Gasparini, Cruces and Tornarrolli, 2016). In the current economic environment, 25-30 million vulnerable Latin Americans might fall back into poverty (UNDP, 2016).

...but investing in youth could ignite endogenous engines of growth and build a solid basis for future progress

Latin America and the Caribbean is still a young region, facing a unique demographic opportunity to prepare for the future by investing in youth. One-quarter of the Latin American population is aged between 15 and 29. The large share of the young population relative to other age groups opens a window of opportunity for the region. This demographic dividend, in full force today in most countries of the region, will not last long (Figure 1.2). Demographic conditions will shift gradually towards a less favourable structure as in OECD member countries; in around three decades, more pressure will fall on the productive share of the population.

Social and economic progress of the last few decades raised expectations, especially among youth, by lifting millions out of poverty and reducing inequality; still, more is needed. Public policies became more inclusive and long-time neglected sectors began participating in society. The consolidated middle class grew by 14 percentage points in the last decade, reaching 35% of Latin Americans. Yet 64% of young Latin Americans – more than 100 million – live in poor or vulnerable households (compared to 57% of adults in 2014) and have been unable to enter the middle class. Simultaneously, most youth, especially those from households in the bottom of the income distribution, have access only to poor quality services, precarious jobs, low and informal savings, and little social mobility. This sharp disconnection between society's expectations and demands on the one hand, and actual socio-economic outcomes on the other has fueled social dissatisfaction and weakened trust levels in democratic institutions. For the first generation born and raised in democracy, this gap widened the distance between societies and their governments, and increased protests and social dissatisfaction in the region.

Figure 1.2. **Youth population in Latin America and the Caribbean**

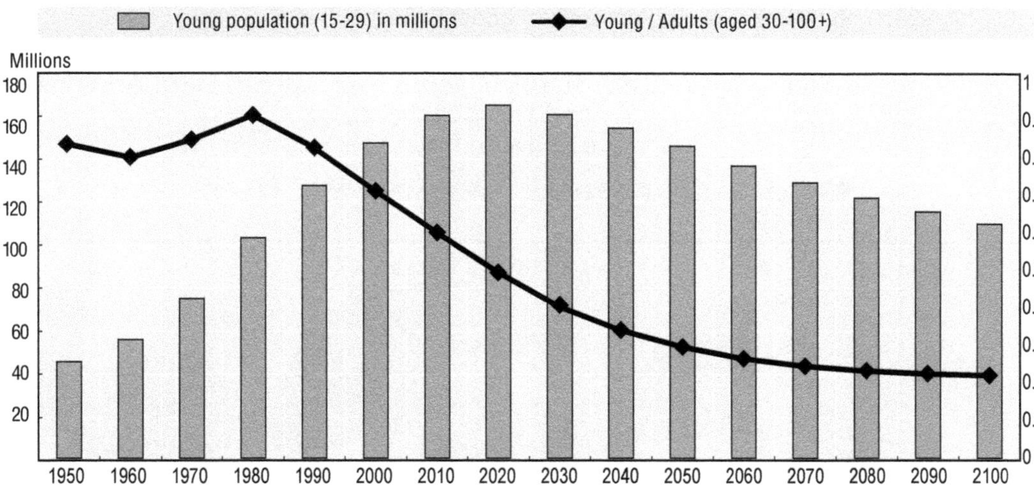

Source: OECD/CAF/ECLAC, based on United Nations, Population Division, (2015), *World Population Prospects*, 2015 Revision.

StatLink http://dx.doi.org/10.1787/888933413653

Economic, political and social inclusion of young people in the region, therefore, remains unfinished, preventing youth from playing a full role in their societies and advancing up the social ladder. Young people are exposed to a remarkable number of vulnerabilities and threats — from poor access to quality education and health services to low civic participation — all of which set the stage for their ability to participate in labour markets and productive activities. Fostering youth inclusion requires recognising the multiple dimensions of exclusion. Limited access to decent employment, education, health services and civic participation all prevent young people from playing a full role in their societies. This is particularly dangerous in countries with high demographic growth and inequality, such as in Latin America, where new generations put pressure on economic and social development (OECD, forthcoming). Good health and living in a safe environment are pre-conditions for studying, working, participating in political life and, ultimately, being included in society. Despite being a demographic group with good health outcomes, youth in LAC face health risks associated with exogenous factors such as mental health, substance abuse and early pregnancy that might affect their transition to adulthood. Likewise, certain youth segments are often stigmatised for supposedly violent tendencies and participation in urban violence, two factors that are both causes and consequences of social isolation and economic exclusion.

Latin American youth lack good employment prospects today

Lack of good employment opportunities is one of the most significant factors hindering the inclusion of youth in society. The jobs that youth in Latin America hold are typically less productive, more insecure and less rewarding than the ones for youth in OECD countries. Latin American youth also hold fewer and worse jobs than adults in the region. One-fifth of the 163 million youth living in Latin America work in informal jobs. An equal share is not engaged in employment, education or training (NEET), compared to

15% among OECD countries. On the other hand, 23% are formal workers and almost 40% are students. Additionally, unemployment rates are almost three times higher for youth (11.2%) than for adults (3.7%) in all countries in Latin America and the Caribbean; this situation is prevalent among the most disadvantaged youth. These poor employment opportunities, which are even worse for young women, result in lower well-being and a pattern of self-reinforcing aspiration gaps (Figure 1.3).

Figure 1.3. **Activity status of youth by gender in Latin America and the Caribbean, 2014**

(percentage of youth aged 15-29)

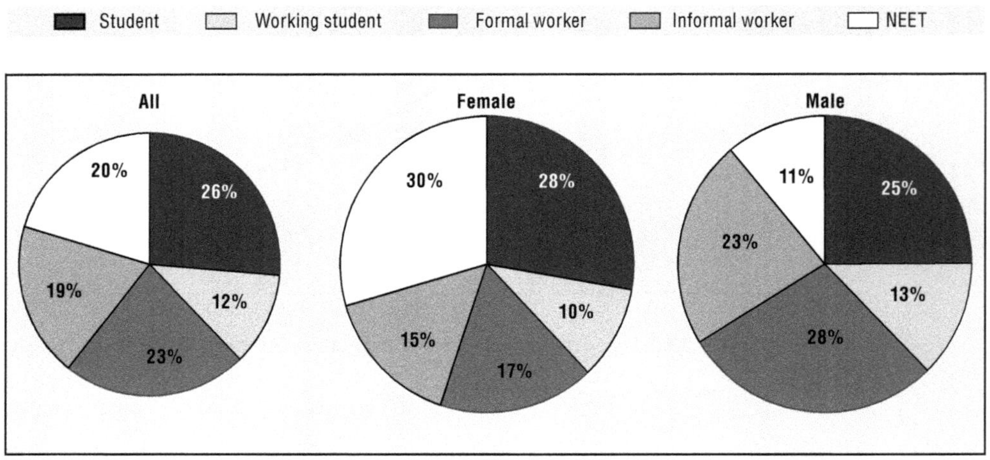

Note: LAC weighted average of 17 countries: Argentina, Plurinational State of Bolivia (hereafter Bolivia), Brazil, Chile, Colombia, Costa Rica, Dominican Republic, Ecuador, El Salvador, Guatemala, Honduras, Mexico, Nicaragua, Panama, Paraguay, Peru and Uruguay.

Source: OECD and World Bank tabulations of SEDLAC (CEDLAS and the World Bank).

StatLink http://dx.doi.org/10.1787/888933413665

The challenges that young Latin Americans face in their path to work are severe, particularly among those from disadvantaged socio-economic backgrounds. The transition from school to work explains the poor labour market outcomes experienced by young people in LAC, especially those from poor and vulnerable households. Youth from these households leave school earlier than their peers in better-off households, and when employed mainly work in informal jobs (Figure 1.4). At age 15, almost seven out of ten youth living in moderate poor households are in school; at age 29, however, almost three out of ten youth in this group are NEET, another four work in the informal sector, only two work in the formal sector and the remaining one is either a working student or a student. In vulnerable households, more than half of young people aged 29 are either working in the informal sector or NEET. In contrast, remarkable differences are observed among consolidated middle-class households: around 85% of youth are in school at age 15, while more than 56% of youth are working in the formal sector at age 29.

Figure 1.4. **Activity status of youth by single year of age and socio-economic status in Latin America and the Caribbean, 2014**

(percentage of youth aged 15-29)

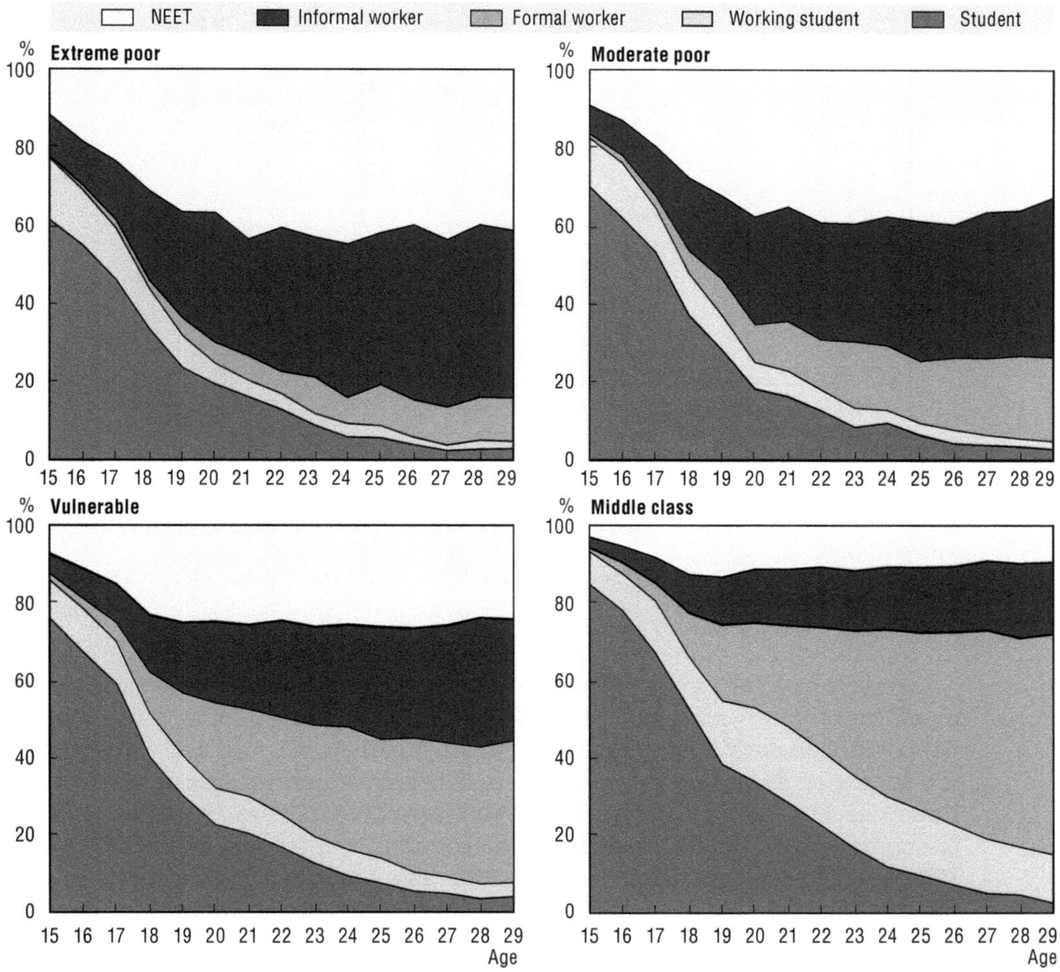

Note: Socio-economic classes are defined using the World Bank classification: "Extreme poor" = youth belonging to households with a daily per capita income lower than USD 2.50. "Moderate poor" = youth belonging to households with a daily per capita income of USD 2.50-4.00. "Vulnerable" = individuals with a daily per capita income of USD 4.00-10.00 "Middle class" = youth from households with a daily per capita income higher than USD 10.00. Poverty lines and incomes are expressed in 2005 USD PPP per day (PPP = purchasing power parity). LAC weighted average of 16 countries: Argentina, Bolivia, Brazil, Chile, Colombia, Costa Rica, Dominican Republic, Ecuador, El Salvador, Guatemala, Honduras, Mexico, Panama, Paraguay, Peru and Uruguay.

Source: OECD and World Bank tabulations of SEDLAC (CEDLAS and the World Bank).

StatLink http://dx.doi.org/10.1787/888933414101

Most youth leaving school enter inactivity or informal low-quality jobs in Latin America (Figure 1.5). Nearly half (47%) of young workers are employed in an informal job. The incidence of informality is much larger for youth from poor and vulnerable households than for those belonging to the middle class. The analysis for Argentina, Brazil, Mexico and Paraguay shows that around 60% of those working in informal jobs will stay in an informal job one year later, while less than 30% will move to a formal job. Similarly, more than 70% of those working in a formal job will stay in a formal job one year later, and only around 5% will move to an informal job. Thus, starting in the informal rather than in the formal sector can lead to very different labour market outcomes. This suggests that a certain degree of labour market segmentation exists in Latin America, making the transition from school to work a particularly relevant stage in young people's careers and futures.

Figure 1.5. **School to labour market transitions of youth in selected Latin American countries, 2005-15**

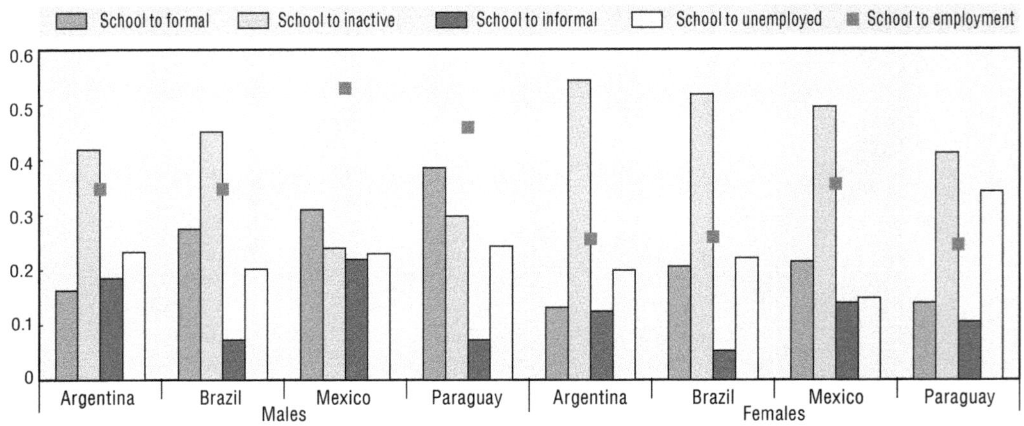

Notes: Yearly transition rates out of school for the pooled period 2005-15. Transition rates are calculated as the ratio between flow of people moving that transitioned from Condition 1 (school) to Condition 2 between time 0 and time 1, over the total stock of people in the population in Condition 1 in time 0 (i.e. in school: only in school, and in school and working). The transitions are year to year. This analysis focuses on urban populations due to data availability.

Source: OECD and World Bank tabulations of Labor Database for Latin America and the Caribbean – LABLAC (CEDLAS and the World Bank).

StatLink http://dx.doi.org/10.1787/888933414116

Around one-fifth of young people in Latin America are neither working nor engaged in education or training (NEET) – nearly 30 million young people. This means they are not positioned within either one of the main channels of social and economic inclusion: the education system or labour markets. The largest percentages of NEETs are found in Honduras, El Salvador, Guatemala and Mexico, where NEET rates surpass 25%. The NEET phenomenon is strongly linked to socio-economic background: 83% of NEET women and 76% of NEET men come from poor or vulnerable households. This status contributes to the intergenerational persistence of inequality, prevents economies in the region from exploiting the demographic window of opportunity and can even be associated with risky behaviour such as crime and violence (de Hoyos et al., 2016).

NEET is primarily a female phenomenon in Latin America, since 76% of NEETs are women; but many of these young women actually contribute to the economy from unpaid jobs. NEET rates for women reach levels of around 30%, much higher than for men (11%). However, some NEETs, particularly young women working in households, are productive and contribute to the total economy. In fact, 70% of NEET women are engaged in unpaid domestic work or caregiving, compared to 10% of NEET men.

More than two-thirds of LAC youth are low-skilled without college, university or high-level technical school education, representing a challenge for structural transformation (Figure 1.6). Many young Latin Americans find themselves out of school too early, as shown by the region's high drop-out and low completion rates for school. As a result, 43 million young Latin Americans aged 15 to 29, or 31% of the youth population, have not completed secondary education and are not enrolled in school. Even those who graduate suffer from poor quality education and transition into adult life with skills far down the ranks in comparative international evaluations such as the Programme for International Student Assessment of the OECD, known as PISA (OECD, 2015a; OECD/CAF/ECLAC, 2014).

Figure 1.6. **Youth population by maximum educational level achieved in Latin America and the Caribbean, 2014**

(percentage of youth aged 25-29)

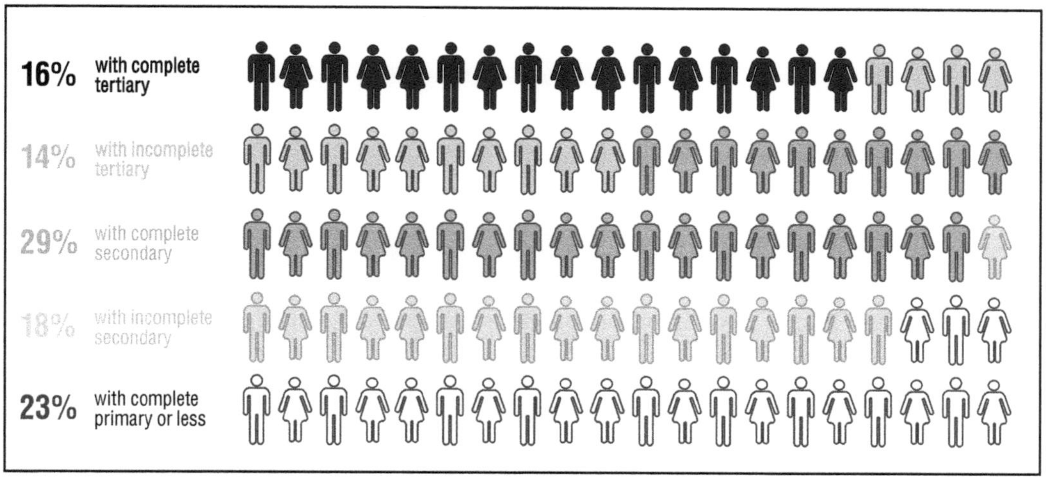

Source: OECD and World Bank tabulations of SEDLAC (CEDLAS and the World Bank).

Skills levels are poor in the region, due to the low quality of primary and secondary education and structural barriers. Young Latin Americans perform poorly in reading, mathematics and science compared to their counterparts in OECD countries. More than half of young Latin Americans enrolled in school do not acquire basic-level proficiency in reading, mathematics and science, according to PISA results (OECD, 2015a). Less than 1% of LAC students perform among the highest levels of proficiency in mathematics, reading or science (OECD, 2016c). This constitutes an obstacle to further develop more specific skills and, at the same time, the small portion of top performers may hamper innovation and entrepreneurship. It also presents a major challenge for LAC countries that are transitioning into knowledge-based economies where citizens need to innovate, adapt and leverage advanced human capital.

LAC has the widest gap between the pool of available skills and those skills that economies and businesses require. In Latin America, around 50% of formal firms do not find the workforce with the skills they need, compared to 36% of firms in OECD countries (Manpower Group, 2015). This is a particularly pressing issue in countries like Peru, Brazil and Mexico (Figure 1.7). As a consequence, one-third of employers need to use foreign talent to meet skills shortages, and firms take longer than in any other region to fill job vacancies (Aedo and Walker, 2012). Among sectors, motor vehicles and machinery shows the most acute skill gaps, accentuating the challenge to diversify into activities deemed more beneficial for development and industrial upgrading (OECD/CAF/ECLAC, 2014; Melguizo and Perea, 2016).

Figure 1.7. **Firms reporting difficulties to hire in Latin America and the Caribbean, China and OECD countries, 2014**

(percentages of formal firms)

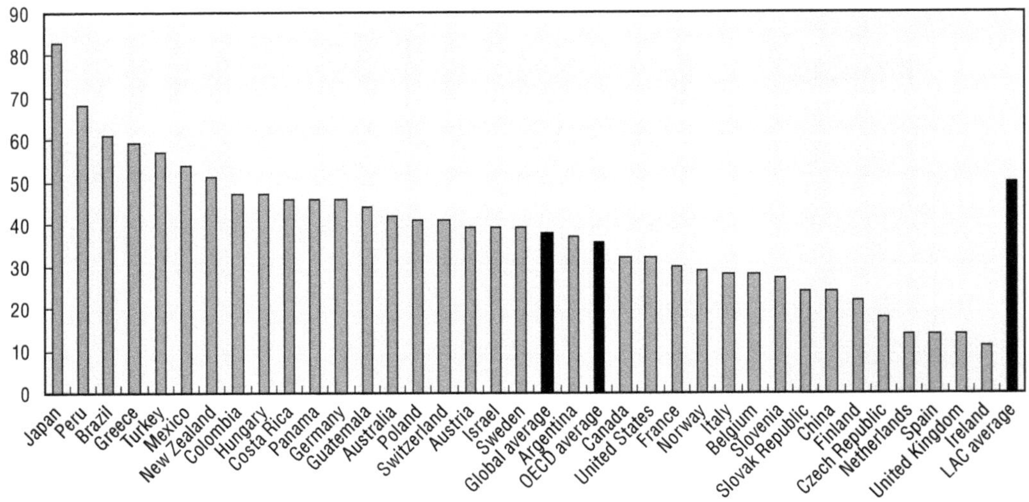

Note: LAC average includes Argentina, Brazil, Colombia, Costa Rica, Guatemala, Mexico and Peru. OECD includes Australia, Austria, Belgium, Canada, Czech Republic, Finland, France, Germany, Greece, Hungary, Ireland, Israel, Italy, Netherlands, New Zealand, Poland, Slovakia, Slovenia, Spain, Sweden, Switzerland, Turkey, United Kingdom and United States. Global average includes the 42 countries in the 2015 Talent Shortage Survey.

Source: Manpower Group (2015).

StatLink http://dx.doi.org/10.1787/888933414533

Investing in skills can improve youth's transition from school to work...

Education and skills are widely recognised as key elements to support youth transition from school to work and inclusive development. Education is central to improve LAC's current low productivity and find new engines to foster long-term growth, reduce poverty, bridge inequalities, and build social stability and cohesion. In fact, education and skills are areas of investment that can support productivity and inclusiveness at the same time and reinforce synergies between the two (OECD, 2016a; OECD/CAF/ECLAC, 2014).

Access to higher education has expanded in LAC during the last decade, but remains below OECD levels. Between 2004 and 2014, enrolment in higher education increased from 29% to 44% of the population aged 15 to 64. However, completion of tertiary education still remains a major problem in LAC, and the potential for higher education remains unrealised. While 41% of the population aged 15-64 began tertiary education, on average, only 14% completed this cycle across LAC countries. This percentage is particularly low compared to OECD countries, where 39% of young people graduate from higher education.

Technical and vocational education (TVET) in LAC rarely train youth in mid- and high-level trade, technical, professional and management skills. National vocational training institutes have expanded and developed better connections with private-sector needs. They play an important role in providing basic technical skills to high school drop-outs and disadvantaged youth, but, with a few exceptions, programmes are limited in size. Public spending in training programmes in LAC ranges from 0.02% of GDP in Peru to more than 0.30% in Colombia and Costa Rica, compared to an OECD average of 0.14%. At secondary and tertiary levels, Argentina, Brazil, Chile, Colombia, Costa Rica, Mexico and Peru are making significant advances in coverage, quality and adequacy of the programmes to meet the needs of the private sector. However, the quality of the technical schools is heterogeneous. High-quality schools that are highly respected and generate positive returns for students and employers coexist with low quality ones. These high-quality schools represent an important source of innovation and experimentation in the design of technical education that benefits the sector as a whole. However, in some countries they are too few to drive change.

Low pertinence of education is another crucial challenge in the region, with few higher education students focusing on science, technology, engineering and mathematics (STEM), disciplines associated with higher earnings. An average of 39% of tertiary education students in LAC are focused on social sciences, business and law. The region lags behind in STEM fields of study, mainly in science, with enrolment rates ranging between 2-7%, compared to an average of 10% in OECD countries, and of 13% and 18% in strong research and innovation economies such as Germany, France, Ireland, United Kingdom and also the People's Republic of China. STEM qualifications and earnings are positively associated in Uruguay, Peru and Panama. On average, STEM graduates earn 20% more than non-STEM tertiary degree holders in Peru and 10% in Uruguay (Cerutti, Crivellaro and De Sousa, forthcoming). Such a premium arises from the fact that the labour market may value some sets of skills more than others, such as those needed for higher productivity tasks. In particular, skill-biased technological changes favour more skilled workers. Given the increasing role of technology and digitisation in driving the demand side of the market for skills, STEM degrees might be particularly relevant for LAC economies.

The lack of skills among youth has led countries to develop programmes to enhance the skills of youth who had dropped out of school or who had poorly integrated into the labour markets and adult life. These programmes disseminated throughout the region deliver new solutions to an old, but growing, problem: youth's economic and social exclusion. Although they provide disadvantaged youth with training and services to find more and better jobs, there are not enough to satisfy the large pool of high school drop-outs in most countries. Still, lifelong learning policies and productive inclusion programmes both for youth and the broader population can pick up from where these small, but effective, programmes left off and provide longer term solutions.

Skills-enhancing programmes for youth that combine classroom teaching, workplace learning and job search services help young Latin Americans transition to employment. Training interventions for youth in the region, such as *Jovenes con más y mejor trabajo* in Argentina, *ProJovem* in Brazil, *Jovenes en Acción* in Colombia and *ProJoven* in Peru, prove that comprehensive interventions have positive results on youth employability, earnings and especially job quality (ILO, 2016) (Table 1.1). At the same time, the interaction between design components and programme implementation is important for their effectiveness.

Training programmes that respond to the needs of the marketplace, thanks to private sector participation in their design and implementation, facilitate youth's transition into quality jobs and better earnings. Impact evaluations of the early experiences of these comprehensive programmes in Latin America show that coordinating course content with the private sector to better satisfy youth needs, as well as providing participants with a stipend, are central for programmes to work well. Although foundational skills are important, individuals should be trained to participate in knowledge-based and skills-based economies. General education and TVET should expand their links with the region's productive sector to underpin on-the-job-training systems, which should be a cornerstone of education and training across the life cycle.

Upgrading human capital by boosting formal education, training programmes and "learning-by-doing" is paramount, and needs to be paired with promoting organisational change and transforming productive structures to maximise the benefits of technology for productivity. Translating technological change into productivity gains will necessitate a range of firm-level organisational changes to increase flexibility, particularly relating to work arrangements, networking and multi-skilling of the labour force.

Table 1.1. **Components and outcomes in youth training programmes in Latin America and the Caribbean**

		Employability	Formality	Earnings
Components	**Labour intermediation services**			
	Information / counselling	Effective	Neutral	Neutral
	Support for job search	Neutral	Effective	Effective
	Job placement	Effective	Effective	Effective
	Public works	Neutral	Neutral	Neutral
	Training for unemployed			
	School based training	Neutral	Neutral	Neutral
	School + work experience	Neutral	Effective	Effective
	Workplace training	Neutral	Effective	Neutral
	For self-employment	Effective	Effective	Effective
	Soft skills training	Effective	Effective	Effective
	Training for active workers	Neutral	Neutral	Neutral
Mechanism	**Service provision**			
	Dual training and labour intermediation	Effective	Effective	Effective
	Dual training	Neutral	Neutral	Neutral
	Single training option	Not effective	Not effective	Not effective
	Demand driven	Effective	Effective	Effective
	Demand and supply driven	Effective	Effective	Effective
	Supply driven	Not effective	Not effective	Not effective
	Stipend to participants			
	Transport/ lunch/health insurance	Effective	Effective	Effective
	Income support	Neutral	Effective	Effective
	Publicly funded training	Effective	Effective	Effective
	Provision of training courses			
	Public	Effective	Effective	Effective
	Private	Effective	Effective	Effective
	Internships arranged by training provider	Neutral	Effective	Effective

Note: = ● Effective ● Neutral given mixed results ● Not effective.

Sources: OECD/CAF/ECLAC, 2016, based on programme evaluations (see Table 4.8).

… and broadening entrepreneurship opportunities can also improve youth's transition from school to work

Youth entrepreneurship is a vehicle for improving employability and social mobility in LAC. Through entrepreneurship, youth can raise their capacity to integrate into labour markets, accumulate skills and improve their own and society's well-being. At the same time, fostering entrepreneurship is fundamental for innovation, which could serve as a driver for much-needed productive transformation and contribute to surpassing the middle-income trap.

Entrepreneurial aptitudes and perceptions are similar among LAC and OECD member countries. Qualities such as creative thinking, management skills, goal-oriented objectives and risk-taking are present among young Latin American entrepreneurs and those in industrialised economies (CAF, 2013). Entrepreneurial activity is highly regarded in both LAC and OECD member countries: among the young, nearly seven out of ten believe that successful entrepreneurs receive high status in their country (GEM, 2016).

Youth entrepreneurship in LAC is characterised by the co-existence of few high-growth and many subsistence entrepreneurs. Despite similar motivations and attitudes towards entrepreneurship than in OECD economies, youth entrepreneurship in Latin America is intrinsically related to the structure of labour markets and the region's business fabric. Young Latin American entrepreneurs are more prone to be own-account workers, less educated and from more disadvantaged socio-economic backgrounds.

Indeed, the share of subsistence entrepreneurship among young workers in Latin America is high. The prevalence of own-account workers among youth (16%) is almost three times the prevalence in the OECD (6%); only 13% of young entrepreneurs in the region possess tertiary education, compared to 33% in OECD economies. Furthermore, entrepreneurial motivation in the region is different than in the OECD: necessity-driven entrepreneurship (e.g. no better options for work) among the young is, on average, higher (26%) than in OECD countries (16%), with significant differences among countries (Figure 1.8).

Figure 1.8. **Entrepreneurial motivation in Latin American and Caribbean countries and OECD, 2015**

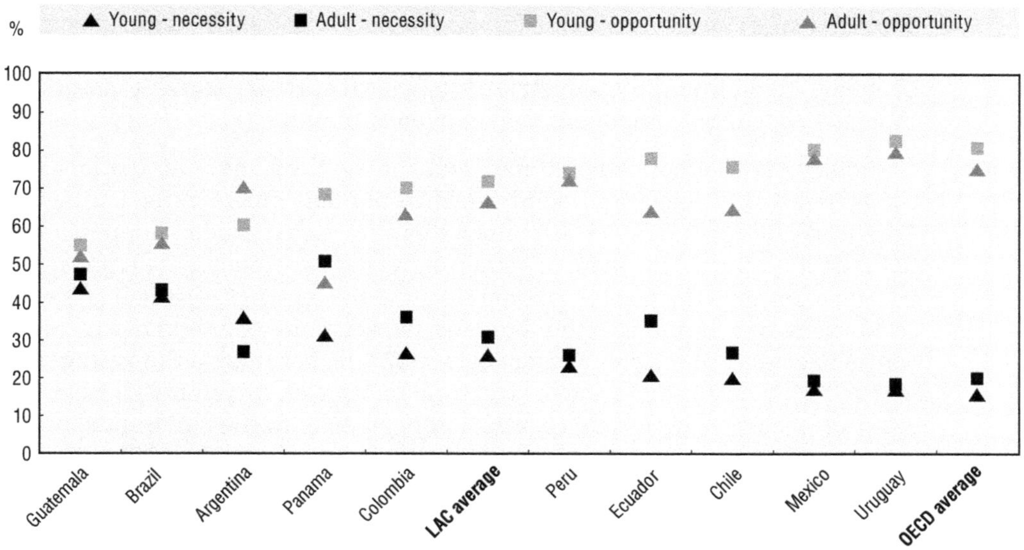

Note: LAC average includes Argentina, Brazil, Colombia, Costa Rica, Ecuador, El Salvador, Mexico, Panama, Peru and Uruguay.

Source: OECD/ECLAC/CAF based on Global Entrepreneurship Monitor individual data 2015.

StatLink http://dx.doi.org/10.1787/888933414605

Entrepreneurship ecosystems for high-growth entrepreneurs in Latin America are developing quickly, but are still nascent. Public spending on entrepreneurship programmes in Latin America is still low (0.04% of GDP), even when only compared to spending on start-up incentives and job creation in OECD countries (0.07% of GDP). Yet, and despite the region's economic downturn, the landscape for start-ups is encouraging (OECD, 2016a). Many countries in the region have consolidated their institutional support for start-ups, and new actors have entered the scene. Together with national governments and academia, the role of local governments and cities in enhancing entrepreneurship ecosystems is noticeable, as shown by *Ruta N* in Medellín and the regional programmes of *Start up Chile* in Valparaíso and Concepción. At the same time, private sector participation has increased, not only from the perspective of financing and investment, but also through new actors supporting the seeding of innovative entrepreneurship activities. Business associations are introducing new forms of collaboration and exchange for start-up support. The *Association of Start-ups of Campinas* in Brazil, several entrepreneurial hubs (*Parques de Emprendimiento*) in Colombia or the *Ibero-American Centre of Entrepreneurship and Innovation* in Costa Rica are good examples. Business-sharing practices and open innovation for large firms are also becoming increasingly common in the region.

Barriers to youth entrepreneurship in LAC are, on average, higher than in other emerging economies and in the OECD, despite recent improvements. Both subsistence and high-growth young entrepreneurs face challenges in accessing financing instruments, building capacity, developing business networks and an entrepreneurial culture, accessing new markets and overcoming regulatory barriers, even more so than their adult counterparts. LAC countries have tried to tackle these dimensions and tailor their policies to young entrepreneurs.

High-growth entrepreneurs can access financing tools in early stages; however, these tools fade away as businesses grow, critically affecting their capacity to mature. Access to finance continues to be a critical constraint for young Latin American entrepreneurs to develop their businesses, as is the case for the OECD. While credit and seed/early stage capital continue to be relevant financing sources, a broader range of instruments is available to suit the diverse needs of entrepreneurs in the region. These include asset-based finance (i.e. factoring), alternative debt (i.e. crowdfunding), hybrid financing instruments and equity finance. In the case of Latin American start-ups, financing support is moving forward rapidly in the early stages of entrepreneurship (such as the *Servicio de Cooperación Técnica* – SERCOTEC – in Chile and *Red Emprender* in Uruguay). In addition to the instruments, youth entrepreneurship programmes with a financial education component have proven successful.

Young Latin American entrepreneurs' integration into international global value changes is still limited, and administrative burdens create extra hurdles. Young Latin American entrepreneurs are less integrated into global production networks than their OECD counterparts. The share of young, early-stage entrepreneurs reporting at least one-quarter of revenues from international clients in the region (10%) is half of the OECD average (21%). Moreover, administrative burdens for start-ups (e.g. number of procedures and bodies to contact to register a company) are 42% higher than in the average OECD country (Figure 1.9). Indeed, advancing in structural reforms on this front can have a considerable effect on economic performance: a 10% improvement in the Barriers to Entrepreneurship Index could represent a 0.3% gain in productivity growth (OECD, 2015b). Countries such as Chile and Mexico have made significant progress by simplifying procedures for creating start-ups with the *Ley de Empresas en un dia*. Similarly, room exists for facilitating greater access to available instruments for youth entrepreneurship in most countries. Internal barriers for providing these instruments (e.g. limits to seed capital and grants due to a higher share of non-performing loans among start-ups) could be changed.

Figure 1.9. **Barriers to entrepreneurship in Latin American countries and OECD**

(Scale 0 to 6 from least to most restrictive, circa 2013)

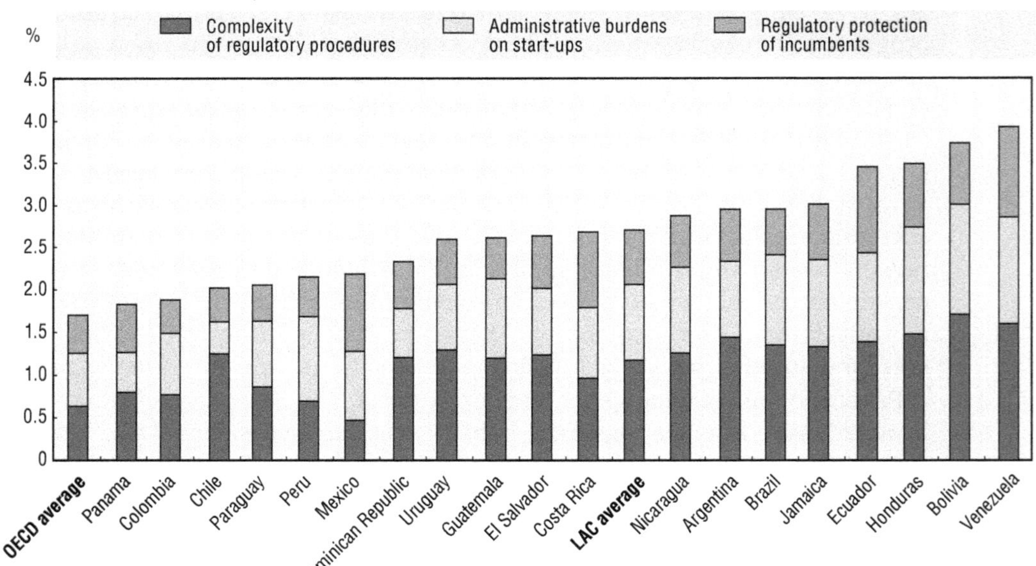

Note: Preliminary results for Bolivia, Ecuador, Guatemala, Panama, Paraguay and Bolivarian Republic of Venezuela (hereafter "Venezuela"). Indicator reflects the state of legislation in 2013 for all countries, with the exception of Uruguay (2014), and Bolivia, Ecuador, Guatemala, Panama, Paraguay and Venezuela (2015).

Source: OECD-WBG product market regulation database for all countries except Brazil, Chile and Mexico; OECD product market regulation database.

StatLink http://dx.doi.org/10.1787/888933414648

Entrepreneurship programmes offering youth business and managerial training, as well as mentoring and counselling services, show the best results in LAC. Existing impact evaluations also show that financial support mechanisms have more limited success (Table 1.2). Moreover, publicly funded programmes in the region are effective, and outcomes are independent of public or private provision of services. A comprehensive approach to entrepreneurship support, encompassing training-financing-mentoring, has produced more effective results. Strengthening these components, and giving them enough flexibility during implementation, can considerably improve programmes' effectiveness and deliver long-term effects.

Table 1.2. **Components and outcomes of youth entrepreneurship programmes in Latin America and the Caribbean**

		Main outcomes			Secondary outcomes		
		Self-employment	Formalisation	Earnings	Firm creation	Psycho-social well-being	Territorial inequality
Components	**Entrepreneurial Training**						
	Technical and vocational	Effective	Effective	Neutral	Not effective		Effective
	Business and managerial training	Effective	Neutral	Effective	Effective	Effective	Neutral
	Financial training				Neutral	Neutral	Neutral
	Financing						
	Credit for business or consumer loans			Neutral	Neutral	Neutral	Neutral
	Cash and in-kind grants				Neutral		Neutral
	Access to financial products			Neutral	Neutral	Effective	
	Counselling						
	Mentoring in business	Neutral	Neutral	Effective	Effective	Effective	
	Psycho-social support	Neutral	Neutral	Neutral			Effective
	Arrangements for on-site advice/consulting		Neutral	Effective	Effective	Neutral	Effective
	Other						
	Support for job search	Effective		Neutral	Effective	Effective	Neutral
	School + work experience	Neutral	Neutral		Effective	Effective	
	For self-employment		Neutral	Effective	Effective	Neutral	Effective
Mechanisms	**Demand driven**	Neutral	Effective	Neutral	Neutral		
	Supply driven	Effective	Neutral	Effective	Effective	Effective	Effective
	Publicly funded	Effective	Effective	Effective	Effective	Effective	Effective
	Provision of services						
	Public	Effective		Effective	Effective	Effective	Neutral
	Private	Neutral		Effective	Effective		

Note: = Effective; Neutral given mixed results; Not effective.
Source: OECD/CAF/ECLAC--, based on programme evaluations (see Table 5.A2.3).

Investing in skills and entrepreneurship also means embracing trends in these areas and mobilising youth to steer – and not be derailed by – social, political and economic changes

Technological and demographic changes, alongside globalisation, are driving major economic, political and social transformations that affect the world of work, the cities youth will live in and the way young Latin Americans participate in politics. The ever-larger penetration of information and communications technologies, artificial intelligence, big data, the expanding power of computing or the *Internet of things* have made the life of youth different than those of their parents. They will further change their way of life as youth become adults.

As adults, youth in LAC will face a different work world than the one adults face today as employment shifts from manufacturing and construction towards services such as trade, wholesale, and information and communications (WEF, 2016). Technological change, the main driver of these trends, is creating a wave of disruptive change understood as the fourth industrial revolution. The net impact of technological change on job creation and destruction is far from certain. Around 9% of jobs in the OECD could be automated (Arntz et al., 2016). In Latin America, less than 2% of jobs (3.4 million jobs) could be lost by 2030, but with a significant shift from traditional sectors, such as manufacturing and construction, to innovative services (WEF, 2016). Latin America must be ready for this change. In a region with high inequalities and a relative abundance of mid-range skills (more prone to be automated), job destruction could be large, while inequalities may widen. For youth to benefit from the opportunities of the digital economy, expanding access to broadband networks in the region will be essential. This involves designing digital strategies at the national level, improving infrastructure deployment and strengthening the accessibility and affordability of broadband services (OECD/IDB, 2016).

New jobs could emerge where complex tasks require genuine human skills; hence, training policies should anticipate and adapt to new demands. As the distribution of tasks between humans and machines changes (with humans performing tasks more specific and exclusive to them), companies will demand workers with skills to work with new information and solve unstructured problems. General cognitive skills, system skills and complex problem-solving skills will become more valuable as the relative importance of manual tasks and routine cognitive tasks declines. The future impact on jobs will be largely determined by both the specific characteristics of the countries and regions, as well as by the capacity to design and implement educational and skills policies to adapt to forthcoming change. Policies to provide youth with stronger foundational and generic skills to support labour mobility and adaptability to change, and mechanisms to anticipate skills demands, will be key to make the most of emerging opportunities.

Young people have the potential and technological possibilities to be drivers of smarter, more sustainable cities in the region. Youth can play a key role in transforming cities so they follow a green path to more sustainable and inclusive living environments. By 2050, LAC youth will live in a region where nine out of ten Latin Americans live in cities (United Nations, 2014). Youth represent a special opportunity as they are more connected and technologically savvy than any other generation; further developing the skills and technological proficiency of youth, while fostering their innovation capacities, will help deliver more efficient and smarter cities. These win-win associations are starting to appear in several cities in Latin America, especially through the use of new technologies (e.g. mobile mapping, user apps). These include apps for improving transport infrastructure in Ecuador and Peru through viability analysis and demand estimates, increasing citizen safety in Mexico, streamlining public procurement in Colombia and fostering sustainable tourism in Chile.

Youth are also using new technological instruments to voice and organise their demands and shape the emerging political developments. This results from the inability of current political institutions to respond satisfactorily to social demands. In 2014, only 36% of Latin American youth expressed confidence in the transparency of election results. This share is lower than for adults (39%), and much lower than the OECD average (62%) (Figure 1.10). Also, the maturity and consolidation of civil society in Latin America has supported social mobilisation. Protest movements bloomed and expanded through social media, rallying against inequality and urban violence and advocating for gender rights. These platforms serve as alternatives to traditional politics and attract many young individuals who have lost trust in current political institutions.

Figure 1.10. **Youth and adults who express confidence in elections in Latin American countries and the Caribbean and OECD, 2014**

(percentage)

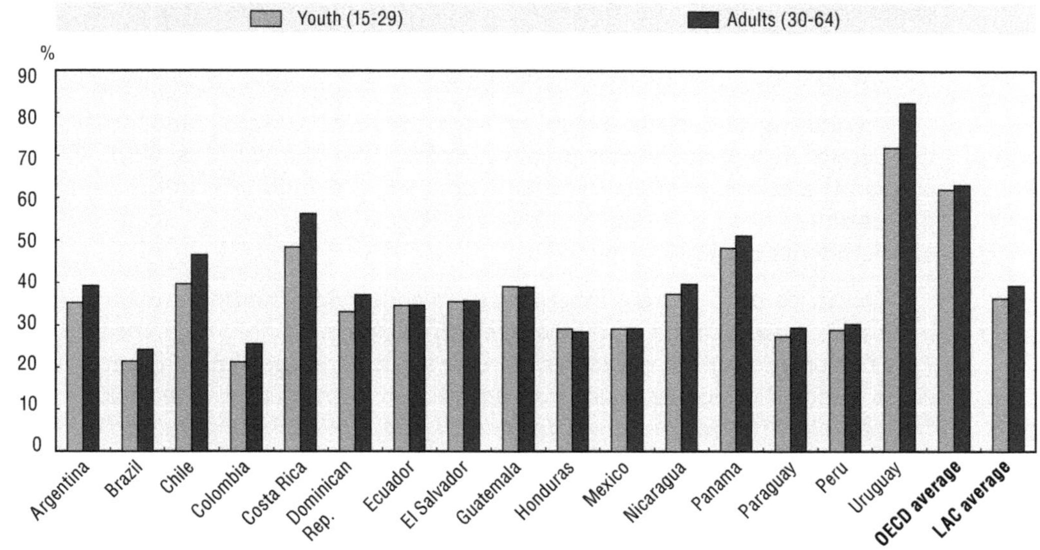

Source: OECD/CAF/ECLAC based on Gallup World Monitor, 2015.

StatLink http://dx.doi.org/10.1787/888933413730

Skills and entrepreneurship can empower youth as social, political and economic actors

Owing to the constantly changing social, political and productive environment, skills and entrepreneurship policies must be flexible and robust enough to embrace future trends proactively. At the same time, policies should provide youth with tailored tools to shape the specific environments in which they live. The economic structure of the country/region, the available pool of skills and the institutional framework, as well as the capacity to implement policies that adapt to forthcoming change, will determine the impact on jobs, cities and politics.

Investments in skills and entrepreneurship must be taken in a credible fiscal framework. The current economic slowdown and fiscal stimuli from previous years have weakened fiscal positions in most Latin American economies. Under this complex scenario, the region's economies must rebuild fiscal space, while protecting key investments that could promote both long-term growth (including a boost in physical, human and technological capital) and short-term growth. Economies with low tax revenues should undertake structural tax reforms to increase revenues. Those with high levels of debt and taxes should reallocate expenditure towards public investment and skills. And economies with low debt should turn to the markets for financing.

Improving Latin American youth's skills involves strengthening the coverage and quality of the education system and promoting lifelong comprehensive skills-enhancing policies. Broader reforms of the education system are expected to increase access to, and quality and pertinence of, primary, secondary and tertiary education. As they do, alternative human capital policies such as the existing training and productive inclusion programmes should support the current generation of low-skilled youth and provide all future adults with training options. Education curricula and skills-enhancing programmes should provide youth with technical training for productive inclusion and foundational skills, which are critical throughout people's lives to favour their mobility and adaptability to changing external conditions. These are key skills for individuals to form a basis to learn new things and adapt to new tasks. At the same time, both traditional and TVET education (including skills training programmes for high school drop-outs) should be more responsive to the needs of the marketplace and provide wider channels for the business sector's participation in the curriculum content. Efforts to strengthen the skills that work today and for the future need to be streamlined and coordinated with private sector demands.

Combining classroom teaching with practical training and other active labour market services helps better prepare students for the world of work. This is relevant beyond the design of short vocational courses. It should inform the design of all TVET programmes from secondary to tertiary education, as well as academic education, to offer students better job prospects.

Countries need more efficient ways to collect information on the skills individuals have and those skills businesses need to design national skills-enhancing strategies. This information helps countries identify skills shortages and gaps and plan for future skills needs to become more productive and competitive. The lack of country-level comparable data hinders governments' capacity to develop policy solutions to address the current skills mismatch.

Latin American and Caribbean countries need to go beyond the current skills mismatch and define long-term strategies that aim to identify and promote new knowledge, linked to the development of the digital economy. To do that, it is essential to encourage public-private work that allows identifying future areas of knowledge and skills that will be needed in the long term, to be promoted today.

Implementing an inclusive entrepreneurship approach with different instruments will increase productivity and equity. Broad, multi-dimensional support, beyond micro-credit, is required for subsistence entrepreneurs to address vulnerabilities outside the labour market. This includes introducing tailored financing instruments adapted to the needs of young entrepreneurs, with more flexible requirements on credit history, collateral and risk. Public financial institutions can play a role in making financing instruments for the young more flexible, both through credit and new instruments. In the case of Latin American start-ups, angel investment and risk capital are still embryonic, and public policy can provide investors with more incentives to participate in the later stages of firm development.

Reducing regulatory barriers and strengthening the link between young entrepreneurs and business networks can help high-growth entrepreneurship. Access to business networks and firm performance are linked closely. They reduce information asymmetries and provide potential access to new markets, while connecting young entrepreneurs with more experienced ones. Reinforcing counselling and mentoring programmes, as shown by recent evaluations, can be effective. Adapting emerging initiatives that connect entrepreneurs to international business networks can also generate synergies for young entrepreneurial communities. Regional associations for entrepreneurs and regional financing platforms can help young entrepreneurs to integrate global production networks.

Strengthening programmes that support business and management training help young entrepreneurs develop the skills needed to develop high-growth enterprises. Entrepreneurship programmes that combine training, financing and counselling produce more effective results. Incorporating a youth perspective in entrepreneurship initiatives in the region will guarantee that these instruments are properly tailored for this population segment.

Integrating a gender perspective into youth policies is essential. Policies can help level the playing field between (young) women and men, ensuring all have the same opportunities to reach their full potential. Scholarships that prevent young women from dropping out of school and that encourage them to study in academic fields that are likely to pay off in future earnings, such as STEM fields, are crucial. Affordable and good-quality childcare, financial aid and teaching methods that do not have a gender bias can help young NEET women in their transition to higher education and employment. Improving entrepreneurship for young women involves providing financial support when they lack experience or collateral, and expanding business support to sectors where women are more concentrated and have a lower survival rate (e.g. manufacturing).

LAC needs to systematically use technical evaluations of youth training and entrepreneurship programmes to identify the most effective components. Even with advances made, few programmes are evaluated properly. Evaluations should be incorporated during the programme design phase to be effective. Moreover, current evaluations of entrepreneurship programmes assess neither their social effects nor their performance in terms of business survival or their international reach. Introducing systematic evaluations of outcomes by group, particularly related to gender and ethnicity, is also important. Evaluations should not only examine the efficiency and cost-effectiveness of programmes, but also consider deadweight (i.e. supporting an entrepreneur who would have behaved in the same way without support) and displacement effects (e.g. when supporting one entrepreneur puts another out of business).

References

Aedo, C. and I. Walker (2012), *Skills for the 21st Century in Latin America and the Caribbean*, Directions in Development, Human Development, World Bank Group, Washington, DC, https://openknowledge.worldbank.org/handle/10986/2236 License: CC BY 3.0 IGO.

Arntz, M., T. Gregory and U. Zierahn (2016), "The risk of automation for jobs in OECD countries: A comparative analysis", *OECD Social, Employment and Migration Working Papers*, No. 189, OECD Publishing, Paris, http://dx.doi.org/10.1787/5jlz9h56dvq7-en.

Alberola, E. et al. (2016), "Fiscal policy and the cycle in Latin America: The role of financing conditions and fiscal rules", *BIS Working Papers*, No. 543, Bank for International Settlements, Basel, http://www.bis.org/publ/work543.pdf.

CAF (2013), *Emprendimientos en América Latina. Desde la subsistencia hacia la transformación productiva.* [Entrepreneurship in Latin America. From Subsistence to Productive Transformation], Development Bank of Latin America, Caracas Reporte de Economía y Desarrollo RED 2013, Bogota.

Cavallo, E. and T. Serebrisky (2016), *Saving for Development: How Latin America and the Caribbean Can Save More and Better*, Development in the Americas Series, Inter-American Development Bank, Washington, DC and Palgrave Macmillan, New York.

CEDLAS and World Bank (2016), *Socio-Economic Database for Latin America and the Caribbean* (http://sedlac.econo.unlp.edu.ar/eng/), (accessed 30 August 2016).

Cerutti P., E. Crivellaro and L. De Sousa (forthcoming), "Returns to STEM education in Latin America", *OECD Development Centre Working Paper*, OECD Publishing, Paris.

de Hoyos, R. et al. (2016), *Out of School and Out of Work: Risks and Opportunities for Latin America's Ninis*, World Bank, Washington, DC.

ECLAC (2016), *Economic Survey of Latin America and the Caribbean 2016: The 2030 Agenda for Sustainable Development and the Challenges of Financing for Development*, Economic Commission for Africa and the Caribbean, Santiago.

Gasparini, L., G. Cruces and L. Tornarrolli (2016), "Chronicle of a deceleration foretold: Income inequality in Latin America in the 2010s", *CEDLAS Working Paper*, No. 198, Center for Distributive, Labor and Social Studies, Universidad Nacional de La Plata, Argentina.

GEM (2016), *Global Entrepreneurship Monitor* (database), www.gemconsortium.org/data (accessed 20 August 2016).

ILO (2016), *Soluciones eficaces: Políticas activas del mercado de trabajo en América Latina y el Caribe* [Efficient Solutions: Active Labour Market Policies in Latin America and the Caribbean], International Labour Organization, Geneva.

IMF (2016), *World Economic Outlook. Too Slow for Too Long*, April, International Monetary Fund, Washington, DC.

Manpower Group (2015), *Talent Shortage Survey Research Results*, Milwaukee.

Melguizo, A. and J.R. Perea (2016), "Mind the skills gap! Regional and industry patterns in emerging economies", *OECD Development Centre Working Papers*, No. 329, Éditions OCDE, Paris, http://dx.doi.org/10.1787/5jm5hkp7v145-en.

OECD (forthcoming), *Youth Well-Being: Towards an Inclusive Agenda. A Toolkit for Evidence-based Policy Making*, OECD Development Centre, OECD Publishing, Paris and European Commission, Brussels.

OECD (2016a), *The Productivity-Inclusiveness Nexus: Preliminary version*, OECD Publishing, Paris, http://dx.doi.org/10.1787/9789264258303-en.

OECD (2016b), *OECD Economic Outlook*, Volume 2016/1, OECD Publishing, Paris, http://dx.doi.org/10.1787/eco_outlook-v2016-1-en.

OECD (2016c), *A Skills Beyond School Review of Peru, OECD Reviews of Vocational Education and Training*, OECD Publishing, Paris, http://dx.doi.org/10.1787/9789264265400-en.

OECD (2015a), *Education at a Glance 2015: OECD Indicators*, OECD Publishing, Paris, http://dx.doi.org/10.1787/eag-2015-en.

OECD (2015b), *Economic Policy Reforms 2015: Going for Growth*, OECD Publishing, Paris, http://dx.doi.org/10.1787/growth-2015-en.

OECD/CAF/ECLAC (2015), *Latin American Economic Outlook 2016: Towards A New Partnership with China*, OECD Publishing, Paris, http://dx.doi.org/10.1787/9789264246218-en.

OECD/CAF/ECLAC (2014), *Latin American Economic Outlook 2015: Education, Skills and Innovation for Development*, OECD Publishing, Paris, http://dx.doi.org/10.1787/leo-2015-en.

OECD/IDB (2016), Broadband Policies for Latin America and the Caribbean: A Digital EconomyToolkit, OECD Publishing, Paris, http://dx.doi.org/10.1787/9789264251823-en.

Pagés, C. (2010), The Age of Productivity: Transforming Economies from the Bottom Up, Development in the Americas Series, Palgrave Macmillan, New York and Inter-American Development Bank, Washington, DC.

Powell, A. (2016), "Time to act: Latin America and the Caribbean facing strong challenges", *2016 Latin American and Caribbean Macroeconomic Report,* Inter-American Development Bank, Washington, DC.

UNDP (2016), *Regional Human Development Report for Latin America and the Caribbean Multidimensional Progress: Well-being Beyond Income,* United Nations Development Programme, Santiago.

United Nations (2014), *World Urbanization Prospects, 2014 Revision*, Department of Economic and Social Affairs, Population Division, New York.

WEF (2016), "The future of jobs: Employment, skills and workforce strategy for the fourth industrial revolution", *Global Challenge Insight Report*, World Economic Forum, Geneva.

World Bank (2013). *Shifting gears to accelerate shared prosperity in Latin America and Caribbean.* Latin America and the Caribbean poverty and labor brief, World Bank, Washington DC.

Chapter 2

Macroeconomic prospects for Latin America and the Caribbean

Latin America must return to the path of strong economic inclusive growth. The prolonged economic slowdown in the region confirms that potential growth is weaker than previously expected. This evolution will test the robustness of the socio-economic progress achieved in the previous decade, especially the strong reduction in poverty levels and the emergence of a middle class. This chapter assesses Latin America's growth prospects in a more challenging international environment and explores its consequences on the region's labour markets and key socio-economic indicators such as poverty and inequality. In addition, it analyses economic policy options with an emphasis on investment in infrastructure and skills to boost inclusive growth under a sustainable and credible fiscal framework.

Introduction

The tailwinds that propelled economic growth in Latin America and the Caribbean (LAC) have dissipated. Global demand growth is sluggish, funding is becoming more expensive and volatile, trade has considerably slowed since 2007 and commodity prices are well below the high levels reached during the past decade. Global growth is expected to gain only modest momentum so no reversal of fortunes is in sight.

After five years of economic slowdown, activity in the region entered negative territory in 2015. Output is expected to contract again in 2016 (between -0.5% and -1% according to different projections) with a modest recovery expected in 2017. The deep contractions in Brazil and the Bolivarian Republic of Venezuela (hereafter Venezuela), which account for nearly 45% of gross domestic product (GDP) in LAC, largely explain aggregate performance in the region.

There are stark contrasts in the cyclical position of countries in Latin America ("*Americas Latinas*" as it was called in previous editions of the *Latin American Economic Outlook*), but fewer differences over the longer term. Short-term economic projections show a more challenging picture for net commodity exporters in South America, particularly for those with weaker policy frameworks, than for Mexico, Central America and the Caribbean. However, mounting evidence points to deterioration of potential output growth in most LAC countries (OECD/CAF/ECLAC, 2015; Aravena, López and Pineda, 2016; IMF, 2016; Box 2.3).

Economic weakness is starting to hit labour markets, which could have a long-lasting impact on equality and well-being (see Annex 2.A1). On average, unemployment rates are rising, the quality of jobs is deteriorating, and wage growth and formality are stalling. Youth and women have been particularly affected since the 2011 economic slowdown.

Heterogeneity across countries precludes a one-size-fits-all approach, but all countries would benefit from policies to boost productivity and potential growth. This calls for active policies favouring inclusive growth, with a long-term view. Policy actions, boosting physical and human capital while strengthening fiscal positions and improving financing conditions, are essential.

Sluggish global context in the short term

Global economic growth remains sluggish, as the prolonged period of low growth has precipitated a self-fulfilling "low-growth trap" (OECD, 2016a). Financial markets are jittery, marked by risk-on and risk-off episodes that are increasing volatility in capital flows to emerging markets, mostly affecting currencies and equity valuations. For their part, commodity markets were hit by lethargic global growth and – in the case of oil – an oversupply in the market.

Global growth is stabilising at a too modest pace

Global growth seems to be stabilising towards a modest 3% (IMF, 2016; OECD, 2016a), although with differences across regions. The weak recovery in developed economies is still fragile, while most developing economies are slowing down. Nevertheless, emerging markets still account for the bulk of global growth (Figure 2.1).

The United States' economy continues to expand at a moderate pace, supported by stronger labour markets, recovery of the housing sector and credit to the private sector. The US dollar appreciation took a toll on manufacturing and industrial exports in 2015, but not enough to derail growth. Activity weakened in the first quarter of 2016, mainly owing to manufacturing and low drilling and mining investment, while services remained more robust. A further drop in investment in the energy sector also dragged output growth. The dollar depreciation in the second quarter should ease some pressure on the manufacturing sector, while the strength of the service sector should support activity in coming quarters. The recovery of oil prices should prevent a further decline of investment in the energy sector, particularly among shale producers; nonetheless, it may not dent consumption, since prices are not expected to soar and the previous low-price windfall was saved rather than spent. As spare capacity diminishes and the economy approaches full employment, real wages are picking up and core inflation is approaching the target of the Federal Reserve (FED). Growth is expected to be around 2% in 2016 and 2017. In spite of recent market volatility, the FED is expected to continue its gradual tightening cycle, by increasing its benchmark interest rates, over the next two years, although it could moderate this approach if growth falters.

Figure 2.1. **Economic growth outlook by groups of economies**

(annual growth, percentage)

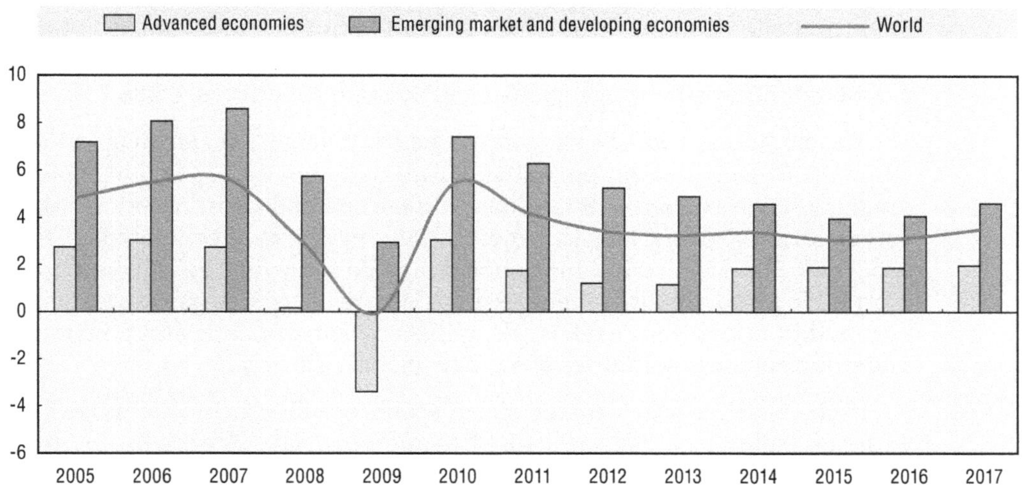

Source: IMF (2016), *World Economic Outlook*, April.

StatLink http://dx.doi.org/10.1787/888933413745

Economic activity remains weaker in the European Union and Japan than in the United States. The European Central Bank (ECB) and Bank of Japan (BoJ) are expected to stimulate their respective economies, but fiscal support will be rather limited. Fiscal consolidation in previous years at least reduced the need for further cuts in the short run. Activity in the European Union is expected to continue its soft-paced recovery, as credit conditions continue to ease and stronger labour markets support domestic demand; this partly compensates for weakened external demand. Lower energy prices have helped consumption in the European Union to a larger extent than in the United States. On the downside, uncertainty generated by the decision of the United Kingdom to leave the European Union ("Brexit") increased market volatility and dampened growth perspectives in both the United Kingdom (UK) and the European Union (EU), as well as increasing risk aversion in global markets. In Japan, the recent strengthening of the yen combined with weaker exports mean the outlook for growth is subdued. Instead, domestic demand will underpin economic activity, owing to monetary and fiscal stimuli and lower energy prices.

Activity in the People's Republic of China (hereafter "China") slowed down in 2015, in line with official projections. Policy stimuli is likely to prevent a hard landing in the short term, but maybe at a cost (as anticipated in OECD/CAF/ECLAC, 2015; OECD, 2015c).

In early 2016, uncertainty about the health of the Chinese economy precipitated capital outflows and increased pressures on the renminbi and other exchange rates in emerging economies. Nonetheless, easing of monetary policy and fiscal stimulus are starting to give some support to activity. Industrial production and retail sales gained momentum, signalling a certain stabilisation of activity during the second quarter of 2016 that should continue during the rest of the year. The pace of capital outflows started to slow down by the second quarter, as sentiment about the economy improved. The revival of the property market in China has played an important role in the country's recovery. Residential property sales have increased since late 2015 thanks to lower mortgage costs and the lifting of certain purchase restrictions. This increase in demand has helped reduce inventories, although an excess supply still remains. Total investment is also stabilising, driven by strong state-sector investment; private sector investment continues to decline. Efforts to keep up with high growth rates in the short run may come at odds with sustainability goals and fuel medium-term risks. The sharp increase in property prices in cities is a concern. In addition, allocating credit largely to state-owned enterprises (with overcapacity but easier access to credit) rather than to more dynamic privately owned enterprises (with limited access to loans) could hinder productivity and growth in the medium term once the credit stimulus loses steam. Therefore, bumps along the transition path cannot be ruled out. In the longer term, however, China is a key partner for other emerging regions, notably Latin America (see Box 2.1).

The situation in other emerging markets is diverse. Expansion in India is picking up, while the Russian Federation and Brazil are undergoing deep and persistent recessions, dragging down the outlook for Emerging Europe and Latin America, respectively. Net commodity exporters are, in general, underperforming compared to manufacturing exporters. Stabilisation in China should provide some footing for commodity prices. But even taking into account recent trends, the loss of income associated with the drop in commodity prices from peak levels will keep denting public and private spending, and undermining the possibilities of a robust global recovery.

In the baseline scenario, the global economy will continue to move forward slowly, with the balance of risks still tilted to the downside. A growth disruption in China and uncertainty due to political and geopolitical events are the biggest risks for global growth and financial markets. Stalling growth in the United States would be another major negative factor for the global economy. Fundamentals, however, seem relatively solid and the FED will tread carefully, increasing interest rates no faster than necessary to avoid derailing recovery.

Box 2.1. **Moving towards a new Latin America-China partnership**

China's economic slowdown, coupled with a rebalancing process from investment to consumption and from an industry-based to a services-driven economy, represents both opportunities and challenges for Latin America (OECD/CAF/ECLAC, 2015).

These challenging transformations may lead to volatility in some local and international financial markets. Still, Latin American economies could benefit from deepening and improving their partnership with China. China's transformation could not only fuel growth in times of economic slowdown in Latin America, but also help the region face its traditional challenges.

China's contribution to world growth is expected to reach 30% for 2016-21, in contrast to LAC's contribution of 5% (Figure 2.2). Trade ties between Latin America and China have soared, with China becoming the largest trading partner for Brazil, Chile and Peru. Financial ties have also increased: Chinese lending to Latin America has become the most important source of external financing (USD 125 billion between 2005 and 2015), surpassing other international financial institutions in the region. This adds to direct investment in infrastructure (mainly energy and transport) and mining.

Box 2.1. **Moving towards a new Latin America-China partnership** (cont.)

To benefit from these trends and face their accompanying challenges effectively, Latin America should diversify and upgrade its production structure, and advance in its integration. China's shift towards consumption, and its changes due to the urbanisation and consolidation of its middle class, will reduce demand for many commodities (notably some metals and energy). However, the changes open opportunities for Latin American exports in agro-food and service sectors. To capture these opportunities fully, Latin America could attempt to position firms in higher value-added stages, incorporating various types of services. Finance (investment and loans) will continue to push the association with China beyond trade, but it requires better regulations, stronger government capacities to develop bankable region-wide projects, environmental sustainability and a stronger commitment to transparency. Finally, technical exchanges between China and Latin America, such as the science and technology schemes with Argentina, Brazil, Chile and Mexico, are mutually beneficial.

Figure 2.2. **Contribution to global GDP growth, by areas**
(percentages)

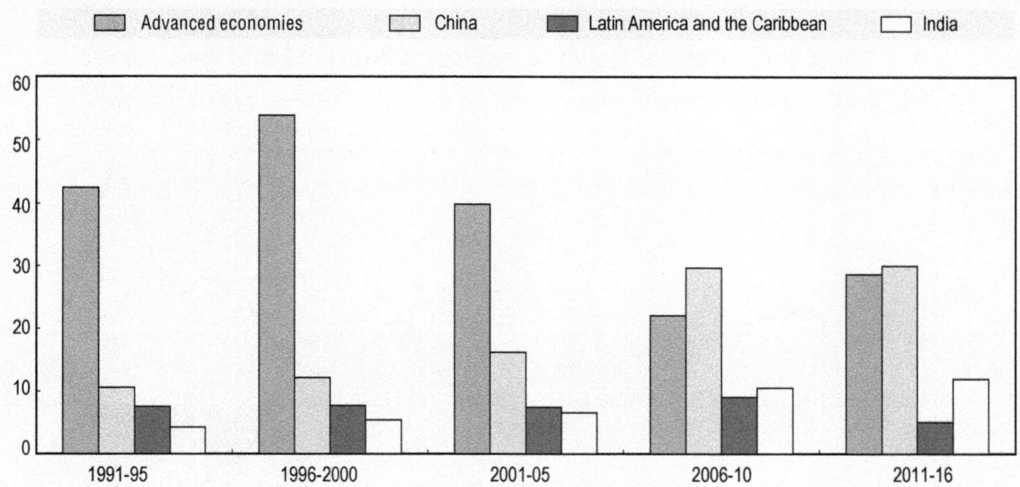

Note: Latin America covers 32 economies from Latin America and the Caribbean. The "advanced economies" category includes 37 countries.

Source: OECD/CAF/ECLAC calculations based on IMF (2016), *World Economic Outlook* database, www.imf.org/external/pubs/ft/weo/2016/01/weodata/weoselgr.aspx .

StatLink http://dx.doi.org/10.1787/888933413753

Financial markets are becoming more volatile

Capital inflows to emerging markets have been receding and becoming more volatile. Net capital inflows to emerging economies reached a multiyear low in 2015. Markets calmly digested the anticipated increase in interest rates by the FED in December 2015. However, investors became jittery in the aftermath of the financial turmoil in China early in 2016 that took place amid deteriorating fundamentals in other emerging economies.

China accounted for a large part of the outflows from emerging markets in 2015 and 2016. To some extent this was due to external debt deleveraging rather than from agents pulling resources out of the country. However, the remaining emerging economies were not immune to swings in risk aversion. Figure 2.3 shows how portfolio inflows to emerging markets drop as risk aversion increases. Capital flows to emerging markets rebounded again in the first quarter of 2016 as fears receded about further deterioration in activity in China.

Financial volatility spiked again in the second quarter in the aftermath of *Brexit*. Sterling plunged to a 31-year low and a record USD 3 trillion was wiped off global shares within hours of the referendum result. Credit markets reacted more calmly, since solvency and counterparty risks are not at the root of the crises, as in the *Lehman episode*. Financial volatility in global markets has had an impact on Latin American economies, where bond spreads, currencies and stock markets have reflected the swings in global risk aversion (Box 2.2). Volatility subsided and losses were reversed in most markets, with only European bank's stock remaining in bearish territory. But the dust will not completely settle in the short run. This is unchartered territory, and the outcome of the negotiations between the UK and the EU will be crucial.

The long-term economic and political implications of *Brexit* remain uncertain, adding to risk aversion. This backdrop heralds a looser stance for global monetary policy; the ECB and BoJ, for example, could ease up on capital inflows, while the FED may have fewer incentives to further tighten monetary policy in 2016. Amid this uncertainty, low interest rates may give some respite for emerging market assets, but conditions for capital inflows will probably be bleaker.

Figure 2.3. **Capital flows to emerging markets and risk aversion**

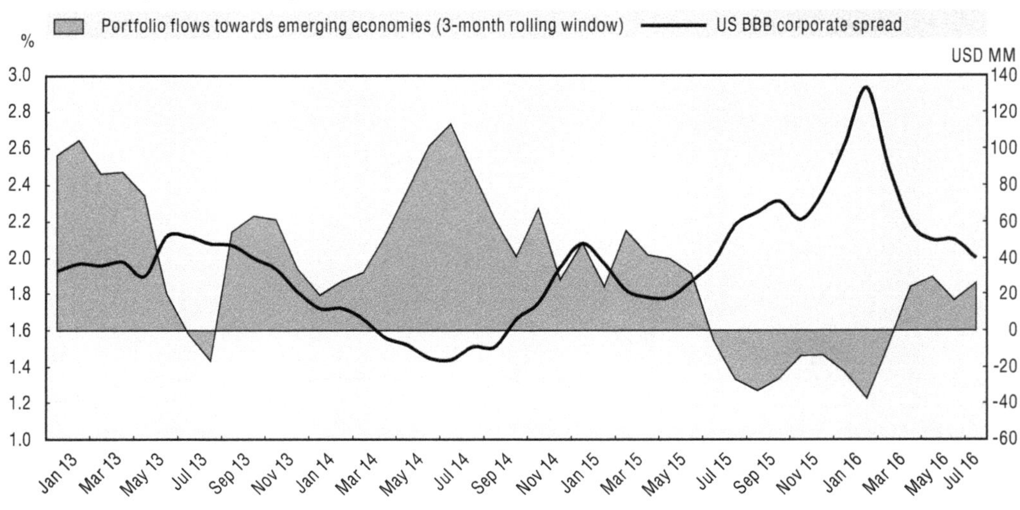

Source: OECD/ECLAC/CAF based on IIF (April 2016) and Bank of America Merrill Lynch.

StatLink http://dx.doi.org/10.1787/888933413762

> **Box 2.2. Global financial markets and volatility in LAC**
>
> Since the summer of 2015, several external and domestic episodes have stirred up volatility in Latin American financial markets. Domestic episodes have mostly been related to Brazil, following the credit downgrade in September 2015 and the political turmoil that triggered the impeachment process in the first semester of 2016 (amid a deep contraction in Brazil and a generalised slowdown in Latin America). The downgrade alone led to significant capital outflows as institutional investors unwound positions in Brazilian assets that no longer met their investment requirements. Among external episodes, the strong volatility in Chinese financial markets in the summer of 2015 and the yuan's devaluation combined with changing perceptions about the timing

Box 2.2. **Global financial markets and volatility in LAC** (cont.)

for an increase in the interest rate by the FED, which finally took place in mid-December 2015. Other external episodes include the 23 June 2016 result of the *Brexit* referendum, where citizens in the United Kingdom voted to leave the European Union.

This box briefly reports the evolution of selected financial indicators since the summer of 2015, comparing them with two major prior episodes for Latin America: the FED's announcement to withdraw quantitative easing in 2013 (tapering episode) and the 2008 Lehman financial crisis.

Since June 2015, volatility in the world markets has surpassed a few times the maximum levels of the tapering episode, but has remained below the maximum levels presented during the financial crisis (Lehman). Panel A uses the VIX Index – the standard market volatility proxy – to show the depth of volatility since 2015 in world markets, which was greater (in some cases) than that experienced in 2013 but less than during 2008. The VIX Index increased points considerably during the Chinese turmoil in local financial markets. Similarly, in the first days of the *Brexit*, the Index was at levels significantly higher than during the tapering episode in 2013. However, volatility has remained lower than during the Lehman crisis, both in levels and variation.

The political turmoil that triggered the impeachment process against President Rousseff in Brazil was an important source of volatility for regional markets. Bond spreads soared in the first quarter of 2016 to their maximum levels since the peak of the Lehman crisis. Panel B shows the evolution of bond spreads or country risk perception using the Emerging Markets Bond Index (EMBI) for Latin America (EMBI Latam). The EMBI Latam reached a maximum of 697 basis points during the impeachment process, versus a maximum of 506 basis points during the 2013 tapering crisis. Again, the volatility remains below the levels of the 2008 Lehman crisis (maximum of 895 basis points).

Figure 2.4. **Volatility index and risk aversion to Latin America 2015-16**

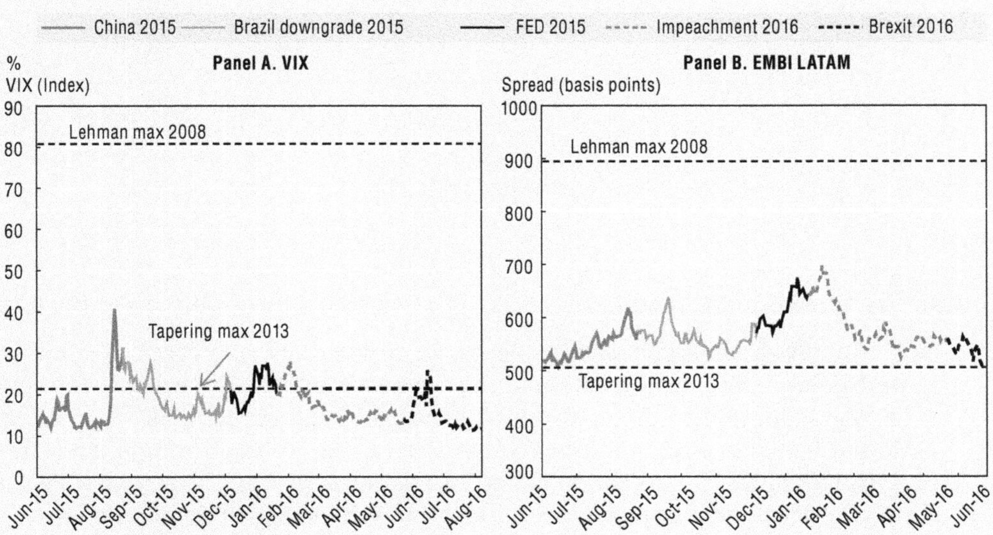

Source: OECD/CAF/ECLAC using Datastream.

StatLink http://dx.doi.org/10.1787/888933413770

Box 2.2. **Global financial markets and volatility in LAC** (cont.)

The impeachment episode in Brazil had a clear contagion effect over regional stocks and bond spreads (Figure 2.5). Latin American currencies also have depreciated since the beginning of 2015, particularly in Brazil and Colombia. The *Brexit* episode seems to have reinforced this trend. In the case of Colombia, the sharp drop in oil prices and the widening of the current account deficit added significant pressure to the currency; in Brazil, political turmoil dampened investors' appetite for Brazilian assets. Markets calmed once the new interim president assumed power in Brazil, and uncertainty abated somewhat regarding economic measures needed to get the economy on track. Some stock markets, however, experienced mild setbacks from the *Brexit* episode. Since the beginning of 2016 the currencies are no longer depreciating as quickly; different interventions by central banks on foreign exchange markets might have helped to restrain volatility.

Figure 2.5. **Financial volatility in selected Latin American economies, 2015-16**

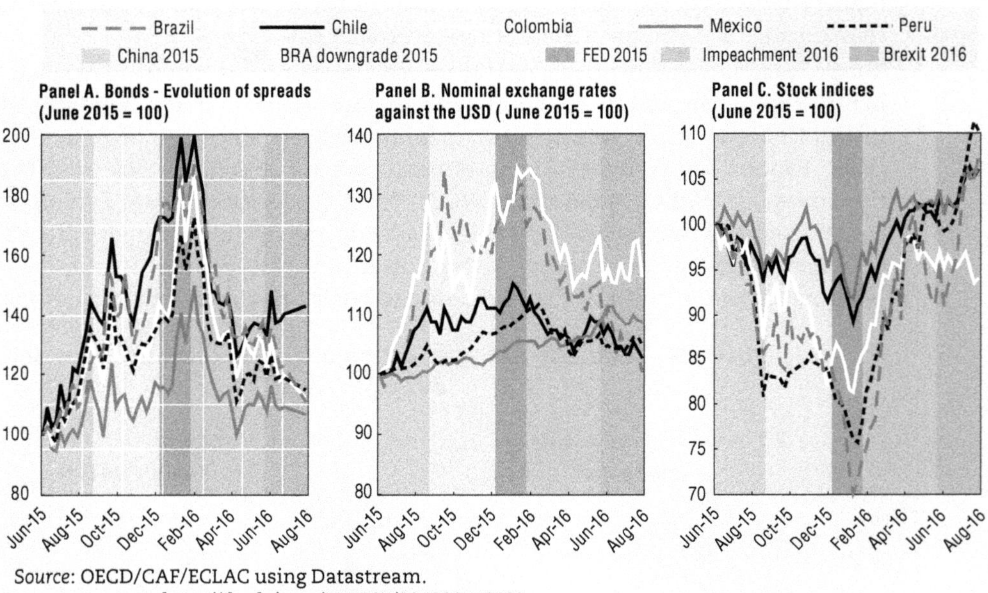

Source: OECD/CAF/ECLAC using Datastream.

StatLink http://dx.doi.org/10.1787/888933413783

Commodity markets are stabilising, but high prices are probably gone for a long time

Supply and demand developments, along with concerns about the Chinese economy, were behind the slump in commodity prices early in 2016. In a context of fragile economic growth, commodity prices dropped because of increased shale oil production in the United States in 2015, additional oil production from Iran and Iraq, and the decision of countries of the Organization of the Petroleum Exporting Countries (OPEC) not to prop up oil prices. Increased production together with sluggish demand created a surplus of about 3.5 million barrels per day (mbd) in 2015, according to the International Energy Agency (IEA), driving prices to 12-year lows in the first quarter of 2016.

Oil prices regained some footing in the second quarter, owing to supply factors. High-grading apparently ran its course and the dramatic decline in investment of the previous year led to a drop in non-conventional crudes in the United States. In addition, supply disruptions in Canada and Nigeria contributed to higher oil prices. Prices, however, receded again in the third quarter as some supply disruptions were short-lived. Aside from fundamentals, commodities have a growing presence in futures markets (including their derivatives), creating greater synchronicity in price movements among them and between their prices and stock markets; this may add volatility to commodity prices. As excess supply clears, commodity prices may start to stabilise. However, the high prices of the past may not be back for some time. No major rebound in global demand is expected. Prices are expected to be between USD 42 and 45 per barrel by the end of 2016, climbing to a range of USD 45 and 55 per barrel in 2017 (Figure 2.6). These higher prices should once more pave the way for non-conventional producers, while production from OPEC countries is expected to increase.

Non-energy commodity prices continued to decline in 2016, although at a much more moderate pace than energy prices. Metal prices also declined owing both to oversupply (as new capacity entered production) and diminishing demand from emerging economies, particularly for industrial metals. Favourable harvests and weaker than expected effects related to *El Niño* also weakened agricultural prices. On the other hand, precious metal prices increased from stronger demand for safe havens during episodes of volatility in financial markets.

Figure 2.6. **Commodity prices outlook**

(index, 2005=100)

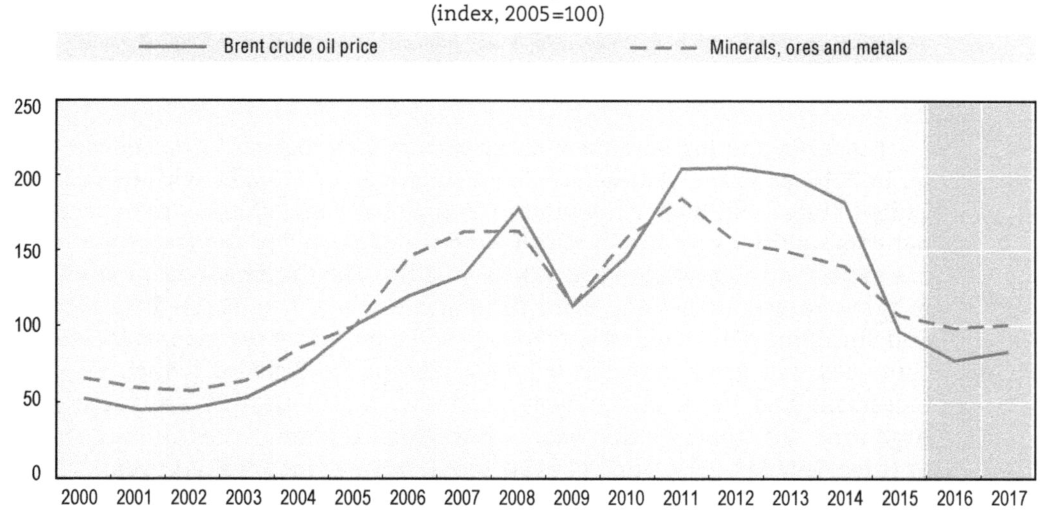

Note: Forecast based on OECD *Economic Outlook* database 99.

Source: OECD *Economic Outlook* 99 database; and International Energy Agency, *Oil Market Report*.

StatLink http://dx.doi.org/10.1787/888933413795

Macroeconomic trends in Latin America: Still looking for potential

A challenging macroeconomic short term

Latin America is undergoing a major slowdown in activity as global growth stabilises at modest rates. While only four countries will show negative GDP growth in 2016 (Argentina, Brazil, Ecuador and Venezuela), there is a general slowing of activity. This reveals not just the exposure of the region to external shocks, but also structural weaknesses that undermine potential output growth. In the baseline scenario, output will contract again in 2016, between -0.5% and -1%, exhibiting a modest rebound in 2017. The balance of risks in Latin America remains tilted to the downside; the main risk is a major drop of growth in China – a so-called hard landing (Figure 2.7). A more subdued recovery in the United States would also dent growth in the region.

Figure 2.7. **GDP growth in Latin American economies with different scenarios for China**

(percentage annual)

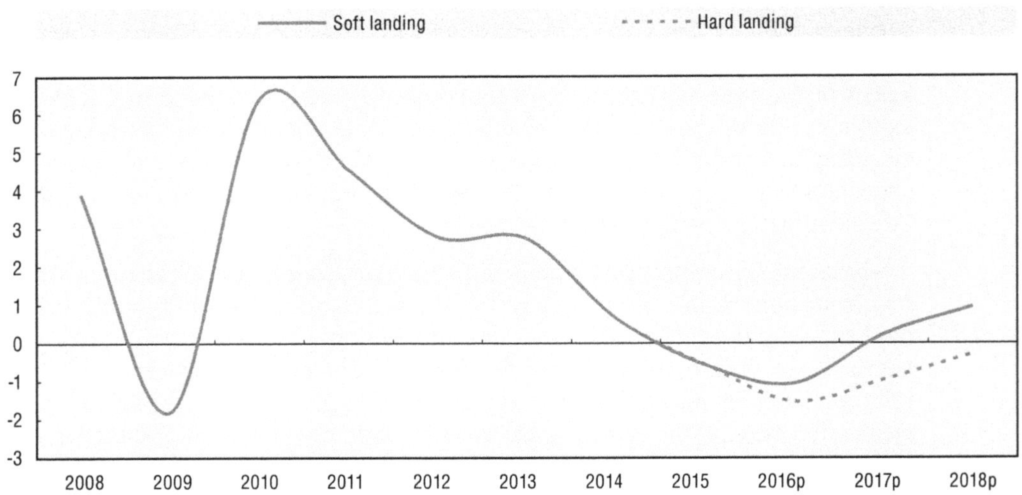

Note: Weighted average for Argentina, Brazil, Chile, Colombia, Mexico, Peru, Uruguay and Venezuela. The soft landing refers to a GDP growth rate in China of 6.6% in 2016, 6.4% in 2017 and 6.0% in 2018. The hard landing refers to a GDP growth rate of 5.8% in 2016, 4.3% in 2017 and 3.6% in 2018. Simulations are from a Bayesian Global VAR for all countries, except for Venezuela, where projections are from an individual model.

Source: OECD/CAF/ECLAC simulations, based on a Global Bayesian VAR model.

StatLink http://dx.doi.org/10.1787/888933413807

However, the region shows an important heterogeneity that needs to be factored in. In 2016, as in the year before, Latin American economies with more linkages to the United States and higher integration into global value chains are expected to outgrow net commodity exporters in South America. Mexico and Central American economies are expected to grow between 2.3-6% in 2016. The Caribbean economies are expected to grow between 0.5-4.4%; Saint Kitts and Nevis will grow slightly above this range, and Suriname and Trinidad and Tobago will experience recessions. Meanwhile, Andean countries will grow between 0.5-4.5%, except for Ecuador (which will experience a recession) and Venezuela (whose economy is still sharply contracting). Activity in Argentina will contract this year, while Brazil remains stuck in its deepest recession in three decades. A rebound is expected in most economies next year, while Venezuela would still be contracting.

This heterogeneity can be illustrated in the cyclical position of countries placed within a stylised economic cycle. Figure 2.8 plots countries' output gap in 2016 based on forecasts of the OECD, Development Bank of Latin America (CAF) and International Monetary Fund (IMF). It places countries to the left or right of the trough depending on the projected variation in 2016 and 2017. Most countries in South America exhibit negative output gaps, notably Argentina, Brazil, Uruguay and Venezuela, but also Chile, Colombia and Ecuador. Weak output still lies ahead until these economies reach a trough in the cycle, although with different intensities. For example, the 2016 contraction in Brazil is expected to be slightly milder than in the previous year, and the economy might grow very modestly at the end of 2017. Activity in Argentina will suffer a mild setback in 2016 as a result of fiscal and relative price adjustments, but it is expected to rebound in 2017. Growth is starting to accelerate in Peru and close the output gap, while signs of a rebound remain elusive in Chile. In contrast, supported by the recovery in the United States and lower energy prices, Central American and Caribbean countries are close to their trend rate of economic growth. English-speaking Caribbean economies seem to be rising to their potential output given their link to the United States and the United Kingdom, with fiscal sustainability being their main risk ahead.

Figure 2.8. **An illustration of the cyclical position of selected Latin American and Caribbean economies**

(2016, deviations from trend using HP filter)

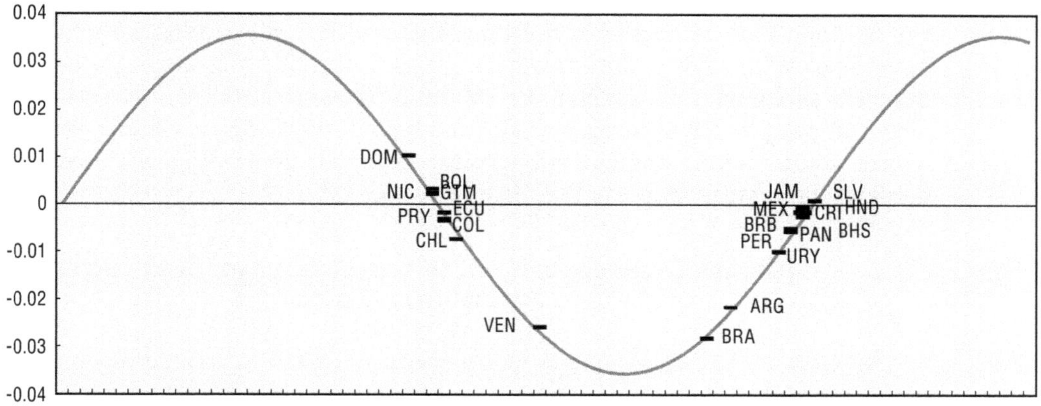

Note: The output gap is calculated as a deviation from trend using Hodrick-Prescott (HP) filter (lambda=6.25). Countries are placed depending on output gap level in 2016 and its projected evolution. The figure depicts a stylised cycle for presentation, and should not be understood as a country forecast.

Source: OECD/CAF/ECLAC calculations based on IMF(2016), *World Economic Outlook* database, www.imf.org/external/pubs/ft/weo/2016/01/weodata/weoselgr.aspx and *OECD Economic Outlook* Vol. 2016/1 for Chile and Mexico.

StatLink http://dx.doi.org/10.1787/888933413812

The slowdown has mostly affected private investment; public investment did not increase to compensate for the decline in private investment. This has negative implications for productivity and competitiveness (OECD/CAF/ECLAC, 2015). In the long term, new investment embedding the latest innovations and technological advances is a key channel through which capital accumulation enhances productivity. Besides, in the short run, investment has a positive impact on other components of aggregate demand through its multiplier effect (Box 2.4).

The policy space and macroeconomic conditions

The current slowdown has reduced space for demand-side policies in Latin America. In many cases the space for both fiscal policy (high fiscal deficits and debt levels) and monetary policy (inflation pressures) has relatively diminished. Nevertheless, different growth performance and distinct policy frameworks also imply significant differences across the region in terms of the policy space.

External conditions differ among sub-regions, but remain challenging

Current account balances improved for net energy importers in Central America and the Caribbean, favoured by a decline in fuel costs, and higher remittances and tourist flows from the United States. In contrast, current account deficits widened substantially for net commodity exporters in South America, surpassing 5% of GDP in several countries. Nonetheless, Central America and the Caribbean still exhibit larger deficits than the South American economies and Mexico. In response, countries with flexible regimes have used the exchange rate to absorb part of the trade shock.

Commodity-linked currencies experienced a large blow from both lower prices and the appreciating US dollar (Figure 2.9). The Colombian peso, the Brazilian real and the Mexican peso have shown the most acute depreciations, while the Argentinean peso was allowed to float by the end of 2015. Central bank intervention is containing the decline of some currencies, most notably the Peruvian sol, but also limiting the possibilities of an adjustment in some fixed regimes such as the Plurinational State of Bolivia (hereafter Bolivia). Most countries with weaker currencies have not gained a competitive edge. On the one hand, since countries hold trade ties with other economies whose currencies have also weakened, competitiveness gains may not be as large as depicted by the bilateral exchange rate against the US dollar (Powell, 2016). On the other hand, even with competitive advantages, soft global demand may limit increasing exports. In other words, adjustment in the current account deficits is generally due to weaker domestic demand dampening imports than from stronger exports.

Figure 2.9. **Exchange rates of selected Latin American currencies against the US dollar**

(100 = 2011)

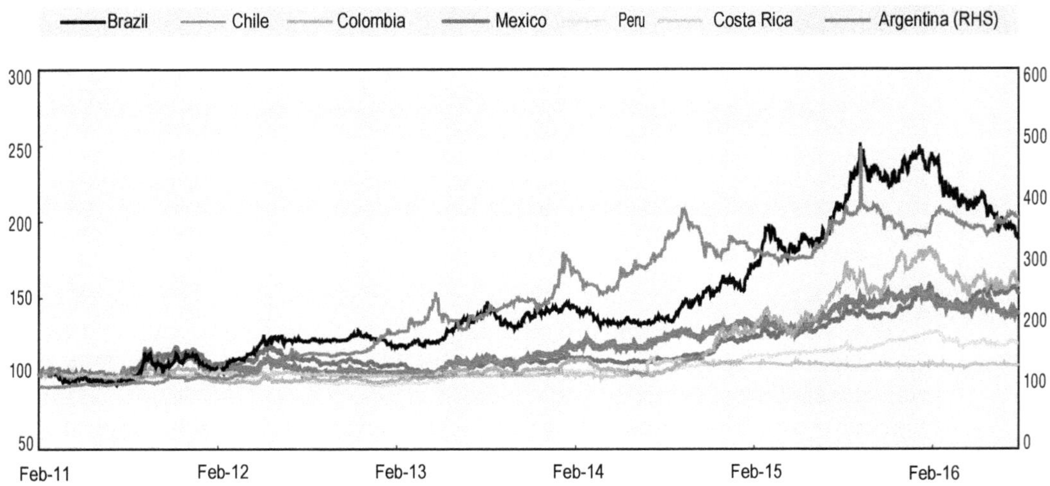

Source: OECD/CAF/ECLAC using Datastream.

StatLink http://dx.doi.org/10.1787/888933413823

Within this scenario of current account deterioration, Chile is so far an exception. The fall in imports started to bottom out in 2015, while exports started to grow as copper exports stabilised and non-copper exports picked up. Trade surpluses in Brazil, conversely, result from a faster fall in imports as the economy continues in recession. Industrial exports remain weak for Brazil in the face of the dramatic fall in commodity exports, although some improvement in the first semester of 2016 is apparent.

In the rest of South America's economies, current account deficits are expected to peak in 2016 or 2017 and gradually reduce to more moderate levels (Figure 2.10). In some countries, foreign direct investment (FDI) is not enough to finance such a deficit, requiring a rebalancing to avoid external instability. The adjustment seems more advanced in non-energy exporters, which suffered a decline in commodity prices earlier on; a deterioration of both exports and FDI related to commodities has affected balance of payments. In Colombia, for instance, recent evidence points to some import substitution, but exports are still falling – although at a slower pace. Trade balances are also narrowing in Central America; weaker energy prices have favoured net energy importers and Caribbean countries have captured larger inflows of tourists. The trade balance is stabilising in Mexico. After a weak first quarter in 2016, exports should gain ground as growth in the United States picks up and oil prices recover.

Figure 2.10. **Current account balances and foreign direct investment for selected Latin American economies**

(percentages of GDP)

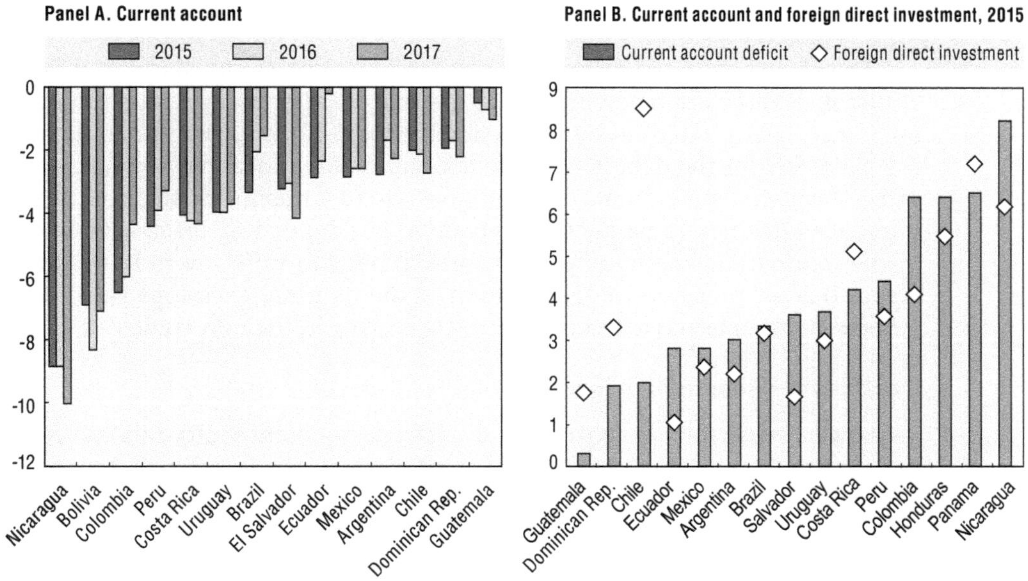

Source: OECD/CAF/ECLAC based on IMF (2016), *World Economic Outlook*, April; *OECD Economic Outlook* 99 database for Chile and Mexico; and CAF projections.

StatLink http://dx.doi.org/10.1787/888933413838

Private financing conditions and external debt deserve attention

Under the current macroeconomic context, the strong increase of Latin American non-financial corporate debt could render firms vulnerable to balance sheet risks. The strong growth of domestic credit coupled with low global interest rates have allowed firms to increase their debt levels considerably (especially international debt) since 2008. Nevertheless, low GDP growth plus low commodity prices and strong depreciations could put strong pressure on the firms' financial situation (Powell, 2016).

Falling commodity prices are affecting the non-financial corporate sector. The corporate sector of emerging economies, including Brazil, China, Mexico and the Russian Federation, has increased borrowing since the global financial crisis, with particularly high leverage in the energy sector. During 2006-14, the global stock of bonds in this sector rose from USD 455 billion to 1.4 trillion (BIS, 2015a, 2015b). In a context of greater indebtedness, falling commodity prices increase the financing costs of firms specialised in these products. The countries may compound the situation yet further if they have secured external debt against the commodity produced and exported. Higher costs and lower revenues reduce profits; when combined with deteriorating assets, this can increase the risk of default. If countries respond by cutting back production and investment in sectors with large ramifications across the rest of the production fabric, they may harm the macroeconomy.

The financial situation of the region's large hydrocarbon-producing firms has deteriorated since the 2008 crisis, particularly since 2011-12. Their return on assets has declined, while their leverage has increased. Total external debt issuance, including corporate private sector and non-financial public sector debt, began to increase in 2009; total external debt and corporate debt have grown, as in other emerging economies.

Total debt issuance rose from USD 20 billion in mid-2009 to more than USD 80 billion in October 2015, peaking at about USD 150 billion (2.8% of regional GDP) in the third quarter of 2014. Between 2010-13, Chile, Peru and Mexico showed the largest volumes of total external debt issuance relative to GDP (3.3%, 2.8% and 2.5%, respectively), while the figure was less than 1% of GDP in Argentina, Venezuela and Bolivia.

The aforementioned depreciation of local currencies can also affect firms' financial situation. Depreciation not only raises the cost of servicing debt, and thus outgoing cash, but it also swells liabilities by increasing the local-currency value of outstanding debt. If the collateral for the debt is likewise denominated in local currency, the asset will lose value through depreciation. This can give rise to a mismatch such that the firm has to purchase currency to balance its accounts. But depending on its size and importance in the market and the number of firms behaving in this way, currency purchases can create further pressure for devaluation of the nominal exchange rate; ultimately, this increases the external debt of the firms operating in the non-tradeable goods sector.

Fiscal stance deteriorates further

Lower economic growth and a setback in commodity-related revenues have deteriorated fiscal balances and increased debt levels in LAC economies. Central governments in the region had average fiscal deficits of 3% of GDP in 2015, and primary fiscal balance slipped to 1%. This represents the fourth consecutive year in which both indicators deteriorated (Figure 2.11).

Figure 2.11. **Overall fiscal and primary fiscal balances in Latin America**

(Central Government, percentages of GDP)

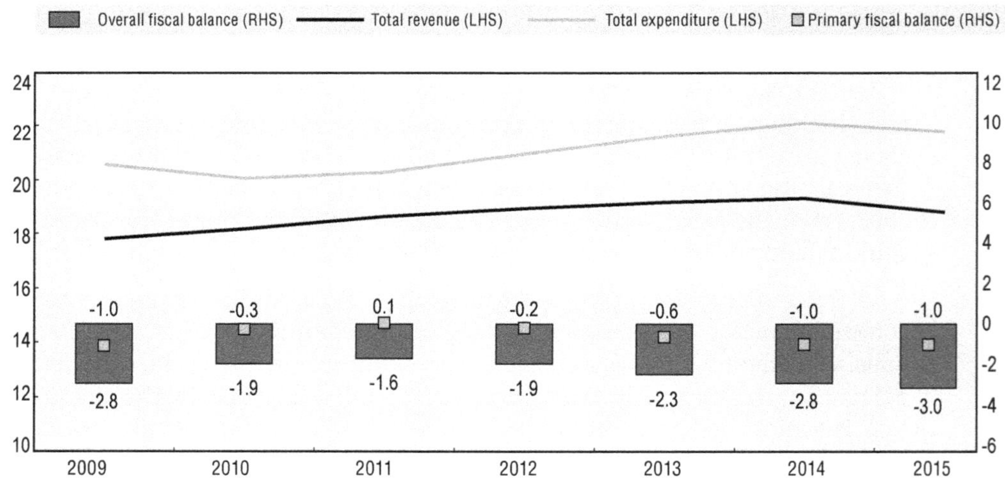

Source: OECD/CAF/ECLAC, using CEPALSTAT and official information.

StatLink http://dx.doi.org/10.1787/888933413848

Expansion of non-financial public sector debt rose by 7.9 percentage points – from 30.8 to 38.7% of GDP during 2008-15 (Figure 2.12). An increasing number of countries in the region find it difficult and costly to raise finance for their public deficits. Lower investor appetite for emerging market assets has worsened conditions for public sector borrowing, a situation unlikely to improve for a lengthy period. Thus, although public debt growth during downturns may be natural and remains below historic levels, its current pace deserves attention and action. On a positive note, the composition of the public debt has shifted. In previous decades the weight of external debt meant that fiscal sustainability depended directly on external conditions (the "twin deficits"). In recent years, domestic financing has accounted for a larger share of public debt, which has eased pressure on fiscal accounts.

Figure 2.12. **Gross public debt in Latin America**

(Central Government and Non-Financial Public Sector, percentages of GDP)

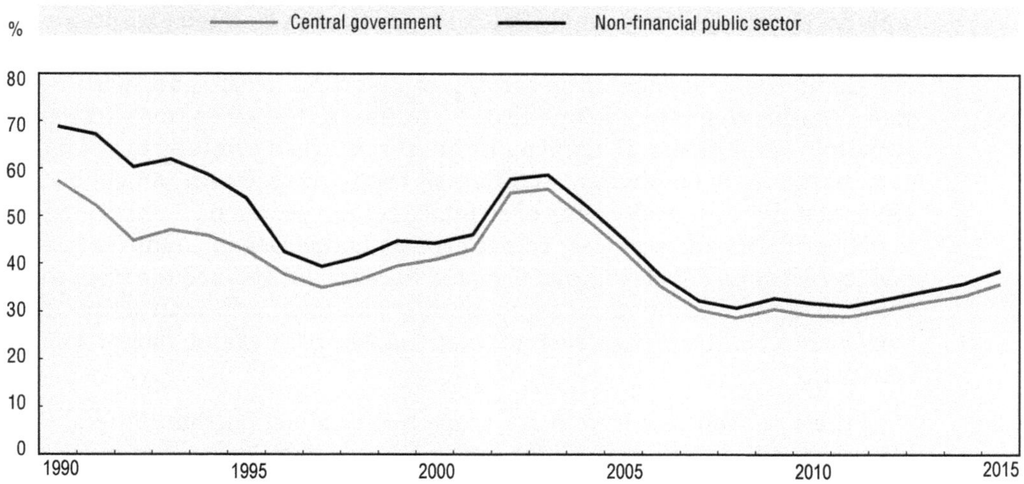

Source: OECD/CAF/ECLAC on the basis of official information.

StatLink http://dx.doi.org/10.1787/888933413859

Latin American economies exhibit significant differences also in fiscal positions. Caribbean economies present high average debt levels, around 70% of GDP, and in the case of Barbados and Jamaica above 100% of GDP, while debt levels in Peru, Chile and Paraguay are below 20% of GDP. Nevertheless, the majority of the region's economies have debt levels between 25-45% of GDP (ECLAC, 2016a). Similarly, Brazil and Venezuela posted near or above two-digit overall fiscal deficits in 2015, while Chile and Paraguay showed deficits of around 2% of GDP (Figure 2.13).

Figure 2.13. **Fiscal balance and debt levels in Latin American countries**

(percentages of GDP)

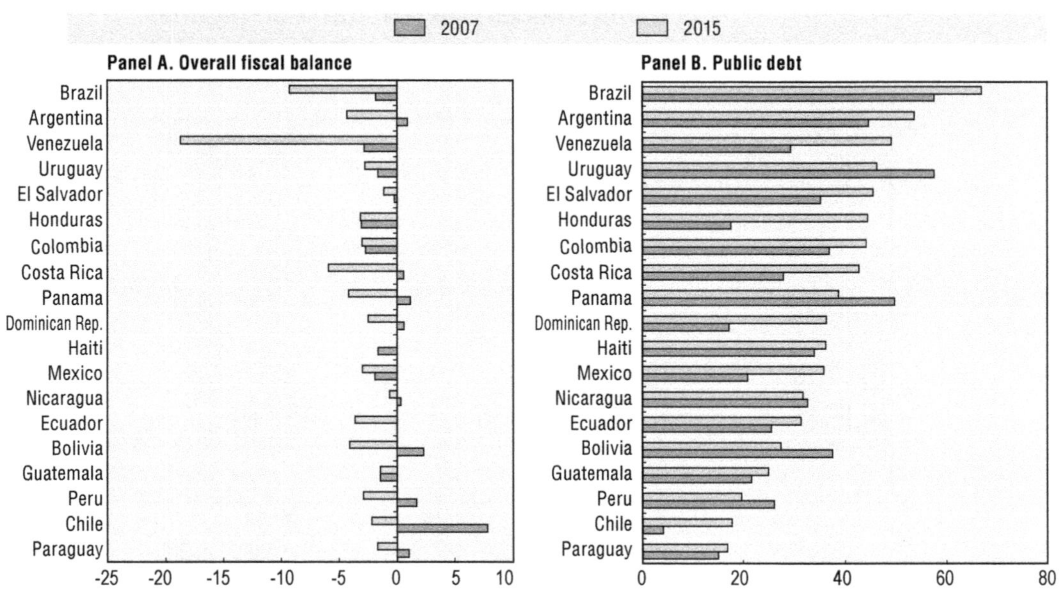

Source: OECD/CAF/ECLAC, based on national official data. For Venezuela data come from IMF (2016), *World Economic Outlook*, April.

StatLink http://dx.doi.org/10.1787/888933413861

A decade ago, stronger fiscal indicators allowed countercyclical stimuli in the aftermath of the global financial crisis in 2009. This was especially the case for countries with fiscal rules (Alberola et al., 2016). However, with counted exceptions, deteriorating fiscal positions have reduced the scope for fiscal stimulus in the region. Governments are facing the challenge of preserving or restoring fiscal space with negative output gaps. As the chapter develops in the section of "Policy options to restore inclusive growth in Latin America", fiscal authorities must tread carefully to avoid large spending cuts, particularly on physical and human capital investment. All countries need more efficient and focused allocation of available resources based on improving state capacity to deliver goods and services. This is especially the case in countries like Brazil, where high deficits and debt levels and elevated fiscal pressure force the state to cut spending. Some governments are resorting to funding schemes for infrastructure that involve the participation of the private sector (Colombia, Peru, Chile and, more recently, Brazil and Ecuador).

Different countries have more scope for fiscal action than others. Chile and Peru have accumulated public savings and moderate debt levels that allow some room to manoeuvre, although they remain bound by structural fiscal rules. The same is true for Bolivia, although the fiscal situation has deteriorated more sharply and debt levels are not as low. Other countries are already undergoing some form of fiscal consolidation, including spending cuts and tax reforms. Finally, given their low fiscal pressure and moderate debt levels, economies such as Colombia and Ecuador have space to strengthen taxation.

Monetary policy space seems limited

The scope for monetary policy is also narrowing as currency depreciations, supply shocks and changes in administrative prices in some countries pushed prices up in most economies in 2015 (Figure 2.14). As the United States moves towards "normalising" monetary policy – raising the target range for the benchmark federal fund – LAC will face an additional challenge, although some countries will cope better than others.

Figure 2.14. **Inflation rates in selected Latin America and the Caribbean economies under different inflation regimes**

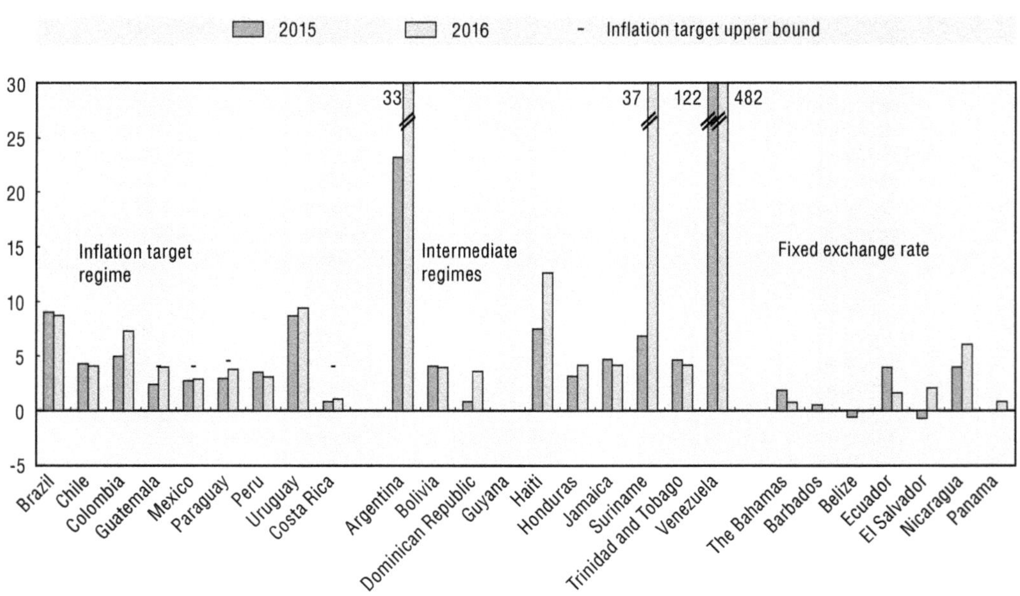

Note: Forecast for 2016 based on IMF WEO database.

Source: OECD/CAF/ECLAC, adapted from Powell (2016) using IMF WEO database.

StatLink http://dx.doi.org/10.1787/888933413871

In particular, the persistence and scale of the depreciation have shored up inflation even in countries with highly credible monetary regimes. Evidence suggests that the *pass through* has declined over the past decades owing to stronger policy (Amador et al., 2015; BDE, 2016; IMF, 2016). However, inflation remains above targets in several countries with inflation-targeting regimes. Again, the situation differs across countries and policy regimes. Inflation is lower in countries with fixed regimes, where weaker demand has absorbed the adjustment to weaker external conditions. Still, inflation rates in countries with inflation targets and fixed regimes are lower than in countries with mixed regimes where fiscal dominance has propped up inflation beyond two digits. On the other hand, some Central American and all the Caribbean economies have benefited by the decline in oil prices, keeping prices contained. Countries using the US dollar in their financial systems face the additional dilemma of avoiding sharp depreciations that can result from external shocks and lead to instability.

Against this backdrop, central banks face the dilemma of negative output gaps and inflation pressures (above the target in some cases). Initially, central banks remained in a "wait and see" mode, waiting for the first round effect of the depreciation (the change in relative prices) abated. But as expectations for medium-term inflation increased and de-anchored in 2015, most central banks became more restrictive, notably in South America. Since 2015, more countries have tightened monetary policy than loosened it or remained neutral (Figure 2.15).

Figure 2.15. **Diffusion index for monetary policy in Latin America**

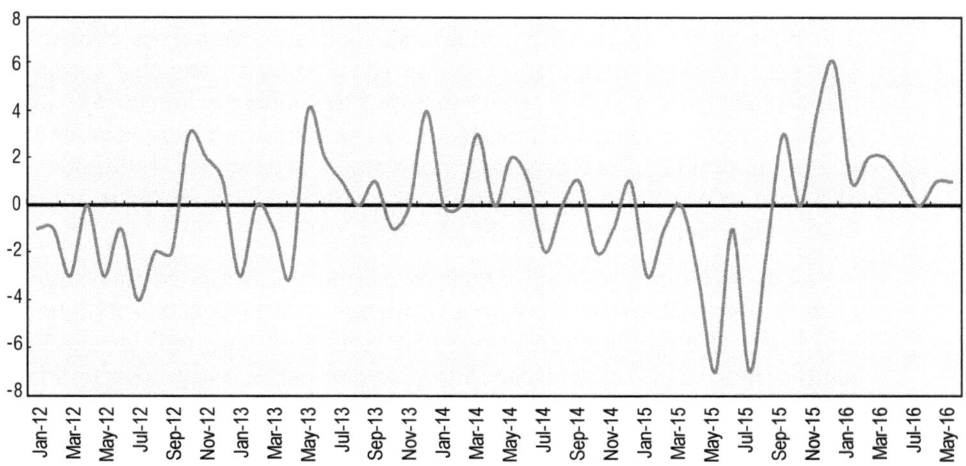

Note: The figure includes Argentina, Bolivia, Brazil, Chile, Colombia, Costa Rica, Dominican Republic, El Salvador, Guatemala, Honduras, Mexico, Nicaragua, Paraguay, Peru, Uruguay and Venezuela. The index is the sum of the number of countries that increase policy interest rates minus the number of countries that cut interest rates each period.

Source: OECD/CAF/ECLAC based on central banks' data.

StatLink http://dx.doi.org/10.1787/888933413887

Most of the currency adjustment may have already taken place, especially in commodity-exporter countries. Therefore, price pressures may start to abate in the second semester of 2016 and 2017 – also aided by soft demand – and prices should continue converging towards lower rates in most countries. This should help rein in expectations and ease pressures for central banks to relax their policy stances. This may not be the case in countries that accumulated large real exchange rate misalignments; their currencies may still slide and fuel inflation. The process of interest rate normalisation in the United States may also limit the ability of countries to loosen policy, particularly those with a larger risk of depreciation that could affect balance sheets.

Labour markets are reflecting the economic slowdown

Sluggish growth and the economic contraction from 2015 are already taking a toll on Latin American labour markets, reversing some positive trends from the previous decade. During the years of the commodity boom high levels of economic growth improved the labour market, decreasing unemployment levels, increasing the participation rate and leading to higher levels of formality and higher employment levels for women and youth (Alaimo et al., 2015). Nevertheless, since the start of the slowdown, progress in the labour market has halted and in some cases partially reversed.

Unemployment rates increased for the first time since the financial crisis, although still at relatively low levels. In 2015, urban unemployment accounted for 6.5% of the total labour force, 0.5 percentage points higher than in 2014 (ECLAC/ILO, 2016). Despite this increase urban unemployment remains below levels presented during the mid-2000s, with an average unemployment rate of 8.2% between 2005-08. The regional average for unemployment masks great diversity across countries. In 2015, unemployment rates varied the most among Caribbean economies – from Jamaica (13.5%) to Trinidad and Tobago (3.4%). In Latin America, the range is smaller – from Colombia (9.8%) to Mexico (4.3%). Similarly, the impact of the 2015 economic setback varied across the region, resulting in unemployment increases in Brazil, Costa Rica, Ecuador, Honduras, Peru, Panama and Uruguay; economies with growth rates above the region's average such as the Caribbean, Mexico or Chile experienced decreases in the unemployment rate (ECLAC/ILO, 2016, OECD, 2016a).

Participation rates have remained fairly stable, even during the commodity boom and bust years, again with considerable differences across countries. Between 2005 and 2012 average participation rate in Latin America and the Caribbean climbed from 59.7% to 60.9%. Since then, participation rates have become relatively stable, closing at 60.0% in 2015. So far this slight decline in participation has prevented steeper increases in unemployment. Participation rates vary widely across the region – from lower than 58% in Argentina, Brazil, Dominican Republic and Honduras to more than 68% in the Bahamas, Colombia and Peru (ECLAC/ILO, 2016).

High inflation rates and weak economic performance have dampened real wage growth, also with variations across countries. In 2015, because of higher levels of inflation and lower GDP growth rates wages increased in commodity-dependent economies in South America at a slower pace than for non-commodity exporters in Central America and Mexico. Specifically, real wage growth rates in those South American economies ranged between -3.2% and 1.8% with a real contraction in Brazil, but were between 1.5% and 4% in Central America and Mexico (ECLAC/ILO, 2016).

A major challenge for Latin America remains the promotion of formal jobs. In 2013, despite high levels of economic growth during the commodity boom years, only 45.2% of workers were formal, measured as those contributing to social security. Nevertheless, there is a wide variation across countries. In 2013, the formal economy provided less than 20% of jobs in Honduras, Nicaragua and Guatemala compared with more than 70% in Chile, Costa Rica and Uruguay (Alaimo et al., 2015).

Long term growth is weak

Potential output in Latin America is less robust than previously thought, as highlighted in previous editions of the *Latin American Economic Outlook*. Over the first half of this decade potential growth increased in most countries, but evidence suggests it has been declining since 2011. This result – which withstands scrutiny from methodologies as varied as real business cycle models and production-based functions (Box 2.3) – stresses the need to increase productivity.

Labour productivity, measured by GDP produced by an hour of labour, has been declining over the past decade in Latin America, relative to more advanced economies. On average, in 2016 it accounts for one-third of the labour productivity of the United States, a share lower than 60 years ago. This is in stark contrast to the performance of high-growth countries in Asia, such as South Korea or more recently China, or even commodity exporters like Australia, where relative productivity remained stable (Figure 2.16). Again, wide differences exist across countries in the region. For instance, Chile exhibited some relative productivity gains in the 1990s, but stagnated over the past decade. In Colombia, the decline in relative labour productivity stopped over the past decade, but the country did not show gains.

Figure 2.16. **Labour productivity in Latin American countries, Australia, China and South Korea**

(percentage productivity of the United States, five-year moving average, PPP)

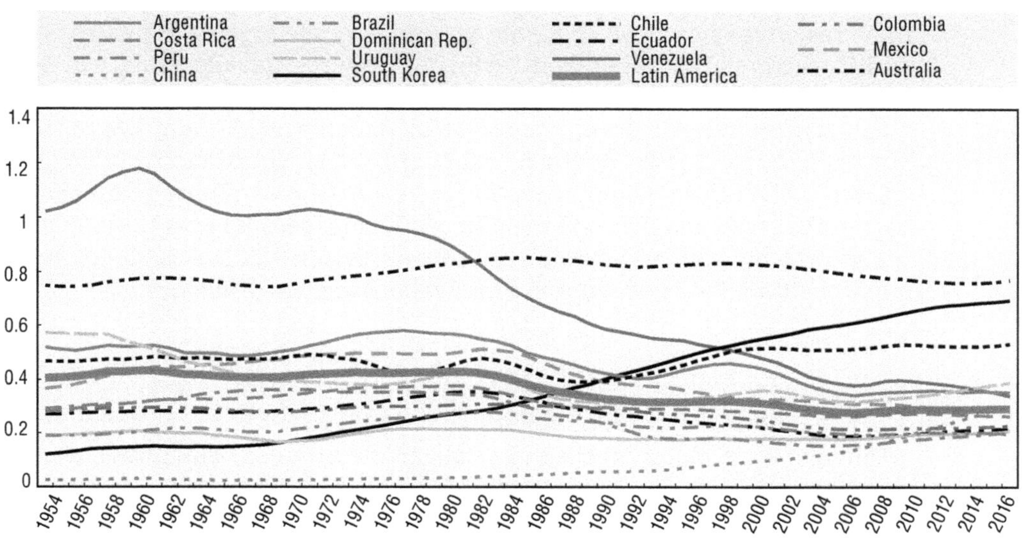

Note: "Latin America" refers to a simple average of Argentina, Brazil, Chile, Colombia, Costa Rica, Dominican Republic, Ecuador, Mexico, Peru, Uruguay and Venezuela. "PPP" refers to purchasing power parity.

Source: OECD/CAF/ECLAC based on "The Conference Board" (2016), *The Conference Board Total Economy Database™*, May.

StatLink http://dx.doi.org/10.1787/888933413896

The lack of productivity convergence stems from a combination of factors; from low savings and poor use of them, to less dynamic capital accumulation, low efficiency in factor utilisation and limited labour contribution to growth (Pagés, 2010; IMF, 2013; Powell, 2015; Carvallo and Serebrisky, 2016). Similarly, poor infrastructure quality has undermined regional integration. In combination with measures to enhance competition, better integrated regional markets can offer opportunities to meet larger consumer demands, achieve economies of scale and attract greater foreign direct investment. Improved infrastructure and logistics performance are needed to bolster structural change and strengthen regional integration (OECD/CAF/ECLAC, 2013). Under-investment in intangible assets (Daude and Fernández-Arias, 2010) such as knowledge-based capital, coupled with poor returns on physical capital and completion, are also at the root of low levels of productivity growth (OECD, 2016b). Skills and innovation are crucial since Latin American firms are 3 times more likely than South Asian firms and 13 times more likely than Pacific Asian firms to face serious operational problems owing to a shortage of human capital (OECD/CAF/ECLAC, 2014; Melguizo and Perea, 2016). In recent years, the dramatic drop in commodity prices curtailed incentives to further increase investment, particularly in the energy and mining sectors. Slower growth also reduced investment incentives in other sectors. At the same time, tighter finance made investment generally more expensive, while currency depreciation increased the cost of imported capital. This can partly be explained by weak demand and excess capacity that give firms little incentive to invest, coupled with public cuts in investment in response to deteriorating public finances (Ollivaud, Guillemette and Turner, 2016).

Subdued prospects for potential growth in the region are also due to a long-standing shortfall in total factor productivity (TFP). In fact, the growth gap between Latin America and emerging Asia during the past decade is attributed largely to lower TFP growth. Latin America's sound macroeconomic management has not been accompanied by significant structural change. An efficient allocation guarantees that factors are employed where their returns are higher, but this is rarely achieved, especially in developing countries. Within industry, dispersion in TFP is larger in Latin America than in developed countries (Hsieh and Klenow, 2010). The region needs to address supply-side bottlenecks and shift more resources from low- to higher-productivity sectors and activities both across and within sectors. The gains from reducing resource misallocation can be substantial. Estimates for Latin America suggest that correcting the misallocation of factor among plants within industries would increase increments of TFP from 45% to 127% depending on the country (Busso, Madrigal and Pagés, 2013). Other factors also affect potential growth in the region. Regulations that increase the cost of hiring formal workers, create barriers to credit and increase the cost of credit (especially over the long term) constrain the growth of small and medium-sized enterprises (OECD/ECLAC, 2012). Similarly, the mentioned low levels of skills and innovation dampen efficiency.

Box 2.3. **Measuring potential output growth in Latin America**

Different estimation methods empirically confirm the decline of potential output growth in Latin America. Box 2.3 presents two original exercises for the region, using widely accepted methodologies: a real business cycle model and a production-based function.

Real business cycle model

Output trend is estimated following a real business cycle (RBC) model for a small open economy, following Alvarez-Parra, Brandao-Marques and Toledo (2013). The model incorporates a stochastic trend as in Aguiar and Gopinath (2007) and Garcia-Cicco, Pancrazi and Uribe (2010).

The model has two sectors that produce durable and non-durable goods. Each sector has a production function $Y_t = A_t K_t^{\alpha} (\Gamma_t L_t)^{1-\alpha}$, where $0 < \alpha < 1$, and K_t and L_t are capital and labour inputs. The variables A_t and Γ_t represent a transitory productivity shock and the stochastic trend, respectively. The latter is given by the nonstationary process $\Gamma_t = \log \Gamma_{t-1} + g_t$, where g_t is the stochastic trend growth rate. We assume that g_t evolves according to the following autoregressive process $g_t = (1-\rho_g)\mu_g + \rho_g g_{t-1} + \varepsilon_t$, where μ_g is the average trend growth rate, and ε_t is an independent and identically distributed (i.i.d) shock normally distributed with mean zero and standard deviation σ_g. The transitory productivity shock A_t is characterised by the following autoregressive process: $\log A_t = \rho \log A_{t-1} + v_t$.

The stochastic trend Γ_t is common to both sectors, but each sector has its own transitory productivity shock (A_{td} and A_{tn}). The shocks are governed by the following seven parameters: ρ_n, ρ_d, ρ_g, σ_n, σ_d, σ_g and μ_g. These first six parameters are estimated by

Box 2.3. Measuring potential output growth in Latin America (cont.)

Bayesian methods and μ_g calibrated to match the observed average quarterly GDP growth rate for each country. We use quarterly data on GDP, aggregate consumption and the net exports-GDP ratio for six Latin American countries (Argentina, Brazil, Chile, Colombia, Mexico and Peru).

As a key feature of the model, countries have a borrowing premium in international financial markets. The interest rate includes a country-risk component that depends on the cyclical conditions of the economy similar to Neumeyer and Perri (2005). A single parameter defines the elasticity of the interest rate to changes in the output gap, which we estimate alongside the six productivity parameters. The remaining parameters of the model are set following Alvarez-Parra, Brandao-Marques and Toledo (2013), and are common across economies.

The (log) trend Γ_t and its growth rate g_t together with its moving average is highlighted for each country (Figure 2.17). These series are built by backing out the implied productivity shocks using the Kalman filter given the estimated parameters.

Figure 2.17. RBC GDP trend and GDP trend growth in selected Latin American economies (in logs)

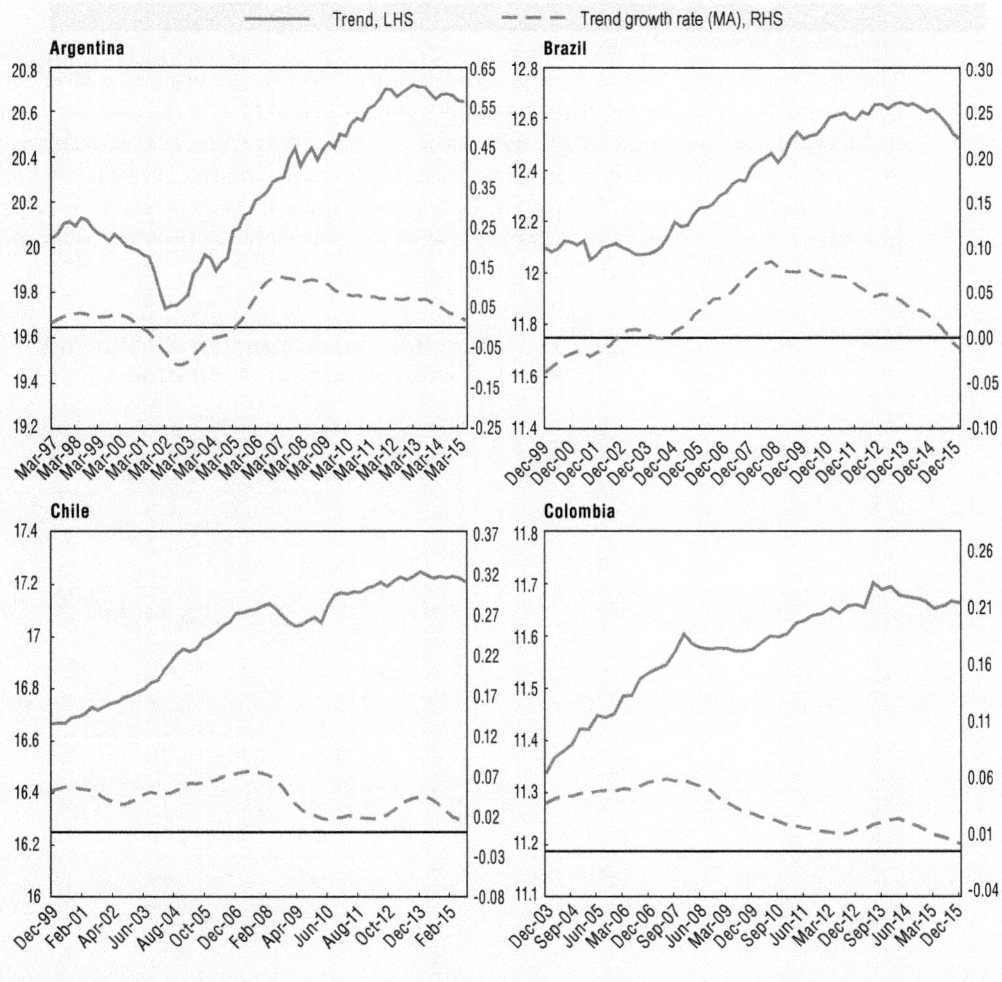

Box 2.3. **Measuring potential output growth in Latin America** (cont.)

Figure 2.17. **RBC GDP trend and GDP trend growth in selected Latin American economies (in logs)** (cont.)

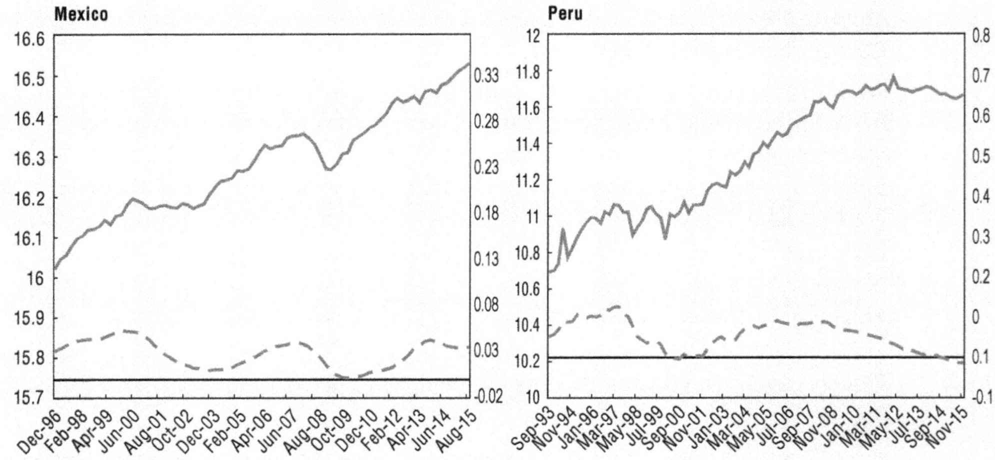

Source: OECD/CAF/ECLAC.

StatLink http://dx.doi.org/10.1787/888933413903

Production-based function

This methodology is based on a production function that incorporates stock of capital and labour, and also corrects for the quality of capital and of labour in the lines suggested by Jorgenson and Khuong (2010). Results show that, on average, the slowdown starts in 2013 and is related to the drop in the stock of capital that, in turn, reflects the drop in the investment rate. As well, the drop in GDP trend shows a major problem in productivity growth. We also observe a different trajectory between South America and Central America and Mexico (Figure 2.18).

Figure 2.18. **Production-based function GDP trend in selected Latin American economies**

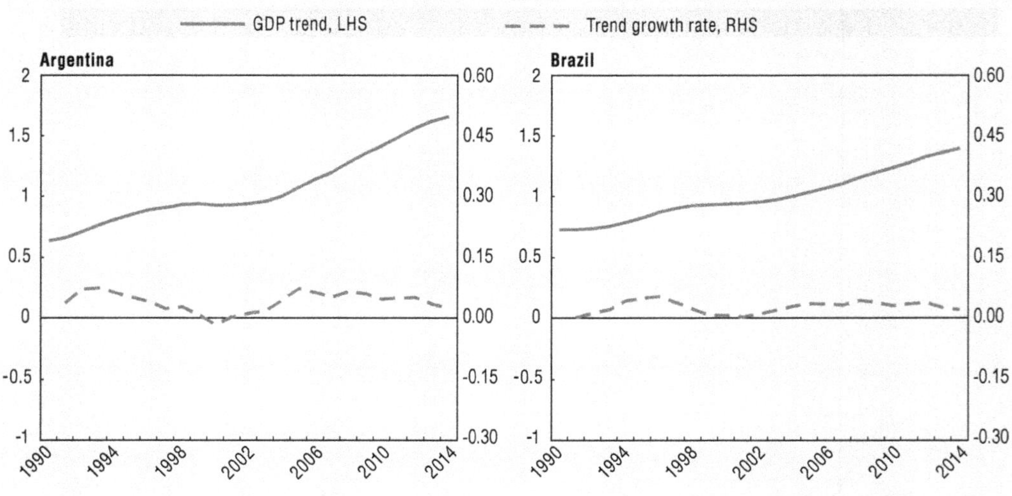

Box 2.3. **Measuring potential output growth in Latin America** (cont.)

Figure 2.18. **Production-based function GDP trend in selected Latin American economies** (cont.)

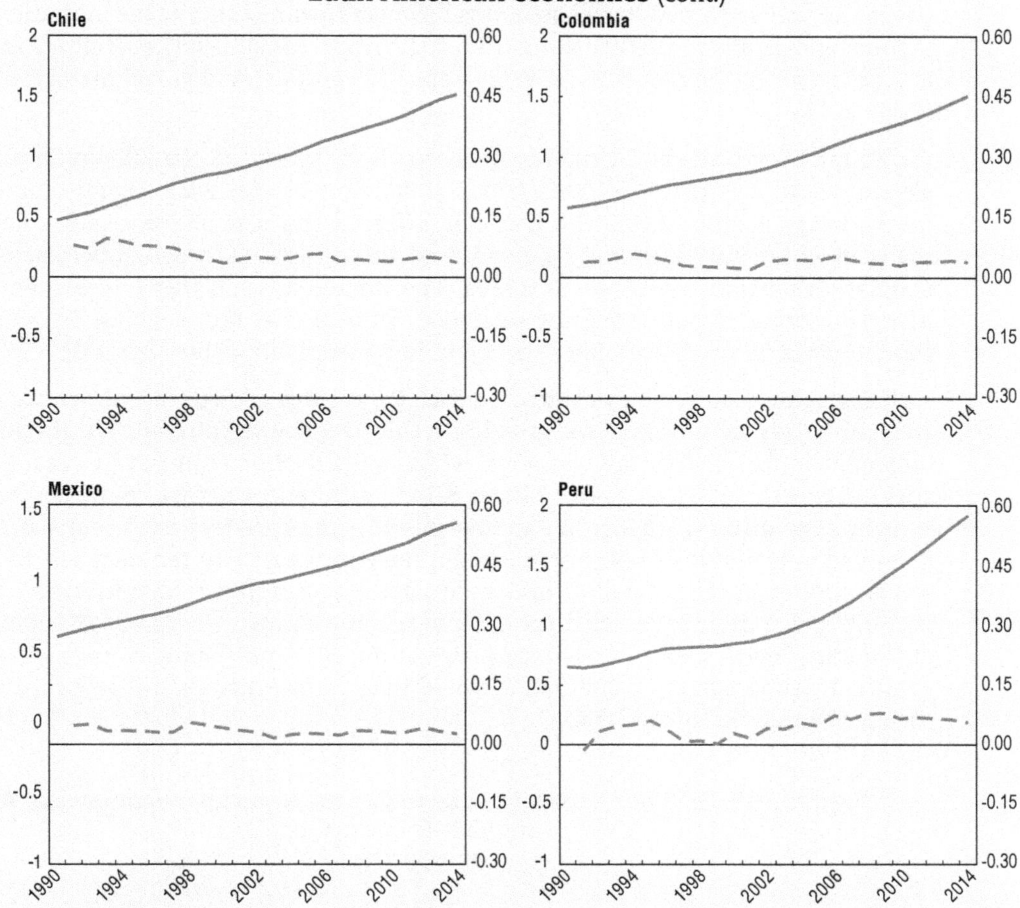

Source: OECD/CAF/ECLAC.

StatLink http://dx.doi.org/10.1787/888933413919

The middle-income trap, a threat for the region

The middle-income trap (MIT) stands as a potential, challenging scenario for Latin American economies. This phenomenon refers to the long-lasting slowdown in growth that many countries endure when they approach middle levels of per capita income. In this scenario, the rapid growth registered by some countries at early stages of development is followed by persistent stagnation (Eichengreen, Park and Shin, 2011; Felipe, Abdon and Kumar, 2012; Zhuang, Vandenberg and Huang, 2012; Aiyar et al., 2013; OECD, 2013a). Growth in low-income countries arises essentially through reallocating labour from low- to high-productivity activities and industries. However, arriving at middle-income levels usually requires new engines of economic growth, which are based on capital- and skill-intensive manufacturing and service industries (Kharas and Kohli, 2011). Economies that successfully transition to these activities have requirements such as a large pool of skilled labour, favourable investment rates, a developed system of national innovation and a macroeconomic and institutional environment conducive to entrepreneurship. Even if countries achieve this foundation, they may struggle to co-ordinate all the elements to reach the goal of productive diversification.

The MIT is traced to the inability of countries to undergo a process of structural change towards innovation and more knowledge-intensive production. Greater technology capacity provides a foundation for long-term productivity and economic growth, which paves the way for broad-based structural change towards high-value activities. In turn, technological capabilities are a function of firm and social level capabilities interacting at a point in time, and over time, within specific national and global historical contexts (Paus, 2014).

So far, only Chile and Uruguay have managed to escape the MIT in Latin America as shown in OECD/CAF/ECLAC (2015), following Felipe, Abdon and Kumar (2012) methodology (Figure 2.19). The trap has affected the rest of the region's economies, many of which have suffered recurrent and pronounced episodes of per capita income stagnation particularly after the 1980s. The middle-income trap is prevalent in Latin America owing to shortcomings related to rule of law, rent-seeking behaviours and productive structures less concentrated in knowledge-intensive activities.

Latin American economies exhibited a 2.5% average growth rate of per capita GDP in 2006-16. If they were to continue growing at this pace the region could stay in the middle-income trap for another four decades, which adds to the nearly seven decades already spent. Nevertheless, this average hides strong differences across countries: economies such as Argentina, Costa Rica or Panama should escape the trap in the early 2020s, while El Salvador, Honduras or Nicaragua might have to wait up to ten decades. In contrast, under similar assumptions, China could aspire to become a high-income country in 2016 (25 years after it reached the middle-income range). Under an alternative, more optimistic growth scenario, assuming 3.4% annual GDP per capita average growth of the commodity boom years (2006-08), it would take Latin America still around 20 years to escape the middle-income trap.

Figure 2.19. **GDP per capita in selected Latin American economies, Asia and OECD countries**

(1990 USD PPP)

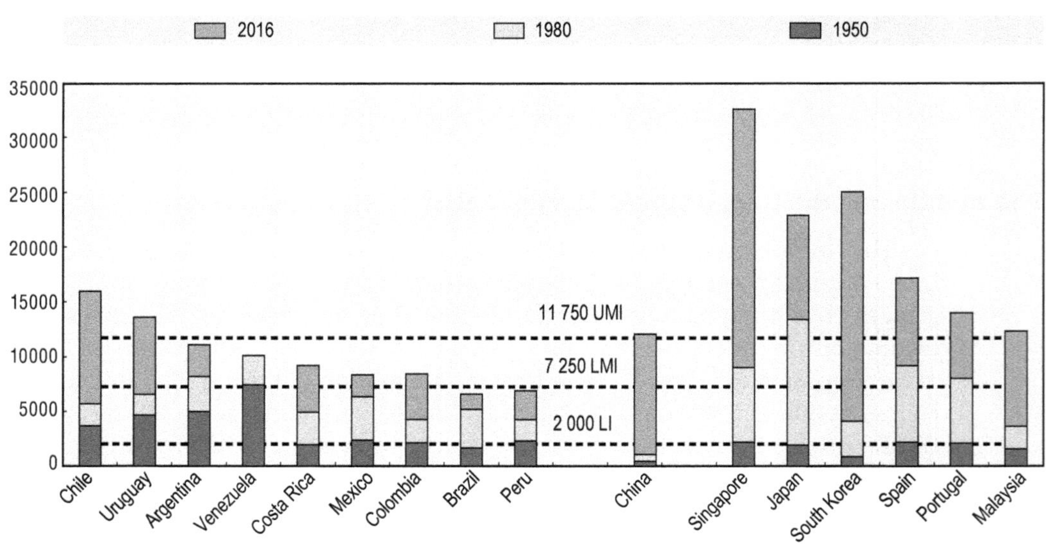

Note: LI = low income; LMI = lower-middle income; UMI = upper-middle income.

Source: OECD/CAF/ECLAC calculations based on the methodology proposed by Felipe, Abdon and Kumar (2012). Data extracted from International Monetary Fund (2016), *World Economic Outlook* database www.imf.org/external/pubs/ft/weo/2016/01/weodata/index.aspx; and Bolt and van Zanden (2014), "The Maddison Project: Collaborative research on historical national accounts".

StatLink http://dx.doi.org/10.1787/888933413924

Socio-economic progress will be tested by macroeconomic weaknesses

Growth matters because it drives improvements in people's lives, but the link between growth and people's well-being is not always straightforward and requires looking across a number of dimensions (see Annex 2.A1, "Beyond growth: measuring well-being in the LAC region"). Overall, socio-economic progress in Latin America during the last two decades has been remarkable. Between 1990-2014, poverty rates decreased from 48.4% to 28.2% of the total population according to the ECLAC definition. Some 60 million people escaped poverty, although 168 million people remain below the poverty line (for poverty and indigence measure, see methodology ECLAC, 2010). The indigence rate also declined to 11.8% in 2014, with 25 million people escaping indigence and 70 million remaining in extreme poverty (ECLAC, 2016a). Similarly, inequality decreased considerably in Latin America as the average Gini coefficient fell below 0.49 in 2010, reflecting a pace of 0.1 points a year since 2002 (Gasparini, Cruces and Tornarrolli, 2016).

In an environment of tighter labour markets and more limited space for demand policies the weaker macroeconomic context is putting this socio-economic progress to the test. Estimates for 2015 show an increase in the poverty and indigence rate as the region faced a contraction and inflation rates increased. A similar result may be expected in 2016 as the recession continues. In 2015, around 7 million Latin Americans became poor, increasing the total regional poverty rate up to 29.2% (175 million people) from 28.2% in 2014 (ECLAC, 2016a) and more than 5 million people became indigent in 2015, increasing the indigence rate by 0.6 percentage points from the year before to 11.4% (75 million people). This represents the largest increase in poverty rates since the late 1980s. More importantly, this reflects a setback in resilience shown by social indicators in Latin America over the last few decades (poverty rates did not increase in the economic slowdown of the early 2000s, nor during the financial crisis; Figure 2.20). Also, income inequality declined at a slower pace since the 2010s in Latin American economies with the exception of Colombia, Ecuador and Uruguay (Gasparini, Cruces and Tornarrolli, 2016). This "deceleration foretold" is due to the anticipated weaker impact of factors that fostered the advance: less expansion of cash programmes and of minimum wage increases, and slowdown of unemployment reduction and fertility rates falling among low-income households.

Figure 2.20. **GDP growth and poverty rates in Latin America and the Caribbean**

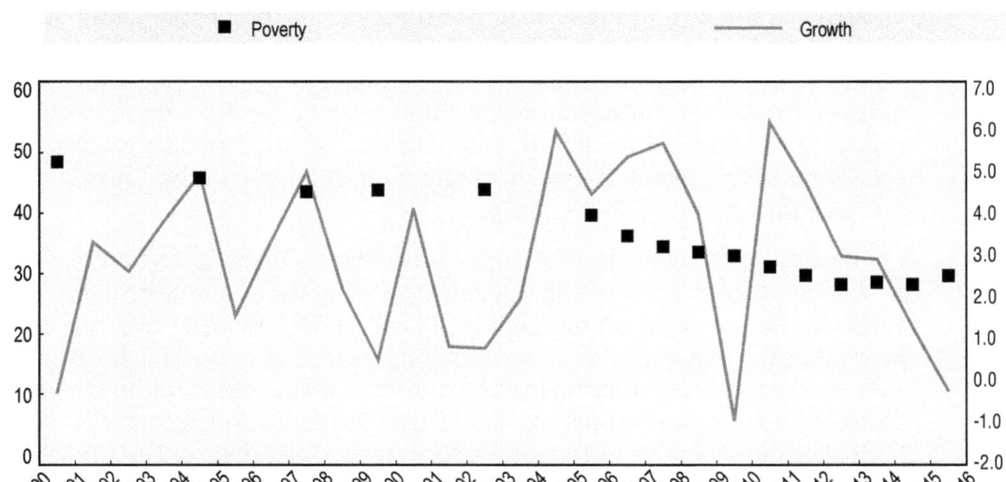

Note: Poverty rates as defined by ECLAC refer to Latin America, and annual GDP growth rates to Latin America and the Caribbean.

Source: OECD/CAF/ECLAC, based on data from ECLAC (poverty) and CEPALSTAT (GDP).

StatLink http://dx.doi.org/ 10.1787/888933413936

This scenario will also test the robustness of the middle class that emerged over the past decade in Latin America and its living standards (as first reflected in the *Latin American Economic Outlook 2011*; OECD, 2010). The percentage of the population in Latin America earning between USD 10-50 (2005 PPP) a day – considered the "consolidated middle class" – reached 35% in 2014, a significant increase from 21% in 2001 (World Bank, 2016). Also, the percentage of Latin Americans living on USD 4-10 (2005 PPP) a day – who are considered "vulnerable" – has increased steadily since 2000, reaching a peak of 39% in 2014 (Figure 2.21). That left 23% of the population living on less than USD 4 (2005 PPP) a day in 2014, which is below the moderate poverty line.

Figure 2.21. **Latin American population by socio-economic groups**

(percentage of total population)

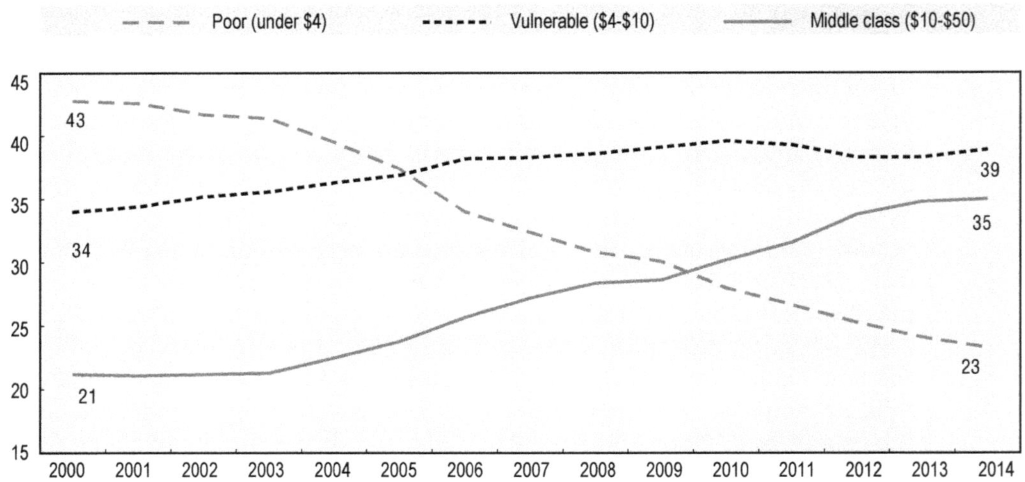

Note: No data available for 2010 and 2013.

Source: OECD and World Bank (2016) *LAC Equity Lab* tabulations of SEDLAC (CEDLAS and the World Bank) and *World Development Indicators*.

StatLink http://dx.doi.org/10.1787/888933413941

The vulnerable and consolidated middle classes emerged thanks to vibrant economic growth, buoyant labour markets and an expansion of public transfers, conditions that no longer exist. Strong macroeconomic growth and high commodity prices provided enough fiscal space to increase social transfers to the people living at the lower end of the distribution, effectively pushing them up the income scale. At the same time, hourly wage increases between 3.9-6.0% annually for those living on less than USD 10 a day pushed many Latin Americans out of poverty. But for a fraction of the population this progress was not enough to enter the consolidated middle classes. In the current economic environment, between 25 and 30 million vulnerable Latin Americans might fall back into poverty (UNDP, 2016).

Related to these socio-economic shifts, the increase in formality rates (measured as workers contributing to social security) during the commodity boom could be under threat in the current economic context. Between 2003 and 2013 informality decreased on average in the region by 7 percentage points, reaching a rate of 54.8% in 2013 (IDB, 2016). However, high informality rates still characterise the region, although with differences across countries (Bosch, Melguizo and Pagés, 2013). In 2013, informality is still relatively high in economies such as Honduras, Nicaragua, Guatemala or Peru, reaching more than 80% of workers. Conversely, informality rates in Chile, Costa Rica and Uruguay are below 40%.

The relevance of the productivity-inclusiveness nexus

There is increasing evidence that productivity and equality are linked, with both trends sharing common root causes. Policy settings and regulations relating to product, financial and labour markets, innovation and skills policies are behind suboptimal outcomes observed in OECD economies in terms of productivity and inclusiveness (OECD, 2016c).

In particular, ample empirical evidence points to the key role of human capital for individual earnings and aggregate productivity growth of countries. Unequal distribution of skills within the population is positively correlated with higher wage inequality. Productivity and inequality in Latin America should therefore be addressed in an integrated way. For the region, addressing these links is crucial, given that unequal access to quality education (see OECD/CAF/ECLAC, 2014, for Latin America), health technology and formal jobs might be responsible for both inequality and low productivity.

Policy options to restore inclusive growth in Latin America

To reignite growth in the region, Latin America needs to combine the emphasis on structural policies with investments in physical and human capital to increase productivity and inclusiveness. Commodity booms and short-term capital inflows have done little to increase the region's potential output (OECD/CAF/ECLAC, 2014). Structural reforms are needed to increase productivity, reduce inequalities and overall boost potential output. For instance, reforms that aim to improve product market regulation and increase knowledge-based capital (KBC) investment could significantly increase competition, boost productivity growth and thus potential output (Koske et al. 2015; ECLAC, 2015; and OECD, 2013b, 2015a, 2016b, 2016d). Similarly, there should be an emphasis on activating credible forward-looking fiscal policies and investments, notably on infrastructure and skills.

Boosting investment in difficult times

Latin America needs efficient schemes that protect investment in order to address macroeconomic volatility in the region, spur long-term growth and advance social inclusiveness. A well-structured policy regime that simultaneously defines the limits of the fiscal space and co-ordinates instruments and resources can multiply the impact of investment incentives. Credibility is fundamental; private agents should have the perception that public investment commitments will be fulfilled and not delayed as a result of financial constraints or discretionary decisions. Fiscal frameworks should therefore aim to create an investment-friendly climate through building organisational capacity and improving institutional arrangements (Carranza, Daude and Melguizo, 2014). In this way, publicly managed investment plans could contain diminishing investment rates while ensuring long-term competitiveness and productivity gains in strategic areas for structural change and support efforts to close infrastructure gaps. Investment plans may combine interactive ventures, mobilising public and private sources of funding, contributing to jobs and growth with a strategic and territorial perspective, and promoting clean and renewable energies.

The public sector can play an important part in fostering potential growth, while stabilising aggregate demand through capital expenditure. Evidence for Latin America (Box 2.4) shows that fiscal multipliers – the effects of fiscal policy on aggregate output – promote both short- and medium-term growth. This effect is even more positive in times of economic contraction, especially in low-taxation economies. As a result, adequately targeted and leveraged fiscal multipliers in the region can help counteract both the current deceleration and the downward trend in potential GDP. Unfortunately, based on fiscal consolidation goals most countries in the region are cutting capital expenditure. This is especially the case for Ecuador, Bolivia and Haiti. The few economies that have increased expenditure, such as Chile, Argentina and some Caribbean countries, have done so through current spending (Figure 2.22).

Figure 2.22. **Change in public primary expenditure in Latin American and Caribbean economies**

(2014 vs. 2015)

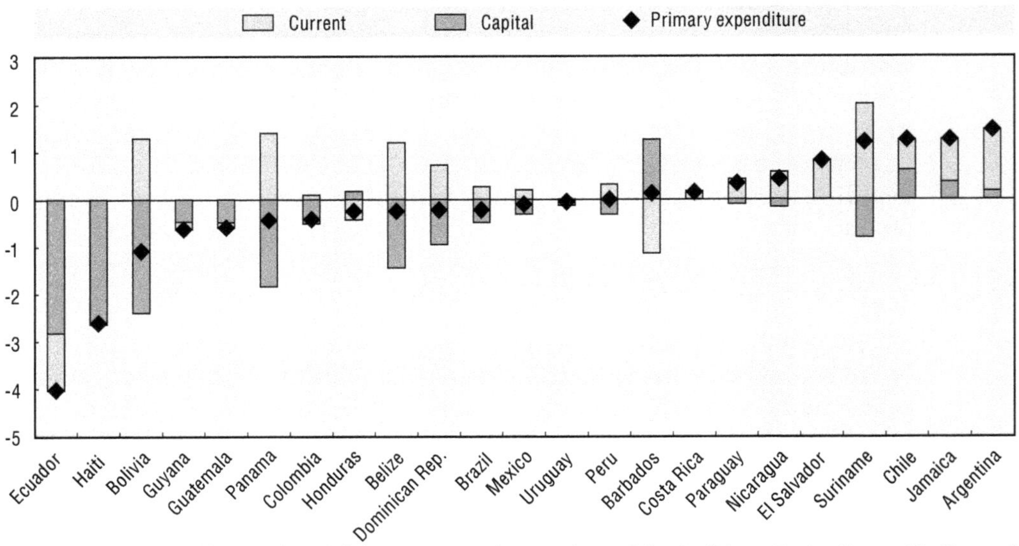

Source: Powell, A., co-ordinator,. (2016), "Time to Act: Latin America and the Caribbean Facing Strong Challenges", *2016 Latin American and Caribbean Macroeconomic Report*.
StatLink http://dx.doi.org/10.1787/888933413951

Box 2.4. Fiscal policy options: The role of fiscal multipliers

Fiscal policy can affect the performance of an economy through different channels, including through the output and income multiplier. As traditionally defined, the multiplier shows the contribution to increasing output and income as a result of an increase in expenditure or change in taxes. The global financial crisis (2007-09) re-opened the debate on the effectiveness of expansionary fiscal policies to mitigate negative effects on output and employment and, more precisely, to pave the way for recovery. The International Monetary Fund (IMF) argued in favour of a "timely, large, lasting, diversified, contingent, collective and sustainable" fiscal stimulus package (Spilimbergo et al., 2008) of 2% of world GDP; the OECD (2016a) entertained a similar view. Opinions regarding the importance of fiscal multipliers have changed over time (Blanchard and Leigh, 2013). More current research has shown it can be a powerful tool to boost short-term and long-term growth (Riera-Crichton, Vegh and Vuletin, 2015a; Riera-Crichton, Vegh and Vuletin, 2015b). Latin American countries should examine the degree to which fiscal policy through the multiplier can be an effective countercyclical tool.

An examination of the literature on the fiscal multipliers for Latin America shows that expenditure multipliers vary widely. This reflects both the use of different methodologies and the size of the fiscal multiplier, which can depend on factors such as degree of openness, exchange rates, the level of public debt and the type of fiscal policy. Similarly, it is also possible that the state of the business cycle, as well as potential "non-linearities" (such as how initial levels of government spending and taxes affect fiscal policy), may also play a role in generating different estimates. Estimates provided by Riera-Crichton, Vegh and Vuletin (2015a) for the mid-1990s until 2014 for 16 countries of Latin America show that the size of the multiplier at the regional level is 1.5 in the long run (after two years) (Figure 2.23).

Box 2.4. Fiscal policy options: The role of fiscal multipliers (cont.)

Figure 2.23. **Public expenditure multiplier for Latin America**

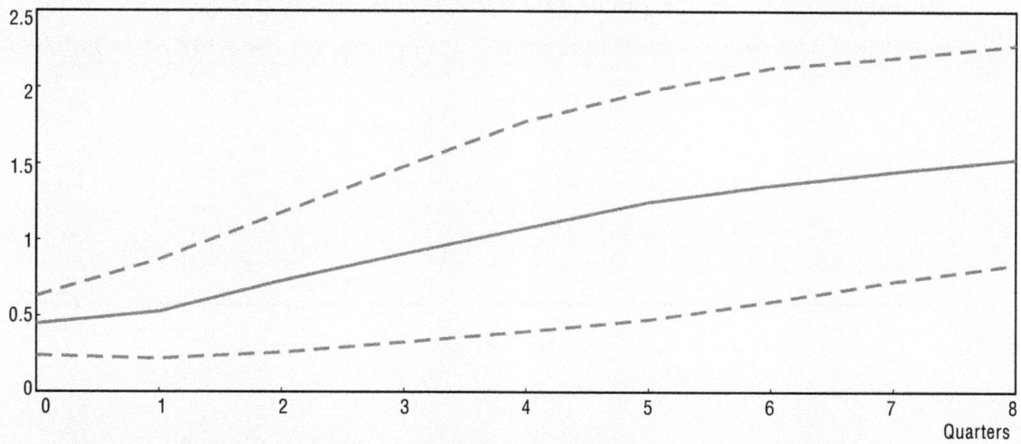

Source: Riera-Crichton, Vegh and Vuletin (2015a), *Fiscal Multipliers in Latin America*, ECLAC.

StatLink http://dx.doi.org/10.1787/888933413963

There is a sizeable heterogeneity in the behaviour of the fiscal multipliers for the 16 economies. For Argentina, the impact multiplier is neutral, but grows to 1.5 after one year, while the coefficient stabilises around 2 in the long run (after two years); this series, however, is quite noisy and cannot reject a neutral multiplier with 95% confidence. The impact multiplier in the Brazilian economy hovers around 0.7 and quickly jumps to 1.1 after half a year before stabilising around 2 in the long run. Meanwhile, the multiplier on impact for Chile is 0.5 and, as in Brazil, quickly grows to 1.1 after half a year. The Chilean multiplier in the long run is larger than in Argentina and Brazil, reaching 3.1. The multiplier on impact is around 2 in Colombia and 4 in Mexico; in both economies, the long-run multiplier ends up being very large (around 5) with series that are less noisy than the ones estimated for the previous countries (Riera-Crichton, Vegh and Vuletin, 2015a).

Riera-Crichton, Vegh and Vuletin (2015b) point out the importance of distinguishing between the effects of fiscal policy along different stages of the business cycle. Latin American economies closely follow results from industrialised countries in that fiscal policy is more effective during bad times than good. Riera-Crichton, Vegh and Vuletin (2015a) show that, on average, increasing (decreasing) USD 1.00 of government expenditure in Latin America leads to a statistically significant increase (decrease) in output of around 80 cents on impact during recessions. On the other hand, during expansions this effect is about half the size (40 cents) and statistically insignificant. While the estimated multipliers in developed countries tend to remain neutral in the long run, the multipliers in the Latin American region are positive and stay significant after two years. Similarly, Riera-Crichton, Vegh and Vuletin (2015b) find that increasing government spending in periods of recession would stimulate output (a USD 1 increase would increase output by around USD 1.25 after two years), whereas increasing it in times of expansion would have essentially no effects.

Moreover, as also shown in Riera-Crichton, Vegh and Vuletin (2015b), countries often contract government spending in bad times (i.e. procyclical fiscal policy) rather than increasing it (countercyclical fiscal policy). Figure 2.24 shows that once the sample is split between increases or decreases in government expenditure, the reaction of output to increases in government expenditure during recessions (countercyclical policy) is much larger. In fact, we observe multipliers as high as 2 (i.e. an increase in USD 2.00 of aggregate output in response to a USD 1.00 shock to government expenditure) after just two years.

Box 2.4. **Fiscal policy options: The role of fiscal multipliers** (cont.)

Figure 2.24. **Public expenditure multiplier for Latin America, and the business cycle**

(economic expansions or recessions and a decrease or increase in government expenditure)

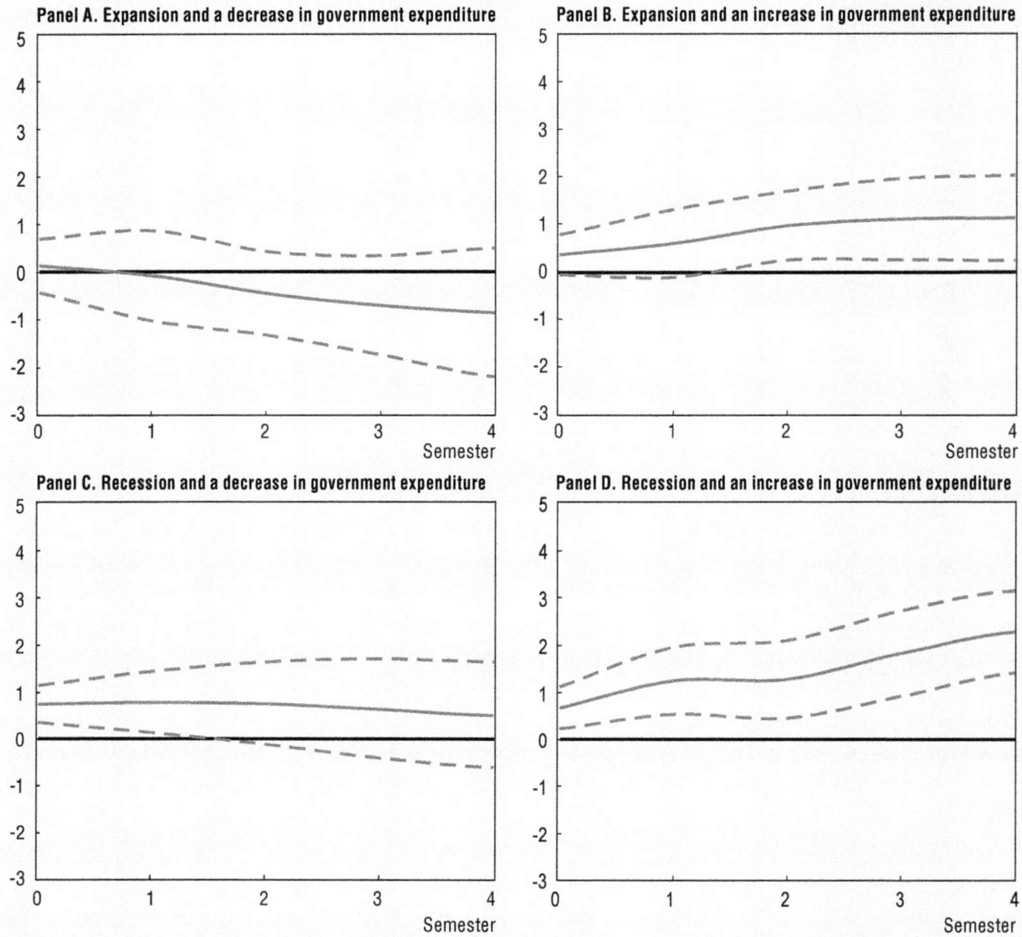

Note: Dashes lines refer to 90% confidence intervals.

Source: Riera-Crichton, Vegh and Vuletin (2015b).

StatLink http://dx.doi.org/ 10.1787/888933413978

Taken together, these results suggest that countries with a sound economy (i.e. no other binding constraints, like Chile) could fight any upcoming recession with increases in public expenditure. On the other hand, a number of recent studies show that countries with no fiscal space (i.e. high debt to GDP ratios) may be unable to reap the benefits of such countercyclical fiscal policies. In particular, Huidrom, Kose and Ohnsorge (2016) show that countries with high debt to GDP ratios have markedly lower multipliers than those with low ratios.

These results also suggest that countries with no fiscal space should prioritise fiscal consolidation packages – tax hikes, expenditure cuts or both – before attempting any countercyclical expenditure measure. Choosing the particular combination that may minimise the negative impact of the fiscal consolidation on output is crucial. Gunter et al. (2016) show that fiscal consolidations based on increases in the value added tax (VAT) rate exhibit, on average, a sizeable negative multiplier of 1.5 that can increase up to 2 after just one year. In addition, policy makers may need to carefully consider

Box 2.4. **Fiscal policy options: The role of fiscal multipliers** (cont.)

the initial level of VAT rates (which could be viewed as an indicator of the initial level of tax distortions) because VAT rate changes have an inherently non-linear effect on aggregate output; that is, the output effect of a given tax increase is larger in countries with a high initial tax rate than in those with a low initial tax rate. Figure 2.25 implies that countries with a low initial tax burden (for example, Costa Rica) would have small (if any) reductions in output, while countries with a high initial tax burden would suffer much larger reductions in output in response to tax increases.

Figure 2.25. **Tax multipliers in Latin America**

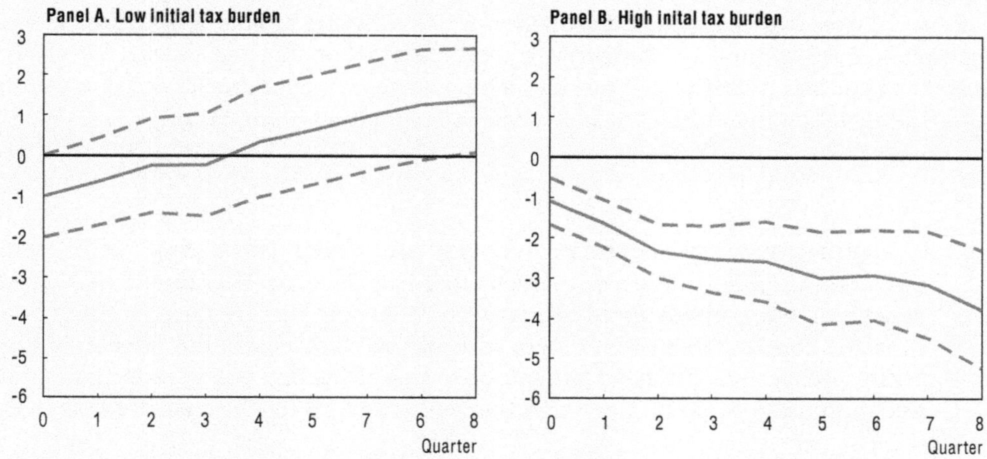

Source: Riera-Crichton, Vegh and Vuletin (2015a), *Fiscal Multipliers in Latin America*, ECLAC.
StatLink http://dx.doi.org/10.1787/888933413986

Figure 2.26. **Fiscal multipliers for government consumption expenditure and investment expenditures in Latin America**

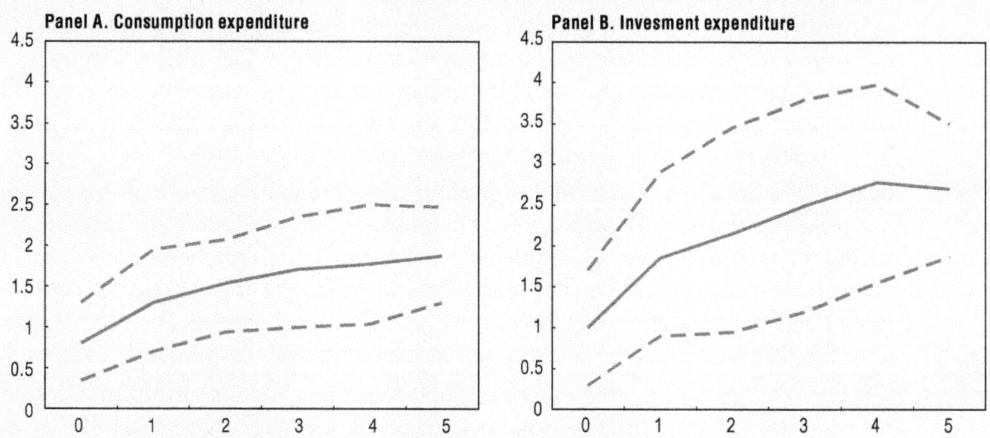

Source: Riera-Crichton, Vegh and Vuletin (2015a), *Fiscal Multipliers in Latin America*, ECLAC.
StatLink http://dx.doi.org/10.1787/888933413990

Box 2.4. Fiscal policy options: The role of fiscal multipliers (cont.)

In light of these non-linearities, countries forced to undergo fiscal consolidations that have already high initial tax burdens may prefer to cut government expenditure rather than increase taxes. Those countries that rely on expenditure cuts still need to minimise the impact on economic activity. Hence, understanding the output effects of different types of expenditure on economic performance should help choose what particular expenditure to cut. Using annual data, the total fiscal expenditure is decomposed into consumption expenditure and investment expenditure. Figure 2.26 shows large differences in multipliers in these categories of expenditure. In general, the investment multiplier is substantially larger than the one for consumption. With respect to impact, a USD 1.00 increase (decrease) in government consumption expenditure increases (decreases) output in USD 0.7. For public investment, the multiplier on impact is very close to 1. After two years, the investment multiplier hovers around 2, while the consumption multiplier hovers around 1.3. Similarly, Izquierdo, Riera-Crichton and Vuletin (2016), show for a global sample that multipliers associated with changes in government capital expenditure are significantly larger than those associated with consumption expenditure.

Latin American countries should also keep advancing with public-private partnerships (PPP) initiatives to invest in infrastructure. This should help demand in the short run, but perhaps more importantly PPPs help increase productivity and potential growth. Considerable room exists to improve fiscal spending efficiency and to focus social policies so that governments can provide public goods to enhance productivity and guarantee equality more effectively (see Box 2.5 for the case of roads in Colombia).

Box 2.5. Fourth generation (4G) of road concessions in Colombia

Inadequate transportation infrastructure is a major bottleneck for growth in Colombia. The country lags behind its competitors in both the quality and quantity of ground transportation. According to the World Economic Forum, Colombia's overall transport infrastructure quality ranks as 110th among 140 countries. This is related to low and ineffective investment in infrastructure. Colombia's average annual investment in roads, railways and ports between 2010 and 2015 was 1.3% of GDP, below the recommended 3.1% of GDP to close the transport infrastructure gap (Fedesarrollo, 2013). Additionally, there are significant planning, design and implementation deficiencies of transport infrastructure policies (Nieto-Parra, Olivera and Tibocha, 2013).

In 2011 Colombia's government designed a ten-year plan to strengthen the transportation institutional framework and attract an estimated USD 55 billion in investment. These resources would double the extension of the four-lane highway network and improve airports, railways and ports. The plan includes creating a national infrastructure agency to oversee the execution of projects through PPPs and passing the Infrastructure Law and the PPPs Law to improve contracting, licensing and carrying out of the projects.

The Fourth Generation (4G) of Road Concessions is a key element of the government's ten-year plan. Colombia depends on its road network for more than 80% of domestic cargo transportation. With an investment of 15 billion, the 4G programme comprises 53 projects, which add up to 8 000 km of new roads to expand the current highway network that connects the main ports with major cities. By June 2016, 26 projects had been awarded and formalised their funding. This first group of projects was expected

Box 2.5. **Fourth generation (4G) of road concessions in Colombia** (cont.)

to start operations during the second semester of 2016, while the remaining 27 projects were to be awarded during the next two years. According to the National Planning Department (DPN, 2016), the 4G projects would add an extra 0.3-0.7 percentage points of GDP growth in 2016-17. As the programme unfolds, its impact will increase, adding an annual average of 1.6 percentage points to growth during 2018-21. Finally, the new infrastructure would raise long-run potential growth by about 0.7%, according to the NPD.

Table 2.1. **4G Road infrastructure programme**

	Number of projects	Km	Investment (USD bn)
First round	10	1.628	4.0
Second round	9	1.827	4.0
Third round	10	1.500	3.7
Private initiative	24	3.600	3.3
Total	53	8.555	15.0

Source: Colombia's Vice Presidency.

The 4G's PPP approach seeks to attract private investment in infrastructure and ensure the quality and timeliness of the projects through a two-stage process. During the construction stage, 4G concession holders should cover the overall capital requirement with equity (20%) and debt (80%). In the operation and maintenance stage, the debt is mainly repaid by toll road revenues, commercial activity revenues in the concession area and payment flows from the government to contractors (USD 19.4 billion). On average, the annual fiscal outlay will be approximately 0.4% of GDP during 2018-42. The PPP approach eases important fiscal constraints by attracting private investment. Otherwise, the central government's investment expenses for the next seven years would rise from the current official estimate of 1.5% of GDP to 2.5% of GDP, which would be unfeasible given the need to comply with the decreasing path of debt set by the fiscal rule.

Through the Intermodal Transportation Master Plan 2015-30, the government complements and strengthens benefits from the 4G programme. This plan bridges local connectivity gaps, prioritising investment (USD 16 billion) in 101 tertiary roads covering more than 12 700 km and in the logistics management of national transport corridors (USD 24.5 billion). Additionally, it includes investment (USD 5.9 billion) in airports and rivers.

Foreign direct investment (FDI) could also be key to reignite growth in a more inclusive manner and promote innovation. FDI can be an important channel for technology transfers and knowledge diffusion (Andrews, Criscuolo and Gal, 2015). As such, Latin America needs to continue improving its business climate to attract and retain further FDI (OECD, 2015b, see OECD FDI Regulatory Restrictiveness Index).

Strengthening human capital and skills

Latin America seems trapped in a "vicious cycle" in which high turnover discourages the education and training of workers, resulting in low productivity. In turn, low labour productivity relative to the costs of formality contributes to a high level of informality in the region. Owing to high turnover and high informality, most workers lack support to withstand a period of unemployment while looking for a good job suited to their skills and training; this leads to inefficient job matches. These inefficient matches, in turn, tend to break up quickly, generating high turnover and completing the vicious cycle (Alaimo et al. 2016).

Latin America has the widest gap between skills supply and demand, which adds to high labour informality: 50% of companies in the formal economy struggle to find a properly trained workforce, compared with a global average of 36% per country and an OECD average of 15% (Manpower Group, 2015). The automotive and machinery sectors, which are sophisticated and complex, struggle the most to find needed skills in Latin America. Yet these sectors could support the region's structural change and transformation towards a knowledge-intensive and technology-intensive development model. To solve the problems of instability, informality and low productivity in the regional labour market, Latin America needs to invest in human capital and skills. This will have significant impacts on both growth and equity.

More than half of the Latin American workforce, including the "emerging middle class" or "middle sectors", work in the informal sector. This makes them vulnerable to drops in income and unemployment caused by lower economic growth and risks posed by illness and old age (Melguizo, 2015). Indeed, some evidence suggests that workers in the informal economy are paid less than workers in the formal economy with comparable jobs and the same level of education.

In addition to the high proportion of low-skilled workers in jobs requiring basic skills, returns to education have been declining. In the short term, the region must invest to improve education programmes and vocational education and training. To achieve these goals, public-private sector co-operation is essential, as shown in this outlook.

Activating sound fiscal policies

A "smart fiscal adjustment" framework should be put in place, combining taxes, debt and reallocation of expenditure. Such a framework would strengthen fiscal positions, while fostering investment in physical and human capital. Actions depend on the initial position of the countries, and the need for debt stabilisation (see Figure 2.27 and Box 2.6).

Figure 2.27. **Tax and debt in selected Latin American and Caribbean countries, 2014**

(percentages of GDP)

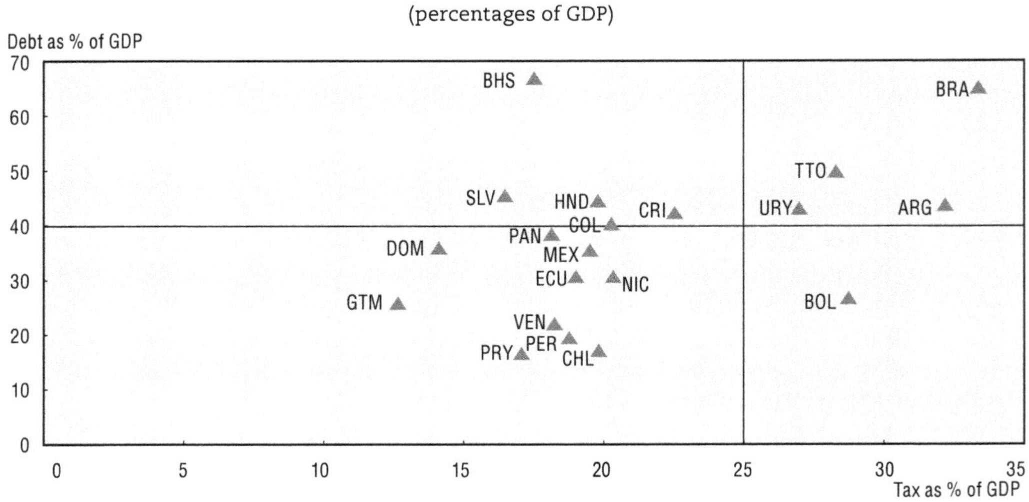

Source: OECD/CAF/ECLAC based on ECLAC (2016b), *Fiscal Panorama of Latin America and the Caribbean 2016: Public Finances and the Challenge of Reconciling Austerity with Growth and Equality*; and OECD/ECLAC/CIAT/IDB (2016), *Revenue Statistics in Latin America and the Caribbean*.

StatLink http://dx.doi.org/10.1787/888933414001

Debt and taxes in Argentina, Brazil, and Trinidad and Tobago are relatively high; the adjustment must come from reallocating expenditure from current to capital. Most Central American countries – notably Costa Rica (see OECD, 2016e), but also Colombia (see OECD, 2015d) and Peru (OECD, 2015f) – the adjustment should incorporate some type of structural tax reform. Peru and other Andean economies (Bolivia, Chile) show some capacity to increase public debt to sustain or increase investment. Finally, in the cases of Chile and Mexico (see OECD, 2015d, 2015e), the full impact of tax reform on collection is expected in the next few years. Debt ratios, meanwhile, are highly sensitive to exchange rate adjustments. In Venezuela, for example, given strong adjustments in the several tiers of the exchange rate regime in 2015, the consolidated public sector debt surpassed 70% of GDP, which is considerably higher.

Box 2.6. **Evolution of public debt in Latin America under different scenarios**

The solvency of the public accounts is threatened by the persistence of a deficit over a lengthy period rather than isolated deficits.

In aggregate terms, the public debt dynamics are represented by the expression:

$$(1)\ \Delta d_t = -sp_t + \frac{(r-n)}{(1+n)} d_{t-1} + sf_t \quad (1)$$

The construction of scenarios to 2025 show public debt on a clear upward path; Table 2.2 summarises the initial conditions. Assuming zero variation in the exchange rate or in other valuation effects (*sf*=0), public debt will rise by 3 GDP points per year, at an implicit interest rate of 5.5%, with trend growth of 3.5% and primary deficit of 1 GDP point (see equation 1). These generic averages and scenarios mask wide heterogeneities; some countries have maintained very solid fiscal positions, having used the gains from the boom period to consolidate stabilisation funds, which can now fulfil their function in the downswing.

In the next ten years, under current parameters, public debt of the central government public debt could reach 54.8% of GDP on average for the region (Figure 2.28). Although such a situation would not be unprecedented, the exercise illustrates the need to correct this trajectory if indebtedness levels are to be controlled. An adjustment of 1 point in primary balance would break the upward spiral of debt; adjustment of 2 points would return the debt-to-GDP ratio to a downward trajectory.

Different routes to reduce gaps have very different consequences. Reducing spending on direct public investment, for example, would certainly lower potential GDP and thus render the adjustment insufficient, leading to rising debt and poor economic growth. This is typical of "self-defeating austerity", where fiscal adjustments worsen macroeconomic conditions and increase public debt. As well, the spending reduction itself would undercut the tax take and thereby widen the gap it was supposed to close. Austerity in the form of public capital expenditure containment alone thus runs the risk of worsening the situation it sets out to resolve.

Growth will not likely be strong enough to close the existing gap in the current scenario. In addition, interest rates hikes on the horizon are auguring the end of cheap financing. These dilemmas have led to multiple efforts to reduce public deficits in the region, including through broad initiatives to cut spending and raise income, as documented in recent publications.

Box 2.6. **Evolution of public debt in Latin America under different scenarios** (cont.)

Table 2.2. **Initial variables used for public debt scenarios**

(percentages)

	Growth rate of potential GDP [a]	Implicit real interest rate [b]	Primary fiscal balance over GDP	Public debt over GDP
		Latest data available		2015
Latin America	3.5	5.5	-1.0	35.9
Argentina	3.7	4.7	-1.1	53.3
Bolivia (Plurinational State of)	6	3.0	-3.3	27.1
Brazil	3	12.5	-2.0	66.5
Chile	3	4.5	-1.5	17.5
Colombia	3.7	6.4	-0.4	43.9
Costa Rica	4	7.3	-3.1	42.4
Dominican Republic	5.6	7.9	0.5	36
Ecuador	5	6.0	-1.9	31
El Salvador	2	5.6	1.3	45.2
Guatemala	4	6.5	0.1	24.4
Haiti	3	0.6	0.3	35.9
Honduras	5	6.1	-0.6	44.2
Mexico	4	5.4	-1.3	35.5
Nicaragua	4	3.1	0.3	31.4
Panama	6	4.6	-2.4	38.4
Paraguay	6	3.8	-1.1	16.6
Peru	5.8	5.7	-1.9	19.5
Uruguay	2.8	5.7	-0.5	46

Notes: a) ECLAC potential growth estimates, from ECLAC (2015). Potential GDP figures differ from results presented in previous sections of the outlook as they are derived from ECLAC (2015). *b)* The implicit real interest rate is defined as the ratio between interest payments (divided by GDP) on the previous period's public debt (divided by GDP).

Source: ECLAC (2015), *Economic Survey of Latin America and the Caribbean 2015: Challenges in boosting the investment cycle to reinvigorate growth.*

Figure 2.28. **Public debt at 2025 in Latin America, under different primary-balance scenarios**

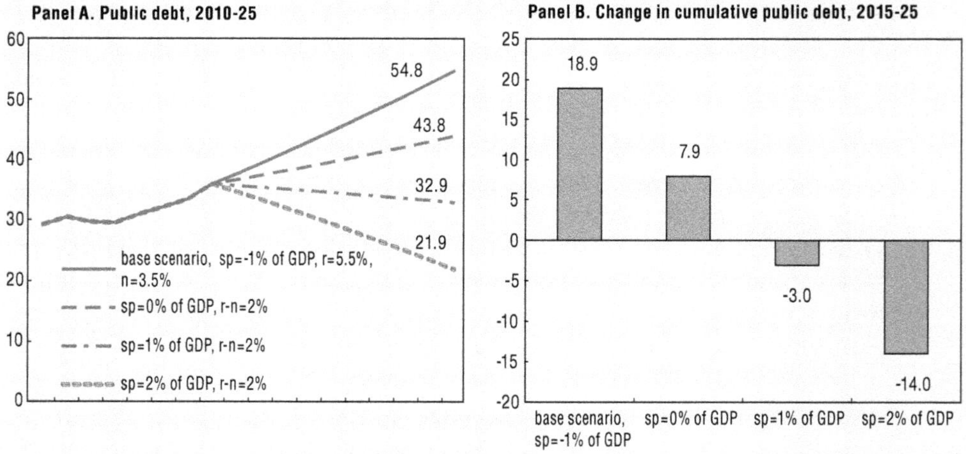

Source: ECLAC (2015), *Economic Survey of Latin America and the Caribbean 2015: Challenges in boosting the investment cycle to reinvigorate growth.*

StatLink http://dx.doi.org/10.1787/888933414011

Conclusion

The pace of Latin American economic growth is expected to disappoint again in 2016. Growth rates for the region will range between -0.5% and -1% in 2016 (compared with 1.2% in 2014 and -0.4% in 2015), before recovering modestly in 2017. External factors are contributing to this weak performance, including lower commodity prices (mainly due to the global economic slowdown), as well as the rising cost of external financing and more restrained capital inflow prospects. Growth levels vary from one country to another, partly because of different economic management strategies. Still, these projections signal the end of a ten-year period during which Latin America has seen higher growth than the OECD average.

Structural reforms must be implemented to boost potential output and inclusiveness. Productivity growth remains modest compared with that of OECD member countries and other emerging economies. Despite recent improvements, Latin America remains the world's most unequal region. Commodity booms and vast short-term capital inflow have not raised the region's growth potential. Reforms to strengthen investment in physical and human capital must foster higher inclusive growth and higher productivity. They can do this by the improvement of workers' skills, infrastructure investment, regional integration and a higher degree of diversification and productive linkages.

Latin America is entering a new electoral cycle, with 18 presidential elections during 2016-18. This should be used as a window of opportunity for the agenda of "productivity-inclusiveness" reforms under "smart adjustment" fiscal scenarios.

References

Aguiar, M. and G. Gopinath (2007), "Emerging market business cycles: The cycle is the trend", *Journal of Political Economy,* Vol. 115, University of Chicago Press, pp. 69-102.

Aiyar, S. et al. (2013), "Growth slowdowns and the middle-income trap", *IMF Working Paper,* No. 13/71, http://www.imf.org/external/pubs/ft/wp/2013/wp1371.pdf .

Alberola, E., I. Kataryniuk, A. Melguizo and R. Orozco (2016), "Fiscal policy and the cycle in Latin America: The role of financing conditions and fiscal rules", *BIS Working Papers,* No. 543, http://www.bis.org/publ/work543.pdf.

Alaimo, V., M. Bosch, D. Kaplan, C. Pages and L. Ripani (2015), *Jobs for Growth,* Inter-American Development Bank, Washington, DC.

Álvarez-Parra, F., L. Brandao-Marques and M. Toledo (2013), "Durable goods, financial frictions and business cycles in emerging economies", *Journal of Monetary Economics,* Vol. 60/6, Elsevier, Amsterdam, pp. 720-736.

Amador, J. et al. (2015), "Ha aumentado el pass-through de tipo de cambio a precios en América Latina?" ["Has the exchange rate pass-through to prices increased in Latin America?"], BBVA Research, *Observatorio Económico Latam,* October 2015.

Andrews, D., C. Criscuolo and P. Gal (2015), "Frontier firms, technology diffusion and public policy: Micro evidence from OECD countries", *The Future of Productivity: Main Background Papers,* OECD Publishing, Paris, http://dx.doi.org/10.1787/5jrql2q2jj7b-en

Aravena, C., G. López and R. Pineda (2016), "Producto potencial de mediano plazo en América Latina" ["Latin America's Potential output in the medium Term"], Economic Commission for Latin America and the Caribbean (ECLAC), Santiago, Chile.

BDE (2016), "Report on the Latin American Economy: First half of 2016", *Economic Bulletin,* April 2016, Bank of Spain, Madrid.

BIS (2015a), *BIS Quarterly Review,* Bank for International Settlements, Basel, September www.bis.org/publ/qtrpdf/r_qt1509.htm (accessed February 2016).

BIS (2015b), "When the financial becomes real", *85th Annual Report: 1 April 2014 - 31 March 2015,* Bank for International Settlements, Basel.

Blanchard, O.J. and D. Leigh (2013), "Growth forecast errors and fiscal multipliers", *American Economic Review,* Vol. 103/3, American Economic Association, Pittsburgh, US, pp. 117-120.

Bolt, J. and J. L. van Zanden (2014). "The Maddison Project: Collaborative research on historical national accounts". *The Economic History Review,* 67 (3): 627–651.

Bosch, M., A. Melguizo and C. Pagés (2013), *Better Pensions, Better Jobs: Towards Universal Coverage in Latin America and the Caribbean,* Inter-American Development Bank, Washington, DC, https://publications.iadb.org/handle/11319/462?locale-attribute=en.

Busso, M., L. Madrigal and C. Pagés (2013), "Productivity and resource misallocation in Latin America", *The B.E. Journal of Macroeconomics,* Vol. 13/1, De Gruyter Online, pp. 903-932.

Carranza, L., C. Daude and A. Melguizo (2014), "Public infrastructure investment and fiscal sustainability in Latin America: Incompatible goals?", *Journal of Economic Studies,* 41(1), pp. 29-50.

Cavallo, E. and T. Serebrisky (2016), *Saving for Development: How Latin America and the Caribbean Can Save More and Better,* Development in the Americas series, Inter-American Development Bank, Washington DC, and Palgrave Macmillan, New York.

Daude C. and E. Fernández-Arias (2010), "On the role of productivity and factor accumulation in economic development in Latin America", *Inter-American Development Bank (IDB) Working Paper Series,* No. 155, Inter-American Development Bank, Washington, DC, www.iadb.org/res/publications/pubfiles/pubIDB-WP-155.pdf.

DNP (2016), *Efectos macroeconómicos de las obras de infraestructura* [*Macroconomic Effects of Infrastructure Works*], Departamento Nacional de Planeación, Colombia.

ECLAC (2016a), *Social Panorama of Latin America 2015,* Economic Commission for Latin America and the Caribbean, Santiago, Chile.

ECLAC (2016b), *Fiscal Panorama of Latin America and the Caribbean 2016: Public Finances and the Challenge of Reconciling Austerity with Growth and Equality,* Economic Commission for Latin America and the Caribbean, Santiago, Chile.

ECLAC (2015), *Economic Survey of Latin America and the Caribbean 2015: Challenges in boosting the investment cycle to reinvigorate growth,* Economic Commission for Latin America and the Caribbean, Santiago, Chile.

ECLAC (2010), *Social Panorama of Latin America, 2009,* Economic Commission for Latin America and the Caribbean, Santiago, Chile.

ECLAC/ILO (2016), "Employment situation in Latin America and the Caribbean: Recent improvements and persistent gaps in rural employment", *Employment Situation in Latin America and the Caribbean,* No. 14, Economic Commission for Latin America and the Caribbean and International Labour Organization, Santiago. Chile.

Eichengreen, B., D. Park and K. Shin (2011), "When fast growing economies slow down: International evidence and implications for China", *NBER Working Paper,* No. 16919, National Bureau of Economic Research, Cambridge, US, www.nber.org/papers/w16919.pdf.

Fedesarrollo (2013), "La inversión en infraestructura en Colombia 2012-2020: Efectos fiscales y requerimientos financieros" ["Infrastructure Investment in Colombia 2012-2020: Fiscal Effects and Financial Requirements"], Fedesarrollo, Bogotá, Colombia. www.cvc.com.ve/docs/2016219124559Inversion%20en%20infraestructura%20Colombia%202013-2020.pdf.

Felipe, J., A. Abdon and U. Kumar (2012), "Tracking the middle-income trap: What is it, who is in it, and why?" *Working Paper,* No. 715, Levy Economics Institute of Bard College, Annandale-on-Hudson, US, www.levyinstitute.org/pubs/wp_715.pdf.

Garcia-Cicco, J., R. Pancrazi and M. Uribe (2010), "Real business cycles in emerging countries?", *American Economic Review,* Vol. 100/5, American Economic Association, Pittsburgh, US, December, pp. 2510-31.

Gasparini, L., G. Cruces and L. Tornarrolli (2016), "Chronicle of a deceleration foretold: Income inequality in Latin America in the 2010s", *CEDLAS Working Paper,* No. 198, Center for Distributive, Labor and Social Studies, Universidad Nacional de La Plata (UNLP), La Plata, Argentina.

Gunter, S., G. D. Riera-Crichton, C. Vegh and G. Vuletin (2016), "Non-linear effect of tax changes on output: A worldwide narrative approach", mimeo.

Hsieh, C.T. and P.J. Klenow (2009), "Misallocation and manufacturing TFP in China and India", *Quarterly Journal of Economics,* Vol. 124/4, Oxford University Press, Cambridge, US, pp. 1403-1448.

Huidrom, R., M.A. Kose and F. Ohnsorge (2016), "Do fiscal multipliers depend on fiscal positions?", *Policy Research Working Paper,* No. 7724, World Bank, Washington, DC.

IMF (2016), *World Economic Outlook,* April 2016 edition, (database), www.imf.org/external/pubs/ft/weo/2015/01/weodata/index.aspx (accessed May 2016).

IMF (2013), *Regional Economic Outlook: Western Hemisphere: Time to Rebuild Policy Space,* International Monetary Fund, Washington, DC., www.imf.org/external/pubs/ft/reo/2013/whd/eng/wreo0513.htm.

Izquierdo, A., D. Riera-Crichton and G. Vuletin (2016), "Public consumption versus public investment multipliers", in *IDB Macroeconomic Report 2016, Time to Act: Latin America and the Caribbean Facing Strong Challenges,* Inter-American Development Bank, Washington, DC.

Jorgenson, D.W. and M.V. Khuong (2010), "Potential growth of the world economy", *Journal of Policy Modeling,* Vol. 32/5, Elsevier, Amsterdam, pp. 615-631.

Kharas, H. and H. Kohli (2011), "What is the middle income trap, why do countries fall into it, and how can it be avoided?", *Global Journal of Emerging Market Economies,* Vol. 3/3, Sage Publications, Thousand Oaks, US, pp. 281-289.

Koske, I. et al. (2015), "The 2013 update of the OECD product market regulation indicators: Policy insights for OECD and non-OECD countries", *OECD Economics Department Working Papers,* No. 1200, OECD Publishing, Paris, http://dx.doi.org/10.1787/5js3f5d3n2vl-en.

Manpower Group (2015), *Talent Shortage Survey Research Results,* Milwaukee.

Melguizo, A. (2015), "Pensions, informality and the emerging middle class", *IZA World of Labor,* Institute for the Study of Labor, Bonn, Germany, pp. 1-10, http://wol.iza.org/articles/pensions-informality-and-emerging-middle-class.

Melguizo, A. and J.R. Perea (2016), "Skill gaps in emerging economies: An empirical analysis", *OECD Development Centre Working Paper,* No. 329, OECD Development Centre, OECD Publishing, Paris, http://dx.doi.org/10.1787/5jm5hkp7v145-en.

Neumeyer, P.A. and F. Perri (2005), "Business cycles in emerging economies: The role of interest rates", *Journal of Monetary Economics*, Vol. 52/2, March, Elsevier, Amsterdam, pp. 345-380.

Nieto-Parra, S., M. Olivera and A. Tibocha (2013), "The politics of transport infrastructure policies in Colombia", *OECD Development Centre Working Papers*, No. 316, OECD Publishing, Paris, http://dx.doi.org/10.1787/5k46n3xqh1hf-en.

OECD (2016a), *OECD Economic Outlook*, Vol. 2016/1, OECD Publishing, Paris, http://dx.doi.org/10.1787/eco_outlook-v2016-1-en.

OECD (2016b), *Economic Policy Reforms 2016: Going for Growth Interim Report*, OECD Publishing, Paris, http://dx.doi.org/10.1787/growth-2016-en.

OECD (2016c), "The productivity-inclusiveness nexus", Meeting at the OECD Council at Ministerial level, 1-2 June 2016, OECD Publishing, Paris, www.oecd.org/global-forum-productivity/library/The-Productivity-Inclusiveness-Nexus-Preliminary.pdf.

OECD (2016d), "Promoting Productivity for Inclusive Growth in Latin America", *Better Policies Series*, OECD Publishing, Paris, June, https://www.oecd.org/latin-america/promoting-productivity-for-inclusive-growth-in-latin-america.pdf.

OECD (2016e), *OECD Economic Surveys: Costa Rica 2016: Economic Assessment*, OECD Publishing, Paris, http://dx.doi.org/10.1787/eco_surveys-cri-2016-en.

OECD (2015a), *OECD Economic Surveys: Brazil 2015*, OECD Publishing, Paris, http://dx.doi.org/10.1787/eco_surveys-bra-2015-en.

OECD (2015b), "FDI regulatory restrictiveness index" (database), in *OECD Factbook 2015-16*, OECD Publishing, Paris, http://dx.doi.org/10.1787/factbook-2015-table67-en.

OECD (2015c), *OECD Economic Surveys: China 2015*, OECD Publishing, Paris, http://dx.doi.org/10.1787/eco_surveys-chn-2015-en.

OECD (2015d), *OECD Economic Surveys: Chile 2015*, OECD Publishing, Paris, http://dx.doi.org/10.1787/eco_surveys-chl-2015-en.

OECD (2015e), *OECD Economic Surveys: Mexico*, OECD Publishing, Paris, http://dx.doi.org/10.1787/eco_surveys-mex-2015-en.

OECD (2015f), *Multi-dimensional Review of Peru: Volume I. Initial Assessment*, OECD Development Pathways, OECD Publishing, Paris, http://dx.doi.org/10.1787/9789264243279-en.

OECD (2013a), "The People's Republic of China – Avoiding the middle-income trap: Policies for sustained and inclusive growth", *Better Policies*, OECD Publishing, Paris, http://dx.doi.org/10.1787/9789264207974-en.

OECD (2013b), *OECD Economic Outlook*, Vol. 2013/1, OECD Publishing, Paris, http://dx.doi.org/10.1787/eco_outlook-v2013-1-en.

OECD (2010), *Latin American Economic Outlook 2011: How Middle-class is Latin America?*, OECD Publishing, Paris, http://dx.doi.org/10.1787/leo-2011-en.

OECD/CAF/ECLAC (2015), *Latin American Economic Outlook 2016: Towards a New Partnership with China*, OECD Publishing, Paris, http://dx.doi.org/10.1787/9789264246218-en.

OECD/CAF/ECLAC (2014), *Latin American Economic Outlook 2015: Education, Skills and Innovation for Development*, OECD Publishing, Paris, http://dx.doi.org/10.1787/leo-2015-en.

OECD/CAF/ECLAC (2013), *Latin American Economic Outlook 2014: Logistics and Competitiveness for Development*, OECD Publishing, Paris, http://dx.doi.org/10.1787/leo-2014-en.

OECD/ECLAC (2012), *Latin American Economic Outlook 2013: SME Policies for Structural Change*, OECD Publishing, Paris, http://dx.doi.org/10.1787/leo-2013-en.

OECD/ECLAC/CIAT/IDB (2016), *Revenue Statistics in Latin America and the Caribbean*, OECD Publishing, Paris, http://dx.doi.org/10.1787/rev_lat_car-2016-en-fr.

Ollivaud, P., Y. Guillemette and D. Turner (2016), "Links between weak investment and the slowdown in productivity and potential output growth across the OECD", *OECD Economics Department Working Papers*, No. 1304, OECD Publishing, Paris, http://dx.doi.org/10.1787/5jlwvz0smq45-en.

Pagés, C. (2010), "The age of productivity: Transforming economies from the bottom up", *Development in the Americas* series, Palgrave Macmillan, New York, and Inter-American Development Bank, Washington DC.

Paus, E. (2014), "Latin America and the Middle-Income Trap", *ECLAC Financing for Development Series*, No. 250, Economic Commission for Latin America and the Caribbean, Santiago, Chile.

Powell, A. (2016), "Time to act: Latin America and the Caribbean facing strong challenges", in *2016 Latin American and Caribbean Macroeconomic Report*, Inter-American Development Bank, Washington, DC.

Powell, A. (2015), "The labyrinth: How can Latin America and the Caribbean navigate the global economy"?, *2015 Latin American and Caribbean Macroeconomic Report*, Inter-American Development Bank, Washington, DC.

Riera-Crichton, D., C. Vegh and G. Vuletin (2015a), *Fiscal Multipliers in Latin America*, Economic Commission for Latin America and the Caribbean (ECLAC), Santiago, Chile.

Riera-Crichton, D., C. Vegh and G. Vuletin (2015b), "Procyclical and countercyclical fiscal multipliers: Evidence from OECD countries," *Journal of International Money and Finance*, Vol. 52, April, Elsevier, Amsterdam, pp. 15-31.

Spilimbergo, A. et al. (2008), "Fiscal Policy for the Crisis", *IMF Staff Note* SPN/08/01, International Monetary Fund, Washington, DC.

UNDP (2016), *Multidimensional Progress: Well-being Beyond Income, Regional Human Development Report for Latin America and the Caribbean*, United Nations Development Programme, Washington, DC.

World Bank Group (2016), *LAC Equity Lab, Tabulations of SEDLAC (CEDLAS and the World Bank) and World Development Indicators, database*, World Bank, Washington, DC, http://www.worldbank.org/en/topic/poverty/lac-equity-lab1/overview (accessed 15 May 2016).

Zhuang, J., P. Vandenberg and Y. Huang (2012), *Growing Beyond the Low-Cost Advantage: How the People's Republic of China Can Avoid the Middle-Income Trap*, Asian Development Bank, Mandaluyong City, Philippines, www.adb.org/publications/growing-beyond-low-cost-advantage-how-peoples-republic-china-can-avoid-middle-income.

Annex 2.A1. Beyond growth: Measuring well-being in the LAC region

Economic growth is a means to an end, that of increasing people's well-being. If growth does not lead to improvements for the majority of people's lives – if it is unequal, unsustainable, or undermines important aspects of quality of life – then it is not serving its purpose.

There is now a widespread recognition of the need to look beyond macro-economic indicators to get a clearer picture of people's experiences across a range of life areas, and to understand whether or not well-being is actually improving in a country or region. In 2011, the OECD launched its *Better Life Initiative* to promote the measurement of well-being and embed the notion at the core of policy-making.[1]

Underpinning this work is a framework for measuring well-being, building on earlier research and collaborations with experts and representatives from national governments.[2] *This How's Life?* framework has been adapted to measure well-being in non-OECD countries, taking into account the literature on measuring development outcomes and reflecting the realities of these countries (Boarini, Kolev and McGregor, 2014). The framework measures well-being outcomes in two broad pillars. The first pillar – material conditions – comprises the dimensions of consumption possibilities, work, housing conditions and infrastructure. The second pillar – quality of life – comprises health status, education and skills, social connections, empowerment and participation, vulnerability and life evaluation, feelings and meaning (i.e. the main aspects of subjective well-being) (Figure 2.A1.1). The framework also encompasses the drivers of sustainability of well-being over time in terms of natural, human, economic and social capital (OECD, 2015a).

Figure 2.A1.1. **The OECD well-being measurement framework for developing countries**

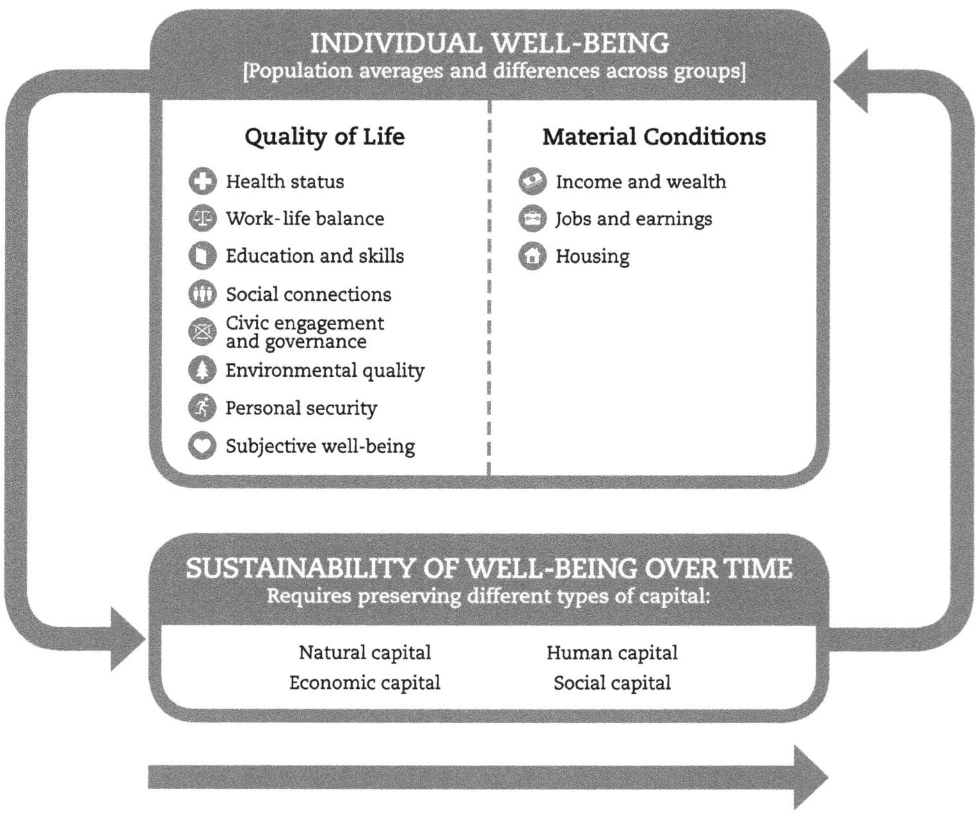

Source: OECD (2015b).

The *How's Life?* framework has four distinct characteristics:

- People (individuals and households), their situation and how they relate to others in the community where they live and work;
- Well-being outcomes (as opposed to well-being inputs or outputs because outcomes provide the best direct information on people's lives);
- Distribution of well-being in the population alongside average achievements (which allows exploration of inequalities across age, gender, socio-economic status and other characteristics);
- Objective and subjective aspects of well-being (since personal experiences and assessments of life circumstances provide important information alongside more objective measures).

An overview of well-being outcomes in Latin America and the Caribbean

The OECD *How's Life?* framework emphasises the multi-dimensionality of well-being. As such, it avoids a single summary measure, aiming for a more nuanced picture of people's life conditions. Applying this framework to Latin American and Caribbean (LAC) countries can suggest areas of strengths and weaknesses for people's well-being. Figure 2.A1.2 presents a selection of headline indicators from the OECD framework for the LAC region, comparing the actual average outcomes against what could be expected given the region's level of gross domestic product (GDP).

According to these indicators, the LAC region performs well in the areas of health, social connections and life evaluations. It has weaknesses, however, in education, vulnerability, and empowerment and participation. Performance across material conditions and environmental conditions are mixed.

Gross national income (GNI) per capita captures the gross flow of income to individuals from earnings, self-employment and income from capital. For its level of economic development, the region could generate GNI of USD 10 434, but falls short of this figure by around USD 1 800. Still, more than two-thirds of people say they are satisfied with living standards.

The ratio of employment to population in the LAC region is 60.5% among individuals over the age of 15, which is slightly higher than could be expected for the level of economic development. But over a third of jobs (36%) are in vulnerable employment (i.e. unpaid family workers and own-account workers). This underlines the importance of job quality and security for the region.

Access to decent housing is a fundamental aspect of well-being. More than three-quarters (80%) of LAC households have access to improved sanitation facilities, which is slightly higher than the expected value. However, only 42% are satisfied with the availability of good, affordable housing, which is lower than the expected value given the region's level of development.

Figure 2.A1.2. **Comparison of actual and expected well-being outcomes for the LAC region, given its level of economic development**

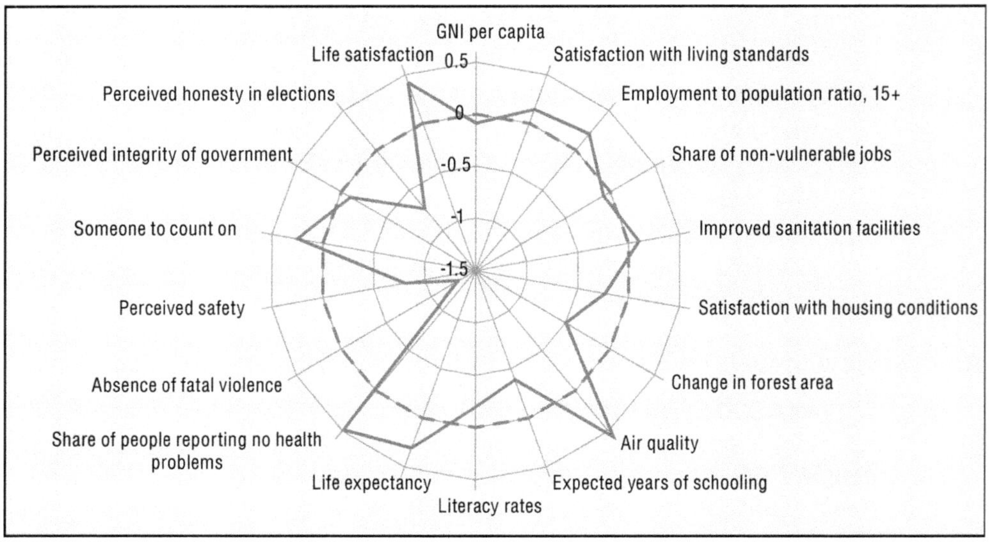

Note: This figure is based on running bivariate regressions where the indicator is the dependent variable and GDP per capita is the independent variable. Applying the coefficient of the bivariate regression to the mean GDP per capita for the LAC region generates the expected value of each indicator. Actual results are then compared to the expected value for each indicator. The difference between the fitted values and the observed values is standardised by the standard deviation of the indicator. Standardising the size of the gap highlights those dimensions in which the performance of the country stands out. The circular line indicates the expected outcomes for the LAC region on the basis of its GDP per capita level and has been calculated using the outcomes for all world countries with a population of over 1 million people. The jagged line indicates the actual average performance in the Latin American region, which has been calculated on the basis of a simple average for 21 Latin American countries with a population of over 1 million people: Argentina, Bolivia, Brazil, Chile, Colombia, Costa Rica, Dominican Republic, Ecuador, El Salvador, Guatemala, Haiti, Honduras, Jamaica, Mexico, Nicaragua, Panama, Paraguay, Peru, Puerto Rico, Trinidad and Tobago and Uruguay. All indicators have been normalised so that a higher score (i.e. movement away from the centre of the circle) indicates an improvement in outcomes. In particular, the 'Absence of fatal violence' indicator shows a normalised value based on homicide rate data, the 'share of non-vulnerable jobs' indicator shows a normalised value based on vulnerable job rate data, the 'Air quality' indicator shows a normalised value based on PM25 concentration data, and the 'Perceived integrity of government' indicator shows a normalised value based on corruption perception data.

Sources: OECD calculations based on Gallup Organization (2014), *Gallup World Monitor* (database); UNDP (2014), *International Human Development Indicators* (database) http://hdr.undp.org/en/data; UIS (2013), *UIS Data Centre* (database); UNESCO, http://data.uis.unesco.org/; United Nations Office on Drugs and Crime (UNODC 2013), www.unodc.org, World Bank (2014), *World Development Indicators* (database), Washington, DC, http://data.worldbank.org/data-catalog/world-development-indicators.

In the area of environmental conditions, the selected indicators show contrasting results, reflecting the complexity of measuring outcomes in this area. Between 1990 and 2011, forest coverage in the region decreased by 7%, which is significantly higher than countries with similar levels of economic development. However, air quality is actually significantly better than could be expected across the region.

Education and skills outcomes highlight this area as a problem for the region. The adult literacy rate is 91%, which is four percentage points lower than could be expected for the level of GDP. Furthermore, expected years of schooling is 13.1 years, a full year lower than the expected outcome. The region shows a comparatively strong performance in health outcomes, however, compared with expected values. The average life expectancy in the region is 74.6 years; 75% of people say they have no health problems that prevent them from doing the things people of their age normally do.

Vulnerability outcomes, as measured by indicators of perceived and actual security are extremely low, and represent one of the most significant weaknesses in well-being performance. Across the region, there were 22 homicides per 100 000 people in 2013, compared to an expected outcome of only 8 homicides per 100 000 for countries of comparable GDP level. Furthermore, less than half of the population (48%) say they feel safe walking alone in their neighbourhood at night. On the other hand, social connections in the region are comparatively strong, with 84% of people saying they have someone to count on for help when needed.

The dimension of empowerment and participation, measured by perceived government integrity, is problematic. More than three-quarters (81%) of people report thinking that corruption is widespread in their government (higher than the expected value); only 32% think that elections are honest.

Despite this mixed performance across the range of well-being dimensions, people in LAC tend to evaluate satisfaction with their overall lives relatively high. On a scale of 0 to 10, the average response across the region for overall satisfaction is 6. This compares to a world average of 5, and an expected value of 5.5 for countries with a similar level of economic development.

Towards a framework for measuring well-being in the LAC region

The OECD and the Economic Commission for Latin America and the Caribbean (ECLAC) are developing a framework and indicators that are adapted to the realities of the LAC region. This initiative aims to meet a real need in the region for meaningful, comparable indicators and deeper analysis on people's well-being and its sustainability, particularly in the context of the Sustainable Development Goals (SDGs) agenda.

Latin American National Statistical Offices have already pioneered work on subjective well-being and quality of life measurement. Projects based on concepts such as *Buen Vivir* in Ecuador or *Vivir Bien* in Bolivia, for example, attest to the relevance of more people-focused approaches in the region. To that end, the OECD/ECLAC initiative will include participation of the statistical agencies of 10 countries: Bolivia, Chile, Costa Rica, Colombia, Dominican Republic, Ecuador, Mexico, Paraguay, Peru and Uruguay. By strengthening collaboration and peer learning between these national efforts, and by developing a common framework for future efforts, the LAC Better Life Initiative aims to:

- promote a broad notion of sustainable and equitable well-being as the focus for policy making in the region;
- develop measures and tools for a better understanding of the drivers, trends and inequalities in well-being, and of the impact of selected policies on people's lives;
- bring issues traditionally absent from the radar of policy makers (such as trust and subjective well-being) into their remit;
- support the SDG monitoring process.

The central output of the initiative will be a scoreboard of performance indicators covering a broad range of areas affecting people's well-being in Latin American countries. In consultation with participating countries, the scoreboard will use the adapted OECD framework as a starting point, but adjust measures and dimensions to the LAC regional context. The scoreboard will be regularly monitored. Future editions of LEO will present regular sections analysing well-being in the region based on these indicators.

Annex notes

1. See www.oecd.org/statistics/better-life-initiative.htm.
2. Key influences on the framework include the capabilities approach, as set out in Sen (1999) and Nussbaum (2001); as well as the recommendations of the Commission on the Measurement of Economic Performance and Social Progress, led by Joseph Stiglitz (2009). In addition to the academic and expert literature, the framework also builds on national and regional experiences, including public consultations, focused on the aim of going 'Beyond GDP', as well as interactions with hundreds of practitioners from all sectors of society in the OECD World Forums on Statistics, Knowledge and Policy held every 2-3 years since 2004. See OECD 2011 and 2013 for more on the background and conceptual underpinnings of the framework.

Annex references

Boarini, R., A. Kolev and A. McGregor (2014), "Measuring well-being and progress in countries at different stages of development: Towards a more universal conceptual framework", OECD *Development Centre Working Paper*, No. 325, OECD Publishing, Paris, www.oecd-ilibrary.org/fr/economics/oecd-statistics-working-papers_18152031.

Gallup Organization (2014), *Gallup World Monitor*, https://analytics.gallup.com (database)

Nussbaum, M. (2001), *Women and Human Development: The Capabilities Approach*, Cambridge University Press, UK.

OECD (2015a), *How's Life? 2015 Measuring Well-being*, OECD Publishing, Paris, http://dx.doi.org/10.1787/how_life-2015-en

OECD (2015b), *Multi-dimensional Review of Peru: Volume 1. Initial Assessment*, OECD Publishing, Paris, http://dx.doi.org/10.1787/9789264243279-en

OECD (2013), *How's Life? 2013 Measuring Well-being*, OECD Publishing, Paris, http://dx.doi.org/10.1787/9789264201392-en

OECD (2011), *How's Life? 2011 Measuring Well-being*, OECD Publishing, Paris, http://dx.doi.org/10.1787/9789264121164-en

Sen, A. (1999), *Development as Freedom*, Oxford University Press, UK.

Stiglitz, J., A. Sen and J-P. Fitoussi (2009), *Final Report of the Commission on the Measurement of Economic Performance and Social Progress, Paris*, http://www.insee.fr/fr/publications-et-services/dossiers_web/stiglitz/doc-commission/RAPPORT_anglais.pdf.

UIS (2013), *UIS Data Centre* (database), UNESCO Institute of Statistics, Montreal, http://data.uis.unesco.org.

UNDP (2014), *International Human Development Indicators* (database), United Nations Development Programme, New York, http://hdr.undp.org/en/data.

World Bank (2014), *World Development Indicators* (database), Washington, DC, http://data.worldbank.org/data-catalog/world-development-indicators.

Chapter 3

Youth inclusion in Latin America and their main challenges

Most countries in Latin America still stand to reap the benefits of the youth dividend because of their demographics. However, for this to happen the Latin America and Caribbean (LAC) region needs greater investments in young people, including their inclusion into economic, political and social processes. This chapter analyses the gaps of youth inclusion in the LAC region. It provides a rich statistical portrait of how the labour market position and social inclusion of youth have evolved along a number of key dimensions, and identifies a comprehensive set of policy levers to tackle these gaps. The chapter is composed of two parts. First, it provides an overview of the labour market performance of youth in the past decade, focusing on both measures of the labour market situation and job quality. Second, it analyses other indicators of inclusion such as health, satisfaction with life and future outlooks, civic and social engagement, and crime and perceived security to give a more complete picture of youth inclusion in the region. Finally, the chapter sketches a set of policy goals and recommendations to foster youth inclusion in Latin American countries.

Introduction

Youth inclusion and exclusion are complex, multi-dimensional concepts. Limited access to decent and formal employment, education, health services and civic participation, for example, all prevent young people from playing a full role in their societies. This is particularly relevant in countries with a high share of youth and inequality, such as countries in Latin America, where new generations put pressure on economic and social development.

The inclusion of young people in the social, economic and political processes of their societies is arguably one of the principal challenges facing countries in the LAC region (Trucco and Ullmann, 2015). This is due not only to the number of young people relative to the general population, but also to their decisive impact on development and progress in the region. Some 163 million people are aged 15-29 years – about a quarter of the region's total population of the region. This is a heterogeneous population with diverse life situations, needs, interests and backgrounds that must be recognised to better target those who are excluded in one or more dimensions. In Latin America, not all young people are excluded; different socio-economic groups face distinct challenges. Still, a large proportion of young people are marginalised and exposed to an increasing number of vulnerabilities and threats.[1] Targeting economic inclusion of youth, defined as broad access to economic opportunities, requires addressing a wide range of political, social and cultural factors.

In light of these considerations, the goal of this chapter is threefold. First, to identify and analyse key barriers to youth inclusion encountered by young Latin American men and women (defined as those aged 15-29) with a special emphasis on economic opportunities, health, participation and active citizenship; second, to characterise youth according to regional disparities, gender differences and socio-economic status; third, it provides orientations for policy on how to address such barriers. To that end, the chapter uses a multi-dimensional approach to identify and address the social, economic, political and cultural barriers encountered by youth in LAC, focusing on a combination of quantitative and qualitative data sources and a set of objective and subjective indicators. Lastly, the chapter is organised along different dimensions of youth inclusion: the first part is devoted to the inclusion of youth in the labour market, while the second part is centred on other measures of inclusion besides employment. Finally, the chapter ends with a set of policy goals and recommendations that address the multi-dimensional nature of the challenges.

Why a focus on youth?

A critical window of opportunity for Latin America...

There are compelling ethical and moral arguments about why governments should aspire to the economic, social, political and cultural inclusion of youth. However, the large share of young people in the region relative to other age groups makes for a strong economic and social argument as well – if youth can acquire the skills needed for tomorrow's job market. Eventually, demographic conditions will become less favourable; more pressure will fall on the productive share of the population, while much of the socio-economic progress achieved in recent times will be in jeopardy. This, then, is the moment to focus on youth.

As a result of marked declines in fertility accompanied by improvements in life expectancy, the age structure of the LAC population has changed significantly (Figure 3.1). All countries in the region are experiencing these transformations, albeit in different ways. Certainly, the social and economic impacts of different age groups of the population vary, depending on their productive contributions and consumption pressures (ECLAC, 2016a).

Figure 3.1. **Latin America and the Caribbean: Population by age groups over time**
(in millions)

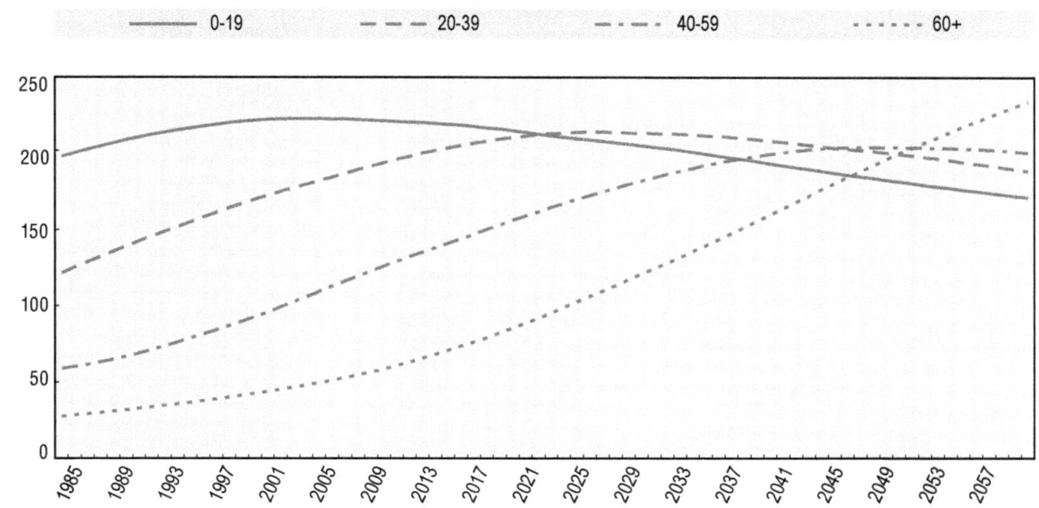

Source: OECD/ECLAC/CAF, based on United Nations Population Division (2015), *World Population Prospects*, 2015 Revision.
StatLink http://dx.doi.org/10.1787/888933414035

The demographic window of opportunity (or "demographic dividend") refers to the period in which the share of the working-age population is larger than the dependent population. It is a particularly favourable period for development because of potential increases in the viability of savings and productivity, as well as the opportunity to invest in economic growth. This bonus can translate into greater economic growth if the necessary policies, markets and institutions are in place to support and promote growth (Bloom, Canning and Sevilla, 2003; Wong and Carvalho, 2006; ECLAC, 2009).[2]

The dependency ratio, used to calculate the demographic window of opportunity, approximates the balance between consumption and the productive contribution of the population.[3] As a first approximation, the demographic dividend occurs when the magnitude of the decrease in dependency ratio equals the percentage reduction of dependence. For most countries in the region the demographic dividend is in full force today (Figure 3.2).[4] Following the end of the demographic dividend, a rapidly ageing population will bring new economic and social challenges that will require public programmes and policy adjustments in various areas; this will include providing long-term care and improving social insurance and security systems for a progressively ageing population.

Demographic change is also affecting the composition of the labour force and the demand for goods and services within the economy. In addition to the demographic transition, environmental change, globalisation and digitisation are also affecting society and the world of work (see Chapter 6). Workplaces and social security systems have to adapt by making it easier for older people to work and by enabling young people to integrate into labour markets. Therefore, in this context, investment must ensure youth have the right skills for future challenges, adequate health services and opportunities for high quality jobs.

Figure 3.2. **Latin America and the Caribbean: Duration of the demographic dividend**
(in years)

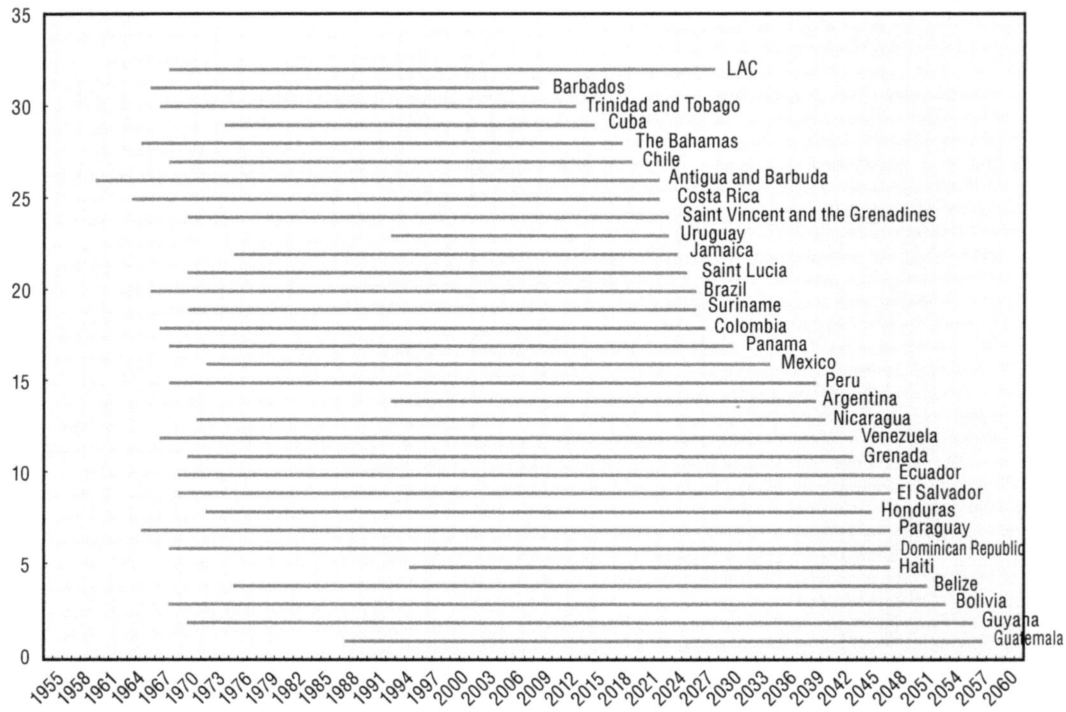

Source: UN "World population prospects: The 2015 revision, key findings and advance tables", *Working Paper*, No. ESA/P/WP.241, División de Población, 2015, http://esa.un.org/unpd/wpp.
StatLink http://dx.doi.org/10.1787/888933414047

… however, opportunities for some youth are scarce

Apart from the demographic transition, LAC countries have all undergone significant social, economic and environmental changes in recent decades. These include increased access to education, more labour market participation and increased income (UNDP, 2016). Millions of people have evaded exclusion and poverty, attaining greater economic and material well-being: during 2004-14 the population living in extreme or moderate poverty dropped from some 40% to a little over 23% (World Bank, 2016).[5] Despite remarkable progress that has witnessed reduced poverty and inequality and the growth of the middle class, many young people still belong to poor and vulnerable households. Particularly, more than half of all youth in the region (around 64%, in 2014) belong to poor and vulnerable households (Figure 3.3 and Figure 3.A1.1 in the annex). The risk of falling back into poverty or vulnerability is high for some of these youth.

Socio-economic differences, relating to areas such as household income, gender and racial/ethnic background,[6] combine with geographical inequalities.[7] These, in turn, translate into wide disparities in labour market, education and health outcomes that can become more pronounced in adulthood. Such inequalities limit the ability of many youth to fulfil their potential and contribute fully to their societies. At the same time, they amplify their marginalisation and exclusion from the economic, social and political processes in place in the region.

In sum, by investing in different dimensions of youth inclusion, countries are preparing the more productive and innovative work force that will be needed to expand formal employment, increase contributions to social security and improve conditions of the active population. This investment must be accompanied by policies that respond to the diversity of young people in the region. Specifically, it must address the main inequalities in the gender, socio-economic and spatial dimensions, providing all youth with the opportunities, knowledge and skills to contribute fully to their societies. Failing to invest in youth can trigger substantial costs, including poor labour market outcomes, social discontent, and crime and violence, as well as poor participation in political and civil society. Public policies must ensure basic conditions and securities to underpin the development of youth capacities and potential.

Figure 3.3. **Youth and socio-economic status in Latin America**

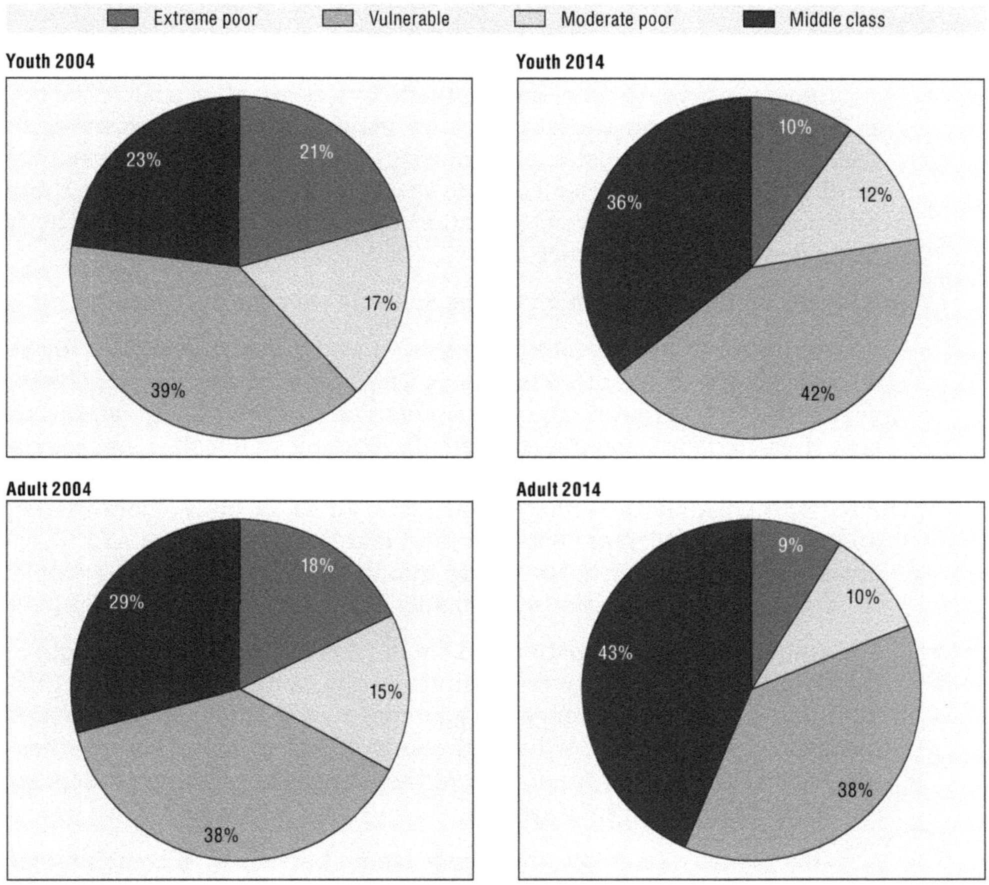

Notes: Youth are people aged 15-29 and adults are aged 30-64. Socio-economic classes are defined using the World Bank classification: "Extreme poor" = youth belonging to households with a daily per capita income lower than USD 2.50. "Moderate poor" = youth belonging to households with a daily per capita income of USD 2.50-4.00. "Vulnerable" = individuals with a daily per capita income of USD 4.00-10.00 "Middle class" = youth from households with a daily per capita income higher than USD 10.00. Poverty lines and incomes are expressed in 2005 USD PPP per day (PPP = purchasing power parity). Latin America weighted average of LAC-17 countries: Argentina, the Plurinational State of Bolivia (hereafter "Bolivia"), Brazil, Chile, Colombia, Costa Rica, Dominican Republic, Ecuador, El Salvador, Guatemala, Honduras, Mexico, Nicaragua, Panama, Peru, Paraguay, Uruguay.

Source: OECD and World Bank tabulations of Socio-Economic Database for Latin America and the Caribbean – SEDLAC (CEDLAS and the World Bank).

StatLink http://dx.doi.org/10.1787/888933414052

Youth labour market outcomes in Latin America

Lack of good employment opportunities is one of the most significant factors hindering the inclusion of youth in society. Furthermore, as labour is one of the most important assets of the poor, helping youth get engaged in productive activities also helps reduce poverty. Growth is translated into higher incomes and greater well-being through productive employment, improvements to real wages, and the coverage and characteristics of workers' social protection (ECLAC, 2016a). This requires enhancing employment opportunities and developing the appropriate skills and abilities to take advantage of those opportunities. This section provides a detailed diagnosis of recent trends in labour market gaps between youth and adult workers, and within different categories of youth. It spans a number of labour market outcomes, including labour force participation, unemployment the status of those not in education, employment or training (NEET), informality and earnings. Moreover, using panel data from select countries, it presents an in-depth analysis of the pace and the modality of the school-to-work and job-to-job transitions.

An overview of youth labour market outcomes in LAC

Integrating youth into development processes is crucial for a more egalitarian society. It is mainly in youth that the link between education and work, which are among the keys to social inclusion and equality, becomes most firmly established: efforts to continue in education often coincide with the need or desire to work and earn a living. Additionally, the move from education to employment represents the transition from dependence to independence (ECLAC, 2014).

Youth labour market participation has been stable over the past decades

Figure 3.4 plots separate participation and employment rates for young men and women across different countries in the region. Some heterogeneity exists across countries; gaps between men and women, for example, are greater in the poorest LAC countries, namely Honduras, Guatemala, Dominican Republic and Nicaragua. However, there are fewer differences between the average in LAC and in the OECD in terms of labour force participation and employment rates. Rates for both labour market participation and employment increase with age (see Figure 3.4 and Figure 3.A1.2 [in the annex]); this is a positive finding since later entry into the labour market gives people valuable time to continue in the education system and improve their credentials (ECLAC, 2014).

Among youth, participation and employment rates are always higher for young men (79.9% and 64.9%, respectively) than for young women (49.6% and 43.3%, respectively). This partly reflects a stronger attachment to the labour force among males. Mostly, however, it reflects higher barriers many young women face in entering the labour market and the greater proportion of them engaged in home production, which is not included in measured employment.

This gap between male and female labour participation is maintained, and in some countries even enlarged, through adulthood. Participation rates for women aged 15-64 (but also for men) seem to have slightly decreased during 2004-14, passing from 50.5% to 49.6% for the LAC weighted average. In many countries more females joined the labour force in the 1990s, but this strong increase contrasted with a substantial decline in the 2000s. Most affected are the most vulnerable women; i.e. those with low education, living in rural areas, with children or married to low-earning spouses (Gasparini and Marchionni, 2015). This trend suggests the emergence of a dual scenario. On the one hand, the number of skilled (richer) women living in large cities reaches the labour participation levels of developed countries. On the other, the labour supply of women in more vulnerable groups remains at substantially lower levels, leading to increasing inequality and poverty cycles.

Over the last decade job opportunities have grown in both urban and rural areas, but at a higher rate in the former. Additionally, a lot of heterogeneity in both employment and participation rates can be observed across different socio-demographic dimensions (see Figure 3.A1.2 in the annex). Youth participation and employment rates also rise with increased education and household income, and are higher in rural than in urban areas. As a rule, the gender gap in labour market participation is much greater in rural areas than in urban zones.

Unemployment rates for youth are systematically higher than for adults

Unemployment patterns differ from those of participation, as rates tend to decline with age (Figure 3.5, Panel A). On average, youth in LAC have more education and higher socio-economic status than in the previous decade. However, youth continue to experience higher levels of unemployment than adults. The average unemployment rate for young men and women in Latin America, in fact, decreased by two percentage points between 2004-14, reaching 11.2%. Although this rate is lower than the OECD average of 13.5% in the first quarter of 2015, the unemployment rate for LAC youth is still on average three times higher than for older workers in the region aged 30-64 (3.7%). This confirms that youth shoulder a disproportionate share of the burden of high joblessness (see OECD, 2014a; Gontero and Weller, 2015). In terms of duration, at least, youth were unemployed on average for five months compared with their adult peers who were unemployed on average eight months.[8]

Figure 3.4. **Labour market situation of youth (aged 15-29)**

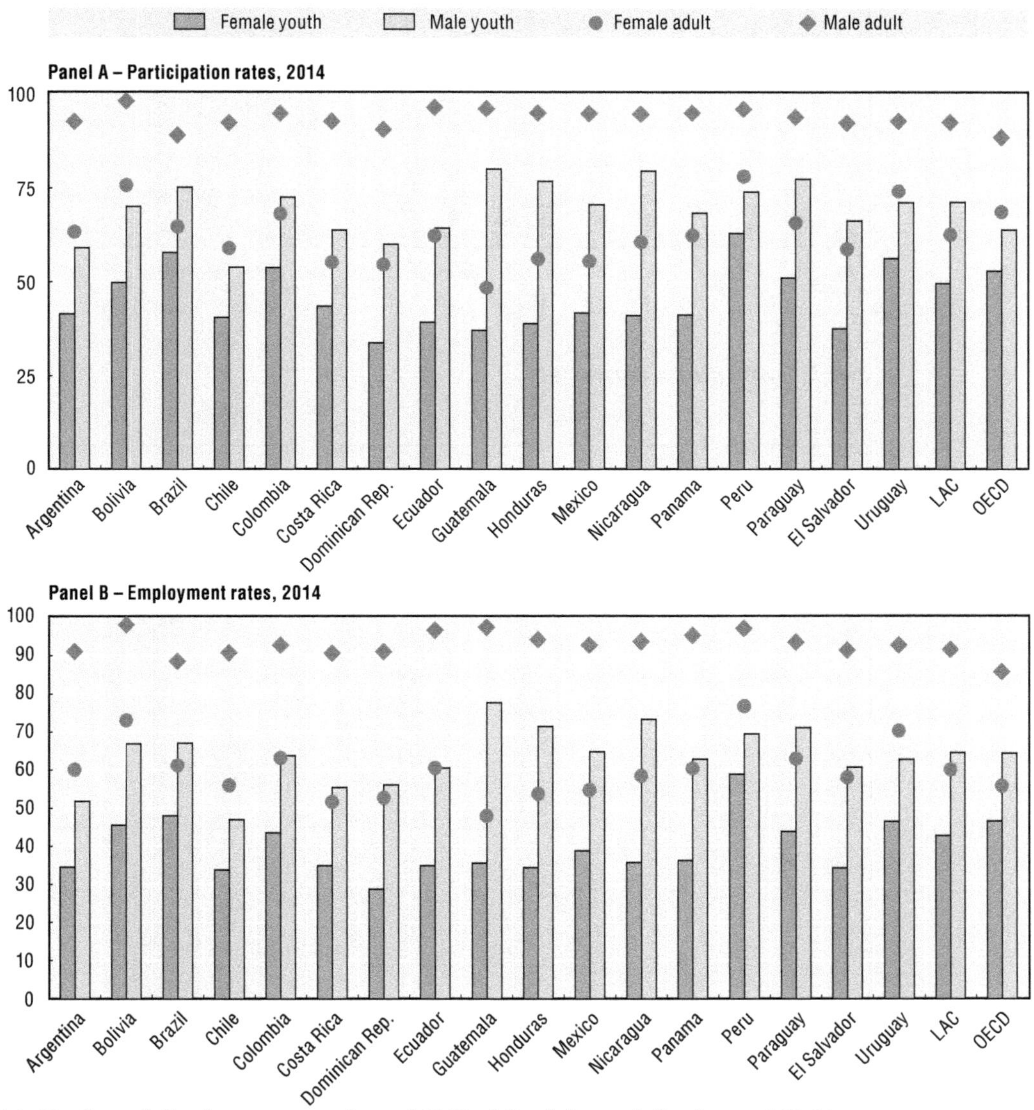

Note: Youth are defined as young people aged 15-29 while adults are defined as aged 30-64.

Source: OECD and World Bank tabulations of SEDLAC (CEDLAS and the World Bank) and OECD – LFS data.

StatLink http://dx.doi.org/10.1787/888933414064

Unemployment patterns are diverse across LAC countries. Lower unemployment rates are observed in the poorest LAC countries, such as Bolivia, Guatemala and Honduras, in less urbanised areas and for lower educated youth. This reflects the need for many people to accept whatever job they can find or to be outside the labour force as working in the household.

Figure 3.5. **Unemployment rates among youth and adult population in LAC and the OECD**

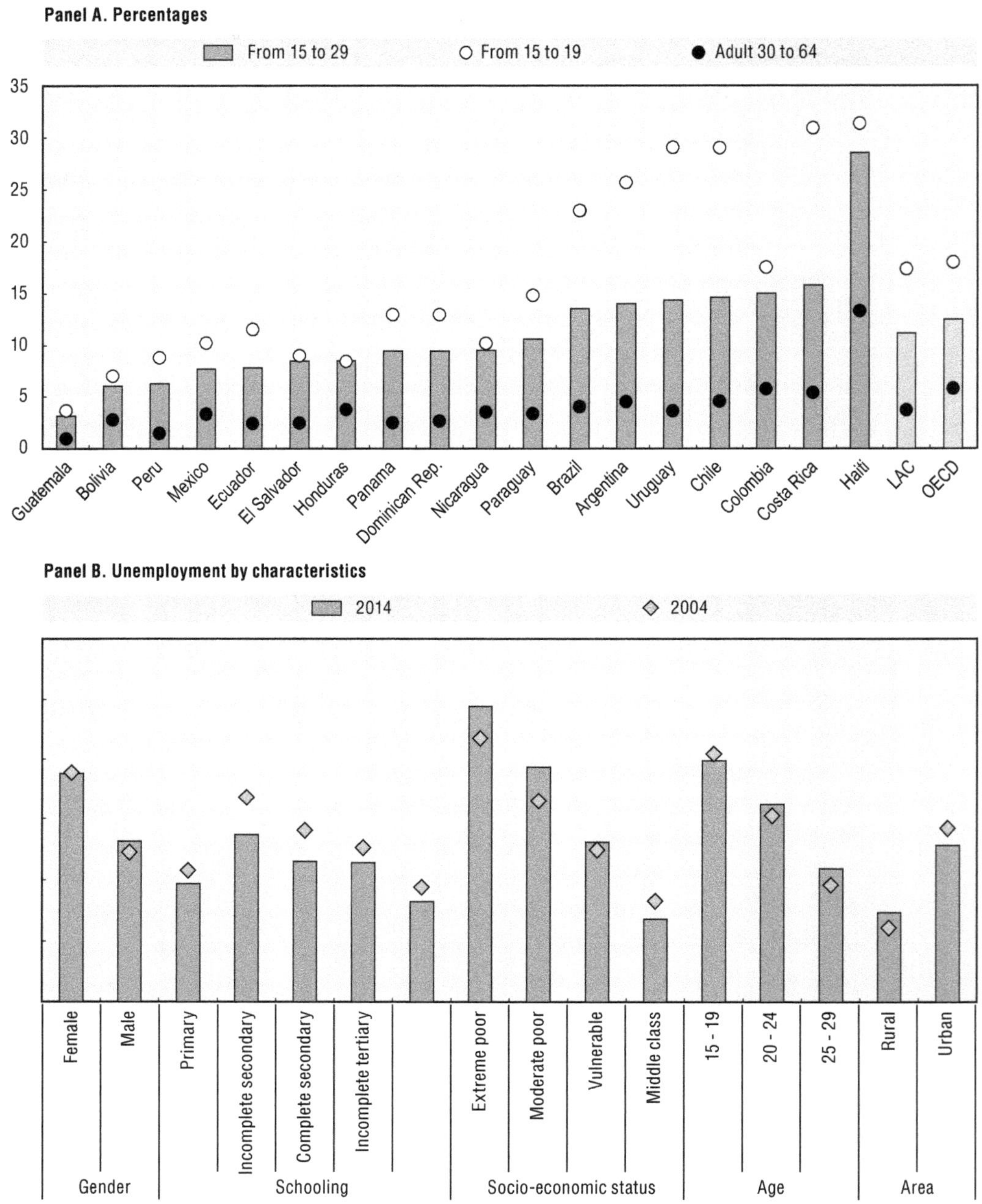

Note: LAC weighted average of 17 countries: Argentina, Bolivia, Brazil, Chile, Colombia, Costa Rica, Dominican Republic, Ecuador, El Salvador, Guatemala, Honduras, Mexico, Nicaragua, Panama, Paraguay, Peru, Uruguay, Bolivarian Republic of Venezuela (hereafter "Venezuela"). Haiti is excluded. OECD unweighted average of 34 OECD countries.

Source: OECD and World Bank tabulations of SEDLAC (CEDLAS and the World Bank) and OECD – LFS data.

StatLink http://dx.doi.org/10.1787/888933414075

Unemployment rates are considerably higher for younger, less-skilled youth from more disadvantaged backgrounds (Figure 3.5, panel B). Poor and vulnerable youth are twice as likely to be unemployed as less vulnerable youth. Unemployment rates are 24.6% for youth belonging to extremely poor households, 20% for moderately poor youth and 13.4% for vulnerable youth compared with 7% for middle-class youth. Youth aged 15-19 face the highest unemployment rates, reach peak at 28% for the extreme poor, 25% for the moderate poor and 19% for the vulnerable compared with 12% for their non-vulnerable peers.

Additionally, the youth unemployment rate is higher in urban than in rural areas, even if disparities by geographical area have narrowed.[9] In 2014, the rate was estimated to be higher for young women (13.4%) than for young men (9.5%), reflecting the particular disadvantage women are facing in the labour market. Despite fewer educational disparities between men and women, traditional gender roles regarding division of work and social norms in LAC remain a major obstacle for women who want to enter the labour market.[10]

Inactivity is a big problem among out-of-school youth

The two main channels for social inclusion are the education system and the labour market. Yet a considerable proportion of youth in Latin America are neither working nor engaged in education nor training (NEET). These activities can help "NEETs" develop skills that will pay off later by making them more employable or opening up better opportunities for career advancement. The NEET rate is a good measure of the youth educational and labour market reality, reflecting both the risk of unemployment and inactivity. As such, it may be more closely connected to the risk of long-run marginalisation in the labour market and social exclusion than youth unemployment, although the two measures overlap considerably. Policy makers also need to focus on NEET both for its relevance as the sole youth-specific target for the post-2015 Sustainable Development Goals (SDGs) and for the adoption of a G20 target on reducing the share of young people most at risk of being left permanently behind in the labour market by 15% by 2025.[11]

In 2014, almost 55% of people aged 15-29 (around 81 million) were employed (including those working while in school); approximately 25% of those people were attending an institution providing primary, secondary or post-secondary education (Figure 3.6, Panel A). Nonetheless, NEET youth remain a sizeable and particularly vulnerable group: in 2014, over one in five youth in the region – 21% of the people in this age group (almost 30 million) – said they were neither in school nor employed. Youth in this group may be stigmatised or linked to vagrancy and violence; long-term NEETs suffer from a high risk of marginalisation. The largest percentages of young people who are neither students nor employed are in El Salvador, Guatemala, Honduras and Mexico – countries with some of the highest levels of poverty and social exclusion in the region (Figure 3.6, Panel B). The share of NEETs has decreased (or remained stable) since 2004 in all LAC countries except for Guatemala and Ecuador; however, for all countries in the region it is well above the OECD area average (15% in 2014).

Inactivity is a problem since it contributes to the intergenerational persistence of inequality, prevents the region from exploiting an emerging demographic window of opportunity and can be associated with risky behaviour such as crime and violence in some contexts (De Hoyos, Halsey and Székely, 2016). When productive options are not available, jobless youth are more likely to damage themselves and society. However, young people are an extremely heterogeneous group requiring distinct paths for integration into society. As will be discussed below, most of these youths, especially young women, provide care and/or perform unpaid domestic work; are currently unemployed but seeking work; are waiting for a job; or have a disability that prevents them from working or studying. Properly distinguishing the reasons for being neither studying nor employed will help identify different strategies for more effective inclusion of youth in the labour market.

Figure 3.6. **Activity rates of youth aged 15-29 in LAC and OECD**

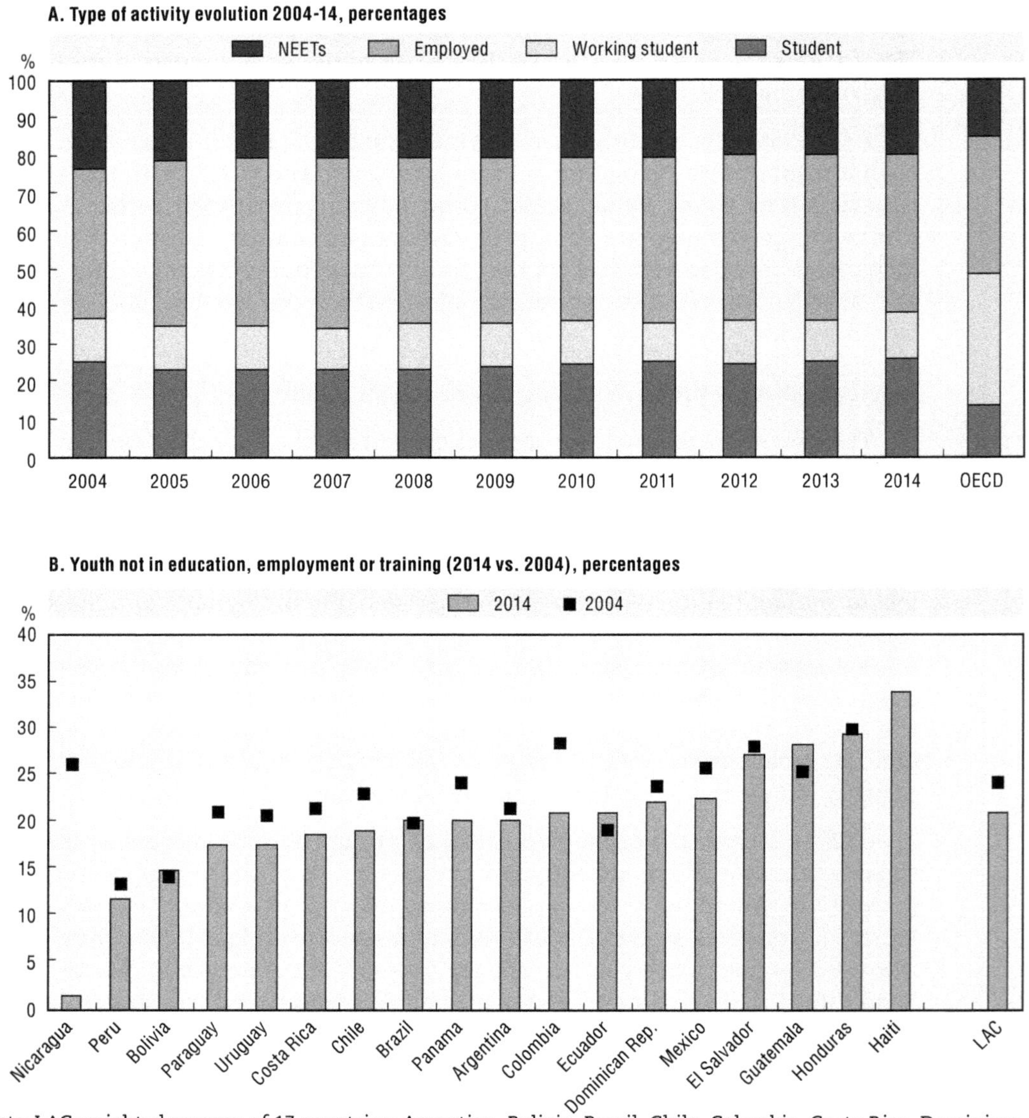

Note: LAC weighted average of 17 countries: Argentina, Bolivia, Brazil, Chile, Colombia, Costa Rica, Dominican Republic, Ecuador, El Salvador, Guatemala, Honduras, Mexico, Nicaragua, Panama, Paraguay, Peru, Uruguay. Haiti is excluded from the LAC average owing to limited data availability. OECD unweighted average of 34 OECD countries for 2014.

Source: OECD and World Bank tabulations of SEDLAC (CEDLAS and the World Bank) and OECD – LFS data.

StatLink http://dx.doi.org/10.1787/888933414082

The proportion of young women and vulnerable NEETs in Latin America is high…

NEET rates are much higher for young women (30% vs. 11% for young men), less-educated youth (33% for youth with primary education vs. about 22% for youth with complete and incomplete secondary and almost 10% for youth with a university degree or some university education and for older age groups (around 30% for ages 20-29). In stark contrast with OECD countries, where male and female youth are equally likely to be NEETs, 76% of youth NEETs in LAC are women (vs. 50% of the total population of youth). In some countries such as Guatemala and Honduras, NEET rates for young women reach 42% and 44%, respectively. The gap between young men and women is smallest among the youngest NEETs (aged 15-19) and increases with age. This suggests that while the school enrolment gender gap has disappeared, the participation gap has not – highlighting the non-transitory nature of this phenomenon for women (Figure 3.7, Panels A and B). It also suggests that the combination of gender roles, limited access to childcare and early fertility are contributing to low participation in the labour force among female youth.

In all LAC countries, NEET youth come from the poorest households in society confirming the relevance of the household situation and socio-economic status (Carcillo et al., 2015). In 2014, nearly 83% of young women and 76% of young men who are NEETs come from poor or vulnerable households with the highest rates of joblessness and lowest level of educational attainment. On the other hand, the reason for being NEETs clearly differs between young men and women (see Box 3.2). Female NEETs have high rates of marriage and young children in the household, as a proxy for family care, while male NEETs show the opposite trend: on average 57% of women NEETs are married compared with 12% of men, while 50% of young women have children under four in the household versus 19% of their male peers.

Box 3.1. **A multivariate perspective on the factors associated with NEET status**

Probit models of the probability for young people to be neither employed nor in education nor training (NEET) help summarise the descriptive findings, while also testing their robustness in a multivariate context. In these models, NEET status is assumed to be influenced by educational attainment, socio-economic status, age and some other household characteristics such as the presence of young people. Table 3.1 shows the results for 2014 separately by gender as the determinants of NEET status might be different for men and women. The estimated marginal effects were obtained from pooled regressions with country-fixed effects across 18 Latin American countries for which data are available from the SEDLAC dataset. A note of caution in interpreting these results: owing to issues of self-selection that are not addressed, causality cannot be established; rather, these are correlations.

Table 3.1. **Relative probabilities of not being in education or employed, LAC 2014**

(marginal effects of selected characteristics on the likelihood of being neither in education nor in employment)

VARIABLES	(1) Men	(2) Men	(3) Women	(4) Women
Incomplete primary	-0.091***	-0.072***	-0.134***	-0.052***
	(0.000)	(0.000)	(0.000)	(0.001)
Primary complete	-0.079***	-0.057***	-0.096***	0.068***
	(0.000)	(0.000)	(0.000)	(0.001)
Some secondary	-0.169***	-0.136***	-0.275***	-0.102***
	(0.000)	(0.000)	(0.000)	(0.001)
Secondary complete	-0.077***	-0.062***	-0.147***	0.175***
	(0.000)	(0.000)	(0.000)	(0.001)
Tertiary income	-0.122***	-0.122***	-0.343***	-0.146***
	(0.000)	(0.000)	(0.000)	(0.001)
Tertiary complete	-0.075***	-0.088***	-0.233***	0.169***
	(0.000)	(0.000)	(0.000)	(0.001)
Poor	-0.026***	-0.026***	-0.019***	-0.012***
	(0.000)	(0.000)	(0.000)	(0.000)
Vulnerable	-0.066***	-0.068***	-0.112***	-0.102***
	(0.000)	(0.000)	(0.000)	(0.000)
Middle class	-0.113***	-0.117***	-0.247***	-0.238***
	(0.000)	(0.000)	(0.000)	(0.000)
Ages 20-24	-0.001***		0.175***	
	(0.000)		(0.000)	
Ages 25-29	-0.037***		0.166***	
	(0.000)		(0.000)	
Number of kids in HH - ages 0-4		-0.004***		0.018***
		(0.000)		(0.000)
Number of kids in HH - ages 5-14		0.000***		-0.007***
		(0.000)		(0.000)
Observations	**64367293**	**64328977**	**64995626**	**64961366**

Box 3.1. A multivariate perspective on the factors associated with NEET status (cont.)

Qualifications and household wealth matter for both young men and women. The probability of being neither in employment, nor education nor training decrease steadily with level of education and socio-economic status. NEET prospects for male youth are also negatively associated with age. However, the opposite is true for young women, for whom NEET status becomes progressively more likely (see columns 1 and 3). Unlike for young men, the probability of being NEET for young women is positively associated with the number of young children in the household; this suggests that women may be more likely to be NEETs because of household obligations and parenthood than men (see columns 2 and 4).

Note: Marginal effects calculated from probit models estimated on a sample of youth aged 15-29 using SEDLAC data for 18 LAC countries. The dependent variable is a dummy variable indicating wherever the young person was NEET in 2014. Additional controls include dummy for urban area, experience and experience squares, country-fixed effects. Reference category for socio-economic status: extreme poor. Standard errors in parentheses *** $p<0.01$, ** $p<0.05$, * $p<0.1$.
Source: OECD and WB estimates using SEDLAC (CEDLAS and the World Bank) microdata.

Figure 3.7. **NEET rates for men and women in LAC, 2014**

A. NEET rates and percentage point differences between women and men in 2014

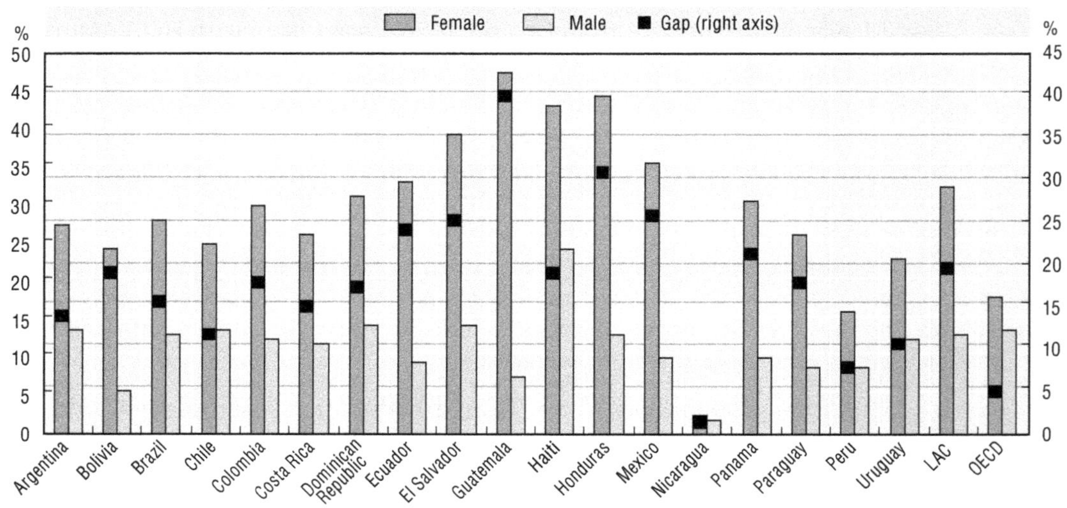

B. NEET rates by characteristics over time

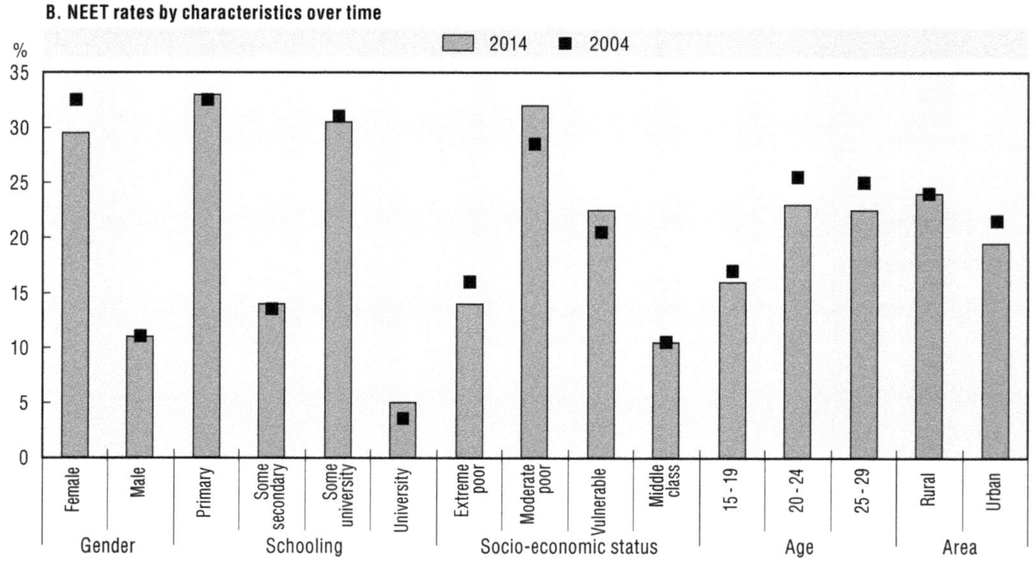

Note: LAC weighted average of 17 countries: Argentina, Bolivia, Brazil, Chile, Colombia, Costa Rica, Dominican Republic, Ecuador, El Salvador, Guatemala, Honduras, Mexico, Nicaragua, Panama, Paraguay, Peru, Uruguay.
Source: OECD and World Bank tabulations of SEDLAC (CEDLAS and the World Bank) and OECD – LFS data.
StatLink http://dx.doi.org/10.1787/888933414091

...but many of these inactive women are contributing to the economy

In OECD countries, relatively few people are engaged in household production compared to emerging economies. Within LAC, some people not employed or in education, in particular young women working in the household, are productive and contributing to the total economy (see Box 3.2). Table 3.2 shows that many young people in LAC who are neither studying nor employed are engaged in unpaid domestic work and caregiving, and the majority of them are women; 70% of female NEETs compared with 10% of male NEETs are engaged in domestic work.

At the same time, some social norms and expectations dictate that young women work in the household, which excludes them from participating in the labour market or in education.[12] As Furlong (2006) states: "the hetereogeneity of NEETs means that both research and policy must begin by disaggregating so as to be able to identify the distinct characteristics and needs of various sub-groups." Therefore, in addition to distinguishing between discouraged youth (i.e. youth who have given up on job searching) and jobless youth, the marginalisation of young women through home-care contributions must be recognised both to promote shared responsibility by men and women for these tasks and to advocate for a work-life balance for both sexes (ECLAC, 2016a). In terms of potential economic growth, a large number of inactive, but educated, women represents an unexploited resource. Policy makers, then, need to understand potential barriers faced by this particular group such as lack of high-quality affordable childcare, labour market discrimination and poor awareness of opportunities, and how to overcome them.

Table 3.2. **Youth (aged 15-29) neither in education nor employment by type of activity in Latin America**

	Male						Female					
Country	Unemployed	Seeking employment for the first time	Pensioners	Unpaid domestic or care work	Disabled	Other inactive	Unemployed	Seeking employment for the first time	Pensioners	Unpaid domestic or care work	Disabled	Other inactive
Argentina	35.6	7.8	2.7	11.2	4.6	38.1	16.1	3.3	1.9	62.9	1.0	14.6
Bolivia	20.2	20.4	0.0	9.1	16.7	33.7	5.8	4.7	0.0	82.2	3.2	4.2
Brazil	24.2	9.1	7.9	19.4	0.0	39.4	12.1	6.8	10.3	64.0	0.0	6.7
Chile	37.3	6.0	1.2	3.2	7.7	44.6	17.2	4.4	0.4	29.0	3.1	46.0
Colombia	50.0	9.9	0.0	9.5	4.1	26.5	24.5	5.9	0.0	62.2	0.7	6.7
Costa Rica	45.7	6.9	4.1	25.3	3.8	14.1	15.9	4.3	1.2	75.4	0.7	2.0
Dominican Rep.	54.4	13.8	0.3	0.4	15.1	16.0	33.0	7.0	0.0	43.2	9.3	7.3
Ecuador	50.1	0.0	0.0	1.2	17.7	30.7	13.4	0.0	0.0	72.1	4.6	9.9
El Salvador	51.0	12.5	0.1	6.8	17.2	12.4	6.4	3.0	0.0	86.2	3.0	1.4
Guatemala	29.6	6.3	0.1	12.2	24.1	27.7	2.8	0.8	0.0	93.9	1.7	0.9
Honduras	27.8	6.1	0.2	23.8	8.2	33.7	5.0	2.5	0.1	87.1	1.1	4.3
Mexico	71.6	0.0	0.0	10.8	8.0	9.5	8.0	0.0	0.0	89.9	0.9	1.1
Nicaragua	41.3	11.1	0.0	9.5	8.2	29.9	6.1	3.2	0.0	86.7	1.8	2.1
Panama	38.8	15.0	0.0	10.3	4.3	31.6	7.0	3.4	0.0	84.3	0.7	4.6
Paraguay	29.5	9.9	0.0	2.5	19.2	38.9	11.6	5.4	0.0	41.9	5.0	36.1
Peru	26.5	5.0	0.0	31.6	10.6	26.2	12.7	3.6	0.0	72.5	3.6	7.6
Uruguay	37.8	6.3	3.5	5.0	8.3	38.9	22.3	4.4	2.0	47.3	3.6	20.2
Venezuela	47.0	8.1	0.0	3.5	5.9	35.6	13.3	4.6	0.0	71.9	1.7	8.4
Latin America	**39.9**	**9.6**	**1.1**	**10.9**	**10.8**	**29.3**	**13.0**	**4.2**	**0.9**	**69.6**	**2.7**	**10.2**

Notes: Data are for 2012, with the exception of Bolivia, Chile, Costa Rica, Panama, Paraguay and Uruguay (2011), Guatemala (2006), Honduras (2010) and Nicaragua (2009). Latin America average is computed as the simple average of results from the 18 countries included in the measurement. The category "pensioners" includes all people who receive some type of pension from the state – for this age group, these are mostly disability pensions or, in fewer cases, widowhood pensions.
Source: ECLAC on the basis of special tabulations of data from household surveys conducted in the respective countries.

Box 3.2. The economic contributions of the NEET population in Argentina

Youth NEETs are commonly considered as "inactive" and "unproductive" and thus connected to the risk of long-run marginalisation in the labour market and social exclusion. However, a large proportion of NEETs perform unpaid housework and produce non-market goods and services that are essential for their households' consumption and well-being. While NEETs performing housework remain unpaid, they can be considered as a substitute to domestic workers and, at the same time, allow other members of the family to work. Additionally, since the output of households' productive activities is not transacted in the market, and therefore carries no monetary value, it is not recorded in national accounts. This exercise uses time-use surveys recording workers' activities in different parts of the day and provides a precise estimate of the time devoted to paid work, unpaid work, leisure and personal care. In this way, it attempts to value NEETs' unpaid household work in monetary terms. Time devoted to non-market production by youth NEETs in Argentina is almost constant across the three age groups, but much higher among young women than young men.

A standard method in the literature of *Household Satellite Accounts* to measure this contribution is imputing a value to the time used in household production, using a wage per hour from the market economy. There are three possibilities within the input approach. First is the "opportunity cost" wage that a person could be paid for working an extra hour in a market job rather than an hour of unpaid household work. The cost of an hour of household work is the forgone opportunity to earn in the market. This method is usually criticised as it yields different values depending on who performs the task. The second method uses the wages of specialist paid workers (i.e. a cleaner, a cook, a nanny, a gardener) to value the same tasks performed by household members. This "specialist replacement cost" method can be criticised as specialised workers might be more efficient than a usual household member, taking less time to perform the same task and thus overstating the value of household production. Finally, a "generalist replacement cost" method uses the wage rate for a generalist worker or housekeeper. This is regarded as more appropriate since the working conditions and range of activities are similar to those of household members.

Given the existence of a minimum wage for household workers in Argentina, this exercise uses the rate as generalist replacement cost. Table 3.3 shows that a large part of those classified as NEETs are not as "unproductive" as they are commonly perceived: if they were participating in the economy they would contribute close to 1.3% of the Argentinean gross domestic product (GDP) in 2013. This contribution is entirely based on female labour with women devoting around 7-10 hours per day to household work.

Table 3.3. Contributions of NEET youth to the Argentinean economy

	Age group	Average hours of work (per day)	Pay	Number of Neets in HH	As % GDP (2013)
Women	15 - 19	6.74	18.6	108 119	0.1%
	20 - 24	8.37	18.6	214 427	0.4%
	25 - 29	9.86	18.6	163 181	0.3%
Men	15 - 19	2.35	18.6	18 252	0.0%
	20 - 24	2.19	18.6	15 345	0.0%
	25 - 29	2.95	18.6	9 206	0.0%
Total				528 530	0.8%

Note: Pay is imputed as the 2013 Argentinean minimum wage for household work. For further information, see www.elsalario.com.ar/main/Salario/salario-minimo-del-personal-domestico.
Source: OECD/ECLAC/CAF based on Encuesta Anual de Hogares Urbanos (EAHU), 2013.

School-to-work transitions are key to social inclusion for youth

The link between education and employment is one of the keys to social inclusion at this stage of life. Leaving school too early is costly for later productivity. The forgone earnings and the lack of skills accumulation can make it much more difficult to escape poverty as an adult. Similarly to OECD countries where transitions from school to work can take time and include spells of unemployment and short-term contracts (OECD, 2015a), Latin America also has many young people who struggle to integrate into the labour market. Over the past 25 years, average educational attainment in Latin America has increased (see Chapter 4). The fact that youth are older when leaving school should have improved the transition to work and led to greater success once employed. Certainly it has, but too many young people still face significant challenges in their path to work. While long-term trends are useful to assess the overall dynamics of youth activities, they tell us little in terms of the actual path that youth follow in their transition to adult life and, in particular, the role that NEET status plays in such a transition. This section aims to use a dynamic approach to measure youth's transition process from education to work.

Figure 3.8 plots the activity status of youth by single year of age in 2014 for LAC-18 average, distinguishing between education; work and study; work in informal job; work in formal job; and neither in education nor employment. Given the differences in labour market outcomes between different household wealth, it is interesting to look at the detailed transition path separately by socio-economic groups. These data provide a useful descriptive portrait of what youth are doing during the transition to adult life, and after leaving school. Unsurprisingly, it emerges that youth from poor households in LAC countries leave school earlier than their peers in other better-off households, and when employed have mainly informal jobs. In addition, poor and vulnerable youth have higher shares of NEET status, which is reflected in differences in employment rates (see previous section). Overall, evidence suggests that vulnerable and poor youth not only tend to leave school earlier, but also experience longer transitions from school to work.

Longitudinal data that follow individuals over time can measure the actual transition of youth into the labour market. Unfortunately, this type of data for Latin America is available for only a reduced set of sample countries (Argentina, Brazil, Mexico, Paraguay). Figure 3.9 presents results of yearly transition rates out of school for the pooled period 2005-15 for youth who were enrolled in school in year *t*-1 and were not in school in year *t*.[13] Transition patterns are quite different for young men and women. While about half of female movers first enter inactivity, this percentage is much lower for men, with the exception of Brazil. A high percentage of young men manage to enter into employment (ranging from 53% in Mexico to 35% in Brazil), but many of them find an informal job, particularly in Argentina. Additionally, a conspicuous percentage (around 20% for both men and women) of young people ends up in unemployment. Overall, this suggests it takes some time to successfully complete the transition from school to work.

Figure 3.8. **Activity status by single year of age, LAC average, 2014**
(percentage of youth aged 15-29)

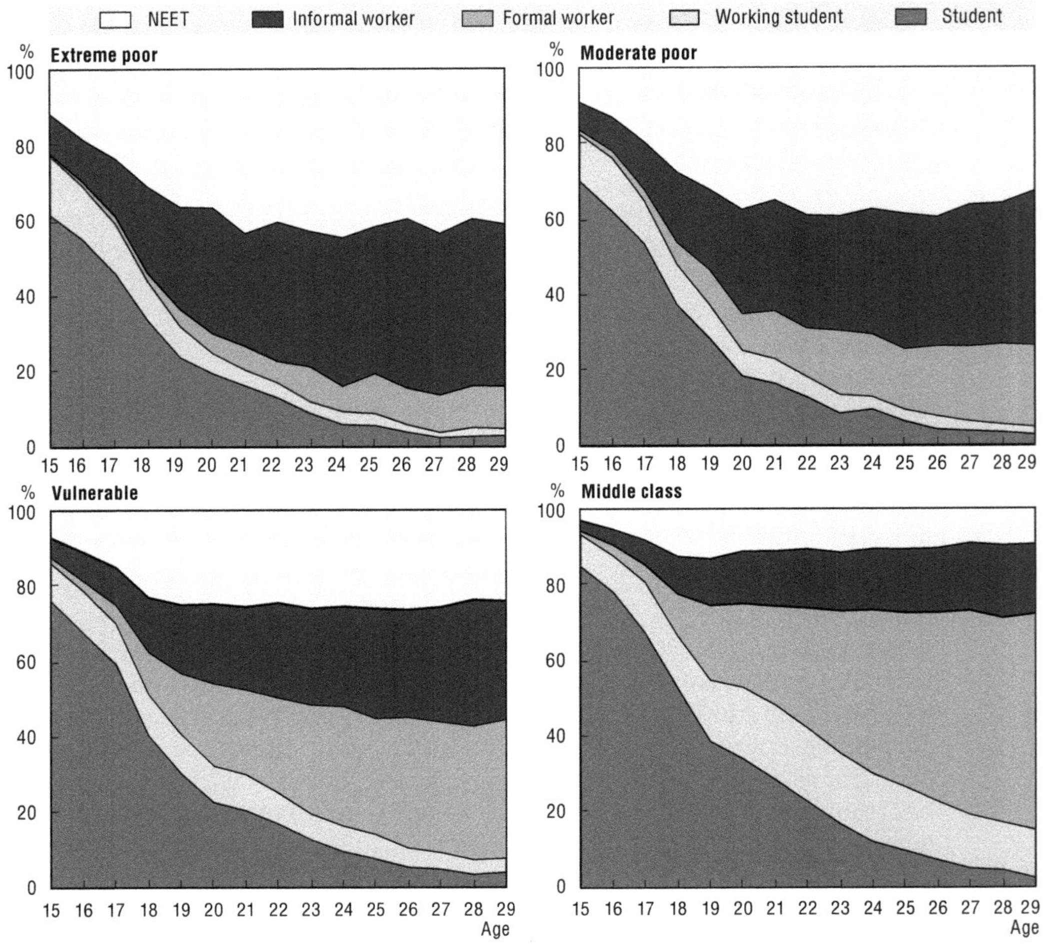

Note: LAC unweighted average of 16 countries: Argentina, Bolivia, Brazil, Chile, Colombia, Costa Rica, Dominican Republic, Ecuador, El Salvador, Guatemala, Honduras, Mexico, Panama, Paraguay, Peru, Uruguay.
Source: OECD and World Bank tabulations of SEDLAC (CEDLAS and the World Bank).
StatLink http://dx.doi.org/10.1787/888933414101

Figure 3.9. **Youth (aged 15-29) school-to-labour market transitions, 2005-15**
(percentages)

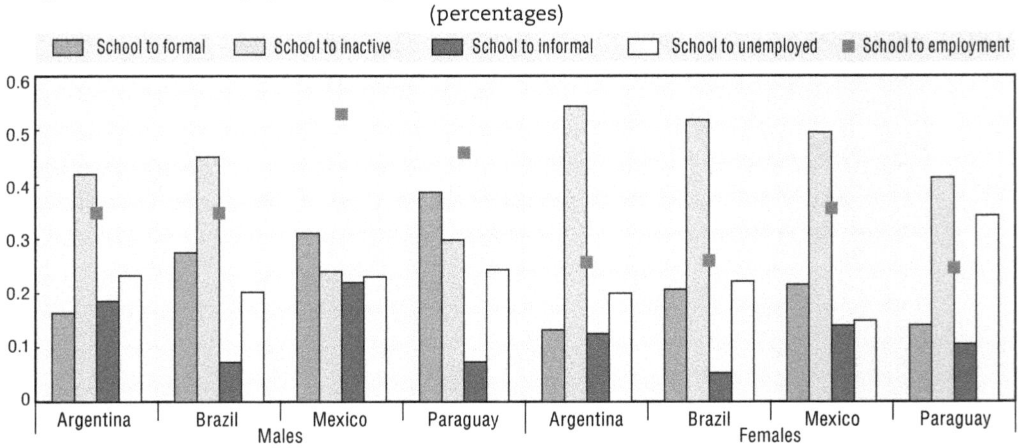

Note: Results show yearly transition rates out of school for the pooled period 2005-15. Transition rates are calculated as the ratio between flow of people moving that transitioned from Condition 1 (school) to Condition 2 between time 0 and time 1, over the total stock of people in the population in Condition 1 in time 0 (i.e. in school: only in school and in school and working). The transitions are year to year (from year t to year t+1). This analysis is limited to urban populations owing to data limitations.
Source: OECD and World Bank tabulations of Labor Database for Latin America and the Caribbean - LABLAC (CEDLAS and the World Bank).
StatLink http://dx.doi.org/10.1787/888933414116

The dynamics of NEET status

In addition to understanding how frequently youth are neither in education nor employment, it is important to understand whether NEET is a temporary or more permanent phase. There is concern that repeated NEET spells and/or longer duration in NEET status can be detrimental to future career prospects (Quintini and Martin, 2007). Based on a sample of LAC countries – Argentina, Brazil, Mexico and Paraguay – for which longitudinal data are available, around one-third of NEET youth on average have moved into employment or school after one year (Figure 3.10). Nonetheless, similarly to the incidence of NEET status, its dynamics are also very different for young males and females. Except for Brazil, where both men and women seem to face difficulties in exiting NEET status, young women are considerably less likely than men to exit NEET after one year (29% vs. 67% in Mexico and 34% vs. 61% in Argentina); this suggests that NEET status can be a trap for young women. In general, exit rates show it is easier to exit from NEET status when younger.

Figure 3.10. **Flows into and out of NEET status in selected Latin America countries – Youth (aged 15-29), 2005-15**

(percentages)

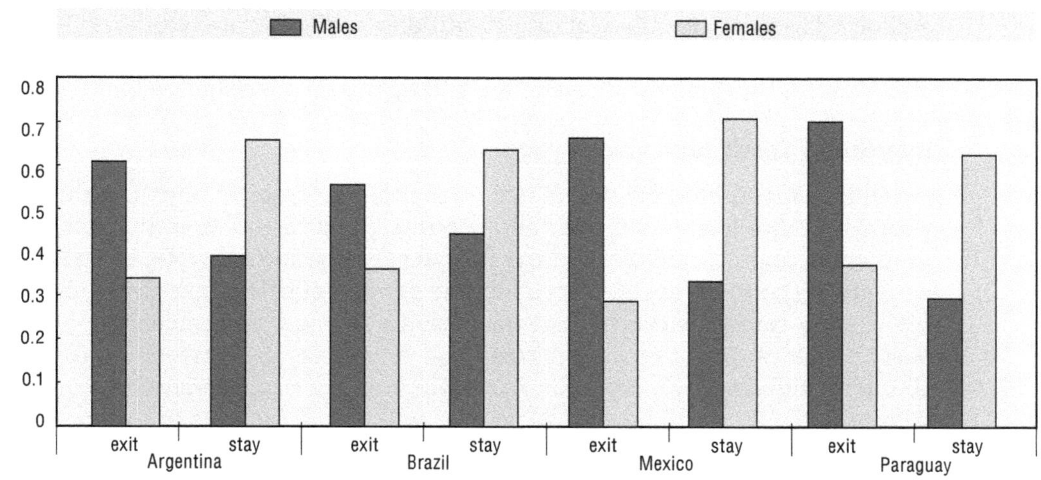

Note: Results show yearly movements out of NEET status after one year for the pooled period 2005-15. This analysis is limited to urban populations owing to data limitations.

Source: OECD and World Bank tabulations of LABLAC (CEDLAS and the World Bank).

StatLink http://dx.doi.org/10.1787/888933414128

Some indicators on the quality of youth jobs

Improving the quality of job opportunities for youth remains a major challenge in Latin America

Previous research shows that young people, even when they do find work, are more likely than prime-age and older people to work in poorer-quality jobs with lower wages and longer working days. They are also less likely to be covered by social security, protection systems and opportunities for training and career progression (Maloney, 2004; Weller, 2007; Bassi and Galiani, 2009). Starting in a low-paying job, or being mismatched early on with the wrong type of employment, would not have severe consequences if youth can move to more productive opportunities. Unfortunately, this does not seem to be the case in the LAC region; young people seem to face particular barriers to entering the labour market, as can be seen in their high unemployment rates, precarious jobs, informality rates and low income. These difficulties can persist and be costly to mitigate, which is why it is crucial to ensure youth are off to a good start.

Low quality of youth entry jobs

When employed, youth in LAC tend to be in poorer-quality jobs than their adult counterparts, with lower wages and longer working days (Box 3.3); this has negative long-term consequences because they are less likely to be enrolled in social protection system (ECLAC, 2014). Nearly half (46%) of young people in LAC report work in low productivity sectors, which particularly affects youth from lower socio-economic levels (Gontero and Weller, 2015).[14] The poorest young people in the region lack capital and skills and toil for others in occupations that others shun. Fixed-term contracts and temporary work agency (TWA) are not common, but more prevalent among youth than among adults: 48.4% of employed youth in some countries in the region have a contract, 32.9% of them have a permanent contract and 82.8% are employed full-time (see Table 3.A1.1 in the annex). Temporary contracts can be seen as a stepping stone to more stable employment for those with low skills and experience; however, many low-skilled youth often get stuck in such jobs or leave the labour market altogether, especially women (OECD, 2014a). In LAC countries, the percentage of low-skilled youth with a temporary contract reached 64% in 2014. For some young people, these indicators reflect a choice for more flexible working conditions, while for many others they reflect the types of obstacles that block full labour insertion. As a consequence of these obstacles, many youth, especially young women, end up working without pay for the family.

Informality is still high among youth

Informality is one of the main factors that can harm job quality in Latin America. LAC youth are more likely than their adult counterparts to end up in informal employment or in other unprotected work in the formal sector. Informal work, by definition, leaves workers without the social protection and general entitlements of the formal sectors.[15] Informality rates, for youth, have decreased by almost ten percentage points over the past ten years. Despite this progress and regardless of enormous differences across countries, informality among youth in Latin America is, on average, still quite high (47%) (Figure 3.12). Young people from poor or vulnerable families are more likely to have informal work than middle-class youth. Informality rates are slightly higher for young women and for younger workers than among older youth and adults. Crucially, and in line with existing evidence, less-educated youth experience higher informality rates (68% for young workers with primary school or less vs. 24% for workers with a university degree).

To the extent that a job in the informal sector constitutes a stepping stone towards a formal career, a high informality rate among youth could not be a major concern. Some recent evidence has suggested that the informal sector may actually serve as informal job training, a "springboard" into the formal sector. Therefore, early experiences in the informal sector need not harm an individual's career path in terms of employment prospects or wages (Bosch and Maloney, 2010; Cunningham and Bustos, 2011). However, Cruces, Ham and Viollaz (2012) show strong and significant scarring effects of this sector in Brazil and Argentina: cohorts exposed to higher levels of unemployment and informality in their youth fare systematically worse in labour markets as adults. Additionally, informal firms generally provide workers with fewer opportunities for human capital accumulation and are less productive (La Porta and Schleifer, 2008). This might thus pose an additional drag on the most vulnerable youth earnings and career advancement at a period that plays a fundamental role for the whole lifelong career path. Being forced into unemployment, informal work or precarious employment conditions, young people find themselves in a vicious circle of poverty; this affects self-esteem, fosters alienation and reduces future prospects.

Box 3.3. Job quality in Latin America

Job quality is an inherently multi-dimensional concept that refers to those job characteristics that contribute to the well-being of workers. The OECD *Job Quality Framework* is structured around three dimensions that are closely related to people's employment situation: earnings quality (a combination of average earnings and inequality); labour market security (capturing the risk of unemployment and extreme low pay); and the quality of the working environment (measured as the incidence of job strain or very long working hours).

Figure 3.11. Job quality and quantity outcomes by socio-demographic groups in Latin America

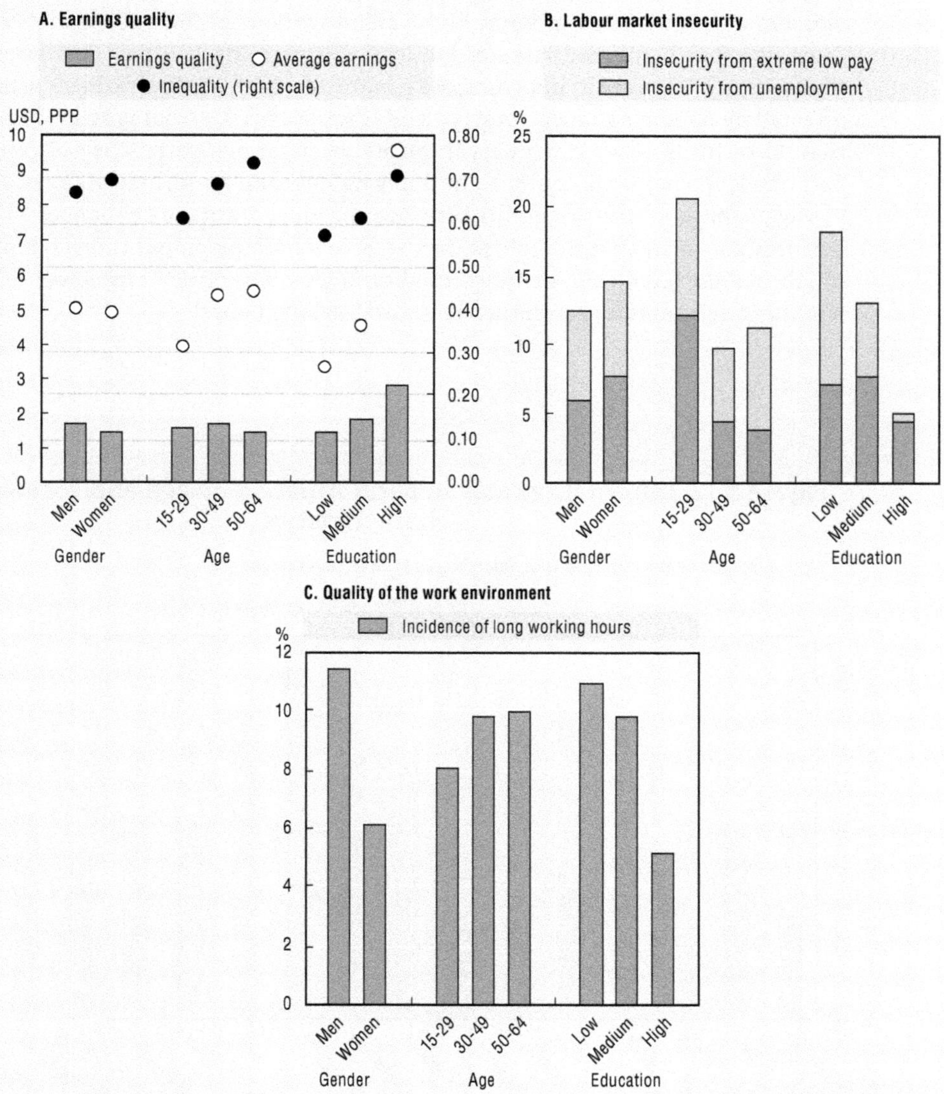

Note: The figures show unweighted country average for six Latin American countries: Argentina, Brazil, Chile, Colombia, Costa Rica and Mexico.

Source: OECD calculations based on national household and labour force surveys (EPH - Argentina, PNAD - Brazil, CASEN - Chile, GEIH - Colombia, ENHAO - Costa Rica, ENIGH - Mexico), in OECD (2015b) "Enhancing job quality in emerging economies", *Employment Outlook 2015*.

StatLink http://dx.doi.org/10.1787/888933414138

Box 3.3. Job quality in Latin America (cont.)

These three dimensions jointly define job quality and should be considered simultaneously, together with job quantity, when assessing labour market performance. OECD (2015b) has adapted the job quality framework to emerging economies by taking into account their labour market specificities, such as the weakness of social protection (inadequacy of benefits and low coverage of social insurance schemes) and high rates of working poverty, and, at the same time, the more limited data available for these countries.

The Latin American countries analysed in OECD (2015b) – Argentina, Brazil, Chile, Colombia, Costa Rica and Mexico – present levels of job quality (in all three dimensions) that are much lower than the OECD average. Data show that, on average, low-skilled workers earn one-third of what high-skilled workers receive for every hour of work; they also face combined risks of job loss and extreme low pay that are almost four times higher. Workers in informal jobs – many of whom are low skilled – are particularly affected by poor job quality: they typically lack access to social protection and earn less than two-thirds of what workers in formal occupations earn. They also face a risk of extreme low pay that is nearly eight times higher than for formal workers. Additionally, young people and low-skilled workers face the most dramatic challenges – they not only perform poorly in terms of job quantity (i.e. lower employment rates) but also in terms of job quality (i.e. lower earnings quality, higher insecurity and lower quality of the working environment, as captured by working long hours).

Figure 3.12. Informality rates in Latin America by age and socio-economic characteristics

A. Youth and adults employed with informal jobs in 2014, percentages

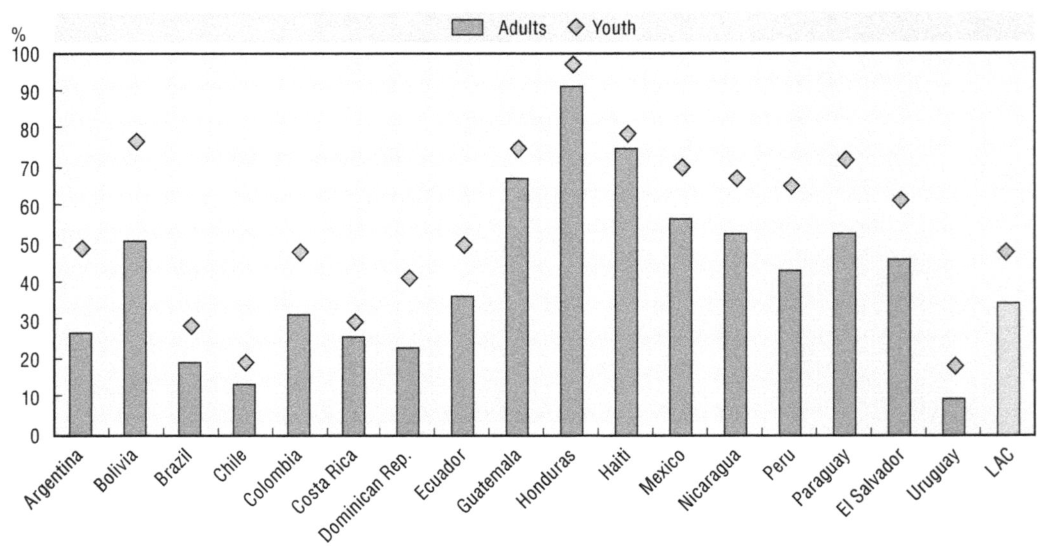

Figure 3.12. **Informality rates in Latin America by age and socio-economic characteristics** (cont.)

B. Informality rates by characteristics – youth (aged 15-29), 2004 vs. 2014

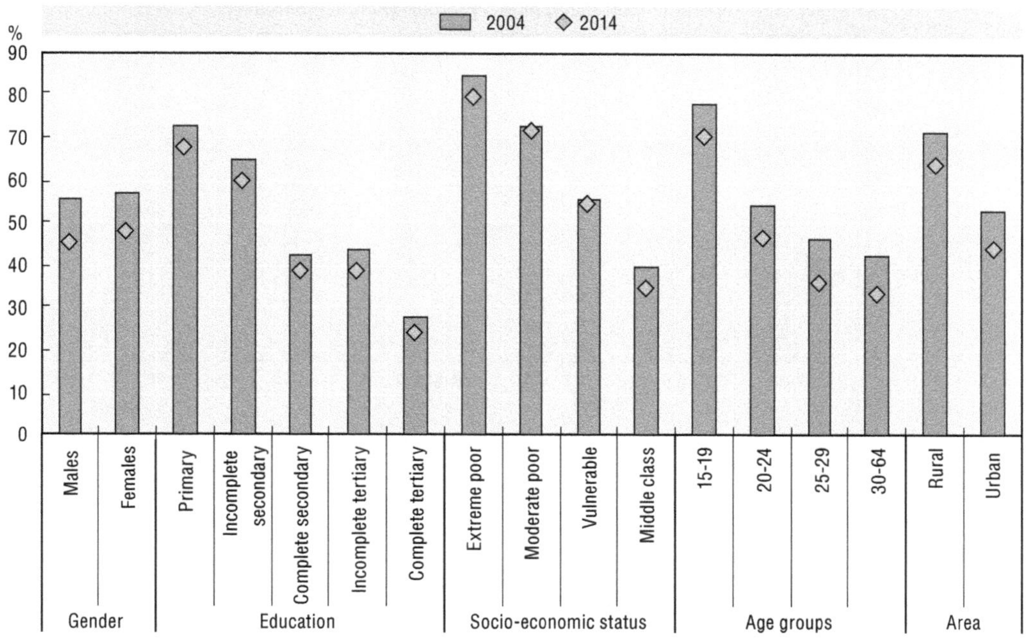

Note: Informality rates are calculated for wage and salary workers using the SEDLAC legislative definition of informality. In this case, access to pension eligibility is the proxy. LAC weighted average of 13 countries: Argentina, Bolivia, Brazil, Chile, Costa Rica, Ecuador, El Salvador, Guatemala, Mexico, Nicaragua, Panama, Paraguay, Peru, Uruguay. Colombia, Dominican Republic, Haiti and Honduras are not included in the LAC average because there is no formality information for 2004.

Source: OECD and World Bank tabulations of SEDLAC (CEDLAS and the World Bank).

StatLink http://dx.doi.org/10.1787/888933414145

Stepping stone or trap?

Only a dynamic perspective of how workers move in and out of informal employment can reveal whether starting "informally" constitutes a real disadvantage and to understand the difficulties of escaping informality. Figure 3.13 plots results from a transition analysis in four countries for which individual panel data are available (Argentina, Brazil, Mexico, Peru). Data show that, for both employed young men and women, informal jobs may be less stable than formal jobs. The retention rate of workers employed in formal jobs is much higher than that among informal workers. Additionally, a substantial fraction of informal workers (ranging from 15% for women in Mexico to 29% of men in Brazil) move to a formal job every year, suggesting that in some cases informal jobs for youth might be a stepping stone.

The instability of informal jobs can also translate into a higher risk of job loss: informal jobs appear to be associated to a higher probability of transitioning into unemployment or inactivity, particularly among young women. Certainly, this can also result from personal choice. Women who are planning to exit the labour force soon for family reasons, for example, may be more likely to look for more flexible work, and thus self-select into informal work. This seems plausible; indeed, transitions into unemployment do not seem much higher for women than men, while transitions from informality to inactivity are quite high. Therefore, informal jobs might be either a stepping stone for some, but a trap for others, particularly more vulnerable low-skilled youth. A reason behind this can be found in the higher cost of formalisation for youth, particularly at the low end of the distribution (see Box 3.4).

Figure 3.13. Flows into and out of informality – Youth (aged 15-29), 2005-15

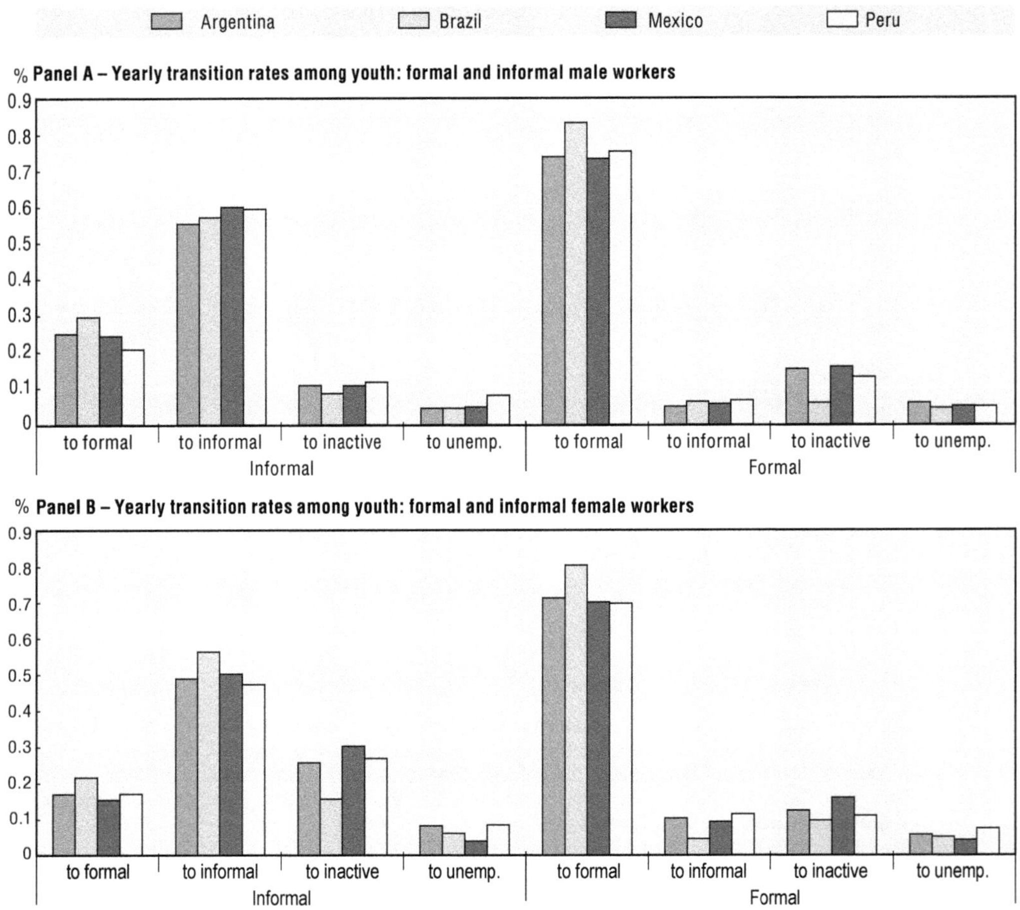

Note: Results show yearly transition rates into and out of informality. This analysis is limited to urban populations in four countries (Argentina, Brazil, Mexico, Peru) owing to data limitations.

Source: OECD and World Bank tabulations of LABLAC (CEDLAS and the World Bank).

StatLink http://dx.doi.org/10.1787/888933414159

Youth earnings still behind prime-time adults

In terms of weekly earnings, young people in LAC earn on average less than prime-age adults. The earnings of youth have been rising faster over time, reducing the gap with their adult counterparts. Overall, during 2004-14, earnings of youth compared with adults aged 30-64 increased from 54% to 76%. However, large differences still exist between different sub-groups (i.e. gender, socio-economic status and ethnicity). A substantial proportion of this gap remains unexplained, indicating possible discrimination in the labour market. The marked income gap between young people and adults is primarily due to the value of work experience. As expected, the gap narrows as workers' age and experience increase (ECLAC/OIJ, 2008). The youngest cohort (15-19 years of age) earns, on average, one-third of the mean earnings of adults; 20-24 year-olds earn approximately half as much; those in the next oldest group (25-29 year-olds) earn more than three-fourths as much as their adult counterparts (see Figure 3.14).

The data also indicate that a sizeable earnings gap remains between men and women. While this phenomenon has been studied extensively, two factors warrant attention. First, there is no gender wage gap when people start their working careers; the gap begins to appear and widens as they grow older. This could be partially explained by the fact that women accumulate less work experience and select employment that allows them to shoulder greater workloads in the home as primary caregivers; with interrupted work histories they typically work in less-productive sectors and hold less-secure jobs (OECD, 2016a). Second, although women, on average, attain higher educational levels than men, this does not translate into higher levels of labour income; this is due to the social and cultural patterns associated with gender-based wage discrimination, since even controlling for all these characteristics an unexplained differential exists (Gontero and Weller 2015; OECD, 2016a).

Figure 3.14. **Latin America average monthly labour income of the employed population, around 2013**

(purchasing power parity in 2005 USD)

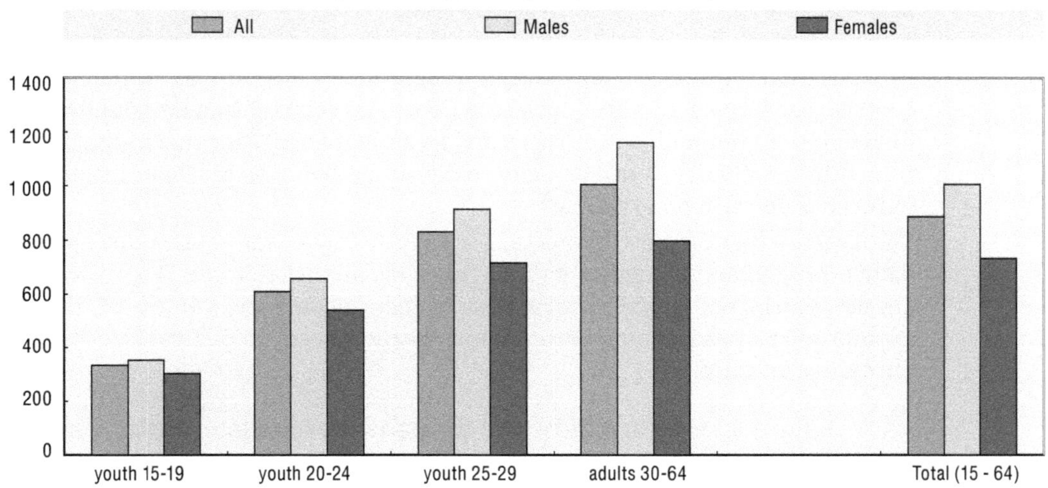

Note: LAC simple average of the following 18 countries: Argentina (2012), Bolivia (2011), Brazil (2013), Chile (2013), Colombia (2013), Costa Rica (2013), Ecuador (2013), Guatemala (2006), Honduras (2010), Mexico (2012), Nicaragua (2009), Panama (2013), Paraguay (2013), Peru (2013), Dominican Republic (2013), El Salvador (2013), Uruguay (2013) and Venezuela (2013).

Source: OECD/ECLAC/CAF special tabulations from single country's household surveys.

StatLink http://dx.doi.org/10.1787/888933414164

The challenge of the "new normal"

Young people's participation in the labour market tends to be characterised by high turnover (between jobs and different labour market status), segmentation and precarious conditions. Many youth view this situation as the "new normal" (OAS, 2012). However, the pattern will undermine the ability of most young people to build upwardly mobile careers or establish stable employment relationships. According to ILO (2013), this poses a political challenge: young people's aspirations to independence through paid employment are thwarted by a labour market with high unemployment and informality. Young people, in fact, aspire and should aspire to high-quality employment. Such opportunities enable them to participate fully in productive and civic development processes and achieve the conditions for personal development and well-being. When they fall short of this aspiration, it translates into a higher sense of discrimination and dissatisfaction. Subjective data from Latinobarometro and LAPOP paint a troublesome picture: 50% of youth aged 16-29 declare themselves to be worried about losing their jobs or being unemployed in the next year; and slightly more than 60% declare to have no guaranteed opportunity of finding employment in the next year. More quality jobs are needed, coupled with the provision of training that will enable youth to take advantage of those expanded opportunities (ECLAC/OIJ, 2008; OECD 2016, 2015a).

Box 3.4. Looking for formal jobs for all in LAC – Calculating the costs

Given that younger populations tend to earn less and are more likely to be employed within informal sectors, a straightforward question is whether the price of social security protection and tax obligations deters this population from becoming formal?

Informality rates among young populations are higher than for adults. Informality, defined as a worker not contributing to social security programmes, can be spurred by several factors. These include, but are not limited to, the cost of social security programmes and taxation. Figure 3.15 shows that informality rates remain high despite more labour income and fewer formalisation costs. Thus, other factors such as job security, institutional issues, how much the young person values the programme or services and the confidence of receiving future benefits, can better explain informality in the region.

As an individual's income moves further from the minimum wage, the cost of formalisation increases. Most social programmes are funded through mandatory contributions levied on wages subject to floors and ceilings. In most countries, floors are linked to the minimum wage. Therefore, as an individual's income moves further away from minimum wage, it will be more costly, as a proportion of labour income, to adhere to social protection programmes.

The average cost of social protection is slightly higher for youth than for prime-aged adults throughout the income distribution. This implies that social security regulations are more stringent on youth regardless of their income level. However, the difference in informality rates among both groups does not seem to decrease despite the lower formalisation costs.

Figure 3.15. **Informality and formalisation costs in Latin America**

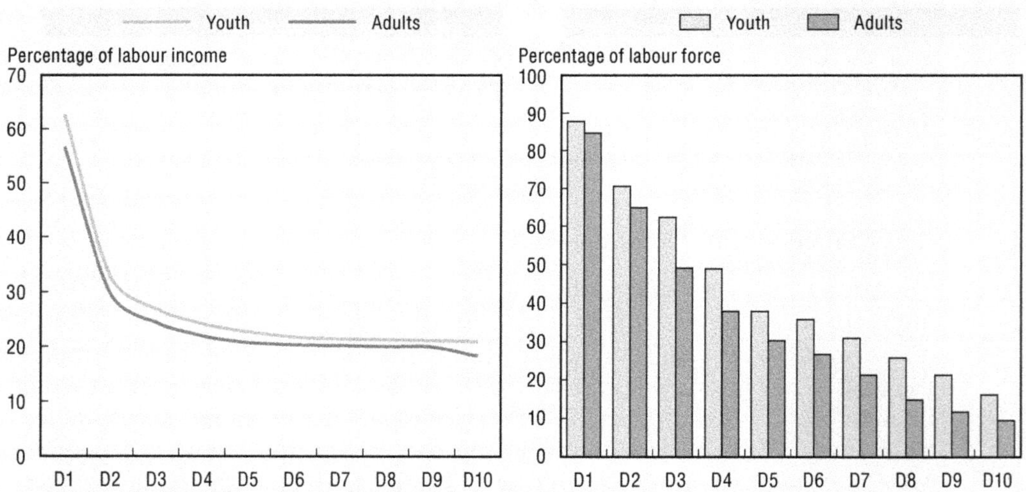

Source: OECD/ECLAC/CAF based on data from IDB and OECD/IDB/CIAT (2016).

StatLink http://dx.doi.org/10.1787/888933414178

The costs of adhering to social security programmes are extremely high for those at the low end of income distribution. For this portion of the population, the price of social security programmes represents a larger than average proportion of labour income earned with respect to their wealthier peers. In these cases, the high cost of these programmes may arguably be influencing the decision of informal workers to remain informal. As income increases, the decision to remain informal has less to do with costs and more with other factors.

Youth social inclusion beyond jobs

Integration of youth must go beyond economic issues. They must also be engaged fully in development processes to help the country progress towards a more egalitarian society. Yet social inclusion of some young people in LAC remains a largely unfinished job. Some youth are exposed to a remarkable number of vulnerabilities and threats that constrain their life choices. In addition to employment, limited access to education, health services and civic participation, for example, all prevent young people from playing a full role in their societies. This can become particularly problematic in countries with high demographic growth and inequality, such as in LAC, where new generations put pressure on economic and social development.

This section aims at understanding the process of youth inclusion in society from a rights-based perspective. It goes beyond the basic pillars of education (covered in the next chapter) and employment to encompass other dimensions of social inclusion. Young people need to progress not only in the objective parameters of inclusion, but also in subjective ones. In this way, they can feel more that they belong to a society they are helping to build.

Good health for youth fosters inclusion and participation

Understanding and addressing the health needs of young people is crucial. Health enables youth to attend school and heightens academic performance, as well as labour market insertion. This, in turn, fosters social inclusion. Moreover, youth who enjoy good health and nutrition are better equipped to participate fully in all spheres of society, not just in education and employment. In this way, health relates directly to overall youth well-being, and also to their future economic and social prospects. That said, health problems during adolescence and youth can leave an indelible mark. Mental health problems, substance abuse and early pregnancy interfere with development processes and can have significant negative long-term consequences. A focus on youth health is also warranted in view of the region's demographics. As the population ages, public resources will be allocated to meet the needs of the older population to the detriment of other age groups, especially in the health sector (Rossel, 2013).

While disease and death rates tend to be lower among young people than other age groups, the health risks youth face associated with external factors are higher. Moreover, many harmful health habits acquired in youth do not manifest as morbidity and mortality until years later (Maddaleno, Morello and Infante-Espínola, 2003). In the health field, the tendency is to perceive youth as a time of risk and transgression (Krauskopf, 2000). This rather negative and limited view narrows the focus to specific problems that young people face and prevents a more comprehensive view of youth health.

Health risks for youth depend on a variety of factors

The subject of youth health is invisible partly because this population generally enjoys good health, including comparatively low mortality rates (Figure 3.16). In general, mortality rates tend to fall during childhood and reach their lowest point at around ten years of age. After that, they gradually climb until age 35 and then turn up more sharply. This pattern holds for both men and women, although men have higher mortality rates at all ages.

In addition to having lower mortality in this age range, the specific causes of mortality fall into particular patterns. Injuries (preventable causes) are the leading cause of death among both young men and women (Figure 3.17). Still, men and women die from different kinds of injuries as do young people and adults. While violence is the leading cause of death due to injury for men, most deaths among women are due to injuries caused by exposure to nature (Ullmann, 2015). Although non-communicable diseases (in particular cardiovascular disease and cancers) are not a main cause of death for young people, their relevance as a cause of death increases with age. These diseases are strongly linked to health behaviours that are often adopted during adolescence and youth, such as a sedentary lifestyle, poor dietary habits, smoking and excess drinking (Baldwin et al., 2013); these two subjects will be analysed further in this sub-section.

Figure 3.16. **Latin America and the Caribbean: Specific mortality rates, by age and sex, 2010**

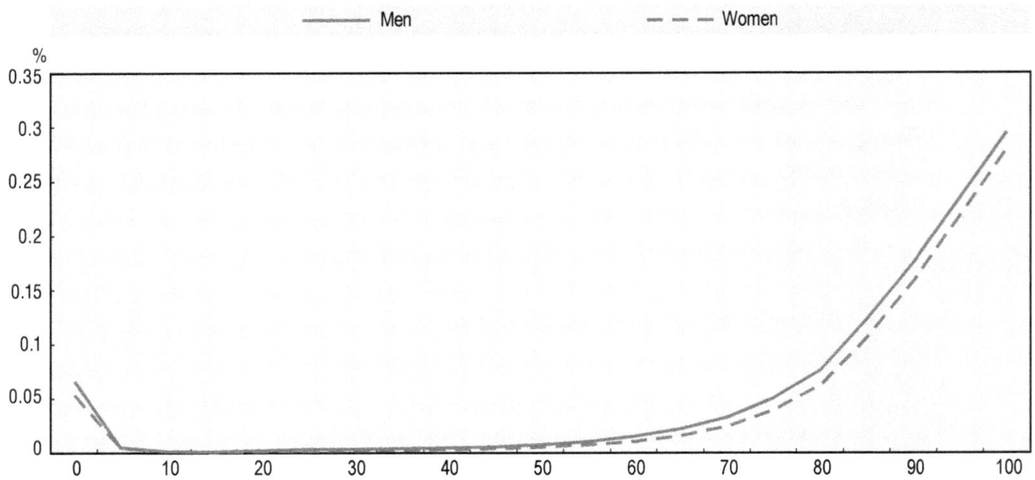

Source: OECD/ECLAC/CAF based on Latin American and Caribbean Demographic Centre (CELADE)-Population Division of ECLAC (2010), "Mortality", Demographic Observatory, No. 9 (LC/G.2490-P), Santiago (Figure 1); Institute for Health Metrics and Evaluation, http://vizhub.healthdata.org/gbd-compare (Figure 2), both in Trucco and Ullmann (2015).

StatLink http://dx.doi.org/10.1787/888933414182

Figure 3.17. **Cause-specific mortality, by age group and sex, in Latin America and the Caribbean, 2010**

(percentages)

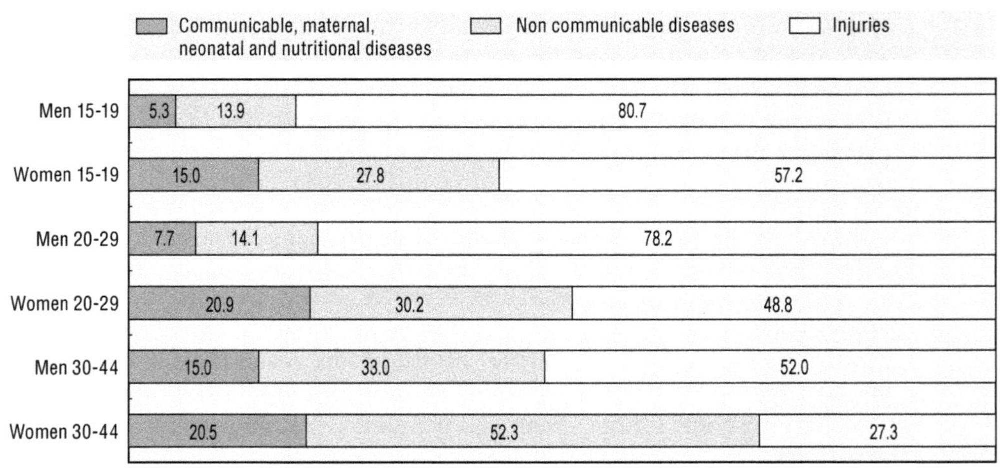

Note: LAC covers 33 countries.

Source: OECD/ECLAC/CAF based on Latin American and Caribbean Demographic Centre (CELADE)-Population Division of ECLAC (2010), "Mortality", Demographic Observatory, No. 9 (LC/G.2490-P), Santiago (Figure 1); Institute for Health Metrics and Evaluation, http://vizhub.healthdata.org/gbd-compare (Figure 2), both in Trucco and Ullmann (2015).

StatLink http://dx.doi.org/10.1787/888933414190

Mortality may well be a reflection of the overall health status of young people in the region. However, it is an incomplete metric as it does not take into account diseases that limit the life potential of young people without leading to death. A disability-adjusted life year (DALY) has been the object of some strong, well-deserved criticism (see Anand and Hanson, 1997), especially with respect to its ethical and value-based underpinnings. Nonetheless, it is a useful metric to measure the health of a given population and to identify causes that keep that population from enjoying full health.

According to recent data (see Table 3.4), DALYs related to mental health account for much of the total burden of disease for the young. DALYs for women aged 15-19 show that mental health problems stand out among the diseases and conditions that contribute the most to the disease burden (unipolar depressive disorders, major depressive disorders and anxiety disorders). This pattern is slightly different for the 20-29 age group, but unipolar depressive disorders still rank first. In the case of men, violence, exposure to nature and road accidents are among the three major diseases and conditions that contribute to the DALY in all age brackets considered.

Table 3.4. **Latin America and the Caribbean (33 countries): Main diseases and disorders contributing to the disease burden, by sex and age, 2010**

Aged 15 to 19	
Men	**Women**
Violence	Unipolar depressive disorders
Exposure to forces of nature	Exposure to forces of nature
Road injuries	Major depressive disorders
Unintentional injuries	Anxiety disorders
Unipolar depressive disorders	Skin and subcutaneous diseases
Aged 20 to 29	
Men	**Women**
Violence	Unipolar depressive disorders
Exposure to forces of nature	Exposure to forces of nature
Road injuries	Major depressive disorders
Drug use disorders	Diabetes and urogenital and endocrine diseases
Unipolar depressive disorders	Anxiety disorders
Aged 30 to 44	
Men	**Women**
Violence	Cardiovascular and circulatory diseases
Exposure to forces of nature	Neoplasms
Road injuries	Diabetes and urogenital and endocrine diseases
HIV/AIDS and tuberculosis	Unipolar depressive disorders
Cardiovascular and circulatory diseases	Lower respiratory infections, meningitis and other common infectious diseases

Source: Institute for Health Metrics and Evaluation, http://vizhub.healthdata.org/gbd-compare.

These data provide a general overview of the health of youth in Latin America and the Caribbean. However, substantial mortality and morbidity disparities exist according to racial/ethnic group, rural/urban residence and socio-economic level. Poverty, lack of education, overcrowding, poor nutrition, lack of water and sanitation, and marginalisation and discrimination influence the exposure of young people to pathogens. At the same time, they create a context of exclusion that may favour the development of or exacerbate health problems. Moreover, social exclusion limits access to medical care, both for diagnosis and treatment of disease. In situations of exclusion, protective factors (such as a stable family life, strong links with school and positive role models) are particularly important for promoting healthy youth development.

Early pregnancy rates are still a burning issue

Reproductive risks faced by young people are a growing concern. Adolescent pregnancy, in particular, has raised concerns at the regional level because of its substantial and wide-ranging negative impacts on the overall development of the women, men, children, families and societies involved. Despite efforts to reduce teenage pregnancy rates, this indicator has stagnated at high levels in many LAC countries (Rodríguez, 2014 in Ullmann, 2015).

Although different paths can lead to adolescent pregnancy, it occurs disproportionately among young women in lower socio-economic strata; adolescent fertility has historically been associated with poverty (Rodríguez, 2008, in Ullmann, 2015). Regardless of the measure used (place of residence, education or household wealth), there is an inverse relationship between adolescent fertility rates and socio-economic status. Figure 3.18 shows the percentage of teenage mothers in seven countries in the region based on the most recent census rounds. It clearly illustrates the social stratification of adolescent fertility in the region.

Figure 3.18. **Latin America (seven countries): Women aged 15 to 19 who are mothers, according to socio-economic quintile and area of residence**

(percentages)

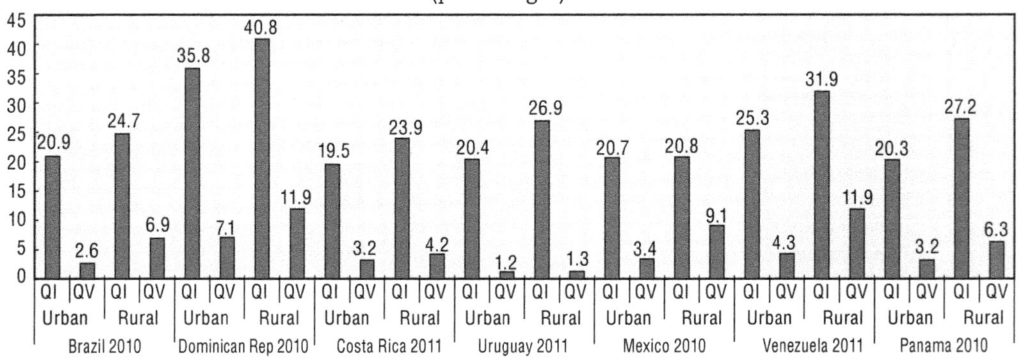

Note: QI = quintile I; QV = quintile V.

Source: Rodríguez, J. (2014), "La reproducción en la adolescencia y sus desigualdades en América Latina. Introducción al análisis demográfico, con énfasis en el uso de microdatos censales de la ronda de 2010" [Reproduction in Adolescence and Inequality in Latin America. Introduction to Demographic Analysis, With Emphasis on Microdata from the 2010 Round], in Santiago, Economic Commission for Latin America and the Caribbean (ECLAC).

StatLink http://dx.doi.org/10.1787/888933414204

Other youth health issues: substance abuse and mental health problems

Licit and illicit drug abuse is a serious public health problem because of its extensive adverse effects at both a personal and a societal level (Ullmann, 2015). The use of tobacco and alcohol has harmful organic health consequences that develop silently during youth; their impacts only become apparent at later stages of life. Alcohol consumption is also linked to aggressive behaviour and violent crime (Parker and Auerhahn, 1998). Moreover, young people with illicit drug dependence may resort to theft and robbery to finance their addiction or engage in specific stages of production and distribution of illicit substances. This may expose them to violence as perpetrators or as victims.

Licit and illicit drug abuse among young people has significant direct and indirect costs for society as well. These can be summed up in years of productive life lost among young people with dependence, costs associated with the criminal justice system, and health care and treatment costs.

The lack of comparable data poses a major problem when discussing substance use among young people in Latin America and the Caribbean. National youth surveys address the issue in detail, but are not necessarily comparable because of methodological differences. Data from the World Health Organization Global School-Based Student Health Survey (WHO, 2010) help shed light on regional trends in this area.[16] This is a useful source of information because substance use at these early ages can signal future problems that can, in turn, interfere with school or employment. However, by definition, the survey does not include data on adolescents not attending school; so the figures likely understate the prevalence of tobacco, alcohol and illicit drug use.

Prevalence of tobacco use varies across countries of the region – from 4.9% in Anguilla to 25.5% in Argentina (Figure 3.19). Similarly, alcohol consumption varies among students across the region (Figure 3.20). However, with few exceptions the prevalence of alcohol consumption tops 30% – that is, one in three students reported having had at least one alcoholic drink in the last 30 days. This ranks alcohol as the substance most consumed by young people in this group of countries.

Figure 3.19. **Latin America and the Caribbean (15 countries): Students who smoked cigarettes at least once in the past 30 days**

(percentages)

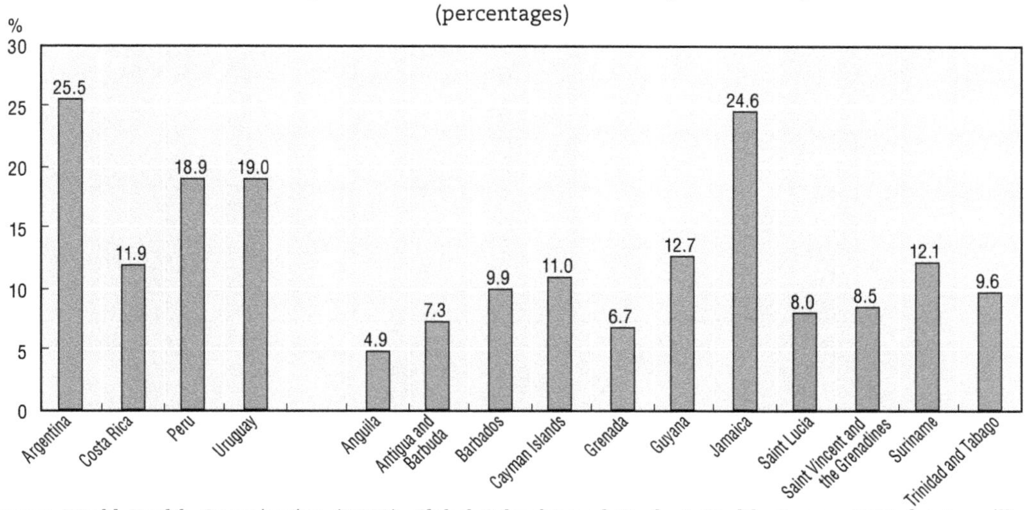

Sources: World Health Organization (WHO), Global School-Based Student Health Survey, 2010 for Anguilla (2009), Antigua and Barbuda (2009), Argentina (2007), Barbados (2011), Cayman Islands (2007), Costa Rica (2009), Grenada (2008), Guyana (2010), Jamaica (2010), Peru (2010), Saint Lucia (2007), Saint Vincent and the Grenadines (2007), Suriname (2009), Trinidad and Tobago (2011), Uruguay (2006).

StatLink http://dx.doi.org/10.1787/888933414212

Figure 3.20. **Latin America and the Caribbean (18 countries): Students who consumed at least one alcoholic drink in the past 30 days**

(percentages)

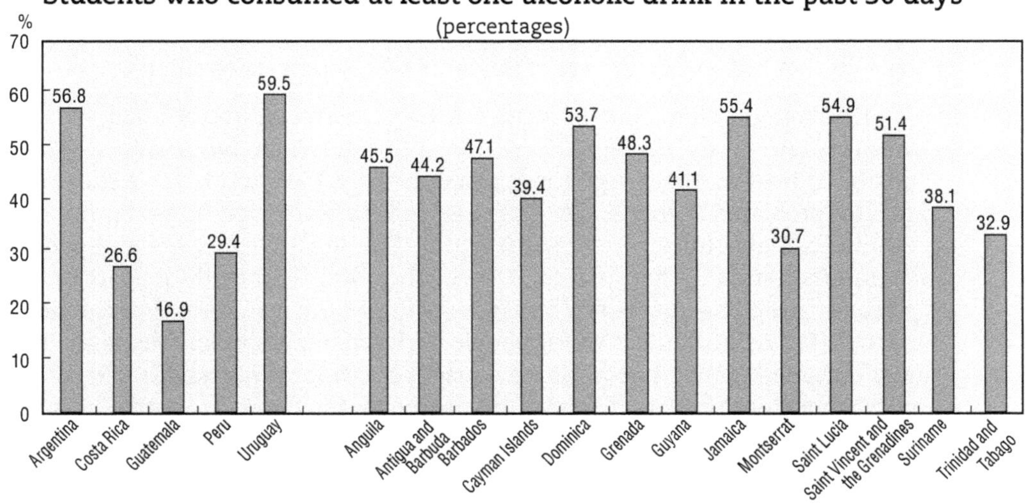

Sources: Figure 3.20: World Health Organization (WHO), Global School-Based Student Health Survey, 2010 for Anguilla (2009), Antigua and Barbuda (2009), Argentina (2007), Barbados (2011), Cayman Islands (2007), Costa Rica (2009), Dominica (2009), Grenada (2008), Guatemala (2009), Guyana (2010), Jamaica (2010), Montserrat (2008), Peru (2010), Saint Lucia (2007), Saint Vincent and the Grenadines (2007), Suriname (2009), Trinidad and Tobago (2011), Uruguay (2006).

StatLink http://dx.doi.org/10.1787/888933414224

According to this same data source, young people who use tobacco or alcohol report having started in most cases before the age of 14. This suggests that prevention messages and public health initiatives against alcohol and tobacco use aimed at teens are coming too late. As illustrated in Figure 3.21, consumption of illicit drugs tends to be higher among students in Caribbean countries than in Latin America.

Figure 3.21. **Students in Latin America and the Caribbean who have used drugs at least once**

(percentages)

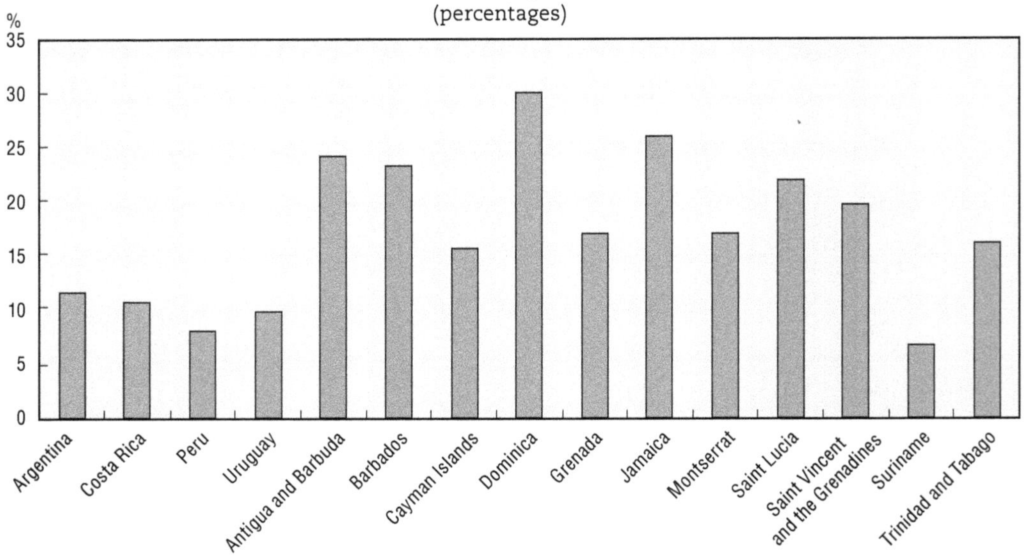

Note: Drugs are defined as marijuana, cocaine and ecstasy.

Sources: World Health Organization (WHO), Global School-Based Student Health Survey, 2010 for Antigua and Barbuda (2009), Argentina (2007), Barbados (2011), Cayman Islands (2007), Costa Rica (2009), Dominica (2009), Grenada (2008), Jamaica (2010), Montserrat (2008), Peru (2010), Saint Lucia (2007), Saint Vincent and the Grenadines (2007), Suriname (2009), Trinidad and Tobago (2011), Uruguay (2006).

StatLink http://dx.doi.org/10.1787/888933414235

In sum, both in Latin America and in the English-speaking Caribbean, alcohol consumption far exceeds tobacco and illicit drug use. In Latin America, tobacco use is more prevalent than illicit drug use; in the English-speaking Caribbean the opposite is true, with a higher percentage of students who report using illicit drugs.

Media and policy makers focus on the problematic use of illicit substances among youth, particularly marijuana and cocaine (and their by-products, such as cocaine paste). However, the drugs most consumed by LAC youth (and those that generate greater problems at this stage of life and in future through non-communicable disease) are alcohol and tobacco (Ullmann, 2015). The legality of these drugs does not make them less harmful; their use can irreversibly alter the health of users and lead to risky situations such as unsafe sex and driving under the influence that can also harm third parties (ECLAC/OIJ, 2008). Young people with substance dependence are also stigmatised and excluded, which has negative consequences for their health and for their chances of receiving appropriate treatment to overcome the dependence (da Silva et al., 2009).

Youth with mental health problems also face enormous challenges in achieving social and economic integration; these conditions have a significant impact across a wide range of developmental outcomes, limiting opportunities for social integration (United Nations, 2014). Moreover, many mental health problems develop in adolescence and have repercussions on subsequent stages of life (Baldwin et al., 2013).

Few epidemiological studies of mental health among young people exist in Latin America and the Caribbean. Further, they are difficult to compare because of differences in measurement instruments, subject age range and periods covered. However, as Table 3.2 shows, mental health disorders are an important issue for young people, especially females in this age group.

Young people with mental illnesses may find it very challenging to complete their studies because of poor academic performance, discipline problems and poor attendance; this may ultimately result in their dropping out (ECLAC, 2014). This school trajectory leaves them ill-prepared to enter the labour market, with adverse effects for their employment situation later on. Mental health issues during adolescence and youth can also affect the development of sound and healthy relationships with peers, parents and others. Mental health difficulties affect young people's self-esteem and social interaction and may even increase the chances of their injuring or harming themselves and others (UNICEF, 2012; Bradshaw, O'Brennan and McNeely, 2008).

By some estimates, around 20% of youth worldwide experience a mental health problem; this means that most young people – even those who face many adversities and multiple risk factors – do not develop mental health disorders (Patel et al., 2007; UNICEF, 2012). This points to the importance of protective elements such as sense of connection and belonging, social support and low levels of conflict that mitigate the impact of risk factors and encourage resilience (Patel et al., 2007). Certainly, family is important too, as the support of parents is essential for building resilience in young people.

Civic participation and political engagement

Along with health, political participation is one of the main, but often neglected, vehicles for the social inclusion of young people. Participation in political affairs is in itself a fundamental human right and the exercise of that right is an essential pathway towards the genuine enjoyment of other human rights (Maldonado, 2015).

A key indicator of youth political participation is voting in the most recent presidential elections (Figure 3.22).[17] Most young people reported they had voted, but the percentage was in most cases much lower than the one for adults. This has partly to do with age restrictions, but self-exclusion is also a factor. The evolution of voting behaviour among youth in the region is mixed. Some countries have witnessed a steep reduction in the past decade of young voters, while others have seen an increase.

Numerous studies have also found that young people are less involved than before in other, non-political types of organisations as well.

The vast majority of young people in Latin America and the Caribbean stand outside existing youth associations and movements (between 5% and 20% participate, depending on the country, with sporting and religious organizations accounting for the overwhelming majority), in what could be seen as a transition to new forms of youth participation and new understandings of civic engagement or action (Maldonado, 2015).

Young people's involvement (or non-involvement) in social movements is an indicator of their engagement, indifference or rejection of public life and democracy (Maldonado, 2015). One way to measure this involvement is youth participation in at least one demonstration during the past year (Figure 3.23). At the regional level, that percentage held at around 26% for 2000-13, which was slightly higher than the figure recorded for persons aged 30 or more.

Figure 3.22. Latin America (17 countries): Young people and adults who report voting in the latest presidential elections, 2000-13*

(percentages)

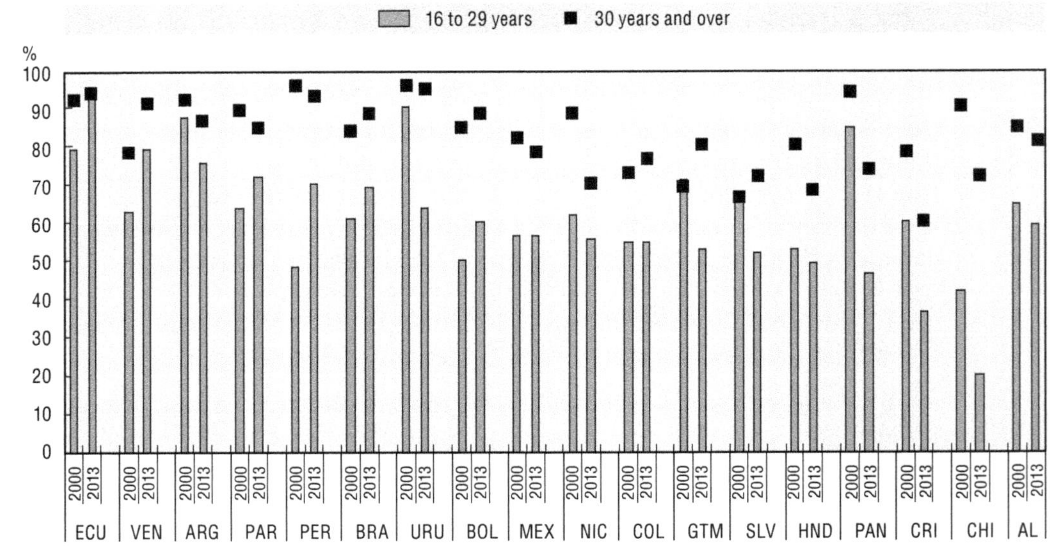

Notes: The percentages that make up the total of non-voters also include those who were unable to get to the polls, those who decided not to vote, and those who did not meet the age requirements, among others. Relating to this last point, young people aged 16-17 were only included in the analysis sample in countries where they were eligible to vote. *The results by country are given in descending order according to the percentage of young people in 2013 who stated that they had voted in the most recent presidential elections.

Source: OECD/ECLAC/CAF based on special tabulations of the results of the 2000 and 2013 Latinobarómetro surveys in Trucco and Ullmann (2015).

StatLink http://dx.doi.org/10.1787/888933414246

Figure 3.23. Latin America (17 countries): Young persons and adults who report having participated in demonstrations at least once during the past year, 2000-13*

(percentages)

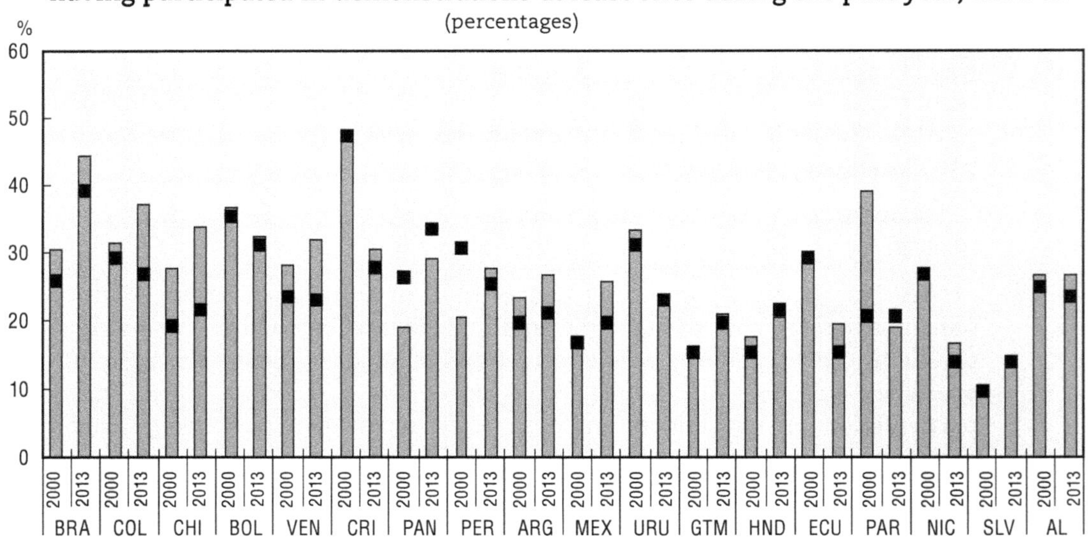

Note: * The countries are listed in descending order of the percentages of young respondents in the 2013 survey who reported that they often worked for a political party or candidate.

Source: OECD/ECLAC/CAF based on special tabulations of the results of the 2000 and 2013 Latinobarómetro surveys in Trucco and Ullmann (2015)

StatLink http://dx.doi.org/10.1787/888933414257

How large is the group of young people who do not vote and do not participate in social movements? A number of different studies have sought to link voting activity and participation in social movements (FLACSO/IDEA International, 2013; Maldonado 2015). This is a means of identifying the groups of young people who i) vote and participate in social movements; ii) vote but do not participate in social movements; iii) do not vote, but do participate in social movements; and iv) do not vote and do not participate in social movements (with this last group being characterised to some extent as those who remain on the sidelines of political life).

The proportion of youth in the fourth group increased between 2000-13 from 27.3% to just over 31.3%. Compared with adults, in 2013, the percentage of youth who refrained from participating in either voting or social movements was more than double the figure for adults (15.4%). Notwithstanding, these data reveal that most Latin American youth, 70%, *did* participate in political processes, as voters, participants in demonstrations, or both.

Figure 3.24. **Latin America (17 countries): Young persons and adults who report having voted in the most recent elections and having taken part in a demonstration at least once in the past year, 2000-13**

(percentages)

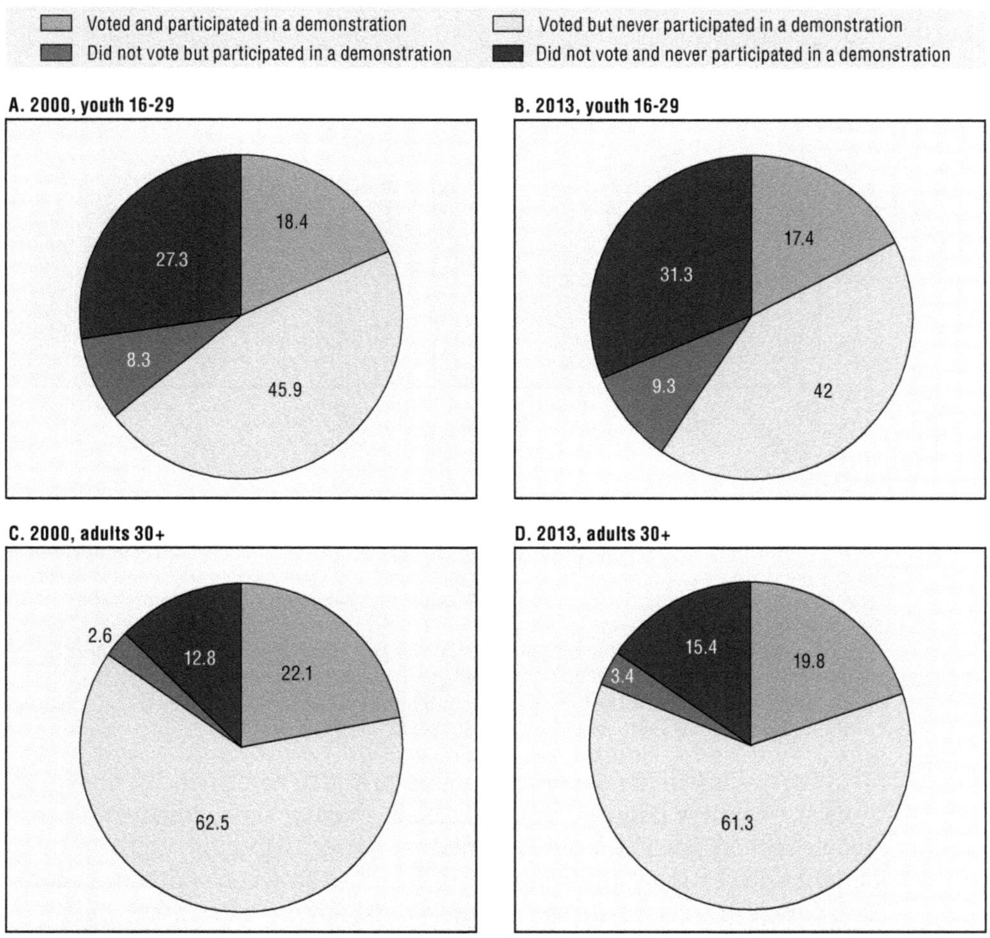

Note: The figures represent those who did not vote because they were unable to go to the polls, those who were not eligible to vote and those who did not wish to vote.

Source: OECD/ECLAC/CAF based on special tabulations of the results of the 2000 and 2013 Latinobarómetro surveys in Trucco and Ullmann (2015).

StatLink http://dx.doi.org/10.1787/888933414268

These data suggest there is scope to promote more political participation among young people. Different channels for participation in social movements and in elections could be sought, especially in countries where young people have been distancing themselves from conventional forms of political activity in the past decade. This also raises the question of how these patterns of political participation tie in with individuals' attitudes, their confidence in institutions or their lack thereof, and their commitment to democracy – all of which may vary quite markedly from one country to another.

A similar percentage of young people and adults regards democracy (at least the form of democracy they have experienced) as the best form of government (see Figure 3.25 and Box 3.5). In Chile and Uruguay, however, more adults than young people display a commitment to democracy.

Figure 3.25. **Latin America (17 countries): Support for democracy as the best form of government by persons between 16-29 years of age and by persons aged 30 and over, 2013**

(percentages)

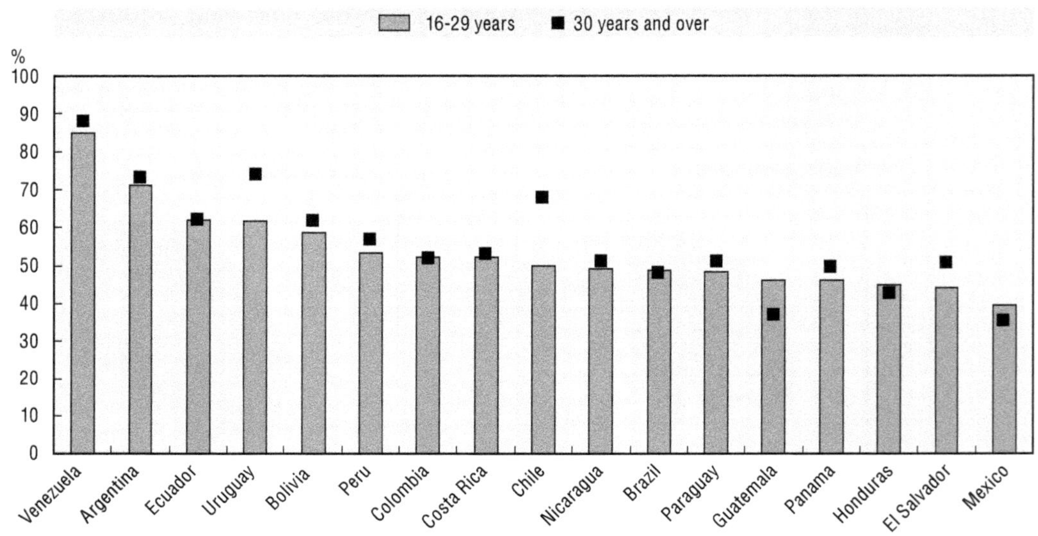

Notes: The question was worded as follows: "With which of the following do you agree the most?" The options were: "Democracy is preferable to any other form of government"; "Under some circumstances, an authoritarian government may be preferable to a democratic one"; and "For people like us, it doesn't matter whether the government is democratic or not". In the 2013 survey, the options "do not know" and "no answer" were added to cover 100% of all cases.

The countries are listed in descending order of the percentages of young respondents in the 2013 survey who said that democracy was preferable to any other system of government.

Source: OECD/ECLAC/CAF based on special tabulations of the results of the 2013 Latinobarómetro survey.

StatLink http://dx.doi.org/10.1787/888933414271

Perceptions of democratic systems are also informed by views on who actually runs the country (Figure 3.26). In 2013, in most of the countries, 70% or more of young people responding to the survey said that powerful groups run the country for their own benefit. Interestingly, there are few differences between youth and adults in this regard. This suggests scepticism about the representative capacity of democratically elected government is quite pervasive.

Although many young people have distanced themselves from conventional political and electoral systems, they are opting for new ways of participating in political affairs; in so doing, they exhibit a growing potential to challenge and influence the public political agenda (Maldonado, 2015). In recent years, forceful, youth-led social movements have appeared that attest to young people's desire to have their voices heard and to play an active part in the development of their societies.

New ways of mobilising and organising members of the younger population are emerging in which technological tools play a key role (e.g. social media). Young university students in Mexico, for example, used Twitter to mobilise during the 2012 presidential campaign. Youth in Brazil and Chile have also expressed social discontent through social media. Five of the 12 countries in the world in which social media are used the most are in the Latin American and Caribbean region, and most users are adolescents and young adults (Maldonado, 2015). Indeed, a recent survey suggests that Latin American youth access social media more than youth from other regions (Telefónica, 2014).

Figure 3.26. **Latin America (18 countries): Persons aged 16-29 and persons aged 30 and over who believe that powerful groups, rather than the people, are running the government of their country, 2013**

(percentages)

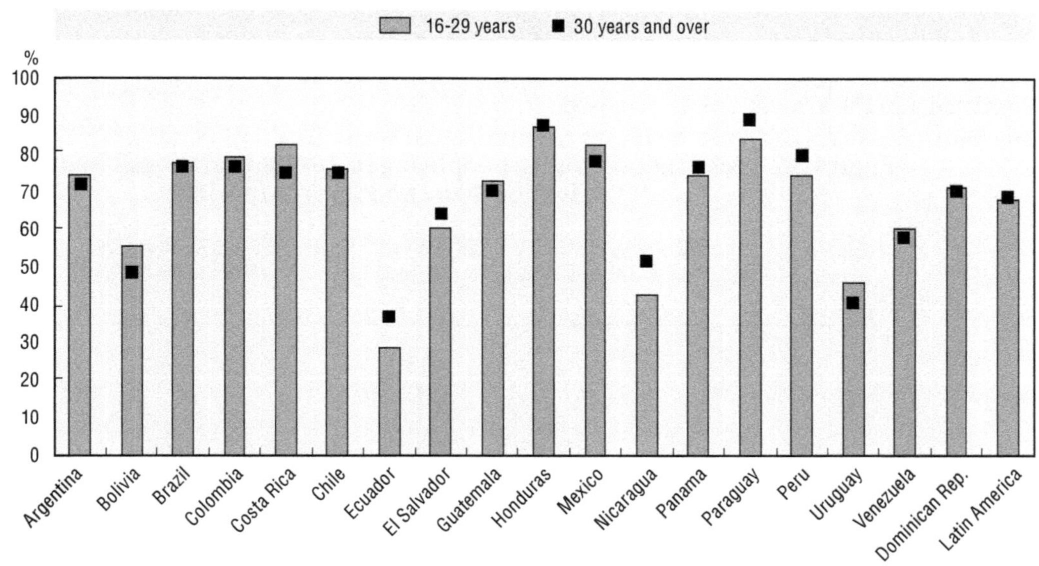

Notes: The survey question was worded as follows: "Generally speaking, would you say that (the country) is governed by a few powerful groups for their own benefit or is governed for the benefit of all?"

The countries are listed in descending order of the percentages of young persons who said that the government was run by powerful groups for their own benefit in 2013.

Source: OECD/ECLAC/CAF based on special tabulations of the results of the 2013 Latinobarómetro survey.

StatLink http://dx.doi.org/10.1787/888933414283

Social media use a different communications model than traditional mass media. Rather than broadcasting a single message to an indefinite group of individuals, social media enable users to create and send out messages (both to an indeterminate number of people and targeted audiences). Interactivity of social media is enhanced by users' ability to create networks and establish contacts. This new model substantially changes how people interact among themselves and with institutions, either as individuals or as members of communities or movements (Pavez, 2014). Social networks are playing an increasingly important role in the way that adolescents and young adults exert influence and make their opinions, concerns and ideas known, and are opening up new pathways for the organisation of social movements and communities (UNDP, 2013; Maldonado, 2015).

Box 3.5. The importance of social capital for youth well-being in El Salvador and Peru: Evidence from the OECD Youth Inclusion project

The *OECD Youth Inclusion* project supports ten countries, including El Salvador and Peru, to improve policies on employment, education, health and civic participation for young people. The project uses a multi-dimensional approach and empirical evidence to shed light on the determinants of youth vulnerabilities and successful transitions to adulthood.

Trust in public institutions and social networks are important social capital for the successful transition of youth into adulthood, but are often neglected when discussing youth well-being. In El Salvador and Peru the project therefore focuses on key issues such as social reintegration of youth in conflict with the law, youth participation in policy making, and the equity and quality of secondary education.

Latin American youth have little trust in their institutions. El Salvador and Peru show a higher degree of mistrust towards official authorities compared with the average Latin American youth (Figure 3.27). This high level of mistrust in elections, political parties and the government is further reflected in the low number of young people regarding democracy as the best form of government. The increasing mistrust over the last decade is especially alarming. In Peru, recent demonstrations against labour market reforms are expressions of this discontent (OECD, 2015c). Indeed, mistrust in political parties and elections strongly increased in Peru. In El Salvador, only mistrust in the armed forces decreased.

Figure 3.27. Mistrust of young people (aged 18-29) in national institutions in El Salvador, Peru and Latin America

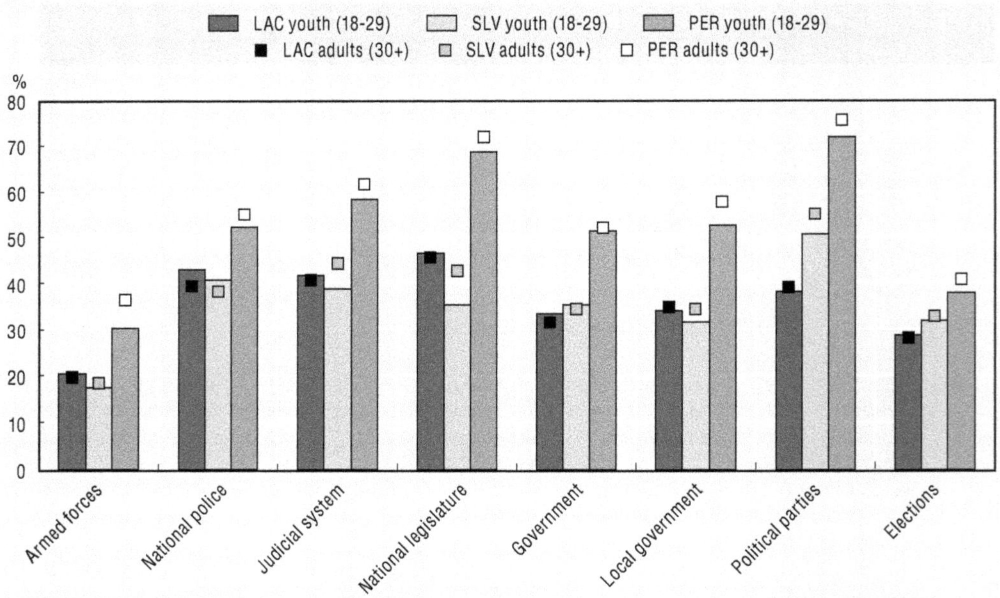

Note: Interviewees had to express their level of trust on a scale from 1 to 7, where 1 means no trust and 7 total trust. Mistrust is defined from 1 to 3.

Source: OECD calculations based on Latin American Public Opinion Project (LAPOP) 2014.

StatLink http://dx.doi.org/10.1787/888933414293

Despite the low level of trust in public institutions, young people have a high sense of community in Peru and El Salvador. Only 9.6% of young Salvadorians and 9.0% of young Peruvians reported they did not trust the members of their community (LAPOP, 2014). Moreover, the majority of young Salvadorians and Peruvians say they can rely on their social network for support: only 10.2% and 9.6% of young Salvadorians and Peruvians, respectively, declared having no relatives

Box 3.5. The importance of social capital for youth well-being in El Salvador and Peru: Evidence from the OECD Youth Inclusion project (cont.)

or friends they can count on in case of need (Gallup World Poll data, 2015). The *OECD Youth Inclusion* project further shows that urban vulnerable youth in Peru rely heavily on their immediate networks to overcome the challenges of transition to adulthood, such as finding employment or raising children. They stressed the importance of such social networks in the absence of state-facilitated support mechanisms. Multiple reasons explain this mistrust in public institutions: lack of information, communication and coverage of youth-specific support programmes generates doubt on the transparency and usefulness of these programmes, and distances young people from the state.

Trust in institutions is essential for social stability, efficient policy implementation, public sector performance and democracy (OECD, 2014b). The high level of interpersonal trust and social networks facilitate youth's transition to adulthood. However, transitions that rely only on interpersonal trust and social networks can be precarious depending on the young person's socio-economic background. The absence of state-facilitated support and low levels of institutional trust hamper youth well-being and signal risks for social stability and democracy. Governments will need to build on the high sense of community and further promote youth participation in official policy processes, and thereby rebuild trust in public institutions.

Youth satisfaction with life and future outlooks

People's subjective perceptions, evaluations and experiences are a crucial component of overall well-being. Unlike the concept of happiness, which only depends on each individual's actions, subjective well-being "has to do with society generating the necessary conditions for people to feel satisfied, both with their lives and with the society where they experience their lives" (UNDP, 2012).

Attitudes and perceptions of young people in LAC countries during the past decade show high satisfaction with their lives – higher than for adults – and a more optimistic view of their countries' economic prospects. However, young people have less trust in social and political institutions and participate less in conventional political channels (as discussed in the previous section). However, they are more optimistic and more enthusiastic than adults about the possibility of taking part in movements to support demands relating to health, education, better jobs and more opportunities.

According to Latinobarómetro data, most (80% youth and 74% of adults) of the population in Latin America declare satisfaction with their lives (Figure 3.28). With the exception of Chile and Venezuela, higher percentages of young people than adults in the other 16 countries declare satisfaction with their lives. No clear trend of the evolution of life satisfaction can be observed over time, but on average the levels of satisfaction are quite high in the entire region.

Young people have a more positive attitude than adults regarding the economic outlook for themselves and their families over the coming 12 months in 2013 (Figure 3.29). In most countries, more than half of respondents thought the situation would improve. El Salvador, Honduras and Venezuela were exceptions in this respect. These positive expectations were more prevalent among young people than among adults, except in Paraguay and Venezuela (Maldonado, 2015).

Figure 3.28. Population declaring satisfaction with their lives in Latin America, 2013

(percentages)

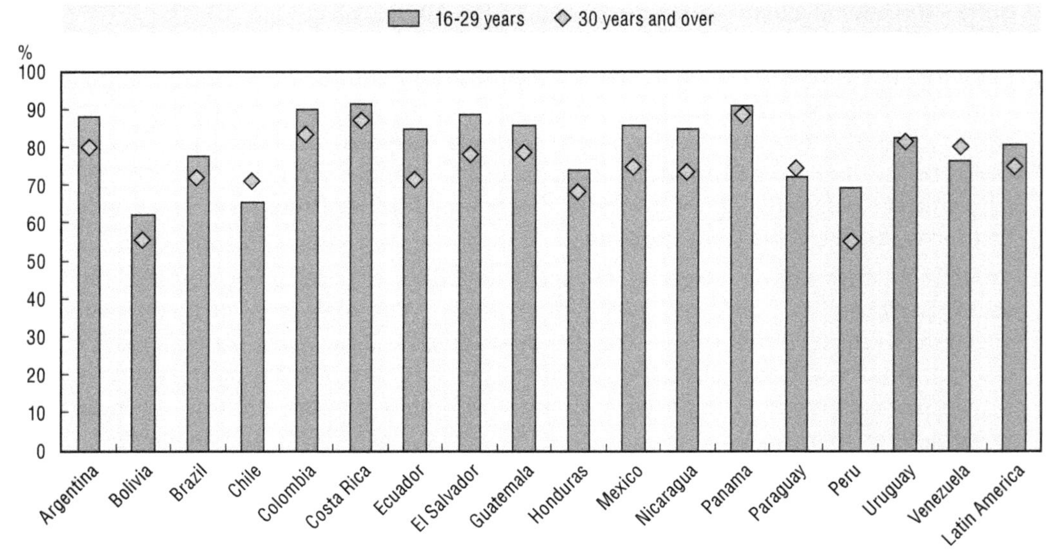

Note: Latin America is simple average of countries' data.

Source: OECD/ECLAC/CAF based on special tabulations of the results of the 2013 Latinobarómetro surveys.

StatLink http://dx.doi.org/10.1787/888933414302

Figure 3.29. Belief that the personal and household economic situation will be better or slightly better in the coming 12 months in Latin America, by country and age group, 2013

(percentages)

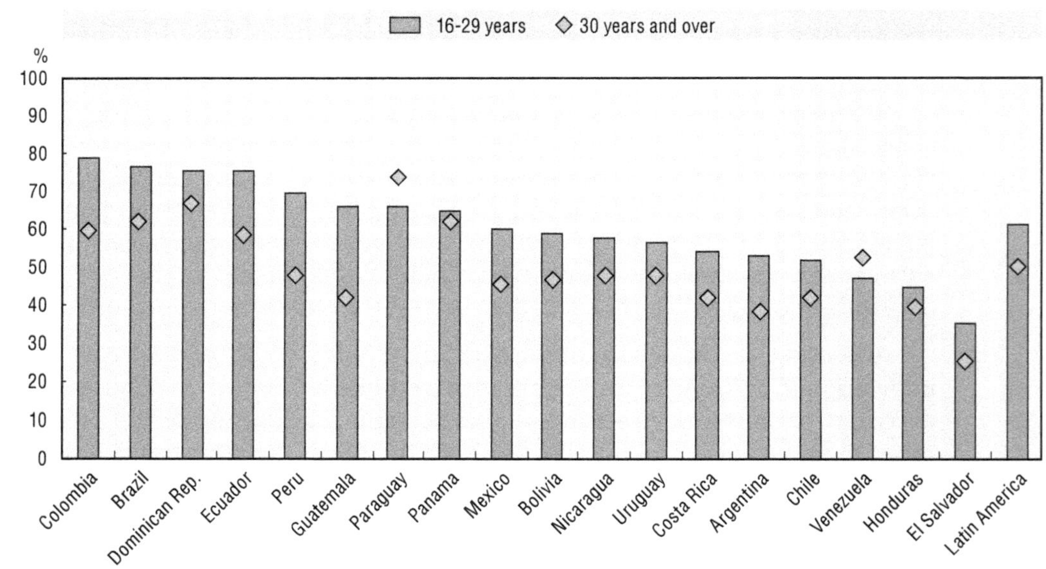

Note: Latin America is simple average of countries' data.

The countries are listed in descending order of the percentages of young respondents who believed that the economic situation would be better or slightly better.

Source: OECD/ECLAC/CAF based on special tabulations of the results of the 2013 Latinobarómetro surveys, in Trucco and Ullmann (2015).

StatLink http://dx.doi.org/10.1787/888933414315

While people are less optimistic about their societies' situation, their confidence nonetheless improved significantly during the last decade; data from Latinobarómetro studies show that only 25% of the population think the economic situation of their country is good. According to Maldonado (2015), young people's assessments of their country's economic situation was more positive in both 2000 and 2013 than those of people aged 30 or over (Figure 3.30). Perceptions of each country's economic situation improved between 2000 and 2013 at the regional level. In both cases, however, fewer young people tend to regard the situation as being poor and more of them tend to evaluate the situation as good or fair in both survey years.

Figure 3.30. **Latin America (simple average of 17 countries): Assessment of the economic situation of the country, 2000-13**

(percentages)

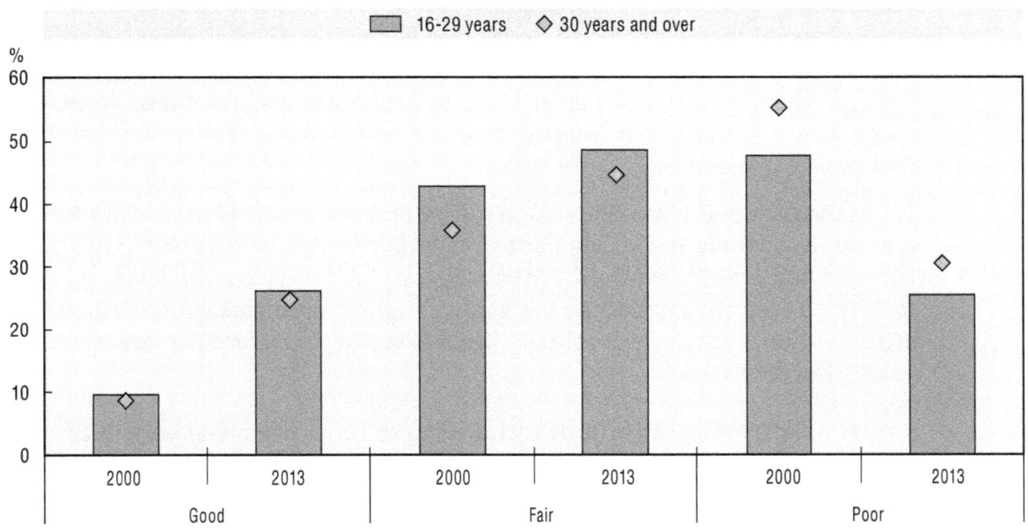

Source: OECD/ECLAC/CAF based on special tabulations of the results of the 2013 Latinobarómetro surveys, in Trucco and Ullmann (2015).

StatLink http://dx.doi.org/10.1787/888933414324

As noted earlier, the optimistic view of youth about their personal situation is accompanied by considerable mistrust and disaffection with regard to various social and, in particular, political institutions. They are much less trustful of national legislatures and political parties than of other institutions that have traditionally been viewed as legitimate, such as the Church (although they are more mistrustful of the Church than in the past) and the media or institutions such as the armed forces or the police (Maldonado, 2015).

As discussed earlier, institutional mistrust does not turn youth away from public issues associated with societal well-being. The results of the 2013 Latinobarómetro survey pinpoint a number of issues that young people appear to be much more willing to champion than older members of the population. The most relevant issues for youth were education and health, followed by higher wages and better jobs, protection of democratic rights, land ownership and harvesting of natural resources. They appear to give more priority to opportunities for individuals (health, education, wages and employment) than to less tangible causes such as the protection of democratic rights. Less enthusiasm was apparent for issues that have traditionally figured prominently in social struggles, such as those relating to land ownership and natural resources (harvesting, appropriation of revenues and environmental impact) (Maldonado, 2015).

Indeed, the priority of issues for youth has shifted in recent years in LAC. In 2000, the main issues were unemployment (21.2%), education (20.7%) and corruption (9.7%), followed by poverty (8.1%) and crime (7.7%). In 2013, the top three issues were crime (23%), unemployment (15.9%), and education and corruption (each with 6.3%).

Crime perceptions and sense of security

The contexts of violence faced by young people in the region influence their life choices. The stigmatisation of youth for its supposedly violent tendencies breaks down social cohesion, heightening their feeling of exclusion. Youth participation in gangs and other organised forms of urban violence has undoubtedly increased as a direct consequence of marginalisation; these offer an alternative form of social inclusion ("inclusion within exclusion") (ECLAC, 2014). Specialists in youth issues have argued for decades that gangs are organisations that provide some Latin American youths with a form of social inclusion: when poverty is widespread, employment options are limited and the state and institutions are near absent, then many young people turn to their peer group in the *barrio* for a sense of inclusion. Gangs give them power, cash income, space and a feeling of belonging that no other social institution provides (Soto and Trucco, 2015).

In the past few years, the region's development progress, including some results that are highly positive for young people, has paradoxically coexisted with high indices of violence and insecurity. Unlike other regions, LAC has extreme levels of violence within society; in fact, the region has the world's highest homicide rate (UNODC, 2014). As seen in the earlier section, crime has climbed to the top of youth concerns in the region during the past decade.

Figure 3.31. **Population claiming to have been the victim of crime in the last 12 months in Latin America and the Caribbean, by age group, 2012**

(percentages)

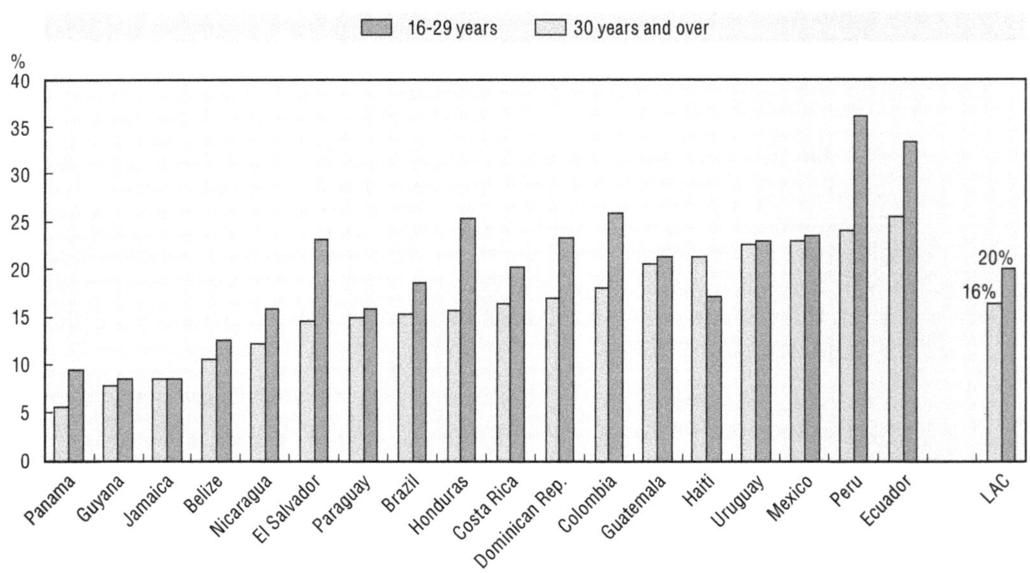

Note: LAC is the simple average of the results for the 18 countries included in the measurement.

Source: OECD/ECLAC/CAF based on special tabulations of the biannual survey of the Latin American Public Opinion Project (LAPOP), 2012.

StatLink http://dx.doi.org/10.1787/888933414330

Violence occurs unevenly throughout the territory, but particularly in deprived urban areas. Shanty towns and slum areas are both poor and violent; this dual burden reproduces and exacerbates social exclusion. As youth in these areas are stigmatised for their supposedly violent way of life, they are denied solidarity and dignity. In these circumstances, young people and adolescents – many of them part of the "hard core" of exclusion – become vulnerable for exploitation in adult-led criminal practices; adults use marginalised youth knowing that minors (under 18 years of age) cannot be held criminally responsible. Since the 1980s, gangs in cities across the continent have become associated with an expression of youth identity linked to violence, substance abuse and illegal acts such as robbery. In this way, young people, including minors, have become part of the complex universe of Latin American law-breaking and the economy of crime. Apart from being involved in adult-led criminality, youth have their own forms of "social integration" associated with law-breaking (ECLAC, 2014).

All this matches people's perception of insecurity. Data from LAPOP (2012) report that some 20% of youth and 16% of adults in the region claimed to have been the victims of some crime (Figure 3.31). The situation varies by country. The youth population is not always disproportionately affected, although it does tend to be more involved where crime is particularly widespread (ECLAC, 2014).

Little is known about the perpetrators of violence and their age distribution. Statistics are few and hard to find, and record-keeping is deficient, partly because so much crime goes unpunished in many of the region's countries. One way to gauge participation in acts of violence is from data on victims of extreme violence, such as homicide; the risk of falling victim to crime is assumed to rise with the degree of participation in violent organisations. In some countries most affected by violence in recent years (in excess of 27 homicides per 100 000 inhabitants), the behaviour of the youth population is variable (Soto and Trucco, 2015). There is no general rule that young people are the main victims of homicide; rather, the situation depends on the country, the time period and the general context of violence facing each society.

The case of Central America bears this out. Increased violence linked to the presence of these actors does not imply a higher level of youth involvement in homicide, as would be expected from the stigma. The cases of El Salvador, Guatemala and Honduras confirm this: up until 2000, young adults (aged 30-44) displayed a slightly higher level of participation, although the difference was not statistically significant (Figure 3.32). In the last decade, as general violence has been increasing, rates of participation for some segments of the youth population have increased in tandem.

The statistical approach to gauge the extent of involvement in violent behaviour based on victim data indicates that stigma attached to violent youth derives from how they participate in violence rather than the degree of participation. Mass media most often highlight organised forms of urban violence among the young (usually males) in gangs by the name of *pandillas*, *maras*, *clicas* or *combos*, depending on the country. Young people of this type are categorised in the collective imagination as "deviants" or "misfits". Table 3.5 shows that around a third of the population perceive their local areas as affected by organisations of this kind, with the proportion being somewhat higher among youth (an average of 35%) than adults (31%). Citizens of the northern triangle of Central America (El Salvador, Guatemala and Honduras), where *maras* have a strong presence in the main cities, are not the ones where gangs are considered most prevalent. In recent years, however, this perception has been growing in other countries, such as Panama and particularly Dominican Republic (ECLAC, 2014).

Figure 3.32. **El Salvador, Guatemala and Honduras: Rate of mortality from interpersonal violence, by age group, 1990-2010**

(deaths per 100 000 inhabitants)

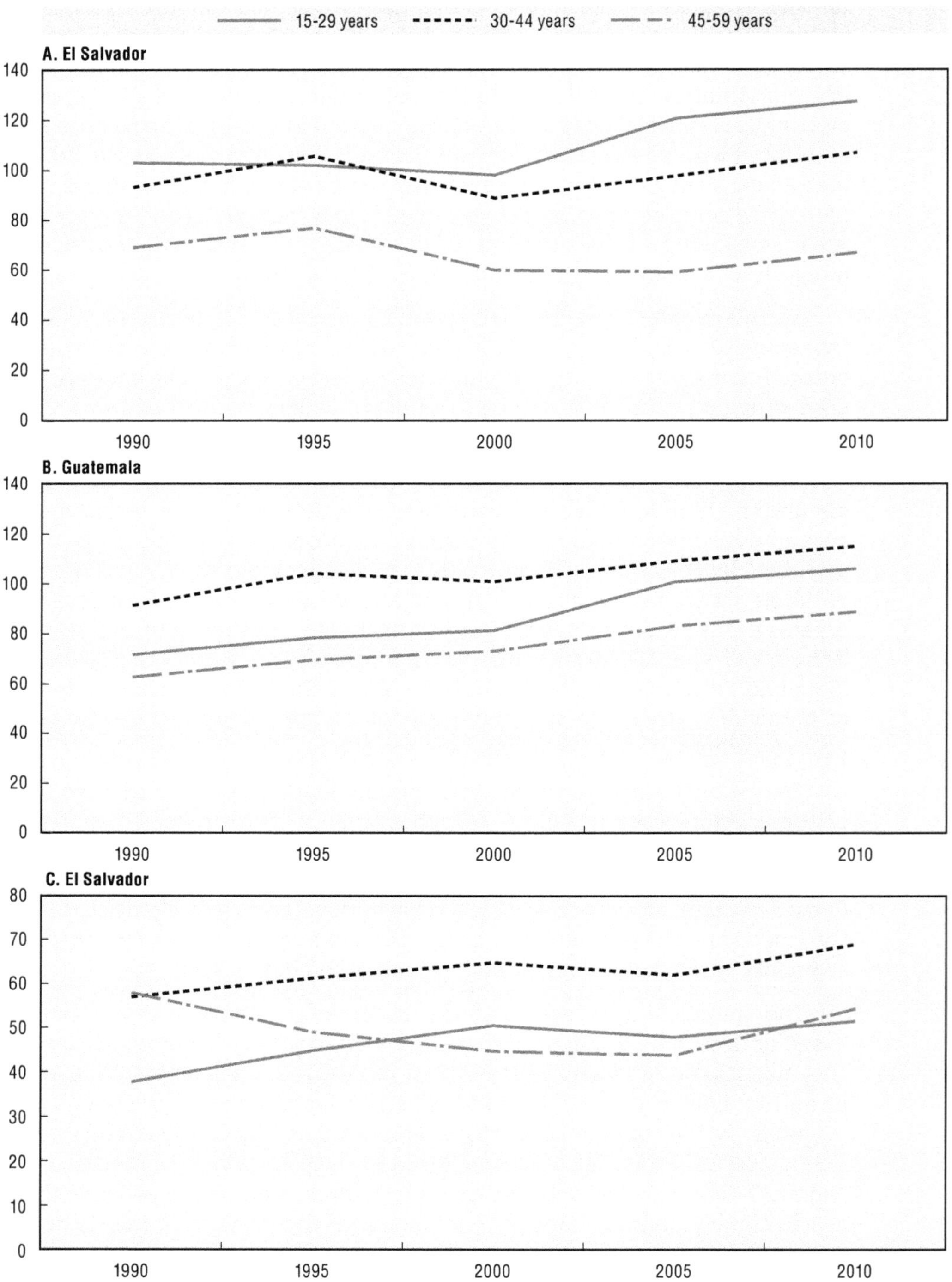

Note: Differences in young people's mortality rates are not statistically different from those of other age groups in any of the countries.

Source: Institute for Health Metrics and Evaluation, http://vizhub.healthdata.org/gbd-compare/ in Trucco and Ullmann, 2015.

StatLink http://dx.doi.org/10.1787/888933414343

Table 3.5. **Residents' perception of the incidence of gangs or maras in their local area in Latin America and the Caribbean, by country and age group, 2012**

(percentages)

Country	16-29 years	30 years and over
Guyana	19	14
Haiti	20	19
Jamaica	25	20
Belize	28	27
Nicaragua	28	24
Paraguay	30	24
Honduras	31	26
Mexico	33	35
Guatemala	36	31
Uruguay	37	35
Brazil	37	40
El Salvador	38	32
Costa Rica	39	32
Peru	40	35
Ecuador	41	38
Colombia	42	33
Panama	43	45
Dominican Rep.	55	48
LAC	35	31

Note: Simple averages of the results from the 18 countries included in the measurement.
Source: Trucco and Ullmann (2015) based on special tabulations of the biannual survey of the Latin American Public Opinion Project (LAPOP), 2012.

The territorial role of gangs within cities is one of the aspects that most creates a feeling of insecurity among the population at large, as it directly affects community life. The scene of gang members standing on a corner, alienated from institutions they should be participating in at this stage of life (traditionally school or work), feeds the stigma of violent youth as a threat to civic order and the city as a cultural project because the gang member's sovereignty is based on the local district or *barrio* (Perea Restrepo, 2008). The division of territories among organised crime is associated with high levels of segregation and creation of ghettos in many Latin American cities.

Gangs have emerged as a direct effect of structural violence, people's exclusion and marginalisation from the development of society. Belonging to a gang operates as a form of "inclusion within exclusion"; many gangs act as microsystems of social integration that reflect, compensate for and reinforce lack of integration into society. However, organisations of this type have changed in recent years from a core space of belonging to one of mutual survival: "Youth groupings in contexts of exclusion and poverty seem to operate for many of their members as a setting that provides a minimum of security and trust, however precarious" (Perea Restrepo, 2008).

The phenomenon of violence, particularly urban violence, cannot be grasped without understanding the socio-political and cultural history of each affected territory. These parameters influence the way groups organise, the power of criminal organisations to recruit young people and the type of dominance exerted. Membership of these groups and levels of violence needed to assert dominance are set within a multiplicity of social processes. These processes, in turn, create space for the alternative social inclusion for some of the region's young people. The literature has identified many risk factors associated with the incorporation of certain sections of youth into violent territorial groups.[18]

Factors that predispose youth to risk

The international literature names eight primary risk factors (or enablers) that can encourage different manifestations of violence in youth (Soto and Trucco, 2015):

(a) *Growing inequality and exclusion*: Although poverty appears to aggravate all types of violence, several studies agree that inequality and growing economic and social polarisation are much more systematically correlated with violence, especially among youth (Cruz, 2004). The most violent communities are those that the state has somehow "abandoned" or neglected, as shown, for example, by infrastructure in poor repair or lack of public services (such as lack of public lighting, of paved streets or of health centres). It may therefore be more appropriate to talk about a social or community setting of poverty rather than household poverty. This is closely related to the tension between the expansion of symbolic consumption and constraints on material consumption. Despite having achieved levels of education and well-being unimagined by their parents, a sizeable part of the youth population is disappointed by the labour options available. These frustrated expectations can trigger violent behaviours.

(b) *The after-effects of civil conflict*: A number of Latin American and Caribbean countries have had violence embedded in their cultures and in people's practices by socio-historical processes. This refers in particular to periods of post-war and post-dictatorship transition, where the idea of political violence begins to be associated with other types of violence. War may have created a culture of violence among the population, breeding a tendency to rely on violence to fix problems which has permeated the youth population. Recent armed conflict may also contribute to higher violence levels through the circulation of firearms and munitions into the sub-region.

(c) *Drug trafficking*: Drug trafficking in the region, particularly of cocaine, has played a key role as a driver of conflict and a multiplier of violence. In the past few decades, drug trafficking has become the dominant illegal market in cities marked by violence in Brazil, Colombia, Mexico and, recently, cities in the northern triangle of Central America comprising El Salvador, Guatemala and Honduras. It is a market that provides large profit margins and around which another set of illegal activities is organised (Perea Restrepo, 2014). In many of these cities there is no hope that the legal market, much less the state, will create economically competitive forms of employment for young people from marginalised populations. In some countries, such as Mexico and those of Central America, the cartels increasingly tend to use gangs to "outsource" abduction and contract killing activities, particularly when they conflict with one another and have to find more recruits quickly and at lower cost. In a specific study of young people from slums in Rio de Janeiro (*favelas*), the initial motivation of youngsters to join gangs is not clear – given that monetary returns are not significantly higher; however, members with weaker attachment to the gang and better outside opportunities were more likely to quit the gang. On the other hand, those with higher previous involvement with violence and aggressive personality traits stayed involved longer and were more likely to die within two years (Carvalho and Soares, 2013).

(d) *Process of migration and deportation*: The case of migration to the United States is particularly important because it is the main destination for emigrants from Latin America and the Caribbean. Migration from Central America to the United States intensified in the 1960s and became even more pronounced during periods of conflict in countries such as El Salvador, Guatemala and Honduras. In the early years of this migratory process, young Central American migrants were socially rejected and segregated upon their arrival in the United States by youth of other nationalities. This led Central American migrants to establish gangs as a violent response to social exclusion. The United States Immigration and Naturalization Service began to deport young gang members at the end of the 1980s, and stepped up these efforts in the 1990s with the establishment of the Violent Gang Task Force. Upon deportation, many young people who had been involved in these gangs replicated the same models of violent organisation in their countries of origin. This was the origin of the majority of the most violent gangs now operating in Central America. Although migration has lessened, it nevertheless continues, with young people forming one of the population segments most likely to migrate; this exposes them to violence, discrimination and health risks at all stages of the migration process.

(e) *Intrafamily violence*: Experts have found intergenerational transmission of mistreatment within the family is associated with violent behaviours (Krauskopf, 2002). Children who witness violent responses by their parents are more likely to follow those response models, as well as the gender role stereotypes in that interaction.

(f) *Lack of sense of belonging among youth*: Lack of a sense of belonging is a major cause of certain manifestations of violence. This is understood as non-adherence to shared values or recognised forms of participation, unwillingness to acknowledge others in relation to perceptions of discrimination or new communicative practices, and lack of trust in social structures and of confidence in the future. This lack of belonging can also be an outcome, and not only a cause, of violence, leading to a vicious cycle that needs to be broken. One of the cultural features embedded in LAC, in some countries more than others, is a tendency towards violent means for conflict resolution. This occurs from the private sphere through to community and collective spaces and shapes practices beginning in childhood. In many countries the media reinforce this image and reward violent behaviour, which viewers learn and later imitate.

(g) *The stigmatisation of youth*: Certain youth groups, such as gang members or youth from vulnerable urban areas, tend to be stigmatised as a potential threat and sign of violence. These expressions of symbolic violence can reinforce processes of exclusion and ultimately become self-fulfilling prophecies: the fact of being born and growing up in certain neighbourhoods deprives young people of opportunities to participate in a society that discriminates against them, and so their route towards integration arises through violent groups and behaviours.

(h) *Alienation from institutions*: Adolescents and young people drop out of school for many reasons, including family financial pressures. Being expelled by a system that does not offer suitable conditions to remain in education can increase risk factors for young people. This is particularly significant when it is associated with a violent setting; inadequate management of conflict among young people or between young people and the staff of educational establishments; failure to address the special needs of students with learning or behavioural difficulties; and use of violence by school authorities against the student body. This, added to the frustration of young people seeking to enter a labour market that fails to offer decent, worthwhile work, heightens their risk of becoming perpetrators of violence. These are young people who see little hope of gaining a good foothold in the labour market. The situation of the hard core of youth exclusion (those young people neither in education nor employment, nor engaged in any other activity) speaks of a rupture of linkages that help build capacity and participation in social capital.

The enablers of violence described are general in nature. Each manifestation of violence can be associated, in turn, with other more specific causal factors. Moreover, none of the youth violence enablers mentioned acts alone or is a sure explanation of violence in itself. Therefore, tackling one factor in isolation from the others is highly unlikely to have the desired effect of reducing violence. On the contrary, it could be counterproductive and ultimately escalate violence. Since the issue involves a combination of national-level factors, such as general economic and social conditions (levels of inequality, drug trafficking, population dynamics, access to education and employment and even a history of civil conflict), and more particular aspects (family and cultural setting, sense of belonging of individuals), it requires an integrated approach that addresses different standpoints (Soto and Trucco, 2015).

Box 3.6. **The Ibero-American Youth Pact Ibero-American International Organisation of Youth**

The Ibero-American Youth Pact is an alliance between governments, the private sector, academia, civil society and requires international co-operation to guide and co-ordinate the development of policies, programmes and projects for the development and protection of young people in the region.

To consolidate and legitimise this process, which involves the formation of high level political agreements, the OIJ has designed a strategy based on participation and collective construction, linking inputs from the following:

a) National Youth Forums in the 21 Ibero-American countries with the same methodology and frameworks for diversity, pluralism and youth participation;

b) Ibero-American Conferences of Ministers that articulate the perspective of youth;

c) The Forum for Intergenerational Dialogue and other participatory spaces with a singular impact on the youth agenda from the perspective of the Ibero-American System of Co-operation;

d) The results from the Digital Ibero-American Consultation;

e) The guidelines and recommendations proposed by the Colombian Government;

f) The content of the OIJ Plan for Action (2016-2021), as well as the diagnostic groundwork used for its elaboration;

g) The National Reports produced by the IOY analysts (Country Reports);

h) Studies and research on youth published by recognised experts in the field;

i) The results from the qualitative study on the realities of youth in Ibero-America, including interviews with key players in the region.

These inputs, methodologically selected, systematised and analysed in depth, will determine an assortment of agreements and thematic statements with regards to the reality that is expected to be transformed (the what) and the concrete action towards this end (the how).

To that effect, the structure of contents within the Pact will allow for the progressive convergence of intersectoral agreements linked to the comprehensive development of youth, education for the improvement of social mobility and entrepreneurship and socio-economic inclusion.

Conclusions and policy recommendations

Youth in Latin America continue to face obstacles to their inclusion in society. Despite significant improvements in a number of areas, the labour market gaps confronting young people in the LAC region continue to be wider than those in OECD countries and those of adults. Furthermore, progress has been uneven across countries. Some groups of youth are particularly vulnerable: young women, NEETs, low-skilled and informal youth, and youth in rural areas. Eliminating disparities in health status, participation and active citizenship is crucial to address both the social and economic inclusion of youth. The main health concerns for youth in Latin America are related to violence, mental health, substance abuse and early pregnancy. The contexts of violence faced by young people in the region also influence their life choices and active participation.

Building the capacities of new generations requires treating young people as essential agents of structural change. Legislation and regulations are needed to safeguard and promote young people's social rights as regards, for example, access to health and education, decent work opportunities and participation in decisions on matters of public interest. A key challenge is to co-ordinate the various public policy sectors involved in an integrated manner; policies that address only one aspect of marginalisation – such as improved access to education – may be too narrow to overcome exclusion more generally (World Bank, 2013). Some initial policy orientations and recommendations are presented below. Additional analysis is needed to tailor policy for the specific needs of each country.

Close remaining gaps in education to improve education-to-work transitions

Strengthening the connection between school and work is key. While youth in Latin America now have the highest educational attainments ever, persistent difficulties remain among the disadvantaged socio-demographic groups and among the poorest. Conditional cash transfers (CCT) have been an effective policy instrument to increase educational attainment. Making social assistance conditional on school attendance can align parents' incentives with students' best interests. Increasing available resources for education, especially in remote areas, should be coupled with advancements in education quality and with graduation strategies and productive inclusion. Young people also need an array of formal and non-formal instruction adapted to their situations, including non-discriminatory programmes that accommodate special needs (e.g. young people with disabilities, pregnant adolescents) and reduce segregation. Modules should encourage young people to stay in school or to return if they have left, and to reconcile their studies with the demands of caregiving and other roles. Linkages among the various educational and training subsystems should accommodate a suitable transition between training, technical education, vocational education and university programmes (Espejo and Espíndola, 2015).

Enhance job quality by promoting effective social protection systems and labour laws

Low quality and informal jobs can leave permanent scars on workers' careers. It is important, therefore, that policy makers help workers get on a good career path early in their working lives; in particular, low-skilled workers who face the highest risk of being trapped in low-productivity and low-quality jobs with limited career prospects. Education and training must be better aligned with labour market needs and provide incentives for investments in training. In particular, policy makers may want to increase the security of youth from the most vulnerable households with lower skills and informal jobs. Priorities are the development of adequate unemployment compensation and social assistance programmes, such as cash transfers and health-care benefits (OECD 2015a). Young people should be encouraged to obtain social security coverage (Espejo and Espíndola, 2015). Well designed and enforced labour laws should balance incentives for youth hiring with social protection and decent work conditions. Beyond social protection, policies should help youth move from first temporary jobs to more stable career paths.

Integrate a gender perspective into youth policies

Adolescent pregnancy and household chores are two key reasons why young women drop out of school and do not enter in the labour market. Public education policies must seek to reduce teenage pregnancy through promotion of sexuality and reproductive rights in public education, as well as high-quality, universal, timely and relevant sexual and reproductive health care. These should be complemented with antidiscrimination legislation to avoid the explicit or implicit school expulsion of pregnant students, and programmes that promote the continuation of studies for mothers (such as free childcare services or flexible school hours and curriculum).[19]

Certainly, another burning issue is the unequal distribution of unpaid work performed by women within households, its economic value and how these activities prevent women from achieving economic autonomy and full integration into the labour market. In this context, it is necessary to reduce gaps in participation, employment and wages (see also OECD [2016a and 2016b] for further discussion). Policies that reconcile work and family life for men and women could produce productivity gains, higher household income and lower levels of socio-economic inequality and household poverty. It would also give impetus to equality in other spheres, such as the full exercise of autonomy, the development of individual capacities and potential, access to contributory social protection and broader participation in society beyond the household (ECLAC, 2014). A range of policies has proved highly successful in freeing women's time and increasing their employment rates. LAC countries could adapt several childcare models already in place in the region, including in Mexico (*Estancias infantiles*) and Colombia (*Hogares comunitarios*), that use public funds to stimulate the provision of childcare in the community.[20] Similarly, the Chilean *Crece Contigo* expands access to childcare, with a focus on the poorest household, combining care and education systems to promote early childhood development. Recently, the national care system of Uruguay has expanded access to childcare, with a focus on the poorest households.

Strengthen health services targeting young people

Prevention, care and treatment services for young people should be tailored to their stage of psycho-emotional development and social, economic, cultural and family environment. Given the interrelationship between youth health issues (e.g. mental health and drug and alcohol abuse), programmes need to be more integrated and transmitted through innovative communication models (e.g. social media and peer education). This more holistic approach should also seek to strengthen protective factors in the lives of young people (especially those facing other conditions of exclusion) instead of just focusing on risk reduction. Demographic changes (an ageing population coupled with proportionately fewer young people in the future) calls for investments that enable young people to reach adulthood with good health so they can fully contribute to the economic and social development of their communities and countries.

Increase the effectiveness of programmes preventing youth engaging in risky behaviours

Policy makers must identify factors to mitigate the most severe risks and help reduce violence to promote contexts of peaceful coexistence at all levels: family, community and social. These policies should consider young people's subjective sense of belonging (Soto and Trucco, 2015). The primary level of prevention should include strategies to reduce risks such as consuming alcohol or carrying weapons, and promote a culture of peace (including assessment of how laws treat violence in youth). Secondary prevention should focus on psycho-social care, support for young people with drug or alcohol addiction problems and demobilisation of young gang members; it should also strengthen strategies to treat violence in schools with protocols that establish roadmaps for care.[21] Tertiary prevention should promote sanctions for crime, but also social reinsertion for youth who break the law. Strengthening justice systems can improve police investigation, processing and reporting, which will benefit both victims and perpetrators.

Strengthen youth participation in political processes

Strengthening youth participation is essential to make all decisions more relevant, sustainable and legitimate (Trucco and Ullmann, 2015). This calls for consultations between youth and youth organisations, effective and sustainable co-operation between ministries, sufficient resource allocation and the integration of national youth policy into national development plans. Reviewing international experiences of engaging youth may provide more pathways for young people to contribute. Potential areas for change include national justice and electoral systems, as well as opening up space for youth at the community level, in political parties and in civil society organisations (including youth-led movements).

Produce relevant information

Better information systems are needed to monitor young people's lives and situations and their perceptions in each country and territory. To that end, governments should generate relevant statistics that can support investment in their country's most vulnerable youth.

Annex 3.A1: Further results

Figure 3.A1.1. **Youth and socio-economic status in Latin America, 2014**

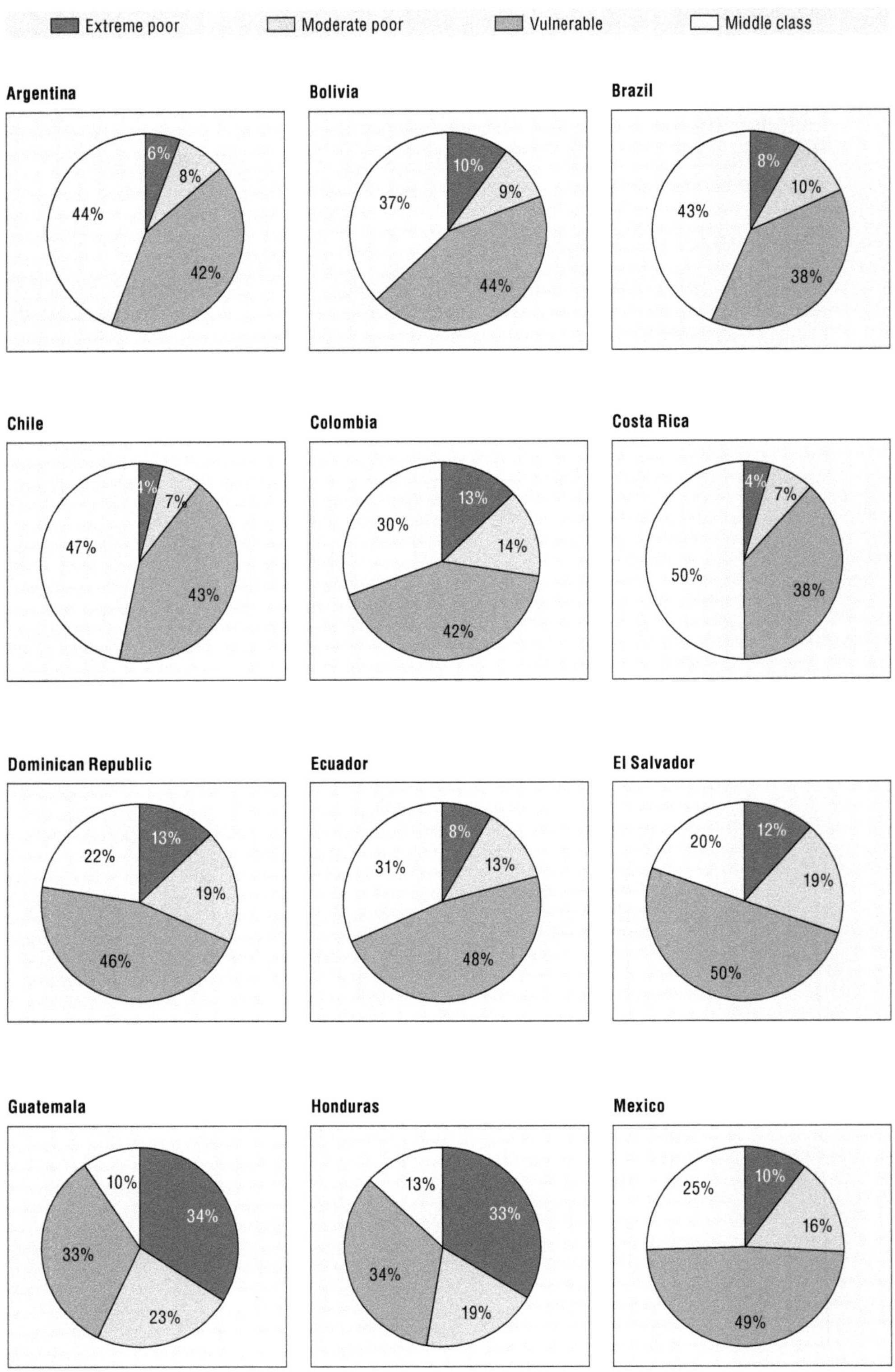

Figure 3.A1.1. **Youth and socio-economic status in Latin America, 2014** (cont.)

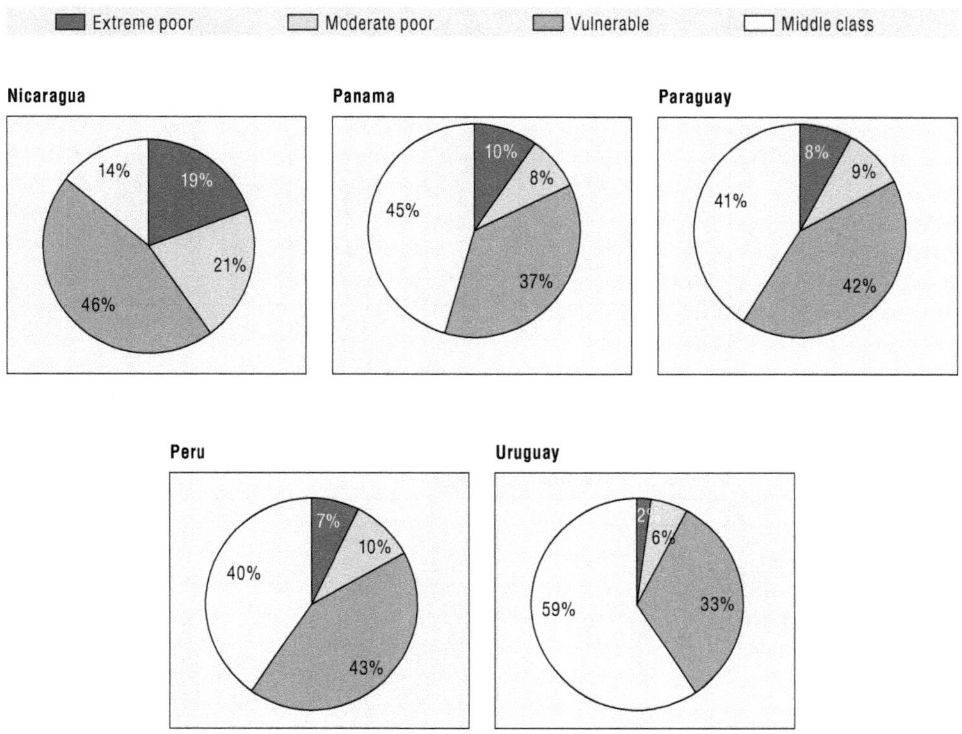

Source: OECD and World Bank tabulations of SEDLAC (CEDLAS and the World Bank) and OECD – LFS data.
StatLink http://dx.doi.org/10.1787/888933414355

Figure 3.A1.2. **Labour market situation of youth in Latin America, 2004 and 2014**

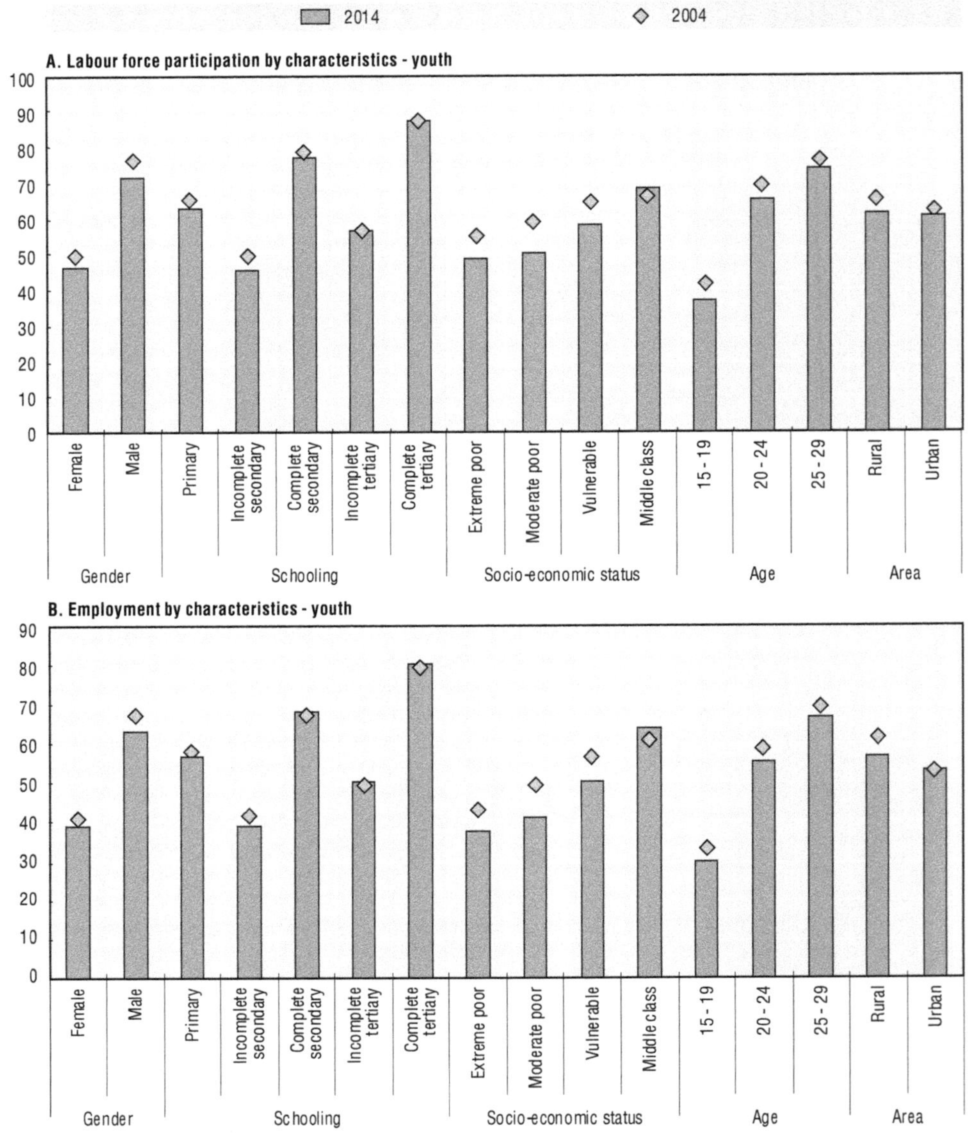

Note: LAC weighted average of 18 countries: Argentina, Bolivia, Brazil, Chile, Colombia, Costa Rica, Dominican Republic, Ecuador, El Salvador, Guatemala, Honduras, Mexico, Nicaragua, Panama, Paraguay, Peru, Uruguay and Venezuela.

Source: OECD and World Bank tabulations of SEDLAC (CEDLAS and the World Bank) and OECD.

StatLink http://dx.doi.org/10.1787/888933414361

Table 3.A1.1. **Type of jobs held by youth, LAC average 2014**

Labour relationship (percentage)		Contract (percentage)		Part-time (percentage)	
Employee	76.85	With a contract	48.4	With full-time job	82.8
Employer	1.53	Without a contract	51.6	With part-time job	19.4
Self-employed	12.76	With permanent contract	32.9		
Unpaid family worker	8.86	With temporary contract	61.0		

Note: LAC weighted average of 18 countries: Argentina, Bolivia, Brazil, Chile, Colombia, Costa Rica, Dominican Republic, Ecuador, El Salvador, Guatemala, Honduras, Mexico, Nicaragua, Panama, Paraguay, Peru, Uruguay and Venezuela.

Source: OECD and World Bank tabulations of SEDLAC (CEDLAS and the World Bank) and OECD.

Notes

1. Other issues affect the social inclusion of youth, such as race and ethnicity, but an analysis of these issues is beyond the scope of this chapter.
2. Evidence indicates that some countries in the region have managed to take advantage of this demographic shift for the benefit of the economy: Rosero-Bixby and Robles (2008) show that almost all economic growth in Costa Rica in the last quarter century is due to the increase in the productive-aged population relative to the dependent population.
3. This indicator establishes the relationship between the potentially inactive population (under the age of 20 years and older than 65 years) in the numerator, and the potentially active population (20-64 years of age), in the denominator. This age grouping differs somewhat from the one typically used in demography, which considers the groups 0-14 years, 15-59 years, and 60 and older. In modifying the age categories, we attempt to reach a better approximation of the dependent population. On the one hand, it includes the entire primary and secondary school-age population. On the other hand, it also reflects the current trend of delaying retirement. In any event, it is a gross indicator. Not all of the population under 20 years stays in the school system and not all people aged 65 and over are removed immediately from the labour market, particularly in countries and socio-economic strata with low social security coverage (ECLAC, 2016a).
4. Only five countries (Barbados, The Bahamas, Chile, Cuba, and Trinidad and Tobago) have completed or are nearing completion of this stage. In ten countries, the demographic window will close during the 2020s, in four countries during the 2030s and in nine others during the 2040s. Lastly, three countries, Guatemala, Bolivia and Guyana, remain at the stage of the demographic bonus until after the middle of this century (ECLAC, 2016a).
5. Unless otherwise noted, poverty estimates are based on comparable data and international poverty lines and hence may differ from official statistics reported by governments and national offices of statistics. Such differences should not be interpreted in any way as a claim of methodological superiority, as both sets of numbers serve the same important objectives: regional comparability and the best possible representation of the facts of individual countries. The welfare aggregate used to measure poverty in this report is the total household per capita income. Since October 2015, the basic World Bank indicator for measuring extreme poverty globally is the percentage of people living on less than USD 1.90 a day in 2011 purchasing parity power (PPP). However, the level of economic development in the LAC region has led analysts to use poverty lines that are higher: USD 2.50 a day (extreme poverty) and a USD 4.00 a day (overall poverty). These lines are based on income aggregates adjusted to 2005 PPP. To measure the middle class and the vulnerable, this report follows Ferreira et al. (2012), defining economic classes based on the concept of economic security: the vulnerable, who have incomes between USD 4.00-10.00 a day; and the middle class, living on between USD 10.00-50.00 a day (2005 PPP). Vulnerable groups are those with a higher probability of falling into poverty in any given year. Internationally comparable numbers in this report are based on two regional data harmonisation efforts known as SEDLAC and LABLAC, joint efforts of the World Bank and CEDLAS at the National University of La Plata in Argentina. Unless otherwise noted, indicators for LAC are calculated using data from Argentina, Bolivia, Brazil, Chile, Colombia, Costa Rica, Dominican Republic, Ecuador, El Salvador, Guatemala, Honduras, Mexico, Nicaragua, Panama, Paraguay, Peru and Uruguay (LAC-17).
6. Although the analysis does not include the racial/ethnic dimension, it is another relevant consideration for discrimination and inequality in LAC. The history of slavery and colonisation still affects growth opportunities.
7. Poverty rates are higher in rural than in urban areas. Although rural poverty fell by a similar percentage to urban poverty in the most recent period, the substantial poverty gap affecting rural areas was left unchanged. The reasons can be numerous: productivity is lower in rural areas; and rural employment typically offers low wages, fewer options for paid work for women, low levels of formal education and weaker labour institutions (evidenced by the limited coverage of social protection systems, substantial non-compliance with minimum wage standards and a high degree of informality).
8. OECD and World Bank elaborations of SEDLAC (CEDLAS and the World Bank) for LAC-17 average (Argentina, Bolivia, Brazil, Chile, Colombia, Costa Rica, Dominican Republic, Ecuador, El Salvador, Guatemala, Honduras, Mexico, Nicaragua, Panama, Paraguay, Peru, Uruguay).
9. Unemployment rates tend to be lower in rural areas than in urban areas because the surplus rural labour supply tends to fuel migratory flows to the cities. This surplus is absorbed in low-paid jobs with less social protection coverage, rather than showing through as open unemployment. Moreover, the chance of obtaining a paid job varies according to the agricultural cycle, which means greater labour inactivity in periods when labour demand is weak.

10. According to Latinobarómetro data(2015), 40% of those interviewed believe that women need to work only if the partner does not earn enough money. Latinobarómetro is an annual public opinion survey that involves some 20 000 interviews in 18 Latin American countries, representing more than 600 million inhabitants.
11. Within Agenda 2030, SDG8 is to "promote sustained, inclusive and sustainable economic growth, full and productive employment and decent work for all". The goal identifies youth in two proposed targets: i) by 2030 achieve full and productive employment and decent work for all women and men, including for young people and persons with disabilities, and equal pay for work of equal value; and ii) by 2020 substantially reduce the proportion of youth not in employment, education or training (NEET). In addition, the 2015 G20 Labour and Employment Ministerial adopted for the first time a quantitative target to reduce the share of young people who are most at risk of being left permanently behind in the labour market by 15% by 2025. Depending on national circumstances, it was proposed to focus on low-skilled youth who are NEET (largely for more developed economies) or who are informally employed (largely for emerging economies).
12. The high future opportunity cost of this situation for women should not be overlooked; their position makes them economically dependent on other people and hampers their entry into the labour market. Young men who leave the education system do not have to pay the same price; they make up for their lack of formal education by amassing more work experience on which the labour market places a fairly high value (Rico and Trucco, 2014).
13. Each bar denotes the proportion who moved between an initial state *i* (in this case, in school) to a final labour market state *j* (i.e. employment, inactivity or unemployment).
14. Gontero and Weller (2015) define employment in low productive sectors as being employees (non-professional nor technical) working in micro firms (fewer than five employees); independent workers without classification (self-employed or unpaid family workers without any professional qualification) and household work.
15. Owing to data comparability limitations, informal workers can be defined using the SEDLAC database using two different approaches. Consistent with previous research, the chapter uses the legislative definition as "those salaried workers who are not affiliated to social security system (do not pay contributions) and those own-account (self-employed) workers whose business is not registered" (Jutting and de Laiglesia, 2009). This information is only available for a subset of SEDLAC countries. Similar results in terms of informality rates are found when using the SEDLAC productive definition that defines informality as workers who are self-employed (excluding those with tertiary degrees) and those who work in firms of fewer than five workers.
16. This survey of middle- and high-school students (aged 13-17) uses a standardised sampling process, a common methodology and modules with standardised questions, facilitating comparisons across countries.
17. Voting is compulsory in the following countries: Argentina, Bolivia, Brazil, Costa Rica, Dominican Republic, Ecuador, Honduras, Mexico, Panama, Paraguay, Peru and Uruguay.
18. Generally speaking, information on the role of women in gangs is limited to the results of certain case studies. With only a few exceptions, women do not play the same roles as men in gang activities. Women involved in gangs usually assume traditional gender roles such as providing food, covering up and protection, concealing arms and tending to injuries. They are generally not consulted in decisions, punished for infidelity and obliged to seek their partner within the gang. They sometimes play a submissive sexual role in a context in which, in most cases, male gang members do not seek stable relationships with women, or do so outside the gang (Lacayo, 2015). However, the few relevant case studies show conclusively how gender inequality is magnified within gangs and reveal the need to analyse the theme of sexual violence against women, mainly adolescents, who become involved with gangs.
19. For example, Law 25273 in Argentina created a system of justified absences for pregnant students; in Brazil, since 1975, Federal Law 6202 has established a special regime for pregnant students that compensate their school absences with homework; in Ecuador the 2008 Constitution and Law 100 (Child and adolescent code), guarantees pregnant women and those in lactation the right to non-discrimination in the education, social and labour spheres.
20. Under these models, community members, frequently poor women, receive a per-child subsidy to transform their spaces into childcare centres.
21. These protocols consider the rights of children and teenagers, and the best interests for children under 18.

References

Anand, S. and K. Hanson (1997), "Disability-adjusted life years: A critical perspective", *Journal of Health Economics*, vol. 16, N° 6, Elsevier, Amsterdam.

Baldwin, W. et al. (2013), "Noncommunicable diseases and youth: A critical window of opportunity for Latin America and the Caribbean", *Policy Brief*, June, Population Reference Bureau, Washington, DC, www.prb.org/pdf13/noncommunicable-diseases-latin-america-youth-policybrief.pdf.

Bassi, M. and S. Galiani (2009), "Labor market insertion of young adults in Chile" (brochure), Inter-American Development Bank, Washington, DC.

Bloom, D.E., D. Canning and J. Sevilla (2003), "The demographic dividend: A new perspective on the economic consequences of population change", *Population Matters Monograph*, No. MR-1274, RAND Corporation, Santa Monica.

Bosch, M. and W.F. Maloney (2010), "Comparative analysis of labor market dynamics using Markov processes: An application to informality", *Labour Economics*,Vol. 17, No.4, pp. 621-631. doi:10.1016/j.labeco.2010.01.005.

Bradshaw, C.P., L. M. O'Brennan and C.A. McNeely (2008), "Core competencies and the prevention of school failure and early school leaving", *New Directions for Child and Adolescent Development*, Vol. 2008, No. 122, Wiley.

Carcillo, S., et al. (2015), "NEET youth in the aftermath of the crisis: Challenges and policies", *OECD Social, Employment and Migration Working Papers*, No. 164, OECD Publishing, Paris, http://dx.doi.org/10.1787/5js6363503f6-en.

Carvalho, L. and R. Soares (2013), "Living on the edge: Youth entry, career and exit in drug-selling gangs", *IZA Discussion Paper*, No. 7189, Institute for the Study of Labor, Bonn.

Cruces, G., A. Ham and M. Viollaz (2012), "Scarring effects of youth unemployment and informality: Evidence from Argentina and Brazil", *CEDLAS Working Paper*, Center for Distributive, Labor and Social Studies (CEDLAS), Universidad Nacional de la Plata, Argentina.

Cruz, J.M. (2004), "Maras y pandillas en Centroamérica: Pandillas y capital social", UCA Editores, Volumen IV, San Salvador; and Briceño & Zuñiga in Posas, M. (2009), "Delincuencia, inseguridad ciudadana y desarrollo humano en Honduras, [Maras and Gangs in Central America: Gangs and Social Capital], *Cuandernos de Desarrollo Humano* No. 4, United Nations Development Programme, Honduras.

Cunningham, W. and J. Bustos (2011), "Youth employment transitions in Latin America", *Policy Research Working Paper*, No. 5521, World Bank, Human Development Network, Children and Youth Unit, Washington, DC.

Da Silva, J. et al. (2009), "Illicit drug use in seven Latin American countries: Critical perspectives of families and familiars", *Rev. Latino-Am. Enfermagem*, Vol.17, Special Issue, http://dx.doi.org/10.1590/S0104-11692009000700002.

De Hoyos, R., R. Halsey and M. Székely (2016), *Out of School and Out of Work: Risk and Opportunities for Latin America's Ninis*, World Bank, Washington, DC.

ECLAC (2016a), *Social Panorama of Latin America 2015*, Economic Commission for Latin America and the Caribbean, Santiago, Chile.

ECLAC (2016b), "Desarrollo social inclusivo. Una nueva generación de políticas para superar la pobreza y reducir la desigualdad en América Latina y el Caribe", Conferencia Regional sobre Desarrollo Social de América Latina y el Caribe. LC.L/4056 Rev.1 ["Inclusive Social Development. A new generation of policies to overcome poverty and reduce inequality in Latin America and the Caribbean"], Economic Commission for Latin America and the Caribbean, Santiago, Chile.

ECLAC (2014), *Social Panorama for Latin America 2014*, Economic Commission for Latin America and the Caribbean, Santiago, Chile.

ECLAC (2009), *Social Panorama of Latin America 2009*, Economic Commission for Latin America and the Caribbean, Santiago, Chile.

ECLAC/OIJ (2008), *Juventud y cohesión social en Iberoamérica. Un modelo para armar* (LC/G.2391) [*Youth and Social Cohesion in Latin America. A Model Kit*], Economic Commission for Latin America and the Caribbean, Santiago, Chile.

Espejo, A. and E. Espíndola (2015), "The master key to the social inclusion of young people: Education and employment", in Trucco, D. and H. Ullmann (eds.), *Youth: Realities and Challenges for Achieving Development with Equality*, Economic Commission for Latin America and the Caribbean, Santiago, Chile.

Ferreira, F. et al. (2012), *Economic Mobility and the Rise of the Latin American Middle Class*, World Bank, Washington, DC.

FLACSO/International IDEA (2013), *Youth and Political Participation in Latin America. Current State and Challenges*, Latin American Faculty of Social Sciences/International Institute for the Development of Electoral Assistance, Santiago, Chile, November.

Furlong, A. (2006), "Not a very NEET solution: Representing problematic labour market transitions among early school-leavers", *Work, Employment and Society*, Vol. 20/3, British Sociological Association, Belmont, UK, pp. 553-569.

Gasparini, L.C. and M. Marchionni (2015), *Bridging Gender Gaps? The Rise and Deceleration of Female Labor Force Participation in Latin America*, Centre for Distributive Labor and Social Studies (CEDLAS), Universidad Nacional de La Plata, La Plata, Argentina.

Gontero, S. and J. Weller (2015), "¿Estudias o trabajas? El largo camino hacia la independencia económica de los jóvenes de América Latina", *Serie Macroeconomía del Desarrollo* ["Do you study or work? The long road to economic independence of young people in Latin America"], Economic Commission for Latin America and the Caribbean, Santiago, Chile.

ILO (2013), *Global Employment Trends for Youth 2013: A Generation at Risk*, International Labour Organization, Geneva.

Jütting, J. and J.R de Laiglesia (2009), *Is Informal Normal? Towards More and Better Jobs in Developing Countries*, OECD Development Centre, OECD Publishing, Paris, http://dx.doi.org/10.1787/9789264059245-en.

Krauskopf, D. (2002), "Juventud en riesgo y violencia. Seminario permanente sobre violencia" ["Youth at risk and violence: Permanent seminar on violence"], United Nations Development Programme, El Salvador, Argentina.

Krauskopf, D. (2000), "El desarrollo psicológico del adolescente" ["Adolescent Psychological Development"], in H. Montenegro and H. Guajardo (eds.), *Psiquiatría del Niño y el Adolescente* Asociación Española de Psiquiatría del Niño y el Adolescente, A Corúna, Spain.

Lacayo, N. (2015), "Inclusión social juvenil en contextos de violencia. Estudio de caso Nicaragua" ["Youth Social Inclusion in Contexts of Violence"], unpublished.

La Porta, R. and A. Shleifer (2008), "The unofficial economy and economic development", *Brookings Papers on Economic Activity, Economic Studies Program*,Vol. 39, No. 2 (Fall), The Brookings Institution, pp. 275-363.

Maddaleno, M., P. Morello and F. Infante-Espínola (2003), "Salud y desarrollo de adolescentes y jóvenes en Latinoamérica y el Caribe: desafíos para la próxima década" ["Health and development of adolescents and youth in Latin America and the Caribbean: Challenges for the next decade"], *Salud Pública de México*, Vol. 45, Cuernavaca, Mexico.

Maldonado Valera, C. (2015), "Political participation, commitment to democracy and priority issues for young people in Latin America, 2000-13", in Trucco, D. and H. Ullmann (eds.) *Youth: Realities and Challenges for Achieving Development with Equality*, Economic Commission for Latin America and the Caribbean, Santiago, Chile.

Maloney, W.F. (2004), "Informality revisited", *World Development*, Vol. 32/7, Elsevier, Amsterdam, pp. 1159-1178, July.

OAS (2012), "Estado del arte sobre empleo juvenil en América Latina y Europa" ["State of the art on youth employment in Latin America and Europe"], presentation at the intersectorial meeting of interchange and programming "Employment of Young People. Innovative Strategies to Facilitate the Transition from School to Work", Washington, DC.

OECD (2016a), *OECD Employment Outlook 2016*, OECD Publishing, Paris, http://dx.doi.org/10.1787/empl_outlook-2016-en.

OECD (2016b), *Gender Equality in the Pacific Alliance: Promoting Women's Economic Empowerment*, OECD Publishing, Paris, http://dx.doi.org/10.1787/9789264262959-en.

OECD (2015a), *OECD Skills Outlook 2015: Youth, Skills and Employability*, OECD Publishing, Paris, http://dx.doi.org/10.1787/9789264234178-en.

OECD (2015b), *OECD Employment Outlook 2015*, OECD Publishing, Paris, http://dx.doi.org/10.1787/empl_outlook-2015-en.

OECD (2015c), *Multi-Dimensional Review of Peru: Volume 1, Initial Assessment*, OECD Development Pathways, OECD Publishing, Paris, http://dx.doi.org/10.1787/9789264243279-en.

OECD (2014a), *Investing in Youth: Brazil*, OECD Publishing, Paris, http://dx.doi.org/10.1787/9789264208988-en.

OECD (2014b), *Social Cohesion Policy Review of Viet Nam*, Development Centre Studies, OECD Publishing, Paris, http://dx.doi.org/10.1787/9789264196155-en.

OECD (2013), "OECD action plan for youth – giving youth a better start in the labour market", presentation at the meeting of the OECD Council at Ministerial Level, Paris, 29-30 May.

OECD/IDB/CIAT (2016), Taxing Wages in Latin America and the Caribbean 2016, OECD Publishing, Paris, http://dx.doi.org/10.1787/9789264262607-en

Quintini, G. and S. Martin (2007), "Same but different: School-to-work transitions in emerging and advanced economies", *OECD Social, Employment and Migration Working Papers*, No. 154, OECD Publishing, Paris, http://dx.doi.org/10.1787/5jzbb2t1rcwc-en.

Parker, R.N. and K. Auerhahn (1998), "Alcohol, drugs, and violence", *Annual Review of Sociology*, Vol. 24.

Patel, V. et al. (2007), "Mental health of young people: A global public-health challenge", *The Lancet*, Vol. 369/9569, London, New York, Beijing, pp. 1302-1313.

Pavez, M.I. (2014), "Los derechos de la infancia en la era de Internet. América Latina y las nuevas tecnologías" ["The rights of children in the Internet age: Latin America and New Technologies"], *Políticas Sociales* series, No. 210 (LC/L.3894), Economic Commission for Latin America and the Caribbean (ECLAC), Santiago, Chile, September.

Perea Restrepo, C. (2014), "La muerte próxima. Vida y dominación en Río de Janeiro y Medellín" [The Next Death: Life and Domination in Rio de Janeiro and Medellin], *Análisis Político*, Vol. 27/80, Universidad Nacional de Colombia, Bogatá, Colombia, pp. 3-25..

Perea Restrepo, C. (2008), "¿Qué nos une? Jóvenes, cultura y ciudadanía", La Carreta, Medellín. ["What unifies us? Youth, culture and citizenship], in *Social Panorama for Latin America 2014*, Economic Commission for Latin America and the Caribbean (ECLAC), Santiago, Chile.

Rico, M.N. and D. Trucco (2014), "Adolescentes: Derecho a la educación y al bienestar futuro", ["Teens: The right to Education and the Future Welfare"], *Políticas Sociales serie*, No. 190 (LC/L.3791), Economic Commission for Latin America and the Caribbean (ECLAC), Santiago, http://www.unicef.org/lac/Adolescentes_derecho_educacion_bienestar_futuro.pdf.

Rodríguez V.J. (2014), "La reproducción en la adolescencia y sus desigualdades en América Latina: Introducción al análisis demográfico, con énfasis en el uso de microdatos censales de la ronda de 2010" ["Reproduction in adolescence and inequality in Latin America: Introduction to demographic analysis, with emphasis on the use of census microdata from the 2010 round"], *Projects Document* (LC/W.605), Economic Commission for Latin America and the Caribbean (ECLAC), Santiago, Chile.

Rodríguez V.J. (2008), *Reproducción adolescente y desigualdades en América Latina y el Caribe: Un llamado a la reflexión y a la acción. [Adolescent Reproductive and Inequalities in Latin America and The Caribbean: A Call to Reflection and Action]*, Comisión Económica para América Latina y el Caribe (CEPAL/ECLAC), Santiago, Chile.

Rosero-Bixby, L. and A. Robles (2008), "Los dividendos demográficos y la economía del ciclo vital en Costa Rica", *Papeles de Población*, Vol. 55, pp. 9-34.

Rossel, C. (2013), "Desbalance etario del bienestar. El lugar de la infancia en la protección social en América Latina" ["Age welfare imbalance: The place of children in social protection in Latin America"], *Políticas Sociales* series, No. 176 (LC/L.3574), Economic Commission for Latin America and the Caribbean (ECLAC), Santiago. Chile.

Soto, H. and D. Trucco (2015), "Inclusion and contexts of violence", in D. Trucco and H. Ullmann (eds.), *Youth: Realities and Challenges for Achieving Development with Equality*, Economic Commission for Latin America and the Caribbean (ECLAC), Santiago, Chile.

Telefónica (2014), "Telefónica global millennial survey – Today's young adults: the leaders of tomorrow" http://survey.telefonica.com/portfolio/global-results-presentation/ (accessed 20 May 2016).

Trucco, D. and H. Ullmann (2015), *Youth: Realities and Challenges for Achieving Development with Equality*, Economic Commission for Latin America and the Caribbean (ECLAC), Santiago, Chile.

Ullmann, H. (2015), "Health and young people in Latin America and the Caribbean", in Trucco, D. and H. Ullmann (eds.), *Youth: Realities and Challenges for Achieving Development with Equality*, Economic Commission for Latin America and the Caribbean (ECLAC), Santiago, Chile.

UNICEF (2012), *Progress for Children – A Report Card on Adolescence*, No. 10, UNICEF, New York, http://www.unicef.org/publications/index_62280.html.

United Nations (2014), *Mental Health Matters: Social Inclusion of Youth with Mental Health Conditions*, Department of Economic and Social Affairs, United Nations, New York, www.un.org/esa/socdev/documents/youth/youth-mental-health.pdf.

UNDP (2016), *Regional Human Development Report for Latin America and the Caribbean Multidimensional Progress: Well-being Beyond Income*, United Nations Development Programme, Santiago, Chile.

UNDP (2013), *Human Development Report for Latin America 2013-2014 – Citizen Security with a Human Face: Evidence and Proposals for Latin America*, United Nations Development Programme, New York, November.

UNDP (2012), *Human Development in Chile 2012 – Subjective Well-being: The Challenges of Rethinking Development*, United Nations Development Programme, Santiago, Chile.

UNODC (2014), *Global Study on Homicide 2013: Trends, Contexts, Data*, United Nations Office on Drugs and Crime, Vienna.

Weller, J. (2007), "Youth employment: Characteristics, tensions and challenges", *ECLAC Review*, Vol. 92, Economic Commission for Latin America and the Caribbean, Santiago, Chile, pp. 61-82.

WHO (2010), "Global school-based student health survey 2010", World Health Organization, Geneva, http://www.who.int/chp/gshs/en. (accessed 20 May 2016).

Wong, L.R. and J.A. Carvalho (2006), "O rápido processo de envelhecimento populacional do Brasil: sérios desafios para as políticas públicas" ["The rapid process of population ageing in Brazil: Serious Challenges for Public Policy]. *Rebep*, Vol. 23/1, Associação Brasileira de Estudos Populacionais, São Paulo.

World Bank (2016), "A slowdown in social gains", *Brief*, No. 105750, Poverty and Inequality Monitoring: Latin America and the Caribbean, World Bank, Washington, DC, http://documents.worldbank.org/curated/en/2016/0 4/26211205/slowdown-social-gains.

World Bank (2013), *Inclusion Matters: The Foundation of Shared Prosperity*, Social Development Department, Washington, DC.

Chapter 4

Education, skills and youth in Latin America and the Caribbean

Skills are essential for youth to make the transition into adult life, to contribute to knowledge-based and skills-based economies, and to participate in society. As such, they allow individuals to become engaged in a country's growth and development. Education serves as one of the main sources of acquiring skills. This chapter analyses the educational attainment and skills endowment of youth in the Latin America and Caribbean (LAC) region by providing a rich statistical portrait of youth education participation and performance. The chapter provides an overview of education attainment, as well as an analysis of the reading, mathematics, science and technology aptitudes of youth in the past decade. It also describes the main results of youth training programmes, one of the region's main policy responses to endow early education leavers with skills to participate in labour markets. Finally, the chapter sketches a set of policy goals and recommendations to improve education and provide better skills to youth in LAC countries.

Introduction

Education and skills are widely recognised as key elements to support inclusive development and favourable labour market outcomes. Improved education leads to economic growth, social inclusion and greater equality. Skills are strongly linked to having access to good quality education, but go much further: they are "the bundle of knowledge, attributes and capacities that can be learned and that enable individuals to successfully and consistently perform an activity or task, and that can be built upon and extended through learning" (OECD, 2012). In this respect, Chapter 4 focuses on skills as the key element for job participation and a crucial determinant of labour market outcomes across the life cycle. In most cases, given limitations on measuring skills in the Latin America and Caribbean (LAC) region, analysis focuses mainly on the education system.

Despite the strong expansion of education in the last two decades in LAC, substantial challenges remain, largely related to completion, quality, pertinence to demands from labour markets, and financing relative to OECD countries (OECD/CAF/ECLAC, 2014). In addition, these deficiencies affect those from disadvantaged social economic groups, those living in rural areas and women more than other groups. As noted in Chapter 2, youth in LAC struggle to join the labour markets, partly because of low levels of skills. Indeed, their poor performance is linked to the many remaining challenges related to education and skills in the region, particularly the school-to-labour transition.

Education coverage in the region has largely expanded for all levels, although it remains low in pre-primary education – 66% in 2012 compared with 83% in the OECD. This is particularly relevant, as pre-primary education has a long-term impact on student performance: secondary-school performance improves by the equivalent of almost a full school year among those who had pre-primary education (OECD/CAF/ECLAC, 2014). Furthermore, disadvantaged students benefit the most since pre-primary education allows them to "catch up", at least partly, with their peers.

Inequalities across different education and skills dimensions, related mainly to quality and access, are the remaining major challenges in the region. The socio-economic background of students and of the school has a marked influence on access to education, performance and completion. Only 56% of those in the lowest income quintile attend secondary school and only 9% continue into tertiary education, compared with 87% and 46%, respectively, for those in the highest income quintile (OECD/CAF/ECLAC, 2014). Also, almost 30% of the variation in students' results in secondary education was associated with socio-economic factors, compared with an average of 26% in OECD countries. Differences related to gender and geographical location are also relevant.

Skills of youth are largely developed at earlier stages of life: what happens at the education cycle before age 15 is crucial. That said, this chapter focuses on the recent evolution of education and skills of young people aged 15-29. It pays particular attention to the challenges of higher education, both university and technical and vocational education and training (TVET). And it examines how these skill levels determine the labour market outcomes of young people.

The chapter is structured in two parts. The first part describes recent trends and challenges in education and skills for youth aged 15-29 in the region. It builds upon the results and recommendations of *Latin American Economic Outlook 2015*, which focused on the challenges faced by the general education system, especially in elementary and secondary education, as well as on the skills of students aged 15 years. The second part reviews the primary results of youth training programmes, one of the region's main policy responses to endow youth without higher or secondary education with skills to participate in labour markets. These programmes are crucial to support those who need an adequate job today, but who have fallen through the cracks of the education system. Still, strengthening the overall education and training systems in the region is fundamental to overcome the medium-to-long-term challenges, and endow the population with the skills necessary to participate in labour markets.

Latin American youth education at a glance

A more skilled workforce, including workers with at least some tertiary experience – both university and post-secondary vocational and technical education – is crucial for LAC countries to enjoy strong and sustainable economic growth and social development. At the same time, quality higher education provides young individuals with tools to better integrate into the productive, political and social life of their countries.

More than 70% of youth are not sufficiently skilled to access good quality jobs

Too many young people leave formal education early or without having acquired the right skills. Only 30% of youth aged 25-29 attended college, university or a technical school and are considered skilled according to classic definitions in the literature (Gasparini et al., 2011; Aedo and Walker, 2012; De la Torre, Levy Yeyati and Pienknagura, 2013). Moreover, only 59% of young people in the region have completed secondary education (Figure 4.1).

Figure 4.1. **Youth population by maximum educational level achieved, Latin America and the Caribbean, 2014**
(percentage of youth aged 25-29)

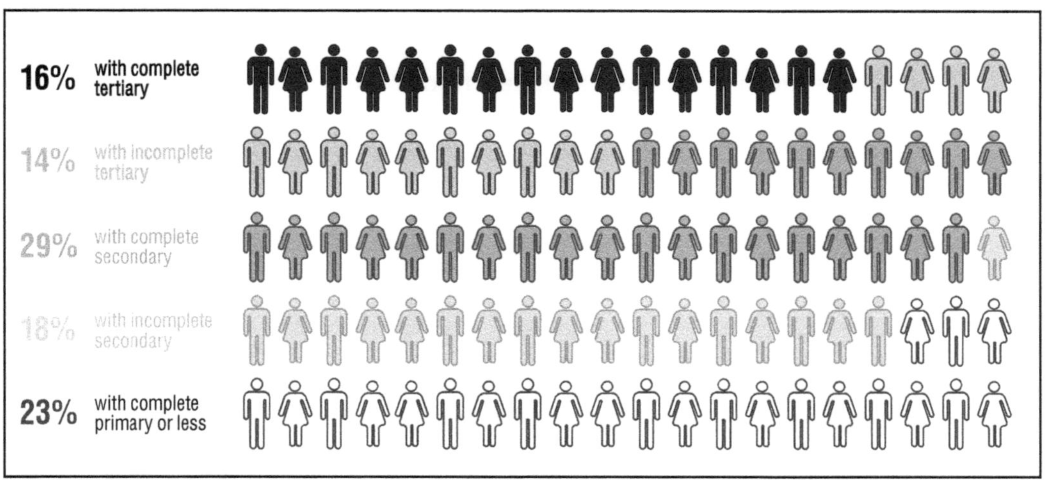

Note: Gender composition is not accurately represented by graphic.
Source: OECD and World Bank tabulations of SEDLAC (CEDLAS and the World Bank).

More than 43 million Latin Americans aged 15-29, 31% of the youth population of the region, have not completed secondary education and are not enrolled in school (Table 4.1). This calls for two areas of policy action. First, policies should address the current problem and equip these individuals with the necessary skills and resources to fully participate in their country's labour markets, politics and social life. Second, policies should improve the education of future generations.

Table 4.1. **Young people with less than secondary education and out of school (aged 15-29), LAC, 2014**

Country	Less than secondary	Share %
Brazil	13 871 335	28
Honduras	12 858 300	42
Colombia	3 014 028	26
El Salvador	2 762 432	54
Argentina	1 654 149	25
Guatemala	1 432 290	59
Panama	1 321 225	19
Ecuador	1 159 725	28
Peru	806 024	44
Bolivia	757 821	28
Dominican Republic	756 999	27
Paraguay	616 897	32
Mexico	560 874	41
Chile	548 896	13
Costa Rica	381 314	30
Uruguay	349 852	46
Nicaragua	292 989	32
LAC 17 Total	43 145 150	31

Note: Figures for Argentina are only representative for urban centres with more than 100 000 habitants.
Source: OECD and World Bank tabulations of SEDLAC (CEDLAS and the World Bank).

Young Latin Americans today are more educated than the previous generation

Educational attainment in LAC has increased in the last decade (2004-14). In ten years' time, the percentage of the population aged 15-64 who have only completed primary education or less has fallen from 34% to 21% (Figure 4.2), to the benefit of higher levels of education. In fact, the percentage of the population with at least some tertiary[1] education increased from 16% to 23% over the decade. "Incomplete secondary education" has taken over "complete primary or less" as the subcategory with the largest percentage of Latin Americans.

Figure 4.2. **Population by maximum educational level achieved, Latin America and the Caribbean, 2004-14**

(percentage of population aged 15-64)

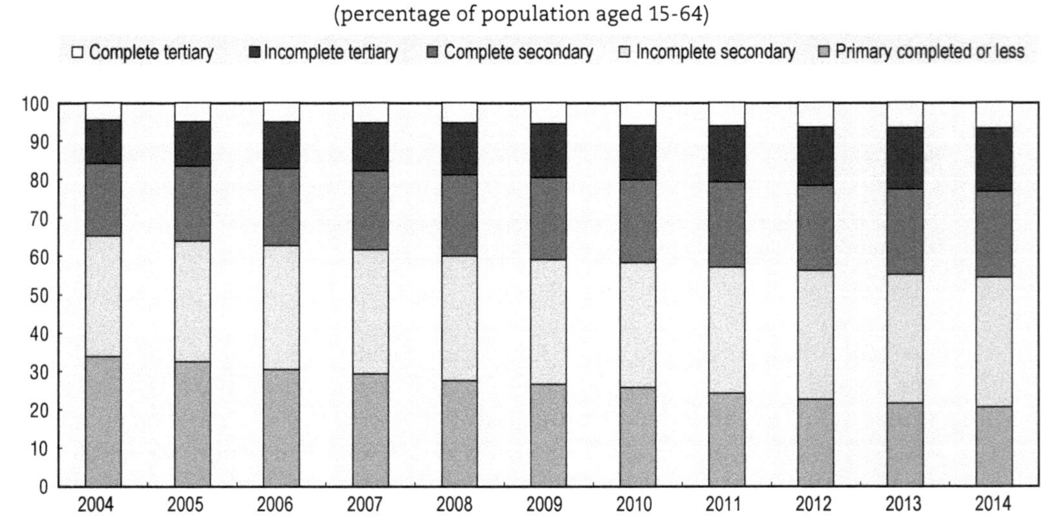

Source: OECD and World Bank tabulations of SEDLAC (CEDLAS and the World Bank).
StatLink http://dx.doi.org/10.1787/888933414381

Still, LAC countries are lagging behind OECD countries. On average, 34% of the population in the OECD had tertiary education in 2014, a 7% increase from 2005. Those with upper secondary and post-secondary non-tertiary education hovered around 43% over the last decade on average (OECD, 2015a).

Moreover, graduation rates are still generally low: 16% of the population has incomplete tertiary education, while 34% has started but not completed secondary education. As quality and access remain key factors to expand education, the region needs policies to retain individuals in the system and support them to finish their studies.

Figure 4.3. **Youth by highest level of education achieved, LAC, 2004, 2009, 2014**
(percentage of youth aged 25-29)

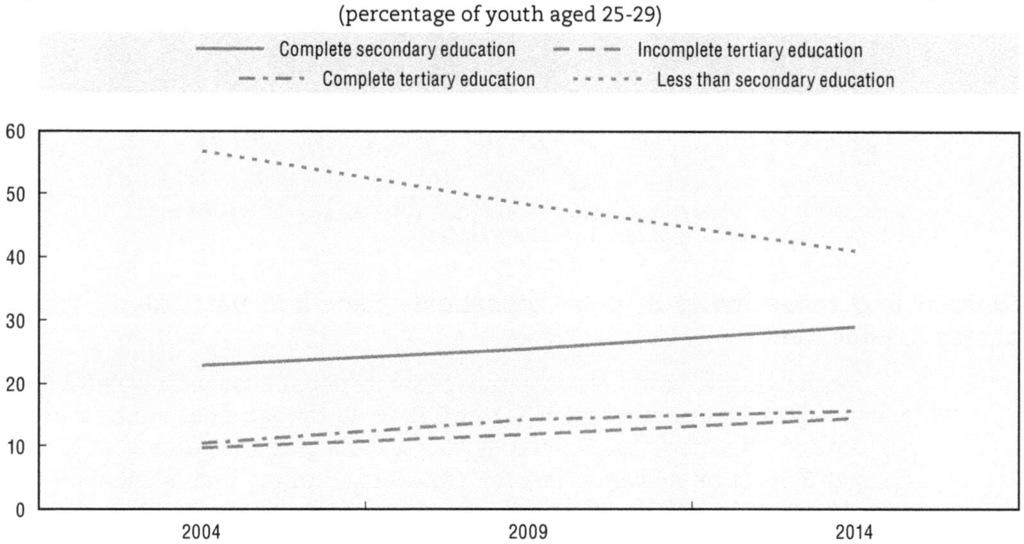

Source: OECD and World Bank tabulations of SEDLAC (CEDLAS and the World Bank).
StatLink http://dx.doi.org/ 10.1787/888933414399

The educational attainment of youth also increased in the last decade (Figure 4.3); young people today are better educated than their peers in previous generations. While the share of young people with incomplete secondary education decreased, the shares of those with complete secondary and tertiary education increased. Yet 41% of the overall LAC population aged 25-29 has less than secondary education. Likewise, completion of higher education increased from just above 10% to 16% over the last decade, but this percentage is still low compared to OECD standards.

The average years of education acquired by the population has increased across all 17 LAC countries for which information is available and across generations (Figure 4.4). Countries such as Costa Rica, Dominican Republic, Ecuador, Guatemala and Honduras have been exceptional for the increase in years of education that youth have attained relative to adults. For its part, Paraguay has improved upon years of education acquired regardless of age, achieving an increase of 1.5 years of education over ten years.

Figure 4.4. **Change in the average years of education for 17 LAC countries, 2004-14**

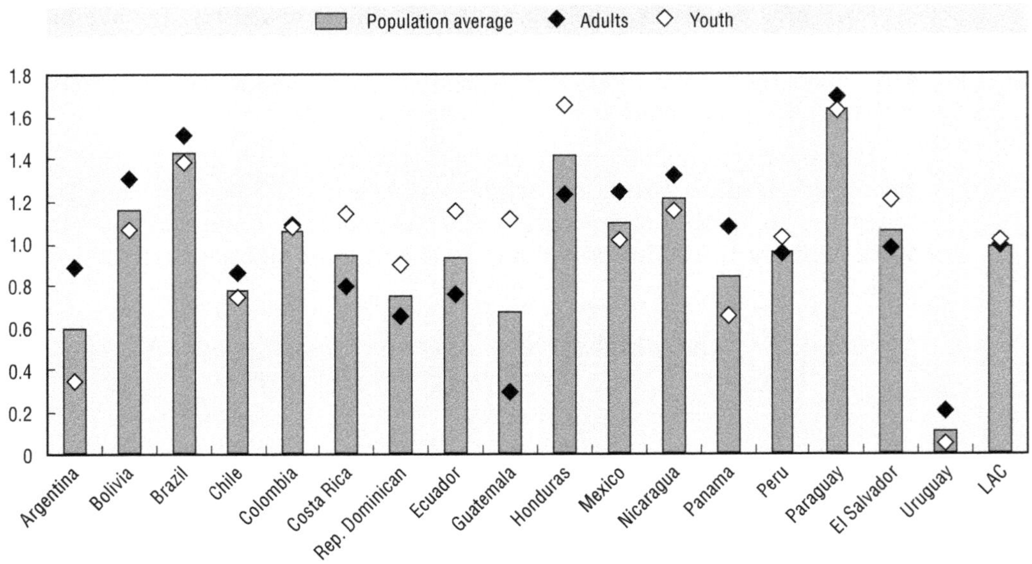

Source: OECD and World Bank tabulations of SEDLAC (CEDLAS and the World Bank).

StatLink http://dx.doi.org/10.1787/888933414404

Women and those living in poor households benefited particularly from expanded access to education

Youth living in extremely poor and moderate poor households benefited the most from expanded education in the region (Figure 4.5). While the extreme poor, on average, completed 5.5 years of education, the moderately poor attained 6.2, the vulnerable 7.7 and the middle class 10.8 years of education in 2014. On average, young individuals living in extremely poor households in 2014 have one extra year of education than the same demographic in 2004, while those in poor and vulnerable households have 0.6 and 0.4 additional years respectively. At the same time, even as the middle class has grown to include households with lower levels of schooling, middle-class youth have more education.

Figure 4.5. **Change in the average years of education by socio-economic group and age group, LAC, 2004-14**

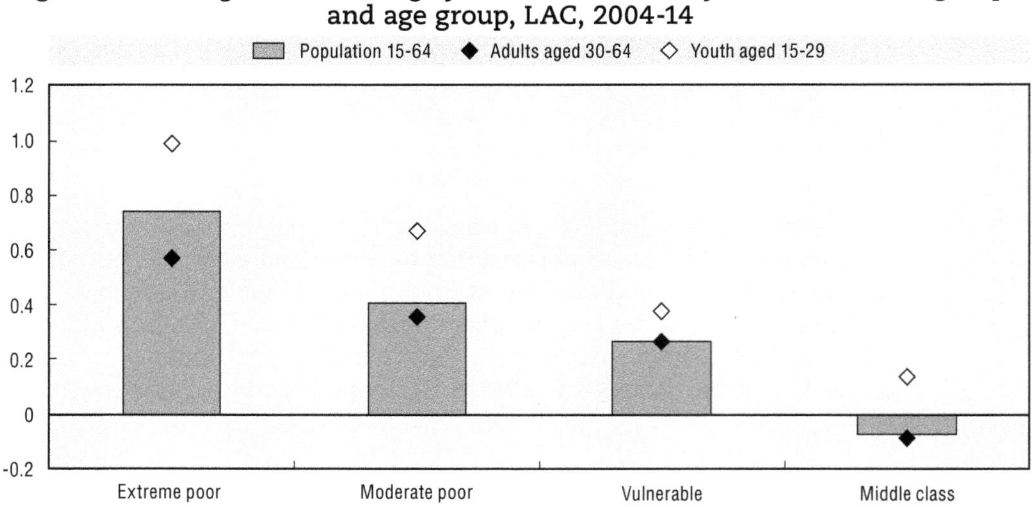

Note: Socio-economic classes are defined using the World Bank classification: "Extreme poor" = youth belonging to households with a daily per capita income lower than USD 2.50. "Moderate poor" = youth belonging to households with a daily per capita income of USD 2.50-4.00. "Vulnerable" = individuals with a daily per capita income of USD 4.00-10.00. "Middle class" = youth from households with a daily per capita income higher than USD 10.00. Poverty lines and incomes are expressed in 2005 USD PPP per day (PPP = purchasing power parity).

Source: OECD and World Bank tabulations of SEDLAC (CEDLAS and the World Bank).

StatLink http://dx.doi.org/10.1787/888933414417

These advances have resulted from a combination of education policies to expand access and improve quality for all students together with social protection policies targeted at those living among the lowest quintiles of income distribution. A large portion of youth benefited from these innovative programmes. In fact, current youth could be known as the Conditional Cash Transfer (CCT) generation. Almost two decades after these programmes were introduced, the results have not been as strong as expected. Still, in terms of skills, this generation has more education and skills than previous ones. These programmes have helped shorten the large education gap between those in the higher and lower ends of income distribution.

Women have benefited to a larger extent than men from this increase in years of education in the region. Breakdown by gender shows that females are outpacing males in all 17 countries for which data are available. In 2014, females had more years of education overall than males in 12 of the 17 countries. The largest gender difference occurred in the Plurinational State of Bolivia (hereafter "Bolivia"), where on average females acquired half a year more of education than males compared with 2004.

A larger percentage of the population has become tertiary-educated over time

Tertiary graduation rates illustrate a country's capacity to provide future workers with specialised knowledge and skills. Incentives to obtain a tertiary degree are strong across LAC countries – from higher earnings to better employment prospects. Expanding access to, improving the quality of and linking tertiary education to labour market demands are essential to move towards knowledge-based economies and reduce income inequality (OECD, 2015a). At the same time, quality higher education provides young individuals with tools for making a better transition into adult life.

In recent decades, access to higher education has expanded in LAC. Between 2004 and 2014, enrolment in higher education increased significantly – from 29% to 44%. This represents an annual growth rate in enrolment of almost 4%.

Figure 4.6. **Gross enrolment ratio, tertiary education, 16 LAC countries, circa 2013**
(percentage)

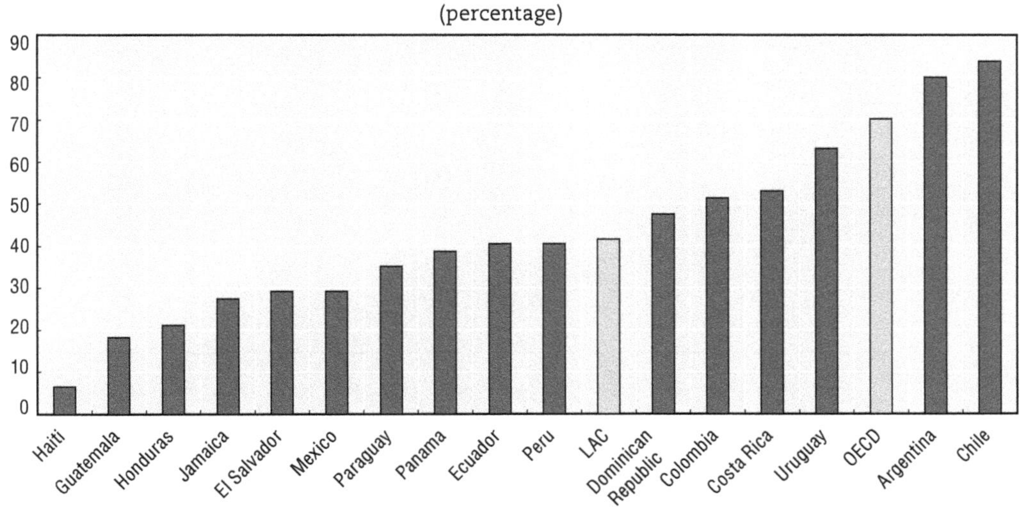

Note: Gross enrolment ratio refers to the number of students enrolled in a given level of education, regardless of age, expressed as a percentage of the official school-age population corresponding to the same level of education. Argentina, Chile, El Salvador, Ecuador, Jamaica, Guatemala, Mexico, OECD and Panama (2013), and Paraguay, Peru and Uruguay (2010).

Source: UNESCO Institute for Statistics. Gross enrolment ratio, tertiary, both sexes (percentage).

StatLink http://dx.doi.org/10.1787/888933414421

Though the growth has been important, most LAC countries still have low enrolment rates compared with OECD countries. Only two countries, Argentina and Chile, the region's leaders, have higher rates of enrolment in tertiary education at 80% and 84%, respectively, than the OECD average of 70% (Figure 4.6). This is not necessarily a sign of wider coverage in these two countries; students may stay longer than expected in university since rates for enrolment in tertiary education account for all students registered in higher education regardless of age, expressed as a percentage of the total population of the five-year age group following on from secondary school. El Salvador, Guatemala, Haiti, Honduras, Jamaica and Mexico are lagging behind, with enrolment rates lower than 30%.

Completion of tertiary education is a major problem in Latin America and the Caribbean

The potential for higher education remains unrealised in LAC. Although enrolment has improved, graduation rates are still low, and higher education institutions face quality and adequacy problems. While 41% of the population aged 15-64 began tertiary education, on average, only 14% completed it across LAC countries.

Tertiary graduation rates vary across LAC countries. Between 2004 and 2014 the percentage of the population who had completed tertiary education increased in 12 of the 17 countries for the population aged 15-64 and in all 17 countries for those aged 25-29 (Figure 4.7). Chile and Ecuador gained 3 percentage points with respect to the population aged 15-64 acquiring tertiary education in ten years. At the same time, the two countries also experienced large gains in the youth population aged 25-29 who had obtained tertiary education. Similarly, Bolivia's overall tertiary education increased by 2 percentage points from 2004-14, and saw great tertiary gains for its youth population aged 25-29.

Figure 4.7. **Youth with complete tertiary education by year, LAC**

(percentage of youth aged 25-29)

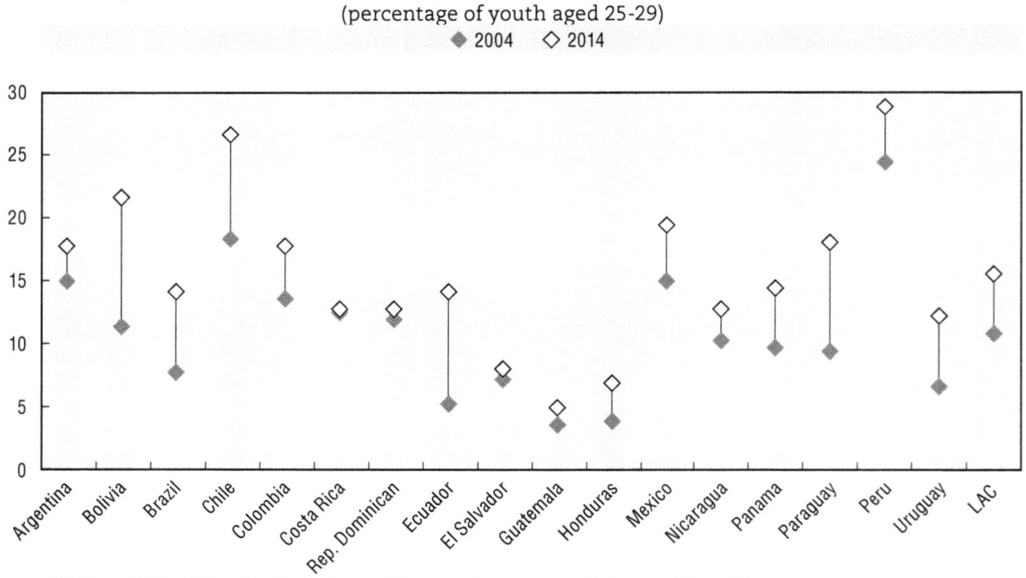

Source: OECD and World Bank tabulations of SEDLAC (CEDLAS and the World Bank).

StatLink http://dx.doi.org/10.1787/888933414430

In spite of advances in the last decade, the region is lagging behind most developed economies with respect to tertiary education. On average, across OECD countries, 39% of young people will graduate from tertiary-type A first-degree programmes (often called bachelor's degrees) and 18% from tertiary-type A second-degree programmes (often called master's degrees). For first-degree programmes, the graduation rate equals or exceeds 50% in Australia, Finland, Iceland, New Zealand, Poland and the Russian Federation (hereafter "Russia"), but is 25% or less in Belgium, Estonia, Greece, Indonesia and Luxembourg (OECD, 2014a).

A small share of students focus on science, technology, engineering and mathematics (STEM) degrees

The region lags behind in terms of science students. Tertiary education students in LAC are heavily focused on social sciences, business and law, averaging 39% across countries – from 25% in Chile to almost half of all students in Colombia (Table 4.2). With the exception of Argentina, science degree enrolment rates range between 2-7% among LAC countries compared with 10% in OECD countries. However, in strong research and innovation economies such as Germany, France, Ireland and the United Kingdom, between 13% and 18% of tertiary students are enrolled in science studies.

Table 4.2. **Students enrolled in tertiary education by type of programme in LAC, circa 2013**

(percentage of total students enrolled)

	Engineering, manufacturing and construction	Sciences	Humanities, arts and education	Health and welfare	Social sciences, business and law	Services	Agriculture	Not known or unspecified
LAC countries								
Argentina	8	10	27	14	35	3	3	n
Brazil	14	6	21	13	41	2	2	n
Chile	19	6	16	22	25	10	2	n
Colombia	23	5	12	8	48	3	2	0
Dominican Republic	10	5	18	14	37	2	1	12
Ecuador	12	7	16	13	44	4	3	0
El Salvador	20	2	19	19	39	n	2	0
Honduras	13	5	23	14	40	1	3	0
Mexico	26	6	14	10	41	1	2	0
Panama	23	7	19	11	35	3	2	n
Selected OECD countries								
France	9	18	19	10	39	4	n	n
Germany	17	13	23	19	23	3	1	n
Ireland	11	17	23	14	23	7	2	2
Israel	23	8	22	7	35	n	n	4
Italy	16	10	21	12	34	4	3	n
Japan	14	2	23	16	27	9	2	7
Korea	25	7	25	14	20	7	1	n
Spain	16	9	23	13	29	8	1	n
United Kingdom	8	15	24	17	28	2	1	6
LAC average	**17**	**6**	**18**	**14**	**39**	**3**	**2**	**1**
OECD average	**15**	**10**	**20**	**13**	**31**	**5**	**2**	**4**

Note: The statistical data for Israel are supplied by and under the responsibility of the relevant Israeli authorities. The use of such data by the OECD is without prejudice to the status of the Golan Heights, East Jerusalem and Israeli settlements in the West Bank under the terms of international law.
Sources: OECD (2014a), Argentina, Brazil, Chile, Colombia, Dominican Republic, Ecuador, El Salvador, Honduras, Mexico, Panama: UNESCO Institute for Statistics, database.

Private firms report shortages of engineers, technicians and skilled trade workers. This is especially true in Argentina, Brazil, Colombia, Costa Rica, Guatemala, Mexico, Panama and Peru where these professions rank among the top ten job titles experiencing talent shortages in 2015 (Manpower Group, 2015). However, the percentage of students studying engineering, manufacturing and construction is similar to that of many OECD countries, averaging between 8% and 26%. Still, this does not fully capture the situation: 27% of doctoral recipients in OECD countries studied sciences and 17% studied engineering, construction and manufacturing (OECD, 2015a).

Few students are enrolled in vocational and technical education programmes at secondary and tertiary level

Technical and vocational education and training (TVET) is crucial to develop a highly skilled labour force, with a range of mid-level trade, technical, professional and management skills alongside those high-level skills associated with university education (OECD, 2014c). In emerging and less developed countries, TVET is increasingly perceived as a tool to respond to changing labour market needs, while at the same time supporting social cohesion. As such, it is – and should be perceived – as a complement to those more academic programmes typically found in universities. Given that poor skills, and hence low productivity, are sometimes seen as one reason for low levels of development, investment in TVET has been argued as a means of promoting a bottom-up labour market transformation (Eichhorst et al., 2012).

Some countries of the region have very small TVET sectors; others have sectors that are of considerable size, at the upper secondary, post-secondary levels or both. The prominence and weight of TVET institutions in secondary education vary greatly across countries (Figure 4.8). In Ecuador and Honduras, almost one-third of those enrolled in secondary education are in TVET programmes. Similarly in Colombia, one-quarter of students are enrolled in vocational programmes at the secondary level and one-fifth of young Costa Ricans choose the vocational track in high school. Conversely, in Nicaragua and Peru this percentage falls to below 1.5%. Because of the low relevance of TVET in educating the general population in LAC countries, youth could benefit from its expansion. In OECD countries, 26% of the population in secondary education are enrolled in TVET programmes, over 10 percentage points higher than the LAC average, with the Netherlands reaching 48% (UNESCO, 2016).

Figure 4.8. **Students in secondary education enrolled in technical and vocational programmes, LAC, circa 2013**

(percentage of total secondary students)

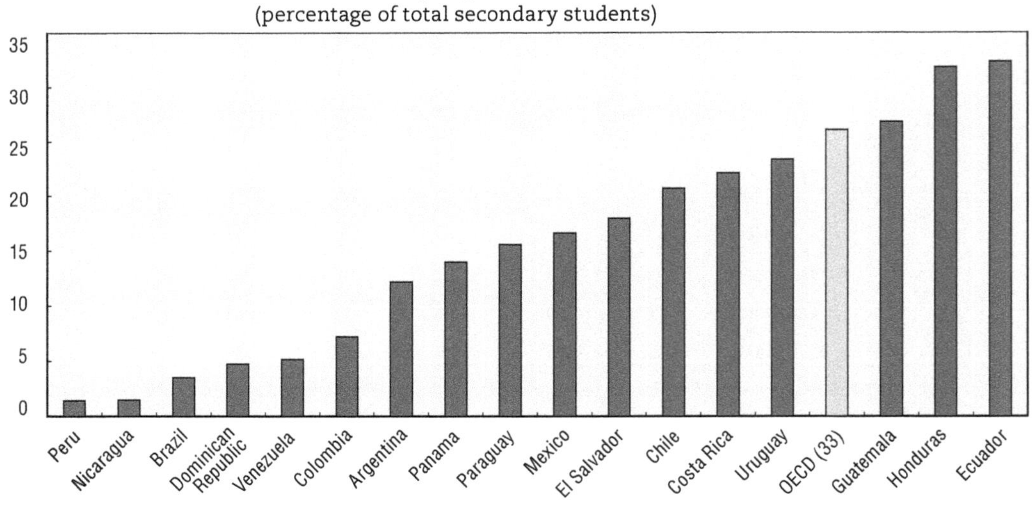

Note: Data from 2014 except for Argentina, Brazil, Ecuador and Uruguay (2013), Mexico, Panama and Paraguay (2012), Nicaragua (2010) and Bolivia (2003).

Source: UNESCO (2016) and DiNIECE, Ministry of Education of Argentina (2013).

StatLink http://dx.doi.org/10.1787/888933414442

Women benefit from TVET in many LAC countries; more than half of students enrolled in secondary TVET in the region are female. Nevertheless, there is wide heterogeneity across countries. In economies such as Dominican Republic or Nicaragua more than 60% of TVET secondary students are women, while in Chile and Uruguay women represent less than half of TVET enrolment (47% and 42%, respectively) (UNESCO, 2016).

As TVET enhances job-related knowledge and prepares young individuals for the workplace, its importance continues beyond secondary education (OECD/CAF/ECLAC, 2014). At the tertiary level, TVET enrolment in the region rose over the last ten years – from 15% to 19% of the total enrolled in tertiary education (UNESCO, 2013a; OECD/CAF/ECLAC, 2014) – but it lags behind OECD standards. Yet Chile, Colombia and Peru have a relatively dynamic post-secondary TVET sector, which engages about 40% of all students enrolled in some form of education and training beyond secondary school (Ministry of Education of Chile, 2014; McCarthy and Musset, 2016; OECD, 2016a). The nature and duration of the programmes vary from country to country, making it too difficult to compare them. Moreover, quality is heterogeneous: high quality schools that are highly respected and generate positive returns for students and employers coexist with low quality ones. Although TVET represents an important source of innovation and experimentation in the design of technical education that benefits the sector as a whole, there are too few programmes to drive a change in quality.

In LAC, TVET serves an important equity function. It caters to the needs of different segments of the population: school-leavers, students looking for more practical education and older individuals seeking to deepen their professional skills, make a sideways career move or return to work after an absence (Quintini and Manfredi, 2009). Alternative training courses can provide high school and tertiary education drop-outs with job skills to increase their employability. High-quality vocational education pathways, particularly in upper secondary education, can help those who have become disaffected with academic education to re-engage with the education system and improve graduation rates. And tertiary education vocational and technical programmes can provide those with no appetite for academic education with practical skills that respond to the needs of the job market. Additionally, TVET programmes in many LAC countries are specifically targeted or favour school leavers or students from poor households. For example, the *Servicio Nacional de Aprendizaje* (SENA) in Colombia provides tuition-free tertiary education. In Mexico, the TVET system provides opportunities for learning in remote regions (Kis, Hoeckel and Santiago, 2012).

Alternative vocational and technical education has expanded in LAC

Vocational and technical programmes to provide youth with workplace skills and bolster lifelong learning have emerged as both an alternative and a complement to formal education. Vocational training institutions (VTIs) in LAC countries play a prominent role in training youth, and almost every LAC country has at least one national VTI. In fact, 65% of the region's VTI course participants are, on average, young individuals.

Apprenticeships are one of the most often-used ways to train youth in LAC countries. They have been particularly effective in fostering skills acquisition and promoting a smooth transition from school to formal employment (Table 4.3). Moreover, apprenticeships revalorise the role played by enterprises in training and lead to the recognition of formal qualifications in the labour market.

Relative to the population, disadvantaged youth are heavily served by VTI programmes. The majority of participants in national VTI programmes are high-school dropouts from households in the lowest quintiles of the income distribution. For example,

61% of the beneficiaries in Peru's SENATI, 81% of the beneficiaries in Colombia's SENA and 84% of the beneficiaries in Mexico's CONALEP belong to the two lowest quintiles of the income distribution (ILO/CINTERFOR, forthcoming).

Table 4.3. **Share of apprenticeships' participants among total participants in VTI programmes, LAC, 2015**

VTI and country	Share %
SENATI Peru	14
SENAC Brazil	13
INFOP Honduras	11
SENA Colombia	9
SENAI Brazil	7
INTECAP Guatemala	5
INADEH Panama	3
SNPP Paraguay	2
INSAFORP El Salvador	1
SENAR Brazil	1

Source: ILO/CINTERFOR (forthcoming).

The participation rate of women in VTIs varies across LAC. With women constituting only 40% of beneficiaries in Guatemala's INTECAP, 44% in Mexico's CONALEP and 47% in Bolivia's INFOCAL, a higher percentage of men clearly are enrolled in VTIs in these countries. This may relate to gender bias in certain professions, particularly those relying on skills from STEM subjects. The limited access to VTIs for women may also result from the cultural environment (ILO/CINTERFOR, 2016a). Yet the gender balance in institutions such as SENAC in Brazil, INEFOP in Uruguay, DGCFT in Mexico, INSAFORP in El Salvador and INFOP in Honduras is almost equal. Furthermore, institutions such as SENA in Colombia and INADEH in Panama have more women enrolled in VTIs than men, with women comprising respectively 56% and 57% of total beneficiaries.

Apprenticeships in LAC suffer from design and implementation problems that could be improved. In some countries programmes are too long (from two to four years) and suffer from high rates of attrition. In other countries, while they offer new and more flexible ways to deliver on-the-job training, it is difficult for participants to secure a job after the programme is over given the low propensity of firms to hire apprentices because of costs.

Efforts to strengthen and develop learning techniques through VTI programmes come from the Global Apprenticeship Network (GAN), a business-driven alliance with the goal of encouraging and linking business initiatives to skills and employment opportunities for youth, most notably through apprenticeships. Currently, national GAN agreements have been implemented in Argentina and Colombia, with additional agreements underway in Brazil and Mexico.

TVET faces similar challenges across Latin American and Caribbean countries, including its primary function to link education with the demands of the labour market

There is little co-ordination between TVET programmes and the general education system. In several countries in the region, such as Argentina, Brazil, Costa Rica, Colombia and Peru, technical TVET is offered by the Ministry of Education, the National Training Institute or the Ministry of Labour and by private schools, companies and organisations. Institutions operate in silos, limiting students' ability to advance academically and sometimes attain university degrees. In Costa Rica, for example, technical degrees offered by the Ministry of Education and the National Training Institute are not harmonised, and neither connect well with the higher education system (Álvarez-Galván, 2015). Skills acquired from TVET often go unrecognised by the traditional education system; many students are unable to proceed to higher levels of general education studies based on TVET certificates. For example, in Peru, students who complete non-formal TVET are often required to repeat coursework in a later general course of study (McCarthy and Musset, 2016). Brazil, where SENAC courses are recognised by Ministry of Education, is an exception and example for the region.

A few countries have started implementing National Qualifications Frameworks to align TVET education with general secondary and tertiary education. National Qualifications Frameworks, which classify qualifications by level based on learning outcomes, standardise qualifications in order to facilitate the evaluation and comparison of skills across systems. *ChileValora* and the Ministry of Education in Chile; INFOTEP and the Ministry of Education in the Dominican Republic; and SENA and the Ministry of Education in Colombia, for example, have implemented these frameworks. Likewise, Costa Rica, Nicaragua and Ecuador are developing co-ordination mechanisms between TVET and general education programmes.

Several countries have identified the need for a national TVET system (UNESCO, 2013b, 2015) and to create institutions responsible for co-ordinating TVET at multiple levels. In Argentina, the *Instituto Nacional de Educación Tecnológica* (INET) oversees public policies related to technical education at secondary, post-secondary and tertiary levels. INET co-ordinates policies and improvements within the TVET system and adapts programmes to specific regional and productivity needs (INET, 2016).

TVET systems in LAC are generally misaligned with the demands of the labour market. Linkages between the TVET system and employers are relatively weak, illustrated by the low level of involvement of employers in TVET policy development. In fact, few countries have institutional bodies where employers are systematically consulted about TVET policy. Even when these bodies exist, interaction is often fragmented or insufficient. Employers' organisations interact with some subsystems and not with others. SENAI and PRONATEC in Brazil, SENA in Colombia and INADEH in Panama consult the private sector, but are only one of many institutions in their countries providing TVET. Likewise, the Ministry of Education of Costa Rica and its National Training Institute consult stakeholders, but these efforts seem insufficient to make the mix of TVET programmes more responsive to labour market needs (Álvarez-Galván, 2015). Additionally, the existing set of TVET qualifications is not regularly updated to meet changing labour market needs.

TVET struggles with quality, prestige and status in various countries. Often, TVET is looked upon less favourably by employers and students than general tertiary education systems. In Colombia, many TVET students were not admitted to university programmes, diminishing the reputation of TVET graduates relative to their university educated peers (OECD/IBRD/WB, 2012). Additionally, the qualification of teachers can differ between TVET and general education. Colombia, Mexico and Peru, in particular, have identified the need to improve monitoring and quality assurance systems (UNESCO, 2015, 2013c; McCarthy and Musset, 2016; OECD, 2016b).

Current TVET programmes in LAC may enhance inequality. Students enrolled in TVET are more likely to be from poor or vulnerable households than those in general education (OECD/CAF/ECLAC, 2014). As noted above, those with TVET certificates have greater challenges in pursuing higher education. As a result, TVET can perpetuate inequality by amplifying the discrepancies in opportunity between those with higher and lower socio-economic status. Additionally, TVET can amplify gender disparities: many of the higher-paying, technical tracks in TVET are male dominated, while women on average focused their studies in low-paying trades (UNESCO, 2010). All of this calls for improving TVET programmes in the region to help ease the associated stigma and contribute towards a more equal education.

Box 4.1. Work-based learning can be a powerful tool

Workplace learning plays an essential role in high quality vocational programmes. It is a powerful tool for developing both hard and soft skills, transitioning students into employment, engaging employers and linking the mix of programmes to employer needs. At the same time, it is too often neglected. On the one hand, education and training organisations find it easier to work on their own without having to involve employers. On the other, employers do not recognise the potential returns from offering work placements to students.

There should be a mandatory work-based learning component in every vocational programme

Evidence from a number of countries suggests that making work-based learning a mandatory element of vocational programmes is feasible and has multiple benefits. Many institutions tend to operate in silos, and education and training institutions are no exception. Reaching out to employers means breaking out of these silos. It also means overcoming the resistance of classroom teachers to the idea that students can learn much in the workplace that they cannot learn so readily in the classroom. Therefore, institutions need strong incentives to establish partnerships with employers for an effective workplace learning element in programmes. But employers also need incentives. Sometimes employers believe (often wrongly) that work placements are an unnecessary cost that they can reasonably avoid; they would prefer simply to recruit graduates of vocational programmes.

Against this background, making work placements mandatory can operate as a game-changer. It means that programmes will only be funded when training institutions develop and maintain the active partnerships that support work placements. Under these conditions, training providers will see employer partnerships as central to their mission. For their part, employers will see that, unless they are willing to offer work placements, their source of recruits may close or contract; government funding may well shift to another sector or another region. Under these conditions, many currently reluctant employers will choose to offer work placements, assuming they value the training programmes.

International examples

It is striking that poorer countries with relatively weak infrastructure (Romania) and weak labour markets (Tunisia), countries with little history of employer engagement in the vocational system (Sweden) and countries with high rates of youth unemployment (Spain) have successfully implemented mandatory arrangements for work-based learning in some of their vocational programmes (OECD, 2014c).

In Romania, all upper secondary and postsecondary vocational programmes include work placements with quality assurance mechanisms (a workplace supervisor, student portfolio and a contract between the school and employers) (Musset, 2013). In Tunisia, vocational programmes under the Ministry of Vocational Training and Employment have a mandatory work-based learning component: about 11% of students are enrolled in apprenticeship programmes where they spend one day a week in a training centre and the remaining days in the workplace. The other 89% of students are enrolled in programmes d'alternance (a combination of school-based and work-based modules), in which the length of the work placement(s) varies, but is never less than one month. Likewise, more than nine out of ten vocational students in Tunisia had benefited from some type of placement with employers in 2011 (OECD, 2015b). In Spain, in both upper secondary and postsecondary programmes, workplace training normally takes place through a compulsory three-month module at the end of the programmes (Field, Kis and Kuczera, 2012).

Such arrangements cannot be implemented overnight. In the early 1990s, for example, Spanish employers had to learn how to make use of students at work, and to appreciate the benefits to their firms (Field, Kis and Kuczera, 2012). South Africa developed tax credits to foster on-the-job training, as well as a simple process for employers to take trainees from vocational programmes OECD (2013a).

Latin American youth skills at a glance

Individuals with similar levels of education do not always have the same level of skills within and across countries. Moreover, attaining a certain level of education or certificate does not guarantee acquiring the associated skills. Acquisition of skills depends on the quality of education systems, as well as other factors, such as the socio-economic context, family, networks or various life experiences. Although employers primarily use education to judge the skill levels of potential employees, especially in the case of inexperienced youth, education is not an unequivocal sign of skill level. Therefore, it cannot be a sufficiently accurate indicator for the development of appropriate skills policies (Hanushek, 2015).

Young Latin Americans still perform poorly in reading, mathematics and science compared to their counterparts in OECD countries

The eight participating LAC countries ranked in the bottom third of the country distribution in all three subjects tested by PISA. In mathematics, 15 year-old students in Latin America and the Caribbean perform almost 100 points lower than OECD students (OECD, 2016c). This is equivalent to 2.4 years of schooling, since, on average, an additional year of schooling is associated with an increase of 41 points in mathematics. All countries rank in the bottom quartile of the score distribution. Chile, the best performer of the region, ranks in the bottom 15 countries and scores 70 points lower than the OECD average. This gap is equivalent to 1.7 years of schooling. Peru is the lowest performer among the 65 countries in the study; its score is more than 125 points lower than the OECD average, which is equivalent to an average performance gap of 3.1 years of schooling.

Figure 4.9. **Students at each level of proficiency in reading, mathematics and science, LAC, 2012**

(percentage)

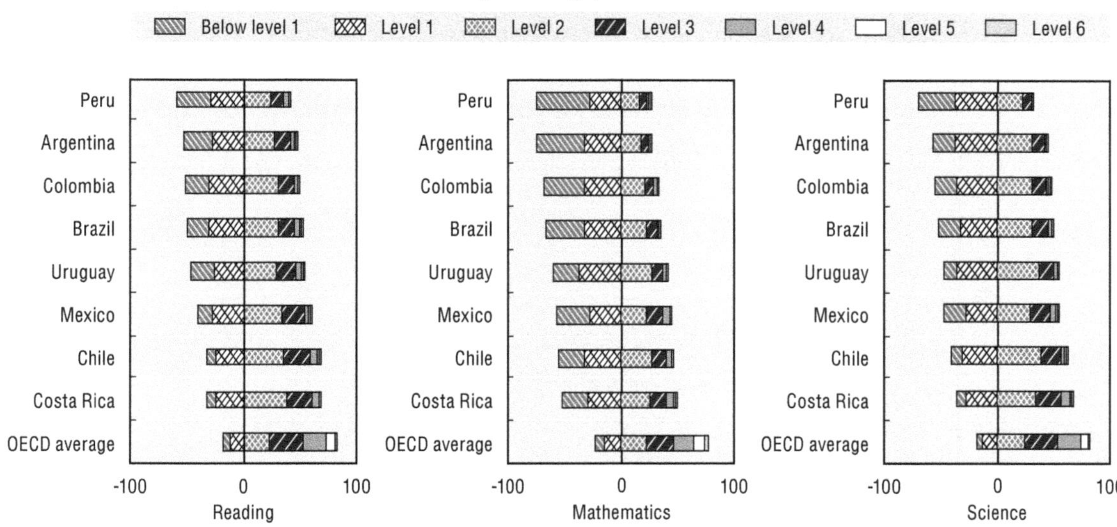

Note: Countries and economies are ranked in descending order of the percentage of students at Levels 2, 3, 4, 5 and 6.

Source: OECD, PISA 2012 (database), www.oecd.org/pisa/pisaproducts/pisa2012database-downloadabledata.htm; OECD (2014b), *PISA 2012 Results: What Students Know and Can Do* (Volume I, Revised edition, February 2014).

StatLink http://dx.doi.org/10.1787/888933414458

LAC countries' performance in reading and science is also poor compared to OECD countries (OECD, 2016c). On average, Latin American students perform almost 80 points lower than OECD students in reading and 90 points lower in science. Costa Rica, the best performer of the region in reading, ranks in the bottom 20 countries and scores 55 points lower than the OECD average. Chile, the best performer of the region in science, ranks in the bottom 15 countries and scores 57 points lower than the OECD average.

More than half of the young Latin Americans enrolled in school do not acquire basic-level proficiency in reading, mathematics and science. The PISA scale ranks student proficiency across 6 levels. Students who perform at level 2 have the basic skills to integrate fully into social and professional life; students who perform below level 2 often face significant disadvantages in their transition into higher education and the labour force. The proportion of students whose score is below the level 2 threshold indicates how educational systems struggle to provide students with a minimum level of proficiency (OECD, 2014b). Around a quarter of 15-year-old students in OECD countries perform below level 2 in mathematics, while in all LAC countries more than half of the students lack basic mathematics skills (Figure 4.9). Some LAC countries even performed worse. In Argentina and Brazil, two-thirds of students are in this situation; three-quarters of students in Colombia and Peru fall below the threshold in mathematics. Similar results were obtained in reading and science. Almost a fifth of 15-year-old students in OECD countries perform below level 2 in both subjects; in LAC countries, between one- and two-thirds of students in reading and between one-third and three-quarters of students in science are below level 2.

Additionally, few LAC students perform very well. Less than 1% of LAC students perform in the highest two PISA proficiency levels – levels 5 or 6 – in mathematics, reading or science. Students at proficiency levels 5 or 6 are able to draw on and use information from multiple and indirect sources to solve complex problems in mathematics; critically evaluate texts and understand details the content or form of which is unfamiliar when reading; and identify the scientific components of many complex life situations and compare, select and evaluate appropriate scientific evidence for responding to these situations. They will be at the forefront of a competitive knowledge-based global economy (OECD, 2012). In contrast, 12% of students in OECD countries perform in the top two levels in mathematics, and 8.5% reach these levels in reading and science. Chile and Uruguay, with respectively 1.6% and 1.4%, are the only countries with more than 1% of top performers in mathematics. Similarly, they both have a share of 1% of top performers in science. However, no LAC country participating in PISA has at least 1% of top performers in reading.

Figure 4.10. **Young student performance in mathematics and equity**

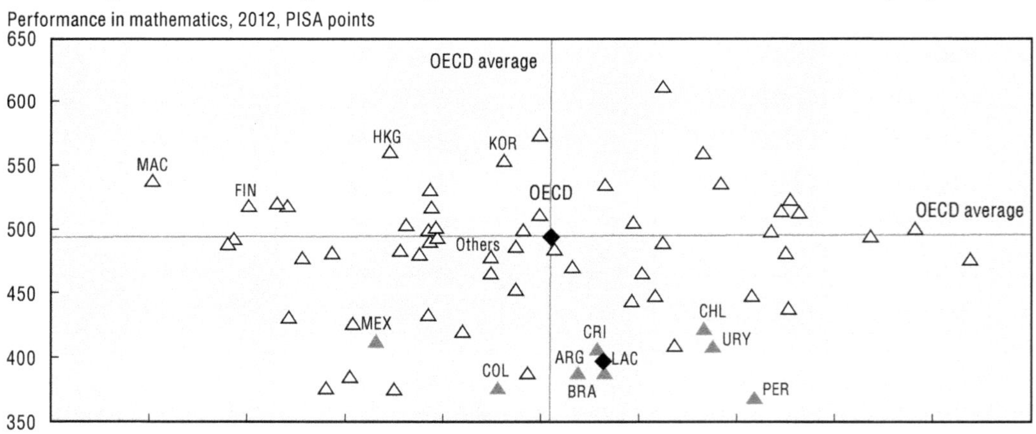

Note: Latin America ("LAC") comprises Argentina, Brazil, Chile, Colombia, Costa Rica, Mexico, Peru and Uruguay. "Others" comprises Albania, Bulgaria, Croatia, Dubai, Hong Kong (China), Indonesia, Jordan, Kazakhstan, Latvia, Liechtenstein, Lithuania, Macao (China), Malaysia, Montenegro, Qatar, Romania, Russia, Serbia, Shanghai (China), Singapore, Chinese Taipei, Thailand, Tunisia and United Arab Emirates. The percentage change in mathematics performance explained by the economic, social and cultural status of students and schools is obtained from a student-level regression where the explanatory variables are the economic, social and cultural status of the student and that of the school.

Source: OECD/CAF/ECLAC (2014).

StatLink http://dx.doi.org/10.1787/888933414464

Education access and quality are reflected in test performance and skills. Latin American countries are subject to strong disparities. The relative performance of students from poor families, with less educated parents and less access to books, compared to better-off students is significantly worse than among students in the same position in other regions of the world (OECD, 2016c). On average, the strength of the relation between the socio-economic status of the students and their performance is much higher than in the OECD. Almost 30% of the variation in students' results in secondary education in LAC was associated with socio-economic factors, compared with an average of 26% in OECD countries (Figure 4.10). As a result of performance differences associated with socio-economic and cultural factors, students in the lowest-income quartile fall two years behind those in the highest-income quartile (OECD/CAF/ECLAC, 2014).

LAC countries are improving their PISA scores faster than OECD countries, but not fast enough to catch up soon

LAC countries improved faster than the OECD average in reading, mathematics and science. Six countries improved faster than the OECD country average in mathematics and science, while five did so in reading. Brazil, Chile, Mexico and Peru showed positive, statistically significant improvements in all three subjects (Figure 4.11); Argentina only did so in mathematics and science. In contrast, the performance of Costa Rica and Uruguay has deteriorated in all three.

Figure 4.11. **Annualised change in performance throughout participation in PISA**

(Reading, Mathematics and Science score-point difference associated with one calendar year)

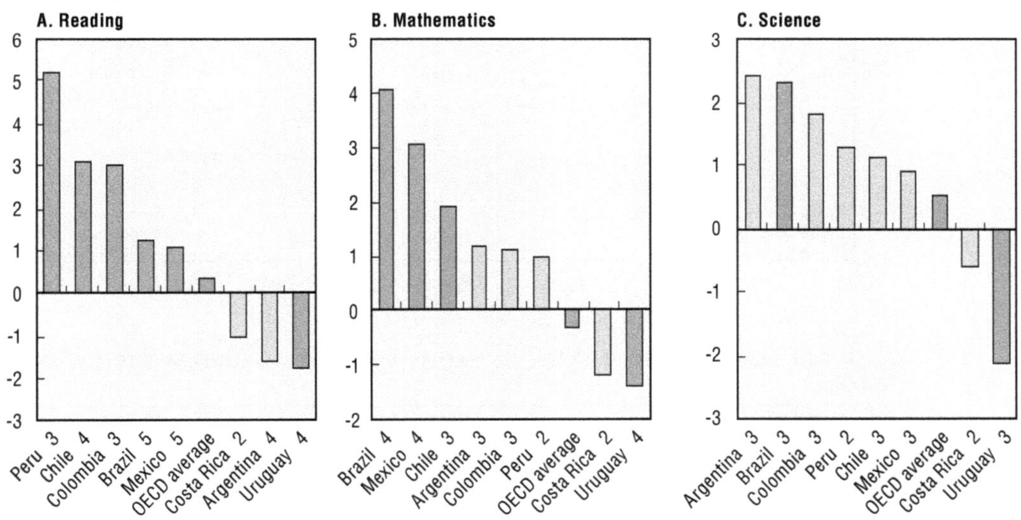

Notes: Statistically significant score point changes are marked in a darker tone.

The number of comparable reading scores used to calculate the annualised change is shown next to the country/economy name. The annualised change is the average annual change in PISA score points from a country's/economy's earliest participation in PISA to PISA 2012. It is calculated taking into account all country's/economy's participation in PISA. "OECD average 2000" compares only OECD countries with comparable reading scores since 2000. Countries and economies are ranked in descending order of the annualised change in reading performance.

Source: OECD, *PISA 2012* (database), Table I.4.3b, www.oecd.org/pisa/pisaproducts/pisa2012database-downloadabledata.htm.

StatLink http://dx.doi.org/10.1787/888933414472

The improvement is significant, but not enough to attain skill levels similar to those in OECD countries in the near future. If the region maintains improvement rates of between 4 and 6 points per year, it would take LAC countries more than 15 years to perform at the current OECD average level.

Moreover, the share of students with basic skills did not improve substantially. Given the low starting level of LAC students, the improvements at the bottom of the PISA score distribution translated mainly as a flow of students from below level 1 to level 1. The share of students at level 2 – the level at which students acquire basic skills – did not rise substantially in most of the region's countries. This is particularly important in the case of Argentina and Colombia, where the share of students at level 5 or 6 decreased simultaneously. Moreover, in Uruguay, the share of students at low levels of performance increased at the expense of top performers (OECD, 2016c).

Work skills build over abilities acquired in high school

The high level of LAC youth below a basic level of proficiency constitutes an obstacle to further development of more specific skills, while the small portion of top performers may hamper innovation and entrepreneurship. Knowledge-based and skills-based economies increasingly depend upon a broad base of technically skilled individuals, as well as a sizeable share of high performers who can produce new knowledge.

Figure 4.12. **Mean numeracy proficiency in PISA (2000 and 2003) and in the Survey of Adult Skills, 2012**

A. Mean mathematics score in PISA 2000 and numeracy score in the Survey of Adult Skills 2012, 26-28 year-olds

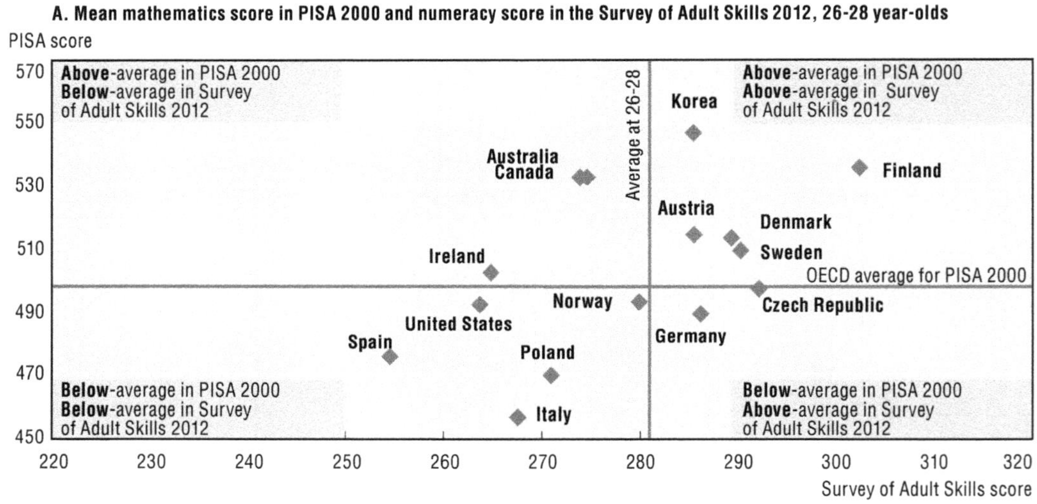

B. Mean mathematics score in PISA 2003 and numeracy score in the Survey of Adult Skills 2012, 23-25 year-olds

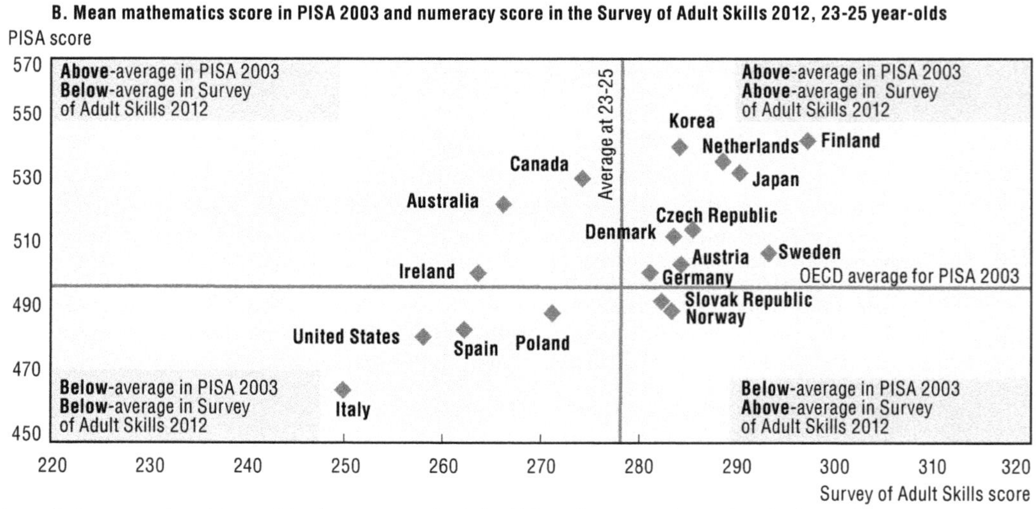

Notes: A three-age band is used in the Survey of Adult Skills to increase size and reliability of estimate. The mix of countries contributing to the average in PISA and the Survey of Adult Skills differs, which may contribute to differences in countries' average scores relative to the overall averages in either study.

Source: Survey of Adult Skills (PIAAC) (2012), OECD, PISA 2000-09 databases, Table A5.6 (N).

StatLink http://dx.doi.org/10.1787/888933414488

Early performance in mathematics is correlated with job-relevant numeracy skills. The results from the 2012 Survey of Adult Skills (PIAAC) show that countries performing well in PISA tend to display a relatively high performance in PIAAC and vice versa (Figure 4.12). Students' performance in PISA will be at least partly reflected in their acquisition of job-related skills later in life. Part of the effect will transit through the ability to pursue further education, the quality of post-secondary training in the different countries and the specialisation chosen.

Box 4.2. **Survey of Adult Skills (PIAAC)**

The Survey of Adult Skills (PIAAC) assesses the proficiency of adults aged 16-65 years in literacy, numeracy and problem solving in technology-rich environments. These skills are "key information-processing competencies" that are relevant to adults in many social contexts and work situations. They are necessary for fully integrating into and participating in the labour market, education and training, and social and civic life.

In addition, the survey collects a range of information on the reading- and numeracy-related activities of respondents. This includes use of information and communication technologies at work and in everyday life, and a range of generic skills, such as collaborating with others and organising one's time, that are required of individuals in their work. Respondents are also asked whether their skills and qualifications match their work requirements and whether they have autonomy over key aspects of their work.

Six proficiency levels are defined for literacy and numeracy (levels 1 through 5 plus below level 1) and four are defined for problem solving in technology-rich environments (levels 1 through 3 plus below level 1). Each level summarises what a person with a particular score can do with a scale of 500 points divided into the levels.

A total of 33 countries/economies participated in PIAAC over two rounds of data collection. Chile collected data as part of the second round, which took place from April 2014 to March 2015. Some 5 212 adults aged 16-65 were surveyed. A third round is underway with Ecuador, Mexico and Peru expected to begin data collection in 2017.

In Chile, PIAAC covers adults born between 1949 and 2000. At one extreme, then, it covers adults who began their studies in the 1950s and, at the other, young people who are still pursuing secondary education.

Source: OECD (2016d).

Youth and adults in LAC perform poorly in literacy, numeracy and technology use compared with their counterparts in OECD countries

More than half of young individuals and adults in LAC do not have basic-level proficiency in reading (Cunningham, Acosta and Muller, 2016; OECD, 2016d). The population aged 25-64 of Chile has the lowest average proficiency in literacy of all the OECD countries participating in PIAAC. Likewise, individuals living in the most important urban centres in Bolivia and Colombia perform below the OECD average in the World Bank Skills Measurement Programme (STEP) survey,[2] which has a testing and scoring system comparable to PIAAC (Cunningham, Acosta and Muller, 2016). According to results of these tests, individuals in these countries have basic capacity to recognise simple vocabulary, evaluate the meaning of sentences and read full paragraphs; however, they lack the ability to understand complex and dense texts. While these tests only cover Chile (PIACC) and Bolivia and Colombia (STEP), they can serve as an approximation to understand some general trends in skills performance in the region and the position relative to OECD countries. On average, Chileans scored 220 points – 48 points below the OECD average score; Colombia scored 235 – 33 points below that the OECD average; and

Bolivia scored 200 – 68 points below the OECD average. Moreover, most individuals at the OECD perform at levels 2 and 3 on the PIAAC proficiency scale, while the majority in Chile, urban Bolivia and urban Colombia performs at levels 1 and below. More than one in two individuals in Chile perform at the lowest proficiency levels in literacy compared to less than one in five on average across OECD countries. In Colombia, 36% scored at level 1 or below, while 41% ranked at level 2. Only 1% of the working-age population performed at level 4 or 5. Bolivia is the worst performer: almost 60% of Bolivians perform at level 1 or below and more than 90% at level 2 or below.

Chilean adults also perform poorly in problem solving. They score 206 points, on average, on the numeracy scale compared with the average 263 points respectively for adults in participating OECD countries. Moreover, almost 62% of Chileans score at or below level 1 in numeracy – 39 percentage points higher than the OECD average of 22.7%. Although 82% of adults in Chile report experience with computers, which is close to the OECD average (90%), 52.4% perform at level 1 or below in problem solving in technology-rich environments; only 2.1% attain level 3, the highest proficiency level in this domain.

Chile is the OECD member country with the second lowest share of young adults and adults scoring at the highest levels of proficiency in literacy, numeracy and problem solving in technology-rich environments. Very few Chileans – only about 1 in 60 adults – attain the highest levels of proficiency in literacy, compared with around 1 in 10 adults across the other OECD countries that participated in the survey. Younger Chileans do not do much better: only 1.5% of 16-24 year-olds perform at this level compared with the OECD average of 11.1%. Concerning numeracy, only 1.8% of adults in Chile attain level 4 or 5, well below the OECD average of 11.3%. Around 1.6% of 16-24 year-olds score at this level, compared with the OECD average of 10.1%. This is the second lowest percentage in the OECD. One in ten adults in Chile attains level 3 in numeracy, below the OECD average of 31.8%. Again, the situation of the younger population is not much better with only one in eight 16-24 year-olds performing at this level.

Youth are better skilled than adults in literacy, numeracy and technology

Young people (aged 16-24 years) in Chile generally perform better than their older counterparts. However, Chilean youth perform poorly compared with youth in other OECD countries. Almost two in five young Chileans are low performers in literacy, and more than one in two in numeracy, while low proficiency among youth in the OECD is less than one in eight in literacy and one in five in numeracy.

Differences by age group are more pronounced for problem solving than for other domains of the assessment in Chile. While access to digital technologies seems to have improved, the challenge of achieving higher skills development remains. Some 69% of Chilean adults aged 55-65 years were unable to take the assessment with a computer compared with 9% of 16-24 year-olds. Nevertheless, only 2.3% of 16-24 year-olds attain the highest level in problem solving – considerably less than the OECD average of 8%.

Individuals aged 15-24 in Bolivia and Colombia are more proficient at reading, evaluating and analysing written texts than their adult counterparts. Peruvian youth (aged 18-24) have better working memory and similar mathematics abilities, but lower verbal skills than adults (Cunningham, Acosta and Muller, 2016).

Youth and adult skills are linked to education attainment, although years of education are not always a good proxy for skills acquired

Skills are the result of a production process in which the level of schooling, as well as families, individual characteristics and social environment, play important roles (Heckman, Stixrud and Urzúa, 2006). Studies such as PIAAC, World Bank STEP and the

Inter-American Development Bank's Skills and Skills Trajectory Survey (STS) confirm that, on average, more-educated individuals show higher levels of both cognitive and socio-emotional skills. However, the distribution of skills proficiency among different levels of education can overlap and are different across countries.

Differences in educational attainment are closely related to skills proficiency in Chile. Tertiary-educated adults (25-65 year-olds) in Chile perform much better than their less-educated compatriots, scoring 77 points higher in literacy than adults who had not attained upper secondary education (the OECD average difference is 61 points). Even though the differences in scores between adults with and without tertiary education are among the largest observed across OECD countries, the proficiency levels of adults with tertiary qualifications in Chile are comparatively low. For example, tertiary-educated Chileans perform at the same level as the least-educated Japanese adults and at the level of upper secondary graduates in the United States.

Among 16-24 year-olds, those who left school without an upper secondary degree in Chile scored 59 points lower in literacy than those either still in school or who had earned an upper secondary degree – the largest difference between the two groups observed across participating OECD countries. It is cause for concern that younger adults in Chile who are in education or who have attained upper secondary education as their highest level of attainment perform at the same level as young adults in most other OECD countries who left school before completing upper secondary education.

Yet the years of education are not always a good proxy for skills acquired. World Bank skills surveys found the distribution of cognitive skills for any educational level heavily overlaps that of other education levels (Cunningham, Acosta and Muller, 2016). Although the distribution of skills increases with education level, the increment in skills does not consistently correlate with years of education. The range of basic cognitive skill levels among adults in Bolivia, Colombia and Peru who completed a particular level of education is wide. Bolivian adults with some secondary education who attained above-average reading proficiency scores do about as well as low-performing Bolivian adults with some university education. In Peru, the distribution of verbal, memory and maths abilities overlaps across all educational levels, although the overlap is smaller between those who completed primary school and people who are less and more educated (Cunningham, Acosta and Muller, 2016). Likewise in Colombia, the survey found wide heterogeneity in reading proficiency scores across educational levels. This suggests that the quality of education in the region is not only crucial for skills development, but also very heterogeneous.

Socio-emotional skills are slightly different among youth and adults, and across education attainment

In terms of socio-emotional skills, there is little difference in the distribution by gender or age group; still, it is noteworthy for policy analysis. Youth (individuals aged 15-24) in Bolivia, Colombia, El Salvador and Peru are less extroverted, persevering and less agreeable – less generous, polite or forgiving – than young adults (individuals aged 25-49) (Cunningham, Acosta and Muller, 2016). However, youth in Bolivia, Colombia and El Salvador are less likely to perceive hostility in others than are adults. Moreover, youth in Peru are as likely as young adults to be co-operative.

Less-educated individuals and their more educated peers have different socio-emotional skills across all three STEP categories: achieving goals, managing emotions and working with others. In Bolivia, Colombia and Peru, people with little or no formal education often have fewer skills for managing emotions, fewer decision-making skills, and less flexibility and ability to work with others (Cunningham, Acosta and Muller, 2016). However, differences across educational levels are much less marked in El Salvador.

Educational attainment and labour markets

Educational attainment often determines labour market participation and employment. To employers, education degrees and certificates signal the level of skills a prospective employee, including a recent graduate, will bring to a job (OECD, 2015c). Empirical evidence suggests that workers in OECD countries need at least an upper secondary diploma to compete effectively in the workforce (Lyche, 2010).

Labour market outcomes of youth in LAC are still poor and strongly linked to educational attainment

As in OECD countries, education increases the chances of being employed in LAC. Individuals with tertiary education are more likely to be employed than those with secondary education. Likewise, those with secondary education are more likely to be employed than those with only primary education. On average, the employment rate for working age adults in LAC is 7 percentage points higher for those with complete tertiary education than for those with complete secondary education. Dispersion among employment outcomes between different education levels is, on average, lower in LAC than in OECD countries.

The trend is slightly less universal among youth. While all countries except Bolivia have higher employment rates among youth with a university degree, employment rates for those with primary and secondary levels of education vary across countries. Because of the age group under consideration, many of those with secondary education may be delaying entry into the labour force to continue their studies.

Formal employment is linked to higher educational attainment. More highly educated youth are more likely to be employed formally, while less educated youth are more likely to work in informal employment. In LAC countries, 90% of those who have completed tertiary education work in formal employment compared with only 30% of those with only primary or less, on average. This pattern is most clear in Colombia and Panama. Colombians who have completed tertiary education are 77% more likely than those with primary education or less to work formally, and Panamanians are 73% more likely to work formally.

Box 4.3. **Skills and youth in the workplace**

For employers, years of education of potential employees signal a certain skill level, yet cognitive and socio-emotional skills are what matter in terms of labour and social inclusion, and to achieve economic and social success (OECD, 2015d). Finding links between skills and employment for LAC youth with a given level of education provides policy makers with tools to design policies to increase employment, labour participation and earnings through skills-enhancing interventions. Yet there is little evidence on the influence of cognitive and socio-emotional skills on labour earnings in Latin America, and developing countries in general.

Data from the World Bank skills surveys for Bolivia, Colombia and Peru, the IDB STS[3] for Argentina and Chile, and PIAAC for Chile highlight the importance of cognitive and socio-emotional skills for youth to succeed in the workplace. Cognitive skills (aptitudes to perform mental tasks such as comprehension or reasoning) and socio-emotional skills (personality traits and behaviours) are central for favourable labour market outcomes such as employability, formality and earnings (Bassi et al., 2012; Acosta, Muller and Sarzosa, 2015; Cunningham, Acosta and Muller, 2016).

In OECD countries, cognitive skills are associated with a higher likelihood of being employed and higher earnings (OECD, 2016d). Among the countries that participated in PIAAC, after the effects of educational attainment are taken into account, an individual who scores 48 points higher than another on the literacy scale (the equivalent to one standard deviation) is 0.8 percentage points more likely

Box 4.3. **Skills and youth in the workplace** (cont.)

to be employed than unemployed. In Chile, an individual who scores 48 points higher than another on the literacy scale is 0.4 percentage points more likely to be employed than unemployed. Likewise, an increase of one standard deviation in literacy proficiency is associated with a 6% increase in hourly wages for salaried employees across OECD countries participating in the PIAAC. In addition, in Chile, the top 25% best-paid workers scoring at level 2 earn less than the median worker scoring at level 4 or 5 suggesting that literacy skills are accurate predictors of higher wages. Still it should be noted that, on average, in the OECD countries that participated in the survey there is a significant overlap in the distribution of wages at a level of competition within and between countries. The top 25% best-paid workers scoring at level 2 earn about the same as the median worker scoring at level 4 or 5 suggesting that other skills or attributes in these countries are also rewarded.

Figure 4.13. **Conditional correlations between labour earnings and measures of skills in Bolivia, Colombia and Peru**

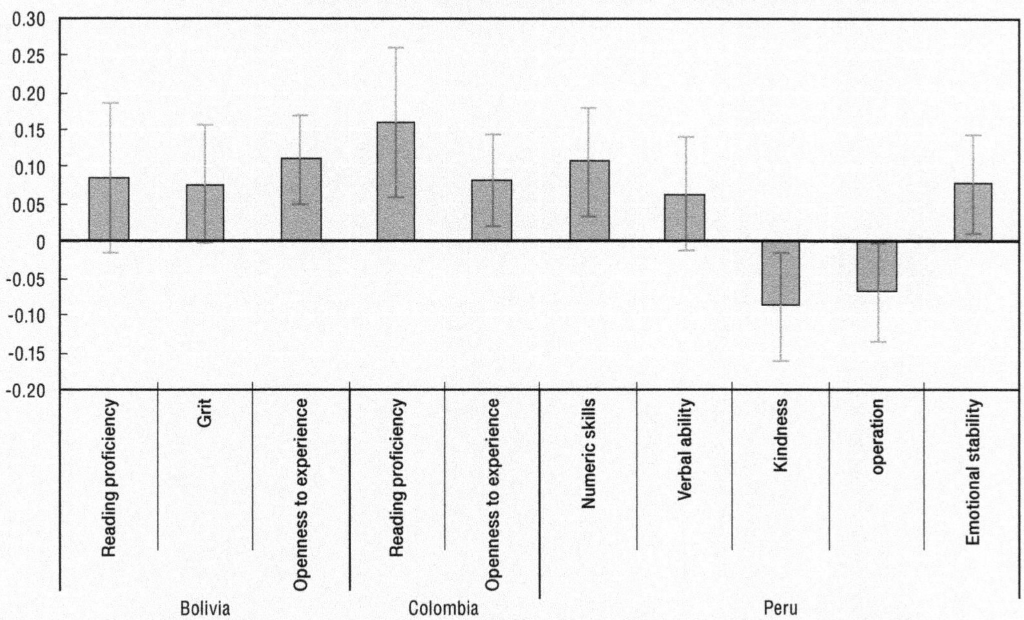

Note: The World Bank STEP Survey defines Grit as "perseverance and passion for long-term goals" (World Bank, 2016). Data are representative of urban areas. Conditional correlations with 95% confidence intervals. The displayed measures of skills show statistically significant associations, positive or negative, with labour earnings (at the 10%, 5% or 1% levels). Conditional correlations were estimated using ordinary least squares and control for background characteristics (such as gender, age, mother's education, place of living, etc.).

Source: Cunningham, Acosta and Muller (2016) based on Bolivia and Colombia STEP Household Surveys (2012) and Peru ENHAB (2010).

StatLink http://dx.doi.org/10.1787/888933414491

In LAC countries, cognitive skills are greatly linked with higher earnings and holding a formal job or a high-qualified occupation (Figure 4.13). In Peru, one standard deviation increase in cognitive skills correlates with a 24% increase in mean log hourly wages. Moreover, one standard deviation increase in cognitive skills increases the probability of employment by 3.5%; increases the chance of being an employee rather than self-employed by 11%; and increases the chance of becoming a white-collar worker by 13% and of holding a formal sector job by 9% (Cunningham, Acosta and Muller, 2016). Verbal fluency is the cognitive skill most associated with labour outcomes, positively related with being employed and with being a white-collar or wage worker. Higher numeric ability is strongly positively correlated with wages and being white collar. In Colombia, for example, reading proficiency proved to be an important predictor of earnings and job quality (Acosta, Muller and Sarzosa, 2015).

Box 4.3. **Skills and youth in the workplace** (cont.)

Along with cognitive skills, socio-emotional skills play an important role in youth schooling decisions, labour participation and transition into the workplace. In Argentina and Chile, self-efficacy stands out as the most highly valued skill in the labour market (Bassi et al., 2012). In Chile, an increase in one standard deviation represents an increase of 6% in the probability of participating in the labour force. Across all methodologies explored by Acosta, Muller and Sarzosa (2015) in Colombia, socio-emotional skills do not seem to play any significant role in explaining wage levels or job quality, but play a stronger role in labour market participation (Figure 4.14). This is consistent with previous findings for the United States such as Bowles, Gintis and Osborne (2001) and Drago (2011). Moreover, socio-emotional skills are a more important predictor of labour force participation among women, youth under 35 years and workers with less than complete secondary education.

Figure 4.14. **Size effects of conditional correlations between measures of skills and labour outcomes in Colombia**

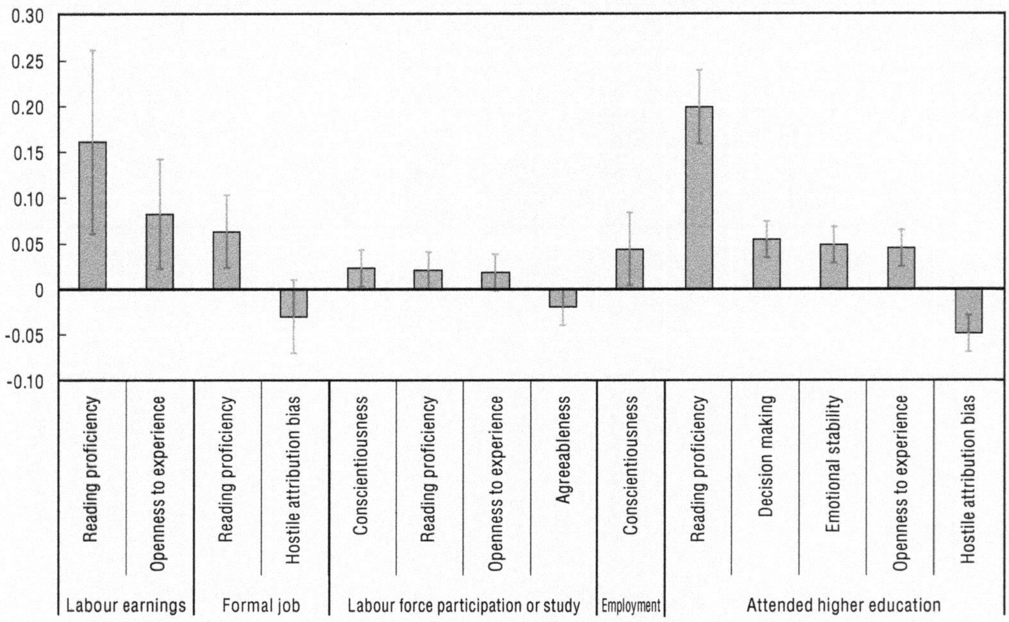

Note: Conditional correlations with 95% confidence intervals. Data are representative of urban areas. The displayed measures of skills show statistically significant associations, positive or negative, with labour earnings (at the 10%, 5% or 1% levels). Conditional correlations were estimated using ordinary least squares and logic and control for background characteristics (such as gender, age, mother's education, place of living, etc.).

Source: Cunningham, Acosta and Muller (2016) based on Colombia STEP Household Surveys (2012).

StatLink http://dx.doi.org/10.1787/888933414506

The results of these initial skills studies in the region underline the importance of a better understanding of the role of skills in employment to improve the education system and facilitate the school-to-work transition of youth. At the same time, they highlight the need to collect more and better data for all countries in the region on the links between education, skills and labour markets.

Earnings are more heavily tied to educational attainment in LAC countries than the OECD average

Education not only leads to better employment rates and job quality prospects, but also to higher earnings. This should serve as an incentive to attain higher education. However, tertiary education varies significantly among countries; graduation rates appear related more to access and flexibility in completing programmes in each country than to returns to such education.

Workers with tertiary education in Brazil, Chile, Colombia, Costa Rica and Mexico make between 186% and 241% of what their counterparts with upper secondary education make (Figure 4.15). This is well above the OECD average of 155%. Additionally, workers with less than upper secondary education make between 60% and 70% of what workers with upper secondary education make, with the OECD average far less at 81%. Brazil and Chile have the largest earnings differentials between workers with varying educational attainment: workers with tertiary education make over two and a half times what those with less than upper secondary education make.

Figure 4.15. **Relative earnings of workers by educational attainment, LAC, 2013**

(adults with income from employment; upper secondary education = 100)

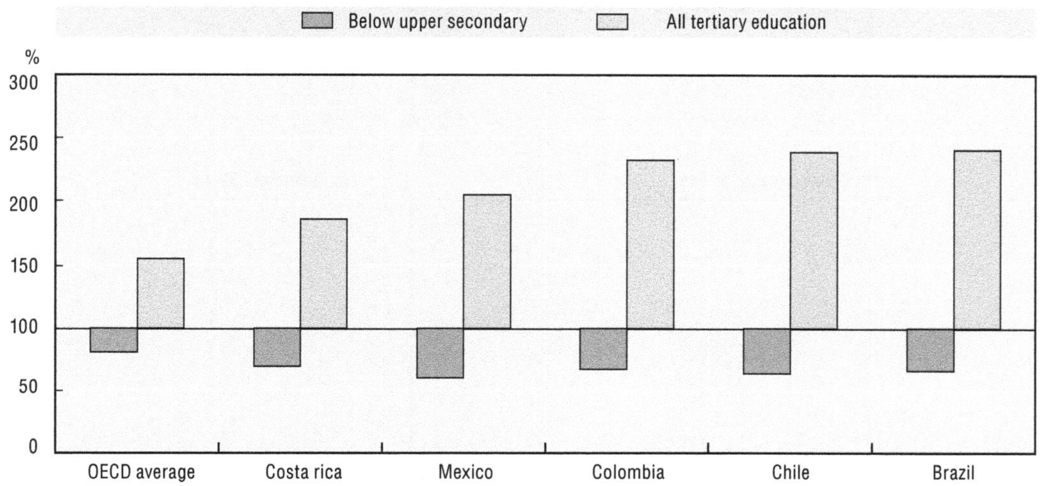

Source: OECD (2016g), *Education at a Glance 2016: OECD Indicators*, OECD Publishing, Paris, http://dx.doi.org/10.1787/eag-2016-en.

StatLink http://dx.doi.org/10.1787/888933414517

Education, therefore, plays a much larger role in determining earnings among workers in LAC countries than in OECD countries. Attending tertiary education or even completing upper secondary education has large impacts on labour market outcomes and well-being. Differences in earning are both a reflection of and a source of high unequal distribution of income in LAC countries. However, they are also a consequence of a low supply of highly educated workers, particularly with tertiary education, and demonstrate that broader investment in education is highly desirable.

The evolution of returns to education can inform how the supply and demand of skills has shifted over time. It can also have a significant impact on the decision of youth to invest in education. They may not pursue further training and skills if they perceive the returns to that investment are not high enough; conversely, they may invest in education if they see it pays off. This has obvious implications for the available talent pool of the future generation, which eventually affects the capacity to strengthen a development model based on knowledge and enhanced productivity (IDB, 2015).

In the past, the economic literature on returns to education in LAC has identified the fall in returns to both secondary and tertiary education from 1990 to 2010 (Gasparini et al., 2011; De la Torre, Levy Yeyati and Pienknagura, 2013). An analysis of 17 LAC countries shows that returns to education have fallen further in the region over 2004-14 for all levels of education. Moreover, the relative supply of skilled workers has increased during the last decade for the six demographic groups analysed; the tertiary education wage premium narrowed, but is still wide (Figure 4.16).

Figure 4.16. **Tertiary education wage premium and relative supply over time, LAC**

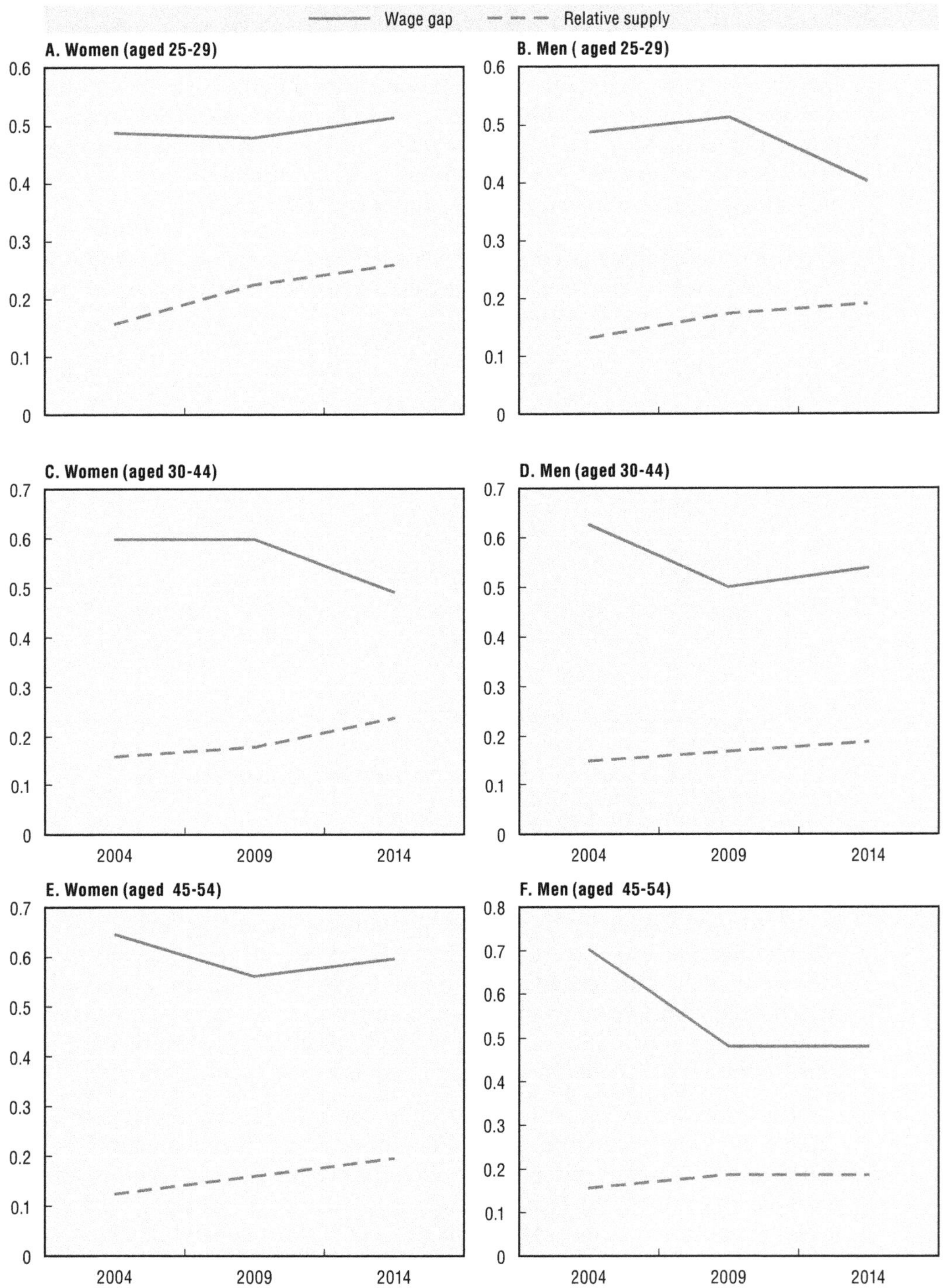

Note: Wage premium is the ratio of the wage rates of individuals with some tertiary education (complete or incomplete), to the wage rates of individuals with up to complete secondary education – but without tertiary education. Relative supply is the ratio of individuals with some tertiary education (complete or incomplete) to individuals with up to complete secondary education. LAC countries: Argentina, Bolivia, Brazil, Chile, Colombia, Costa Rica, Dominican Republic, Ecuador, El Salvador, Honduras, Mexico, Nicaragua, Panama, Paraguay, Peru and Uruguay.

Source: OECD and World Bank tabulations of SEDLAC (CEDLAS and the World Bank).

StatLink http://dx.doi.org/10.1787/888933414520

There could be many reasons for high-but-falling returns to education and skills, from both the supply and demand sides. Several explanations are noted below, but deserve further analysis that goes beyond the scope of this report.

From the supply side, the fall in returns to education could emerge from a larger pool of educated people due to the expansion of education in the region. It could also come from a deteriorating quality of education, which would lead to skills being less relevant – and thus less valued – for existing demand. Such deteriorating quality could have been linked to expanded access to education; this may have put pressure on existing resources or may have led to newcomers lowering the overall level of foundational and general skills (OECD/CAF/ECLAC, 2014). From the demand side, structural transformation in the region over the last decade could have created demand for sectors requiring low skills (De La Torre, Messina and Pienknagura, 2012).

Box 4.4. Returns to STEM education

The graduate's field of study can also affect returns to education. More technical and quantitatively focused disciplines, commonly known as STEM (science, technology, engineering and mathematics) are associated with higher educational returns than humanities; the difference appears to be due to both higher wages and a higher probability of being employed. However, it is unclear how much these findings are due to unmeasured differences in, for example, productivity or ability that may influence choice of field and wages.

Table 4.4 uses data from the *Encuesta Nacional de Hogares* (ENAHO) of Peru and the *Encuesta Continua de Hogares* (ECH) of Uruguay to estimate a modified version of the standard Mincer equation augmented for STEM tertiary education. It shows returns to STEM education for male and female workers aged 25-55. Results for 2014 reveal that a positive association between the wage returns and tertiary-level STEM qualifications could be quite substantial, particularly in Peru.

Such a premium can exist for many reasons. The labour market may value some sets of skills more than others, for example, such as those needed for higher productivity tasks. There may also be technical changes that favour workers with more skills. Given the important role of technology and digitisation (see also Chapter 6) in driving the demand side of the market for skills, STEM degrees might be particularly relevant.

Table 4.4. Returns to STEM education in Uruguay and Peru, 2014

	Peru	Uruguay
STEM degree holders (tertiary, college and graduate)	0.208***	0.116***
	-0.056	(0.023)
Urban dummy	0.287***	0.034
	(0.040)	(0.049)
Male dummy	0.233***	0.138***
	-0.028	(0.019)
Tertiary STEM degree * Male dummy	-0.173	0.039
	-0.065	(0.035)
Observations	7 468	6 521
R-squared	0.133	0.140

Notes: The sample includes youth aged 25-55 years in Uruguay and Peru. Standard errors in parentheses *** p<0.01, ** p<0.05, * p<0.1. Additional controls include age, age squared, tenure, dummy for informal job, dummies for educational attainment (6 categories – baseline is no education) and dummies for activity sectors (17 categories – baseline is "agriculture").
Source: OECD and World Bank tabulations of SEDLAC (CEDLAS and the World Bank).

LAC is among the regions that show the greatest problems in matching the private sector demand for skills

Latin America and the Caribbean is the region with the widest gap between the available pool of skills and those skills that economies and societies require (OECD/CAF/ECLAC, 2014). Current skills mismatches could be aggravated in a context where technological change, globalisation and trade are responsible for job destruction and new types of job creation. The capacity of countries to improve the skills of their population and adjust to these changes will partially determine labour market outcomes, economic growth, productivity and competitiveness.

Five of the top ten countries where firms identify difficulty filling jobs in the Manpower Group Talent Shortage Surveys are from Latin America: Peru (68%), Brazil (61%), Mexico (54%), Colombia (47%) and Costa Rica (46%). In fact, the share of firms identifying difficulty filling jobs is larger in all LAC countries than for the average of OECD countries (Figure 4.17). Further, 32% of employers use foreign talent to meet skills shortages (Manpower Group, 2015).

Figure 4.17. **Firms identifying difficulty filling jobs, 2015**

(percentage of formal firms)

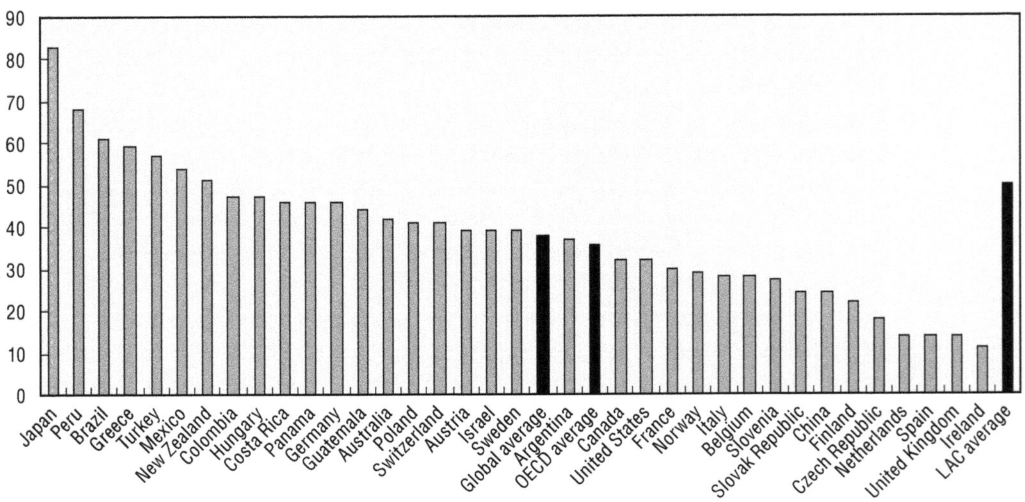

Source: Manpower Group (2015).

StatLink http://dx.doi.org/10.1787/888933414533

LAC firms take longer to fill job vacancies than firms in any other region (Figure 4.18). On average, Latin American employers take almost four weeks to fill a job vacancy with external talent, compared with three weeks in South Asia or Africa (Aedo and Walker, 2012).

Since the time to fill a job vacancy is an indicator of an economy's efficiency, it can be used to assess the degree of skills mismatch in the labour market (Aedo and Walker, 2012). This analysis assumes that firms take a longer time to hire when the skills and competencies of available workers do not match the technical requirements of the unfilled jobs. However, job vacancies could also be due to proxy-matching problems between firms and workers or poor adjustment between supply and demand due to occupational or geographical immobility.

Job vacancies for skilled workers take almost three times longer to fill than for unskilled workers. On average, firms take 2.1 weeks to fill a vacancy for unskilled labour, and 6.5 weeks for skilled labour. Brazil tops the list of LAC countries that take the longest number of weeks (eight) to fill a job vacancy (Figure 4.19). For all countries for which information is available, skilled job vacancies take longer to fill than unskilled vacancies, providing extra evidence of possible skills misalliance in the region. This variance is probably related to skills mismatch. However, firing and other costs of labour are greater for skilled workers, requiring more thorough screening of candidates (Aedo and Walker, 2012). Furthermore, skilled workers can perform skilled and unskilled occupations, while unskilled workers can only work on unskilled jobs (Albrecht and Vroman, 2002).

Figure 4.18. **Average time to fill job vacancy, regions of the world, circa 2012**
(weeks)

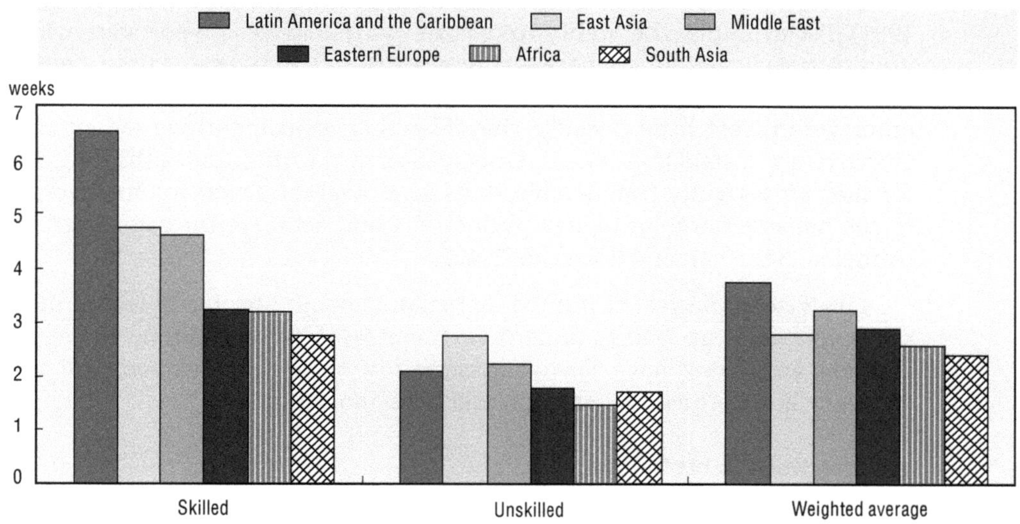

Source: Aedo and Walker (2012).
StatLink http://dx.doi.org/10.1787/888933414549

Figure 4.19. **Average time to fill job vacancy, selected LAC countries, circa 2012**
(weeks)

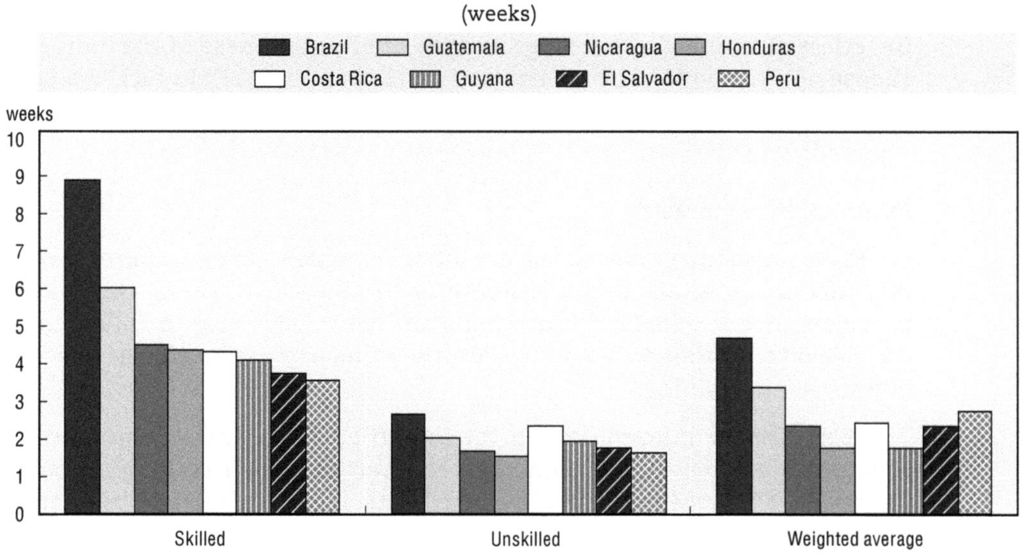

Source: Aedo and Walker (2012).
StatLink http://dx.doi.org/10.1787/888933414556

Low levels of investments in and misallocation of skills arise from market failures

Youth participation in labour markets can bring benefits in terms of productivity, growth and well-being. Young individuals are confronted by the same market failures as regular adults, as well as barriers relative to age and inexperience. In terms of skills, as described in this chapter, they face suboptimal levels of investments in education, training and/or misallocation of skills, which arise from imperfections in both labour markets and capital markets, and information asymmetry.

Imperfections in labour markets

Technical skills are sector specific and partially transferable (Acemoglu and Pischke, 1999). For example, the ability to operate particular design software can be useful to architecture firms, but not necessarily to a hospital. At the same time, neither employers nor firms can fully appropriate the returns from their investments in skills. As a result, employers invest little because they fear that, in competitive labour markets, other employers will steal their talent. Employees invest little because the limited competition for their imperfectly transferable skills gives market power to employers who can fail to compensate fairly for higher productivity and decrease the rate of return in training (Almeida, Behrman and Robalino, 2012).

Likewise, imperfect or limited information about how much labour markets value a particular skill can lead to underinvestment in skills acquisition. Usually, job seekers, workers and firms have partial information on a country's demand and supply of different skills (Almeida, Behrman and Robalino, 2012).

Imperfections in capital markets

Education and training costs – tuition, books, lodging, food and transportation – can negatively affect students' ability to succeed or even prevent them from further investing in skills. Adequate finance is often a constraint for young people, especially those in poor and vulnerable households, to attend school, university or training. In theory, they could borrow as long as the rate of return on the investment surpasses the interest rate. In practice, financial institutions usually have little information on the effect of training on earnings and the creditworthiness of the individual, and may choose not to lend (Almeida, Behrman and Robalino, 2012). In fact, the offer of student loans in the region is very limited and confined to households in the upper quintiles of income distribution.

Information asymmetry

Skills investment decisions are often complex. They require several pieces of information, especially in terms of returns to education/training and quality of training providers. Households and individuals are not always able to collect and process all the relevant information. As a result, they underinvest or choose the wrong type of investment in training.

Lack of clear information on returns to education mean that perceived returns sometimes are more important than real returns when making schooling decisions (Jensen, 2010). Perceptions may be inaccurate, based on partial observations of labour market outcomes in the local economy. They may also reflect the experience of peers, friends and family, which might be unrepresentative (Almeida, Behrman and Robalino, 2012). Perceptions can thus lead to investments in education and training that are too low, too high or assigned to the wrong skills.

Moreover, even if individuals have improved information on returns to education, they also need information on the quality of training providers. Lack of information and inability to compare the quality of different courses may lead individuals to low-quality providers or those who are not a good fit for their needs. In the long run, the market should separate good providers from bad ones; however, the process can be long and costly (Almeida, Behrman and Robalino, 2012).

All in all, the problems described above call for some government participation, in co-ordination with private actors, in education and training to partially compensate or fully correct these failures. The following section will study some interventions developed to confront the lack of skills in youth, especially among those in disadvantaged households and with low education attainment.

Skills-enhancing interventions for low-educated youth in LAC

The persistency of low-income, low-skilled youth in the labour market is a major concern for LAC countries. The poor quality of education together with early school dropouts resulted in a large group of low-skilled youth with poor labour market prospects. The region's insufficient formal education and the large reported mismatch between skills supply and demand highlight the need to strengthen skills training programmes. These can improve employability prospects and help LAC youth make the transition into labour markets.

In the last two decades, LAC countries significantly augmented their public spending on social programmes to reduce poverty and increase equality. However, most beneficiaries did not successfully make the transition into the labour market. As a result, countries started working on a new wave of "active inclusion" and "productive inclusion". These interventions link income support programmes, such as Conditional Cash Transfers, with services that equip beneficiaries with the tools needed to participate in economic activities, including active labour market policies and training. Programmes such as the *Ingreso Ético Familiar* in Chile, *Socio Empleo* in Ecuador, *PATI* in El Salvador and the *Brasil Sem Miséria* strategy, together with a number of regional pilot initiatives, provide integrated packages of services. In addition to providing income support, for example, the programmes feature technical and vocational guidance, entrepreneurship support, job placement and other services to improve beneficiaries' labour market and economic participation (World Bank and GIZ, 2015).

As these integrated programmes scale up, they co-exist with individual labour market and social assistance programmes from which they feed, among them training and entrepreneurship programmes. Lessons from the first generation of early training and entrepreneurship programmes are key to designing and implementing the new wave of productive inclusion initiatives.

Training programmes in LAC expanded as public spending increased

Training programmes are the most used active labour market policy (ALMP) in LAC and youth employment intervention worldwide (Betcherman et al., 2007). In the early 2000s, LAC countries, except for Colombia, spent less than 0.1% of gross domestic product (GDP) on all training programmes (Cerutti et al., 2014). In the 2010s, spending in Brazil, Chile, Costa Rica, Honduras and Panama surpassed that mark. Moreover, four LAC countries currently spend a larger share of their GDP on training programmes than the average of OECD countries (Figure 4.20).

Figure 4.20. **Public spending on training programmes, LAC**
(percentage of GDP)

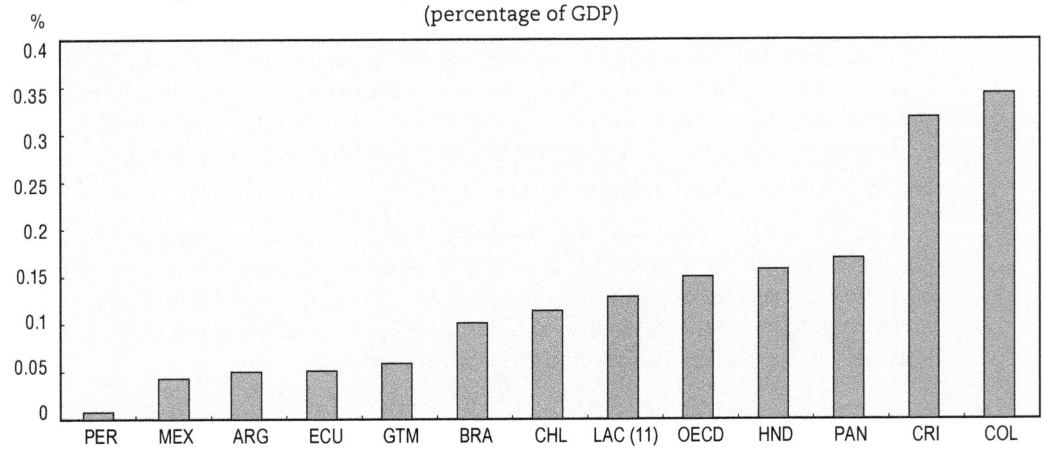

Note: Year 2014 for Argentina, Brazil, OECD and Panama, 2013 for Costa Rica, Guatemala, Nicaragua and Peru, 2012 for Dominican Rep, Honduras and Mexico, 2011 for Chile and Ecuador, and 2010 for Colombia.
Source: World Bank (2015), *LAC Social Protection* (database); OECD.Stats (2015), http://stats.oecd.org.
StatLink http://dx.doi.org/10.1787/888933414568

Almost all LAC countries offer training and first employment programmes for youth. Traditionally, training programmes in LAC offered either classroom preparation or on-the-job placement, similar to OECD countries. However, in past decades, to address the growing problem of youth's lack of skills and unemployment, especially among the poor and vulnerable, LAC combined classroom training with practical experience in the formal labour market and other interventions to boost employability and access to quality jobs (Fares and Puerto, 2009).

Youth training programmes in LAC have a distinctive design, incorporating traditional elements with novel design features and other labour market services

LAC has seen a big wave of the "Jovenes" programmes since the creation of *Chile Joven* in 1991 and Mexico's *Probecat* in 1984. *Chile Joven* combined its existing class training programmes with a full-time internship at a firm for three to six months. After three months of classroom learning, participants continue training at a private firm arranged by the training centre. The labour ministry was primarily responsible for implementation; while private vocational training centres took over fundamental aspects of the operation (UNESCO, 2014). Mexico's *Probecat* does not target youth or disadvantaged populations, although in practice eligibility criteria favour these groups. Similar to *Chile Joven*, it offers short-term, demand-driven courses matched with internships to provide beneficiaries with on-the-job training. Additionally, the programme offers job search services that help provide disadvantaged youth with skills to look for work. Private firms offer both the courses and the internships (World Bank, 2012).

These models were later replicated across LAC (Table 4.5): The Bolivarian Republic of Venezuela (hereafter "Venezuela") (1993), Argentina (1993), Paraguay (1994), Uruguay (1996), Peru (1996), Dominican Republic (1999), Colombia (2000), Panama (2002), El Salvador (2005), Haiti (2005) and Honduras (2006).

"Jovenes" programmes across LAC targeted urban youth considered to be "at risk" because of their low likelihood of insertion into the formal labour market: vulnerable or disadvantaged young workers or first-time job seekers such as those living in poor households, unemployed, underemployed or low-skilled. In practice, this generally means young school dropouts unlikely to return to formal education. To assist young people in making a more successful transition into the world of work, they typically offer short skills training courses in occupations, trade-specific abilities or basic job readiness skills demanded by the private sector (UNESCO, 2014).

Table 4.5. "Jovenes" type of youth training programmes, LAC

Country	Programme name	Implementation period	Ages	Average number of beneficiaries per year
Argentina	Proyecto Joven	1993-2001	16-30	25 455
	Jóvenes con Futuro	2006-	18-24	400
	Jóvenes por Más y Mejor Trabajo	2008-	18-24	185 016
Bolivia	Mi Primer Empleo Digno	2009-	18-24	4 333
Brazil	Programa Nacional De Estímulo Ao Primeiro Emprego	2003-2007	16-24	120 000
	Pro Jovem	2005-	15-29	1 127 133
	Educação para a nova indústria	2007-2013	14-24	n
Chile	Chile Joven	1991-2002	16-30	13 705
	Especial de Jóvenes	1997-2013	18-29	1 679
	Jóvenes Bicentenario	2008-2012	18- 29	6 667
Colombia	Jóvenes en Acción	2002-2006	18-25	21 958
	Jóvenes Trabajando Unidos	2011-2013	18-26	n
Costa Rica	Construyendo Alternativas Juveniles	2000-	18-25	4 000
	Empleate	2011-	17-24	n
Dominican Republic	Juventud y Empleo	1999-	16-29	7 602
El Salvador	Programa Empresa Centro	1996-2013	18-29	4 198
	Empleo Joven	2005-2008	14-25	n
Guatemala	Programa Jóvenes Protagonistas	2012-	16-24	35 000
	Guatemala Joven	2009-	16-24	4 222
Honduras	Honduras Proempleo	2004-2011	18-29	1 563
	Mi primer empleo	2006-2010	15-19	1 200
	Projoven	2014-	16-30	n
	Chamba Joven	2016-	16-30	n
Mexico	Probecat/SICAT/Becate	1984-	16-64	294 118
Nicaragua	Desarrollo de las capacidades nacionales para mejorar las oportunidades de empleo y autoempleo	2009-2012	15-24	2 211
Panama	ProCaJoven	2002-	16-29	136 832
Paraguay	SAPE'A	2015-	15-24	8 000
Peru	Projoven	1996-	18-29	6 375
Uruguay	Opción Joven (Pilot)	1994-1997	15-24	n
	Projoven	1996-	15-29	2 234
	Yo Estudio y Trabajo	2012	16-20	700
Venezuela	Plan Empleo Joven	1993-	15-29	n

Sources: OECD/ECLAC/CAF based on Minowa and Wodon (1999); Cohen, Martinez and Navarrete (2001); Cayapa (2002); Naranjo Silva (2002); Rosas (2006); Aguayo (2007); Ibarrarán and Rosas (2007); Puentes and Urzúa (2010); IDB (2011); Portal Brasil (2012); Ministry of Finance of Argentina (2014); World Bank (2014); World Bank (2015), LAC Social Protection (database); INADEH (2015); INEFORP (2015); INSAFORP (2015); CEPAL (2016); Ministry of Labour of Argentina (2016); ILO/CINTERFOR (2016a, 2016b, 2016c, 2016d, 2016e, 2016f, 2007); Youth Employment Inventory (2016); Ministry of Social Development of Guatemala (2016a, 2016b. 2016c); Ministry of Labour of Bolivia (2016); CEDLAS (2016).

The model for Chile and Mexico, as well as most "Jovenes" programmes (Table 4.6), has three main characteristics. First, these programmes combine an initial classroom-training phase with workplace training, usually in the form of an internship in a firm; these are complemented by labour market services such as job search information, counselling and support or job placement. Second, the private sector helps define the menu of skills training courses to ensure market-oriented and demand-driven training that reduces countries' skills mismatch and boosts employability. Third, the programmes separate financing from training. Governments select training providers through competitive biddings where both private and public training firms and institutions can participate; providers receive incentive payments based on trainees' outcomes (Ibarrarán and Rosas Shady, 2009).

Table 4.6. Characteristics of selected youth training programmes in LAC

	ARG: Projecto Joven	ARG: Jóvenes con Futuro	ARG: Jóvenes con Más y Mejor Trabajo	ARG: Entra 21 and ADEC	BOL: Mi primer empleo digno	BRA: Programa Nacional de Estímulo Ao Primeiro Emprego	BRA: Pro Jovem	BRA: Entra 21 and CEPRO	CHL: Chile Joven	CHL: Jóvenes Bicentenario
Main characteristic										
Coverage										
National	x	x	x		x	x	x		x	x
Regional				x				x		
Local										
Employment/employability	x	x	x	x	x	x	x	x	x	x
Increase wages								x		
Promote social insertion	x	x	x	x	x	x	x	x	x	
Enhance labour market efficiency	x									x
Raise productivity	x				x			x		
Develop a private market for training services	x								x	
Components										
Labour intermediation services										
Information/counselling	x			x	x	x	x	x		x
Support job search										x
Job placement				x	x	x	x	x		x
Public works										
Training for unemployed		x	x							
School-based training	x				x		x			
School + work experience	x			x	x	x	x	x	x	x
Workplace training						x				x
For self-employment		x	x						x	
For at-risk population								x		
Soft skills training		x	x	x				x	x	
Training for active workers	x			x		x				x
Institutional strengthening	x								x	x
Mechanisms										
Demand-driven	x			x	x			x	x	x
Supply-driven	x			x			x			
Stipend to participants										
Transport/lunch/health insurance	x								x	x
Income support		x	x	x	x		x	x		
Wage subsidy						x				
Publicly funded training	x	x	x	x			x	x	x	x
Provision of training courses										
Public	x	x	x	x	x	x	x	x	x	x
Private	x	x		x	x	x	x	x	x	x
Internships arranged by training provider	x	x		x		x		x	x	x
Institutional basis										
Executing agency										
Existing institution	x		x	x	x	x	x	x	x	x
New, parallel to regular bureaucracy										

Table 4.6. Characteristics of selected youth training programmes in LAC (cont.).

	COL: Jóvenes en Accion	COL: Proyecto de Servicios Integrados para Jóvenes	DR: Juventud y Empleo	MEX: Probecat	MEX: Inserción Laboral de Jóvenes	PAN: ProCaJoven	PER: Projoven	PER: Entra 21 and Alternativa Partnership	URY: Opción Joven	URY: ProJoven
Main characteristic										
Coverage										
National	X		X	X	X	X	X	X	X	X
Regional										
Local										
Employment/employability	X	X	X	X	X	X	X	X	X	X
Increase wages		X					X		X	X
Promote social insertion	X	X			X				X	X
Enhance labour market efficiency				X				X		
Raise productivity				X		X				
Develop a private market for training services	X					X	X			
Components										
Labour intermediation services								X		
Information/counselling		X	X	X	X	X	X	X	X	X
Support job search			X	X						
Job placement	X	X			X					
Public works	X				X					
Training for unemployed										
School-based training		X		X				X		
School + work experience	X	X	X	X	X	X	X	X	X	X
Workplace training										
For self-employment	X	X	X	X	X			X		
For at-risk population			X		X	X				
Soft skills training		X					X		X	X
Training for active workers				X		X				
Institutional strengthening	X		X	X		X	X			X
Mechanisms										
Demand-driven	X	X	X	X	X	X	X	X	X	X
Supply-driven				X						
Stipend to participants										
Transport/lunch/health insurance	X		X	X		X	X			X
Income support	X		X	X	X				X	X
Wage subsidy										
Publicly funded training	X	X	X	X	X	X	X		X	X
Provision of training courses								X		
Public	X	X		X						
Private	X	X	X	X		X	X		X	X
Internships arranged by training provider	X	X	X		X	X	X		X	X
Institutional basis										
Executing agency										
Existing institution		X		X	X	X		X	X	X
New, parallel to regular bureaucracy	X		X				X			

Sources: OECD/ECLAC/CAF based on Ibarrarán and Rosas (2009), updated with World Bank (2015); Youth Employment Inventory (2016).

Several other training services in LAC targeted at youth are similar to "Jovenes" programmes (Table 4.6). The Entra 21 programme promoted by the International Youth Foundation (IYF) provided disadvantaged youth aged 16-29 with job placement and vocational training in information technology, communication and life skills. Entra 21-type programmes, implemented by local and central governments, expanded to most LAC countries during the 2000s (Puerto, 2007). Other programmes in the region combine training in occupational and entrepreneurship skills for youth. This last group is further described and discussed in the entrepreneurship chapter (Chapter 5).

Evaluations and evidence of training programmes' performance are increasing in LAC; still, information remains limited, especially to determine which components work best

Job training programmes, including those targeted at youth, have been evaluated widely around the world. In fact, past literature on impact evaluation has identified evaluations of training programmes as a catalyst to develop and apply cutting-edge evaluation methods. This led to the development of a sizeable body of worldwide evidence on what does and does not work (Ibarrarán and Rosas, 2009).

Table 4.7. **Evidence available on the impact of youth training programmes, LAC**

Country/ Programme/ Year	Classification	Result
Colombia / Jóvenes en Acción/ 2002-05	****	(+)
Uruguay/ProJoven/1996-97	****	(+)
Dominican Republic/Juventud y Empleo/1999	****	(+)
Chile/ Jóvenes Bicentenario	****	(+)
Dominican Republic/Juventud y Empleo/1999	****	(+0)
Argentina/ Entra 21 Córdoba	****	(+0)
Peru/ ProJoven / 1996 -	****	(+0)
Chile/ Chile Joven/ 1995-97	***	(+)
Argentina/Proyecto Joven/1994-98	**	(+0)
Chile/ Chile Joven/ Fase I 1991-95 y Fase II 1996-2002	**	(+)
Peru/ ProJoven / 1996 -	**	(+)
Panama / ProCaJoven/2002-	**	(+0)
Argentina/Programa Joven/1996-97	**	(+)
Mexico/ Probecat/ 1984-	**	(+)
Mexico/ Probecat/ 1984-	**	(+0)
Mexico/ Probecat/ 1984-	**	0
Bolivia/Mi Primer Empleo Digno / 2008-	**	0
Bolivia/Entra 21 - alianza Quipus/ 2004 -05	**	0
Brazil-São Paulo/Entra 21 - alianza CEPRO/ 2003 -05	**	0
Brazil-Salvador/Entra 21 - alianza Instituto de Hospitalidade / 2003 -	**	0
Chile / Formación de Oficios para Jóvenes de Escasos Recursos/ 1998-2000	**	(-0)
Colombia - Medellín /ENTRA 21 y alianza COMFENALCO / 2002-05	**	0
Colombia - Cartagena /ENTRA 21 y alianza INDUSTRIAL /2002-05	**	0
Dominican Republic / ENTRA 21 y alianza ISA / 2003-06	**	0
El Salvador / ENTRA 21 y alianza AGAPE / 2003-05	**	0
Mexico / ENTRA 21 y alianza CIPEC / 2004-07	**	0
Honduras / ENTRA 213 y alianza COSPEA / 2004-05	**	0
Paraguay / ENTRA 213 y alianza CIRD / 2003-05	**	0
Peru / ENTRA 213 y alianza Alternativa / 2003-05	**	0
Uruguay / Opción Joven / 1994-97	**	(+)
Chile/ Chile Joven/ 1991-95	*	(+)
Honduras / ENTRA 21 y alianza CARDEH / 2004-05	*	0
Brazil / Programa Primero Empleo /1999-	*	0
Colombia / Proyecto de Servicios Integrados para Jóvenes / 2000-03	*	0

Note: **** experimental; *** experimental with limited number of results; ** non-experimental; * non-experimental with limited number of results. (+) Positive, robust and significant results; (+0) Combination of positive, robust and significant and neutral results; 0 Neutral or non-significant results; (-0) Combination of negative, robust and significant and neutral results; (-) Negative, robust and significant results.

Sources: OECD/ECLAC/CAF based on Puentes and Urzúa (2010), updated with Card et al. (2011), Alzúa, Cruces and Erazo (2015), Herani-Limarino and Villarroel (2015), Ibarrarán et al. (2015), Díaz and Rosas (2016) and Kluve (2016).

The general trend for evaluations of job training programmes in LAC has been promising (Table 4.7). Evidence on youth interventions in the region is developing, while the design of impact evaluations is improving. As in most of the developing world, the past decade has witnessed a surge in rigorous programme evaluation in LAC with randomised control trials or crafted quasi-experimental design studies.

Still, there is room for improvement. Evidence on youth training programmes for developing countries and LAC is limited. While most programmes in developed countries are evaluated extensively, only a few programmes were rigorously evaluated in LAC. Evaluations focus on a small group of programmes, look mainly at short-term impact and rarely incorporate analysis on the impact of specific components and design features.

What have we learned from individual programme evaluations? Evidence on youth training programmes

While impact evaluations are still scarce in the region and show some deficiencies, a growing body of evidence hints at what has been working and possible areas for further improvement. This section looks at individual impact evaluations of 12 job training programmes – Argentina, *Entra 21* and *Proyecto Joven*; Brazil, *Entra 21*; Bolivia, *Mi Primer Empleo Digno*; Chile, *Chile Joven* and *Jóvenes Bicentenario*; Colombia, *Jóvenes en Acción*; Dominican Republic, *Juventud y Empleo*; Mexico, *Probecat/Bécate*; Panama *ProCaJoven*; Peru, *ProJoven*; and Uruguay, *Opción Joven* (Table 4.8). It summarises some of the main results of each individual evaluation, and provides some conclusions of what does and does not work according to certain programme characteristics.

Youth training programmes in the region share similar designs, especially among those that have been evaluated. All evaluated programmes combine in-class and on-the-job training with some type of labour intermediation or placement, except *Chile Joven*. Therefore, it is difficult to assess if any of these components is responsible for the overall effect, which has the largest impact or even if the impact results from the interaction of its components. Furthermore, several programmes – *Proyecto Joven, Jovenes en Accion, Juventud y Empleo, ProJoven Peru* and *Probecat* and its successors – have been evaluated multiple times, using different methods (Table 4.8).

Employment, formality and earnings effects

Results are heterogeneous across programmes and different evaluations of the same programme. Although each individual impact evaluation assesses the influence of the programme on a particular set of labour, education and welfare outcomes, almost all look at the effect on employability, job quality and labour earnings.

Youth training programmes in the region aim at providing unemployed young people at the bottom of the income distribution with improved skills to access jobs. Although the effects of such programmes on beneficiaries' likelihood to get employed are diverse, most evaluations show no significant impact on the employment rates of participants. The early programmes, *Chile Joven* and Uruguay's pilot *Opción Joven*, had a positive and significant impact on youth employability. In Argentina, Bolivia, Dominican Republic and Panama, the programme had a negligible impact on employment, while for Peru and Mexico different studies report different results. Still, almost half of the programmes show improvements in the likelihood of employability for specific groups. This is partly due to the low unemployment, high informality and presence of disadvantaged groups that characterise the Latin American and the Caribbean labour market.

Table 4.8. Evidence available on the impact of youth training programmes, LAC, selected programmes

	Publication year	Observation period	Evaluation method	Employment effect		Formality effect		Earnings effect		Authors
				Women	Men	Women	Men	Women	Men	
ARG: Entra 21 Cordoba	2015	18 months	Experimental			Neutral	Positive	Neutral	Positive	Alzúa, Cruces, and Lopez Erazo (2015)
		3 years	Experimental			Neutral	Positive	Neutral	Positive	
ARG: Projecto Joven	2006	11, 12 & 19 months	Non experimental	Positive	Neutral	Positive	Neutral	Neutral	Neutral	Alzua and Brassolio (2006)
	2001	1 year	Non experimental	Positive	Neutral			Positive	Positive	Aedo and Nuñez (2004)
BRA: Entra 21	2006	1 year	Non experimental	Negative	Negative			Negative	Negative	Alzua et al. (2007)
BOL: Mi Primer Empleo Digno	2015	3 months	Non experimental	Positive	Positive	Neutral	Neutral	Positive	Positive	Hernani-Limarino and Villarroel (2015)
		6 months	Non experimental	Neutral	Neutral	Neutral	Neutral	Neutral	Neutral	
CHL: Chile Joven	2004	12 months	Non experimental	Positive	Positive	Positive	Positive	Neutral	Neutral	Aedo and Pizarro Valdivia (2004)
CHL: Jóvenes Bicentenario	2010	6 months	Experimental	Positive	Positive	Positive	Positive			Acero et al. (2009)
COL: Jóvenes en Accion	2015	10 years	Experimental			Positive	Neutral	Positive	Neutral	Attanasio et al. (2015)
	2015	8 years	Experimental			Positive	Positive	Positive	Neutral	Kugler et al (2015)
	2011	19 & 21 months	Experimental	Positive	Neutral	Positive	Positive	Positive	Neutral	Attanasio et al. (2011)
	2008	19 & 21 months	Experimental	Positive	Neutral	Positive	Positive	Positive	Positive	Attanasio et al. (2008)
DR: Juventud y Empleo	2016	12-18 months	Experimental	Positive	Negative			Positive	Neutral	Acevedo et al. (forthcoming)
		42-48 months	Experimental	Neutral	Neutral	Neutral	Negative	Neutral	Neutral	
	2015	6 years	Experimental	Neutral	Neutral	Neutral	Positive	Neutral	Positive	Ibarrarán et al. (2015)
	2012	18 to 24 months	Experimental	Neutral	Neutral	Neutral	Positive	Positive	Neutral	Ibarrarán et al. (2014)
	2011	10-14 & 22-24 months	Experimental	Neutral	Neutral	Positive	Positive	Positive	Positive	Card et al. (2011)
MEX: Probecate/ Becate	2010	3-6 months	Non experimental	Positive	Positive			Positive	Positive	Van Garmeren (2010)
	2006	3-6 months	Non experimental	Neutral	Neutral	Positive	Positive	Neutral	Neutral	Delajara et al. (2006)
	2001	16-20 months	Non experimental					Positive	Positive	Calderon-Madrid and Trejo (2001)
	1999	1 year	Non experimental	Neutral	Neutral			Neutral	Neutral	Wodon and Minowa (1999)
PAN: ProCaJoven	2007	9-20 months	Natural Experiment	Neutral	Neutral	Neutral	Neutral	Positive	Positive	Ibarrarán and Rosas(2007)
PER: ProJoven	2016	3 years	Experimental	Neutral	Neutral	Positive	Neutral	Neutral	Neutral	Díaz and Rosas (2016)
	2006	6, 12 & 18 months	Non experimental	Positive	Positive	Positive	Positive	Neutral	Neutral	Diaz and Jaramillo (2006)
	2002	12 & 18 months	Non experimental	Positive	Positive	Positive	Positive	Positive	Positive	Ñopo and Saavedra (2002)
URY: Opcion Joven	2002	1 year	Experimental	Positive	Positive	Positive	Positive	Positive	Positive	Naranjo Silva (2002)

Note: ● Positive, robust and significant results, ● Neutral or non-significant results, ● Negative, robust and significant results. Author- preferred results were used.

Sources: OECD/ECLAC/CAF based on Wodon and Minowa (1999); Calderon-Madrid and Trejo (2001); Naranjo Silva (2002); Aedo and Nuñez (2004); Aedo and Pizarro Valdivia (2004); Alzúa, Nahirñak, and Alvarez de Toledo (2007); Alzúa and Brassolio (2006); Ñopo and Saavedra (2002); Delajara, Freije and Soloaga (2006); Díaz and Jaramillo (2006); Ibarrarán and Rosas (2007) ; Acero, C., et al. (2009); Ibarrarán and Rosas (2009); Card et al. (2011), Puentes and Urzúa (2010); Van Garmeren (2010); Robalino et al. (2013); Vezza (2014); Attanasio, Kugler and Meghir (2015, 2011, 2008); Hernani-Limarino and Villarroel (2015); Ibarrarán et al. (2015, 2014); Kugler et al. (2015); Alzúa, Cruces and Lopez Erazo (2015); Acevedo et al. (forthcoming); CAF (2016); Díaz and Rosas (2016).

Programmes that offer training for self-employment and entrepreneurship, combine technical skills with soft skills training and operate in parallel to the regular bureaucracy seem to have a better impact on employability than programmes without these elements. Almost two-thirds of programmes that offered soft skills training had positive effects on employment, which is similar to the results of programmes operating in parallel to the regular bureaucracy. Moreover, half of the programmes that offer training for entrepreneurship and self-employment boost employability of the beneficiary group.

While youth training programmes focus mainly on employment, it is also interesting and relevant to consider their effects on job quality. The impact evaluations analysed in this section show that youth training programmes have been more successful at offering beneficiaries higher probability of formal employment than at leading to employment itself. Both the evidence of experimental and non-experimental impact evaluation programmes find positive and statistically significant effects on the quality of employment (formal employment), with a few exceptions. Job quality turned into one of the most important aspects of these programmes. This is especially relevant given that labour markets are becoming increasingly divided between formal and informal workers, and that informality is higher for youth than for adults.

In Dominican Republic, for example, the programme had a positive impact on job formality for men of about 17% (Ibarrarán et al., 2015). In Peru, the probability of having a job with health insurance and of having a pension increased by 3.8 and 3.3 percentage points, respectively, for the treatment group when compared to the control group (Díaz and Rosas, 2016). Moreover, the *Jovenes en Acción* evaluation shows that those who had lower average education before the programme benefited substantially more from training in terms of formal sector employment (Kugler et al., 2015).

Working at firms, support for job search and job placement services emerge as particularly important in terms of formality. This might imply that singling out employability and having better information on current openings help beneficiaries gain insight into the hiring process of the formal sector and to accessing quality jobs. Moreover, out of the four programmes evaluated that offer training for entrepreneurship and self-employment, three have positive impacts on job quality for the entire beneficiary group and one has positive impact for a subgroup (making entrepreneurship skills relevant for providing better jobs to youth).

Considering the programmes' effects on labour earnings is equally important since youth training interventions target youth at the lower distribution quintiles. Impact evaluations show mixed results both among programme results and demographic groups. While the programme evaluation in Mexico found small positive wage effects for salaried workers, *Chile Joven* had positive and significant effects on labour earnings with differences across gender. While male earnings were higher in absolute terms in Chile, the post-treatment increase proved to be more important for women since it represented a larger percentage of their initial income (Aedo and Pizarro Valdivia, 2004). In Panama, the evaluation observed a significant impact related to both gender and region: women living in Panama City increased labour earnings (Ibarrarán and Rosas, 2007). And, in Colombia, the earnings impact was only positive and statistically significant for women (Attanasio, Kugler and Meghir, 2015; Kugler et al., 2015). Moreover, lower bound estimates of the impact of training on formal sector earnings are strongest not only for women, but also among applicants with below-average educational attainment (Kugler et al., 2015).

The average earnings of those beneficiaries employed could have increased for several reasons. The programme training may have increased worker productivity; or the intervention may have increased employability and changed the composition of those working towards higher rates in the formal sector. Results from Colombia suggest that about two-thirds of the rise in salaries can be attributed to the increased earnings among those employed who participated of the programme relative to those who did not

(Attanasio, Kugler and Meghir, 2008). Likewise, the 2015 evaluation of *Jóvenes en Acción* suggests the programme might have improved productivity in the formal sector of the female youth who participated in the programme (Attanasio, Kugler and Meghir, 2015).

Studies find complementarity between vocational training and formal education, especially among trainees with above-average baseline education. This result underlines the notion that skills build upon skills (Heckman, 2000). However, evaluations show very strong long-term effects on employment and earnings outcomes among applicants with below-average baseline education; among this group, training did not affect tertiary education enrolment or retention after participation.

Overall, the literature on impact evaluations reviewed in this section shows that combining dual training – especially providing youth with a first on-the-job experience – and labour intermediation services has positive results for employability, formality and earnings. Early experiences have also shown it is essential to engage the private sector in developing course content to ensure that graduates have learned useful skills for the workplace. Although these interventions have been more successful at increasing formality than employability and earnings, some components contribute to improving these outcomes (Table 4.9). At the same time, the interaction of the design components and programme implementation is important for success.

Table 4.9. **Components and outcomes in youth training programmes in Latin America and the Caribbean**

		Employability	Formality	Earnings
Components	**Labour intermediation services**			
	Information / counselling	Effective	Neutral given mixed results	Neutral given mixed results
	Support for job search	Neutral given mixed results	Effective	Effective
	Job placement	Effective	Effective	Effective
	Public works	Neutral given mixed results	Neutral given mixed results	Neutral given mixed results
	Training for unemployed			
	School based training	Neutral given mixed results	Neutral given mixed results	Neutral given mixed results
	School + work experience	Neutral given mixed results	Effective	Effective
	Workplace training	Neutral given mixed results	Effective	Neutral given mixed results
	For self-employment	Effective	Effective	Effective
	Soft skills training	Effective	Effective	Effective
	Training for active workers	Neutral given mixed results	Neutral given mixed results	Neutral given mixed results
Mechanism	**Service provision**			
	Dual training and labour intermediation	Effective	Effective	Effective
	Dual training	Neutral given mixed results	Neutral given mixed results	Neutral given mixed results
	Single training option	Not effective	Not effective	Not effective
	Demand driven	Effective	Effective	Effective
	Demand and supply driven	Effective	Effective	Effective
	Supply driven	Not effective	Not effective	Not effective
	Stipend to participants			
	Transport/ lunch/health insurance	Effective	Effective	Effective
	Income support	Neutral given mixed results	Effective	Effective
	Publicly funded training	Effective	Effective	Effective
	Provision of training courses			
	Public	Effective	Effective	Effective
	Private	Effective	Effective	Effective
	Internships arranged by training provider	Neutral given mixed results	Effective	Effective

Note: = ● Effective ● Neutral given mixed results ● Not effective.
Sources: OECD/ECLAC/CAF, 2016, based on programme evaluations (see Table 4.8).

Differences across demographic groups

Programme impacts differ across gender, age, education attainment and place of residence. For most programmes, employability, formality and earning effects were different among subgroups. Youth training programmes had greater impact on the most disadvantaged such as women, youngest and lowest educated.

Women seem to benefit more in terms of employability and earnings, while men benefit from job quality. The impact of Chile Joven on the probability of employment was particularly important for women, while the impact on the probability of obtaining a formal job appears to be greater for men (Aedo and Pizarro Valdivia, 2004). Similarly, evidence from Argentina's *Entra 21* experimental evaluation, which focuses exclusively on formal employment, showed stronger effects for males and for younger participants over the whole period than the average effect for the full sample (Alzúa Cruces and Erazo, 2015).

Evaluations of *Jóvenes en Acción* showed the programme had a strong impact on labour market outcomes for women: higher employment, higher earnings and higher formality rates; while its impact on males was unclear (Attanasio, Kugler and Meghir, 2011). Likewise, Acevedo et al. (forthcoming) found that women participants of Dominican Republic's *Juventud y Empleo* benefited more than men in terms of employment and wages. Moreover, women had substantially higher soft skills and better labour market outcomes than men three years after programme completion.

Location plays an important role, too. In Panama and Dominican Republic the programmes had little impact outside the big cities. This is partly because those areas do not have fully functioning labour markets (Ibarrarán and Rosas, 2007; Diaz and Rosas, 2016).

Long-term effects

A new wave of impact evaluations brings light to the question of whether effects are sustained over time. Contrary to results of other long-term impact evaluations in the United States and Europe, several evaluations in LAC have shown positive and significant results after several years of treatment. Still, results vary among LAC countries and demographic groups within countries.

In Colombia, gains of youth training programmes proved to be stable over time and seem to be permanent (Attanasio, Kugler and Meghir, 2015). Training programmes showed positive impact on formal earnings in the short term that do not diminish in the medium and long term. As for short-term results, the effects on being employed in the formal sector and duration of formal employment are larger for women than for men. In addition, those who started with less education benefit most from the training lottery in terms of their formal employment in the medium to long term (Kugler et al., 2015). Likewise, the likelihood of formal employment is the same in the short and long term for women and men. For those with baseline educational attainment below the average, the effect also persists over time. However, for those with above average education at baseline, the effect becomes smaller over time, showing evidence of decline; perhaps this is because the group has a higher fraction of lottery winners that attends and remains in tertiary education (Kugler et al., 2015).

The first experimental and long-term impact evaluation of Peru's *ProJoven* programme showed a long-term positive impact on formality: the programme increased the opportunities of finding a formal job in a context of high labour informality (Díaz and Rosas, 2016). According to the authors, the results in formality levels are noteworthy for their magnitude and longevity; impacts were observed three years after beneficiaries completed the programme.

In Dominican Republic, one of the the long-term impact evaluations of the *Juventud y Empleo* programme found the intervention supports formal employment of males. It also has a positive impact on earnings for women and men living in Santo Domingo, the main urban centre that has a dynamic economy; this suggests that impact is more positive where there is an actual demand for skills (Ibarrarán et al., 2015). Additionally, the study revealed that the higher likelihood of participants having formal jobs in the short term seems to gain strength over time. Acevedo et al. (forthcoming), in another long-term evaluation, found strong and lasting effects on soft skills and expectations with differences between young men and young women. Shortly after completing the programme, both male and female participants experienced a strong increase in their soft skills and employment expectations. Three years later, women still exhibited higher levels of soft skills while results are reversed for male participants.

Similarly, in Colombia, Kugler et al. (2015) demonstrate that the employment and earnings impacts of training participation amplify rather than diminish over time, at least for the eight years after randomisation. Additionally, the earnings effects are also persistent for women and the less educated. In contrast, the results show depreciation of earnings gains over the long term for men and for those with above-average educational attainment at baseline. This could be because men, and those more educated to begin with, end up attending, and staying in, university; thus, this may be a group that is working and studying simultaneously and whose earnings capture employment in temporary jobs (Kugler et al., 2015).

Estimates of impact three years after programme completion in Argentina show that the sizeable and statistically significant effects in the short term decrease over time. The stronger effect found for males and for younger participants in the medium term seem to wind down in the long run (Alzúa, Cruces and Erazo, 2015).

Long-term evaluations also find that skills acquisition and changed expectations from vocational training complement, rather than substitute, formal educational investments, particularly in tertiary education. Training participation also has positive spillover effects on participants' family members (Kugler et al., 2015).

Cost-benefit analysis

Several impact evaluations found that direct benefits exceed direct cost. The cost-benefit exercise by Aedo and Nuñez (2004) for *Proyecto Joven* in Argentina suggested that, all things being equal, a longer time period for benefits generated a smaller discount rate, a lower ratio of indirect to direct costs and a greater net present value (NPV). Young males and adult females, who present higher and statistically significant earning impacts, required only nine years of programme benefits to achieve a positive NPV. After 12 years, all beneficiaries had reached a positive NPV.

The cost-benefit analysis suggests Colombia's programme generated a large net gain, much larger than that found in developed countries, especially for women. Attanasio,Kugler and Meghir (2011) concluded that no skill depreciation attributes a 29% internal rate of return. Kruger et al. (2015) found that the implied internal rates of return are 19.1% for females and 30.1% for males.

It is difficult to extract common conclusions from programmes that have many particularities, both in their design, components and target groups, as well as in the context for application. Still, some elements are worth highlighting. Most of the evaluated LAC youth training programmes have been successful with sustained effects either in terms of employment, formality or labour earnings. The findings discussed in this section underline that training by itself has benefits for disadvantaged groups.

Overall, results suggest that youth training programmes that combine classroom and apprenticeship time with pay-for-performance incentives are an attractive social investment and a potential avenue for social mobility (Kugler et al., 2015). Youth training programme evaluations in LAC serve as useful policy evidence for future policy design. However, impact evaluation and cost-benefit analysis fail to compare their results with the potential outcomes of reinserting youth back into the formal education system.

Evidence on youth training programmes: General findings from the metadata analysis

Identifying the specific characteristics that explain the success of a particular set of labour market interventions is difficult. Yet meta-regression analysis reports and comprehensive reviews of active labour market policies (ALMPs) – including youth training programmes – have jointly examined individual impact evaluations to identify potential elements that can positively affect beneficiaries of ALMPs. These studies are valuable because they use individual experimental and quasi-experimental impact evaluations that assess labour market performance of individual participation in ALMPs and identify what does and does not work.

With respect to overall programme type, evidence from worldwide ALMP studies suggests that, in the long run, programmes that emphasise human capital accumulation have larger gains (Card, Kluve and Weber, 2015; ILO, 2016; Kluve, 2016). In fact, work-first programmes tend to have more significant short-term effects, while training programmes have small, or even negative, short-term impacts, but larger impacts in the medium or longer term – two to three years after programme completion (Card, Kluve and Weber, 2015; Kluve, 2016).

Analysis of training programmes adds further evidence on programme design. Programmes that show better results target a specific group, provide integrated services with multiple skills training (including in-class, work place and non-cognitive skills training), establish market mechanisms to define the demand for training services and use private providers (Puentes and Urzúa, 2010). Other important elements are participation incentives and social protection support, particularly for young beneficiaries (Puentes and Urzúa, 2010).

Across these studies, the most salient aspect to highlight is the positive effect of integrated training systems. Lack of integration among the various training activities potentially offered to participants (in-class and workplace skills; cognitive, technical and social skills) undermines effectiveness (Puentes and Urzúa, 2010). Training activities should be organised to allow a systemic progression of beneficiaries at different levels; each activity should offer a variety of services focused on specific deficiencies. Such a structure would improve the chances for better results.

Meta-analysis suggests that programme duration is central for successful training programmes (ILO, 2016; Kluve, 2016).Within training interventions in LAC, programme duration emerged as a key design factor to enhance effectiveness, even more important than individual components. Evidence shows that interventions shorter than four months are less likely to show positive treatment effects. This pattern seems to hold regardless of whether there were one, two, three or more training components included in the intervention (Kluve, 2016).

Similar results were found when analysing interventions that target youth specifically. In general, ALMPs worldwide targeting youth proved to be effective tools for improving labour market outcomes for young people (Betchmerman et al., 2007; Kluve et al., 2014; Card, Kluve and Weber, 2015). The systematic review of 97 ALMP programmes targeted at youth worldwide by Kluve et al. (forthcoming) shows that investing in youth through skills training programmes pays off and leads to positive employment and earning outcomes. Moreover, comprehensive training interventions tend to increase the probability of positive labour market outcomes for trainees compared with in-classroom training only (Fares and Puerto, 2009).

Furthermore, strong evidence supports the view that youth skills training interventions in low- and middle-income countries have positive labour market outcomes for beneficiaries, especially women. In particular, interventions that combine services tend to be more successful than single training programmes (Kluve et al., forthcoming). The six studies reviewed for this report showed that youth programmes in low- and middle-income countries increased the probability of employment, increased job quality and led to higher earnings; female participants benefited more than males. However, evidence is less clear on employment duration (Fares and Puerto, 2009; Puentes and Urzúa, 2010; Kluve et al., 2014; Card, Kluve and Weber, 2015; ILO, 2016; Kluve, 2016).

The "Jovenes" programmes in Latin America and the Caribbean, Job Corps in the United States and the New Deal in the United Kingdom all enjoyed relatively good performance. This provides further evidence to support the argument that integrated skills training services can have a significant impact on the employability of trainees, particularly among youth.

Improved impact evaluations of training programmes will allow for better analysis of key programme design aspects

Six issues need better answers before governments can improve youth training programmes. Studies have not conveyed enough evidence to assess the quality of training programmes; the impact of specific components, their duration and interaction among them; the importance of profiling mechanisms; the impact of soft skills training on labour market outcomes; the spillovers and general equilibrium effect of training programmes; and cost-effective analysis.

Meta-analysis studies and comprehensive reviews of both training programmes and ALMPs generally conclude that the impact evaluation design method (experimental or quasi experimental) has no statistical impact on results obtained. Similar outcomes are observed using both methods (Card, Kluve and Weber, 2015; ILO, 2016; Kluve et al., forthcoming).

Additionally, most of them agree the quality of these evaluations needs to be improved (Puentes and Urzúa, 2010). Evaluation should be planned as a central element during the programme design phase, and not added at the end. International evidence is particularly important in this matter. Experiences from around the world show that including evaluations in the initial design and considering long-term monitoring for beneficiaries – and a control group – are key to collecting quality data (Puentes and Urzúa, 2010).

Conclusions and policy recommendations

Education and skills are a significant engine of economic growth and source of equality and social mobility. Latin American inequity is a cause and consequence of uneven access to and quality of education and – later in life – labour market participation. Education is the main source of skills acquisition. Primary and secondary education are the necessary building blocks to acquire skills. Meanwhile, tertiary education provides specialised skills playing an important role in the development process of countries. In fact, skills and education are among the determining factors to help countries overcome the middle-income trap.

Education and skills are critical to support youth inclusion and successful labour market participation. Quality education, which provides foundational and technical skills, endows youth with tools to participate in and enjoy adult life fully. It is one of the main instruments to ensure that youth are socially, politically and productively included in society.

Despite significant progress, overall education and skills endowment of the population in LAC remain poor. Quality and pertinence of education and skills offered by educational systems in the region are still a major issue. There are indications of a dearth of skills required by employers. While traditional education lags behind in terms of basic reading, mathematics and science skills, TVET is still too underdeveloped, focused on outdated sectors and of low quality to offer a viable solution to the skills deficiencies of the young population. Additionally, the lack of linkages between tertiary education and skills demanded by the labour markets remains a major cause of concern.

Many young Latin Americans leave school too early. The region's high secondary school dropout rates and low tertiary education completion rates call for policy action.

Training for youth in the region has tried to solve failures in the education system rather than to offer practical skills and update capabilities of workers. The huge education gap among youth compared with the relatively low size of training programmes calls for rethinking the role of training interventions in the region. Should youth training continue trying to make up for a lack of formal education? Or is it more efficient and cost-effective to reroute youth back into the education system? In the meantime, more than 43 million young individuals aged 15-29 lack the skills to fully participate in labour markets. As broader reforms of the education system improve its coverage, quality and pertinence, alternative human capital policies should support the current generation of low-skilled youth who are out of the formal education system.

These challenges call for policies for promoting youth education and skill acquisition. Some recommendations emerging from the chapter follow below:

Put in place efficient skills supply and demand data collection systems. Lack of country-level comparable data on both individual skills and those demanded by enterprises hinders governments' capacity to solve the current skills mismatch. With only few individual efforts from countries and international organisations, there is little knowledge on literacy, numeracy, problem solving and technical skills capacity in LAC. Information is also lacking on what types of higher level technical and professional skills businesses in the region require now and in future. This information is the building block for countries to identify skills shortages and gaps, and plan for future skills needs to become more productive and competitive.

Enforce clear quality standards for public and private education. Quality primary and secondary education will provide all students with the chance of continuing their path towards higher education studies. Clear standards are needed to ensure all students access quality education. Moreover, countries should invest more resources and better train teachers in schools attended by children of disadvantaged households to further narrow the education quality and skills gap.

Improve school and teacher mechanisms to identify students who are low performers and those who are struggling academically, economically and socially. Students who struggle are likely to drop out and have a smaller chance of advancing to higher education. Identifying these students early and offering solutions to their problems would help close learning gaps and avoid early exit.

Strengthen vocational and technical education by investing in better and more modern infrastructure, teacher training and mechanisms to identify labour market needs. Quality vocational and technical education is crucial to develop a highly skilled labour force. At the same time, practical and work-based vocational programmes can be more effective at appealing to youth disenchanted by academic education. TVET should, therefore, provide instruction in foundational skills and build mechanisms for TVET graduates to participate in higher education. At the same time, higher education curricula should be more flexible both to incorporate these students and allow for academic career changes.

Expand access to higher education. The region's education systems are struggling to supply enough skilled workers to raise productivity. In order to boost economic growth, improve social mobility and reduce inequality, LAC must invest in skilled youth. To do so, countries have to expand access to high-quality education by providing financing solutions that make quality higher education more affordable and accessible to all socio-economic groups.

Improve coherence and links between secondary and tertiary education to facilitate the transition from school to higher education. Such mechanisms can ensure that more young people in LAC who enrol in tertiary education attain a degree.

Develop education programmes that are more responsive to the needs of the marketplace. Training and education institutions should work with companies to ensure that occupational requirements are matched through adequate education and training. Demand-driven training programmes proved to be more successful than supply-driven throughout the region. This is a valuable lesson for future short training programmes, as well as for the overall education system. From early stages in life, youth should be exposed to the skills needed to participate in knowledge-based and skills-based economies. As such, academic education and TVET need to create more spaces to receive input from those who will demand skills in the future and further co-ordinate teaching curricula with business to align some of the content to the future demand for skills.

Expand programmes that combine classroom teaching with practical training and other active labour market services. The impact evaluations of youth skills interventions revealed the most successful programmes have a comprehensive design and offer institutional education, on-the-job training and intermediation services. The success of combining classroom with workplace learning of both soft and technical skills is relevant beyond the design of short vocational courses. It should inform the design of all TVET programmes from secondary to tertiary education, as well as academic tertiary education.

Systematise the use of robust impact evaluations in the early stages of education and training programmes. The lack of clear evidence of what specifically make academic, TVET and training programmes effective calls for better impact assessment strategies for future programmes. Evaluation should be planned as a central element of programmes during their design phase. International evidence is particularly important in this matter. Experiences from around the world show that including evaluations in the initial design and monitoring beneficiaries – and a control group – over the long term are key to collecting quality data.

Notes

1. Throughout this report, tertiary education refers to both university and post-secondary technical and vocational education.
2. STEP is a survey that measures skills in low- and middle-income countries (World Bank, 2016). It collects data on both employed and unemployed adults between the ages of 15 and 65 living in urban areas (World Bank, 2016). It is composed of two surveys – a household-based survey and an employer-based survey – to measure the supply and demand of skills to improve the understanding of skills and their connection with employability and productivity (World Bank, 2016). The household-based survey assesses reading proficiency; job-related skills possessed and used by the interviewee; and self-reported information on personality, behaviour, and time and risk preferences. To that end, it randomly selects an individual in the household to complete the individual questionnaire (Pierre, 2014). The employer-based survey evaluates the structure of the labour force; job-related skills being used; skills that employers look for when hiring new workers; training provided by employers; the link between skills and employee compensation; firms' background characteristics; and level of satisfaction with available education and skills training (Pierre, 2014; World Bank, 2016).

   STEP evaluated 2 435 individuals from Bolivia and 2 617 individuals from Colombia (World Bank, 2013a, 2013b). The sample population for Bolivia was taken from La Paz, El Alto, Cochabamba and Santa Cruz de la Cierra in which 0.11% of the eligible population were surveyed, ranging from 0.09% in El Alto to 0.14% in Cochabamba (World Bank, 2013a). In Colombia, the urban areas Bogota, Medellin, Cali, Barranquilla and Bucaramanga were included in the survey, as well as a probabilistic stratum composed of samples from the cities Cucuta, Ibague, Manizales and Villavicencio (World Bank, 2013b). In each of the five certainty metropolitan areas, 0.02% of the eligible population was included in the sample; 0.05% of the eligible population in each city was included in the probabilistic stratum (World Bank, 2013b). In El Salvador, where the reading assessment is not conducted, 2 335 individuals were surveyed (Cunningham, 2016).

   Peru conducts a similar survey, the *Encuesta Nacional de Habilidades* (National Skills Survey), which measures cognitive skills through verbal ability, verbal fluency, math and memory and socio-emotional skills through self-reported personality traits (World Bank, 2011; Cunningham, 2016). In 2010, this survey was given to 1 394 adults between the ages of 18-50 living in urban areas, on the coast and in the highlands, the jungle and Metropolitan Lima (World Bank, 2011; Cunningham, 2016).
3. The Skills and Trajectory Survey (STS), a survey to assess the relationship between education and the labour market, measures cognitive ability and socio-emotional skills, which include social skills, meta-cognitive strategies and self-efficacy (Bassi, 2012). The survey evaluates the association between education and skills to determine if higher educational attainment is related to greater cognitive abilities, as well as the relationship between skills and labour market outcomes (Bassi, 2012). It was administered to individuals between the ages of 25 and 30 in Argentina and Chile (Bassi, 2012). In 2010, 4 497 individuals in Argentina completed the survey (Bassi, 2012). At least 1 000 participants were from Buenos Aires, while the remaining were from Cordoba and Mendoza, with at least 300 individuals surveyed from each city (Bassi, 2012). In Chile, 1 800 individuals from the cities of Arica, Iquique, Antofagasta, Copiapo, La Serena, Coquimbo, the Valparaiso Metropolitan Area, Rancagua, Talca, the Concepción Metropolitan Area, Temuco, Padre Las Casas, Valdivia, Puerto Montt, Punta Arenas and the Santiago Metropolitan Area completed the survey in 2008 (Bassi, 2012).

References

Acemoglu, D. and J. Pischke (1999), "Beyond Becker: Training in imperfect labour markets", *The Economic Journal*, No. 109/453, Royal Economic Society, St. Andrews, pp. 112-142.

Acero, C. et al. (2009), "Evaluación de Impacto del Programa Jóvenes al Bicentenario para la cohorte de participantes en el año 2008", *PNUD*, Chile.

Acevedo, P. et al. (forthcoming), "Soft skills and hard skills in youth training programs: Long-term experimental evidence from the Dominican Republic", *CEDLAS Working Paper Series*, Universidad Nacional de La Plata, La Plata.

Acosta, P., N. Muller and M. Sarzosa (2015), "Beyond qualifications: Returns to cognitive and socio-emotional skills in Colombia", *Policy Research Working Papers*, No. WPS 7430, World Bank Group, Washington, DC.

Aedo, C. and S. Nuñez (2004), "The Impact of Training Policies in Latin America and the Caribbean: The Case of Programa Joven", *Working Paper (Research Network)*, Inter-American Development Bank, Research Department, Washington, DC.

Aedo, C. and M. Pizarro Valdivia (2004), "Rentabilidad económica del programa de capacitación laboral de Jóvenes Chile Joven" ["Economic performance of the training programme for youth, Chile Joven"], NACAP and Mideplan, Santiago de Chile.

Aedo, C. and I. Walker (2012), *Skills for the 21st Century in Latin America and the Caribbean*, Directions in Development, Human Development, World Bank Group, Washington, DC, https://openknowledge.worldbank.org/handle/10986/2236.

Aguayo, Y. (2007), *An Evaluation of Active Labor Market Policies in Developing Economies: The Mexican Case*, Digital Repository at the University of Maryland, University of Maryland, College Park, http://drum.lib.umd.edu/handle/1903/7330 (accessed 25 July 2016).

Albrecht, J. and S. Vroman (2002), "A matching model with endogenous skill requirements", *International Economic Review*, Vol. 43/1, Department of Economics, University of Pennsylvania and Osaka University Institute of Social and Economic Research Association, pp. 283-305.

Almeida, R., J. Behrman and D. Robalino (2012), *The Right Skills for the Job? Rethinking Training Policies for Workers*, Human Development Perspectives, World Bank Group, Washington, DC, https://openknowledge.worldbank.org/handle/10986/13075

Álvarez-Galván, J. (2015), "A skills beyond school r eview of Costa Rica", *OECD Reviews of Vocational Education and Training*, OECD Publishing, Paris, http://dx.doi.org/10.1787/9789264233256-en.

Alzuá, M.L. and P. Brassiolo (2006), *The Impact of Training Policies in Argentina: An Evaluation of Proyecto Joven*, Office of Evaluation and Oversight, Inter-American Development Bank, Washington, DC.

Alzúa, M.L., G. Cruces and C.L. Erazo (2015), "Youth training program beyond employment. Evidence from a randomized controlled trial", *CEDLAS Working Paper Series*, No. 177, Universidad Nacional de La Plata, La Plata.

Alzúa, M.L., P. Nahirñak and B. Alvarez de Toledo (2007), "Evaluation of Entra 21 using quantitative and qualitative data", *Q-Squared Working Paper*, No. 41, University of Toronto.

Attanasio, O., A. Kugler and C. Meghir (2015), "Long term impacts of vouchers for vocational training: Experimental evidence for Colombia", *Borradores de Economiá*, No. 896, Economic Studies Department, Central Bank of Colombia, Bogotá, www.banrep.gov.co/sites/default/files/publicaciones/archivos/be_896.pdf.

Attanasio, O., A. Kugler and C. Meghir (2011), "Subsidizing vocational training for disadvantaged youth in Colombia: Evidence from a randomized trial", *American Economic Journal: Applied Economics*, Vol. 3/3, American Economic Association, Pittsburgh, pp. 188-220.

Attanasio, O., A. Kugler and C. Meghir (2008), "Training disadvantaged youth in Latin America: Evidence from a randomized trial", *NBER Working Paper*, No. 13931, National Bureau of Economic Research, Cambridge, US.

Bassi, M. et al. (2012), *Disconnected: Skills, Education and Employment in Latin America*, Inter-American Development Bank, Washington, DC, https://publications.iadb.org/bitstream/handle/11319/427/Disconnected.%20Skills%2c%20Education%2c%20and%20Employment%20in%20Latin%20America.pdf?sequence=11.

Betcherman, G. et al. (2007), "A review of interventions to support young workers: Findings of the Youth Employment Inventory", *Social Protection Discussion Paper*, No. 0715, World Bank Group, Washington, DC.

Bowles, S., H. Gintis and M. Osborne (2001), "The determinants of earnings: A behavioral approach", *Journal of Economic Literature*, Vol. 39/4, American Economic Association, Pittsburgh, pp. 1137-1176, http://dx.doi.org/10.1257/jel.39.4.1137.

CAF (2016), *Más Habilidades para el Trabajo y la Vida: Los Aportes de la Familia, la Escuela, el Entorno y el Mundo Laboral* [More Skills for Work and Life: The Contributions of Family, School, Environment and Workplace], Development Bank of Latin America, Caracas.

Calderón-Madrid, A. and B. Trejo (2001), "The impact of the Mexican training programme for unemployed workers on re-employment dynamics and on earnings", *Research Network Papers*, Inter-American Development Bank, Washington, DC.

Card, D., J. Kluve and A. Weber (2015), "What works? A meta analysis of recent active labour market programme evaluations", *NBER Working Paper*, No. 21431, National Bureau of Economic Research, Cambridge, US.

Card, D., J. Kluve and A. Weber (2010), "Active labour market policy evaluations: A meta-analysis", *The Economic Journal*, Vol. 120/548, Royal Economic Society, St. Andrews, pp. F452–F477.

Card, D. et al. (2011), "The labour market impacts of youth training in the Dominican Republic", *Journal of Labour Economics*, Vol. 29/2, Elsevier, Amsterdam, pp. 267-300.

Cayapa (2002), "Empleo juvenil o reproducción de la pobreza en Venezuela," ["Youth employment or reproduction of poverty in Venezuela], *Revista Venezolana de Economía Social*, Vol. 2/3, pp. 1-23, www.saber.ula.ve/bitstream/123456789/18624/1/articulo3-4.pdf.

CEDLAS (2016), *Mapa de iniciativas laborales para jóvenes, [Map of Youth Labour Initiatives]*, www.labor-al.org/mapa-de-iniciativas-laborales-para-jovenes.html (accessed 12 August 2016).

CEPAL (2016), *Programas de Inclusión Laboral y Productiva [Programmes for Labour and Productive Inclusion]*, http://dds.cepal.org/bdilp (accessed 20 July 2016).

Cerutti, P. et al. (2014), "Social assistance and labour market programmes in Latin America: Methodology and key findings from the social protection database", *Social Protection and Labour Discussion Paper*, No. 1401, World Bank Group, Washington, DC.

Cohen, E., R. Martínez and C. Navarrete (2001), *Gestión de Programas Sociales en América Latina, Análisis de Casos [Management of Social Programmes in Latin America, Case Analysis]*, Vol. I: Proyecto Joven de Argentina, CEPAL, http://repositorio.cepal.org/bitstream/handle/11362/6001/1/S0102142_es.pdf.

Cunningham, W., P. Acosta and N. Muller (2016), *Minds and Behaviors at Work: Boosting Socioemotional Skills for Latin America's Workforce*, Direction in Development – Human Development, World Bank Group, Washington, DC.

Delajara, M., S. Freije and I. Soloaga (2006), "An evaluation of training for the unemployed in Mexico", *Working Paper*, OVE/WP-09/06, Inter-American Development Bank, Washington, DC.

De la Torre A., E. Levy Yeyati and S. Pienknagura (2013), "Latin America and the Caribbean as Tailwinds Recede: In Search of Higher Growth", *LAC Semiannual Report*, World Bank Group, Washington, DC.

De la Torre, A., J. Messina and S. Pienknagura (2012), *The Labor Market Story Behind Latin America's Transformation*, Semiannual Report, Regional Chief Economist Office, Latin America and the Caribbean, World Bank Group, Washington, DC.

Díaz, J.J. and M. Jaramillo (2006), "An evaluation of the Peruvian 'youth labour training programme' Projoven", Working Paper, OVE/WP-10/06, Inter-American Development Bank, Washington, DC.

Díaz, J.J. and D. Rosas (2016), "Impact evaluation of the Job Youth Training Programme Projoven", *Working Paper Series*, No. IDB-WP-693, Inter-American Development Bank, Washington, DC.

Drago, F. (2011), "Self-esteem and earnings", *Journal of Economic Psychology*, Vol. 32/3, Elsevier, Amsterdam, pp. 480-488.

Eichhorst, W. et al. (2012), "A roadmap to vocational education and training systems around the world", *IZA Discussion Papers*, No. 7110, Institute for the Study of Labor, Geneva.

Fares, J. and O.S. Puerto (2009), "Towards comprehensive training", *Social Protection Discussion Paper*, No. 0924, World Bank Group, Washington, DC.

Field S., V. Kis and M. Kuczera (2012), "A Skills Beyond School Commentary on Spain", *OECD Reviews of Vocational Education and Training*, OECD Publishing, Paris, www.oecd.org/education/vet.

Gasparini, L. et al. (2011), "Educational upgrading and returns to skills in Latin America: Evidence from a supply-demand framework, 1990-2010", *Policy Research Working Paper*, No. 5921, World Bank Group, Washington, DC.

Hanushek, E. (2015), "Why standard measures of human capital are misleading", *KDI Journal of Economic Policy*, Vol. 37/2, Korea Development Institute, Sejong, pp. 22-39.

Heckman, J. (2000), "Policies to foster human capital", *Educational Studies*, Issue 3, National Research University Higher School of Economics, Moscow, pp. 73-137.

Heckman, J., J. Stixrud and S. Urzúa (2006), "The effects of cognitive and noncognitive abilities on labor market outcomes and social behavior", *Journal of Labor Economics*, No. 24, Elsevier, Amsterdam, pp. 411-482.

Herani-Limarino, W. and P.M. Villarroel (2015), "Capitación Laboral y Empleabilidad, Evidencia de Mi Primer Empleo Digno" ["Job training and employability: Evidence from *Mi Primer Empleo Digno*], *Fundación ARU, Working Paper Series*, March, www.aru.org.bo/REPEC/pdf/capacitacion_laboral_y_empleabilidad.pdf.

Ibarrarán, P. et al. (2014), "Life skills, employability and training for disadvantaged youth: Evidence from a randomized evaluation design", *IZA Journal of Labour & Development*, Vol. 3/10, Springer, http://dx.doi.org/10.1186/2193-9020-3-10.

Ibarrarán, P. and D. Rosas (2009), "Evaluating the impact of job training programmes in Latin America: Evidence from IDB funded operations", *Journal of Development Effectiveness*, Vol. 1/2, International Initiative for Impact Evaluation (3ie), New Delhi, London, Washington, pp. 195-216.

Ibarrarán, P. and D. Rosas (2007), *Impact Evaluation of a Labour Training Programme in Panama*, Inter-American Development Bank, Washington, DC.

Ibarrarán, P. et al. (2015), "Experimental evidence on the long-term impacts of a youth training programme", *Working Paper Series*, No. IDB-WP-657, Inter-American Development Bank, Washington, DC.

IDB (2015), *Jobs for Growth*, Inter-American Development Bank, Washington, DC.

IDB (2011), PROEMPLEO: *Turning Challenges into Jobs in Honduras*, Inter-American Development Bank, Washington, DC, www.iadb.org/en/news/webstories/2011-12-20/proempleo-changes-challenges-to-jobs-in-honduras,9763.html, (accessed 25 July 2016).

ILO (2016), *Soluciones eficaces: Políticas activas de mercado de trabajo en América Latina y el Caribe [Effective Solutions: Active Labour Market Policies in Latin America and the Caribbean]*, International Labour Organization, Geneva.

ILO/CINTERFOR (forthcoming), *Vocational and Training Insitutions Survey*, Organización International del Trabajo/International Labour Organization and Centro Interamericano para el Desarrollo del Conocimiento en la Formación Profesional Montevideo.

ILO/CINTERFOR (2016a), *Programa Jóvenes con Futuro [Youth with a Future Programme]*, Organización International del Trabajo/International Labour Organization, Centro Interamericano para el Desarrollo del Conocimiento en la Formación Profesional and Ministry of Labor, Employment and Social Security, Argentina, www.oitcinterfor.org/experiencia/programa-j%C3%B3venes-futuro-mteyss-argentina (accessed 27 July 2016).

ILO/CINTERFOR (2016b), *Programa Jóvenes con Más y Mejor Trabajo [More and Better Jobs for Youth Programme]*, Organización International del Trabajo/International Labour Organization, Centro Interamericano para el Desarrollo del Conocimiento en la Formación Profesional and Ministry of Labour, Employment and Social Security, Argentina, www.oitcinterfor.org/experiencia/programa-j%C3%B3venes-m%C3%A1s-mejor-trabajo-mteyss-argentina (accessed 27 July 2016).

ILO/CINTERFOR (2016c), *Jóvenes en Acción [Youth in Action]*, SENA (National Training Service, Colombia), Organización Internacional del Trabajo/International Labour Organization, Centro Interamericano para el Desarrollo del Conocimiento en la Formación Profesional, Colombia, www.oitcinterfor.org/en/experiencia/j%C3%B3venes-acci%C3%B3n-youth-action-sena-colombia (accessed 21 July 2016).

ILO/CINTERFOR (2016d), *Programa de Formación Inicial: Modalidad Empresa-centro, [Initial Training Programme : Company – Center Modality]*, INSAFORP (Salvador Institute of Vocational Training), Organización Internacional del Trabajo/International Labour Organization and Centro Interamericano para el Desarrollo del Conocimiento en la Formación Profesional, El Salvador, www.oitcinterfor.org/experiencia/programa-formaci%C3%B3n-inicial-modalidad-empresa-centro-insaforp-salvador (accessed 18 July 2016).

ILO/CINTERFOR (2016e), *Bécate - Programa Becas para la Capacitación para el Trabajo, [Grants for Job-Training Programme]*, STPS (Secretariat of Labour and Social Provision, Mexico), Organización Internacional del Trabajo/International Labour Organization and Centro Interamericano para el Desarrollo del Conocimiento en la Formación Profesional, México, www.oitcinterfor.org/experiencia/b%C3%A9cate-programa-becas-capacitaci%C3%B3n-trabajo-stps-m%C3%A9xico (accessed 19 July 2016).

ILO/CINTERFOR (2016f), *Projoven. Ministerio de Trabajo y Promoción del Empleo - Perú [Pro-Youth, Ministry of Labor and Employment of Peru]*, Organización Internacional del Trabajo/International Labour Organization and Centro Interamericano para el Desarrollo del Conocimiento en la Formación Profesional, www.oitcinterfor.org/experiencia/projoven-ministerio-trabajo-promoci%C3%B3n-del-empleo-per%C3%BA (accessed 21 July 2016).

ILO/CINTERFOR (2007), *Chile Joven: Una Experiencia Pionera Revisada [Young Chile : A Groundbreaking Experience Revised]*, www.oitcinterfor.org/sites/default/files/file_articulo/bol139g.pdf (accessed 22 July 2016).

INADEH (2015), Instituto Nacional de Formación Profesional y Capacitación para el Desarrollo Humano, Panama, http://panamatramita.gob.pa/institucion/instituto-nacional-de-formaci%C3%B3n-profesional-y-capacitaci%C3%B3n-para-el-desarrollo-humano (accessed 14 July 2016).

INEFORP (2015), *Projoven, Programa de Capacitación Laboral para Jóvenes, [Pro-Youth, Youth Training Programme]*, Instituto Nacional de Empleo y Formación Profesional, Uruguay, www.inefop.org.uy/uc_28_1.html (accessed 17 July 2016).

INET (2016), Instituto Nacional de Educación Tecnológica [National Institute of Technological Education], Argentina, www.inet.edu.ar (accessed 20 June 2016).

INSAFORP (2015), "Programas de Formación Profesional para Jóvenes" ["Youth vocational training programmes"], El Salvador, www.insaforp.org.sv/index.php/programas-de-formacion-profesional/formacion-para-jovenes (accessed 15 July 2016).

Jensen, R. (2010), "The (perceived) returns to education and the demand for schooling", *The Quarterly Journal of Economics*, Vol. 125/2, Oxford University Press, pp. 515-548.

Kis, V., K. Hoeckel and P. Santiago (2012), *OECD Reviews of Vocational Education and Training: A Learning for Jobs Review of Mexico 2009*, OECD Publishing, Paris, http://dx.doi.org/10.1787/9789264168688-en.

Kluve, J. (2016), "A review of the effectiveness of active labour market programmes with a focus on Latin America", *ILO Research Department Working Paper*, No. 9, International Labour Organization, Geneva.

Kluve, J. et al. (forthcoming), *Interventions to Improve the Labour Market Outcomes of Youth: A Systematic Review of Training, Entrepreneurship Promotion, Employment Services and Subsidized Employment Interventions*, The Campbell Collaboration, Oslo.

Kluve, J. et al. (2014), *Interventions to Improve Labour Market Outcomes of Youth: A Systematic Review of Training, Entrepreneurship Promotion, Employment Services, Mentoring, and Subsidized Employment Interventions*, The Campbell Collaboration, Oslo, www.campbellcollaboration.org/lib/project/306.

Kugler, A. et al. (2015), "Long-term direct and spillover effects of job training: Experimental evidence from Colombia", *Working Paper*, No. 21607, National Bureau of Economic Research, Cambridge, US, www.nber.org/papers/w21607.pdf.

Lyche, C. (2010), "Taking on the completion challenge: A literature review on policies to prevent dropout and early school leaving", *OECD Education Working Papers*, No. 53, OECD Publishing, Paris, http://dx.doi.org/10.1787/5km4m2t59cmr-en.

Manpower Group (2015), *Talent Shortage Survey Research Results*, ManpowerGroup, Milwaukee, US.

McCarthy and Musset (2016), "A Skills Beyond School Review of Peru", *OECD Reviews of Vocational Education and Training*, OECD Publishing, Paris, http://dx.doi.org/10.1787/9789264265400-en.

Ministry of Education, Argentina (2013), *La Educación de Argentina en Cifras* (database), Dirección Nacional de Información y Evaluación de la Calidad Educativa (DINIECE), http://diniece.me.gov.ar (accessed 17 June 2016).

Ministry of Education, Chile (2014), *Publicaciones Estadísticas* (database), Unidad de Estadísticas, Centro de Estudios, División de Planificación y Presupuesto, http://centroestudios.mineduc.cl/tp_modulos/tpm_seccion/contVentana.php?cc=2196, (accessed 16 June 2016).

Ministry of Finance, Argentina (2014), Ministry of Housing and Public Finance, www.economia.gob.ar (accessed 18 July 2016).

Ministry of Labour, Argentina (2016), Youth programme, www.trabajo.gov.ar/jovenes (accessed 12 July 2016).

Ministry of Labour, Bolivia (2016), Ministry of Labour, http://empleo.gob.bo (accessed 19 July 2016).

Ministry of Social Development, Guatemala (2016a), Social programmes, http://mides.gob.gt/programas/blue/beca.html (accessed 21 July 2016).

Ministry of Social Development, Guatemala (2016b), Ministry of Social Development, http://mides.gob.gt/programas/blue/jovenes.html (accessed 21 July 2016).

Ministry of Social Development, Guatemala (2016c), *Jóvenes Protagonistas inicia talleres 2016*, http://mides.gob.gt/jovenes-protagonistas-inicia-talleres-2016 (accessed 21 July 2016).

Minowa, M. and Q. Wodon (1999), *Training for the Urban Unemployed: A Reevaluation of Mexico's Probecat*, World Bank, Washington, DC.

Musset, P. (2013), "A Skills Beyond School Commentary on Romania", *OECD Reviews of Vocational Education and Training*, OECD Publishing, Paris, www.oecd.org/education/vet.

Naranjo Silva, A. (2002), *Capacitación y formación profesional para Jóvenes en Uruguay: Los programmeas Opción Joven y ProJoven a través de sus experiencias de evaluación [Vocational Training for Youth in Uruguay: Assessment Experience from the Opción Joven and ProJoven Programmes]*, International Labour Organization, Geneva.

Ñopo, H. and J. Saavedra (2002), "Evaluación del impacto de mediano plazo de Projoven: Resultados de las mediciones realizadas a los seis, doce y dieciocho meses de culminado el programa" ["Medium -term impact assessment of Projoven: Measurements at six, twelve and eighteen months of programme culmination"], GRADE report, GRADE, Lima, Peru.

OECD (2016a), *Education in Colombia*, OECD Publishing, Paris, http://dx.doi.org/10.1787/9789264250604-en.

OECD (2016b), *A Skills Beyond School Review of Peru, OECD Reviews of Vocational Education and Training*, OECD Publishing, Paris, http://dx.doi.org/10.1787/9789264265400-en.

OECD (2016c), *Skills in Ibero-America Insights from PISA 2012*, OECD Publishing, Paris, www.oecd.org/latin-america/Skills-IberoAmerica.pdf.

OECD (2016d), *Skills Matter: Further Results from the Survey of Adult Skills*, OECD Publishing, Paris, http://dx.doi.org/10.1787/9789264258051-en.

OECD (2016e), *PISA Products* (database), www.oecd.org/pisa/pisaproducts (accessed 1 June 2016).

OECD (2016f), *Survey of Adult Skills (PIAAC)* (database), www.oecd.org/skills/piaac (accessed 1 June 2016).

OECD (2016g), *Education at a Glance 2016: OECD Indicators*, OECD Publishing, Paris, http://dx.doi.org/10.1787/eag-2016-en.

OECD (2015a), *Education at a Glance 2015: OECD Indicators*, OECD Publishing, Paris, http://dx.doi.org/10.1787/eag-2015-en.

OECD (2015b), *Strengthening the Employability of Youth during the Transition to a Green Economy, Investing in Youth: Tunisia*, OECD Publishing, Paris, http://dx.doi.org/10.1787/9789264226470-en.

OECD (2015c), *OECD Employment Outlook 2015*, OECD Publishing, Paris, http://dx.doi.org/10.1787/empl_outlook-2015-en.

OECD (2015d), *Skills for Social Progress: The Power of Social and Emotional Skills*, OECD Publishing, Paris, http://dx.doi.org/10.1787/9789264226159-en.

OECD (2014a), *Education at a Glance 2014: OECD Indicators*, OECD Publishing, Paris, http://dx.doi.org/10.1787/eag-2014-en.

OECD (2014b), *PISA 2012 Results: What Students Know and Can Do (Volume I, Revised edition, February 2014): Student Performance in Mathematics, Reading and Science*, OECD Publishing, Paris, http://dx.doi.org/10.1787/9789264208780-en.

OECD (2014c), "Skills Beyond School: Synthesis Report", *OECD Reviews of Vocational Education and Training*, OECD Publishing, Paris, http://dx.doi.org/10.1787/9789264214682-en.

OECD (2014d), *Investing in Youth: Brazil*, OECD Publishing, Paris, http://dx.doi.org/10.1787/9789264208988-en.

OECD (2013), *OECD Economic Surveys: South Africa 2013*, OECD Publishing, Paris, http://dx.doi.org/10.1787/eco_surveys-zaf-2013-en.

OECD (2012), *Better Skills, Better Jobs, Better Lives: A Strategic Approach to Skills Policies*, OECD Publishing, Paris, http://dx.doi.org/10.1787/9789264177338-en.

OECD/CAF/ECLAC (2014), *Latin American Economic Outlook 2015: Education, Skills and Innovation for Development*, OECD Publishing, Paris, http://dx.doi.org/10.1787/leo-2015-en.

OECD/IBRD/WB (2012), *Reviews of National Policies for Education: Tertiary Education in Colombia 2012*, OECD, International Bank for Reconstruction and Development and World Bank, OECD Publishing, Paris, http://dx.doi.org/ 10.1787/9789264180697-en.

Organización Internacional del Trabajo, Centro Interamericano para el Desarrollo del Conocimiento en la Formación Profesional (Cinterfor), www.inet.edu.ar (accessed 20 June 2016).

Pierre, G. et al. (2014), *STEP Skills Measurement Surveys, Innovative Tools for Assessing Skills*, The World Bank, Washington, DC, http://documents.worldbank.org/curated/en/516741468178736065/pdf/897290NWP0P132085290B00PUBLIC001421.pdf

Portal Brasil (2012), Brazil Ministry of Justice, www.brasil.gov.br/cidadania-e-justica/2012 (accessed 1 June 2016).

Puentes, E. and S. Urzúa (2010), "La Evidencia del impacto de los programmeas de capacitación en el desempeño en el mercado laboral" ["Evidence of the impact of training programmes in labour market performance], *Technical Note*, No. 268, Inter-American Development Bank, Washington, DC.

Puerto, O. (2007), *Labor Market Impact on Youth: A Meta-analysis of the Youth Employment Inventory*, World Bank, Washington, DC.

Quintini, G. and T. Manfredi (2009), "Going separate ways? School-to-work transitions in the United States and Europe", *OECD Social, Employment and Migration Working Papers*, No. 90, OECD Publishing, Paris, http://dx.doi.org/10.1787/221717700447.

Robalino, D. et al. (2013), "Youth employment: A human development agenda for the next decade", *Social Protection and Labour Discussion Paper*, No. 1308, World Bank Group, Washington, DC.

Rosas, D. (2006), "Impact Evaluation of PROJoven Youth Labor Training Program in Peru", Office of Evaluation and Oversight, Inter-American Development Bank, Washington, DC.

UNESCO (2016), *Education*, (database), UNESCO Institute of Statistics, Montreal, http://data.uis.unesco.org/Index.aspx?DataSetCode=EDULIT_DS (accessed 15 June 2016).

UNESCO (2015), *World TVET Database Mexico*, UNESCO-UNEVOC International Centre for Technical and Vocational Education and Training (database), www.unevoc.unesco.org/wtdb/worldtvetdatabase_mex_en.pdf (accessed 8 June 2016).

UNESCO (2014), *TVETipedia Glossary*, 2014, UNESCO-UNEVOC International Centre for Technical and Vocational Education and Training, www.unevoc.unesco.org/go.php?q=TVETipedia+Glossary+A-Z&article=What%2Bis%2BTVET (accessed 1 June 2016).

UNESCO (2013a), *Status Report on the Education Management Information Systems (EMIS) of Technical and Vocational Education and Training (TVET) in 12 Countries in Latin America and the Caribbean*, OREALC/United Nations Educational, Scientific and Cultural Organization, Santiago.

UNESCO (2013b), *World TVET Database Paraguay*, UNESCO-UNEVOC International Centre for Technical and Vocational Education and Training (database), www.unevoc.unesco.org/wtdb/worldtvetdatabase_pry_en.pdf (accessed 1 June 2016).

UNESCO (2013c), *World TVET Database Colombia*, UNESCO-UNEVOC International Centre for Technical and Vocational Education and Training (database), www.unevoc.unesco.org/wtdb/worldtvetdatabase_col_en.pdf, (accessed 8 June 2016).

UNESCO (2010), "Gender Issues and TVET", *TVETipedia*, UNESCO-UNEVOC International Centre for Technical and Vocational Education and Training, www.unevoc.unesco.org/tvetipedia.0.html?&tx_drwiki_pi1%5Bkeyword%5D=Gender%20issues%20and%20TVET (accessed 1 June 2016).

Van Gameren, E. (2010), *Evaluación de Impacto del Programa de Apoyo al Empleo,* [*Impact Evaluation of the Employment Support Programme*], Centro de Estudios Económicos el Colegio de México, www.stps.gob.mx/bp/secciones/evaluaciones_externas/internas/evaluaciones4/igPAE.pdf.

Vezza E. (2014), "Policy scan and meta-analysis: Youth and employment policies in Latin America", *CEDLAS Working Paper Series*, No. 156, Universidad Nacional de La Plata, La Plata.

Werner, L. et al. (2015), "Capacitación Laboral y Empleabilidad Evidencia de Mi Primer Empleo Digno" [Job Training and Employability Evidence from *Mi Primer Empleo Digno* Programme], *Working Paper Series,* Fundación Aru Publishing, www.aru.org.bo/REPEC/pdf/capacitacion_laboral_y_empleabilidad.pdf.

Wodon, Q. and M. Minowa (1999), "Training for the urban unemployed: A reevaluation of Mexico's PROBECAT, Government Programmes and Poverty in Mexico", *Report,* No. 19214-ME, Vol. II, World Bank, Washington DC.

World Bank (2016), *The STEP Skills Measurement Program*, World Bank, Washington, DC, http://microdata.worldbank.org/index.php/catalog/step/about (accessed 11 August 2016).

World Bank (2015), *World Bank Social Protection & Labor* (database), World Bank, Washington, DC, www.worldbank.org/en/topic/socialprotectionlabor (accessed 15 July 2016).

World Bank (2014), *A More Promising Future for Poor Youth in the Dominican Republic*, World Bank, Washington, DC, www.worldbank.org/en/results/2014/04/08/more-promising-future-poor-youth-dominican-republic (accessed 26 July 2016).

World Bank (2013a), *STEP Survey Weighting Procedures Summary, Bolivia*, World Bank, Washington, DC, http://microdata.worldbank.org/index.php/catalog/2011/related_materials, (accessed 12 August 2016).

World Bank (2013b), *STEP Survey Weighting Procedures Summary, Colombia*, World Bank, Washington, DC, http://microdata.worldbank.org/index.php/catalog/2012, (accessed 12 August 2016).

World Bank (2012), *Youth Employment Programmes: An Evaluation of World Bank and International Finance Corporation Support*, World Bank Group, Washington, DC, https://openknowledge.worldbank.org/handle/10986/12225.

World Bank (2011), *Strengthening Skills and Employability in Peru, Final Report*, https://openknowledge.worldbank.org/bitstream/handle/10986/12533/616990ESW0whit0ficial0Use0Only00090.pdf?sequence=1&isAllowed=y.

World Bank and GIZ (2015), *Linking Social Assistance and Productive Inclusion*, World Bank, Washington, DC.

Youth Employment Inventory (2016), Inventory website, www.youth-employment-inventory.org/inventory/browse/entrepreneurship/14 (accessed 12 July 2016).

Chapter 5

Youth entrepreneurship in Latin America and the Caribbean

Youth entrepreneurship can be a vehicle for enhancing individuals' employability and social mobility, while also inducing productive transformation. Whereas attitudes towards entrepreneurship are similar, Latin American young entrepreneurs tend to be less educated and come from more disadvantaged socio-economic backgrounds than in OECD economies. With fewer resources, skills and experience, they face higher barriers for business creation in accessing finance, acquiring entrepreneurial skills, integrating business networks, creating new markets and overcoming regulatory barriers. Public policy in these areas has improved entrepreneurship prospects to some extent. Programme evaluations suggest that youth entrepreneurship programmes have been effective for improving labour market outcomes. Strengthening those programme components which are most effective, such as business training, counselling and mentoring, can substantially improve the effectiveness of future programmes.

Introduction

Entrepreneurship and firm creation – important drivers of a country's productive structure – also enhance employment and social mobility. Entrepreneurs' activity is related, on the one hand, to technological progress, innovation, the adoption of better productive processes, access to new markets and efficiency gains in production and management. A country's productive structure and, ultimately, its productivity, rely largely on its capacity for linking entrepreneurship to key objectives of productive transformation. On the other hand, fostering entrepreneurship is a policy priority for improving employability and earning opportunities. It can tap into unexploited potential among specific groups, including youth, and be a driver of social mobility.

Entrepreneurship is particularly important for improving employment and living conditions among the young. With more than 163 million individuals aged 15-29 years, and only half of them employed, Latin America faces a challenge of creating work opportunities for this age group, particularly in the formal sector. Youth unemployment in Latin America remains twice as high as the overall global rate and three times that of adults in the region. Moreover, economic downturns are more likely to affect young individuals, given their higher propensity to temporary work.

Through entrepreneurship, young people can improve their capacity to integrate labour markets and bring about other positive externalities in the medium-term. Even if youth do not possess the experience or financial resources for entrepreneurship, for example, engaging in these activities can help them to acquire new skills and improve their well-being (Blanchflower and Oswald, 1998; Bandeira et al., 2013). Youth entrepreneurship can also counteract the detrimental effects of unemployment, which tends to increase the likelihood of poorer wages and unemployment in later life (OECD/EC, 2012). Besides creating jobs and enhancing innovation, young entrepreneurs in the region may become role models to their peers, providing direction to deprived communities or groups facing social exclusion.

The purpose of this chapter is threefold. First, it aims to compare the main characteristics of young entrepreneurs in Latin America with those of their counterparts in OECD economies. Besides looking at education, occupational and gender traits, the chapter contrasts the features of subsistence and high-growth entrepreneurs. Second, it describes the main barriers faced by youth when engaging in entrepreneurial activities, and the policies that have been implemented to tackle them, compared with the OECD experience. Third, it explores the evaluations of youth entrepreneurship programmes in Latin America and their implications for the programmes' design and implementation in the future. Finally, the chapter concludes with policy recommendations to make the most of public policies in this direction.

The face of young entrepreneurs in Latin America and OECD

Youth entrepreneurship is an important policy tool for improving material conditions and youth opportunities in Latin America. Just as developing the right set of skills can bring long-term benefits for an individual's job prospects and social mobility, youth entrepreneurship interventions can help build human capital, as well as increase innovation and create jobs (OECD, 2016). Policy makers have also supported youth entrepreneurship programmes to tap unexploited potential for entrepreneurship among young people (Green, 2013). Indeed, among Latin Americans, around one-fifth of the population between 15-29 years-old plans to start a business in the next 12 months (Gallup, 2016).

Youth entrepreneurship in Latin America is intrinsically related to the structure of the business fabric in the region. Small and medium-sized enterprises (SMEs) account for more than 80% of employment and more than 90% of firms in Latin America. However, large firms still contribute nearly 70% to the region's gross domestic product (GDP). These asymmetries between the distribution of employment and productivity – with a large share of workers concentrated in less dynamic firms – is also reflected in the structure of entrepreneurship projects in the region. Such "structural heterogeneity" can also be seen in persistent gaps for both enterprises and entrepreneurs in key areas including skills, adoption of technical developments and access to international networks (OECD/ECLAC, 2012).

Entrepreneurship in Latin America is extremely diverse, characterised by both subsistence and high-growth entrepreneurs (See Box 5.1 for definition of entrepreneurship). The difficulty of employability in Latin American countries – analysed in the first part of the report – becomes an obstacle for the creation, survival and growth of enterprises. More often than not, entrepreneurship creation is associated to informal micro-entrepreneurship; the region has not yet tackled the barriers that encourage the development of productive entrepreneurs. This trend is also observable for young entrepreneurs, who are confronted by similar barriers as their adult counterparts. If Latin America is known as a region of entrepreneurs, its large informal sector, the prevalence of subsistence entrepreneurs and the high turnover of firms in the region offers a mixed landscape. Still, subsistence entrepreneurship is largely a vehicle to help lower-middle-class households and the poor to cope with informality, scarce jobs in middle- and lower-end occupations, and public sector regulations and taxation (IDB/WB, 2014).

Box 5.1. **What we talk about when we talk about entrepreneurs**

Although consensus exists on the significant role of entrepreneurs for improving efficiency and market competition, the definition of entrepreneurial activity is less clear. Three main conceptions of entrepreneurship are presented in the literature. The first considers entrepreneurship as an enhancer for market creation through technology diffusion, innovation or market coordination. In this sense, the entrepreneur is a catalyst for economic growth, employment creation and competitiveness. The second focuses on risk-taking as the fundamental characteristic of the entrepreneur. The third stresses the individual's labour decisions; this considers entrepreneurs as people who administer their own business, and focuses on the definition of independent entrepreneurs (Hebert and Link, 1989). A challenge in the field is to employ a definition of entrepreneurship that remains as close as possible to these three concepts.

For this report, all self-employed persons are considered entrepreneurs (business owners) in one of two different categories: self-employed with no employees (own-account workers with no employees) and self-employed who employ other workers (self-employed who are employers).

The household surveys used in this report to identify labour decisions list (at least) five categories for the active population: i) employers (self-employed with at least one employee); ii) own-account workers without employees; iii) employees; iv) unemployed (actively searching for a job, but not finding one); and v) unpaid family workers. To be consistent with the definition above, and in line with recent entrepreneurship research (Praag and Versloot, 2007; Praag and Stel, 2011; Gasparini, Gluzmann and Jaume, 2012), entrepreneurs are defined as those individuals in the first two categories (employers and own-account workers).

The term *subsistence* entrepreneur, as opposed to *opportunity, high growth* or *transformational* entrepreneur, refers to those individuals who engage in entrepreneurial activity, but would prefer salaried employment to business ownership (Schoar, 2010). In this framework, subsistence entrepreneurs encompass a number of own-account workers, but also small family business structures. Not all own-account workers are "subsistence entrepreneurs", as self-employed include semi-skilled trades (e.g. carpenter, plumber) or individual consultants working for a larger company. On the other hand, the OECD defines *high*

Box 5.1. What we talk about when we talk about entrepreneurs (cont.)

growth firms as those companies with more than 10 employees and with an average growth of sales or employees above 20% in the last three years. This definition may change for some countries in the region.

Data from the Global Entrepreneurship Monitor (GEM) are also presented in this chapter, covering individuals who report they are planning to start or are already operating their own business or any type of self-employment. These differ from the self-employment data from labour and household surveys, as they include, for instance, owner-managers of incorporated businesses and individuals who may be running a business as a secondary activity (Figure 5.A1.2).

In contrast to OECD economies, a large number of young entrepreneurs in Latin America are own-account workers. If the share of employees and entrepreneurs who employ people is relatively similar in both Latin America and the OECD, workers in Latin America are more prone to being subsistence entrepreneurs than in OECD countries (16% of own-account workers to 6% on average, respectively, Figure 5.1). Not surprisingly, business ownership increases with age (Figure 5.A1.1) and the share of young entrepreneurs is lower than the share of adult entrepreneurs for all countries. Individuals who are own-account workers own businesses that tend to be smaller, employ fewer workers and are less productive (CAF, 2013; OECD, 2016b).

Figure 5.1. **Distribution of employed population by occupational category in Latin America and the OECD (aged 15-29 years)**

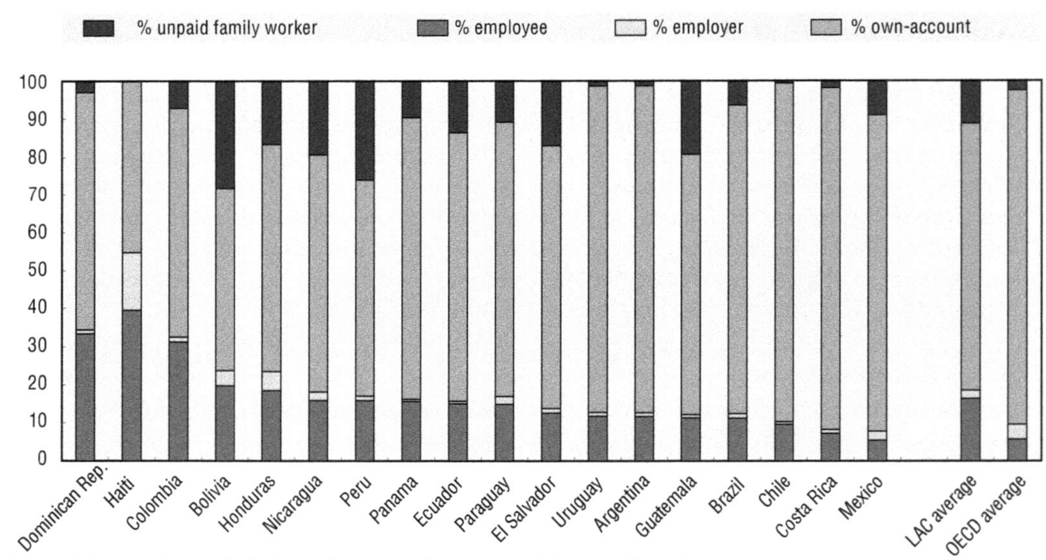

Source: OECD and WB tabulations of SEDLAC (CEDLAS and the World Bank).

StatLink http://dx.doi.org/10.1787/888933414575

Youth entrepreneurs from lower socio-economic backgrounds tend to face higher barriers than those from more advantaged households. In general, young Latin American entrepreneurs from low and middle-income households have fewer resources, skills and networks than those from more advantaged households, who tend to have had more exposure to business experience at an early stage, both from family and schooling. In comparison with entrepreneurs from middle-income households in other regions, Latin American entrepreneurs are believed to have less entrepreneurial role models (IDB/WB, 2014). As a result, they tend to rely on a support network that is poorly qualified for entrepreneurial activities.

Young Latin American entrepreneurs tend to be less educated, on average, than their counterparts in OECD economies. A comparison of entrepreneurs' educational background by age group shows that young entrepreneurs tend to be more educated than adults in both regions. The share of Latin American entrepreneurs having reached secondary schooling is comparable to OECD levels. However, the gap in tertiary education is pronounced, with only 13% of young entrepreneurs having some form of tertiary education in Latin America against 33% in OECD countries (Figure 5.2)[1]. Moreover, the distribution of young entrepreneurs in Latin America is also related to the socio-economic background (Figure 5.2, Panel C) with almost two times the share of own-account workers in extreme poverty than in the middle class. Heterogeneity in the entrepreneurs' profile in the region is associated with a complex interaction of factors, including family background, quest for independence, education, need for economic survival and risk-taking.

Figure 5.2. **Distribution of entrepreneurs by educational and socio-economic background**

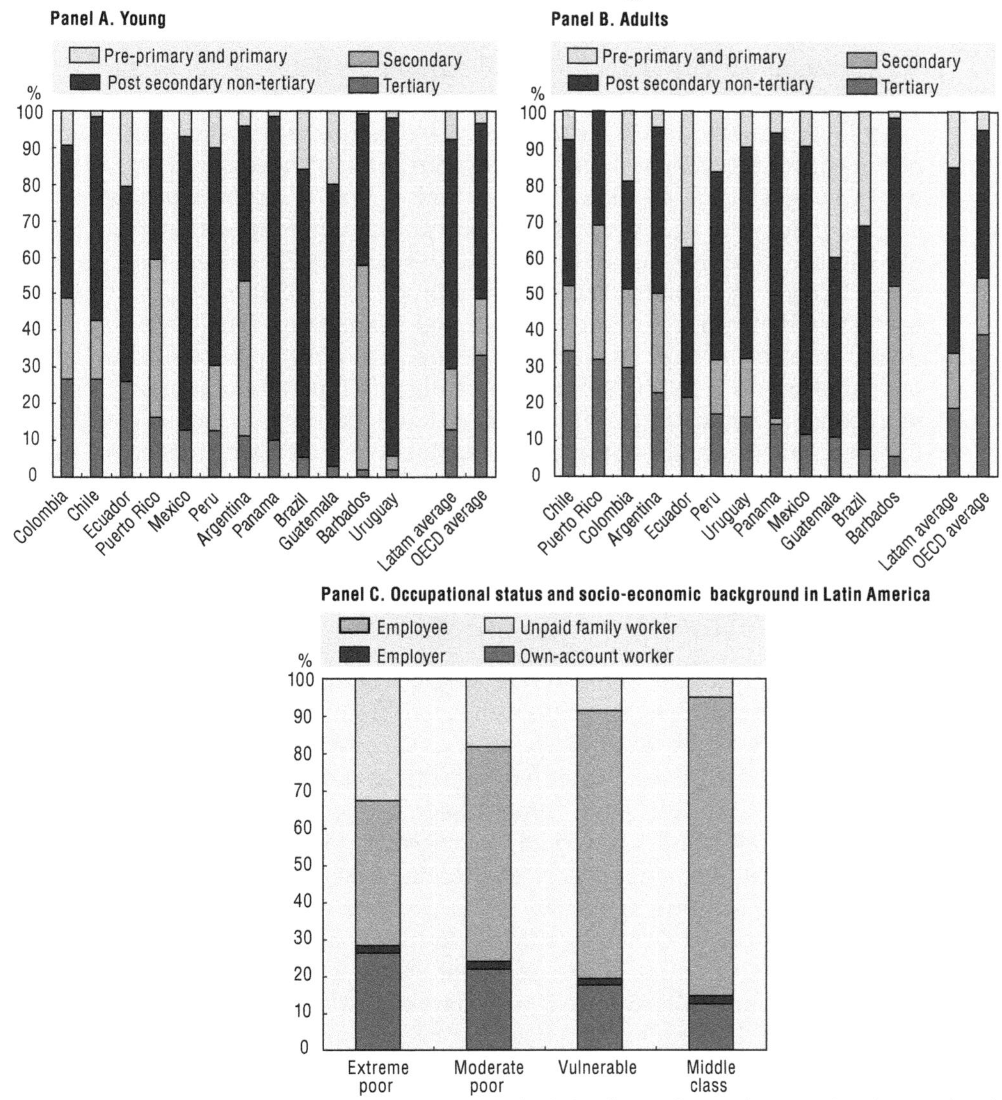

Note: Secondary includes lower and upper levels. Tertiary includes first and second stages of tertiary. Estimations of young (18-29 years) and adult (30-64) education levels for all TEA (Total Entrepreneurial Activity) in sample.

Source: OECD/ECLAC/CAF based on Global Entrepreneurship Monitor individual data, 2015 (Panels A and B) and OECD and WB tabulations of SEDLAC (Panel C).

StatLink http://dx.doi.org/10.1787/888933414582

The landscape for women entrepreneurs in Latin America and the Caribbean is mixed. Strong rates of female entrepreneurship in LAC, well above OECD averages, suggest the region's women perceive entrepreneurship as a potential and practical pathway to economic autonomy. Women are less likely than men to engage in entrepreneurship, but when they do they are more likely to do so out of necessity. Women entrepreneurs are also more likely to be own-account workers than employers, and have less education. Whereas in OECD economies over 10% of women are entrepreneurs, Chile (29%), Mexico (25%) Colombia (45%) and Peru (39% in urban areas) have significantly higher percentages (OECD, 2016c). Women in LAC experience greater difficulties, both perceived and real, in starting their own business compared with their counterparts in the OECD; however, regional gender gaps that favour men are relatively small across key areas of entrepreneurship, such as access to credit, access to business training or perceptions of difficulties in starting a business (OECD 2016c; Kelley et al., 2014). High confidence also reigns: half of women in the region believe they have the ability to start a business. All told, 75% of women entrepreneurs (at early-stage) work in the consumer, culture and society sectors, with smaller percentages working in extractive, business and transforming sectors.

Entrepreneurship is not fully delivering on its potential for economic autonomy and empowerment for women of the region, in particular for young women. Young women aged 25-29 globally, as well as regionally, are more likely to start their own business than other age cohorts. The reduced, and even reverse, gender gap in education in the region might suggest that women and men enjoy similar economic opportunities through entrepreneurship. Motivations and outcomes, however, differ by gender. This helps explain the lower impact and survival rates of female-run businesses. First, women are more likely to be concentrated in less productive sectors (e.g. manufacturing, public sector), which reflects other occupational segregation challenges in these economies linked in part to lower percentages of girls studying science, technology, engineering or mathematics (STEM). Second, entrepreneurship for women is often an antidote to workplace discrimination and other related barriers to access formal employment linked to discriminatory perceptions against young working mothers. Entrepreneurship is often perceived as a means of balancing work and care responsibilities: across the region, women perform over twice as much time on unpaid care work than men and, with both unpaid and paid work combined, work longer hours.

Similar attitudes in Latin America and the OECD towards entrepreneurship

Attitudes towards entrepreneurship in Latin America and OECD countries are similar. Recent studies on entrepreneurial talent have identified certain personality characteristics to be associated with a successful entrepreneur: creative thinking, management skills, goal-oriented objectives and a certain degree of risk-taking. At the same time, the environment seems to play an important role in enhancing entrepreneurial traits and could be relevant for understanding the differences in entrepreneurial behaviour between Latin America and other regions (Aboal and Veneri, 2016). Adverse or weaker environments could better allow the expression of personality traits, and therefore favour or hinder entrepreneurship behaviour. However, no significant differences are observed between Latin America and industrialised countries around allocation of entrepreneurial characteristics (CAF, 2013). Lack of entrepreneurial attitude, then, does not explain the difference in firms' distribution by size and productivity observed between Latin American and OECD countries. Rather, market failures and other factors explain the difference.

Both Latin American and OECD economies perceive entrepreneurial activities as enhancers of social status. The social status of occupational activities, which is associated with high social esteem, shows that job choice is affected by peers' perception. The group status of the profession "entrepreneurship" tends to shape people's occupational preferences and thus their choice behaviour. In this case, the status of the entrepreneur is associated with hard work and potentially high income, but lower education (Van Praag, 2009). The perception that successful entrepreneurs receive high social status applies to both Latin America and OECD economies, and the difference between youth and adults is relatively small (Figure 5.3). As most countries perceive entrepreneurship positively as an occupational choice, attitudes towards entrepreneurship alone do not explain the contrast in entrepreneurial activity between LAC and the OECD.

Figure 5.3. **Percentage of the population who agree with the statement that, in their country, successful entrepreneurs receive high status**

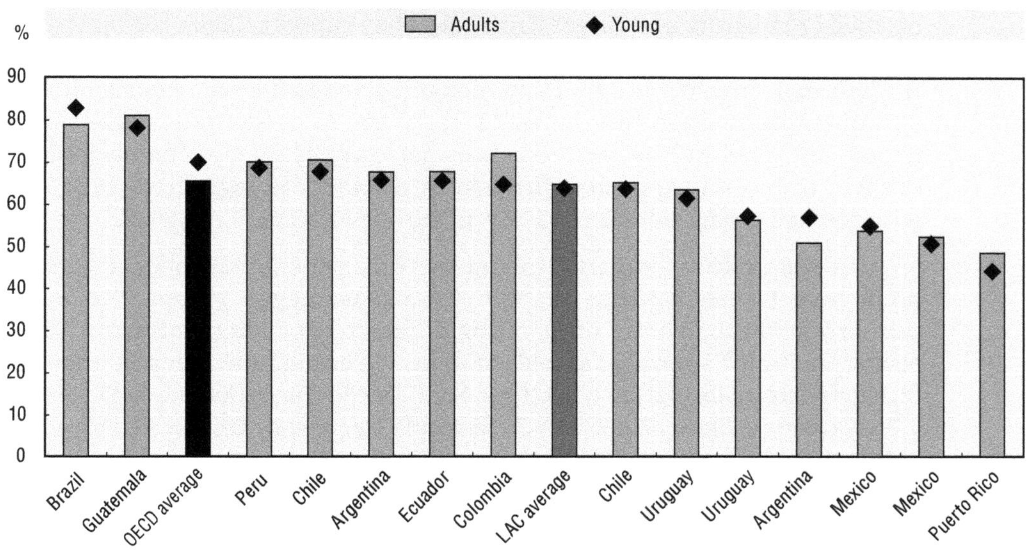

Source: OECD/ECLAC/CAF based on Global Entrepreneurship Monitor individual data, 2015.
StatLink http://dx.doi.org/10.1787/888933414593

Figure 5.4. **Entrepreneurial motivation in Latin American and Caribbean countries and OECD, 2015**

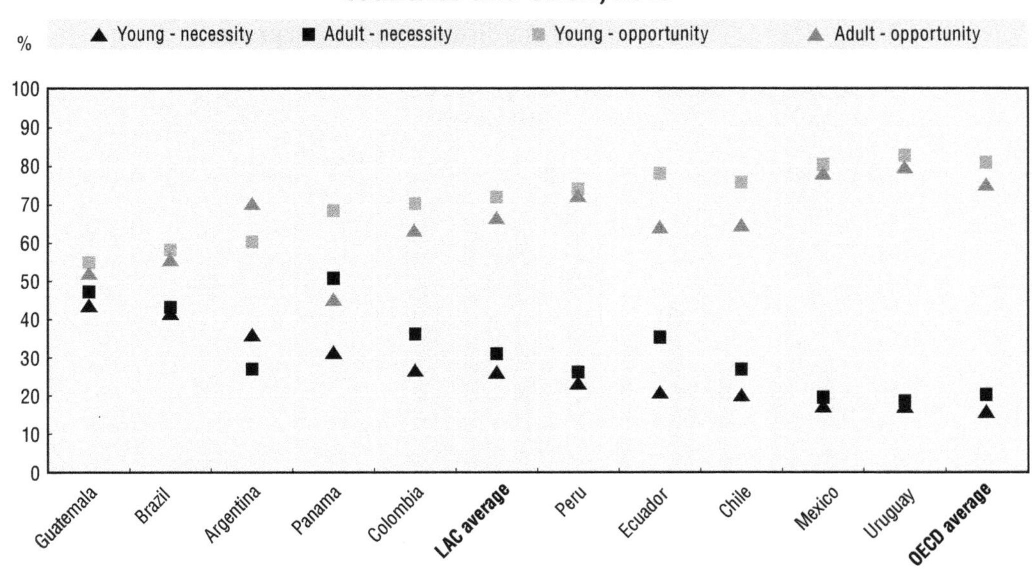

Source: OECD/ECLAC/CAF based on Global Entrepreneurship Monitor individual data, 2015 and Herrington, Kelley and Singer (2016).
StatLink http://dx.doi.org/10.1787/888933414605

In contrast, entrepreneurial activity in the region is more associated with lack of other employment alternatives in Latin America than it is in OECD economies (Figure 5.4). Indeed, entrepreneurial motivation in the region is different in Latin America from in OECD economies: necessity-driven entrepreneurship (e.g. no better options for work) among the young is, on average, higher than OECD countries (26% to 16%). Differences among countries remain significant.

Better targeting needed for youth entrepreneurship policies

While Latin America's entrepreneurial landscape is a complex one, the debate on the policy support for firms and entrepreneurs has gained importance in recent years. The heterogeneity observed among the region's entrepreneurs has raised questions about the best way to identify and target firms for policy support. Given the barriers small firms confront, they have generally been considered natural recipients of policy instruments. At the same time, while small and medium-sized firms are responsible for more than 80% of employment in Latin America, they tend to be less productive than large firms (Figure 5.5, Panel A). The gap tends to be narrower in OECD economies; the productivity of small firms relative to large firms in Latin America ranges from 16 to 36% compared with relative productivities of 63-75% in Europe (OECD/ECLAC, 2012).

If firm growth is an important dimension to consider, other policy objectives – including productive transformation, support for disadvantaged groups and inclusiveness – can also guide the choice of targeting different populations of firms. The technology sector illustrates several examples of fostering entrepreneurship in areas aligned with productive transformation objectives. For FONTEC (*Fondo Nacional de Desarrollo Tecnológico y Productivo*) in Chile or SENATYC (*Secretaria Nacional de Ciencia, Tecnologia e Innovacion*), policy support has been critical to promote clusters in certain industries. Policies could also be targeted at enhancing entrepreneurship among disadvantaged groups, including young, seniors or ethnic minorities. Fostering entrepreneurship among youth groups can also be instrumental in some countries of the region to be more inclusive. In Colombia, current peace negotiations underline the need to promote a smooth transition to the labour market for former conflict participants and victims. Entrepreneurship initiatives that expand job prospects and promote effective integration can be critical at this stage.

Figure 5.5. **Relative productivity and firm size of small and medium-sized enterprises**

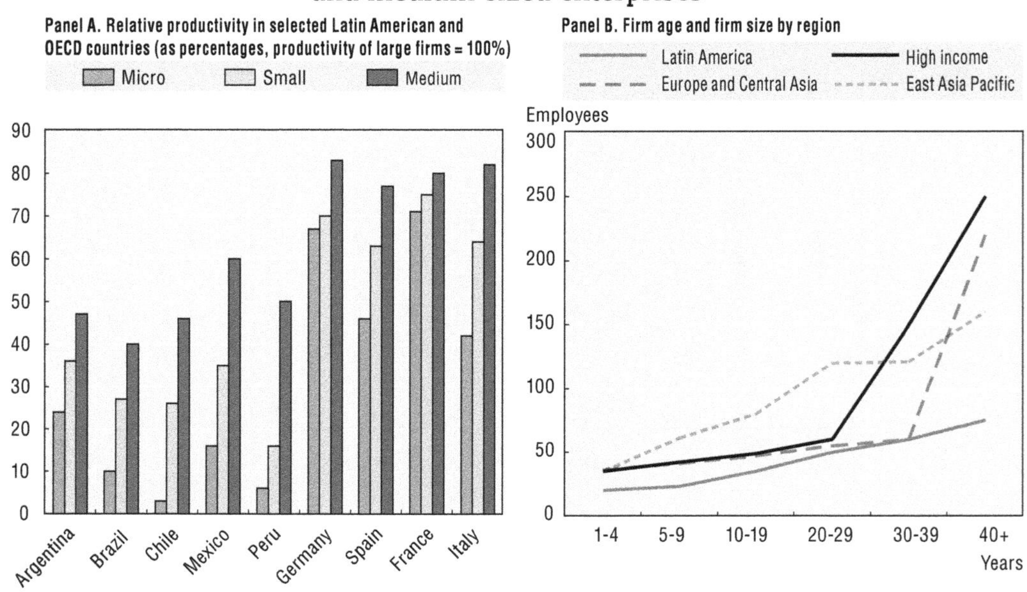

Source: OECD/ECLAC, 2012 and Lederman et al. (2014).

StatLink http://dx.doi.org/10.1787/888933414616

Besides size and employment share, other dimensions, such as firm age, could be considered when targeting active policies for firms. If firm size is a prominent factor for identifying companies that face more barriers to operability and profitability, other factors seem to be relevant for targeting those policies. Latin American firms tend to grow at a slower rate than those in other regions (Lederman et al., 2014; Figure 5.5, Panel B). Recent evidence on OECD economies suggests that a firm's age is an important factor to explain employment growth, sales growth and productivity growth (Box 5.2; OECD, 2015b). Indeed, young firms (less than five years old) tend to perform better than mature firms with respect to all these indicators (Ayyagari, Demirguc-Kunt and Maksimovic, 2011). This evidence suggests that firm age could be important when considering the allocation of policy instruments towards small firms and entrepreneurship.

Policy instruments and incentives targeting young firms, and not only small ones, have been introduced in some countries. Between 2010 and 2014, for example, Colombia implemented 1429 Law to support fledgling entrepreneurs and small firms with no more than 50 workers. The law's benefits included no income tax for the first two taxable years of operation; the benefit was gradually phased out (from 6.25% income tax in the second year rising to 25% after the sixth year following the company's registration). Moreover, beneficiary companies were not subject to the presumptive income system for the first five taxable years. Importantly, companies benefiting from the law had to act as direct employers, meaning they must hire employees. Evidence suggests this instrument reducing fixed costs of operating formally had a moderate and temporary effect on formalisation (Galiani, Meléndez and Navajas, 2015).

Box 5.2. **Entrepreneurship and job creation: Evidence from OECD economies**

Entrepreneurship is regarded as an important contributor to job creation, both in the OECD and Latin America. After the 2008 financial crisis, OECD countries struggled to create better jobs and understand the effectiveness of policies in this regard. Evidence from the OECD suggests that young firms can be critical for creating jobs, but are also more sensitive to income shocks (Criscuolo, Gal and Menon, 2014; Calvino, Criscuolo and Menon, 2015; OECD, 2016e). The age profile of firms, therefore, becomes critical when analysing their effects as job creators. Young firms played an important role for employment growth before and after the financial crisis. This is explained by the entry of start-ups, as well as higher growth rates of young firms that survive.

Figure 5.6. **Net employment growth rates by surviving young and old firms, 2001-11**

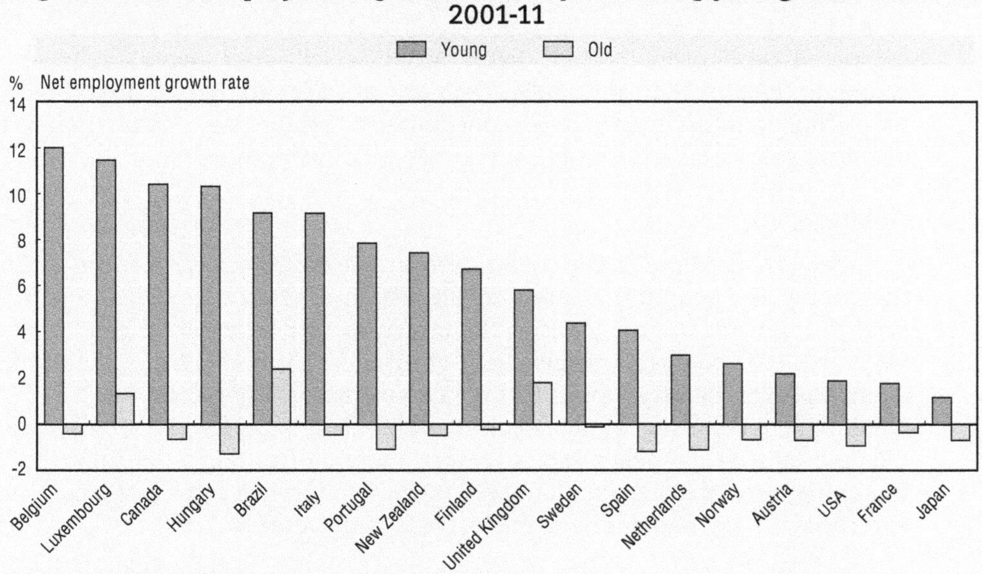

Source: Criscuolo, Gal and Menon (2014).

StatLink http://dx.doi.org/10.1787/888933414626

Box 5.2. Entrepreneurship and job creation: Evidence from OECD economies (cont.)

The 2008 financial crisis hit young firms harder than older ones, as reported in a number of OECD countries (Criscuolo, Gal and Menon, 2014). The contribution to net employment growth of start-ups and young firms remained positive during the crisis, confirming their importance for job creation during the business cycle. Interestingly, the contribution of older firms to job destruction is considerably larger than their share in total employment. The disproportionate contribution of young firms to employment creation prevails for all economies, sectors and years considered (Figure 5.6). These findings underscore the importance of considering the age dimension of firms. Although differences in productivity between small and large businesses have been highlighted, most studies ignore systematic cross-country differences in the age profile across firms of different sizes. Recent research also points out differences across countries in the contribution of new firms to job creation; different components, such as the average size of firms at entry and the survival rate, interact (Calvino, Criscuolo and Menon, 2015). Interestingly, evidence suggests the survival rate of young firms after three years is nearly 60%, underlining a strong heterogeneity.

The analysis also suggests the important role of public policy on the efficiency of resource allocation. Well-functioning product, labour and capital markets, along with efficient judicial systems and bankruptcy laws that do not overly penalise failure, can raise the returns to innovative activity. Young firms are more likely to experiment with disruptive technologies and rely on external financing to implement and commercialise their ideas. Consequently, they may disproportionately benefit from reforms to labour markets and more developed markets for credit and seed and early-stage finance.

Source: Criscuolo, Gal and Menon, (2014), "The Dynamics of Employment Growth: New Evidence from 18 Countries", *OECD Science, Technology and Industry Policy Papers*, No. 14, OECD Publishing, Paris, http://dx.doi.org/10.1787/5jz417hj6hg6-en.

Public policies for enhancing youth entrepreneurship

Public policies for entrepreneurship in the face of market and government failures

If young entrepreneurs can bring benefits in terms of employment, earnings and productivity and other dimensions, they are confronted with the same market failures faced by regular entrepreneurs and small and medium-sized businesses. In addition, compared with other regions Latin America still has several cultural, social and economic factors that adversely affect the entrepreneurial context. Five main areas where policy intervention could contribute to reduce these distortions are identified below, in particular within the context of youth entrepreneurship.

Financing

Adequate finance is a key constraint for developing entrepreneurial activities among the young. The scarcity of funds in the region is often the outcome of a low level of financial intermediation. SMEs in the region receive only 12% of the total credit, while SMEs in OECD countries receive 25% of total credit; one-third of small businesses in Latin America identify access to finance as a serious restriction (OECD/ECLAC, 2012). Small firms, which rely almost exclusively on bank loans for external funding, are more affected by this financing gap, and even more so for long-term financing. Long-term financing is more expensive for SMEs, with high interest rates when compared to large enterprises, a phenomenon not exclusive to Latin America.

Structural factors on both the demand and supply sides explain the persistent and growing difficulty for firms in general, and SMEs in particular, to access credit. On the demand side, access to finance tends to be more difficult than for large firms because of credit standards, technical and formal loan eligibility requirements (including requests for collateral and guarantees) and higher evaluation and monitoring unit transaction costs. Underlying these requirements are information asymmetries in financial transactions. When they have little information on a firm's solvency, banks refuse to lend or will require a very high interest rate. Among the most common reasons for excessive financing costs or even outright credit rationing are lack of a track record; lack of transparency in accounting often associated with weak disclosure capacity; and insufficient capital to offer collateral for the loan.

On the supply side, recent trends in the banking business model also help explain these gaps. The transition from relationship lending to multiservice banking has had adverse implications on the provision of credit (OECD, 2013b). Small and young firms, because of high fixed issuance costs and limited scale, cannot compensate by borrowing in capital markets. Multiservice banking placed the focus on standardised products with less costly screening mechanisms (and a lower premium on loans to small businesses). Credit risk assessment and credit scoring models were in most cases detrimental to SMEs as they were based solely on risk.

Public policies to tackle financing constraints for small businesses and entrepreneurs have been gradually introduced. The importance of funding and market imperfections combined with structural shifts that are leaving non-standard borrowers increasingly underfinanced in relation to large companies, underline the need for public intervention to provide guarantees, offer technical assistance and diminish information gaps. To tackle these barriers, public policy, and in particular development banks, have expanded their role in the region. Recent programmes are targeting young entrepreneurs, providing credit guarantee schemes to reduce the financing gap for young individuals with no collateral. They are also extending their range of products to credit cards, electronic transaction systems and invoicing.

In the case of nascent companies and start-up businesses, and to facilitate the creation of new enterprises that encounter financing difficulties due to their lack of credit history, governments in the region have designed initiatives for the distinct stages of a business's development (incubation, initiation, growth and consolidation). Programmes such as *Financiadora de Estudios y Proyectos* (FINEP) or Empretec managed by SEBRAE in Brazil (Box 5.7), Fondo Emprender in Colombia, *Nacional Financiera* (NAFIN) in Mexico and *Corporación de Fomento de la Producción* (CORFO) in Chile combine different instruments and actors (incubators, seed capital, angel investors and venture capital) to promote long-term investment (OECD, 2013a, 2013b).

Instruments targeting young entrepreneurs also include grants, the most common instrument for financing this population in the European Union. Finland, for instance, offers grants to support start-ups for the under-30s (OECD/EU, 2015). Italy provides up to half of the required start-up investment as a grant. The most successful youth entrepreneurship programmes in OECD economies, such as the United Kingdom's *Prince's Trust Enterprise Programme*, provide staged financing. They start with a small grant and then offer a range of loan products, paired with mentoring. The integrated nature of the support, including coaching and financial instruments, seems to be a key factor for its success.

Capacity building and entrepreneurial skills

The region's lack of skills undermines both the prospects for young workers to integrate into the labour market, as well as their capacity to seize entrepreneurial opportunities (see Chapter 4). In addition, the region has a significant shortage of management skills and business leadership. Many SMEs are limited by their management's inability to lead processes of development, technology adoption and innovation, as well as expansion into new sectors and markets – which is definitely a barrier to increasing productivity (OECD/ECLAC, 2012). For the case of start-ups, a number of OECD countries (e.g. France, Canada) have introduced regulation to facilitate visa requirements for entrepreneurs bringing financial investments or developing innovative projects.

Market access and internationalisation

Latin American SMEs do not generally integrate into global production networks; most participate in local or national, rather than supranational, production systems. This is due to the nature of their goods produced and the types of markets served, as well as other reasons such as management and production capabilities, quality, scale and pricing. While most major companies export directly, SMEs have low participation in exports. They seek to access foreign markets indirectly, through partnership schemes, consortia, sales groups and market operators. Small firms in Latin America are less internationalised than those in other regions; direct and indirect export levels of Latin American SMEs are only half of those recorded in Europe and one-third less than in four East Asian countries (OECD/ECLAC, 2012). Young entrepreneurs in Latin America seem, on average, to have fewer international linkages than young entrepreneurs in the OECD (Figure 5.7), although there are some exceptions (e.g. Colombia, Panama). Moreover, both young and adult entrepreneurs in LAC countries are "disconnected" from international business networks; in the OECD, young entrepreneurs seem more prone than adults to develop these global linkages.

Figure 5.7. **Percentage of entrepreneurs with at least 25% of revenues from international customers**

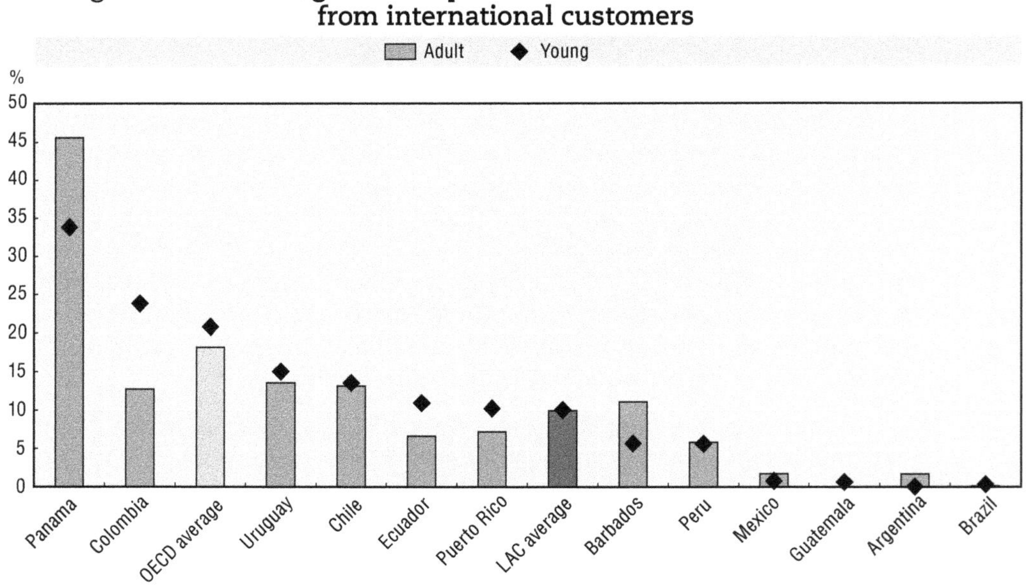

Source: OECD/ECLAC/CAF based on Global Entrepreneurship Monitor individual data, 2015.
StatLink http://dx.doi.org/10.1787/888933414632

Support programmes based on production linkages have become widespread in Latin American countries. Some examples include the Development Partnership Projects (PROFOs) (Chile), business development centres (Argentina, El Salvador), outsourcing exchanges (Argentina, Brazil, Colombia, Mexico), supplier development schemes (Argentina, Brazil, Chile, Mexico), horizontal network programmes (Honduras), clusters and production chains (Peru), clusters (El Salvador, Nicaragua, Uruguay) and export consortia (El Salvador, Uruguay). Despite these programmes, the region needs to go from individually successful projects to national development strategies applicable to a broader segment of businesses.

Different instruments tackle the lack of production linkages between small firms and global value chains. Subsidies, in the form of grants to boost competitiveness, have been the primary instruments used to foster production linkages among firms in Latin America. These instruments include business association projects (such as PROFO in Chile, or the Latin American Association of Entrepreneurs ASELA, created in 2013 in the framework of the Pacific Alliance), export consortia programmes (Argentina, Uruguay) and technology funds and agencies (Argentina, Chile). Other tools include professional technical assistance to support the creation and launch of partnership projects; fiscal support through favourable tax conditions associated with the development of clusters; and credit through special paths to incorporate or develop shared assets (such as effluent treatment plants and joint purchasing of machinery). Regional efforts to tackle the barriers faced by startups in are worth highlighting. Networks like *Pacific Angels* (Angeles del Pacífico) or Xcala, created in 2013 and 2014 by different angel investment funds, aim at transferring the knowledge in this sector across countries in the region (OECD, 2016d).

Entrepreneurial culture and business networks

Business networks have been another priority for improving small firms' linkages to global production networks. For young entrepreneurs, they seem to be even more critical. The region has made efforts to provide entrepreneurs options for consolidating their professional networks and improve business performance. Joint activities include buying consumables to cut costs or improve terms with suppliers; hiring consulting firms to access knowledge that businesses could not afford on their own; selling products jointly to achieve economies of scale and access high-volume markets; and sharing use of costly, highly productive facilities and equipment that groups of small, and especially medium-sized, enterprises, can buy collectively and, above all, use efficiently. Some examples in the region include the tannery and ceramics SME networks in Guanajuato, Mexico; the fashion networks in Gamarra, Peru; the craft networks in Guatemala, Honduras and Nicaragua; and the furniture and fashion networks in Dominican Republic. Other examples of networks are the supplier-development programmes, in which larger private companies promote linkage projects with their network of suppliers to improve particular aspects of the production chain.

Some initiatives in the region have been effective at business networks among young entrepreneurs. The Youth Entrepreneurs programme of the *Fundación Banhcafé* in Honduras, for example, puts young entrepreneurs in contact with local business networks. This involves inviting entrepreneurs to evaluate business plans for the programme before providing seed capital. Fairs and meetings enable young entrepreneurs to promote their initiatives among a group of experienced business leaders. Another example is the *Colectivo Integral de Desarrollo (CID)* in Peru, established in 1990, that provides mentorship, assistance and access to business networks to young entrepreneurs. As part of the Prince's Trust, the *Youth Business International* has also been operating in Argentina, Brazil, Colombia and Mexico. It provides a similar set of instruments for young entrepreneurs: mentorships, business networks and seed capital. The initiative involves the presentation of potentially successful projects to investment networks. In Central America, *CiEmprender* (Ibero-American Centre for Entrepreneurship and Innovation) has also played a role in developing entrepreneurial networks in Costa Rica, particularly in innovation sectors.

Regulatory barriers

Regulations can pose a significant barrier for young entrepreneurs. Procedures and policies that stifle competition and excessive administrative burdens may all conspire to frustrate the entry of entrepreneurs into product markets. Conversely, a competitive product market environment that allows new firms to challenge incumbents, efficient firms to grow and inefficient ones to exit can help boost sustainable economic growth and living standards.[2]

Box 5.3. **Entrepreneurship barriers: A comparison of Product Market Regulation indicators**

The OECD's *Indicators of Product Market Regulation* (PMR) are a set of comprehensive and internationally comparable indicators that measure the degree to which policies promote or inhibit competition in many areas of the product market. Alongside the pillars of state control and barriers to trade and investment, barriers to entrepreneurship are the third pillar with which to analyse product market regulation in the OECD framework (Barbiero et al., 2015).

The World Bank and the OECD have jointly compiled quantitative indicators measuring the extent to which regulation in emerging-market economies promotes or inhibits competition in product markets. This has been achieved based on the PMR indicators, extensively used in OECD countries and now available for a large number of non-OECD economies (De Serres, Egert and Wanner, forthcoming). The PMR indicators measure the economy-wide regulatory and market environments in 34 OECD countries and in another 33 non-OECD countries. In addition to Chile and Mexico – the Latin American members of the OECD – the PMR indicator was specifically developed for Argentina, Brazil, Colombia, Costa Rica, Dominican Republic, El Salvador, Honduras, Jamaica, Nicaragua and Peru. In addition, a PMR indicator has been compiled through a collaboration between the World Bank, the Inter-American Development Bank and the OECD for six other countries from Latin America (Plurinational State of Bolivia [hereafter Bolivia], Ecuador, Guatemala, Panama, Paraguay and the Bolivarian Republic of Venezuela [hereafter "Venezuela"]). The results reported for these six countries (Figure 5.8) are preliminary.

Source: De Serres, Egert and Wanner (2016), "How competition-friendly is regulation in emerging economies? Insights from the OECD indicator of product market regulation".

The "barriers to entrepreneurship" component measures the extent to which regulations facilitate or inhibit the entry of new firms. This component captures a) the complexity of regulation related to license and permit systems, and to communication of those rules and procedures; b) the administrative burdens on start-ups (e.g. number of procedures and bodies needed to contact to register a company); and c) the regulatory protection of incumbents through legal barriers to entry and antitrust exemptions (Barbiero et al., 2015).

Barriers to entrepreneurship are higher on average across Latin American economies than among other emerging economies and the OECD average (Figure 5.8). However, there are variations across the Latin American countries covered. Regulation in this area is friendliest to competition in Chile, Colombia and Panama where the scores are close to the average of OECD economies. Conversely, regulatory barriers to firm entry are particularly high in Bolivia, Ecuador, Honduras and Venezuela.

The variations of Latin American economies with respect to the OECD are mostly reflected in differences in the complexity of regulatory procedures and to a lesser extent in the administrative burdens on start-ups. Compared with the rest of non-OECD countries, regulatory procedures related to entrepreneurship in LAC are particularly restrictive and complex. Above all, the differences among the least to most restrictive countries in Latin America are explained by the complexity of regulatory procedures and the administrative burdens on start-ups. Regarding the licence permits system – a key item in the complexity of regulatory procedures index – several countries in the region have a high restrictive index, including Argentina, Brazil, Bolivia, Chile, Dominican Republic, Ecuador, Jamaica and Venezuela.

Figure 5.8. **Barriers to entrepreneurship index**
(index: scale 0 to 6 from least to most restrictive, 2013)

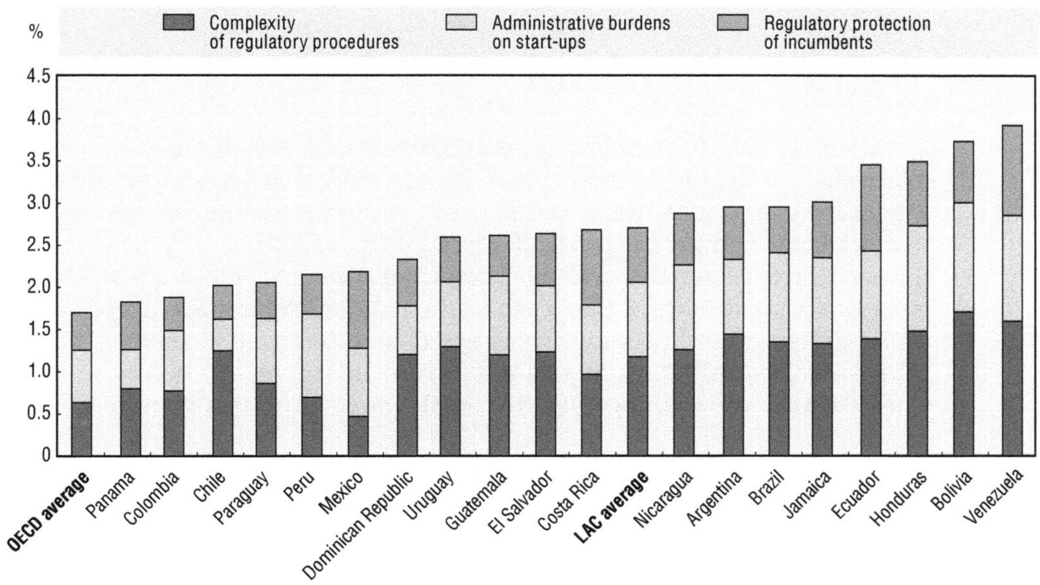

Note: In the case of six countries from Latin America (Bolivia, Ecuador, Guatemala, Panama, Paraguay and Venezuela, a PMR indicator has been compiled through a collaboration between the World Bank, the Inter-American Development Bank and the OECD. The results for these six countries reported are preliminary.

Source: OECD-WBG product market regulation database for all countries except Brazil, Chile, India, Mexico and South Africa, OECD product market regulation database. The indicator reflects the state of legislation in 2014 for Kenya, Philippines, Rwanda and Uruguay; in 2015, for Bolivia, Ecuador, Guatemala, Panama, Paraguay and Venezuela; in 2013, for all others.

StatLink http://dx.doi.org/10.1787/888933414648

Different examples of "red tape" illustrate the problems with which entrepreneurs are confronted for the creation and operation of their business. The cost and time needed to register and start up a business in Latin America are among the main obstacles to their development. LAC also still lags behind other regions and the global average. These problems translate into higher business costs, which as a percentage of per capita income are almost eight times higher in Latin America than in OECD countries. Latin American regulations hinder creating and liquidating businesses and encourage micro and small enterprises to operate informally (Capelleras and Kantis, 2009). The regional average, however, hides how different countries have developed distinct regulations to enhance entrepreneurship. These initiatives confirm the gradual trend towards greater inclusion of SMEs in countries' strategies and more precise definitions of their role. In some countries, these new laws enabled existing initiatives to be consolidated and organised, or laid the foundations for adopting a new strategy of action. Besides facing administrative costs, entrepreneurs can lose certain social security benefits. This can discourage young individuals to pursue entrepreneurial activities; they prefer the stability and social protection benefits of being an employee.

Some OECD economies have encouraged policies to reduce labour costs to enhance youth entrepreneurship. Members of the European Union, for example, have phased out social security contributions for the self-employed. Contributions for entrepreneurs under the age of 30 who register for the first time are reduced from 80% after the first six months to 30% after the first year. Since 2006, Germany's "start-up premium" (*Gründungszuschuss*) has provided unemployment benefits plus a lump sum social security insurance contributions to unemployed individuals with an approved business plan. New Zealand Enterprise Allowance Programme, introduced in the 1990s, also helps unemployed individuals in self-employment through a grant for starting a business; participants have been shown less likely to return to unemployment.

Financing and targeting of youth entrepreneurship programmes in Latin America

As in the OECD, spending on entrepreneurship programmes in Latin America is relatively low compared with other labour market programmes. Estimating public expenditure in youth entrepreneurship can be cumbersome given that programmes are scattered across different levels of government, ministries and government agencies. However, recent estimates in selected countries show that entrepreneurship programmes represent a small share of the expenditure in other labour market programmes such as training (Figure 5.9). Spending on entrepreneurship-related activities in OECD countries (which involves direct job creation and start-up incentives) is also low on average (0.07%) when compared to training (0.15%) or employment (0.11%) programmes.[3]

Figure 5.9. **Estimated spending of entrepreneurship programmes in Latin America (percentage of GDP, 2010-14)**

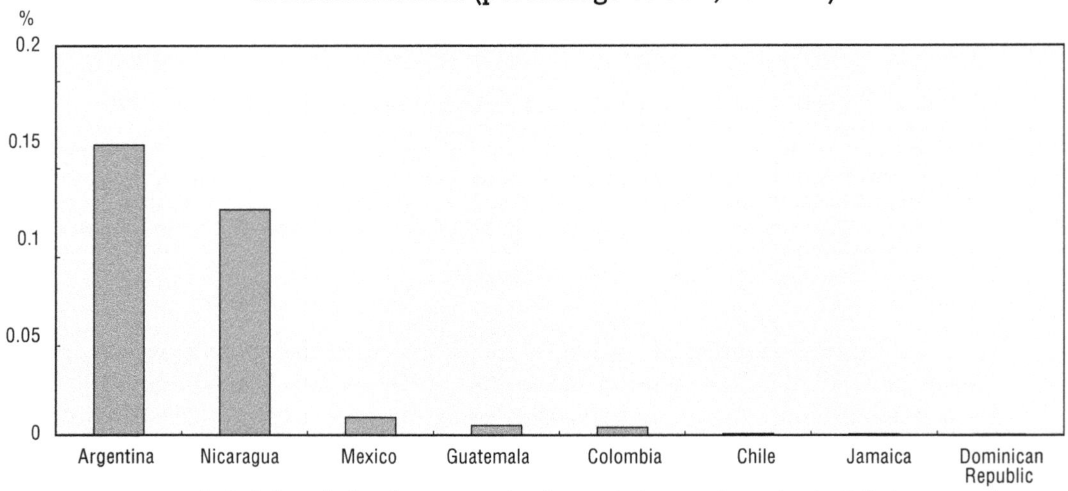

Note: Programmes included are in brackets. Argentina (*Agregado* Start-up incentives), Chile (*Programa de Apoyo a Emprendimientos Sociales; Programa Emprende Más; Programa Generación Microemprendimiento Indigena Urbano; Subsidio al Fomento de la Economía Indígena Urbana y Rural*), Colombia (*Fondo Emprender;*), Dominican Republic (*Promoción, Orientación y Ubicación Puestos de Trabajo*), Guatemala (*Creciendo Seguro*), Honduras (*Fomento Empresas Autogestionarias para Mujeres en zonas Rurales; Jóvenes emprendedores*), Jamaica (Youth Empowerment Strategy Programme; Rehabilitation Grants Public Assistance; Economic Empowerment and Assistive Aids Grant), Mexico (*Fideicomiso del Fondo de Microfinanciamiento a Mujeres Rurales; Fondo para el Apoyo a Proyectos Productivos; Programa de Coordinación para el Apoyo a la Producción Indígena; Programa de Fomento y Desarrollo de las Culturas Indígenas; Programa Organización Productiva para Mujeres Indígenas*) and Nicaragua (*Cooperativas juveniles; Desarrollo de las MIPYMES; Fomento de la pequeña y mediana empresa familiar urbana y rural; Programa Productivo Alimentario; Usura Cero*). Average expenditure over the period 2010-14 for all countries.

Source: OECD/ECLAC/CAF calculations based on Cerutti et al. (2014) and World Bank LAC Social Protection Database (2015); OECD/EU (2015).

StatLink http://dx.doi.org/10.1787/888933414655

Apart from specific programmes, allocated budgets show that entrepreneurship institutions are still incipient in the region and vary according to the employed financing mechanisms. For instance, entrepreneurial programmes sponsored by the SENA in Colombia are financed through earmarked taxation on the payroll, while entrepreneurship programmes in Peru employ a mix of loans and outlays from the central government. Differences on revenue sources could explain the large differences of estimated entrepreneurship budgets across countries. Chile's estimated annual budget for institutions supporting entrepreneurship activities (USD 21 million) is comparable to that of Colombia (USD 38 million), and lower than countries such as Mexico (USD 79 million) or Peru (USD 116 million) or Argentina (USD 273 million).[4] However, some countries have increased their allocation for high-growth entrepreneurs. This is the case of Chile, which increased its budget line to this segment from 10.5% in 2012 to 13% in 2014 (OECD, 2016d).

Although most youth entrepreneurship programmes in the region aim to reach disadvantaged sectors by income, there is little evidence they are reaching this population. Information on the distribution of entrepreneurship programmes and tools in the region is relatively scarce. A number of programmes have an explicit mandate for reaching disadvantaged groups by socio-economic background, education, location or ethnic origin. Almost 70% of the programmes analysed in this chapter (see Table 5.A2.1) targeted primarily low-income individuals; in nearly half of this group, the intervention focused on individuals with low levels of education attainment and high drop-out levels. Programmes also have some common characteristics linked to the targeted population (i.e. youth in cities with low socio-economic background and level of education). Most programmes targeted cities and only two focused on rural areas (Financially Self-Sufficient School Programmes in Colombia and Paraguay); seven programmes covered both cities and rural areas; and seven programmes focused exclusively on cities. Only two programmes considered gender: PREJAL in Argentina and *Programa Juventud y Empleo* in Dominican Republic. None of the programmes included disability or ethnic considerations.

In contrast, more *inclusive entrepreneurship* programmes have been introduced in some OECD countries. After the 2008 financial crisis, entrepreneurship among under-represented and disadvantaged groups in OECD countries has become a policy priority. In 2014, the European Union accounted for 30 million self-employed individuals, of whom 24 million were women, youth (15-24 years-old) or seniors (50-64 years-old) (OECD/EC, 2015). Entrepreneurs from disadvantaged and under-represented groups in the OECD tend to have lower quality businesses in terms of income, revenue or firm survival. *Inclusive entrepreneurship* policies aim at tackling these issues by supporting both business creation and business growth; building entrepreneurship networks; providing coaching and mentoring that include sensitivity to disadvantaged entrepreneurs; and increasing use of evaluations to measure the impact of inclusive entrepreneurship.

Policies targeting high-growth entrepreneurs and start-ups

Despite the economic downturn of the region in the past two years, the landscape for start-ups in the region is more encouraging than in 2012 (OECD, 2016d). Start-ups certainly face specific challenges in their creation, development and expansion that are different from other traditional companies. This is due to the high risks and uncertainty involved, especially in their earlier operation stages. However, many countries offer support to start-ups in relation to their institutional framework, territorial governance and scientific and productive networks (OECD, 2013b; Primi, 2013). The institutional governance generally comprises those agencies responsible for the innovation and productive development policies. These include both public and private institutions focused on innovative entrepreneurship such as networks of angel investors, incubators and accelerators.

Public policies for start-ups generally cover five different areas: financing, services and capacity building, market creation, diffusion of entrepreneurial culture and regulatory framework (Figure 5.10). The creation and development of start-ups requires support tools for each of these areas, adapted to different development stages. An emerging challenge for public policy is to take advantage of new trends for open innovation and to generate incentives that increase public-private collaboration and enhance the impact of public policy for creation and development of start-ups (OECD, 2016d).

Figure 5.10. **Taxonomy of instruments for start-ups support, 2016**

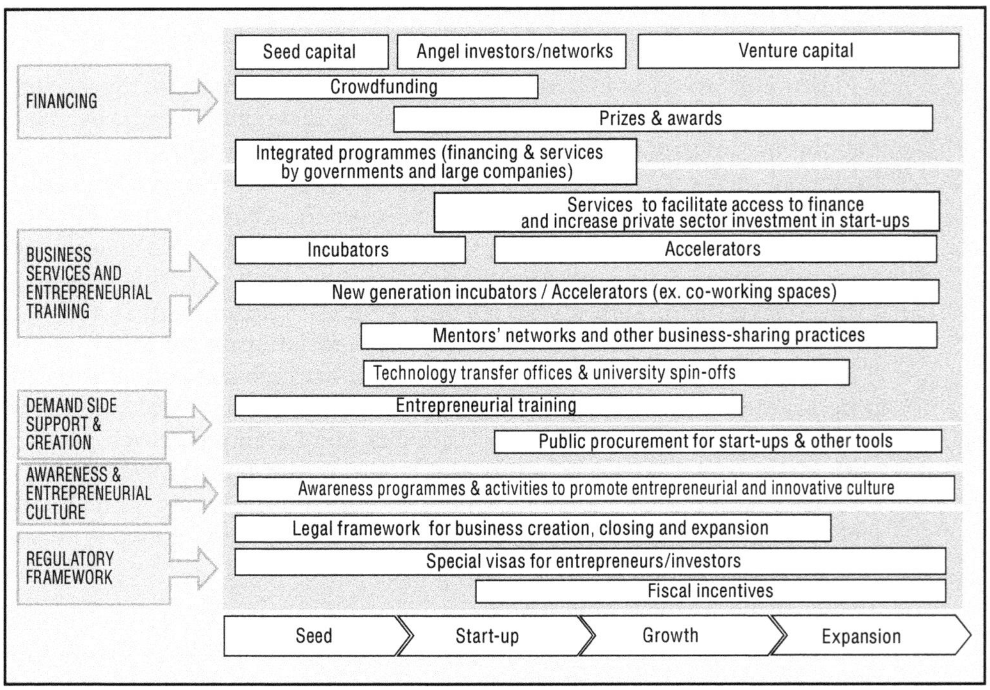

Source: OECD (2016d): *Start-up America Latina 2016: Construyendo un futuro innovador*, OECD Publishing, Paris.

New actors have entered the scene for the support of start-ups. Together with national governments, universities and research centres, the role of local governments and cities for the enhancement of entrepreneurship ecosystems is noticeable. The case of Medellín and Bogotá in Colombia has brought worldwide attention recently. At the same time, the private sector has increased its role, not only from the perspective of financing and investment, but also through new actors to support the seeding of new and innovative entrepreneurship activities. In Mexico, for instance, foundations like Walmart, PepsiCo and Haciendas del Mundo Maya have strengthened their support to small suppliers and local communities (OECD/AMEXCID/GIZ/Cemefi, 2016). The innovation strategies of large companies are also playing a key role in the creation and development of start-ups. One example is the start-up accelerator *Wayra*, created in 2011 as part of Telefonica's innovation strategy, which supports digital base start-ups in Argentina, Brazil, Chile, Colombia, Mexico, Peru and Venezuela. The private sector is developing new forms of collaboration and exchange of good practices that play an important role for start-up support. The Association of Start-ups of Campinas in Brazil, a non-profit organisation created in 2010, has ten technological start-ups for knowledge exchange and events directed to innovative entrepreneurs; it favours dialogue with private sector and financial markets (OECD, 2013a). At the same time, although still incipient, communities and groups associated with crowdfunding activities support the creation of innovative entrepreneurship with high-growth potential, innovative content and capacity to solve concrete issues. This has allowed Latin American start-ups have to gain a prominent role in new sectors, including financial technology, agri-business and biotechnology.

Support to start-ups in Latin America is moving from experimentation to consolidation. Several countries have introduced policies to support start-ups since 2010, including Chile, Colombia, Mexico and Peru (OECD, 2013a), but also Uruguay and Panama (OECD, 2015a). These policies, in contrast with more traditional interventions for innovation and competitiveness, have evolved rapidly; in just three years, they have generated significant transformations in their focus and structure. Latin America is accumulating learning experience for the management and support of start-ups that could be used to expand these activities.

The matrix of direct instruments to support start-ups in Latin America is modernising. The range of instruments to support start-ups in the region grew significantly between 2012 and 2015, and is adapting to the increasingly complex needs of the entrepreneurial ecosystem. Besides the traditional instruments in seed capital, and angel and capital investors, Chile, Colombia, Mexico and Peru are introducing more efficient mechanisms and implementing other tools from the "collaborative economy" (Box 5.4.). Business-sharing practices and open innovation for large firms are becoming increasingly common in the region.

Financing support is moving forward rapidly in early stages of entrepreneurship, but angel investment and venture capital are still embryonic (ILO, 2015; OECD, 2016c). Simplifying the procedures for start-up creation is increasingly important. Chile and Mexico have moved in this direction through a law (*Ley de Empresas en un Dia*) that recognises the use of electronic signature for business creation. Chile has also introduced other reforms to facilitate negotiations with creditors and debtors. Argentina, Colombia and Peru have introduced some reforms to simplify business creation, but procedures are still burdensome, in particular for start-ups.

Box 5.4. **Implementing specialised financing tools for start-ups: The case of iNNpulsa Colombia**

Nearly four years ago, iNNpulsa Colombia identified the need to develop new funding sources for entrepreneurship and innovation, as well as to create a venture capital industry in the country. To this end, iNNpulsa has worked in three fundamental financing sources: grants, credit and private investment. Through calls to award grants as seed capital (funding granted to companies without a minimum viable product developed and without commercial validation) and early-stage capital (funds granted to companies with a minimum viable product with commercial validation), nearly 120 firms have benefited from the grants programme with a total investment of USD 13 million.

Regarding strategies to improve access to credit, Bancoldex developed three lines, implemented through first-tier banking, which benefited 366 firms with an investment by iNNpulsa of USD 5 million. Similarly, an awareness strategy targeting banking institutions was put forward to highlight the high-growth firms with potential and new credit products have been developed in association with banks.

The National Network of Angel Investors (Red Nacional de Ángeles Inversionistas) was created to address the need to develop a venture capital industry in Colombia. The network is led by the Bavaria Foundation and private venture funds (Velum Ventures, Mountain Nazca, Atom Ventures and Promotora II), investing in early-stage firms. Thirty firms in early stages of development were also furnished with grant funds

Box 5.4. Implementing specialised financing tools for start-ups: The case of iNNpulsa Colombia (cont.)

through events such as the *Great Investment Challenge* (*Gran Desafío de la Inversión*). These instruments have benefited 68 firms with an investment by iNNpulsa of more than USD 4 million. While *rediscount* lines and the support of venture capital networks enable a greater leverage for early-stage firms (for each Colombian peso invested by iNNpulsa, between 13 and 27 pesos are leveraged by the private sector), seed capital awarded through grants has lower leverage levels (for each peso invested, between 0.35 and 1 peso are leveraged by the private sector, Figure 5.11).[5]

Figure 5.11. INNpulsa financing instruments and external leveraged capital (2011-15)

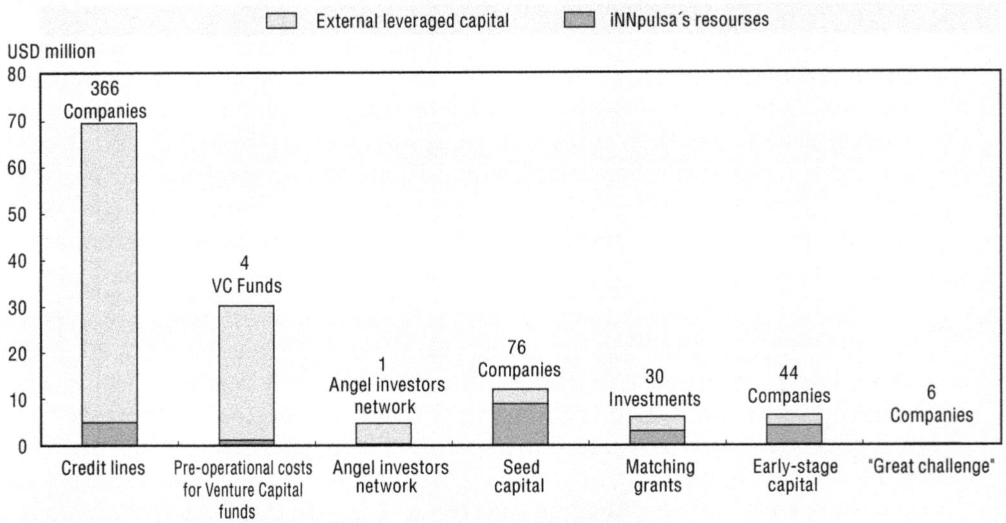

Source: Authors' elaboration, based on iNNpulsa's annual reports.

StatLink http://dx.doi.org/10.1787/888933414670

Over the past four years, iNNpulsa Colombia sheds some insights in developing new funding sources for entrepreneurship and creating a venture capital industry: i) Grant schemes to new businesses need to be complemented with monitoring and support to ensure not only the proper use of resources, but also the company's growth. Clear guidelines in the amount of resources and in the use of funds so as not to distort needs of capital of the companies are required; ii) *Rediscount* lines are not instruments that guarantee new firms' access to funding, despite financing some innovative firms. In this respect, new credit products are required to target firms with high-growth potential. These firms should be assessed not on a historical basis but in function to the firm's human capital and growth and market prospects; iii) A venture capital industry in which not only the creation of private equity funds is promoted (currently greater regulatory restrictions make them less profitable than in other countries in the region) but also the formation of new investment managers and the creation of other investment vehicles that ensure greater availability of investment funds for the group of high-potential companies that is flourishing; iv) It is necessary to develop a financing scheme that considers *complementarity* with other sources: investment, credit and grants.

Support to encourage demand has emerged as an instrument in Latin America to contribute to start-up activities. Some instruments, recently introduced, aim to generate a market for start-ups and to take advantage of their flexibility. INADEM's programme on *Retos Publicos*, for example, envisages the possibility of hiring start-ups for digital services in the federal public administration and the private sector. Mechanisms to help start-ups participate in tenders and public procurement activities have been improving, and have room to develop further. International examples in this area include Barcelona's Open Challenge, a programme oriented to attract startups in areas of urban transport or cultural management.

Box 5.5. **High potential on youth entrepreneurship: The case of Endeavor**

One of the largest high-impact entrepreneurship organisations in the region over the past two decades, Endeavor has aimed to build a network of enterprises and mentors to support high-growth entrepreneurs. The company started in Argentina and Chile, and later expanded to Brazil, Uruguay, Mexico and Colombia. Today, it has regional offices in 25 countries around the world. The Endeavor Foundation selects firms according to growth potential and sustainability. It also considers whether the firm's business model is replicable, innovative and capable of scaling up. It requires participating firms to have business transactions between USD 1-25 million.

Within participating countries, Endeavor considers the potential for high-growth entrepreneurs, a dynamic private sector and leaders interested in the network. The model has five stages: launch, selection, support, expansion and reinvestment. The selection is made through personal interviews in front of an international panel. The support focuses on different services offered by the network, including access to global mentors, consultancies with private sector and academia, and networking.

The expansion stage, which gives visibility to entrepreneurs' projects, is focused on five areas: access to capital markets, leadership programmes, education and capacity building, and providing a proper institutional setting. Finally, the reinvestment stage is divided into different mentorship and corporate social responsibility programmes. Successful Endeavor initiatives include *Bodytech*, a chain of health and fitness centres in Colombia; *MercadoLibre*, an online merchandising company with a large presence in the region; and *Beleza natural* in Brazil, a personal care company. As other initiatives in the region, Endeavor's approach has contributed to strengthen entrepreneurship ecosystems in Latin America while accumulating a useful know-how for the region.

Latin America is accumulating knowledge for improving start-ups' support policies and could do better to target youth in this sector. The lessons learned highlight the importance of aligning support to start-ups with a broader productive transformation strategy, and acknowledging the fact that start-ups operate in a complex and demanding ecosystem. Among the current challenges for defining public policies to the sector are the need to a) maintain the region's image as a cluster for global innovation (Box 5.5); b) overcome gaps for the development of angel investors and venture capital markets; c) increase capacity to design support frameworks that consider the global dimension of start-ups; and d) identify new forms of regional co-operation to strengthen the activity of emerging start-ups and new entrepreneurial talents (Box 5.6).

The encouraging development of start-up ecosystems in the region suggests these instruments could start targeting broader sectors of the population. Although the requirements to participate in some start-up programmes are inclusive in nature, there is evidence of a self-selection effect in the type of entrepreneurs who apply. For Start-up Chile and Innpulsa Colombia, for instance, nearly half of instruments are granted in capitals (Eesley and Leatherbee, 2014; CAF, 2015; Box 5.4). In these two cases, the average recipient tends to be from a more advantaged socio-economic and urban background. Programmes oriented to high-growth firms should also consider targeting more disadvantaged sectors and be more inclusive.

Box 5.6. **Ruta N: Medellín's Business and innovation Centre**

With the aim of creating an innovation ecosystem for the city, Medellín's local authorities developed *Ruta N*, a business and innovation centre for entrepreneurship promotion in technology and knowledge-based sectors. *Ruta N* focuses on four elements as enablers of innovation: entrepreneurial talent, strong networks both inside and outside the ecosystem, available capital for innovation and adequate and sufficient infrastructure for start-ups and innovative companies within the city's innovation district.

The search for **entrepreneurial talent** has been one of the driving forces of the initiative, by developing capabilities, especially among the youth, for addressing the city's biggest challenges. With initiatives such as *Horizontes*, created in 2014, more than 7 000 unprivileged students (11-17 years old) have joined training programmes in technology sectors, including robotics, nanotechnology and engineering. Another example is *Web Bootcamp*, a fast-track training programme to develop aptitudes in programming and software development, skills highly demanded in the ICT sector and with little supply in the city. Nearly 150 students have benefited from the programme. Connecting universities' knowledge with businesses is also a priority. For this, *Ruta N* started the *Innovation Challenge*, an initiative that connects undergraduate students and firms to jointly solve industry challenges.

Another priority for *Ruta N* has been to promote **innovative capital** solutions to young entrepreneurs in the city. Emerging projects require appropriate financial instruments that consider their inherent risk, and the current offer of the financial sector is limited. To close this gap, *Ruta N* has structured *Ruta N Capital*, a mechanism with flexible financing and specialised mentoring services to support projects with potential. *Ruta N Capital* selects projects using a "scoring for innovation" evaluation tool to measure the risk, "novelty" degree and social impact of the project, allowing to determine the amount and conditions of financing. The mechanism can incorporate both private and public resources. It also combines flexible financing, with low interest rates and grace periods, with the specialised mentoring service from experts.

Ruta N has also introduced a **local development** strategy to link its initiatives to the city. The centre has articulated a *market access network (MAN)*, with more than 50 allies, that offers knowledge and specialised services to facilitate innovative businesses to reach new markets and increase exports. Other networks, such as the *smart capital network* that gathers 14 venture capital funds and connects them to startups, the *co-working spaces network* and the *business accelerator network*, have been introduced. Finally, citizen participation has also been encouraged in these initiatives. In 2015 Medellín created the *Cities for Life* global platform to connect with other innovation ecosystems. In recent years, the city facilitated the landing of more than 135 companies from 21 different countries, creating more than 2 000 qualified new jobs and laying the grounds for a 172 hectare innovation district.

Medellín's efforts to reinvent itself have shown that innovation, entrepreneurship and the empowerment of the youth can be valuable tools to enhance local development.

An evaluation of youth entrepreneurship programmes in Latin America

Although entrepreneurship programmes in Latin America are a popular way to improve labour market outcomes and business practices, there is little evidence on their effectiveness owing, in part, to methodological challenges. Impact evaluations suggest that programmes directed towards market failures in innovation, entrepreneurial talent and financing have the highest potential for efficiency and productivity (CAF, 2013). Earlier evaluations for youth programmes in Latin America, focused on vulnerable youth sectors, suggested that skills training and work experience could also enhance self-employment (Attanasio, Kugler and Meghir, 2011).[6] Positive effects on psycho-social well-being have also been found in other regions, while the evidence for labour market outcomes is more nuanced (Cho and Honorati, 2014). As programmes become more comprehensive, covering several areas of entrepreneurship (financial guidance, mentoring, business networks), the net effect of specific policies is more difficult to assess. Moreover, the same type of programme can have different effects in different populations (Cho and Honorati, 2014).

The evaluation of youth entrepreneurship programmes is also important to set proper incentives among beneficiaries. Despite the broad scope of entrepreneurship programmes in the region, they do not always have the expected effect. Furthermore, certain policy instruments (tax exemptions, credit subsidies, labour policies) could undermine the growth of formal/high-productivity firms, while promoting subsistence firms with little value added for the economy (CAF, 2013). Policies alone cannot explain the differences in growth and performance among entrepreneurs; subsistence entrepreneurs tend not to grow because of lack of financing, human capital or entrepreneurial qualities. Evaluation of entrepreneurship programmes in OECD economies distinguishes clearly between national and local policies, and between direct and indirect entrepreneurship policies. Different forms of evaluation are commonly practised: formative evaluations during operation and summative evaluations to assess impact. While evaluation of programmes is required, peer reviews are also common among OECD countries to provide a full picture of the range of entrepreneurship and SME policies (OECD, 2008).

Defining outcomes for youth entrepreneurship programmes

Areas of intervention and a broader set of indicators to measure the effectiveness of entrepreneurship programmes need to be identified. Traditionally, programme evaluations in Latin America have focused on measures of employability and earnings. Different barriers to entrepreneurship and market failures, however, suggest that other additional indicators should be considered. Firm *survival* is a basic dimension often overlooked in evaluations, as most focus on short- and medium-term outcomes. Firm *productivity* is an obvious dimension for analysis, although measurement is not straightforward. Little research has been devoted to analysing the effects of public policies on productivity enhancement for firms, with some exceptions (Eslava, Maffioli and Meléndez, 2012; OECD, 2014). Quantifiable measures directly related to firms' performance after intervention, such as *internationalisation* or investment in *innovation* could also be considered as proxies for the success of policy interventions. In the case of start-up programmes, it is not uncommon to have a pool of applicants with previous experience in setting up a firm; *failure* rates could be considered a measure of *experience* in firm creation and development, and should be valued as an important outcome of entrepreneurship programmes.

Recent efforts to measure the impact of entrepreneurship programmes have shed some light on the most effective interventions (McKenzie and Woodruff, 2012; Cho and Honorati, 2014; Kluve et al., 2016). Although effects could vary depending on the outcomes of interest and targeted groups, overall entrepreneurship programmes are perceived to have a positive (and large) effect for youth and on business knowledge and practice (Cho and Honorati, 2014; Kluve et al., 2016). Yet the results are more nuanced when considering different outcomes and targeted populations. There is, for example, little evidence that entrepreneurship programmes in the region affect firm *survival* (Lederman et al., 2014).

Business training, on the other hand, can have positive short-run effects on *start-up* and most studies in the region find a positive effect on business practices. The effectiveness of programmes depends as much on design as on implementation. A combination of different interventions (or components) seems to matter more for some contexts (Table 5.1). Evidence from meta-analyses shows that vocational and business training is more effective than financial training; business training seems to be cost-effective for promoting business performance. The effect of the programmes by outcome groups also highlights the need to customise them to specific requirements.

Table 5.1. **Areas of intervention (components) in entrepreneurship programmes**

Area	Component
Training	Technical and vocational
	Business and managerial training
	Financial training
Financing	Credit for business or consumer loans
	Cash and in-kind grants
	Access to financial products
Counselling	Mentoring in business
	Psycho-social support
	Arrangements for on-site advice and consulting
Other	Support for job search
	School + work experience
	For self-employment

Source: Based on Cho and Honorati (2014).

Entrepreneurship programmes for youth in Latin America have focused on aspects linked to capacity building, entrepreneurial culture and, to some extent, financing for young entrepreneurs. Youth programmes have combined several interventions to boost employability and youth's access to quality jobs. In particular, regarding capacity building, programmes have covered training and apprenticeship schemes. Regarding policies linked to entrepreneurial culture, most programmes have focused on entrepreneurship training and advisory services (e.g. mentoring, business development services or business formalisation). Few programmes have also covered cross-cutting services, such as search assistance, access to labour market information or job counselling. Finally, some programmes have included financing and, in most cases, have been linked to access to microfinance. In Peru, for example, these include the *Calificacion de jóvenes creadores de microempresas* (Certificate of Youth Entrepreneurship) and *Formación empresarial de la juventud* (Youth Entrepreneurship Programme) and *Projoven emprendedor.*

Most programmes have targeted socio-economically disadvantaged youth in the region, while largely ignoring gender considerations. The interventions targeted primarily low-income individuals with low levels of education and drop-outs. Some also covered young people having problems with drug abuse or violence. In contrast, few programmes primarily targeted women. Promoting Youth Employment in Latin America (PREJAL) in Argentina or Promotion of Employment and Entrepreneurship and the Management of Juvenile Labour Migration in Peru are rare exceptions. A few other programmes primarily targeted specific ethnic groups (such as the Youth Employment Programme in Honduras or the JUVSOL Art and Technology Centre in Peru).

When empirical assessment is available, most youth entrepreneurship programmes have had a positive impact on labour market outcomes, as well as on employment, earnings, creation of firms and formalisation. However, with few exceptions most impact evaluations have not included a cost-benefit analysis. This highlights the increasing need for monitoring costs related to their execution and monitoring (Urzúa and Puentes, 2010). Results of analysis show that benefits of the intervention are greater than its cost (e.g. Planfor – National Plan of Professional Education in Brazil (Box 5.7), the Life-long Learning and Training Project in Chile, and the *Programa juventud y empleo* in Dominican Republic). Reported gender differences on entrepreneurship programmes are not conclusive, although some financing programmes appear to be more effective for women.

Box 5.7. **Enhancing entrepreneurial behaviour: The case of Empretec in Brazil**

The *Empretec* training workshops, developed by the United Nations (UN), focuses on the development of entrepreneurial qualities through workshops. *Empretec* aims to develop several entrepreneurial competencies: opportunity seeking, persistence, fulfilling commitment, quality and efficiency, calculated risk-taking, goal setting, information seeking, systematic planning, networking, independence and self-confidence.

In Brazil, *Empretec* is managed by SEBRAE and has trained over 230 000 beneficiaries in 27 states. New training materials and product upgrades are tested before they are replicated in other countries. Brazil also boasts the largest number of certified national trainers and international master trainers working within the *Empretec* programme. Overall satisfaction with the *Empretec* in 2015 is positive, with an average score of 9.1 points (out of 10), and 74% of participants reporting to be very satisfied. A recent evaluation confirmed that half of the participants who attended *Empretec* training with no previous experience in business became entrepreneurs. Also, 73% of entrepreneurs that had already established businesses registered sales expansion.

Identifying effective components in youth entrepreneurship programmes

The set programme evaluations considered suggest a large heterogeneity in the effectiveness of different components across final outcomes. Results in Table 5.2 illustrate the components that had a positive effect on programme evaluations for a set of six outcomes: self-employment, formalisation, earnings, firm creation, psycho-social skills and territorial inequality. The table also provides information on the mechanisms and programme characteristics. The programmes studied below were carried out in Argentina, Brazil, Chile, Colombia, Costa Rica, Dominican Republic, Mexico and Peru (see Table 5.A2.3 for details).

The effectiveness of programme components for self-employment highlights the supportive role of job search. Nearly three out of four programmes containing a job search component had a positive effect on self-employment. The training component of the programmes generates success on self-employment half the time, while grants or other forms of financial compensation tend to have no effect on this outcome. In the case of formalisation, the vocational and training component seems to be the more effective in three of four cases analysed. The programmes that considered formalisation as an outcome (PREJAL in Argentina, *Primero emprego* in Brazil and *Escuelas auto-suficientes* in Paraguay) also had a strong component in business and managerial training, although no effects were observed in the first programme. The programme components with the largest effects on earnings are more related to business and managerial training, as well as mentoring and advising activities (a two-thirds success rate in both cases). In line with previous analyses, these results suggest that counselling and mentoring activities tend to have a significant effect on earnings (Cho and Honorati, 2014; Kluve et al., 2016).

Table 5.2. **Components and final outcomes in youth entrepreneurship programmes**

		Main outcomes			Secondary outcomes		
		Self-employment	Formalisation	Earnings	Firm creation	Psycho-social well-being	Territorial inequality
Components	**Entrepreneurial Training**						
	Technical and vocational	Effective	Effective	Neutral	Not effective		Effective
	Business and managerial training	Effective	Neutral	Effective	Effective	Effective	Neutral
	Financial training				Neutral	Neutral	Neutral
	Financing						
	Credit for business or consumer loans			Neutral	Neutral	Neutral	Neutral
	Cash and in-kind grants				Neutral		Neutral
	Access to financial products			Neutral	Neutral	Effective	
	Counselling						
	Mentoring in business	Neutral	Neutral	Effective	Effective	Effective	
	Psycho-social support	Neutral	Neutral	Neutral			Effective
	Arrangements for on-site advice/consulting		Neutral	Effective	Effective	Neutral	Effective
	Other						
	Support for job search	Effective		Neutral	Effective	Effective	Neutral
	School + work experience	Neutral	Neutral		Effective	Effective	
	For self-employment		Neutral	Effective	Effective	Neutral	Effective
Mechanisms	**Demand driven**	Neutral	Effective	Neutral	Neutral		
	Supply driven	Effective	Neutral	Effective	Effective	Effective	Effective
	Publicly funded	Effective	Effective	Effective	Effective	Effective	Effective
	Provision of services						
	Public	Effective		Effective	Effective	Effective	Neutral
	Private	Neutral		Effective	Effective		

Note: = ● Effective ● Neutral given mixed results ▨ Not effective.

Source: OECD/ECLAC/CAF, based on programme evaluations (see Table 5.A2.3).

In addition to the basic outcomes considered, some youth entrepreneurship programmes report effects on three secondary outcomes for entrepreneurship: firm creation, psycho-social well-being and territorial inequality. In the case of firm creation, business and managerial training, together with mentoring in business, tend to have the largest effects (significant in almost all cases) on firm creation for the evaluations considered. Interestingly, financial support and financial incentives such as credit for business or cash and in-kind grants tend to have a relatively low effect on firm creation; this suggests that financial constraints are not necessarily the most important barrier to setting up a firm. Psycho-social well-being is more related to access of financial products and mentoring, and support for job search and advice than other factors. These results suggest that components with more "active support" schemes tend to have a positive impact on recipients' well-being.

This descriptive analysis of programme components and outcomes is in line with several meta-analyses (Cho and Honorati, 2014; Kluve et al., 2016), suggesting that vocational and business training programmes and counselling are more effective than financial training. Business training, in particular, seems to be cost-effective for promoting business performance (i.e. earnings).

Conclusions and policy recommendations

Youth entrepreneurship, one of many Latin American youth opportunities, reflects today many of their vulnerabilities, its barriers for integrating into the labour market and the segmentation between subsistence and high-growth entrepreneurs. Young Latin American entrepreneurs tend to be own-account workers, less educated and from more disadvantaged socio-economic backgrounds than in OECD economies. Having fewer resources, skills and experience, they are more vulnerable and face higher barriers than core-age entrepreneurs (aged 25-49) in areas such as financing, capacity building, business networks, internationalisation and regulatory requirements. In addition, Latin America still has cultural, social and economic factors that adversely affect the entrepreneurial context. These gaps justify the existence of public intervention for promoting youth entrepreneurship. Recommendations for this purpose are the following:

Indicators and targeting

Put in place efficient data services collection and information systems at the country level to have comparable data on entrepreneurial activity. Although countries in the region have introduced data collection including for labour market decisions (i.e. labour force surveys) and perceptions on entrepreneurship, the region can have more systematic information on firms regarding performance (growth, employment) and demographics (birth rate, survival). Digital platforms ca be useful for tracking the activity of firms, especially start-ups. More detailed information on public investment for entrepreneurship programmes is also needed to evaluate its effect. The region could exchange practices and technical assistance with OECD countries that have introduced more efficient information systems for this purpose.

Invest in strategies to target better those young entrepreneurs who will capitalise the most on policy support. Novel indicators, which guide choice for targeting specific firms, can be introduced to help target young entrepreneurs who will capitalise the most on policy support. Firm age is increasingly relevant to measure business potential and employment growth in entrepreneurship programmes, but other dimensions could be considered. In countries such as Brazil, where young firms account for more than half of the economy's total job creation, public policy targeting young firms can be critical. The alignment of targeted firms with key productive transformation objectives is another example. Developing better indicators to target the right recipients is essential to maximise the effectiveness of youth entrepreneurship programmes.

Overcoming market failures

Introduce tailored financing instruments adapted to the needs of young entrepreneurs, with more flexible requirements on credit history, collateral and risk. Access to finance continues to be a critical constraint for young Latin American entrepreneurs to develop their business, as is the case for the OECD. While credit and seed/early stage capital continue to be relevant financing sources, a broader range of instruments is available to suit the diverse needs and typologies of firms in the region. These include asset-based finance (i.e. factoring), alternative debt (i.e. crowdfunding), hybrid financing instruments and equity finance. In the case of Latin American start-up firms, the financing support is moving forward rapidly in early stages of entrepreneurship such as the *Servicio de Cooperación Técnica* (SERCOTEC) in Chile or *Red emprender* in Uruguay. However, angel investment and venture capital are still embryonic and highly concentrated. While Brazil and Mexico attract 57% and 15% of total venture capital in the region, other countries (Colombia, 3.5%) are still consolidating investment in this sector. Public policies for attracting these actors have been implemented in some countries, but can be intensified. In addition to the instruments, youth entrepreneurship programmes with a financial education component have proved successful. Developing financial skills among the young, and raising awareness about the available financing sources and programmes to support young initiatives, should be encouraged.

Strengthen the link of young entrepreneurs with business networks by supporting mentoring programmes. Programme evaluations in the region have highlighted the strong link between access to business networks and firm performance. Besides reducing information asymmetries in the sector and providing potential access to new markets, business networks connect young entrepreneurs with individual support and mentoring from more experienced peers. Counselling and mentoring programmes, such as those developed by the Start-up Association of Campinas (Brazil) or Entrepreneurship Parks (*Parques de Emprendimiento*) in Medellín (Colombia), should be encouraged. To improve their effectiveness, these initiatives should promote the participation of the local business community and provide training to coaches and mentors that includes sensitivity to issues faced by young entrepreneurs. In the case of growth-oriented young entrepreneurs, good matching between mentor and firm, which considers defined criteria such as age, gender and business sector, can have significant effects over the long term.

Reduce regulatory barriers for young entrepreneurs to help generate a significant impact on firm creation and access to entrepreneurship programmes. Barriers to entrepreneurship in Latin America are higher than in other emerging economies and the OECD. These barriers are measured by the complexity of regulatory procedures, the administrative burdens on start-ups (e.g. number of procedures and bodies to contact to register a company) and the regulatory protection of incumbents through legal barriers to entry. Countries such as Chile and Mexico have made significant progress in this direction, as shown, for instance, by the simplifying procedures for start-up creation with the *Ley de Empresas en un dia*. In Colombia, the CONPES 3834 law establishes a fast-track system for innovation firms to receive tax exceptions for investment in science and technology. Similarly, there is room for facilitating access to available instruments for youth entrepreneurship in most countries. Internal barriers for providing these instruments (e.g. limits to seed capital and grants due to higher share of non-performing loans among start-ups) could be adapted.

Towards inclusive entrepreneurship

Implement *inclusive entrepreneurship* policies to enhance the quality of businesses created by young entrepreneurs. Young entrepreneurs are an under-represented group in the entrepreneurship universe, and within this group those from socially disadvantaged groups tend to have lower quality businesses in terms of income, revenue and survival. More active support policies towards young entrepreneurs with higher barriers in educational background, finance and networks, are needed. Entrepreneurship policies towards disadvantaged sectors, including youth, can not only have positive spillovers for equity, but can also be critical for enhancing productivity (OECD, 2016a). The fragmentation of entrepreneurship initiatives, with subsistence entrepreneurs on one side and high-growth entrepreneurs on the other, suggests that a differentiated approach for each group may be needed. A broader, multi-dimensional support, beyond micro-credit, is required for subsistence entrepreneurs to address vulnerabilities outside the labour market. Given the high share of informal workers in this group, incentives towards their formalisation should be encouraged. High-growth entrepreneurs, on the other hand, should have access to a comprehensive support to address different constraints in financing, entrepreneurial skills and business networks, regardless of their socio-economic background. The distribution of youth entrepreneurship instruments can be enhanced by improving the screening mechanisms for identifying youth potential. In this sense, enhancing policies that can make entrepreneurial activities promote intergenerational equity is important for the region.

Expanding evaluations

Systematise the use of robust evaluations of youth entrepreneurship programmes for identifying the most effective components. Existing evaluations of youth entrepreneurship programmes in the region point out positive effects on outcomes such as self-employment, earnings and formalisation. It is important to strengthen the components that are more effective to improve these outcomes. The evidence analysed in this chapter suggests that business and managerial training, mentoring in business and counselling are the components with the clearest effect on most entrepreneurship outcomes, with financial support mechanisms being more limited. Other components, such as support for job search, can also have a positive impact. Overall, an integrated approach to entrepreneurship support, encompassing training-financing-mentoring, has produced more effective results. Strengthening these components and giving them enough flexibility when they are implemented can considerably improve programmes' effectiveness and deliver long-term effects. Evidence suggests that publicly funded programmes in the region are effective and programme outcomes are independent of public or private provision of services.

Expand the range of outcomes considered when implementing youth entrepreneurship programmes. Although most youth entrepreneurship programmes have focused on archetypal labour market outcomes (employment, earnings), other dimensions could be considered when evaluating programme effectiveness. Secondary outcomes include measures of firm performance, including firm creation, business survival and firm internationalisation, but also social effects of entrepreneurship programmes, such as psycho-social well-being or territorial inequality. Introducing systematic evaluations of outcomes by group, in particular related to gender and ethnicity, is also important. Evaluations could not only examine the efficiency and cost-effectiveness of programmes, but also consider *deadweight* (i.e. supporting an entrepreneur who would have behaved in the same way without support) and *displacement* effects (e.g. when supporting one entrepreneur puts another out of business).

Notes

1. The GEM database is a commonly used dataset for analysing entrepreneurship trends. See Annex 5.A2 for a detailed description.
2. For more information, see: www.oecd.org/eco/growth/indicatorsofproductmarketregulationhomepage.htm .
3. OECD.Stat database on direct expenditure and participant stocks on Labour Market Programmes, 2016. Start-up incentives in OECD countries refer to programmes that promote entrepreneurship by encouraging the unemployed and target groups to start their own business or to become self-employed.
4. Information from national budgets for corresponding institutions between brackets in latest available year: Argentina (FONCyT, FONTAR, FONSOFT, FONARSEC and D-TEC), Colombia (SENA Entrepreneurship programmes and Innpulsa Colombia), Chile (CORFO, Start-up Chile, *Desarrollo Emprendedor*, SSAF), Mexico (INADEM available grants for entrepreneurship) and Peru (Innovate Peru, which encompasses the FINCYT and FOMITEC funds).
5. Rediscount refers to the act of discounting a debt or money market instrument for a second time. A central (or public) bank may lend funds to a commercial bank in this way – the commercial bank buys the short-term paper at a discount then rediscounts it with the central bank (i.e. the central bank buys the paper from the commercial bank) to boost its reserves.
6. For country-specific studies see Alzúa and Brassiolo (2006) in Argentina; Castañeda, González and Rojas (2010) and Rubiano (2003) in Colombia; Card et al. (2011) in Dominican Republic; and Jaramillo and Parodi (2003) in Peru. Additional information on regional programmes is available in Chakroun, Holmes and Marope (2015) and ILO (2013). A complete compilation of different evaluation programmes for entrepreneurship in Latin America is provided in YEI (2016).

References

Aboal, D. and F. Veneri (2016), "Entrepreneurs in Latin America", *Small Business Economics*, Vol. 46/3, SpringerLink, pp. 503-525.

Alzúa, M.L. and P. Brassiolo (2006), "The impact of training policies in Argentina: An evaluation of Proyecto Joven", *Working Paper*, No. OVE/WP-15/06, Inter-American Development Bank, Washington, DC.

Attanasio, O., A. Kugler and C. Meghir, (2011), "Subsidizing vocational training for disadvantaged youth in developing countries: Evidence from a randomized trial", *American Economic Journal, Applied Economics* 3, pp. 188-220.

Ayyagari, M., A. Demirguc-Kunt and V. Maksimovic (2011), "Small vs. young firms across the world: Contribution to job creation, employment and growth", *Policy Research Working Paper*, No. 5631, World Bank, Washington, DC.

Bandeira, O. et al. (2013), "Can basic entrepreneurship transform the economic lives of the poor?" *Iza Discussion Paper*, No. 7386, Institute for the Study of Labor, Bonn.

Barbiero, O. et al. (2015), "The 2013 update of the OECD's database on product market regulation: Policy insights for OECD and non-OECD countries", *OECD Economics Department Working Papers*, No. 1200, OECD Publishing, Paris, http://dx.doi.org/10.1787/5js3f5d3n2vl-en.

Blanchflower, D. and A.J. Oswald (1998), *Entrepreneurship and the Youth Labour Market Problem: A Report for the OECD*, www.dartmouth.edu/~blnchflr/papers/OECD.pdf

CAF (2015), "El caso de iNNpulsa Colombia. La evolución de una política pública para el crecimiento empresarial extraordinario" [The Case of iNNpulsa Colombia: the Evolution of a Public Policy for a True Entrepreneurial Growth.], Development Bank of Latin America, Caracas, www.innpulsacolombia.com/sites/default/files/caf_n19_4.pdf

CAF (2013), "Emprendimientos en América Latina. Desde la subsistencia hacia la transformación productiva" ["Entrepreneurship in Latin America. From subsistence towards productive transformation"], Development Bank of Latin America, Caracas.

Calvino, F., C. Criscuolo and C. Menon (2015), "Cross-country evidence on start-up dynamics", *OECD Science, Technology and Industry Working Papers*, Vol. 2015/06, OECD Publishing, Paris, http://dx.doi.org/10.1787/5jrxtkb9mxtb-en.

Capelleras, J. and H. Kantis, (2009), "Nuevas empresas en América Latina: factores que favorecen su rápido crecimiento" [New Firms in Latin America: High-growth Enhancing Factors], Departament d'Economia de l'Empresa Universitat Autònoma de Barcelona, Barcelona.

Card, D. et al. (2011), "The labour market impacts of youth training in the Dominican Republic", *Journal of Labour Economics*, Vol. 29/2, Elsevier, Amsterdam, pp. 267-300.

Castañeda, C., J.L. González and N. Rojas (2010), "Evaluación de impacto: Programa Jóvenes Rurales Emprendedores del SENA" ["Impact evaluation: Rural Youth Programme], *Fedesarrollo Working Paper*, No. 53-2010-2, Centro de Investigación Económica y Social, Bogotá.

Cerutti, P. et al. (2014), Social Assistance and Labor Market Programs in Latin America Methodology and Key Findings from the Social Protection Database, *World Bank Discussion Paper* No. 1401. Washington, D.C.

Chakroun, B., K.P. Holmes and P.T.M. Marope (2015), *Unleashing the Potential: Transforming Technical and Vocational Education and Training*, UNESCO Publishing, Paris.

Cho, Y. and M. Honorati (2014), "Entrepreneurship programs in developing countries: A meta-regression analysis", *Labour Economics*, Vol. 28, Elsevier, Amsterdam, pp. 110-130.

Criscuolo C., P.N. Gal and C. Menon (2014), "The dynamics of employment growth: New evidence from 18 countries", *OECD Science, Technology and Industry Policy Papers*, No. 14, OECD Publishing, Paris, http://dx.doi.org/10.1787/5jz417hj6hg6-en.

De Serres A., B. Egert and I. Wanner (forthcoming), "How competition-friendly is regulation in emerging economies? Insights from the OECD indicator of product market regulation", *OECD Notes*, Paris.

Eesley, C. and M. Leatherbee (2014), "Boulevard of broken behaviors: Cognitive and behavioral effects of Start-Up Chile", *Working Paper*, Stanford University, Stanford, US.

Eslava, M., A. Maffioli and M. Meléndez (2012), "Second-tier government banks and firm performance: Micro-evidence from Colombia", *Working Papers Series*, No. IDB WP 294, Inter-American Development Bank, Washington, DC.

Fazio M. V. (2011), "Programa Juventud y Empleo en República Dominicana: Análisis de la percepción de los empleadores acerca de las pasantías y de las perspectivas de inserción laboral de los jóvenes" ["Youth and Employment Programme in Dominican Republic: Analysis of employers' perception on internships and youth employability"], *Notas Técnicas*, IDB-TN-240, Inter-American Development Bank,, Washington, DC.

Galiani, S., M. Meléndez and C. Navajas (2015), "On the effect of the costs of operating formally: New experimental evidence", ["Sobre los Efectos de los Costos de Ser Formal: Nueva evidencia Experimental"] *NBER Working Paper*, No. 21292, National Bureau of Economic Research, Cambridge, US.

Gallup (2016), *Gallup* (database), www.gallup.com (accessed June 2016).

Gasparini, L., P. Gluzmann and D. Jaume (2012), "Decisiones laborales en América Latina: El caso de los emprendedores" [Labour Market Decisions in Latin America: The Case of Entrepreneurs], *Documento de trabajo*, No. 2012/06, Development Bank of Latin America, Caracas.

GEM (2016), *Global Entrepreneurship Monitor* (database for 2015), Global Entrepreneurship Research Association, London, UK, www.gemconsortium.org/data (accessed August 2016).

Green, F. (2013), *Youth Entrepreneurship: A Background Paper for the OECD Centre for Entrepreneurship, SMEs and Local Development*, OECD Publishing, Paris.

Hebert, R. and A. Link (1989), "In search of the meaning of entrepreneurship," *Small Business Economics*, Vol. 1/1, Springer, pp. 39-49.

Herrington, M., D. Kelley and S. Singer (2016) *Global Entrepreneurship Monitor 2015/2016 Global Report*. www.gemconsortium.org/report/49480.

IDB-WB (2014), *Entrepreneurship in Latin America: A Step Up the Social Ladder?* Lora E. and F. Castellani (eds.), Inter-American Development Bank and World Bank, Washington, DC.

ILO (2015), *Promoción de la iniciativa empresarial y el empleo independiente de los jóvenes en América Latina y El Caribe: experiencias innovadoras*, Oficina Regional para América Latina y el Caribe, Lima.

ILO (2013), "Buenas practicas para el empleo juvenil" ["Good Practices for Youth Employment"], International Labour Organization, Geneva.

Jaramillo, M. and S. Parodi (2003), "Jóvenes emprendedores" ["Young entrepreneurs"], Instituto Apoyo, Lima.

Kelley, D. et al. (2014), *Special Report: Women's Entrepreneurship*, Global Entrepreneurship Monitor, Global Entrepreneurship Research Association, London.

Kluve J. et al. (2016), "Interventions to improve the labour market outcomes of youth: A systematic review of training, entrepreneurship promotion, employment services, and subsidized employment interventions", *Campbell Systematic Reviews*, International Labour Organization, Geneva.

Lederman, D. et al. (2014), "Latin American entrepreneurs: Many firms but little innovation", *World Bank Latin American and Caribbean Studies*, World Bank, Washington, DC, https://openknowledge.worldbank.org/handle/10986/16457.

McKenzie, D., C. Woodruff, (2012), "What are we learning from business training and entrepreneurship evaluations around the developing world?", *World Bank Policy Research Working Paper* No. 6202, World Bank, Washington, DC.

OECD/AMEXCID/GIZ/Cemefi, (2016), Engagement between foundations and governments: Mexico's experience. OECD Development Centre, Paris.

OECD (2016a), "The productivity-inclusiveness nexus", Meeting at the OECD Council at Ministerial level, 1-2 June 2016, OECD Publishing, Paris, www.oecd.org/global-forum-productivity/library/The-Productivity-Inclusiveness-Nexus-Preliminary.pdf.

OECD (2016b), *OECD Employment Outlook 2016*, OECD Publishing, Paris, http://dx.doi.org/10.1787/empl_outlook-2016-en.

OECD (2016c), *Gender Equality in the Pacific Alliance: Promoting Women's Economic Empowerment*, OECD Publishing, Paris, http://dx.doi.org/10.1787/9789264262959-en

OECD (2016d), *Start-up Latin America 2016: Building an Innovative Future*, OECD Publishing, Paris (forthcoming).

OECD (2016e), "No country for young firms? Policy failures and regulations are a greater obstacle for start-ups than for incumbents", *STI Policy Note*, OECD Publishing, Paris, June, www.oecd.org/sti/ind/Policy-Note-No-Country-For-Young-Firms.pdf

OECD (2015a), *New Approaches to SME and Entrepreneurship Financing: Broadening the Range of Instruments*, OECD Publishing, Paris, http://dx.doi.org/10.1787/9789264240957-en.

OECD (2015b), *Entrepreneurship at a Glance 2015*, OECD Publishing, Paris, http://dx.doi.org/10.1787/entrepreneur_aag-2015-en.

OECD (2014), *Perspectives in Global Development: Boosting Productivity to Meet the Middle-Income Trap*, OECD Publishing, Paris, http://dx.doi.org/10.1787/persp_glob_dev-2014-en.

OECD (2013a), "Startup América Latina: Promoviendo la innovación en la region" ["Promoting innovation in the region"], OECD Development Centre Studies, OECD Publishing, Paris, http://dx.doi.org/10.1787/9789264202306-en.

OECD (2013b), *Perspectives in Global Development 2013: Industrial Policies in a Changing World*, OECD Publishing, Paris, http://dx.doi.org/10.1787/persp_glob_dev-2013-en.

OECD (2008), *OECD Framework for the Evaluation of SME and Entrepreneurship Policies and Programmes*, OECD Publishing, Paris, http://dx.doi.org/10.1787/9789264040090-en.

OECD/ECLAC (2012), *Latin American Economic Outlook 2013: SME Policies for Structural Change*, OECD Publishing, Paris, http://dx.doi.org/10.1787/leo-2013-en.

OECD/EU (2015), *The Missing Entrepreneurs: Policies for Self-employment and Entrepreneurship*, OECD and European Union, OECD Publishing, Paris, http://dx.doi.org/10.1787/9789264226418-en.

OECD/EU (2012), *Policy Brief on Youth Entrepreneurship: Entrepreneurial Activities in Europe*, OECD Publishing, Paris, www.oecd.org/cfe/leed/Youth%20entrepreneurship%20policy%20brief%20EN_FINAL.pdf.

Primi, A. (2013), "The evolving geography of innovation: A territorial perspective", in *The Global Innovation Index 2013: The Local Dynamics of Innovation*, Cornell University, INSEAD, World Intellectual Property Organization, Geneva, Ithaca and Fontainebleau.

Rubiano, N. (2003), "Evaluacion de impacto del proyecto servicios integrados Para Jóvenes" ["Impact evaluation of youth's integral services project"], Consolidado Nacional Universidad Externado De Colombia - Centro De Investigaciones Sobre Dinamica Social, Bogotá.

Schoar, A. (2010), "The divide between subsistence and transformational entrepreneurship" in Lerner, J. and S. Stern (eds.), *Innovation Policy and the Economy*, Vol. 10, pp. 57-81.

Urzúa S. and E. Puentes (2010), "La evidencia del impacto de los programas de capacitación en el desempeño en el mercado laboral" ["Evidence on the Impact of Training Programmes on Labour Market Performance"], *Notas Técnicas IDB-TN-268*, Banco Interamericano de Desarrollo, Unidad de Mercados Laborales y Seguridad Social,

Van Praag, M. (2009), "Who values the status of the entrepreneur?" *Iza Discussion Paper*, No. 4245, Institute for the Study of Labor, Bonn.

Van Praag, M. and A. Stel (2011), "The more business owners the merrier? The role of tertiary education", *Scales Research Reports*, No. H201010, EIM Business and Policy Research, Zoetermeer, The Netherlands, http://ondernemerschap.panteia.nl/pdf-ez/h201010.pdf.

Van Praag, M. and P. Versloot (2007), "What is the value of entrepreneurship? A review of recent research", *Iza Discussion Paper*, No. 3014, Institute for the Study of Labor, Bonn.

YEI (2016), *Youth Employment Inventory* (database), www.youth-employment-inventory.org/ (accessed June 2016).

Annex 5.A1. Business ownership and job creation among young and adults in Latin America

Figure 5.A1.1. **Share of population who currently own a business by age group**

Latin America and the OECD

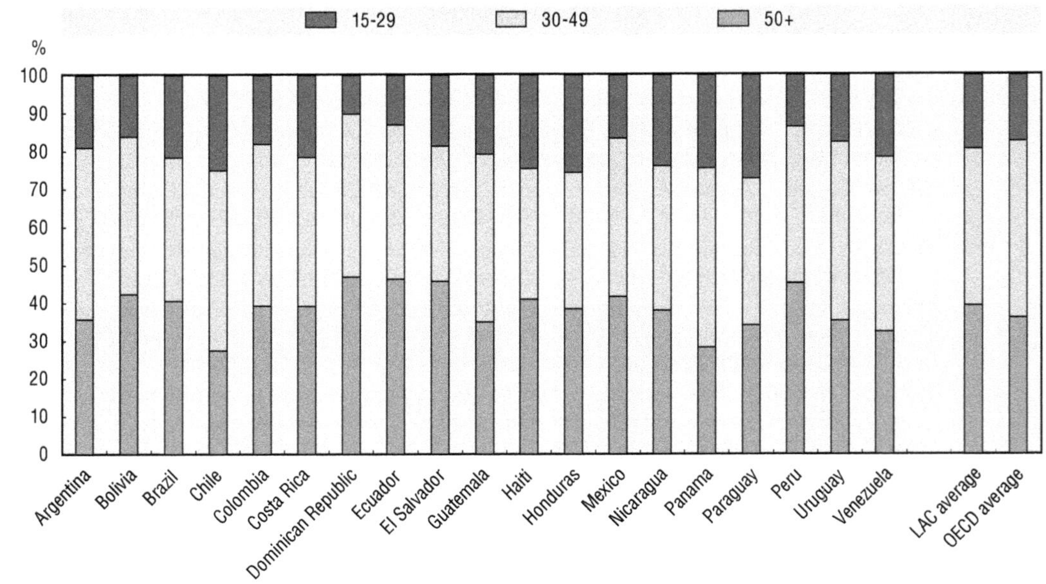

Source: OECD/ECLAC/CAF based on Gallup (2016).

StatLink http://dx.doi.org/10.1787/888933414683

Figure 5.A1.2. **Job creation among young and adult entrepreneurs in Latin America and the OECD**

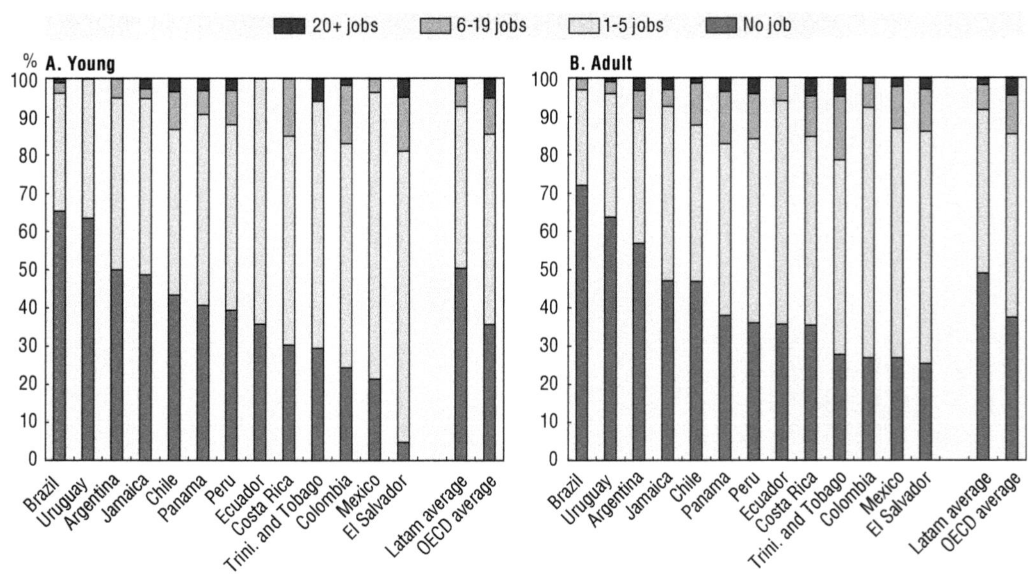

Note: Data corresponding to current number of jobs in Total Entrepreneurial Activity (TEA) for young (18-29) and adults (30-64 years).

Source: OECD/ECLAC/CAF based on Global Entrepreneurship Monitor individual data, 2012 and 2015.

StatLink http://dx.doi.org/10.1787/888933414694

Annex 5.A2. Global Entrepreneurship Monitor Database

The Global Entrepreneurship Monitor (GEM) database is one of the leading vehicles to understand the entrepreneurial behaviour and attitudes of individuals and, in so doing, shed light on the national context affecting entrepreneurship decisions. GEM collects a wealth of primary data on entrepreneurship from individual interviews, in accordance with its own conceptual framework and methodology. The survey provides responses from interviewed adults on their reported attitudes towards entrepreneurship, their pre-start-up activities and their work at different stages of the firm. Initiated in 1997, the project is conducted on nearly 100 economies. Among other organisations, it is used by the United Nations, World Bank, World Economic Forum and the OECD. The data collection engine powering GEM research has two complementary tools: the Adult Population Survey (APS), which tracks entrepreneurial attitudes, activity and aspirations of individuals; and the National Expert Survey (NES), which monitors factors believed to have a significant impact on entrepreneurship and is administered to national experts. As a primary source of information on entrepreneurs, GEM is based on individual surveys, not on firm-level data. Therefore, it is important to contrast results with other sources. The GEM dataset tracks informal entrepreneurship activity, which official statistics do not always capture.

Table 5.A2.1. **Youth entrepreneurship programmes and evaluations**

Programme	Country	Status	Start	End
Jóvenes con Más y Mejor Trabajo	Argentina	Ongoing	2008	Ongoing
Promoción del Empleo Juvenil in Latin America	Argentina	Completed	2005	2009
Programa Primeiro Emprego In Rio Grande Do Sul	Brazil	Completed	1999	2007
Entra 21 And Cepro Partnership	Brazil	Completed	2003	2005
Chile Joven (I and II)	Chile	Completed	1991	2002
Programa Jóvenes Rurales Emprendedores del SENA	Colombia	Ongoing	2003	
Proyecto de Servicios Integrados para Jóvenes	Colombia	Completed	2000	2003
Programa Juventud, Empleo y Migración	Costa Rica	Completed	2009	2012
Programa Juventud y Empleo	Dominican Republic	Ongoing	2008	2012
Autoempleo Juvenil	Mexico	Ongoing	2012	Ongoing
Foro Emprezando (Mexico)	Mexico	Ongoing	2007	Ongoing
Programa de Escuelas Auto-suficientes	Paraguay	Ongoing	2003	Ongoing
Calificación de Jóvenes Creadores De Microempresas	Peru	Completed	1999	2001
Formación Empresarial De La Juventud	Peru	Completed	1999	2001
Projoven Emprendedor	Peru	Completed	2010	2011
Creer para Crear	Peru	Completed	2000	2005

Source: Based on YEI (2016), and national programme evaluations.

Table 5.A2.2. Youth entrepreneurship programmes and outcomes

Country	Programme	Employment	Self-employment	Formalisation	Firm survival	Firm creation	Earnings	Productivity	Internationalisation	Innovation	Psycho-social well-being	Gender	Territorial inequality
Argentina	Jóvenes con Más y Mejor Trabajo												
	Promoción del Empleo Juvenil in Latin America												
Brazil	Programa Primeiro Emprego In Rio Grande Do Sul												
	Entra 21 and Cepro Partnership												
Chile	Chile Joven (I and II)												
Colombia	Programa Jóvenes Rurales Emprendedores del SENA												
	Proyecto de Servicios Integrados para Jóvenes												
Costa Rica	Programa Juventud, Empleo y Migración												
Dominican Rep.	Programa Juventud y Empleo												
Mexico	Autoempleo Juvenil												
	Foro Emprezando (Mexico)												
Paraguay	Programa de Escuelas Auto-suficientes												
Peru	Calificación de Jóvenes Creadores De Microempresas												
	Formación Empresarial De La Juventud												
	Projoven Emprendedor												
	Creer para Crear (start-up)												

Effective = Mixed = Not effective =

Note: This table summarises outcomes and results from studies described in Table 5.A2.1
Source: Authors' elaboration, based on national evaluations and YIE (2016).

Table 5.A2.3. **Unevaluated youth entrepreneurship programmes**

Country	Title	Start date	Location
Argentina	Manos Platenses	1999	Urban
Colombia	Future of ANDI (Asociación Nacional de Empresarios de Colombia)	2005	Rural
Colombia	Rural Entrepreneurship Programme	2003	Rural
Dominican Republic	Into Employment	2009	Both
Dominican Republic	Programa Juventud y Empleo (2008-2012)	2008	Both
El Salvador	Socio-laboral Management Programme	2009	Urban
Guatemala	Youth Enterprises (Empresas Juveniles)	2010	Rural
Honduras	National Work Education Center, CENET	2008	Both
Honduras	YES Honduras	2005	Both
Mexico	El Ingenio - Center for Learning and Developing Creativity	2006	Both
Mexico	Foro Emprezando	2007	Both
Mexico	Self-Employment for Youth - Public Plan for Young Entrepreneurs	2012	Both
Nicaragua	YES Nicaragua	2005	Urban
Paraguay	Financially Self-Sufficient School Programme	2003	Rural
Peru	Promotion of Employment and Entrepreneurship and the Management of Juvenile Labour Migration	2008	Both
Peru	Youth at Work	2011	Both

Source: Authors' elaboration.

Chapter 6

The future of work, politics and cities

Strong transformations – mainly driven by technological change – are taking place in the world of work, politics and cities. Technologies applied to jobs are replacing some tasks as well as creating new ones, thus shifting demand for skills. New ways of voicing social demands are emerging, playing a catalyst role to current discontent and detachment from the political system mainly shown by youth in LAC. The process of urbanisation continues in the region, and cities in the near future will be more densely populated, diverse, interconnected, economically vibrant and complex than the ones today. All these transformations are bringing about challenges and opportunities, picturing a future that will be very different in nature to the world we know today. Policies should prepare youth to embrace change, face new challenges and make the most of emerging opportunities.

Introduction

Today's youth are witnessing how technology, in conjunction with other forces, is paving the way to an era of "disruptive creation" in all areas of social, political and economic participation. This new generation will capitalise on these changes tomorrow, and will live and work in a different world from the one we know. This raises key questions as to the kind of future that youth can expect, and how this will affect different areas such as their productive activities, their decision processes and political participation, and the cities where they will live.

Latin America has the largest youth population of its history, and thus has the opportunity – and the challenge – of preparing young people to be the drivers of future progress and their own aspirations. This chapter examines three trends that could transform the lives of youth and affect their economic, political and social participation. First, the *future of work*, shaped by technology, demographics and globalisation, could largely transform the nature of jobs and change the skill set needed by the young to successfully participate in the labour market. The potential creation and destruction of jobs, alongside the change in tasks performed by humans, are transformational forces that could have large socio-economic consequences in Latin America. Policies, specifically related to skills and entrepreneurship, must begin to prepare for these future scenarios today. Second, the *future of politics* will probably be different. Technology, which is already opening new channels for civic engagement and political participation, will help reinvent democratic interaction and participation; today's youth are and will be at the forefront of these changes. Finally, the *future of cities* adds a territorial dimension to public policies that can support opportunities for youth. By 2050, approximately 90% of Latin America's population will be established in urban regions. This will result in numerous challenges related to financing, public services, transport and infrastructure, including deployment of broadband to accelerate development of information and communication technologies (ICTs). Other issues will revolve around sustainability, climate change, health and well-being. At the same time, the new urban landscape will create opportunities for entrepreneurs to respond with innovative approaches.

A shift in policies today is required to meet these challenges and provide youth with the right skills and opportunities for entrepreneurship. Policies should thus be oriented to help younger generations improve their economic, political and social participation in the coming world and support them as key drivers of further socio-economic progress in the region.

The *future of work*: Implications for skills, jobs and the nature of work

Three main structural trends are shaping the world of work: ageing, globalisation and technological change. Ageing creates imbalances across countries with different demographics that will eventually lead to further labour mobility, as well as challenges related to migration and wages. A new phase of globalisation will continue to fragment production stages, which in turn changes not only the type of jobs performed by workers, but also the range of tasks performed. Finally, technology advances are calling into question the kind of jobs we can expect for the future and who will perform them (Scarpetta, 2016).

Technological change is reaching a new era worthy of the label "fourth industrial revolution". New cycles of innovation are expected to transform the way we understand the world of work with potential to be both more creative and more destructive than many previous technological surges (*Financial Times*, 2016). The ever-larger penetration of ICTs, artificial intelligence, big data, the expanding power of computing and the Internet of Things (IoT) are some notable examples of this recent trend.

The impact of technology on jobs is unclear, but there will be a shift in tasks demanded and education and skills policies should be ready to adapt to it

The impact of technological change on jobs is far from certain. According to some authors, almost half of the jobs in the United States are at risk of being automated in the short term (Frey and Osborne, 2013). A more positive view is based on different arguments. First, the destruction of jobs could be much lower since technology will only replace certain tasks, not the full jobs or occupations (Levy and Murnane, 2013; Brynjolfsson and McAfee, 2014; Arntz, Gregory and Zierahn, 2016). In this sense, only around 9% of jobs would become automated in OECD member countries (Arntz, Gregory and Zierahn, 2016). Second, technology could create large numbers of new jobs where complex tasks still require genuine human skills. Humans will continue to perform many existing and emerging tasks where they have a "comparative advantage" relative to machines (*The Economist*, 2014). Finally, potential increases in productivity could release humans from certain tasks, enabling them to perform more productive tasks or reduce the burden of work; this could also liberate resources that might lead to investment in other activities and further job creation.

The future impact of technology on jobs will be largely determined by the specific characteristics of countries and regions, as well as by their capacity to adapt educational and skills policies. Thus the economic structure of the country/region, the available pool of skills, the institutional framework, as well as the capacity to implement policies that adapt to forthcoming change, will determine the final impact on jobs.

Latin America could witness significant employment shifts, mainly from the manufacturing and construction sectors to trade-related services (WEF, 2016a). By 2030, around 3.4 million net jobs could be lost (Figure 6.1), which represents a mere 1-2% of total employment in the region. While the absolute number remains relatively low, however, the shift in employment from some sectors to others could be much more disruptive.

Figure 6.1. **Projections of job creation and destruction by sectors by 2030 in Latin America**

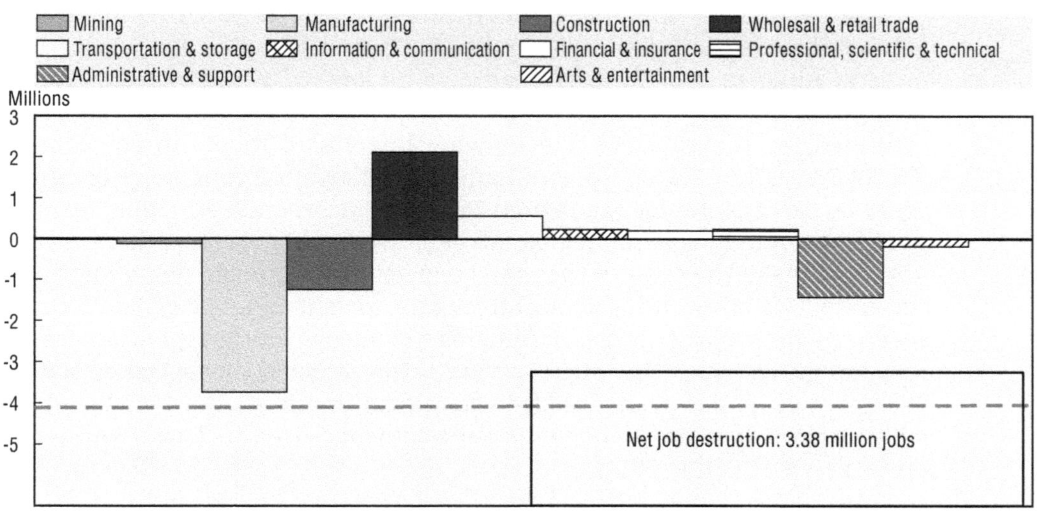

Source: OECD/ECLAC/CAF based on WEF (2016a) and ILO KILM dataset.
StatLink http://dx.doi.org/10.1787/888933414708

While the disruptive impact on full occupations may be lower than initially feared, a major shift could occur in the core set of skills that become in high demand. The distribution of tasks between humans and machines is already transforming work today, suggesting more changes ahead in the type of skills required for jobs. A popular quote claims that 65% of children entering the education system today will work in jobs that do not yet exist. In addition, by 2020, "more than a third of the desired core skills sets of most occupations will be comprised of skills that are not yet considered crucial to the job today" (WEF, 2016a). Increasingly demanded skills will be those more specific and exclusive to humans, and those needed for effective interaction with machines. A trend already observed over the last few decades in the United States could be accentuated: a decline in the relative importance of routine and non-routine manual tasks and routine cognitive tasks, and the increasing relevance of skills to work with new information and solve unstructured problems (Levy and Murnane, 2013). The largest growing demand will be for cognitive abilities, systems skills and complex problem-solving skills along with a stable demand for technical skills; fewer than one in three new jobs will require a larger demand of physical skills.

A trend with a strong impact on future jobs and the role of labour market institutions is the "sharing economy" or "gig economy". This trend, in which many workers complement their income with additional work in other jobs, creates new job opportunities and businesses, and fosters innovation. But it also raises questions about workplace protection and about the future of jobs. Workers may have more flexibility and autonomy, but these extra jobs are largely based on non-standard work arrangements that tend to offer fewer rights to social protection. In addition to less training and fewer opportunities to advance their careers, such workers have less access to credit and face greater insecurity. Further, having multiple unconventional jobs and income sources automatically challenges the traditional role of labour market institutions (working hours, minimum wages, unemployment insurance, taxes and benefits, collective agreements).

Better skills and technology are needed to help Latin America embrace opportunities

Low technology adoption in Latin America relative to OECD member economies will not impede the significant impact of ICTs on the region. Knowledge-based capital in Latin America and the Caribbean may be low (OECD/CAF/ECLAC, 2014), but rapid technological change could soon have a deeper impact. In fact, automation has already increased, as suggested by the growing imports of robots in some LAC countries (OECD/CAF/ECLAC, 2014). In addition, not participating fully in technological change could be detrimental for the region. Failing to incorporate emerging technologies into production could make the region fall behind in terms of competitiveness; it would be unable to make the most of the many opportunities brought about by change. Indeed, access to ICTs is becoming critical to ensure current and new generations take part in socio-economic opportunities. It remains a challenge for the region, where access is not only low but unequal (the "digital divide"). The United Nations (United Nations General Assembly, 2015) has acknowledged the critical importance of broadband to the three pillars of development – economic development, social inclusion and environmental protection (OECD/IDB, 2016).

Job polarisation associated with technological change could be particularly harmful in LAC, which has a relative abundance of workers with a mid-range of skills. In developed economies, technological change is destroying more jobs in the middle skills range, while increasingly creating jobs that require either low or high skills (Acemoglu and Autor, 2011). In Latin America, the recent expansion of education has led to a much larger enrolment and completion in secondary education, while enrolment rates in tertiary education are still very much below OECD levels. The educational structure of the labour force could be particularly affected by the job polarisation process.

Large inequalities in Latin America could be widened by job polarisation through further wage dispersion; this could affect particularly those working in the informal sector, including the emerging middle class. In recent years, the middle class – which is composed mainly of people with skills at the mid-range – has greatly expanded in the region. The size of the middle class (35%) and of the vulnerable (38.9%) suggests that job destruction in the mid-skilled range could have an impact on a large share of the population (World Bank, 2015). In addition, high levels of informal employment in Latin America – almost 50% (Chapter 1) – could be another source of concern; informal, less productive jobs can be the first ones to be displaced by technological change.

Poor education and skills levels may also make it difficult for the region to adapt and adopt change. Generally low levels of foundational skills in the region, as confirmed by poor results of the OECD's Programme for International Student Assessment (PISA), as well as the concentration of university graduates in fields of study other than science, technology, engineering or mathematics (STEM) (only one out of five students graduates from STEM [OECD//CAF/ECLAC, 2014]) suggest the region is not well prepared for the foreseeable shift in demand for skills, and that training and education systems may provide students with skills that will soon be outdated. The Programme for the International Assessment of Adult Competencies (PIAAC) sheds some light on how adults consistently score low in key competencies, including technology-rich environments, in Chile (OECD, 2016a).

The "sharing economy" could face particular challenges in the region, such as the still relatively low penetration of the Internet (just over half of the population has access to it); low levels of trust among citizens; and low levels of banking services and weakness of payment systems (IDB, 2016a). Good governance is critical to promoting regulatory frameworks that balance job security, while supporting innovation and enhancing the business environment. In any case, its dimension cannot be overstated (Cañigueral, 2015).

Finally, the digital divide may leave many on the sidelines from opportunities brought about by ICTs. Access to broadband platforms that ensure participation in this new technology wave has room for improvement. With almost half of the LAC population not connected to the Internet, 301 million people are considered to be offline. Brazil, Mexico and Colombia together, given their size and population, still need to connect around 180 million people – almost three times the population of France. In addition, this estimate does not yet classify the type or quality of Internet access available (OECD/IDB, 2016).

Skills policies, particularly for youth, should adapt to changing demands

All the above challenges can be turned into opportunities if policies are well designed to embrace change and to prepare the population to get the most out of an evolving world of work. New technologies offer the possibility of bringing about social and economic gains. First, technological advances could narrow labour productivity gaps between the region and developed economies. Second, technologies can foster productive diversification and the creation of new sectors within the economies of the region. As a corollary, these new trends could drive structural change. Finally, policies to enhance ICTs can improve access of traditionally isolated and disadvantaged groups to opportunities through the use of technology.

Some areas of policy, mainly related to skills for youth, seem particularly relevant to make the most of technological change and prepare current and coming generations for the future world of work. Current skills systems have to adapt for future challenges: existing policies should already be preparing youth for a world that changes fast. Some strategic policy areas are noted below:

- Curricula should have a stronger focus on foundational and generic skills, which are critical to help people learn and adapt to new tasks throughout their lives. This will also support labour mobility and help people adapt to changing labour market conditions.
- Life-long learning mechanisms need to be strengthened to help retrain or re-skill workers across the life cycle so they can adapt to changing conditions. Governments should co-ordinate with the private sector to underpin on-the-job-training systems, which should be a cornerstone of lifelong training.
- More focus should be given to providing the right incentives, both through better and clearer information on existing demand and returns, to enrol in STEM fields of study and in technical vocational education and training (TVET) programmes. These are oriented towards skills that are relatively scarce in the region. They are key to developing a more balanced pool of skills in LAC that can help the region benefit from the emerging demands in jobs of the future.
- More mechanisms need to be embedded in the education system to help respond to changing skills needs, anticipate demands and foster constant dialogue between the public, the private and the education sectors. Co-ordination among stakeholders, production of good data and sharing of results to inform policy making are relevant areas to support better adaptation to changes in skills demand.[1]
- Labour market institutions must be strengthened and rethought, as new jobs may bring about strong transformations related to hours worked, sources of labour income, or flexibility and transitions from employed to unemployed status, among other areas.
- Connecting schools and training centres is essential if ICTs are to equip citizens for the new economy (OECD/IDB, 2016).

The *future of politics:* Reconnecting emerging social demands and the political system

In a fast-changing world, social and political demands are evolving, and so are the tools and channels to voice them. In LAC, young generations are at the centre of these dynamics and represent one of the key agents shaping emerging political developments in the region. In addition, they are the future generation of adults who will live in a world where the relationship between the political system and the society is expected to be different. This section explores the evolving link between social demands and the political system given that trust and confidence in democratic institutions are low in the region. It also analyses emerging mechanisms to voice demands and to mobilise social groups, as well as some innovative examples on how to respond to them. It ends with the main policy conclusions that can help embrace the opportunities of change.

Trust in democratic institutions is low in the region

Confidence in democratic institutions is rather low in Latin America and the Caribbean, and has decreased recently. Almost 60% of Latin Americans stated in 2015 they were not at all satisfied (19%) or not very satisfied (37.5%) with the functioning of democracy, with only 10% being very much satisfied (Figure 6.2, Panel A). While evidence about government performance worsening in recent years is scarce, confidence in the functioning of democracy and in most democratic institutions (state, government and political parties, among others) has deteriorated. Between 2010-15, those with little or no confidence in the government jumped from around 55.5% to about 65% (Figure 6.2, Panel B). Overall, indicators that gauge trust do not seem to differ much across generations, with similar results for young people and adults.

Lack of trust in governments has also risen in recent years outside LAC. Only around 40% of citizens in OECD countries trust their governments (OECD, 2015a), for example. This indicator has deteriorated significantly since 2007, mainly related to the impact of the economic crisis and its political management. This suggests the economic slowdown in LAC may potentially be a source of further discontent and detachment from the political system in coming years.

Figure 6.2. **Perceptions of youth towards democracy and government in LAC**

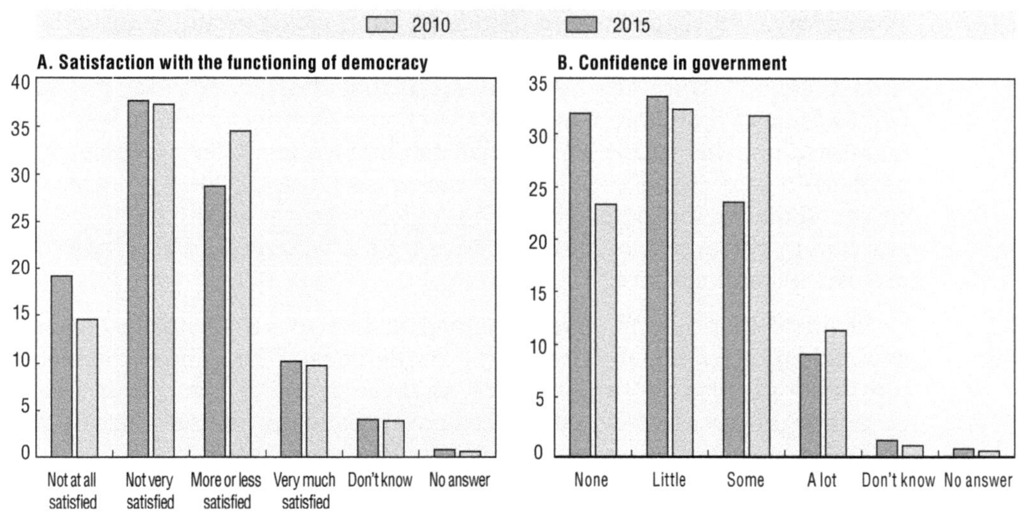

Source: OECD/CAF/ECLAC based on Latinobarómetro, 2016.
StatLink http://dx.doi.org/10.1787/888933414712

New and evolving social demands are strongly disconnected from the political system

The region faces increasing disconnection between the demands of society and responses by governments. Low levels of trust in democratic institutions, coupled with greater expectations and new and emerging demands, have widened the gap between society and governments in Latin America and the Caribbean. This has translated, among other things, to an increase of protests and social movements in the region in recent years. Lower voter turnout, as well as disenchantment with political parties, gives some indication of this broadening disconnection (Bianchi, 2016).

Social demands have evolved rapidly, alongside socio-economic progress and the expansion of the middle class. Between 2003 and 2013, the middle class grew from 20-35% and almost 40% of the population was considered to be vulnerable (World Bank, 2015). The middle-class expansion has been one of the most relevant socio-economic advances in the region in recent years. It has entailed deep transformations in the political demands of a class that usually seeks stable and predictable policies. When the middle class reaches at least 30% of the population, its members "can start to identify with one another and use their collective power to demand that the state spend their taxes to finance public services, security and other public goods" (Birdsall, 2016).

A generation of young people born and raised in democracy with new instruments – mainly technology-related – to voice and organise their needs is another key driver of the shift in social demands in LAC. Latin America has the largest number of young people (aged 15-29) in its history, reaching around 163 million. They represent the first generation growing up in a context of democracy, which has had an impact on their expectations and demands. In this context, technological progress has emerged as a catalyst of these new demands. Young people – though not exclusively – have found new ways to organise and mobilise around some of these technologies, using them as tools to voice their political discontent (Bianchi, 2016). The maturity and consolidation of civil society in Latin America have also encouraged social mobilisation.

Social demands in the short term could be influenced by the current economic slowdown, but looking ahead they will continue to revolve around preserving and generating socio-economic progress and more equal opportunities. Economic progress of recent years raised expectations, leading to certain frustration and social discontent as these were not fully satisfied. However, two elements associated with the economic slowdown could shape current demands. First, losing ground is usually seen as more problematic by citizens than never gaining it – something that behavioural studies call "loss aversion". This may heighten social mobilisation. Second, the nature of social demands in an economic slowdown can change as citizens will be less ready to support long-term reforms and more inclined to embrace short-term policies as long as they promise to protect their socio-economic status (Birdsall, 2016). In recent years, beyond citizen demands for socio-economic progress, other issues in the region are related to reaction to corruption or lack of justice for all, which could continue to be a focus of protests in coming years.

Political institutions have remained unable to satisfactorily respond to shifting demands, as shown by the rise in protests, demonstrations and social mobilisation. This remains a paradox in Latin America, as these demands come after a decade of socio-economic progress marked by reduced poverty and inequalities (Justino and Martorano, 2016). The paradox is very much linked to two phenomena mentioned above. First, the rise of expectations led to greater frustration for unachieved goals; indeed, subjective assessments of inequality rather than objective measures seem to drive social protests (Justino and Martorano, 2016). Second, new ways of organising and mobilising social movements have emerged, mainly boosted by technological progress and the associated higher level of connectedness.

Protests and social mobilisation have intensified in recent years

New ways of organising and voicing social demands have translated into a new wave of social movements across the globe and in Latin America. Different social movements at the global level have stood out in recent years, mainly ignited by the impact of the global economic crisis. #Occupy in the United States, the 15M movement in Spain and the Arab Spring are some of the most remarkable and influential examples. LAC has witnessed various social movements and protests that share many features with those seen in the international sphere, including #YaMeCansé or #YoSoy132 in Mexico, #NiUnaMenos in Argentina and Peru, #Yasunidos in Ecuador and #VemPraRua in Brazil (Bianchi, 2016). These represent social and political innovations based on technologies, usually emerging in urban contexts and mainly among youth, and where traditional political institutions have not played an adequate role. Some of these movements have already had specific impacts. In fact, through the use of technology these movements can give voice to minorities (e.g. indigenous and Afro communities) or populations with disabilities (e.g. El Salvador) at low cost; they contribute to the creation of regional networks (e.g. equal marriage in Argentina in 2010 generated campaigns in each Latin American country) and can raise international solidarity (e.g. students protests in Chile), with impacts on policies (e.g. free university) and on the political system (some protest leaders ended up as political representatives); and they can favour real time control of political authorities through fact-checking initiatives.

The new social movements in Latin America are emerging as an alternative to traditional politics. Indeed, these movements appear to be creating a new paradigm of political participation, which has strongly benefited from the digital revolution through the Internet, mobile phones and social networks (Bianchi, 2016). The movements share some common features. First, they bring together different interests since they result from the interaction of people who may participate in other movements and other causes and are not exclusively dedicated to that specific movement. Second, each is constructed as a network. As such, they can connect different people with similar sensitivities in diverse parts of the world, but do so in an informal way that can be more fragmented. Finally, each is based on open participation, decentralised and built up on collaboration; the ethics of collective action, which have been evolving alongside the development of these movements and networks, define how they function.

These social movements in Latin America contrast strongly with traditional political parties and institutions. They are more participative, horizontal and decentralised with a focus on present and specific challenges (Bianchi, 2016). In this context, the political system seems to be outdated and incapable of responding to certain social demands and adapting to emerging models of political participation. In order to restore the connection between social demands and the political system, some emerging trends must be institutionalised as part of the broader political system.

These emerging political practices face strong challenges and need support to become part of the broader political system. First, more complex democracies, with a higher degree of political participation and with more channels to participate, demand more and better educated citizens who also need to be better connected through access to technology. Many disadvantaged groups in the region have low levels of education and limited access to technologies. Yet these are precisely the groups in greater need of a political channel to voice their demands; they risk being left behind. Second, many movements do not seem to have had a real impact in decision making at the political level. Thus, mechanisms are needed to better integrate them into formal institutions and into public policies.

To make the most of these emerging movements and restore the connection between emerging demands and existing political institutions, social mobilisation needs to translate into more effective laws and stronger institutions; at the same time, existing institutions must be more open to social demands and make specific efforts to restore legitimacy. The political system needs to support social initiatives that improve civic engagement. In addition, current and future generations of youth must be ready to actively participate in politics and political life, taking full advantage of new opportunities. To this end, government transparency and openness should be enhanced to promote citizen participation (OECD, 2014), while supporting initiatives to strengthen education in citizenship, civic participation and leadership. Policies to support access to technologies for all must be fostered as a key mechanism for social and political participation.

The *future of cities*: The urban dimension of policies for youth

Young people have the potential and technological possibilities to build smarter, more sustainable cities for the future based on new skills and high-growth entrepreneurship. The new generation is already actively shaping the urban landscape in many Latin American cities. To build on these achievements, younger generations need opportunities to drive change, the right skills and favourable conditions for entrepreneurship and innovation.

Latin American cities in the future will be more densely populated, diverse, interconnected, economically vibrant and more complex than the ones today. This will exacerbate present challenges and bring about new ones. Rapid urbanisation will require not only accommodating an orderly expansion, but improving the quality of life by adopting smarter and more efficient strategies that lead to sustainable cities. However, daunting questions related to governance, inclusiveness, public safety and green practices should be addressed today.

Increasing levels of urbanisation will bring new challenges and opportunities alike

In 2015, approximately 80% of the LAC population lived in cities, making the region one of the most urbanised in the world. Cities have attracted the vast majority of citizens owing to higher prospects of employment, a more diverse and better paying pool of jobs (high and low quality) and increased access to public services. Although Latin America is a middle-income region, urbanisation levels are similar to those in advanced economies and almost twice as high as economies in Southeast Asia (47%) (Figure 6.3). Urbanisation was spurred by the rural-urban migration experienced between 1950 and 2000. During this period, an average population of 40% migrated to cities (United Nations, 2014).

Figure 6.3. **Urbanisation in Latin America and other regions of the world**
(percentage of the population)

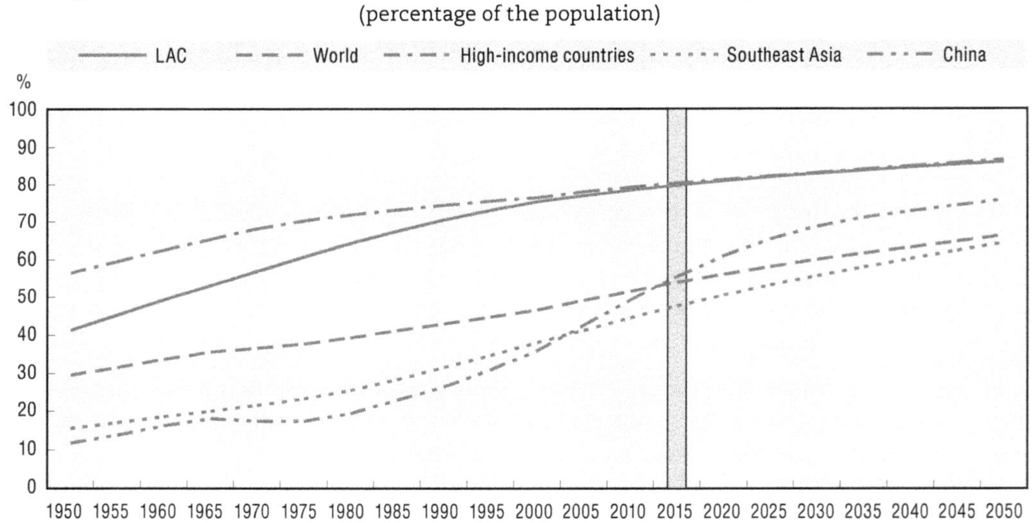

Source: United Nations (2014).
StatLink http://dx.doi.org/10.1787/888933414728

By 2050, almost nine out of ten Latin Americans will live in cities. Most urban-rural migration, in fact, took place over the last five decades; by 2050, only 6.4% of the population is expected to migrate to the cities. Given the high levels of urbanisation, the majority of population growth will take place in cities. In 2015, more than 500 million Latin Americans lived in cities; by 2050, this figure is expected to rise to more than 673 million (34% increase) with 86% of Latin Americans living in cities.

Latin America already has one of the highest levels of concentration in densely populated metropolises, and this will increase over time. In 2015 more than 14% of the urban population lived in densely populated metropolises. By 2030 population density within large cities will increase up to more than 17% to the detriment of smaller cities.

In 2015 the region also showed levels of density considerably superior to those in high-income economies (11.7% of urban population) and in Southeast Asia (7.7% of urban population) (Figure 6.4). These differences are expected to increase considerably with respect to high-income countries and decrease compared with economies in Southeast Asia. Cities and settlements of different sizes will both face urbanisation challenges; however, these issues will differ between large and smaller cities. Densely populated metropolises (i.e. more than 10 million people) are more likely to face issues like lack of capacity to meet demand for basic services and the ability to adapt and accommodate urban expansion and further population growth. For smaller cities, challenges might be more concentrated in connectivity (outside the cities) and competitiveness. A common challenge for small and large cities alike will be dealing with inequalities and social exclusion that might ensue owing to high levels of population concentration.

Figure 6.4. **Distribution of population in cities by 2030 by size**

(percentage of urban population)

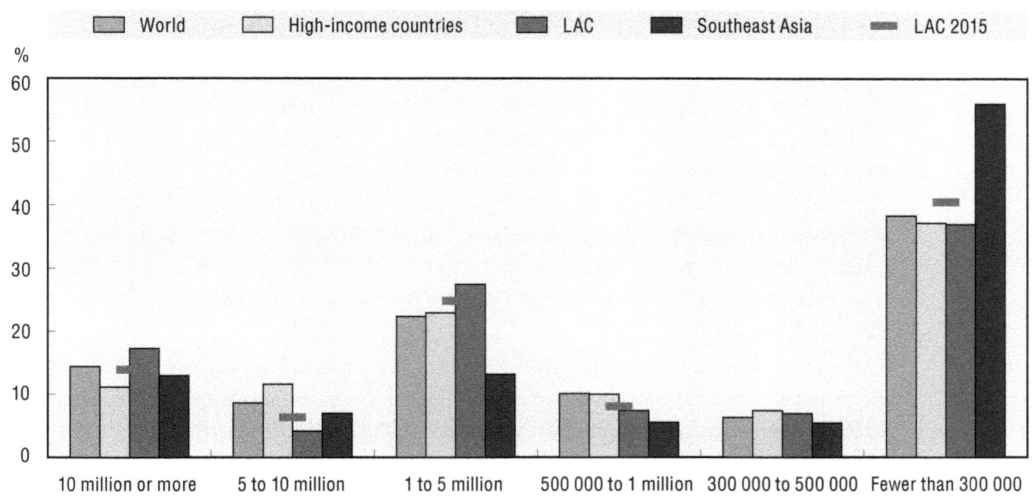

Source: United Nations (2014).

StatLink http://dx.doi.org/10.1787/888933414735

Increased urbanisation levels and population growth may exacerbate current challenges in cities, even as new challenges emerge. On the one hand, cities must respond to existing urban sprawl, pollution, poverty, unemployment and informality. The key to sustainable urban centres will be the use of new technologies, clean energy sources, innovation and a broader urban development strategy that includes improved transportation infrastructure, land-use and housing. This approach will reduce environment impact and increase productivity and liveability (WEF, 2016b, 2016c). On the other hand, climate change and higher levels of urbanisation in the future could complicate the ability of some cities to deliver public services (e.g. water, waste management, transportation, health care, energy). For example, increasing water demand could push up prices and accelerate the depletion of water available for agriculture or ecosystems. Similarly, health problems could increase because of air pollution caused by energy production or transportation. Bigger cities would also produce higher levels of solid and liquid waste that, if not properly treated, could translate into health and environmental problems. This will require more co-ordination within all levels of government, especially of local governments, and becoming more efficient as a way of ensuring sustainability. Also, these challenges will only be addressed by investing in new technologies and innovation that could allow the cities of the region to leapfrog and boost productivity and economic growth. Similarly, further investment in human capital could create the necessary skills to amplify the characteristic of cities as centres of creativity and innovation in order to mitigate climate change shocks and to ensure long-term planning with a sustainable view (UN-HABITAT, 2011).

Young people can be key drivers of smarter, more sustainable cities in Latin America. In the future, LAC youth will live in a more urbanised region and play a key role in addressing associated challenges, including delivery of public services. The participation of youth in Latin America's path towards sustainable urban development can also be a unique opportunity to boost inclusive economic growth (Box 6.1), enhance productivity and increase overall living standards. To support these efforts, policies for skills and entrepreneurship will need to acknowledge the transformative role of youth in moving towards smarter and more sustainable cities. Policy makers must also understand the main challenges for sustainability in cities, including those related to climate change, use of space and finite resources, and provision of services.

Box 6.1. **OECD Inclusive Cities Initiative**

Cities and metropolises are critical to foster inclusive growth in the developed and developing world alike. The OECD initiative for inclusive growth within cities acknowledges this fact and with the support of the Ford Foundation the OECD launched an initiative on Inclusive Growth in 2012 to help governments analyse rising inequalities, monitor material living standards and broader well-being, and design policies that promote equity and growth. The OECD approach to inclusive growth is multi-dimensional, going beyond income to see how people are faring in other areas of life, such as jobs and health.

Champion Mayors for Inclusive Growth is a global coalition of local leaders who committed to promote a more inclusive form of economic growth in cities (OECD, 2016b). The initiative, launched in March 2016, articulates policies towards achieving inclusive economic development; inclusive housing, transportation and sustainable urban environments; and partnerships and new sources of financing for inclusive growth in cities. The cities of Medellín (Colombia), Curridabat (Costa Rica), Quillota and Santiago (Chile), Kingston (Jamaica), Merida, Ciudad de Mexico and Tijuana (Mexico), Cuzco and Lima (Peru) participate from Latin America.

To become sustainable, cities must be ready to face climate change

The impact of climate change, both locally and globally, is one of the main challenges the region's cities face. At the global level, cities are responsible for 40-60% of greenhouse gas (GHG) emissions produced by industry, as well as 60-70% of emissions generated by consumption – a main culprit of global warming (Kohli, 2016). These emissions have contributed considerably to global warming, including higher worldwide temperatures and sea level, and more acidic oceans. At the local level, poorly planned cities have reduced air quality, depleted water sources, polluted water and created traffic jams among other negative externalities that have lowered quality of life and created serious health problems.

Climate change will have different impacts on cities in Latin America depending on their characteristics, location (coast or inland cities) and ability to adapt. Coastal cities might be more prone to negative impacts as rising sea levels or higher natural disasters could pose a serious risk. Similarly, cities exposed to droughts might find it harder to maintain water supply. On the other hand, cities might also become more vulnerable to higher precipitation levels that could result in strong floods or increases in diseases such as Zika or dengue fever. Some cities face multiple risks. In 2010, for example, the city of Rondônia in Brazil suffered the driest event recorded in the Amazon; four years later it recorded the largest flood in 106 years. Both events had dreadful consequences on the economy, environment and society (OECD, 2015b).

Better urban planning and more investments are required to reduce the footprints of cities on the environment and decrease health risks, while increasing well-being through the use of clean and smart transportation systems. For instance, lack of urban planning (among other factors) has led to an inefficient urban sprawl, population growth and policies that favoured private vehicle ownership. As a result, the current transportation network in Latin America consists mainly of privately owned cars run on fossil fuels that create constant traffic jams and generate high GHG emissions. In fact, after power generation, transport is the second highest source of GHG emissions (IEA, 2015).

A shift towards public transport within cities, alongside more efficient and clean vehicle technologies for public and private vehicles, is key to producing environmental and health benefits in the region (ITF, 2015).To explore further the prospects of different types of internal mobility policies in the region, the ITF (2015) compares public and private transport-oriented urbanisation scenarios under high and low road infrastructure perspectives. In the baseline scenario for Latin America, the car fleet in urban centres with more than 500 000 habitants would grow 5 times, while the two-wheeler fleet would grow 21 times. This represents an average annual growth rate of 4% and 8% for cars and two-wheelers, respectively. Thus, urbanisation that promotes private transport yields mobility scenarios with highly intensive CO_2 emissions. Conversely, policy scenarios that focus on public transportation would allow cities to reduce CO_2 emissions to 17% relative to baseline scenario levels, generating a lower marginal cost of mobility.

The development and use of clean energy is crucial to reduce GHG emissions and guarantee a sustainable path for cities in Latin America. As in transport, energy used by industries and households (electricity, heating and cooling) depends on fossil fuels, producing high levels of GHG emissions, air pollution and health problems. To reduce both dependency on fossil fuels and GHG emissions Latin American economies could benefit further from other energy sources complemented by local sources (such as solar rooftops) and smarter grid management that maximises energy efficiency. Investments in clean energies generate economic as well as environmental and health benefits. Solar or Eolic energy are economically competitive and a feasible alternative to fossil fuels. In this regard, Brazil has invested in a successful low-carbon energy mix. The use of renewable energy sources has increased steadily to reach 41% of total primary energy supply in 2012 (more than four times the OECD average) (OECD, 2015d). Renewables account for 83% of electricity generation, far above the OECD average of 21% (IEA, 2015). Similarly, Costa Rica covers more than 99% of electricity demands with clean energy.

Investment in better water management and governance will also be necessary to address growing urbanisation demands, climate change and water scarcity. Non-existent or ageing infrastructure is common in LAC countries, leading to inefficiency, particularly with respect to water (OECD, 2016c, 2015c). Moreover, further population density could result in additional water pollution and other stresses on water resources and infrastructure, while climate change is likely to threaten water availability for different uses. Better governance would improve the level of service provision and water security, creating a much-needed balance between urban and rural water supply of future cities (OECD, 2012). Coping with present and future water-related challenges will be possible only through coherent policy, engaged stakeholders, well-designed regulatory frameworks, adequate and accessible information, and sufficient capacity, integrity and transparency (OECD, 2016c, 2015b).

Countries must furnish the right incentives to sway cities on to a green path of environmentally friendly transportation, energy use and water treatment. Among available instruments, taxes on energy use play an important role. Such taxes will induce households to alter consumption, which will reduce GHG emissions and support more environmentally friendly transportation and energy use. LAC countries typically levy taxes on energy use at lower rates than OECD member economies; for instance, the simple average of the effective tax rates on CO_2 from energy use in Argentina, Brazil, Chile and Mexico is 12%,[2] compared to 52%[3] in OECD member countries (OECD, 2015d). The tax revenues raised may also help economies in Latin America and the Caribbean to finance the necessary public investment to achieve more sustainable cities.

Smart cities: Building sustainable cities requires smarter use of space and finite resources, and more efficient services

The advent and expansion of ICTs, artificial intelligence, the growth of the IoT and the big data revolution have fundamentally changed the ways in which individuals, especially youth, engage with one another in a globalised world economy. Data have fundamentally changed how companies approach customers; technology has altered the way we communicate and participate in society; and the IoT is revamping how resources are used at home and at work. Cities have not been immune to these trends; the amalgamation between ICT, IoT, big data and cities is creating "smart cities".

Cities around the world are becoming smarter by better using technology and data to become more resource-efficient, and to provide better quality and sustainable services in a dynamic and rapidly changing environment. Several cities around the globe are using technology and data in innovative ways to build smarter infrastructure (smart buildings), improve energy provision (smart grid) and engage in sustainable and environmentally friendly practices (smart transportation systems). Successful smart cities are ubiquitous in Europe, Japan and South Korea. For instance, Stockholm covers 80% of its heating demand through combustion and waste management. Hamburg has installed 200 000 low energy consumption bulbs in 400 public buildings that save EUR 3.4 million per year. Seoul constructed photovoltaic systems on to buildings to reduce GHG emissions and its heavy dependence on nuclear energy (Ecointelegencia, 2012).

Latin American cities rank low in terms of sustainability, efficiency and urban development. Although data metrics are still in their infancy and scarce with respect to smart cities, three systems can be highlighted. The City Prosperity Index (Box 6.2) is a composite indicator that analyses several aspects of cities and is a monitoring framework for the Sustainable Development Goals (SDGs) at the level of cities (UN-Habitat, 2015). The Ericsson Networked Society Index (Ericsson, 2014) appraises the maturity of ICTs in association with the economic, social and environmental performance of 40 cities throughout the world. The Cities in Motion Index (IESE, 2016) uses a multi-dimensional approach to build a synthetic gauge that captures 50 indicators on 10 different dimensions for 135 cities throughout the globe. In all these systems, Latin American and Caribbean cities are ranked at the bottom in a static dimension, but several are ranked as highly promising in a dynamic setting (Figure 6.5). IESE (2016) shows that some Latin American and Caribbean cities have experienced rapid progress in their smart city scores since 2011 but are still vulnerable; this rapid change stresses the further developments still required for the near future.

Cities in LAC are a hub of smart innovations that present entrepreneurship opportunities for the young, although they still require nurturing. Cities such as Rio de Janeiro are pioneering models of data collection to become more efficient in the use of municipal resources (Ericsson, 2014); Centro de Operaçõnes compiles 30 different types of data from several district sources. Neighbouring cities are replicating the Rio model as a form of inter-city collaboration that should serve as a best practice for the region. Also, Santiago has a pilot project within its Enterprise District that promotes electric vehicles in public transportation. Bogotá is also a pioneer in transportation solutions such as Bus Rapid Transit. Smaller cities are also innovating (IDB, 2016b), but require more support from the central or federal branches of government.

Box 6.2. **The City Prosperity Initiative: A tool to measure sustainable urban development**

In 2012, UN-Habitat created a tool to measure the sustainability of cities known as the City Prosperity Index, which was accompanied by a conceptual matrix, the Wheel of Urban Prosperity. In 2013, however, UN Habitat received numerous requests from local authorities and central governments to estimate their respective prosperity indexes. Mayors and other decision makers wanted to know how their cities compared others. In particular, they sought knowledge on how to improve ratings and measurements of cities towards the prosperity path, including critical insights into which programmes and policies work, and their possible impacts. In response, UN-Habitat transformed the City Prosperity Index into the City Prosperity Initiative (CPI) to offer cities from developed and developing countries alike the possibility to create indicators, baseline targets and goals that can support ambitious, but measurable, long-term plans.

CPI is an integral part of the Data Revolution for Sustainable Development. Apart from integrating new sources of data and increasing their usefulness, CPI also enables city authorities, as well as local and national stakeholders, to identify opportunities and potential areas of intervention for their cities to become more prosperous.

Further development of smart cities in Latin America and Caribbean economies is constrained by infrastructure deficits, as well as by unplanned and improvised expansion of urban centres. The infrastructure gap amounts to over 6% of annual regional GDP between 2012 and 2020 (ECLAC, 2014). The large number of informal urban settlements that have proliferated within the region's cities lack many basic services, including sanitation. To cope with highly populated and polluted urban centres, public administrations must become more efficient and effective. Key areas include more inclusive participation; better governance; sustainable and environmentally friendly utilities, mobility and transportation; and effective public safety and disaster management.

To the extent that current policy makers are able to empower youth and encourage their creativity and entrepreneurship, the younger generation will lead the transition towards smarter, more interconnected and sustainable cities. The potential of Latin American and Caribbean youth remains largely untapped. The youth cohort is more connected and technologically savvy than any other generation; with the right skills and incentives they can shine a light on difficult issues of both today and tomorrow.

The cities of the future will need to address the SDGs holistically. With populations increasingly urbanised, achieving the SDGs within cities will greatly contribute to reaching these goals on a broader national level. Therefore, SDGs should be seen as a web of interconnected and interdependent goals that require a multi-dimensional approach in which all levels of government and society are actively involved.

Figure 6.5. **Cities in Motion Index 2015**

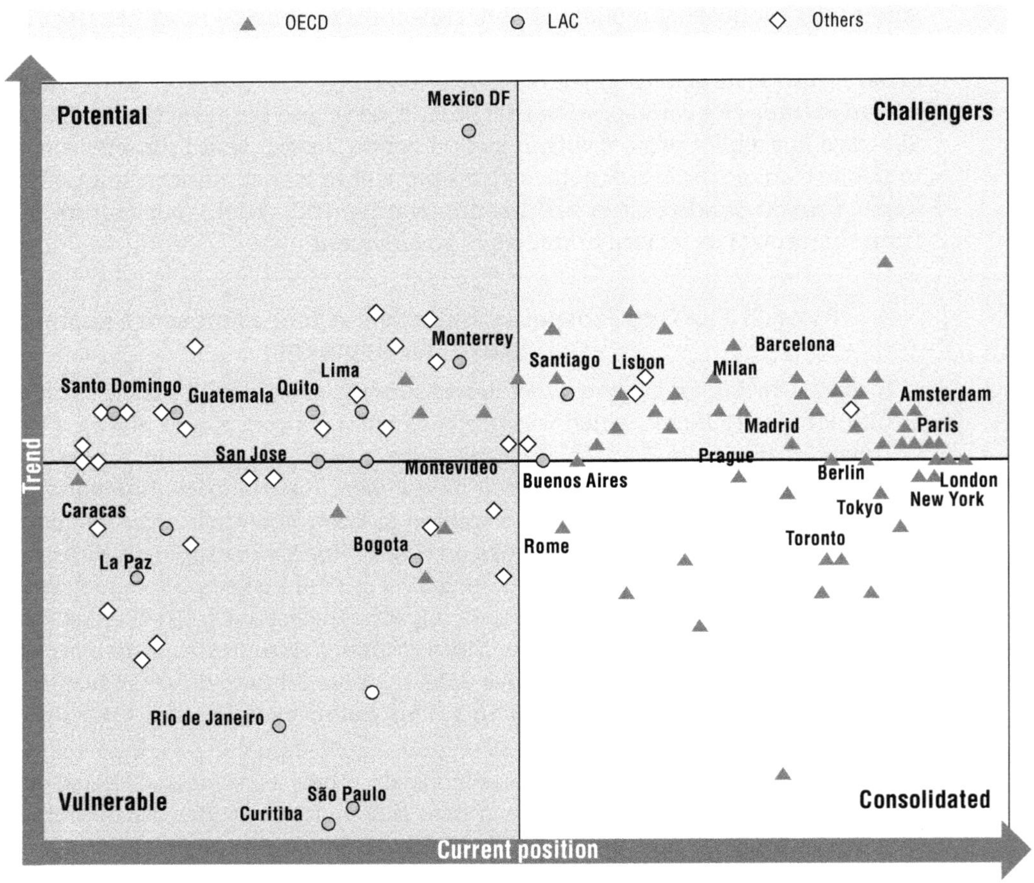

Source: IESE (2016), Cities in Motion Index.
StatLink http://dx.doi.org/10.1787/888933414745

Concluding remarks

Deep transformations are taking place in the field of work, politics and cities that will shape tomorrow's world. These must be taken into account when designing policies for youth today, particularly regarding skills and entrepreneurship. Technological change is one of the main drivers of these trends. In the world of work a shift in the tasks demanded is expected to take place owing to automation of jobs, which in the OECD could reach 9% of total jobs (Arntz et al. 2016). New opportunities are expected to emerge, in jobs where complex tasks require genuine human skills such as working with new information, solving unstructured problems, or certain cognitive and socio-emotional skills. In Latin America, between 1% and 2% of jobs (3.4 million jobs) could be destroyed by 2030, with a significant reallocation of jobs across sectors, mainly from manufacturing and construction towards wholesale and retail trade and the information and communication sectors. Latin America must be ready for this change: in a region with high inequalities and a relative abundance of skills at the mid-range (more prone to be automated), the impact in terms of job destruction can be large, which could widen inequalities. Policies to provide youth with stronger foundational and generic skills to support labour mobility and adaptability to change, to reskill workers throughout the life cycle, and mechanisms to anticipate skills demands, will be key to embrace change and make the most of emerging opportunities in the world of work.

Social and political demands are rapidly evolving, and the tools and channels to voice them are also experiencing significant transformations. Youth in Latin America are playing a relevant role in shaping emerging political developments. Recent progress has lifted expectations about well-being. But youth have not particularly benefited from these advancements, and the distance between reality and expectations of the first generation born and raised in democracy has widened. In 2015, almost 60% of Latin Americans stated they were not at all satisfied (19%) or not very satisfied (37.5%) with the functioning of democracy, and 65% said they had little or no confidence in the government (Latinobarómetro, 2016). Technological advancements have played the role of a catalyst, through which young generations have found new ways to organise and mobilise, using them as tools to voice their political discontent. LAC has witnessed various social movements and protests recently, including #YaMeCansé or #YoSoy132 in Mexico, # NiUnaMenos in Argentina and Peru, #Yasunidos in Ecuador, and # VemPraRua in Brazil. These social and political innovations are emerging as an alternative to traditional politics, and appear to be creating a new paradigm of political participation, in a context where the political system seems to be outdated and incapable of responding to certain social demands. In order to restore the connection between social demands and the political system, some emerging trends must be institutionalised as part of the broader political system. Mobilisation needs to translate into more effective laws and stronger institutions; at the same time, existing institutions must be more open to social demands and make specific efforts to restore legitimacy.

By 2050, LAC youth will live in a region where nine out of ten Latin Americans live in cities. Young people have the potential and technological possibilities to be key drivers of smarter, more sustainable cities in the region. They can play a key role in transforming cities so they follow a green path into more sustainable, sanitary and inclusive living environments. An avenue to overcome these challenges is to invest in smarter cities by better using available technology and through better urban planning. Similarly, to achieve a sustainable path, investment must be undertaken to address current infrastructure gaps, increase the use of clean energies, improve water treatment and provide more and better public transport. Youth represent a special opportunity as they are more connected and technologically savvy than any other generation; with the right skills and incentives, they can shine a light to overcome present and future challenges and build cities that offer opportunities and favour inclusion. Thus it will be crucial to further develop skills and technological savviness of youth in Latin America, while fostering their innovation and entrepreneurship capacities to deliver more efficient, smarter cities.

Notes

1. OECD (2016d) is an exhaustive report on effective strategies for improving labour market information on skills needs and ensuring this information helps develop the right skills in OECD member countries.
2. Unweighted average for Argentina, Brazil, Mexico and Chile.
3. Unweighted average for 34 OECD economies.

References

Acemoglu, D. and D.H. Autor (2011), "Skills, tasks and technologies: Implications for employment and earnings", in O. Ashenfelter and D.E. Card (eds.) *Handbook of Labor Economics*, Vol. 4B, pp. 1043-1171, Elsevier, Amsterdam.

Arntz, M., T. Gregory and U. Zierahn (2016), "The risk of automation for jobs in OECD countries: A comparative analysis", *OECD Social, Employment and Migration Working Papers,* No. 189, OECD Publishing, Paris.

Bianchi, M. (2016), "Youth and the new political paradigm in Latin America", *OECD Development Centre Working Papers*, OECD Publishing, Paris.

Birdsall, N. (2016), "Middle-class heroes: The best guarantee of good governance", Centre for Global Development, www.cgdev.org/publication/ft/middle-class-heroes-best-guarantee-good-governance (accessed 16 February 2016).

Brynjolfsson E. and M. McAfee (2014), *The Second Machine Age: Work Progress and Prosperity in a Time of Brilliant Technologies*, W.W. Norton & Company, New York.

Cañigueral, A. (2015), "Can digital sharing economy platforms pull Latin America's informal sector into the mainstream? Yes", *Americas Quarterly*, Summer, Americas Society and Council of the Americas, New York.

ECLAC (2014), "The economic infrastructure gap and investment in Latin America", *FAL Bulletin,* Vol. 332/4, Economic Commission for Latin America and the Caribbean, Santiago.

Ecointeligencia (2012), *Ciudades Ecointeligentes* (1), www.ecointeligencia.com/documents/ciudades-ecointeligentes-1.pdf.

Ericsson (2014), *Networked Society City Index 2014,* Ericsson, Stockholm, www.ericsson.com/res/docs/2014/networked-society-city-index-2014.pdf.

Financial Times (2016), "Bring on the robots but reboot our societies too", 6 May 2016, *FT View, Financial Times*, London.

Frey, C. and M. Osborne (2013), "The future of employment: How susceptible are jobs to computerisation?", *Working Paper,* Oxford Martin Programme on Technology and Employment, University of Oxford.

IDB (2016a), "Economía Colaborativa en América Latina" ["The Collaborative Economy in Latin America"], Instituto de Empresa, Fondo Multilateral de Inversiones, Inter-American Development Bank and Government of Spain, Madrid, http://idbdocs.iadb.org/wsdocs/getDocument.aspx?DOCNUM=40259423.

IDB (2016b), *Emerging and Sustainable Cities Initiative* website, Inter-American Development Bank, Washington, DC, www.iadb.org/en/topics/emerging-and-sustainable-cities/sustainable-cities-publications,18715.html (accessed 15 June 2016).

IEA (2015), *Energy Statistics of OECD Countries 2015*, International Energy Agency, OECD Publishing, Paris, http://dx.doi.org/10.1787/energy_stats_oecd-2015-en.

IESE (2016), *Cities in Motion – Index 2016*, IESE Business School-University of Navarra and Center for Globalisation and Strategy, Navarra, Spain, www.iese.edu/research/pdfs/ST-0396-E.pdf.

ILO (2016), *Key Indicators of the Labour Market (KILM), Ninth Edition*, International Labour Organization, Geneva.

ITF (2015), *ITF Transport Outlook 2015*, International Transport Forum, OECD Publishing, Paris, http://dx.doi.org/10.1787/9789282107782-en.

Justino, P. and B. Martorano (2016), "Inequality, distributive beliefs and protests: A recent story from Latin America", *IDS Working Paper*, No. 467, Institute of Development Studies, University of Sussex.

Kohli, H. (2016), "El mundo en el año 2050. En busca de una sociedad más próspera, justa y armoniosa" ["The world in the year 2050. Seeking a more prosperous, fair and harmonious society"], Emerging Markets Forum, Washington, DC.

Latinobarómetro (2016), *Latinobarómetro Análisis de Datos* (database), www.latinobarometro.org/latOnline.jsp (accessed 10 June 2016).

Levy, F. and R.J. Murnane (2013), "Dancing with robots: Human skills for computerized work", 17 July, *Third Way*, Washington, DC, www.thirdway.org/report/dancing-with-robots-human-skills-for-computerized-work.

OECD (2016a), "Skills matter: Further results from the Survey of Adult Skills", *OECD Skills Studies*, OECD Publishing, Paris, http://dx.doi.org/10.1787/9789264258051-en.

OECD (2016b), "Proceedings from the Launch of the Inclusive Growth in Cities Campaign" OECD and Ford Foundation, OECD Publishing, Paris, www.oecd.org/inclusive-growth/events/IGIC%20Launch%20Proceedings_FINAL.pdf.

OECD (2016c), "Water Governance in Cities", *OECD Studies on Water*, OECD Publishing, Paris, http://dx.doi.org/10.1787/9789264251090-en.

OECD (2016d), *Getting Skills Right: Assessing and Anticipating Changing Skill Needs*, OECD Publishing, Paris, http://dx.doi.org/10.1787/9789264252073-en.

OECD (2015a), *Government at a Glance 2015*, OECD Publishing, Paris, http://dx.doi.org/10.1787/gov_glance-2015-en.

OECD (2015b) "Water resources governance in Brazil", *OECD Studies on Water*, OECD Publishing, Paris, http://dx.doi.org/10.1787/9789264238121-en.

OECD (2015c), *OECD Principles on Water Governance*, OECD Publishing, Paris, www.oecd.org/gov/regional-policy/OECD-Principles-on-Water-Governance-brochure.pdf.

OECD (2015d), *Taxing Energy Use 2015: OECD and Selected Partner Economies*, OECD Publishing, Paris, http://dx.doi.org/10.1787/9789264232334-en.

OECD (2014), *Open Government in Latin America*, OECD Publishing, Paris, http://dx.doi.org/10.1787/9789264223639-en.

OECD (2012), "Water governance in Latin America and the Caribbean: A multi-level approach", *OECD Studies on Water*, OECD Publishing, Paris, http://dx.doi.org/10.1787/9789264174542-en.

OECD/CAF/ECLAC (2015), *Latin American Economic Outlook 2016: Towards a New Partnership with China*, OECD Publishing, Paris, http://dx.doi.org/10.1787/9789264246218-en.

OECD/CAF/ECLAC (2014), *Latin American Economic Outlook 2015: Education, Skills and Innovation for Development*, OECD Publishing, Paris, http://dx.doi.org/10.1787/leo-2015-en.

OECD/IDB (2016), *Broadband Policies for Latin America and the Caribbean: A Digital Economy Toolkit*, OECD and Inter-American Development Bank, OECD Publishing, Paris, http://dx.doi.org/10.1787/9789264251823-en.

Scarpetta, S. (2016), "What future for work?", *OECD Observer*, No. 305/1, OECD Publishing, Paris, http://dx.doi.org/10.1787/e0e110b2-en.

The Economist (2014), "The third great wave", *Special Report, The World Economy*, 4 October.

UN-HABITAT (2015), *The City Prosperity Initiative: 2015 Global City Report, UN-Habitat and International City Leaders*, UN-Habitat, Nairobi.

UN-HABITAT (2011), *Cities and Climate Change: Global Report on Human Settlements 2011*, UN-Habitat, Nairobi.

United Nations (2014), *World Urbanization Prospects, 2014 Revision*, Department of Economic and Social Affairs, Population Division, New York.

United Nations General Assembly (2015), "Transforming our world: The 2030 Agenda for Sustainable Development", Resolution Adopted by the General Assembly on 25 September 2015, United Nations, New York, https://sustainabledevelopment.un.org/post2015/transformingourworld.

WEF (2016a), "The future of jobs: Employment, skills and workforce strategy for the fourth industrial revolution", *Global Challenge Insight Report*, World Economic Forum, Geneva, http://www3.weforum.org/docs/WEF_Future_of_Jobs.pdf .

WEF (2016b) *Inspiring Future Cities and Urban Services: Shaping the Future of Urban Development & Services Initiative*, World Economic Forum, Geneva, www3.weforum.org/docs/WEF_Urban-Services.pdf.

WEF (2016c), *Shaping the Future of Urban Development & Services*, website, www.weforum.org/global-challenges/projects/future-of-urban-development-services/ (accessed 31 May 2016).

World Bank (2015), *Equity Lab, LAC Equity Lab Tabulations of SEDLAC* (database), CEDLAS and the World Bank, Washington, DC, www.worldbank.org/en/topic/poverty/lac-equity-lab1/overview (accessed 15 May 2016).

Country notes

Argentina

Recent trends

Labour market conditions in Argentina continue to improve, but are still below the Latin America and Caribbean (LAC) average. The recovery from the 2001 crisis remains uneven across different groups within the workforce. Unemployment rates for adults (aged 30-64), which have been declining since 2004, fell to 4.5% in 2014; this is still above the LAC average (3.3%), but below the OECD average (5.8%). Between 2004 and 2014, informality rates for adults decreased by almost 15 percentage points – from almost 42% to around 27%. These figures are from the Socio-Economic Database for Latin America and the Caribbean (SEDLAC) data based on Argentina's National Household Survey (EPH).

Despite considerable progress, gaps in youth inclusion in the labour market and society persist throughout the region and are especially marked in Argentina. Youth unemployment is on a slow downward trend, dropping from 21% to 14% over 2004-14, but still remains higher than the LAC average (10%) and OECD average (12%). Informality rates for youth (50% in 2014) are improving, but are as twice as high as those for adults.

Activity status of youth by single year of age in Argentina, 2014

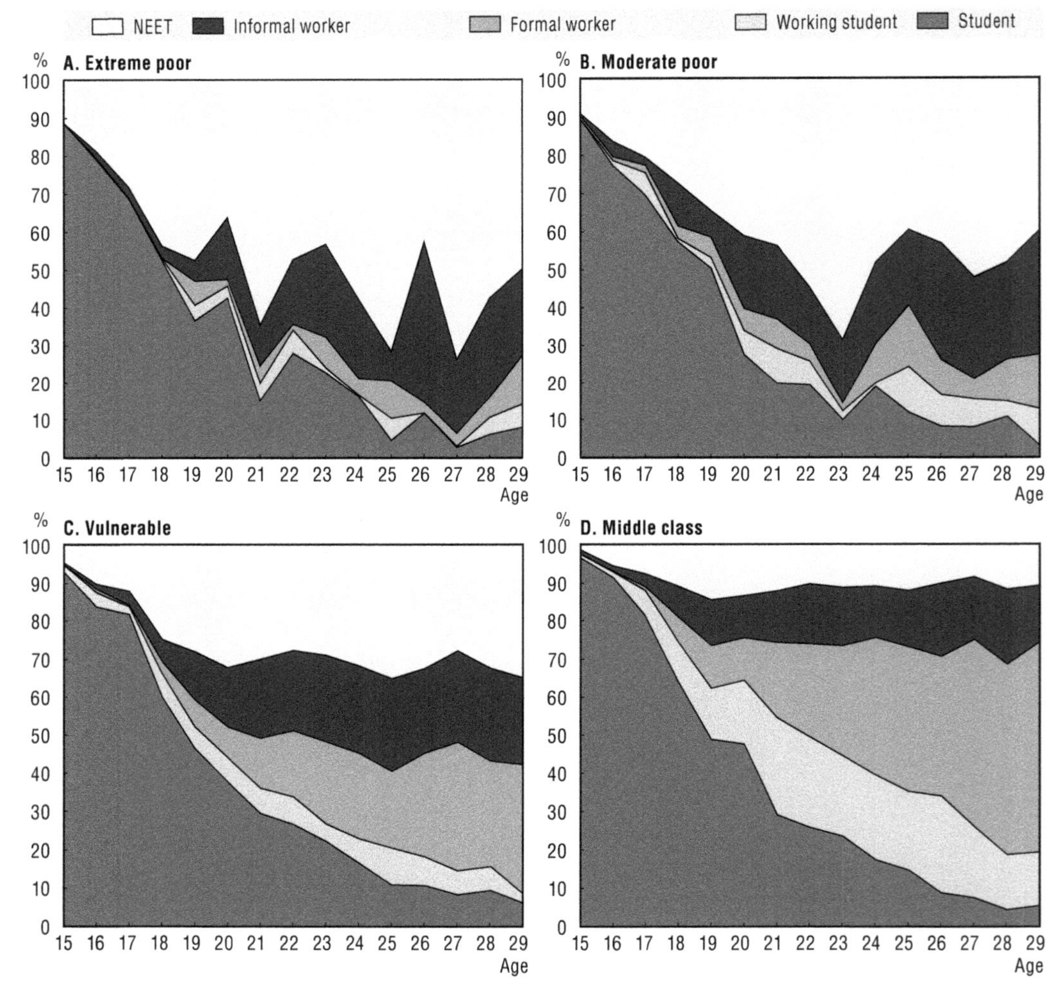

Source: OECD and World Bank tabulations of SEDLAC (CEDLAS and the World Bank).
StatLink http://dx.doi.org/10.1787/888933415421

More than a third of young people in Argentina are studying – 37% vs. 25% in the LAC region – and more than 40% are working or working students. Young people who are neither employed nor in education nor training ("NEETs") risk being permanently left behind in the labour market. This risk is especially high for the relatively large share of poor and vulnerable NEETs. In Argentina, more than 20% of young people aged 15-29 are NEETs compared with 15% in the OECD as a whole.

The poor and vulnerable account for more than three-quarters of all NEETS. There is also a 15 percentage point gender gap between women and men considered NEETs.

Youth confidence in the transparency of election results (35.3%) is lower than that of adults (39.2%). However, young Argentineans feel slightly safer (42.5%) compared with adults (41.9%), according to the Gallup World Monitor survey.

Educational attainment in Argentina is higher than average for the region. In 2014, 67% of youth (aged 25-29) completed secondary education (vs. 55% for the LAC average) and 17% completed tertiary education (vs. 15% for the LAC average). However, along with other countries in the region Argentina faces high drop-out and low completion rates for school: 25% of youth (aged 15-29) have not completed secondary education and are out of school, while 12% of secondary education students are enrolled in technical and vocational education and training (TVET) programmes. Argentina's spending on TVET – 0.05% of gross domestic product – stands well below both LAC and OECD averages.

In terms of entrepreneurship in Latin America, the majority of self-employed are own-account workers (12%) rather than employers (1% for young workers). Additionally, data from the Global Entrepreneurship Monitor (GEM) show that the share of youth in Argentina (aged 18-29) who become entrepreneurs out of necessity (compared to all early-stage entrepreneurs) is higher (about 36% in 2015) than the regional (26%) and OECD averages (16%).

Barriers to entrepreneurship are almost twice as high in Argentina than the OECD average. The most important barriers faced by young entrepreneurs seem to be the complexity of regulatory procedures and administrative burdens on start-ups.

Recent developments in Argentinean youth policies

Argentina has a long history of lifelong learning and training programmes. Currently, *Jóvenes con Más y Mejor Trabajo* [Youth with more and better jobs] promotes formal employment among youth between the ages of 18 and 24 who have not completed secondary school, particularly those living in poverty. The programme enables young people to attend a course oriented to the world of work, learn a job, complete primary or secondary school, start-up a business or undertake an apprenticeship.

Since 2014, the *Programa de Respaldo a Estudiantes de Argentina* [Support Programme for Argentinian Students], or *Prog.res.ar*, has offered cash support to almost 703 000 students; 63% of them are women and 78% are between 18-22 years of age. The programme provides an income transfer to young people between 18 and 24 years of age who are unemployed, have informal jobs or receive a salary below the minimum wage. The beneficiaries must regularly attend public education (secondary, tertiary or university) or labour training programmes and perform annual medical checkups.

There are also youth-oriented policies focused on education, aimed at preventing dropouts and stimulating young adults to re-enrol in school. Among the former are the *Programa Nacional de Becas Estudiantiles* [National Student Grants Programme], the *Becas para el Estímulo de la Educación Técnica - BET* [Programme to Stimulate Technical Education] and the *Programa de Apoyo para Estudiantes Embarazadas y Estudiantes con Hijos* [Programme to Support Pregnant Students and Students with Children]. As far as re-enrolment programmes are concerned, the *Finalización de Estudios Primarios y Secundarios- FinEs* [Completing Primary and Secondary Studies] and the *Pensá en la Secundaria* [Think about School] programmes play a distinctive role. Tertiary education programmes include the *Programa Nacional de Becas Universitarias PNUB* [National University Grants Programme] and *Programa Nacional de Becas Bicentenario – PNBB* [National Bicentennial Grants Programme].

In 2016, the government of Argentina presented to Congress the *Primer Empleo* [First Job] law project and a package of law projects that aim to promote entrepreneurship, including the *Ley de Emprendedores* [Law of Entrepreneurs]. The First Job law, being discussed in Congress, seeks to raise employment among young people by providing tax exemptions, subsidies and incentives to employers who hire workers aged 18 to 24 with fewer than 36 months of social security contributions. The Law of Entrepreneurs aims to cut red tape by allowing new enterprises to complete registration on line in a single day.

Key indicators: Argentina

Labour market developments[i] (%)	Argentina 2004	Argentina 2014	LAC 2004	LAC 2014	OECD 2004	OECD 2014
Unemployment rates - adults (30-64)	8.6	4.5	4.8	3.4	4.6	5.8
Unemployment rates - youth (15-29)	20.9	14.0	12.4	10.3	8.0	12.5
Informality rates - adults (35-64)	41.6	26.6	47.0	38.3		
Informality rates - youth (15-29)	59.8	49.1	62.3	52.3		

Youth and socio-economic status (%)	Argentina Extreme poor	Argentina Moderate poor	Argentina Vulnerable	Argentina Middle class	LAC (17) Extreme poor	LAC (17) Moderate poor	LAC (17) Vulnerable	LAC (17) Middle class
Youth (15-29)	5.7	8.2	41.9	44.3	15.1	12.4	39.4	33.1

Activity rates for youth (15-29)[i] (%)	Argentina 2004	Argentina 2014	LAC 2004	LAC 2014	OECD 2014
Student	34.2	37.4	23.0	25.3	13.2
Working student	10.5	10.1	11.3	11.2	35.5
Working	33.5	31.9	43.6	43.1	36.2
NEET	21.8	20.5	22.2	20.3	15.1

Activity rates for youth (15-29)[i] by socio-economic status (%)	Argentina Extreme poor	Argentina Moderate poor	Argentina Vulnerable	Argentina Middle class	LAC (17) Extreme poor	LAC (17) Moderate poor	LAC (17) Vulnerable	LAC (17) Middle class
Student	41.3	40.7	40.3	34.1	27.0	29.7	30.0	30.7
Working student	2.2	4.5	5.4	16.5	7.8	7.5	8.9	15.0
Working- formal	3.2	5.4	13.8	26.2	4.8	9.6	18.4	28.8
Working- informal	11.7	13.8	15.1	12.6	25.2	22.0	19.1	13.3
NEET	41.6	35.6	25.5	10.6	35.1	31.2	23.7	12.2

Distribution of youth employed[i] (%)	Argentina	LAC	OECD
Employee	86.1	70.0	88.0
Employer	1.1	2.2	3.9
Own-account worker	11.6	16.3	5.7
Unpaid family worker	1.2	11.2	24.0

Trust in elections[ii] (%)	Argentina Youth (16-29)	Argentina Adults (30-64)	LAC Youth (16-29)	LAC Adults (30-64)	OECD Youth (15-29)	OECD Adults (30-64)
Share of population that expresses confidence in the transparency of election results	35.3	39.2	36.3	39.3	62.1	63.2
Feeling of safety[ii] (%)						
Share of population that feels safe in their city or area	42.5	41.9	47.0	46.0	70.9	71.3

Skills[iii] (%)	Argentina Youth (25-29)	Argentina Adults (30-64)	LAC Youth (25-29)	LAC Adults (30-64)	OECD Adults (25-64)
Population with complete secondary education	67.3	57.2	55.4	38.6	76.0
Population with complete tertiary education[a]	17.0	21.8	14.6	13.4	34.0

	Argentina (2013)	LAC (18)	OECD (33)
Students in secondary education enrolled in vocational programme[b]	12.2	14.5	26.1

	Argentina (2014)	LAC	OECD (2014)
Public spending in training programmes (% of GDP)[c]	0.05	0.12	0.15

Entrepreneurship[iv] (%)	Argentina	LAC	OECD
Necessity as entrepreneurial motivation (share of 18-29 in total early-stage entrepreneurial activity)	36.1	26.2	16.0

Barriers to entrepreneurship index[v]	Argentina	LAC	OECD
Complexity of regulatory procedures	1.4	1.2	0.6
Administrative burdens on start-ups	1.1	0.9	0.6
Regulatory protection of incumbents	0.5	0.6	0.4
Total	2.9	2.7	1.7

Table notes : i) Latin America weighted average of LAC-17 countries: Argentina, Bolivia, Brazil, Chile, Colombia, Costa Rica, Dominican Republic, Ecuador, El Salvador, Guatemala, Honduras, Mexico, Nicaragua, Panama, Peru, Paraguay, Uruguay. OECD weighted average for 34 OECD member countries; ii) Latin America unweighted average of LAC-16 countries: Argentina, Brazil, Chile, Colombia, Costa Rica, Dominican Republic, Ecuador, El Salvador, Guatemala, Honduras, Mexico, Nicaragua, Panama, Paraguay, Peru, Uruguay, OECD simple average of OECD 35 member countries; iii) Latin America unweighted average of LAC-17 countries: Argentina, Bolivia, Brazil, Chile, Colombia, Costa Rica, Dominican Republic, Ecuador, El Salvador, Guatemala, Honduras, Mexico, Nicaragua, Panama, Peru, Paraguay, Uruguay. OECD unweighted average for 34 OECD member countries; iv) Share of population that see start-up as a necessity (no other options for work) rather than an opportunity. Latin America (10) non-weighted average of Argentina, Brazil, Chile, Colombia, Ecuador, Guatemala, Panama, Mexico, Peru, and Uruguay. OECD (27) non-weighted average of Australia, Belgium, Chile, Estonia, Finland, Germany, Greece, Hungary, Ireland, Israel, Italy, Latvia, Luxembourg, Mexico, Netherlands, Norway, Poland, Portugal, Slovakia, Slovenia, South Korea, Spain, Sweden, Switzerland, United Kingdom and United States; v) The Entrepreneurship Barriers Index is composed of three sub-indices: 1) Complexity of regulatory procedures: measures the licences and permits system, such as the communication and simplification of rules and procedures. 2) Administrative burdens on start-ups: measures the burdens that are faced by corporations and sole proprietor firms, and the barriers in services sectors. 3) Regulatory protection of incumbents: measures legal barriers to entry, anti-trust exemptions and barriers in network sectors. The three indicators are based on the 2013 Product Market Regulation questionnaire available at: http://www.oecd.org/eco/reform/PMR-Questionnaire-2013.pdf. The indicator reflects the state of legislation in 2014 for Kenya, Philippines, Rwanda and Uruguay; in 2015 for Bolivia, Ecuador, Guatemala, Panama, Paraguay and Venezuela; in 2013 for all others. Scale 0 to 6 from least to most restrictive. See methodological note for further details.

Table sources: i) SEDLAC (CEDLAS and the World Bank) for Latin American countries and OECD-LFS data for the OECD (2014); ii) OECD calculations based on Gallup Organization (2014), *Gallup World Monitor* (database); iii) (a) SEDLAC (CEDLAS and the World Bank) for Latin American countries (2014); and OECD (2014), *Education at a Glance 2014: OECD Indicators*; (b) UNESCO (2016) and DiNIECE. Ministerio de Educación (2013) for Latin American countries and OECD (2014) *Education at a Glance 2014: OECD Indicators* for the OECD; (c) World Bank LAC Social Protection Database (2015) and OECD/EC Labour Market Programme Database; iv) Global Entrepreneurship Monitor individual data (2015); v) OECD-WBG product market regulation database for all countries except Brazil, Chile, India, Mexico and South Africa; OECD product market regulation database (2014).

Brazil

Recent trends

In 2014, unemployment rates in Brazil (4%) were lower than the OECD average, but still slightly above the Latin America and Caribbean (LAC) average (3%), according to Socio-Economic Database for Latin America and the Caribbean (SEDLAC) data based on the Pesquisa Nacional por Amostra de Domicílio [National Household Survey] (PNAD). Informality rates for adults decreased by almost 10 percentage points between 2004 and 2014, dropping from 28% to around 19%; this is much lower than the LAC average.

In comparison to overall unemployment, youth unemployment in Brazil remains relatively high (13% in 2014). The proportion of unemployed youth in Brazil is at levels similar to the OECD average (12%), but still remains higher than the LAC average (10%). On the other hand, informality rates for youth are lower than the LAC average of 52% despite being higher than for their adult counterparts.

Activity status of youth by single year of age in Brazil, 2014

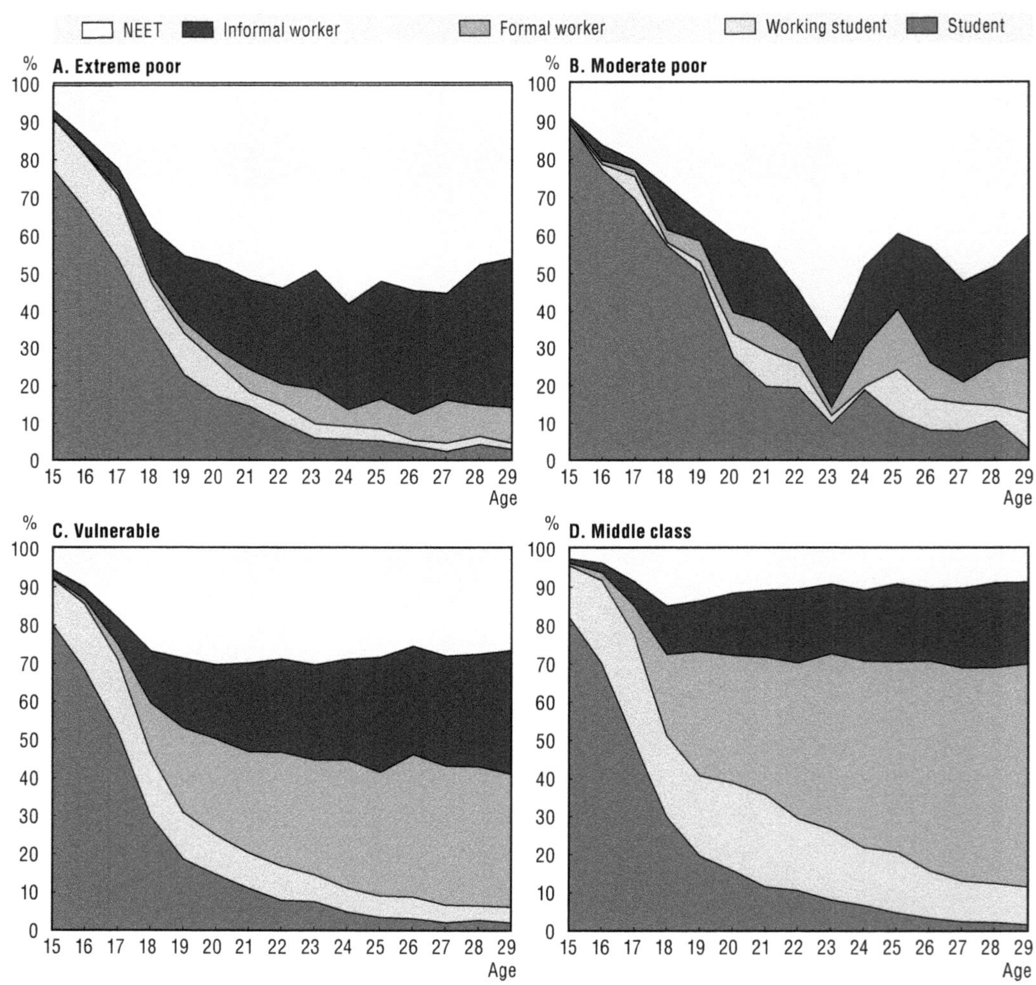

Source: OECD and World Bank tabulations of SEDLAC (CEDLAS and the World Bank).
StatLink http://dx.doi.org/10.1787/888933415439

Data from SEDLAC based on PNAD provide some insights into labour conditions for young people in Brazil. In 2014, more than one in five young people (22%) were studying in Brazil vs. 25%

in the LAC region; more than half of youth were working or were working students. Young people who are neither employed nor in education nor training ("NEETs") risk being left permanently behind in the labour market. This risk is especially high for the relatively large share of poor and vulnerable NEETs. In the same year, around 20% of young people aged 15-29 were NEET in Brazil, which was in line with the LAC average, but higher than in the OECD (15%). The poor and vulnerable account for almost 80% of all young NEETs. Moreover, there is also a 20 percentage point gender gap between young women and men NEETs.

According to the Gallup World Monitor survey, youth confidence in the transparency of election results (21%) is lower than for adults (24%) and lower than the regional average. However, the share of young Brazilians who feel safe in their local community is the same as for adults (41%) and lower than the LAC average (47% for youth).

Higher education attainment in Brazil is slightly lower than the average for the region. In 2014, 63% of youth (aged 25-29) completed secondary education (vs. 55% for the LAC average); only 13% completed tertiary education (vs. 15% for the LAC average). However, just as in other countries in the region, Brazil faces high dropout and low completion rates in schools: 28% of youth (aged 15-29) have not completed secondary education and are out of school. At the same time, the share of students in secondary education who are enrolled in technical and vocational education and training programmes (TVET) is remarkably low. On the other hand, in 2014 Brazil spent 0.10% of its gross domestic product on training programmes, which is more or less in line with both LAC and OECD averages.

In terms of entrepreneurship in Brazil, the majority of self-employed are own-account workers rather than employers (11% of young workers are own account while 1% of them are employers).

Additionally, data from the Global Entrepreneurship Monitor (GEM) show that the share of youth in Brazil (aged 18-29) who become entrepreneurs out of necessity (compared with all early-stage entrepreneurs) is higher (42% in 2015) than the regional (26%) and OECD averages (16%).

Barriers to entrepreneurship are higher in Brazil than across the LAC region and the OECD average. The most important barriers facing young entrepreneurs seem to be the complexity of regulatory procedures and administrative burdens on start-ups.

Recent trends in youth employment policies

The high unemployment rate for young workers is particularly worrisome in Brazil. According to PNAD 2015, the unemployment rate for 15-24 year-olds reached 16.8%, while the average rate for all ages was 9.0%. Hence, the government has developed a large number of programmes with high and low impact to offset this structural problem. They range from traditional apprenticeship programmes (driven by public training institutions) to programmes focused on critical segments of youth (such as those belonging to poor households and school dropouts).

The Apprenticeship Act (*Lei do Aprendiz*), which became law in 2000, is implemented by the Labour Ministry. It provides young workers with opportunities for dual training – academic and practical experience. The applicants must be between 14 and 24 years old and enrolled in elementary or high school. Medium and large firms are encouraged to have apprentices (young workers) occupy at least 5% of the total payroll in return for discounts on the employer's contribution to FGTS (*Fundo de Garantia por Tempo de Serviço*), a job-separation fund. Firms deposit only 2% of the basic wage in this fund instead of a rate of either 8% or 8.5%. The main objective is to place participants in a formal job and help them stay in the formal segment of the labour market in the future.

Alternatively, the National Youth Inclusion Programme (*Programa Nacional de Inclusão de Jovens –ProJovem*), introduced by an Act in 2005 and restructured in 2008, is implemented in partnership with the federal government, states, municipalities and the third sector. *ProJovem* offers formal education courses to specific targets: adolescents (focused on reintegrating young people aged 15-17 years into the education system); urban (focused on youth aged 18-29 years who did not finish elementary school); farm (focused on young farmers excluded from the formal education system); and workers (focused on preparing young people for the labour market, as well as alternative income-generating occupations and offering financial assistance for minimum attendance).

Recent trends in training programmes

The National Programme for Access to Technical Education and Employment (*Programa Nacional de Acesso ao Ensino Técnico e Emprego – Pronatec*) was created in 2011 to expand access to vocational and technological education for young people, workers and beneficiaries of national income transfers. Between 2011 and 2014, 8.1 million people in 4 300 municipalities registered for *Pronatec*, with 1.3 million people registering in 2015 alone. In 2016, the number of people registered in *Pronatec* was expected to increase to 1.6 million.

There are five initiatives within *Pronatec*. First, the expansion of the Federal Network of Professional Education, Science and Technology (*Rede Federal de Educação Profissional, Científica e Tecnológica*) included the construction of 422 federal education institutions between 2003 and 2014 for a total of 562 campuses in operation. Second, the Brazil Professional Programme (*Programa Brasil Profissionalizado*), which intends to expand the supply and strengthen the integration of professional education to high schools, transfers funds from the federal government to vocational education networks. Approximately BRL 2 billion will go towards the construction, renovation and expansion of state schools, installing laboratories for technical courses and training teachers. Third, the e-Tec network Brazil (*Rede e-Tec Brasil*) offers free technical courses and professional training for distance learning. Fourth, the Gratuity Agreement with the National Learning Service (*Acordo de Gratuidade com os Serviços Nacionais de Aprendizagem*) aims to distribute resources so that low-income people, particularly students and workers, can attend technical courses and receive professional qualifications. Lastly, the Training Grant (*Bolsa-Formação*), created by *Pronatec*, offers technical courses, initial and continuing training courses or professional qualification to students in high school, students who have completed high school and adults.

Reference

Instituto Brasileiro De Geografia E Estatística (IBGE) (2015), *Pesquisa Nacional por Amostra de Domicílios (PNAD)* (National Household Survey), http://www.ibge.gov.br/home/estatistica/pesquisas/pesquisa_resultados.php?id_pesquisa=40 [accessed on 16 August 2016].

Key indicators: Brazil

Labour market developments[i] (%)	Brazil 2004	Brazil 2014	LAC 2004	LAC 2014	OECD 2004	OECD 2014
Unemployment rates - adults (30-64)	5.4	4.0	4.8	3.4	4.6	5.8
Unemployment rates - youth (15-29)	15.3	13.5	12.4	10.3	8.0	12.5
Informality rates - adults (35-64)	28.0	19.0	47.0	38.3		
Informality rates - youth (15-29)	42.7	28.5	62.3	52.3		

Youth and socio-economic status (%)	Brazil Extreme poor	Brazil Moderate poor	Brazil Vulnerable	Brazil Middle class	LAC (17) Extreme poor	LAC (17) Moderate poor	LAC (17) Vulnerable	LAC (17) Middle class
Youth (15-29)	8.2	10.2	38.2	43.4	15.1	12.4	39.4	33.1

Activity rates for youth (15-29)[i] (%)	Brazil 2004	Brazil 2014	LAC 2004	LAC 2014	OECD 2014
Student	21.6	22.5	23.0	25.3	13.2
Working student	15.6	13.1	11.3	11.2	35.5
Working	43.1	44.5	43.6	43.1	36.2
NEET	19.7	20.0	22.2	20.3	15.1

Activity rates for youth (15-29)[i] by socio-economic status (%)	Brazil Extreme poor	Brazil Moderate poor	Brazil Vulnerable	Brazil Middle class	LAC (17) Extreme poor	LAC (17) Moderate poor	LAC (17) Vulnerable	LAC (17) Middle class
Student	28.6	27.1	24.0	18.7	27.0	29.7	30.0	30.7
Working student	8.1	7.7	10.2	17.4	7.8	7.5	8.9	15.0
Working- formal	4.6	9.6	22.3	38.0	4.8	9.6	18.4	28.8
Working- informal	20.2	20.4	19.2	15.8	25.2	22.0	19.1	13.3
NEET	38.4	35.1	24.4	10.1	35.1	31.2	23.7	12.2

Distribution of youth employed[i] (%)	Brazil	LAC	OECD
Employee	81.2	70.0	88.0
Employer	1.2	2.2	3.9
Own-account worker	11.2	16.3	5.7
Unpaid family worker	6.4	11.2	24.0

Trust in elections[ii] (%)	Brazil Youth (16-29)	Brazil Adults (30-64)	LAC Youth (16-29)	LAC Adults (30-64)	OECD Youth (15-29)	OECD Adults (30-64)
Share of population that expresses confidence in the transparency of election results	21.4	24.2	36.3	39.3	62.1	63.2
Feeling of safety[ii] (%)						
Share of population that feels safe in their city or area	40.9	41.0	47.0	46.0	70.9	71.3

Skills[iii] (%)	Brazil Youth (25-29)	Brazil Adults (30-64)	LAC Youth (25-29)	LAC Adults (30-64)	OECD Adults (25-64)
Population with complete secondary education	63.6	44.5	55.4	38.6	76.0
Population with complete tertiary education[a]	13.3	12.9	14.6	13.4	34.0

	Brazil (2013)	LAC (18)	OECD (33)
Students in secondary education enrolled in vocational programme[b]	3.5	14.5	26.1

	Brazil (2014)	LAC	OECD (2014)
Public spending in training programmes (% of GDP)[c]	0.10	0.12	0.15

Entrepreneurship[iv] (%)	Brazil	LAC	OECD
Necessity as entrepreneurial motivation (share of 18-29 in total early-stage entrepreneurial activity)	41.7	26.2	16.0

Barriers to entrepreneurship index[v]	Brazil	LAC	OECD
Complexity of regulatory procedures	1.3	1.2	0.6
Administrative burdens on start-ups	1.0	0.9	0.6
Regulatory protection of incumbents	0.6	0.6	0.4
Total	2.9	2.7	1.7

Table notes: i) Latin America weighted average of LAC-17 countries: Argentina, Bolivia, Brazil, Chile, Colombia, Costa Rica, Dominican Republic, Ecuador, El Salvador, Guatemala, Honduras, Mexico, Nicaragua, Panama, Peru, Paraguay, Uruguay. OECD weighted average for 34 OECD member countries; ii) Latin America unweighted average of LAC-16 countries Argentina, Brazil, Chile, Colombia, Costa Rica, Dominican Republic, Ecuador, El Salvador, Guatemala, Honduras, Mexico, Nicaragua, Panama, Paraguay, Peru, Uruguay, OECD simple average of OECD 35 member countries; iii) Latin America unweighted average of LAC-17 countries: Argentina, Bolivia, Brazil, Chile, Colombia, Costa Rica, Dominican Republic, Ecuador, El Salvador, Guatemala, Honduras, Mexico, Nicaragua, Panama, Peru, Paraguay, Uruguay. OECD unweighted average for 34 OECD member countries; iv) Share of population that see start-up as a necessity (no other options for work) rather than an opportunity. Latin America (10) non-weighted average of Argentina, Brazil, Chile, Colombia, Ecuador, Guatemala, Panama, Mexico, Peru, and Uruguay. OECD (27) non-weighted average of Australia, Belgium, Chile, Estonia, Finland, Germany, Greece, Hungary, Ireland, Israel, Italy, Latvia, Luxembourg, Mexico, Netherlands, Norway, Poland, Portugal, Slovakia, Slovenia, South Korea, Spain, Sweden, Switzerland, United Kingdom and United States; v) The Entrepreneurship Barriers Index is composed of three sub-indices: 1) Complexity of egulatory procedures: measures the licences and permits system, such as the communication and simplification of rules and procedures. 2) Administrative burdens on start-ups: measures the burdens that are face by corporations and sole proprietor firms, and the barriers in services sectors. 3) Regulatory protection of incumbents: measures legal barriers to entry, anti-trust exemptions and barriers in network sectors. The three indicators are based on the 2013 Product Market Regulation questionnaire available at: http://www.oecd.org/eco/reform/PMR-Questionnaire-2013.pdf. The indicator reflects the state of legislation in 2014 for Kenya, Philippines, Rwanda and Uruguay; in 2015 for Bolivia, Ecuador, Guatemala, Panama, Paraguay and Venezuela; in 2013 for all others. Scale 0 to 6 from least to most restrictive. See methodological note for further details.

Table sources: i) SEDLAC (CEDLAS and the World Bank) for Latin American countries and OECD-LFS data for the OECD (2014); ii) OECD calculations based on Gallup Organization (2014), *Gallup World Monitor* (database); iii) (a) SEDLAC (CEDLAS and the World Bank) for Latin American countries (2014); and OECD (2014), *Education at a Glance 2014: OECD Indicators*; (b) UNESCO (2016) and DiNIECE. Ministerio de Educación (2013) for Latin American countries and OECD (2014), *Education at a Glance 2014: OECD Indicators* for the OECD; (c) World Bank LAC Social Protection Database (2015) and OECD/EC Labour Market Programme Database; iv) Global Entrepreneurship Monitor individual data (2015); v) OECD-WBG product market regulation database for all countries except Brazil, Chile, India, Mexico and South Africa, OECD product market regulation database (2014).

Chile

Recent trends

Following the recent economic slowdown, Chile's unemployment rate has been increasing since 2014 and is expected to surpass the OECD average, peaking at 7.1% in 2016 Q4 (OECD, 2016). Informality – defined as all employed persons not paying social contributions – for adults has decreased in the last decade, reaching 13% in 2014 which is much lower than the Latin America and Caribbean (LAC) average.

Despite considerable progress, gaps in youth inclusion in the labour market and society persist throughout the region and in Chile as well. The labour market situation of Chile's youth is particularly challenging. Socio-Economic Database for Latin America and the Caribbean (SEDLAC) data based on the national socio-economic survey CASEN (*Caracterizacion Socioeconomica Nacional*) show that youth unemployment remained high at around 15% in 2014, slightly above the OECD average of 13% and the regional average of 10%. On the other hand, informality rates for youth, at 19% in 2014, are the second lowest in the region, less than half of the LAC average of 52%.

Activity status of youth by single year of age in Chile, 2014

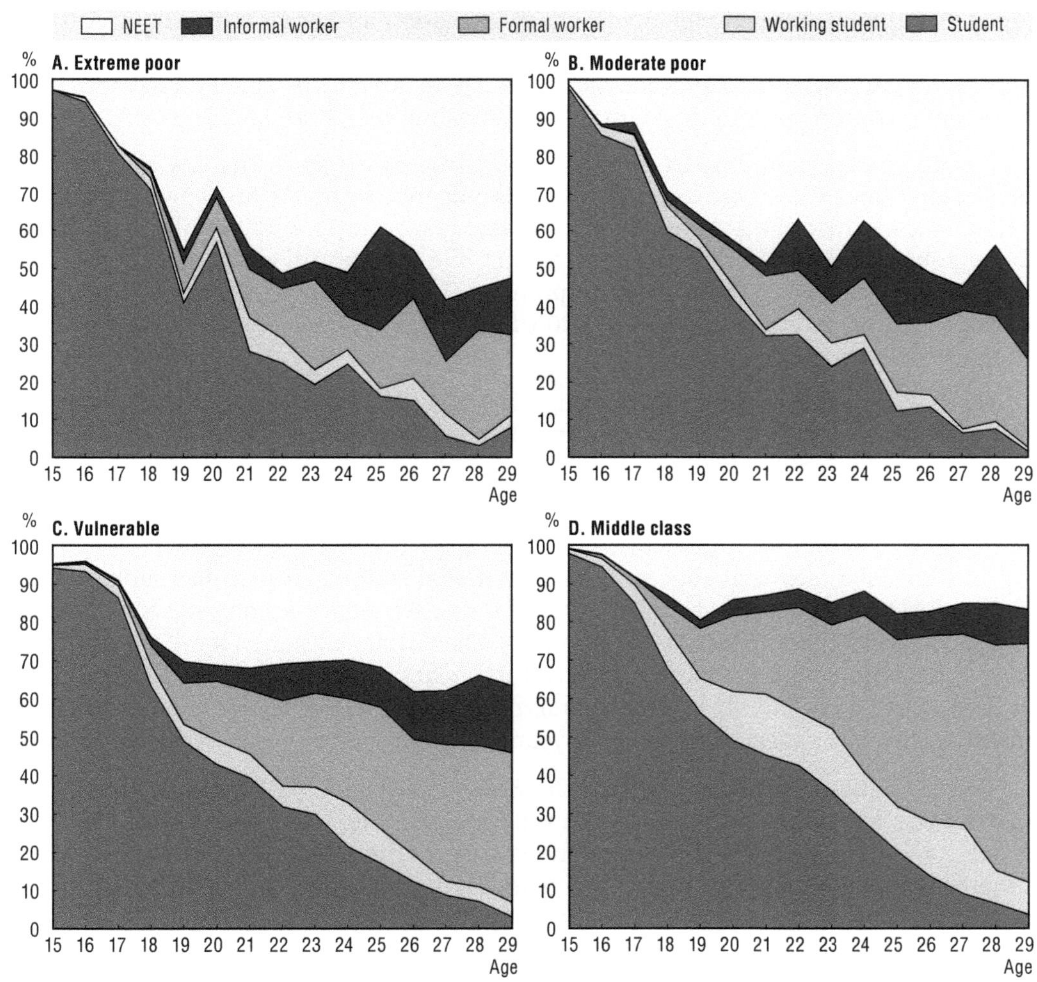

Source: OECD and World Bank tabulations of SEDLAC (CEDLAS and the World Bank).

StatLink http://dx.doi.org/10.1787/888933415441

In 2014, 44% of young people in Chile were studying against 25% in the LAC region; more than 36% were working or working students. Young people who are neither employed nor in education nor training ("NEETs") risk being permanently left behind in the labour market. This risk is especially high for the relatively large share of poor and vulnerable NEETs. Despite being in line with the LAC average, the percentage of youth NEETs in Chile (20% in 2014) is among the highest in the OECD. Contrary to many other countries in the region, more than half of young NEETs come from vulnerable households (52%) and almost 30% belong to middle-class families, while only around 18% come from extremely and moderately poor households. The 12% gender gap between young women and men NEETs in Chile is lower than the average for the LAC region. Informality rates for youth are lower in Chile than in the LAC region: 19% vs. 52%.

The share of the youth population that expresses confidence in the transparency of election results (39%) is lower than that of adults in Chile, but higher than the average for the region (36%) (Gallup World Monitor survey). Youth safety perception in Chile is slightly higher than that of adults and the regional average for youth (48% of youth in Chile vs. 47% for the LAC average).

Educational attainment in Chile is much higher than the average for the region. In Chile, 82% of youth (aged 25-29) completed secondary education in 2014 (vs. 55% for the LAC average). Furthermore, 25% of youth (aged 25-29) and 20% of adults (aged 30-64) completed tertiary education in 2014 (vs. 15% and 13%, respectively, for the LAC average). However, similar to other countries in the region, Chile faces a high dropout rate from schools and a low completion rate: 25% of youth (aged 15-29) have not completed secondary education and are out of school. At the same time, 21% of students in secondary education are enrolled in vocational training programmes (vs. 15% across the LAC region and 26% across the OECD). In 2011, Chile spent 0.11% of its gross domestic product on training programmes, more or less in line with both LAC and OECD averages.

Youth entrepreneurship in Chile is less widespread than in the LAC average. In Chile, 10% of working youth are own-account workers and not even 1% are employers compared with 16% and 2% across the LAC region on average, respectively. Additionally, data from the Global Entrepreneurship Monitor (GEM) show that in Chile the share of young entrepreneurs (18-29 years old) where necessity is the main entrepreneurial motivation (as percentage of total early-stage entrepreneurial activity), estimated in 20% for 2015, is below the regional average (26%) and close to the OECD average (16%).

Barriers to entrepreneurship are slightly higher in Chile than the OECD average, but lower than in the LAC region. The complexity of regulatory procedures is one of the most relevant barriers faced by youth entrepreneurs.

Recent trends in Chile's training and labour market insertion policies

In Chile, the technical education and vocational training system has multiple training levels and paths. In the formal education system, upper-secondary schools account for two branches: humanistic scientific and technical (four years). The tertiary education level has three possible paths: post-secondary technical education, which takes place in the centres for technical training (*centros de formación técnica: CFT*) (two-three years); higher technical education offered by the professional institutes (*institutos profesionales: IP*) (four years); and university education (five years or more).

Chile's national training institute the Servicio Nacional de Capacitación y Empleo (SENCE) offers basic vocational training programmes of short to medium duration (200 to 800 hours) to adults and young people entering the labour market. An example is the "+ *Capaz*" [+ Able] programme, which aims to help inactive and vulnerable people, including youth, to enter and stay in the labour market. It provides the target group with technical qualifications, transferable skills and placement services to improve employability. Men aged 18-29 and women aged 18-64 in the most vulnerable 60% of the population with little or no work experience are eligible for the programme (SENCE, 2016).

In 2011, Chile implemented "*Programa Formación en Puesto de Trabajo*" [On-the-Job Training Programme] through the SENCE. The goal was to help young people gain entry into the labour market in order to increase the overall percentage of working young people. This programme targets those between 15 and 25 who are unemployed or searching for work for the first time and who do not have access to vocational or technical training. The programme helps link the supply and demand of labour by encouraging firms to hire young and vulnerable workers. The training for youth is meant to focus on the job for which they are being hired (PROPYME, 2013).

Recent developments in Chile's entrepreneurship policies

One of the current goals of Chile's Entrepreneurism Policy is to democratise access to entrepreneurship programmes among its population. The Chilean Economic Development Agency (CORFO) leads policies in that area; its "*Nueva Política de Emprendimiento 2014-18*" [New Entrepreneurship Policy 2014-18] aims to improve the Chilean business ecosystem to develop dynamic ventures.

Since 2014, Chile has been trying to integrate support to entrepreneurship through incubators (for national ventures) and StartUp Chile (to attract foreign talents). As a consequence, in 2014 Chile doubled funds available for entrepreneurship and created a National Policy Platform that finances co-working spaces throughout the country, extending mentoring networks and entrepreneurship contests, both at the national and regional levels. Funds were also created through the entire entrepreneurship chain via crowdfunding and angel investors, enabling Chile to scale up subsidies and create technological early inversion funds. Instruments were improved and modernised, with investments in inclusion and consideration for gender, regional ventures and social entrepreneurism.

The national entrepreneurship policy is geared towards entrepreneurs of all ages, but a large number of beneficiaries have been young people. These programmes benefit 40 000 youths per year through more than 20 000 projects, 850 of them supported directly.

Along with CORFO's efforts, the Instituto Nacional de la Juventud (INJUV) [National Youth Institute] supports social entrepreneurship by youth, aimed at youth development. Together with Microsoft and the Organismo Internacional de Juventud para Iberoamérica (OIJ) [Iberoamerican Youth International Organisation], the Institute launched a web platform *#YoPuedoEmprender* [#Icanstart] to facilitate access to information for young entrepreneurs.

References

OECD (2016), *OECD Employment Outlook 2016*, OECD Publishing, Paris, http://dx.doi.org/10.1787/empl_outlook-2016-en.

PROPYME (2013), El "*Programa Formación en el Puesto de Trabajo*" es una las nuevas apuestas del SENCE, http://www.propymechile.com/noticias/4863-pymes-innovacion-emprendimiento-programa-formacion-puesto-de-trabajo-nueva-apuesta-sence.html (accessed 24 August 2016).

SENCE (2016), *Programa +Capaz* [+ Able Programme], Servicio Nacional de Capacitación y Empleo, http://www.sence.cl/portal/Perfil/Personas/Jovenes;Oportunidades/Capacitacion/+Capaz/ (accessed 24 August 2016).

Key indicators: Chile

Labour market developments[i] (%)	Chile 2004	Chile 2014	LAC 2004	LAC 2014	OECD 2004	OECD 2014
Unemployment rates - adults (30-64)	7.2	4.6	4.8	3.4	4.6	5.8
Unemployment rates - youth (15-29)	16.9	14.6	12.4	10.3	8.0	12.5
Informality rates - adults (35-64)	19.4	13.3	47.0	38.3		
Informality rates - youth (15-29)	28.9	18.6	62.3	52.3		

Youth and socio-economic status (%)	Chile Extreme poor	Chile Moderate poor	Chile Vulnerable	Chile Middle class	LAC (17) Extreme poor	LAC (17) Moderate poor	LAC (17) Vulnerable	LAC (17) Middle class
Youth (15-29)	3.9	6.7	42.6	46.8	15.1	12.4	39.4	33.1

Activity rates for youth (15-29)[i] (%)	Chile 2004	Chile 2014	LAC 2004	LAC 2014	OECD 2014
Student	39.3	43.9	23.0	25.3	13.2
Working student	5.1	8.1	11.3	11.2	35.5
Working	32.3	27.8	43.6	43.1	36.2
NEET	23.3	20.2	22.2	20.3	15.1

Activity rates for youth (15-29)[i] by socio-economic status (%)	Chile Extreme poor	Chile Moderate poor	Chile Vulnerable	Chile Middle class	LAC (17) Extreme poor	LAC (17) Moderate poor	LAC (17) Vulnerable	LAC (17) Middle class
Student	42.4	44.8	46.4	42.4	27.0	29.7	30.0	30.7
Working student	3.6	3.5	5.1	11.2	7.8	7.5	8.9	15.0
Working- formal	10.9	10.4	16.6	28.2	4.8	9.6	18.4	28.8
Working- informal	6.9	7.0	6.5	4.9	25.2	22.0	19.1	13.3
NEET	36.2	34.3	25.3	13.3	35.1	31.2	23.7	12.2

Distribution of youth employed[i] (%)	Chile	LAC	OECD
Employee	89.3	70.0	88.0
Employer	0.7	2.2	3.9
Own-account worker	9.6	16.3	5.7
Unpaid family worker	0.5	11.2	24.0

	Chile Youth (16-29)	Chile Adults (30-64)	LAC Youth (16-29)	LAC Adults (30-64)	OECD Youth (15-29)	OECD Adults (30-64)
Trust in elections[ii] (%)						
Share of population that expresses confidence in the transparency of election results	39.7	46.5	36.3	39.3	62.1	63.2
Feeling of safety[ii] (%)						
Share of population that feels safe in their city or area	48.5	46.2	47.0	46.0	70.9	71.3

Skills[iii] (%)	Chile Youth (25-29)	Chile Adults (30-64)	LAC Youth (25-29)	LAC Adults (30-64)	OECD Adults (25-64)
Population with complete secondary education	82.6	57.8	55.4	38.6	76.0
Population with complete tertiary education[a]	25.8	20.3	14.6	13.4	34.0

	Chile (2014)	LAC (18)	OECD (33)
Students in secondary education enrolled in vocational programme[b]	20.7	14.5	26.1

	Chile (2011)	LAC	OECD (2014)
Public spending in training programmes (% of GDP)[c]	0.11	0.12	0.15

Entrepreneurship[iv] (%)	Chile	LAC	OECD
Necessity as entrepreneurial motivation (share of 18-29 in total early-stage entrepreneurial activity)	23.1	26.2	16.0

Barriers to entrepreneurship index[v]	Chile	LAC	OECD
Complexity of regulatory procedures	1.2	1.2	0.6
Administrative burdens on start-ups	0.4	0.9	0.6
Regulatory protection of incumbents	0.4	0.6	0.4
Total	2.0	2.7	1.7

Table notes: i) Latin America weighted average of LAC-17 countries: Argentina, Bolivia, Brazil, Chile, Colombia, Costa Rica, Dominican Republic, Ecuador, El Salvador, Guatemala, Honduras, Mexico, Nicaragua, Panama, Peru, Paraguay, Uruguay. OECD weighted average for 34 OECD member countries; ii) Latin America unweighted average of LAC-16 countries: Argentina, Brazil, Chile, Colombia, Costa Rica, Dominican Republic, Ecuador, El Salvador, Guatemala, Honduras, Mexico, Nicaragua, Panama, Paraguay, Peru, Uruguay, OECD simple average of OECD 35 member countries; iii) Latin America unweighted average of LAC-17 countries: Argentina, Bolivia, Brazil, Chile, Colombia, Costa Rica, Dominican Republic, Ecuador, El Salvador, Guatemala, Honduras, Mexico, Nicaragua, Panama, Peru, Paraguay, Uruguay. OECD unweighted average for 34 OECD member countries; iv) Share of population that see start-up as a necessity (no other options for work) rather than an opportunity. Latin America (10) non-weighted average of Argentina, Brazil, Chile, Colombia, Ecuador, Guatemala, Panama, Mexico, Peru, and Uruguay. OECD (27) non-weighted average of Australia, Belgium, Chile, Estonia, Finland, Germany, Greece, Hungary, Ireland, Israel, Italy, Latvia, Luxembourg, Mexico, Netherlands, Norway, Poland, Portugal, Slovakia, Slovenia, South Korea, Spain, Sweden, Switzerland, United Kingdom and United States; v) The Entrepreneurship Barriers Index is composed of three sub-indices: 1) Complexity of regulatory procedures: measures the licences and permits system, such as the communication and simplification of rules and procedures. 2) Administrative burdens on start-ups: measures the burdens that are face by corporations and sole proprietor firms, and the barriers in services sectors. 3) Regulatory protection of incumbents: measures legal barriers to entry, anti-trust exemptions and barriers in network sectors. The three indicators are based on the 2013 Product Market Regulation questionnaire available at: http://www.oecd.org/eco/reform/PMR-Questionnaire-2013.pdf. The indicator reflects the state of legislation in 2014 for Kenya, Philippines, Rwanda and Uruguay; in 2015 for Bolivia, Ecuador, Guatemala, Panama, Paraguay and Venezuela; in 2013 for all others. Scale 0 to 6 from least to most restrictive. See methodological note for further details.
Table sources: i) SEDLAC (CEDLAS and the World Bank) for Latin American countries and OECD-LFS data for the OECD (2014); ii) OECD calculations based on Gallup Organization (2014), *Gallup World Monitor* (database); iii) (a) SEDLAC (CEDLAS and the World Bank) for Latin American countries (2014); and OECD (2014), *Education at a Glance 2014: OECD Indicators*; (b) UNESCO (2016) and DiNIECE. Ministerio de Educación (2013) for Latin American countries and OECD (2014), *Education at a Glance 2014: OECD Indicators* for the OECD; (c) World Bank LAC Social Protection Database (2015) and OECD/EC Labour Market Programme Database; iv) Global Entrepreneurship Monitor individual data (2015); v) OECD-WBG product market regulation database for all countries except Brazil, Chile, India, Mexico and South Africa, OECD product market regulation database (2014).

Colombia

Recent trends

Colombia has experienced strong and sustained economic growth over the past 15 years, apart from a short slowdown in 2008 and 2009; labour market outcomes have improved significantly. Unemployment has also dropped considerably in recent years. However, based on Colombia's official household survey (ECH), data from the Socio-Economic Database for Latin America and the Caribbean (SEDLAC) report unemployment at 6% in 2014 for adults. This was above the Latin America and Caribbean (LAC) average (3%), but in line with the OECD average.

Despite considerable progress, gaps in youth inclusion in the labour market and society persist throughout the region and are especially marked in Colombia. Although youth benefited from the positive labour market climate, their unemployment rate of 15% in 2014 remained more than double that of the total unemployment rate in Colombia and above the LAC (10%) and OECD (12%) averages.

Activity status of youth by single year of age in Colombia, 2014

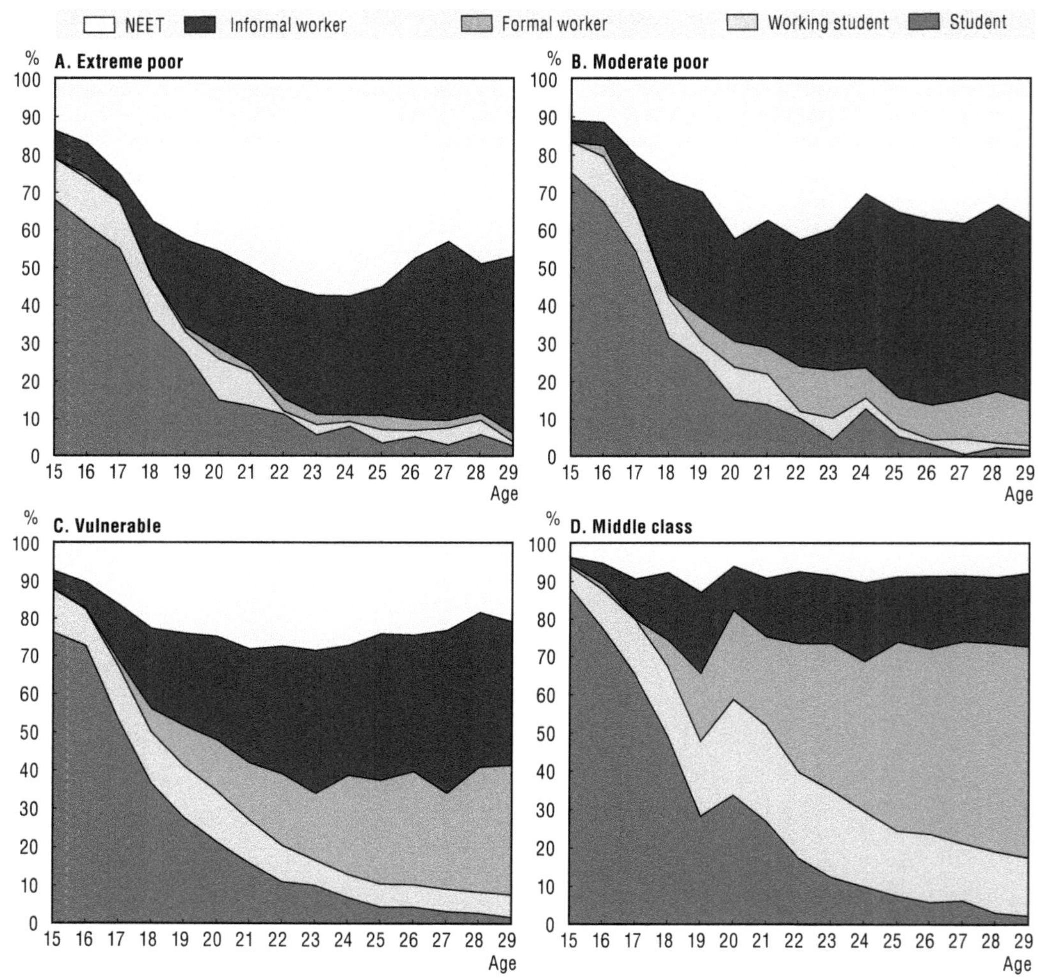

Source: OECD and World Bank tabulations of SEDLAC (CEDLAS and the World Bank).
StatLink http://dx.doi.org/10.1787/888933415455

In Colombia, around one-quarter of young people are studying and more than half are working or working students. Young people who are neither employed nor in education nor training ("NEETs") risk being permanently left behind in the labour market. The risk is especially high for the relatively large share of poor and vulnerable NEETs. In 2014, according to SEDLAC data, more than 20% of young people aged 15-29 in Colombia were NEET; this was similar to the LAC average, but higher than the OECD average of 15%. Furthermore, the poor and vulnerable account for almost 90% of all young NEETs and young women exhibit higher NEET rates. The gender gap between young women and men NEETs accounted for around 20 percentage points in 2014.

In spite of recent improvements, Colombia still has a high incidence of youth informality, defined as all employed persons not paying social contributions. In 2014, almost 48% of working youth held an informal job, which jumped to 95% and 83% of youth belonging to extreme poor and moderately poor households (vs. 57% and 30% of youth in vulnerable and middle class households).

The share of the youth population that expresses confidence in the transparency of election results is lower than that of adults in Colombia, and is slightly lower than the average for the region (21% vs. 36% for the LAC average). Safety perception of youth in Colombia is close to the regional average (46% of youth in Colombia vs. 47% for the LAC average).

Educational attainment in Colombia is higher than the regional average. In 2014, 70% of youth (aged 25-29) completed secondary education (vs. 55% for the LAC average) and 17% completed tertiary education (vs. 15% for the LAC average). Still, just as in other countries in the region, Colombia faces a high dropout rate and a low completion rate in schools: 26% of youth (aged 15-29) have not completed secondary education and are out of school.

Colombia's spending in training programmes (0.34% of gross domestic product) is the highest in the region (0.12%) and even higher than the OECD average (0.15%). This is partially explained by the active role of its National Training Institute (Servicio Nacional de Aprendizaje – SENA), which offers students a vast variety of technical and vocational education and training (TVET) programmes. Although SENA is important to the provision of TVET post-secondary and alternative education, TVET secondary education is not highly developed and few students in secondary education are enrolled in TVET (7% vs. 14% in LAC and 26% in the OECD).

In terms of entrepreneurship in Colombia, the majority of self-employed are own-account workers rather than employers: 31% of working youth report being own-account workers, while only 1% define themselves as entrepreneurs.

Barriers to entrepreneurship are lower in Colombia than the LAC average. The most important barriers faced by young entrepreneurs seem to be the complexity of regulatory procedures and administrative burdens on start-ups.

Recent developments in Colombian youth policies

The promotion of formal employment, including reducing youth unemployment, is a priority for Colombia's government, and in 2010 Colombia's Congress approved the Law of Job Creation and Formalisation (Law 1429/10).[1] Regarding the promotion of youth employment, this law provides tax discounts to enterprises that hire new personnel from several groups, including youth up to age 28.

Additionally, in April 2015 the government launched the programme "40 000 First Jobs".[2] In partnership with 850 enterprises, the programme promotes the hiring of secondary school graduates, young professionals or technicians with no experience. The government will invest USD 100 million to cover the remuneration and social obligations of these workers, as well as a six-month transport subsidy. The enterprise agrees to keep at least 60% of youth hired and on payroll through the subsidy programme for a minimum of six additional months.[3]

Finally, in May 2016, Congress approved the Pro-Youth Law (Law 1780/16).[4] This law creates new benefits for young entrepreneurs and youth employment. First, it exempts entrepreneurs under the age of 35 from paying the fees associated with registering new ventures at the chambers of commerce. Second, it exempts enterprises from paying contributions to the Family Compensation Fund when they hire youth up to age 28.[5] Third, the government will promote youth employment in public entities and state-owned enterprises, prioritising the ex-combatants of the FARC guerrilla army. Fourth, the law creates a regulatory framework for internships in the public sector. Finally, the law removes barriers to the labour market by withdrawing the mandate of attaining military clearance as a requirement to participate in the labour market.

Key indicators: Colombia

Labour market developments[i] (%)	Colombia 2004	Colombia 2014	LAC 2004	LAC 2014	OECD 2004	OECD 2014
Unemployment rates - adults (30-64)	7.8	5.8	4.8	3.4	4.6	5.8
Unemployment rates - youth (15-29)	20.5	15.0	12.4	10.3	8.0	12.5
Informality rates - adults (35-64)		31.5	47.0	38.3		
Informality rates - youth (15-29)		47.5	62.3	52.3		

	Colombia				LAC (17)			
Youth and socio-economic status (%)	Extreme poor	Moderate poor	Vulnerable	Middle class	Extreme poor	Moderate poor	Vulnerable	Middle class
Youth (15-29)	13.0	14.4	42.1	30.5	15.1	12.4	39.4	33.1

Activity rates for youth (15-29)[i] (%)	Colombia 2004	Colombia 2014	LAC 2004	LAC 2014	OECD 2014
Student		25.6	23.0	25.3	13.2
Working student		11.5	11.3	11.2	35.5
Working		42.1	43.6	43.1	36.2
NEET		20.7	22.2	20.3	15.1

	Colombia				LAC (17)			
Activity rates for youth (15-29)[i] by socio-economic status (%)	Extreme poor	Moderate poor	Vulnerable	Middle class	Extreme poor	Moderate poor	Vulnerable	Middle class
Student	29.6	26.9	24.7	25.1	27.0	29.7	30.0	30.7
Working student	7.4	6.4	9.4	18.0	7.8	7.5	8.9	15.0
Working- formal	1.6	6.5	16.1	32.1	4.8	9.6	18.4	28.8
Working- informal	23.1	30.3	27.7	16.2	25.2	22.0	19.1	13.3
NEET	38.3	29.9	22.0	8.6	35.1	31.2	23.7	12.2

Distribution of youth employed[i] (%)	Colombia	LAC	OECD
Employee	60.3	70.0	88.0
Employer	1.3	2.2	3.9
Own-account worker	31.2	16.3	5.7
Unpaid family worker	7.2	11.2	24.0

	Colombia		LAC		OECD	
Trust in elections[ii] (%)	Youth (16-29)	Adults (30-64)	Youth (16-29)	Adults (30-64)	Youth (15-29)	Adults (30-64)
Share of population that expresses confidence in the transparency of election results	21.3	25.6	36.3	39.3	62.1	63.2
Feeling of safety[ii] (%)						
Share of population that feels safe in their city or area	45.9	48.4	47.0	46.0	70.9	71.3

	Colombia		LAC		OECD
Skills[iii] (%)	Youth (25-29)	Adults (30-64)	Youth (25-29)	Adults (30-64)	Adults (25-64)
Population with complete secondary education	69.0	46.1	55.4	38.6	76.0
Population with complete tertiary education[a]	16.9	13.9	14.6	13.4	34.0

	Colombia (2014)	LAC (18)	OECD (33)
Students in secondary education enrolled in vocational programme[b]	7.2	14.5	26.1

	Colombia (2010)	LAC	OECD (2014)
Public spending in training programmes (% of GDP)[c]	0.34	0.12	0.15

Entrepreneurship[iv] (%)	Colombia	LAC	OECD
Necessity as entrepreneurial motivation (share of 18-29 in total early-stage entrepreneurial activity)	26.8	26.2	16.0

Barriers to entrepreneurship index[v]	Colombia	LAC	OECD
Complexity of regulatory procedures	0.8	1.2	0.6
Administrative burdens on start-ups	0.7	0.9	0.6
Regulatory protection of incumbents	0.4	0.6	0.4
Total	1.9	2.7	1.7

Table notes: i) Latin America weighted average of LAC-17 countries: Argentina, Bolivia, Brazil, Chile, Colombia, Costa Rica, Dominican Republic, Ecuador, El Salvador, Guatemala, Honduras, Mexico, Nicaragua, Panama, Peru, Paraguay, Uruguay. OECD weighted average for 34 OECD member countries; ii) Latin America unweighted average of LAC-16 countries Argentina, Brazil, Chile, Colombia, Costa Rica, Dominican Republic, Ecuador, El Salvador, Guatemala, Honduras, Mexico, Nicaragua, Panama, Paraguay, Peru, Uruguay, OECD simple average of OECD 35 member countries; iii) Latin America unweighted average of LAC-17 countries: Argentina, Bolivia, Brazil, Chile, Colombia, Costa Rica, Dominican Republic, Ecuador, El Salvador, Guatemala, Honduras, Mexico, Nicaragua, Panama, Peru, Paraguay, Uruguay. OECD unweighted average for 34 OECD member countries; iv) Share of population that see start-up as a necessity (no other options for work) rather than an opportunity. Latin America (10) non-weighted average of Argentina, Brazil, Chile, Colombia, Ecuador, Guatemala, Panama, Mexico, Peru, and Uruguay. OECD (27) non-weighted average of Australia, Belgium, Chile, Estonia, Finland, Germany, Greece, Hungary, Ireland, Israel, Italy, Latvia, Luxembourg, Mexico, Netherlands, Norway, Poland, Portugal, Slovakia, Slovenia, South Korea, Spain, Sweden, Switzerland, United Kingdom and United States; v) The Entrepreneurship Barriers Index is composed of three sub-indices: 1) Complexity of regulatory procedures: measures the licences and permits system, such as the communication and simplification of rules and procedures. 2) Administrative burdens on start-ups: measures the burdens that are face by corporations and sole proprietor firms, and the barriers in services sectors. 3) Regulatory protection of incumbents: measures legal barriers to entry, anti-trust exemptions and barriers in network sectors. The three indicators are based on the 2013 Product Market Regulation questionnaire available at: http://www.oecd.org/eco/reform/PMR-Questionnaire-2013.pdf. The indicator reflects the state of legislation in 2014 for Kenya, Philippines, Rwanda and Uruguay; in 2015 for Bolivia, Ecuador, Guatemala, Panama, Paraguay and Venezuela; in 2013 for all others. Scale 0 to 6 from least to most restrictive. See methodological note for further details.

Table sources: i) SEDLAC (CEDLAS and the World Bank) for Latin American countries and OECD-LFS data for the OECD (2014); ii) OECD calculations based on Gallup Organization (2014), *Gallup World Monitor* (database); iii) (a) SEDLAC (CEDLAS and the World Bank) for Latin American countries (2014) and; OECD (2014), *Education at a Glance 2014: OECD Indicators*; (b) UNESCO (2016) and DiNIECE. Ministerio de Educación (2013) for Latin American countries and OECD (2014), *Education at a Glance 2014: OECD Indicators* for the OECD; (c) World Bank LAC Social Protection Database (2015) and OECD/EC Labour Market Programme Database; iv) Global Entrepreneurship Monitor individual data (2015); v) OECD-WBG product market regulation database for all countries except Brazil, Chile, India, Mexico and South Africa, OECD product market regulation database (2014).

Notes

1. http://www.mintrabajo.gov.co/empleo/abece-ley-de-primer-empleo.html.
2. http://es.presidencia.gov.co/logros/Paginas/logros-2015.aspx.
3. http://www.ilo.org/americas/publicaciones/observatorio-de-la-crisis/WCMS_LIMD3_2_EN/lang--en/index.htm.
4. http://es.presidencia.gov.co/normativa/normativa/LEY%201780%20DEL%2002%20DE%20MAYO%20DE%202016.pdf.
5. This is a mandatory payroll contribution used to finance entities that provide a variety of health, education, housing and recreational services to employees.

Costa Rica

Recent trends

Labour market conditions have been worsening in Costa Rica in recent times. Even though Costa Rica's labour market performance has been better in comparison with other countries in the region, the informality trend has been increasing. Unemployment rates remained in line with OECD average in 2014, still slightly above the Latin America and Caribbean (LAC) average (5% in Costa Rica vs. 3% in LAC). Despite having increased over the last decade informality rates for adults, defined as all employed persons not paying social contributions, have remained much lower than the LAC average (26% in Costa Rica vs. 38% in the LAC region).

According to Socio-Economic Database for Latin America and the Caribbean (SEDLAC) data based on Costa Rica national household survey ENAHO, in comparison to overall unemployment youth unemployment (15-29 years old) in Costa Rica remains relatively high, at 16% in 2014, well above the OECD average and highest among LAC countries (10% LAC average). In contrast, at 30% in 2014 (compared with 52% across the LAC average) the informality rate for youth has been declining over the past decade. However, this percentage jumps to 89% and 71% for youth belonging to extreme poor and moderate poor households, respectively (vs. 42% and 21% for youth in vulnerable and middle class households).

Activity status of youth by single year of age in Costa Rica, 2014

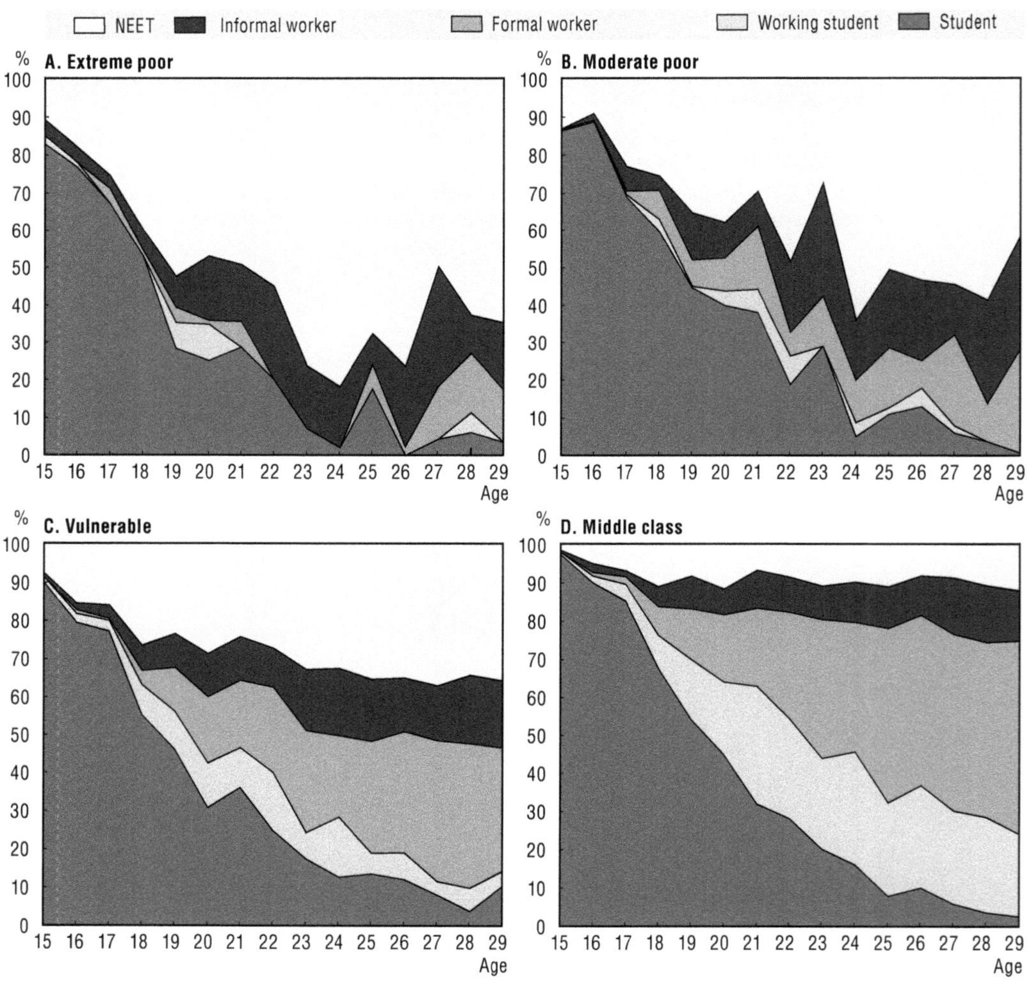

Source: OECD and World Bank tabulations of SEDLAC (CEDLAS and the World Bank).
StatLink http://dx.doi.org/10.1787/888933415466

According to SEDLAC data based on ENHAO, in Costa Rica 37% of young people are enrolled in the educational system (vs. 25% in the LAC region) and around 45% of youth are part of the workforce or working students. Young people who are neither employed nor in education or training ("NEETs") risk being left behind permanently in the labour market. This risk is especially high for the relatively large share of poor and vulnerable NEETs. In Costa Rica around 19% of young people aged 15-29 are NEET compared with 15% in the OECD as a whole but slightly below the LAC average. The poor (extreme and moderate) and vulnerable youth account for more than three-quarters of all young NEETs. Similarly to all the other countries in the region, in Costa Rica there is also a quite big (around 17 percentage points) gender gap between young women and men NEETs.

The share of the youth population who express confidence in the transparency of election results is lower than that of adults in Costa Rica, but higher than the average for the region (48% vs. 36% for the LAC average). Youth safety perception in Costa Rica is higher than for adults and the regional average for youth, (50% of youth in Costa Rica vs. 47% for the LAC average).

Educational attainment in Costa Rica is slightly lower than the average for the region, 54% of the youth (aged 25-29) have completed secondary education in 2014 (vs. 55% for the LAC average) and 12% of the youth (aged 25-29) have completed tertiary education in 2014 (vs. 15% for the LAC average). However, as in other countries in the region, Costa Rica faces high school dropout and low completion rates: 30% of youth (aged 15-29) have not completed secondary education and are out of school, as of 2014. Technical and vocational education and training (TVET) has a good status in Costa Rica and is a priority in the country's policy agenda (Álvarez-Galván, 2015). It is no surprise that the share of students in secondary education who are enrolled in vocational training programmes is quite high: 22% compared with 14% in the LAC region. Moreover, the share of gross domestic product spent by Costa Rica in training programmes in 2013, 0.32%, is higher than the LAC and OECD averages.

In Costa Rica youth entrepreneurship is less widespread than in the LAC average: 7% of the working youth are own-account workers and 1% are employers compared with 16% and 2% across the LAC average. Additionally, data from the Global Entrepreneurship Monitor (GEM) show that in Costa Rica the share of young entrepreneurs (18-29 years old) where necessity is the main entrepreneurial motivation (as percentage of total early-stage entrepreneurial activity), estimated at 15% for 2012, is similar to the OECD average (16%) and below the regional (26%). Around 46% of Costa Rican entrepreneurs are 35 years old or younger, but the average age is 36 years old (GEM 2014). Men and women tend to create new ventures at around the same rate, with a small inclination towards men.

According to OECD data on product market regulation, barriers to entrepreneurship in Costa Rica are in line with the LAC average. Even though, the government is committed to improving regulatory conditions through the implementation of 75 measures included in the Inter-Institutional National Plan on Procedure Simplification, one of the most relevant barriers young entrepreneurs face to their activity is the complexity of the regulatory procedures. Additional initiatives, such as the development banking system (*sistema banca de desarrollo*), created by Law No. 8634 of 23 April 2008, and their respective reforms have allowed the relaxation of requirements, improving the accession of entrepreneurs to credits in the bank system. In addition, the National Learning Institute (INA) will start additional programmes for startups, with the recent approval of more than 150 teaching positions.

Recent trends in Costa Rica's youth inclusion policies

The Costa Rican government is conducting important efforts to promote the inclusion of the youth population into the educational system and workforce through three main programmes. First, *Avancemos* [Let's Advance] was introduced in 2006 and offers a conditional cash transfer to poor and vulnerable families with young children between 12 and 25 years old, who require an economic incentive to stay in the secondary education system instead of entering the labour market. It started in 2006 as a pilot plan in vulnerable urban communities, providing scholarships to 8 000 students. In 2015, it benefited 169 030 students, after the Mixed Institute of Social Assistance (IMAS), the institution in charge of the programme, changed the structure because it had observed higher dropout rates in 7th grade. *Empleate* [Employ Yourself], is a programme that provides conditioned subsidies or transfers to young people (aged 17-24, and up to 35 years old if the person has a disability) who do not study or work and are in a condition of poverty, to be trained in technical-occupational careers and improve their employability. Finally, *Mi Primer Empleo* [My First Job] provides a benefit to hiring companies which aims to boost inclusion of women, young people (aged 18-35 years) and people with disabilities in the labour market.

Recent trends in Costa Rica's vocational training policies

Costa Rica has two paths for technical education and vocational training: technical education offered at the upper-secondary education (third cycle) by the Ministry of Education and non-formal vocational training offered by the National Apprenticeship Institute (Instituto Nacional de Aprendizaje: INA) as well as by companies and other organisations to a smaller extent (Álvarez-Galván, 2015). The national system offering technical education services is complemented by the Technical Education School (Escuela de Educación Técnica) of the Technology Institute (Instituto Tecnologico de Costa Rica), which is mainly in charge of teacher training, and the National Technical University (Universidad Técnica Nacional: UNT), which was created to facilitate a higher level of training to graduates from technical secondary schools. Between 2011 and 2012, 60 new services were created to increase the coverage of technical education; 24 of them were new colleges and 36 night modules. Finally, a proposal for the implementation of a dual system in TVET is currently under discussion in Costa Rica.

Recent developments in Costa Rica's entrepreneurship policies

Costa Rica Government has the *Política de Fomento al Emprendimiento de Costa Rica 2014-2018* [Policy to Boost Entrepreneurship in Costa Rica], which aims to strengthen the institutional offer and the service chain, with innovative and inclusive instruments, and fostering entrepreneurship and its culture in the country. Among its goals, the policy considers youth and women as important pillars, encouraging social inclusion and environmental responsibility. It also aims at fostering associativity and public private partnership.

The Ministry of Economy, Industry and Commerce (MEIC), the Ministry of Science, Technology and Telecommunications (MICITT) and the Ministry of Public Education (MEP) have together developed the *Programa de Emprendedores Jóvenes, Tour de Emprendimiento e Innovación* to support young entrepreneurs and to develop an entrepreneurial culture among youth. In addition, the *Feria Encuentro de Personas Jóvenes Emprendedoras* is an initiative co-ordinated jointly with the Ministry of Culture and Youth (MCJ).

In 2014, the MICITT, the MEIC and Telefónica Movistar launched OpenFuture, a platform aimed at supporting entrepreneurism in the country by creating an open space where entrepreneurs can work, know each other and exchange ideas, and a platform that brings together entrepreneurs, investors and other key stakeholders for the sector.

Reference

Álvarez-Galván, J. (2015), "A skills beyond school review of Costa Rica", *OECD Reviews of Vocational Education and Training*, OECD Publishing, Paris, http://dx.doi.org/10.1787/9789264233256-en.

Key indicators: Costa Rica

Labour market developments[i] (%)	Costa Rica 2004	Costa Rica 2014	LAC 2004	LAC 2014	OECD 2004	OECD 2014
Unemployment rates - adults (30-64)	3.8	5.4	4.8	3.4	4.6	5.8
Unemployment rates - youth (15-29)	11.3	15.8	12.4	10.3	8.0	12.5
Informality rates - adults (35-64)	23.8	25.8	47.0	38.3		
Informality rates - youth (15-29)	35.9	29.9	62.3	52.3		

Youth and socio-economic status (%)	Costa Rica Extreme poor	Costa Rica Moderate poor	Costa Rica Vulnerable	Costa Rica Middle class	LAC (17) Extreme poor	LAC (17) Moderate poor	LAC (17) Vulnerable	LAC (17) Middle class
Youth (15-29)	4.4	7.3	38.2	50.1	15.1	12.4	39.4	33.1

Activity rates for youth (15-29)[i] (%)	Costa Rica 2004	Costa Rica 2014	LAC 2004	LAC 2014	OECD 2014
Student	29.9	36.7	23.0	25.3	13.2
Working student	12.8	13.3	11.3	11.2	35.5
Working	35.7	31.2	43.6	43.1	36.2
NEET	21.5	18.7	22.2	20.3	15.1

Activity rates for youth (15-29)[i] by socio-economic status (%)	Costa Rica Extreme poor	Costa Rica Moderate poor	Costa Rica Vulnerable	Costa Rica Middle class	LAC (17) Extreme poor	LAC (17) Moderate poor	LAC (17) Vulnerable	LAC (17) Middle class
Student	34.2	42.0	38.9	34.1	27.0	29.7	30.0	30.7
Working student	1.7	2.1	7.4	19.8	7.8	7.5	8.9	15.0
Working- formal	4.8	8.9	17.1	28.0	4.8	9.6	18.4	28.8
Working- informal	12.3	12.5	10.3	8.9	25.2	22.0	19.1	13.3
NEET	47.1	34.4	26.3	9.2	35.1	31.2	23.7	12.2

Distribution of youth employed[i] (%)	Costa Rica	LAC	OECD
Employee	90.0	70.0	88.0
Employer	1.0	2.2	3.9
Own-account worker	7.2	16.3	5.7
Unpaid family worker	1.8	11.2	24.0

	Costa Rica Youth (16-29)	Costa Rica Adults (30-64)	LAC Youth (16-29)	LAC Adults (30-64)	OECD Youth (15-29)	OECD Adults (30-64)
Trust in elections[ii] (%)						
Share of population that expresses confidence in the transparency of election results	48.4	56.3	36.3	39.3	62.1	63.2
Feeling of safety[ii] (%)						
Share of population that feels safe in their city or area	50.4	45.0	47.0	46.0	70.9	71.3

Skills[iii] (%)	Costa Rica Youth (25-29)	Costa Rica Adults (30-64)	LAC Youth (25-29)	LAC Adults (30-64)	OECD Adults (25-64)
Population with complete secondary education	54.8	38.0	55.4	38.6	76.0
Population with complete tertiary education[a]	11.8	12.7	14.6	13.4	34.0

	Costa Rica (2014)	LAC (18)	OECD (33)
Students in secondary education enrolled in vocational programme[b]	22.1	14.5	26.1

	Costa Rica (2013)	LAC	OECD (2014)
Public spending in training programmes (% of GDP)[c]	0.32	0.12	0.15

Entrepreneurship[iv] (%)	Costa Rica	LAC	OECD
Necessity as entrepreneurial motivation (share of 18-29 in total early-stage entrepreneurial activity)	14.8	26.2	16.0

Barriers to entrepreneurship index[v]	Costa Rica	LAC	OECD
Complexity of regulatory procedures	1.0	1.2	0.6
Administrative burdens on start-ups	0.8	0.9	0.6
Regulatory protection of incumbents	0.9	0.6	0.4
Total	2.7	2.7	1.7

Table notes: i) Latin America weighted average of LAC-17 countries: Argentina, Bolivia, Brazil, Chile, Colombia, Costa Rica, Dominican Republic, Ecuador, El Salvador, Guatemala, Honduras, Mexico, Nicaragua, Panama, Peru, Paraguay, Uruguay. OECD weighted average for 34 OECD member countries; ii) Latin America unweighted average of LAC-16 countries Argentina, Brazil, Chile, Colombia, Costa Rica, Dominican Republic, Ecuador, El Salvador, Guatemala, Honduras, Mexico, Nicaragua, Panama, Paraguay, Peru, Uruguay, OECD simple average of OECD 35 member countries; iii) Latin America unweighted average of LAC-17 countries: Argentina, Bolivia, Brazil, Chile, Colombia, Costa Rica, Dominican Republic, Ecuador, El Salvador, Guatemala, Honduras, Mexico, Nicaragua, Panama, Peru, Paraguay, Uruguay. OECD unweighted average for 34 OECD member countries; iv) Share of population that see start-up as a necessity (no other options for work) rather than an opportunity. Latin America (10) non-weighted average of Argentina, Brazil, Chile, Colombia, Ecuador, Guatemala, Panama, Mexico, Peru, and Uruguay. OECD (27) non-weighted average of Australia, Belgium, Chile, Estonia, Finland, Germany, Greece, Hungary, Ireland, Israel, Italy, Latvia, Luxembourg, Mexico, Netherlands, Norway, Poland, Portugal, Slovakia, Slovenia, South Korea, Spain, Sweden, Switzerland, United Kingdom and United States; v) The Entrepreneurship Barriers Index is composed of three sub-indices: 1) Complexity of regulatory procedures: measures the licences and permits system, such as the communication and simplification of rules and procedures. 2) Administrative burdens on start-ups: measures the burdens that are face by corporations and sole proprietor firms, and the barriers in services sectors. 3) Regulatory protection of incumbents: measures legal barriers to entry, anti-trust exemptions and barriers in network sectors. The three indicators are based on the 2013 Product Market Regulation questionnaire available at: http://www.oecd.org/eco/reform/PMR-Questionnaire-2013.pdf. The indicator reflects the state of legislation in 2014 for Kenya, Philippines, Rwanda and Uruguay; in 2015 for Bolivia, Ecuador, Guatemala, Panama, Paraguay and Venezuela; in 2013 for all others. Scale 0 to 6 from least to most restrictive. See methodological note for further details.

Table sources: i) SEDLAC (CEDLAS and the World Bank) for Latin American countries and OECD-LFS data for the OECD (2014); ii) OECD calculations based on Gallup Organization (2014), *Gallup World Monitor* (database); iii) (a) SEDLAC (CEDLAS and the World Bank) for Latin American countries (2014) and; OECD (2014), *Education at a Glance 2014: OECD Indicators*; (b) UNESCO (2016) and DiNIECE. Ministerio de Educación (2013) for Latin American countries and OECD (2014), *Education at a Glance 2014: OECD Indicators* for the OECD; (c) World Bank LAC Social Protection Database (2015) and OECD/EC Labour Market Programme Database; iv) Global Entrepreneurship Monitor individual data (2015); v) OECD-WBG product market regulation database for all countries except Brazil, Chile, India, Mexico and South Africa, OECD product market regulation database (2014).

Dominican Republic

Recent trends

Dominican Republic has experienced strong and sustained economic growth over the past two decades, and labour market outcomes improved. Unemployment is low, at 2.7% in 2014 according to Socio-Economic Database for Latin America and the Caribbean (SEDLAC) data (this goes to 4.4% if calculated using data from the National Labour Force Survey [ENFT]). The unemployment rate for adults is in line with the Latin America and Caribbean (LAC) average (3.3%), and below the OECD average. Dominican Republic is among LAC countries with the lowest rates of informality, defined as all employed persons not paying social contributions. This group represents 22.5% of the 30-64 year-old workers' population, well below the 38% LAC average.

Activity status of youth by single year in Dominican Republic, 2014

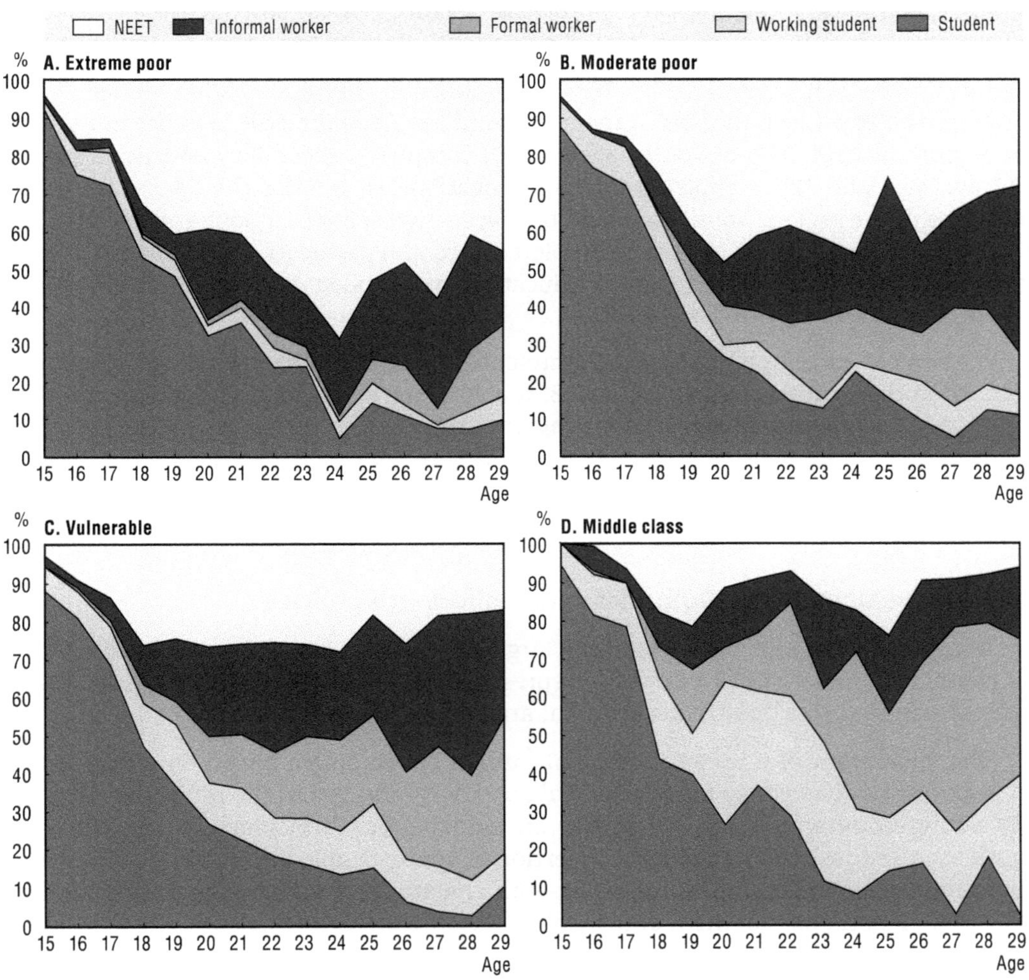

Source: OECD and World Bank tabulations of SEDLAC (CEDLAS and the World Bank).
StatLink http://dx.doi.org/10.1787/888933415473

Despite considerable progress, gaps in youth inclusion in the labour market and society persist throughout the region and also in Dominican Republic. Youth benefited from the positive labour market climate; however, in 2014, their unemployment rate was at 9.5% according to SEDLAC data (11.4% with ENFT/BCRD data), slightly lower than the LAC and OECD average (10% and 12% respectively) but more than three times the total unemployment rate in Dominican Republic.

In Dominican Republic, more than one-third of young people are studying and more than 42% are working or working students. Young people who are neither employed nor in education nor training ("NEETs") risk being left permanently behind in the labour market. This risk is especially high for the relatively large share of poor and vulnerable NEETs. In Dominican Republic, between 2004 and 2014, the number of young people aged 15-29 who were NEETs dropped from 24-22% compared with 15% in the OECD as a whole. Poor and vulnerable NEETs account for almost 90% of all young NEETs.

Dominican Republic also has a high incidence of youth engaged in informal jobs: almost 41% of working youth hold an informal job and this percentage jumps to 66% and 52% for youth belonging to extremely poor and moderately poor households, respectively (vs. 45% and 31% of youth in vulnerable and middle-class households).

According to Gallup World Monitor Survey, the share of the youth population that expresses confidence in the transparency of election results is lower than that of adults in Dominican Republic and lower than the average for the region (33% vs. 36% for the LAC average). Youth safety perception in Dominican Republic is slightly higher than that of adults, but lower than the regional average for youth (41% of youth in Dominican Republic vs. 47% for the LAC average).

In terms of educational attainment, Dominican Republic still lags behind the average for the region: in 2014, 54% of youth (aged 25-29) completed secondary education (vs. 55% for the LAC average) and 12% completed tertiary education (vs. 15% for the LAC average). As in other countries in the region, Dominican Republic faces high school dropout and low completion rates: 27% of youth (aged 15-29) have not completed secondary education and are out of school. At the same time, few students in secondary education are enrolled in vocational training programmes (5% vs. 14% in LAC and 26% in the OECD).

In terms of entrepreneurship, in Dominican Republic, the majority of self-employed are own-account workers rather than employers: 33% of working youth report being own-account workers, while only 1% define themselves as entrepreneurs.

The barriers to entrepreneurship in Dominican Republic are as high as in the LAC average. The most important barrier faced by young entrepreneurs seems to be the complexity of regulatory procedures and the administrative burdens on start-ups.

Recent developments in Dominican Republic youth policies

Dominican Republic concentrates a large proportion of people in productive ages, so that its youth population (15-29 years old) represents approximately 22%; this explains why public policies aimed at this population segment are particularly important.

The generation of a broad process of human development based on social development is an important public policy for youths. This policy is reflected in the project *Mi Communidad Joven* (My Young Community), which focuses on reducing youth violence, promoting integration of youth associations, encouraging the insertion of young people into national education processes and stimulating leadership skills, along with the study of priority areas such as demography, education, health, employment and housing.

The consolidation of institutions directed towards youth is another key element of public policy in Dominican Republic. The National Program for Establishment of Youth Councils aims to strengthen public policies in this area at the local level, enhancing the integration, operation and actions of the Ministry of Youth through the creation and installation of youth councils in each municipality, as well as strengthening provincial youth councils.

In 2009, Dominican Republic established the *Programa Juventud y Empleo* to improve the employability of young people from low income and vulnerable households. It offers theoretical and practical vocational training in classrooms combined with an internship. In addition to a first job experience the programme prepares young people by providing foundational and technical skills that can be used in a trade of their choice.

The training of individuals and enhancing their potential for successful insertion into the labour market is another element of public policy, which focuses mainly on entrepreneurship and innovation. With this in mind, the Program of Entrepreneurial Skills, which includes the University Chair of Entrepreneurship and New Ideas for Development, along with the National Entrepreneurship Program, are the main projects considered in this area.

Public policy intended for training young people for employment has been implemented to improve the professional qualifications of youth, as well as their ability to enter the labour market. The National and International Scholarship Program offers the opportunity to access undergraduate, graduate and diploma education, in addition to technical and professional education. This programme, along with the National Literacy Plan, helps reduce low levels of education and increase specialisation, as well as improve quality of life of individuals.

Finally, the Strategic Plan (2015-19) of the Ministry of Youth establishes guidelines to carry out the public policy elements described above, together with various projects that these include, through an updated diagnosis of the social, economic and political situation of youth in Dominican Republic.

Key indicators: Dominican Republic

Labour market developments[i] (%)	Dominican Republic 2004	Dominican Republic 2014	LAC 2004	LAC 2014	OECD 2004	OECD 2014
Unemployment rates - adults (30-64)	2.9	2.7	4.8	3.4	4.6	5.8
Unemployment rates - youth (15-29)	7.0	9.5	12.4	10.3	8.0	12.5
Informality rates - adults (35-64)		22.5	47.0	38.3		
Informality rates - youth (15-29)		41.0	62.3	52.3		

Youth and socio-economic status (%)	Dominican Republic: Extreme poor	Moderate poor	Vulnerable	Middle class	LAC (17): Extreme poor	Moderate poor	Vulnerable	Middle class
Youth (15-29)	12.8	18.8	46.0	22.4	15.1	12.4	39.4	33.1

Activity rates for youth (15-29)[i] (%)	Dominican Republic 2004	Dominican Republic 2014	LAC 2004	LAC 2014	OECD 2014
Student	32.3	35.1	23.0	25.3	13.2
Working student	14.1	12.0	11.3	11.2	35.5
Working	29.8	31.0	43.6	43.1	36.2
NEET	23.7	21.9	22.2	20.3	15.1

Activity rates for youth (15-29)[i] by socio-economic status (%)	Dominican Republic: Extreme poor	Moderate poor	Vulnerable	Middle class	LAC (17): Extreme poor	Moderate poor	Vulnerable	Middle class
Student	44.1	37.4	33.9	31.7	27.0	29.7	30.0	30.7
Working student	4.5	7.4	11.0	21.9	7.8	7.5	8.9	15.0
Working- formal	3.6	9.3	14.6	22.1	4.8	9.6	18.4	28.8
Working- informal	12.9	16.2	20.0	12.8	25.2	22.0	19.1	13.3
NEET	34.8	29.7	20.5	11.5	35.1	31.2	23.7	12.2

Distribution of youth employed[i] (%)	Dominican Republic	LAC	OECD
Employee	62.8	70.0	88.0
Employer	1.0	2.2	3.9
Own-account worker	33.3	16.3	5.7
Unpaid family worker	2.9	11.2	24.0

Trust in elections[ii] (%)	Dominican Republic: Youth (16-29)	Dominican Republic: Adults (30-64)	LAC: Youth (16-29)	LAC: Adults (30-64)	OECD: Youth (15-29)	OECD: Adults (30-64)
Share of population that expresses confidence in the transparency of election results	33.1	37.1	36.3	39.3	62.1	63.2
Feeling of safety[ii] (%)						
Share of population that feels safe in their city or area	40.6	38.8	47.0	46.0	70.9	71.3

Skills[iii] (%)	Dominican Republic: Youth (25-29)	Dominican Republic: Adults (30-64)	LAC: Youth (25-29)	LAC: Adults (30-64)	OECD: Adults (25-64)
Population with complete secondary education	54.6	33.5	55.4	38.6	76.0
Population with complete tertiary education[a]	11.8	13.5	14.6	13.4	34.0

	Dominican Republic (2014)	LAC (18)	OECD (33)
Students in secondary education enrolled in vocational programme[b]	4.8	14.5	26.1

Barriers to entrepreneurship index[iv]	Dominican Republic	LAC	OECD
Complexity of regulatory procedures	1.3	1.2	0.6
Administrative burdens on start-ups	0.8	0.9	0.6
Regulatory protection of incumbents	0.5	0.6	0.4
Total	2.6	2.7	1.7

Table notes: i) Latin America weighted average of LAC-17 countries: Argentina, Bolivia, Brazil, Chile, Colombia, Costa Rica, Dominican Republic, Ecuador, El Salvador, Guatemala, Honduras, Mexico, Nicaragua, Panama, Peru, Paraguay, Uruguay. OECD weighted average for 34 OECD member countries; ii) Latin America unweighted average of LAC-16 countries Argentina, Brazil, Chile, Colombia, Costa Rica, Dominican Republic, Ecuador, El Salvador, Guatemala, Honduras, Mexico, Nicaragua, Panama, Paraguay, Peru, Uruguay, OECD simple average of OECD 35 member countries; iii) Latin America unweighted average of LAC-17 countries: Argentina, Bolivia, Brazil, Chile, Colombia, Costa Rica, Dominican Republic, Ecuador, El Salvador, Guatemala, Honduras, Mexico, Nicaragua, Panama, Peru, Paraguay, Uruguay. OECD unweighted average for 34 OECD member countries; iv) The Entrepreneurship Barriers Index is composed of three sub-indices: 1) Complexity of regulatory procedures: measures the licences and permits system, such as the communication and simplification of rules and procedures. 2) Administrative burdens on start-ups: measures the burdens that are face by corporations and sole proprietor firms, and the barriers in services sectors. 3) Regulatory protection of incumbents: measures legal barriers to entry, anti-trust exemptions and barriers in network sectors. The three indicators are based on the 2013 Product Market Regulation questionnaire available at: http://www.oecd.org/eco/reform/PMR-Questionnaire-2013.pdf. The indicator reflects the state of legislation in 2014 for Kenya, Philippines, Rwanda and Uruguay; in 2015 for Bolivia, Ecuador, Guatemala, Panama, Paraguay and Venezuela; in 2013 for all others. Scale 0 to 6 from least to most restrictive. See methodological note for further details.

Table sources: i) SEDLAC (CEDLAS and the World Bank) for Latin American countries and OECD-LFS data for the OECD (2014); ii) OECD calculations based on Gallup Organization (2014), *Gallup World Monitor* (database); iii) (a) SEDLAC (CEDLAS and the World Bank) for Latin American countries (2014); OECD (2014), *Education at a Glance 2014: OECD Indicators*; (b) UNESCO (2016) and DiNIECE. Ministerio de Educación (2013) for Latin American countries and OECD (2014), *Education at a Glance 2014: OECD Indicators* for the OECD; iv) OECD-WBG product market regulation database for all countries except Brazil, Chile, India, Mexico and South Africa, OECD product market regulation database (2014).

Mexico

Recent trends

Unemployment for adults in Mexico has been declining since the end of 2009. Although lower than the OECD average, unemployment rates remain in line with the Latin America and Caribbean (LAC) average (at 3% in 2014) according to the Socio-Economic Database for Latin America and the Caribbean (SEDLAC). At the same time, informality – defined as all employed persons not paying social contributions – remains high for adults over the last decade (57%), which is still higher than the LAC average (38%). However, informality rates have been decreasing since 2013 owing to labour market reforms introduced in 2012. These reforms aim to stimulate formal employment by adding new types of contracts that give access to social benefits.

Despite considerable progress, gaps in youth inclusion in the labour market and society persist throughout the region and also in Mexico. Youth unemployment – at 8% in 2014 according to SEDLAC data – increased slightly from 2004. However, it remains lower than the LAC average (10%) and OECD average (12%). Informality rates for youth are improving (70%), but were still higher than for adults (57%) in 2014.

Activity status of youth by single year of age in Mexico, 2014

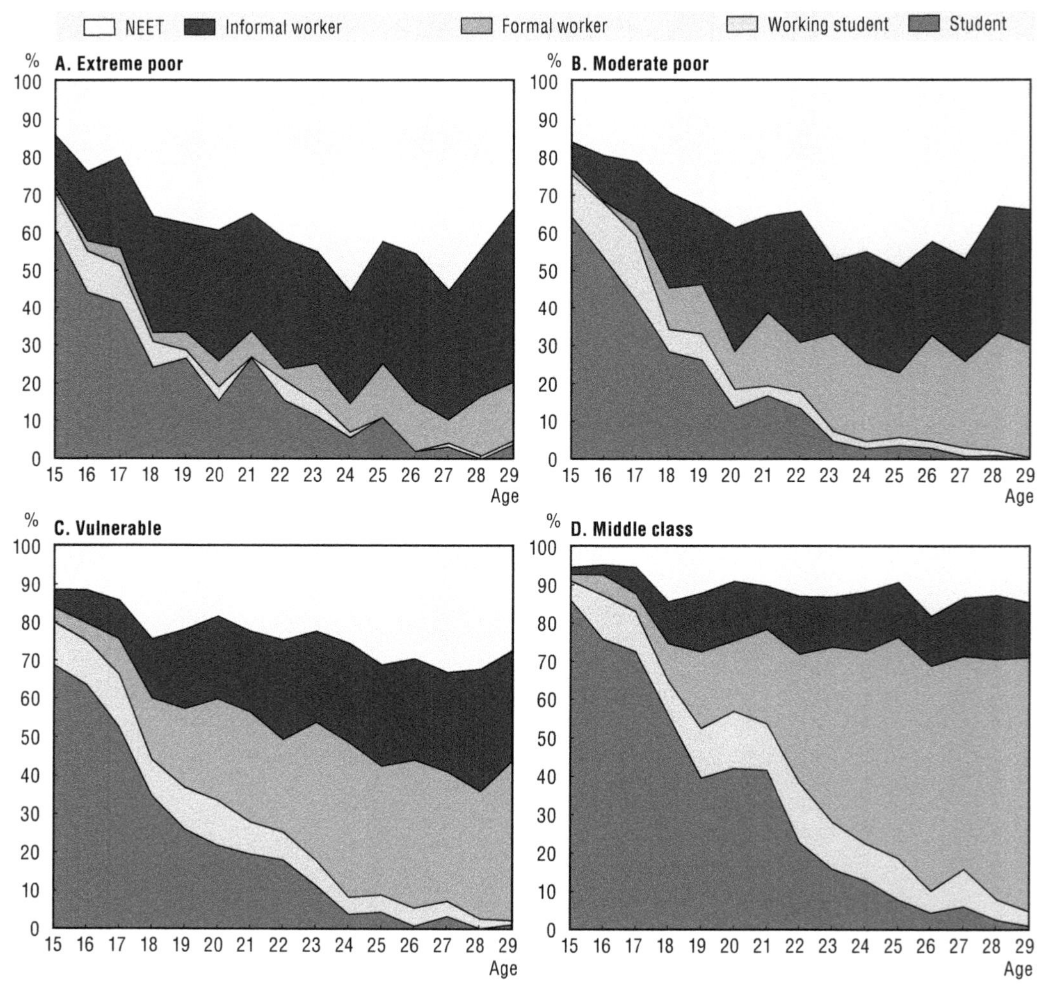

Source: OECD and World Bank tabulations of SEDLAC (CEDLAS and the World Bank).

StatLink http://dx.doi.org/10.1787/888933415523

In Mexico, more than a fourth of young people are studying (26% vs. 25% in the LAC region); more than half are working or are working students. Young people who are neither employed nor in education nor training ("NEETs") risk being left permanently behind in the labour market. This risk is especially high for the relatively large share of poor and vulnerable NEETs. Although the total number of NEETs in Mexico has decreased over the last decade, Mexico continues to be among the OECD countries with the highest rates of youth NEETs. This group represents 22% of the 15-29 year-old population, well above the 15% OECD average. Poor (extreme and moderate) and vulnerable youth account for more than 87% of all young NEETs. There is also a large gender gap as young women are three times more likely to be NEET as young men; however, NEET rates for women decreased from 39% to 35% between 2012 and 2014. These young women are generally working in the household, suggesting the gender gap may be largely related to cultural norms.

According to Gallup World Monitor survey, the share of the youth population that expresses confidence in the transparency of election results (29%) is lower than that of adults in Mexico and of LAC average (36%). However, youth safety perception in Mexico (50%) is higher than that of adults and the regional average (47%).

Educational attainment in Mexico is lower than average for the region in secondary education, but higher in tertiary education. In 2014, 45% of youth (aged 25-29) completed secondary education (vs. 55% for the LAC average) and 18% completed tertiary education (vs. 15% for the LAC average). As in other countries in the region, Mexico faces high dropout and low completion rates for school: 41% of youth (aged 15-29) have not completed secondary education and are out of school. Technical and vocational education and training (TVET) in Mexico plays an important social role by providing learning opportunities to students at risk of dropping out or in remote regions (Kis, Hoeckel and Santiago, 2012). Almost 17% of students in secondary education are enrolled in vocational training programmes (vs. 15% across the LAC region and 26% across the OECD). Mexico spent 0.04% of its gross domestic product in 2012 on training programmes, well behind both LAC and OECD averages. It is the country spending the least on active labour market policies in the OECD.

Youth entrepreneurship is less widespread in Mexico than the LAC average. In Mexico, 5% of working youth are own-account workers and 2% are employers compared to 16% and 2% across LAC. Additionally, data from the Global Entrepreneurship Monitor (GEM) show that in Mexico the share of young entrepreneurs (18-29 years old) where necessity is the main entrepreneurial motivation (as percentage of total early-stage entrepreneurial activity), estimated in 17% for 2015, is below the regional average (26%) and close to OECD levels (16%).

Barriers to entrepreneurship are slightly higher in Mexico than the OECD average, but lower than in the LAC region. Regulatory protection and administrative burdens on start-ups are among the most important barriers faced by young entrepreneurs. To reduce these burdens, the Mexican government created a new legal entity in March 2016: the simplified stock company, which allows entrepreneurs to create and register a small firm (even if it has a single proprietor) in less than 24 hours and at no cost for the entrepreneur.

Recent trends in technical and vocational training programmes

In Mexico, technical education at a medium-high level takes place in four types of school: technical schools in agriculture, industry and sea fishing, as well as colleges for professional technical education. There are two options for vocational training: 1) School training offered by the training centres for industrial work (*centros de capacitación para el trabajo Industrial: CECATI*) and the vocational training institutions (*Institutos de capacitación para el trabajo: ICAT*). Both provide several types of courses based on occupational competencies or on education-based competencies. The courses are short and aim at expanding and/or improving technical skills and training in new technologies; 2) Training out of school for unemployed persons, which is managed by the Ministry of Labour and Social Security. An example is "*Bécate*", which enables job seekers with short training courses to access employment or develop a self-employment activity. This programme is not exclusively for young people, but approximately 44% of its beneficiaries are between 16 and 25 years old.

Recent trends in entrepreneurship policies

In 2013, the Mexican government established the National Institute of the Entrepreneur (INADEM), a decentralised body responsible for fostering the innovation and competitiveness of micro, small and medium-sized enterprises on a national level. In addition, to help develop an entrepreneurial culture in the country, the institute supports national ventures to grow and to access international markets. To that end, INADEM created *Red de Apoyo al Emprendedor* [Support Network for Entrepreneurs], a network to support entrepreneurs and help them find relevant programmes, products and services provided by the institute.

Along with these initiatives, the Mexican government created the *Crédito Joven* [Credit for Youth] programme in 2015. With support from the state, the programme aims at providing credit to young people to create their business. It is a joint initiative between INADEM (through its entrepreneurial network) and Nacional Financiera (NAFIN), one of Mexico's development banks.

The National Council of Science and Technology (CONACYT) supports technological innovation in established and new ventures through the *Fondo de Innovación Tecnológica* [Technology Innovation Fund], a fund that fosters innovative ideas, both in small and medium-sized enterprises and in start-ups. The *Programa de Estímulo a la Innovación* [Programme to Stimulate Innovation] is another tool CONACYT offers to strengthen the technological foundation of Mexican firms.

The Mexican Institute for Youth (IMJUVE) has its *Programa Nacional de Juventud 2014-2018* (ProJuventud) [National Programme for Youth], which targets entrepreneurism as an important pillar to bring youth into the labour market.

More recently, *Oportunidades*, Mexico's flagship anti-poverty programme, was transformed into PROSPERA. The programme's new objective is to link poor households with productive assets, employment opportunities and financial products offered by various government initiatives. As part of the new approach, *Jóvenes Emprendedores Prosperando* [Prospering Youth Entrepreneurs] was developed with INADEM to foster entrepreneurship among young PROSPERA beneficiaries. Another programme under development will link PROSPERA high-school graduates to employment opportunities in partnership with the Ministry of Labour and Social Security.

In May 2013, the government established the National Productivity Commission (CNP), which includes federal ministries and the National Science and Technology Council, as well as representatives from the private sector, labour unions and education institutions. The CNP contributed to the administration's Productivity Programme, which includes the government's strategy for raising productivity in an inclusive way. More recently, the CNP has identified cross-cutting policy areas (such as labour training and innovation in specific sectors) in which co-ordinated actions are deemed crucial for boosting productivity.

Recent progress in fighting informality

In addition to labour market reforms in 2012, the Mexican government has other initiatives to tackle informality. The Go Formal programme aims to stimulate formal employment by facilitating the participation of informal firms in the formal economy, including easing of social benefit obligations. At the same time, tax measures included in the 2013 fiscal reform have helped promote the formalisation of the workforce, with a new Incorporation Regime that reduces taxes for up to ten years. Mexico's new fiscal regime for small firms (RIF), which began in January 2014, replaced an earlier small-taxpayer regime (REPECOS). It includes substantially reduced personal, social security, value added and excise tax obligations in the initial decade of operation, to induce informal firms to formalise their status and start paying taxes.

Reference

Kis, V., K. Hoeckel and P. Santiago (2012), *OECD Reviews of Vocational Education and Training: A Learning for Jobs Review of Mexico 2009*, OECD Publishing, Paris, http://dx.doi.org/10.1787/9789264168688-en.

Key indicators: Mexico

Labour market developments[i] (%)	Mexico 2004	Mexico 2014	LAC 2004	LAC 2014	OECD 2004	OECD 2014
Unemployment rates - adults (30-64)	1.9	3.3	4.8	3.4	4.6	5.8
Unemployment rates - youth (15-29)	7.2	7.7	12.4	10.3	8.0	12.5
Informality rates - adults (35-64)	54.7	56.7	47.0	38.3		
Informality rates - youth (15-29)	66.1	69.5	62.3	52.3		

	Mexico				LAC (17)			
Youth and socio-economic status (%)	Extreme poor	Moderate poor	Vulnerable	Middle class	Extreme poor	Moderate poor	Vulnerable	Middle class
Youth (15-29)	10.3	15.5	48.8	25.4	15.1	12.4	39.4	33.1

Activity rates for youth (15-29)[i] (%)	Mexico 2004	Mexico 2014	LAC 2004	LAC 2014	OECD 2014
Student	22.5	26.3	23.0	25.3	13.2
Working student	6.4	8.1	11.3	11.2	35.5
Working	45.6	43.0	43.6	43.1	36.2
NEET	25.5	22.6	22.2	20.3	15.1

	Mexico				LAC (17)			
Activity rates for youth (15-29)[i] by socio-economic status (%)	Extreme poor	Moderate poor	Vulnerable	Middle class	Extreme poor	Moderate poor	Vulnerable	Middle class
Student	22.8	22.4	25.3	31.1	27.0	29.7	30.0	30.7
Working student	4.7	6.2	8.1	10.1	7.8	7.5	8.9	15.0
Working- formal	7.0	14.8	24.1	34.7	4.8	9.6	18.4	28.8
Working- informal	29.5	23.4	19.9	12.4	25.2	22.0	19.1	13.3
NEET	36.0	33.2	22.5	11.7	35.1	31.2	23.7	12.2

Distribution of youth employed[i] (%)	Mexico	LAC	OECD
Employee	83.1	70.0	88.0
Employer	2.4	2.2	3.9
Own-account worker	5.5	16.3	5.7
Unpaid family worker	9.1	11.2	24.0

	Mexico		LAC		OECD	
Trust in elections[ii] (%)	Youth (16-29)	Adults (30-64)	Youth (16-29)	Adults (30-64)	Youth (15-29)	Adults (30-64)
Share of population that expresses confidence in the transparency of election results	29.1	29.2	36.3	39.3	62.1	63.2
Feeling of safety[ii] (%)						
Share of population that feels safe in their city or area	50.0	49.4	47.0	46.0	70.9	71.3

	Mexico		LAC		OECD
Skills[iii] (%)	Youth (25-29)	Adults (30-64)	Youth (25-29)	Adults (30-64)	Adults (25-64)
Population with complete secondary education	45.8	31.9	55.4	38.6	76.0
Population with complete tertiary education[a]	18.5	14.0	14.6	13.4	34.0

	Mexico (2012)	LAC (18)	OECD (33)
Students in secondary education enrolled in vocational programme[b]	16.6	14.5	26.1

	Mexico (2012)	LAC	OECD (2014)
Public spending in training programmes (% of GDP)[c]	0.04	0.12	0.15

Entrepreneurship[iv] (%)	Mexico	LAC	OECD
Necessity as entrepreneurial motivation (share of 18-29 in total early-stage entrepreneurial activity)	17.3	26.2	16.0

Barriers to entrepreneurship index[v]	Mexico	LAC	OECD
Complexity of regulatory procedures	0.5	1.2	0.6
Administrative burdens on start-ups	0.8	0.9	0.6
Regulatory protection of incumbents	0.9	0.6	0.4
Total	2.2	2.7	1.7

Table notes: i) Latin America weighted average of LAC-17 countries: Argentina, Bolivia, Brazil, Chile, Colombia, Costa Rica, Dominican Republic, Ecuador, El Salvador, Guatemala, Honduras, Mexico, Nicaragua, Panama, Peru, Paraguay, Uruguay. OECD weighted average for 34 OECD member countries; ii) Latin America unweighted average of LAC-16 countries Argentina, Brazil, Chile, Colombia, Costa Rica, Dominican Republic, Ecuador, El Salvador, Guatemala, Honduras, Mexico, Nicaragua, Panama, Paraguay, Peru, Uruguay, OECD simple average of OECD 35 member countries; iii) Latin America unweighted average of LAC-17 countries: Argentina, Bolivia, Brazil, Chile, Colombia, Costa Rica, Dominican Republic, Ecuador, El Salvador, Guatemala, Honduras, Mexico, Nicaragua, Panama, Peru, Paraguay, Uruguay. OECD unweighted average for 34 OECD member countries; iv) Share of population that see start-up as a necessity (no other options for work) rather than an opportunity. Latin America (10) non-weighted average of Argentina, Brazil, Chile, Colombia, Ecuador, Guatemala, Panama, Mexico, Peru, and Uruguay. OECD (27) non-weighted average of Australia, Belgium, Chile, Estonia, Finland, Germany, Greece, Hungary, Ireland, Israel, Italy, Latvia, Luxembourg, Mexico, Netherlands, Norway, Poland, Portugal, Slovakia, Slovenia, South Korea, Spain, Sweden, Switzerland, United Kingdom and United States; v) The Entrepreneurship Barriers Index is composed of three sub-indices: 1) Complexity of regulatory procedures: measures the licences and permits system, such as the communication and simplification of rules and procedures. 2) Administrative burdens on start-ups: measures the burdens that are face by corporations and sole proprietor firms, and the barriers in services sectors. 3) Regulatory protection of incumbents: measures legal barriers to entry, anti-trust exemptions and barriers in network sectors. The three indicators are based on the 2013 Product Market Regulation questionnaire available at: http://www.oecd.org/eco/reform/PMR-Questionnaire-2013.pdf. The indicator reflects the state of legislation in 2014 for Kenya, Philippines, Rwanda and Uruguay; in 2015 for Bolivia, Ecuador, Guatemala, Panama, Paraguay and Venezuela; in 2013 for all others. Scale 0 to 6 from least to most restrictive. See methodological note for further details.

Table sources: i) SEDLAC (CEDLAS and the World Bank) for Latin American countries and OECD-LFS data for the OECD (2014); ii) OECD calculations based on Gallup Organization (2014), *Gallup World Monitor* (database); iii) (a) SEDLAC (CEDLAS and the World Bank) for Latin American countries (2014) and; OECD (2014), *Education at a Glance 2014: OECD Indicators*; (b) UNESCO (2016) and DiNIECE. Ministerio de Educación (2013) for Latin American countries and OECD (2014), *Education at a Glance 2014: OECD Indicators* for the OECD; (c) World Bank LAC Social Protection Database (2015) and OECD/EC Labour Market Programme Database; iv) Global Entrepreneurship Monitor individual data (2015); v) OECD-WBG product market regulation database for all countries except Brazil, Chile, India, Mexico and South Africa, OECD product market regulation database (2014).

Panama

Recent trends

Panama's economic growth over the past decade was inclusive and led to a significant reduction in poverty and the expansion of shared prosperity. Panama has made significant progress in reducing poverty in recent years (poverty and extreme poverty decreased by more than 10 percentage points over the decade 2004-14) and as a percentage of the total population (29% in 2014). Panama has now one of the largest middle-class populations in the region. This positive period of strong growth also was reflected in the labour market.

According to the Socio-Economic Database for Latin America and the Caribbean (SEDLAC), unemployment has decreased by more half since 2004, reaching 2.5% in 2014, below the Latin America and Caribbean (LAC) average (3.3%) and well below the OECD average (5.8%).

Activity status of youth by single year in Panama, 2014

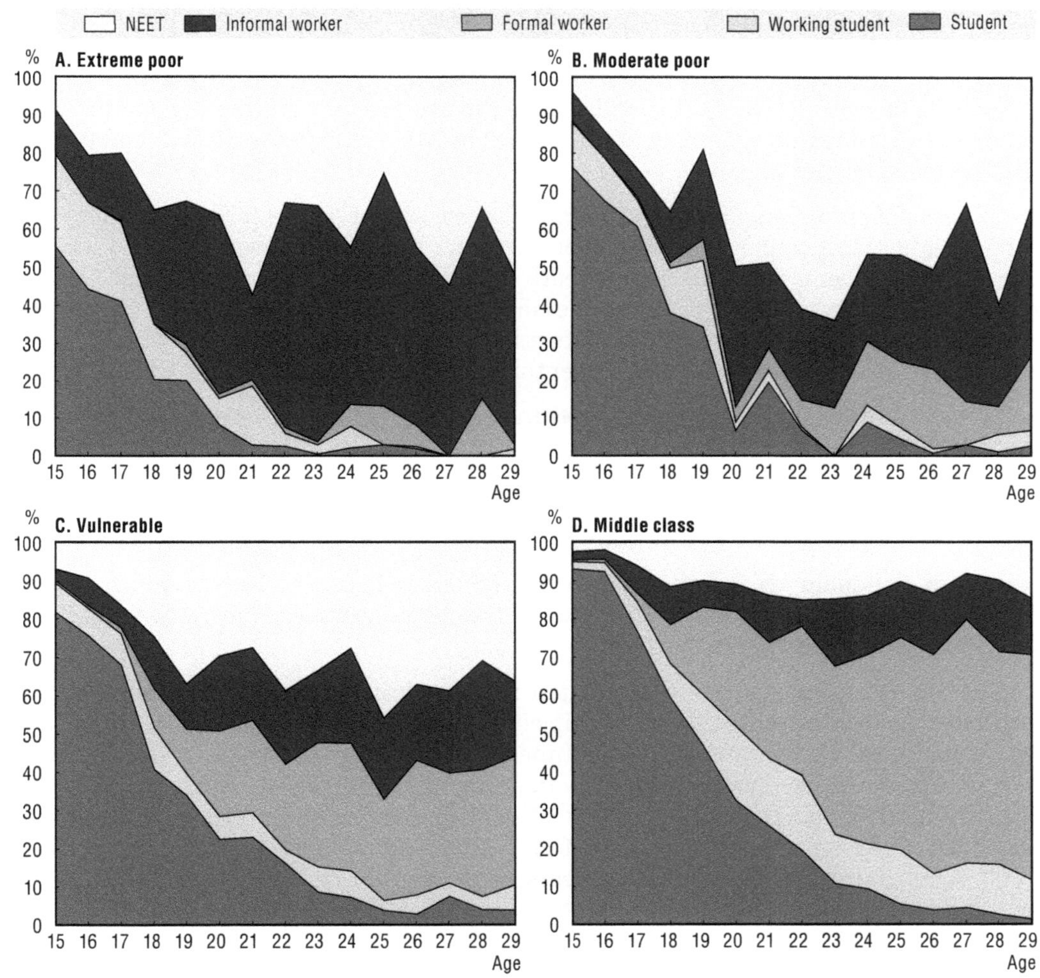

Source: OECD and World Bank tabulations of SEDLAC (CEDLAS and the World Bank).

StatLink http://dx.doi.org/10.1787/888933415509

Despite considerable progress, gaps in youth inclusion in the labour market and society persist throughout the region and also in Panama. Youth benefited from the positive labour market climate, but at 9.4%, their unemployment rate remains more than three times the total unemployment rate in Panama – still below the LAC and OECD average (10% and 12%, respectively).

In Panama, around 31% of young people are studying and more than 49% are working or working students. Young people who are neither employed nor in education nor training ("NEETs") risk being left permanently behind in the labour market. In Panama, in line with the regional average, around 20% of young people aged 15-29 are NEET compared with 15% in the OECD as a whole. Risk is especially high for the relatively large share of poor and vulnerable NEETs, who have much higher NEET rates (32%, 33% and 27% for extreme poor, moderate poor and vulnerable youth, respectively). In addition, consistent with other countries in the region, there is a wide gender gap (around 21 percentage points) in NEET rates between young women and men.

According to Gallup World Monitor survey, the share of the youth population that expresses confidence in the transparency of election results is lower than that of adults in Panama, but higher than the average for the region (48% vs. 36% for the LAC average). Youth safety perception in Panama is slightly higher than for adults and higher than the regional average for youth, (51% of youth in Panama vs. 47% for the LAC average).

The significant advances over the past decade have benefited secondary educational attainment over tertiary education in Panama. In 2014, 60% of young Panamanians (aged 25-29) completed secondary education compared with 55% for the LAC average, while 14% completed tertiary education, which is slightly below the LAC average (15% for the LAC average). Technical and vocational education and training (TVET) is gaining importance in the country; 14% of students in secondary education are enrolled in TVET programmes in line with the LAC average (14%), but still below the OECD average (26%). At the same time, the country offers a wide variety of training opportunities through its national training institute, *Instituto Nacional de Formación Profesional y Capacitación para el Desarrollo Humano (INADEH)*. It spends above the average for both the region and OECD member countries in training programmes (0.17% of GDP in 2014 compared with 0.12 and 0.15 for LAC and OECD, respectively).

In terms of entrepreneurship, in Panama, the majority of self-employed youth are own-account workers rather than employers: 16% of working youth report being own-account workers, while less than 1% define themselves as entrepreneurs. Additionally, data from the Global Entrepreneurship Monitor (GEM) show that in Panama, the share of young entrepreneurs (18-29 years old) where necessity is the main entrepreneurial motivation (as percentage of total early-stage entrepreneurial activity), estimated at 32% for 2015, is higher than both the regional average (26%) and the OECD (16%).

Barriers to entrepreneurship are lower in Panama than the LAC average. The most important barriers faced by young entrepreneurs are the complexity of regulatory procedures and the regulatory protection of incumbents.

Recent developments in youth policies

One of the main objectives of Panama's labour policy is to reduce youth unemployment. There are two main programmes targeted at this population: the *Pro Youth* programme and the *New Employment Opportunities* programme.

The *Pro Youth* programme was created in 2015 by the Ministry of Labour to promote the employability of youth through internships in enterprises. The beneficiaries are youth in the last year of technical and vocational programmes. Participating enterprises must develop a training plan, which is evaluated and approved by the ministry. Enterprises receive a government subsidy for hiring interns, and should hire at least 50% of the young workers once their internship contract has ended. It is expected that during its first year of operation 2015-16 the programme will cover 1 000 beneficiaries. In the following years, the programme may be expanded to include all youth who receive technical/vocational degrees annually (currently some 11 000 young people). Additionally, INADEH, the public entity in charge of technical and vocation training, is developing a comprehensive training programme designed to create the skills that the productive sector needs, in order to increase the pool of prospective candidates for this programme.[1]

The *New Employment Opportunities* programme is an initiative of the Multilateral Investment Fund (MIF). Its main objective is to offer job training and placement services to the low income population aged 16 to 29 years old from Panama City, David, Penonome and Colon.[2] The programme was created in 2012 and started its implementation phase in mid-2015. It is funded by the Government, MIF, the International Youth Foundation (IYF) and the private sector.[3] It is expected that by the end of 2016 there will be 75 companies offering internships and jobs and 10 000 youths accessing counselling and training services.[4]

Key indicators: Panama

Labour market developments[i] (%)	Panama 2004	Panama 2014	LAC 2004	LAC 2014	OECD 2004	OECD 2014
Unemployment rates - adults (30-64)	5.4	2.5	4.8	3.4	4.6	5.8
Unemployment rates - youth (15-29)	15.7	9.5	12.4	10.3	8.0	12.5
Informality rates - adults (35-64)			47.0	38.3		
Informality rates - youth (15-29)			62.3	52.3		

Youth and socio-economic status (%)	Panama Extreme poor	Panama Moderate poor	Panama Vulnerable	Panama Middle class	LAC (17) Extreme poor	LAC (17) Moderate poor	LAC (17) Vulnerable	LAC (17) Middle class
Youth (15-29)	9.8	8.2	36.5	45.5	15.1	12.4	39.4	33.1

Activity rates for youth (15-29)[i] (%)	Panama 2004	Panama 2014	LAC 2004	LAC 2014	OECD 2014
Student	29.6	30.6	23.0	25.3	13.2
Working student	8.4	9.7	11.3	11.2	35.5
Working	37.9	39.6	43.6	43.1	36.2
NEET	24.1	20.1	22.2	20.3	15.1

Activity rates for youth (15-29)[i] by socio-economic status (%)	Panama Extreme poor	Panama Moderate poor	Panama Vulnerable	Panama Middle class	LAC (17) Extreme poor	LAC (17) Moderate poor	LAC (17) Vulnerable	LAC (17) Middle class
Student	19.7	33.4	32.1	31.9	27.0	29.7	30.0	30.7
Working student	11.3	7.1	6.3	11.8	7.8	7.5	8.9	15.0
Working- formal	2.4	6.4	18.5	34.4	4.8	9.6	18.4	28.8
Working- informal	34.5	19.6	15.5	11.1	25.2	22.0	19.1	13.3
NEET	32.0	33.5	27.5	10.8	35.1	31.2	23.7	12.2

Distribution of youth employed[i] (%)	Panama	LAC	OECD
Employee	74.2	70.0	88.0
Employer	0.6	2.2	3.9
Own-account worker	15.6	16.3	5.7
Unpaid family worker	9.6	11.2	24.0

	Panama Youth (16-29)	Panama Adults (30-64)	LAC Youth (16-29)	LAC Adults (30-64)	OECD Youth (15-29)	OECD Adults (30-64)
Trust in elections[ii] (%)						
Share of population that expresses confidence in the transparency of election results	48.3	51.2	36.3	39.3	62.1	63.2
Feeling of safety[ii] (%)						
Share of population that feels safe in their city or area	51.6	50.3	47.0	46.0	70.9	71.3

Skills[iii] (%)	Panama Youth (25-29)	Panama Adults (30-64)	LAC Youth (25-29)	LAC Adults (30-64)	OECD Adults (25-64)
Population with complete secondary education	59.9	50.1	55.4	38.6	76.0
Population with complete tertiary education[a]	13.6	15.9	14.6	13.4	34.0

	Panama (2012)	LAC (18)	OECD (33)
Students in secondary education enrolled in vocational programme[b]	14.0	14.5	26.1

	Panama (2014)	LAC	OECD (2014)
Public spending in training programmes (% of GDP)[c]	0.17	0.12	0.15

Entrepreneurship[iv] (%)	Panama	LAC	OECD
Necessity as entrepreneurial motivation (share of 18-29 in total early-stage entrepreneurial activity)	31.5	26.2	16.0

Barriers to entrepreneurship index[v]	Panama	LAC	OECD
Complexity of regulatory procedures	0.8	1.2	0.6
Administrative burdens on start-ups	0.5	0.9	0.6
Regulatory protection of incumbents	0.6	0.6	0.4
Total	1.8	2.7	1.7

Table notes: i) Latin America weighted average of LAC-17 countries: Argentina, Bolivia, Brazil, Chile, Colombia, Costa Rica, Dominican Republic, Ecuador, El Salvador, Guatemala, Honduras, Mexico, Nicaragua, Panama, Peru, Paraguay, Uruguay. OECD weighted average for 34 OECD member countries; ii) Latin America unweighted average of LAC-16 countries Argentina, Brazil, Chile, Colombia, Costa Rica, Dominican Republic, Ecuador, El Salvador, Guatemala, Honduras, Mexico, Nicaragua, Panama, Paraguay, Peru, Uruguay, OECD simple average of OECD 35 member countries; iii) Latin America unweighted average of LAC-17 countries: Argentina, Bolivia, Brazil, Chile, Colombia, Costa Rica, Dominican Republic, Ecuador, El Salvador, Guatemala, Honduras, Mexico, Nicaragua, Panama, Peru, Paraguay, Uruguay. OECD unweighted average for 34 OECD member countries; iv) Share of population that see start-up as a necessity (no other options for work) rather than an opportunity. Latin America (10) non-weighted average of Argentina, Brazil, Chile, Colombia, Ecuador, Guatemala, Panama, Mexico, Peru, and Uruguay. OECD (27) non-weighted average of Australia, Belgium, Chile, Estonia, Finland, Germany, Greece, Hungary, Ireland, Israel, Italy, Latvia, Luxembourg, Mexico, Netherlands, Norway, Poland, Portugal, Slovakia, Slovenia, South Korea, Spain, Sweden, Switzerland, United Kingdom and United States; v) The Entrepreneurship Barriers Index is composed of three sub-indices: 1) Complexity of regulatory procedures: measures the licences and permits system, such as the communication and simplification of rules and procedures. 2) Administrative burdens on start-ups: measures the burdens that are face by corporations and sole proprietor firms, and the barriers in services sectors. 3) Regulatory protection of incumbents: measures legal barriers to entry, anti-trust exemptions and barriers in network sectors. The three indicators are based on the 2013 Product Market Regulation questionnaire available at: http://www.oecd.org/eco/reform/PMR-Questionnaire-2013.pdf. The indicator reflects the state of legislation in 2014 for Kenya, Philippines, Rwanda and Uruguay; in 2015 for Bolivia, Ecuador, Guatemala, Panama, Paraguay and Venezuela; in 2013 for all others. Scale 0 to 6 from least to most restrictive. See methodological note for further details.
Table sources: i) SEDLAC (CEDLAS and the World Bank) for Latin American countries and OECD-LFS data for the OECD (2014); ii) OECD calculations based on Gallup Organization (2014), *Gallup World Monitor* (database); iii) (a) SEDLAC (CEDLAS and the World Bank) for Latin American countries (2014) and; OECD (2014), *Education at a Glance 2014: OECD Indicators*; (b) UNESCO (2016) and DiNIECE. Ministerio de Educación (2013) for Latin American countries and OECD (2014), *Education at a Glance 2014: OECD Indicators* for the OECD; (c) World Bank LAC Social Protection Database (2015) and OECD/EC Labour Market Programme Database; iv) Global Entrepreneurship Monitor individual data (2015); v) OECD-WBG product market regulation database for all countries except Brazil, Chile, India, Mexico and South Africa, OECD product market regulation database (2014).

Notes

1. https://www.thebusinessyear.com/panama-2015/the-necessary-talent/vip-interview.
2. http://www.iadb.org/en/news/news-releases/2015-04-09/job-training-program-benefits-1-million-youths,11125.html.
3. Mainly Arcos Dorados, Caterpillar, CEMEX, Microsoft, and Walmart.
4. http://idbdocs.iadb.org/wsdocs/getdocument.aspx?docnum=40249929.

Paraguay

Recent trends

Paraguay labour market outcomes have improved significantly in the last decade. According to the Socio-Economic Database for Latin America and the Caribbean (SEDLAC), unemployment has also dropped considerably in recent years, and, at slightly more than 3% in 2014, the unemployment rate for adults is in line with the Latin American and Caribbean (LAC) average and well below the OECD average. Informality – defined as all employed persons not paying social contributions – among adults has been declining since 2004, although it remains much higher (at 53% in 2014) than the LAC average (38%).

Activity status of youth by single year of age in Paraguay, 2014

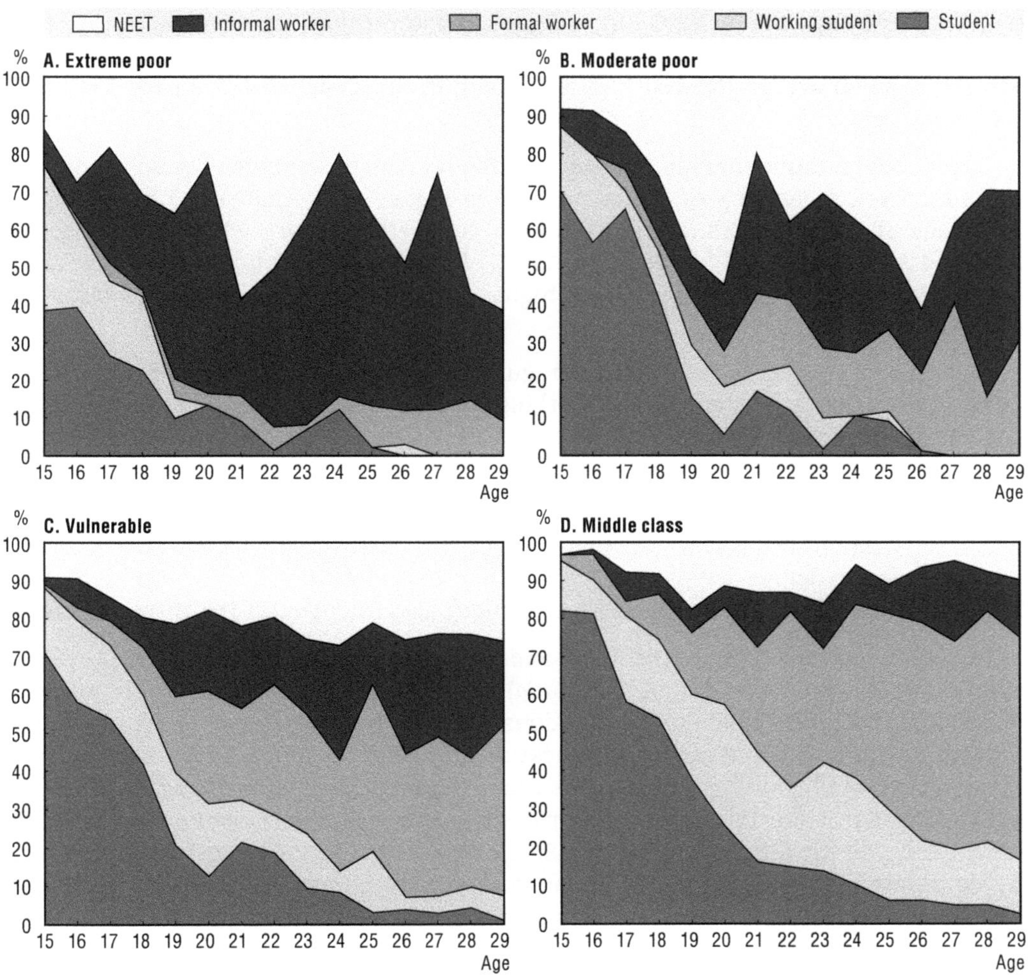

Source: OECD and World Bank tabulations of SEDLAC (CEDLAS and the World Bank).
StatLink http://dx.doi.org/10.1787/888933415499

Youth has benefited from the positive labour market climate, but at almost 11%, their unemployment rate remains more than three times the total unemployment rate in Paraguay (although in line with the LAC average of 10%). In Paraguay, in 2014, around one-quarter of young people are studying and more than 56% are working or working students. Paraguay continues to be among the LAC countries with the lowest rates of youth neither in employment nor in education nor training (NEETs). In Paraguay, around 17% of young people aged 15-29 are NEETs compared with 20% in the LAC and with 15% in the OECD as a whole.

Young people who are NEETs risk being left permanently behind in the labour market. This risk is especially high for the relatively large share of poor and vulnerable NEETs, who have much higher NEET rates (almost 80% of all young NEETs). NEET rates in Paraguay jump to 33% among the extreme poor and 29% among the moderate poor. Consistent with other countries in the region, there is a wide gender gap (around 17 percentage points) in NEET rates between young women and men.

Paraguay is also one of the countries in the LAC region with the highest incidence of youth engaged in informal jobs. Almost 72% of working youth hold an informal job, around 20 percentage points higher than the LAC average of 52%. In addition, this percentage jumps to 99% and 94% for youth belonging to extremely poor and moderately poor households, respectively (vs. 82% and 61% of youth in vulnerable and middle-class households).

The share of the youth population that expresses confidence in the transparency of election results is lower than that of adults in Paraguay and lower than the average for the region (27% vs. 36% for the LAC). Youth safety perception in Paraguay is slightly higher than that of adults, but lower than the regional average for youth (41% of youth in Paraguay vs. 47% for the LAC) (Gallup World Monitor Survey).

Educational attainment is improving in Paraguay: the percentage of young people (aged 25-29) with completed secondary education in 2014 is higher (59%) than the LAC average (55%). The percentage of young people (aged 25-29) with completed tertiary education is also higher (17%) than the LAC average (15%). In addition, 15.6% of students in secondary education are enrolled in vocational training programmes; this is higher than the LAC average (14.5%), but still below the OECD average (26%).

In terms of entrepreneurship, in Paraguay, the majority of self-employed are own-account workers rather than employers: 15% of working youth report being own-account workers, while only 2% define themselves as entrepreneurs.

Barriers to entrepreneurship are slightly lower in Paraguay than the LAC average. The most important barriers faced by young entrepreneurs seem to be the complexity of regulatory procedures and administrative burdens on start-ups.

Recent developments in Paraguay's technical and vocational training policies

Paraguay has four types of technical and vocational training: 1) the Agricultural Professional Initiation (*Iniciación Profesional Agropecuaria*) that addresses the third-cycle student in basic education; 2) technical schools and vocational training programmes that address students of the medium education level; 3) technical education offered at the tertiary education level; and 4) non-formal (vocational) training programmes that are part of lifelong learning. The last is part of the National System of Professional Promotion (*Sistema Nacional de Promoción Profesional: SNPP*) under the responsibility of the Ministry of Labour, Employment and Social Security and aims at promoting and developing the training and skills of workers. The courses offered encompass the areas of agriculture, industry and services. Furthermore, the National System for Skill Formation and Vocational Training (*Sistema Nacional de Formación y Capacitación Laboral: SINAFOCAL*) also provides various kinds of training and skill learning opportunities. Other training programmes of public-private partnerships are New Employment Opportunities for Young People (*Nuevas Oportunidades de Empleo para Jóvenes: NEO*) and SAPE'A Skills, Employment and Youth Entrepreneurship, which provides young people with vocational training and skill learning opportunities, as well as internships and facilities for entrepreneurial development.

In 2013, a law to facilitate the insertion of young people into the labour market was passed, and was fully implemented in 2015. Through establishing legal incentives for employers to hire young people, such as by subsidising workers between the ages of 18 and 29, firms face lower costs for hiring young workers. The law is especially helpful for youth as they need to acquire work experience before joining a company. The law also establishes the legal terms for job training, grants to workers, apprenticeship contracts and first job contracts (SNNP 2015).

Recent developments in Paraguay's youth entrepreneurship policies

The *Política de Empleo Juvenil* [Youth Employment Policy] of Paraguay aims to develop and implement initiatives that allow youths to have a decent job trajectory. It also seeks to develop programmes that encourage entrepreneurial culture in the country and create more and better jobs through entrepreneurship.

Since 2013, the National Secretary of Youth of Paraguay, together with other organisations such as the Peace Corps and the Association of Young Businessmen, have the "*Paraguay Emprende*" [Paraguay Entrepreneurs] programme, which aims to give youths tools to help them start their own businesses. As a first step, it holds regional and national workshops, mentoring and consulting to entrepreneurs aged 18-30 years. It then holds a contest where selected ventures compete for the funding assigned to the winners.

Along with this programme, the Science, Technology and Innovation Policy guidelines aim at developing the entrepreneurial culture in Paraguay, focusing on social innovation and entrepreneurship, as well as technological ventures and public-private partnerships.

Reference

SNPP (Servicio Nacional de Promoción Profesional) (2015), *Gobierno reglamenta ley para inserter jóvenes al mercado laboral*, Ministerio de Trabajo, Empleo y Seguridad Social, http://www.snpp.edu.py/noticias-snpp/569-gobierno-reglamenta-ley-para-insertar-j%C3%B3venes-al-mercado-laboral.html (accessed 24 August 2016).

Key indicators: Paraguay

Labour market developments[i] (%)	Paraguay 2004	Paraguay 2014	LAC 2004	LAC 2014	OECD 2004	OECD 2014
Unemployment rates - adults (30-64)	4.6	3.4	4.8	3.4	4.6	5.8
Unemployment rates - youth (15-29)	11.7	10.6	12.4	10.3	8.0	12.5
Informality rates - adults (35-64)	67.8	52.6	47.0	38.3		
Informality rates - youth (15-29)	84.7	72.2	62.3	52.3		

Youth and socio-economic status (%)	Paraguay Extreme poor	Paraguay Moderate poor	Paraguay Vulnerable	Paraguay Middle class	LAC (17) Extreme poor	LAC (17) Moderate poor	LAC (17) Vulnerable	LAC (17) Middle class
Youth (15-29)	8.0	9.3	41.8	41.0	15.1	12.4	39.4	33.1

Activity rates for youth (15-29)[i] (%)	Paraguay 2004	Paraguay 2014	LAC 2004	LAC 2014	OECD 2014
Student	19.5	25.5	23.0	25.3	13.2
Working student	14.0	16.8	11.3	11.2	35.5
Working	45.4	40.5	43.6	43.1	36.2
NEET	21.1	17.2	22.2	20.3	15.1

Activity rates for youth (15-29)[i] by socio-economic status (%)	Paraguay Extreme poor	Paraguay Moderate poor	Paraguay Vulnerable	Paraguay Middle class	LAC (17) Extreme poor	LAC (17) Moderate poor	LAC (17) Vulnerable	LAC (17) Middle class
Student	17.6	30.9	26.5	25.4	27.0	29.7	30.0	30.7
Working student	12.4	10.1	13.8	21.2	7.8	7.5	8.9	15.0
Working- formal	4.6	11.3	23.1	34.3	4.8	9.6	18.4	28.8
Working- informal	33.2	19.8	16.9	9.3	25.2	22.0	19.1	13.3
NEET	32.2	27.9	19.7	9.9	35.1	31.2	23.7	12.2

Distribution of youth employed[i] (%)	Paraguay	LAC	OECD
Employee	72.2	70.0	88.0
Employer	2.1	2.2	3.9
Own-account worker	14.9	16.3	5.7
Unpaid family worker	10.8	11.2	24.0

	Paraguay Youth (16-29)	Paraguay Adults (30-64)	LAC Youth (16-29)	LAC Adults (30-64)	OECD Youth (15-29)	OECD Adults (30-64)
Trust in elections[ii] (%)						
Share of population that expresses confidence in the transparency of election results	27.4	29.4	36.3	39.3	62.1	63.2
Feeling of safety[ii] (%)						
Share of population that feels safe in their city or area	40.7	39.7	47.0	46.0	70.9	71.3

Skills[iii] (%)	Paraguay Youth (25-29)	Paraguay Adults (30-64)	LAC Youth (25-29)	LAC Adults (30-64)	OECD Adults (25-64)
Population with complete secondary education	60.0	36.6	55.4	38.6	76.0
Population with complete tertiary education[a]	17.3	12.5	14.6	13.4	34.0

	Paraguay (2012)	LAC (18)	OECD (33)
Students in secondary education enrolled in vocational programme[b]	15.6	14.5	26.1

Barriers to entrepreneurship index[iv]	Paraguay	LAC	OECD
Complexity of regulatory procedures	0.7	1.2	0.6
Administrative burdens on start-ups	1.0	0.9	0.6
Regulatory protection of incumbents	0.5	0.6	0.4
Total	2.2	2.7	1.7

Table notes: i) Latin America weighted average of LAC-17 countries: Argentina, Bolivia, Brazil, Chile, Colombia, Costa Rica, Dominican Republic, Ecuador, El Salvador, Guatemala, Honduras, Mexico, Nicaragua, Panama, Peru, Paraguay, Uruguay. OECD weighted average for 34 OECD member countries; ii) Latin America unweighted average of LAC-16 countries Argentina, Brazil, Chile, Colombia, Costa Rica, Dominican Republic, Ecuador, El Salvador, Guatemala, Honduras, Mexico, Nicaragua, Panama, Paraguay, Peru, Uruguay, OECD simple average of OECD 35 member countries; iii) Latin America unweighted average of LAC-17 countries: Argentina, Bolivia, Brazil, Chile, Colombia, Costa Rica, Dominican Republic, Ecuador, El Salvador, Guatemala, Honduras, Mexico, Nicaragua, Panama, Peru, Paraguay, Uruguay. OECD unweighted average for 34 OECD member countries; iv) The Entrepreneurship Barriers Index is composed of three sub-indices: 1) Complexity of regulatory procedures: measures the licences and permits system, such as the communication and simplification of rules and procedures. 2) Administrative burdens on start-ups: measures the burdens that are face by corporations and sole proprietor firms, and the barriers in services sectors. 3) Regulatory protection of incumbents: measures legal barriers to entry, anti-trust exemptions and barriers in network sectors. The three indicators are based on the 2013 Product Market Regulation questionnaire available at: http://www.oecd.org/eco/reform/PMR-Questionnaire-2013.pdf. The indicator reflects the state of legislation in 2014 for Kenya, Philippines, Rwanda and Uruguay; in 2015 for Bolivia, Ecuador, Guatemala, Panama, Paraguay and Venezuela; in 2013 for all others. Scale 0 to 6 from least to most restrictive. See methodological note for further details.
Table sources: i) SEDLAC (CEDLAS and the World Bank) for Latin American countries and OECD-LFS data for the OECD (2014); ii) OECD calculations based on Gallup Organization (2014), *Gallup World Monitor* (database); iii) (a) SEDLAC (CEDLAS and the World Bank) for Latin American countries (2014) and; OECD (2014), *Education at a Glance 2014: OECD Indicators*; (b) UNESCO (2016) and DiNIECE. Ministerio de Educación (2013) for Latin American countries and OECD (2014), *Education at a Glance 2014: OECD Indicators* for the OECD; iv) OECD-WBG product market regulation database for all countries except Brazil, Chile, India, Mexico and South Africa, OECD product market regulation database (2014).

Peru

Recent trends

Apart from a short slowdown in 2014, Peru has experienced strong and sustained economic growth over the past 15 years, and labour market outcomes improved significantly. Unemployment has also dropped considerably in recent years, reaching 1.5% in 2014 according to Socio-Economic Database for Latin America and the Caribbean (SEDLAC) data; the unemployment rate for adults is among the lowest among the Latin American and Caribbean (LAC) countries (LAC average 3.3%) and keeps well below the OECD average. Informality, defined as all employed persons not paying social contributions, has also been declining since 2004. Despite these favourable developments, the incidence of informal work remains high in Peru at 43% in 2014, still slightly above the LAC average (38%).

Youth benefited from the positive labour market climate, but at 6% their unemployment rate remains more than three times higher than the adult unemployment rate in Peru, although still below the LAC and OECD average (10% and 12%, respectively).

Activity status of youth by single year of age in Peru, 2014

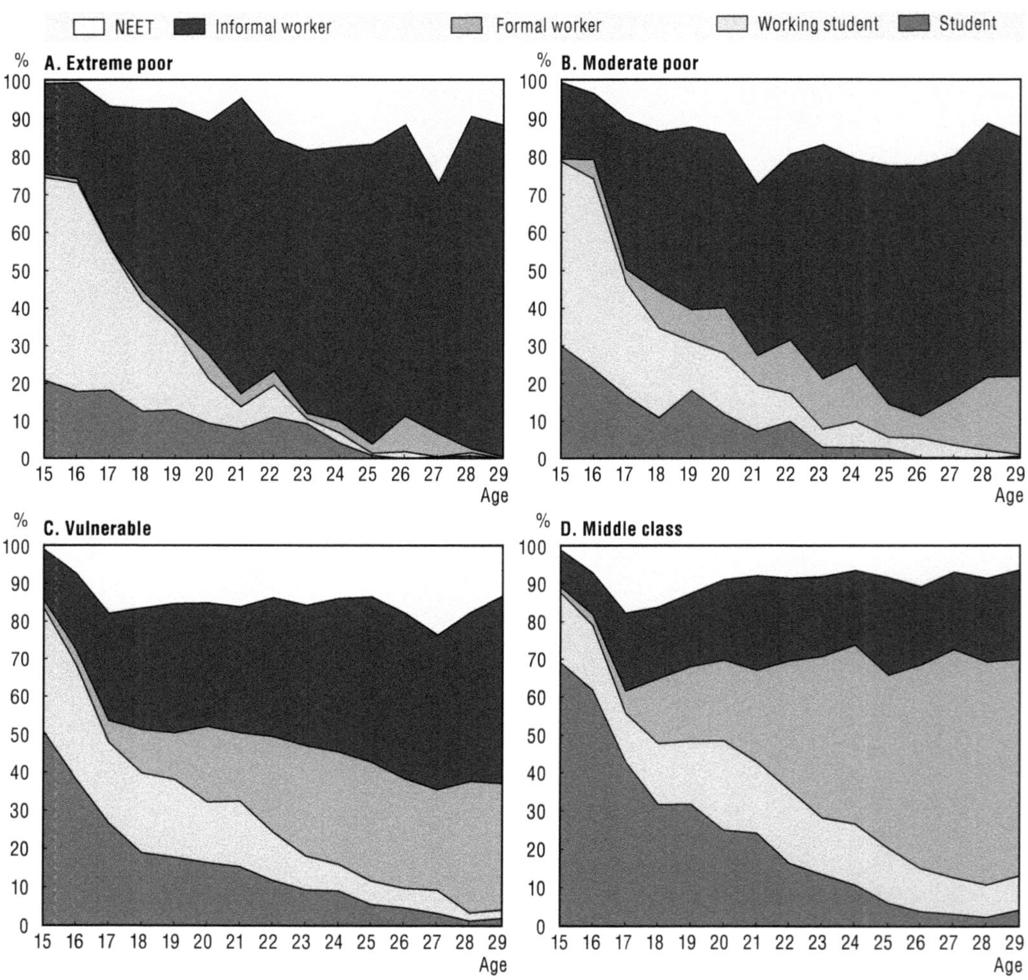

Source: OECD and World Bank tabulations of SEDLAC (CEDLAS and the World Bank).
StatLink http://dx.doi.org/10.1787/888933415519

In Peru, around 19% of young people are studying and more than 67% are working or working students. Peru continues to be among the LAC countries with the lowest rates of youth neither in employment nor in education nor training (NEETs). In Peru, around 12% of young people aged 15-29 are NEETs compared with 20% in the LAC and with 15% in the OECD as a whole. Young people who are NEETs risk being left permanently behind in the labour market. This risk is especially high for the relatively large share of poor and vulnerable NEETs (almost 70% of all young NEETs). The gender gap between young women and men NEETs is lowest in Peru (8%) than in other LAC countries.

Despite some progress over the last decade, informal young workers account for more than 65% of all young workers in Peru, well above the LAC average of 52%. This percentage jumps to 99% and 93% for youth belonging to extremely poor and moderately poor households, respectively (vs. 77% and 51% of youth in vulnerable and middle-class households).

According to Gallup World Monitor survey, the share of the youth population that expresses confidence in the transparency of election results is lower than that of adults in Peru (29%) and the average for the region (36%). Likewise, youth safety perception in Peru (42%) is lower than that of adults and the regional average for youth (47%).

Peru's significant improvement in education has made the country one of the best performers of the region. In 2014, education attainment in Peru was higher than average for the region, with 76% of youth (aged 25-29) having completed secondary education (vs. 55% for the LAC average) and 28% having completed tertiary education (vs. 15% for the LAC average). Peru has a vibrant technical and vocational education and training (TVET) sector with many providers and programmes (OECD, 2016). Still, very few students in secondary education are enrolled in TVET programmes (1.4% vs. 14% in LAC and 26% in the OECD). Moreover, the country has a low public expenditure in training programmes (0.01% of gross domestic product in 2014, compared with 0.12 and 0.15 for the LAC and OECD average, respectively).

In terms of entrepreneurship, in Peru, the majority of self-employed are own-account workers rather than employers: 16% of working youth report being own-account workers, while only 1% define themselves as entrepreneurs.

Barriers to entrepreneurship are lower in Peru than the LAC average. The most important barriers faced by young entrepreneurs seem to be the complexity of regulatory procedures and administrative burdens on start-ups.

Youth skills development and entrepreneurship programmes and policy

A handful of programmes are oriented towards the development of skills and job market insertion at the national level, including *Trabaja Peru* [Work Peru], where 30% of beneficiaries are between 18 and 29 years of age; there are also platforms to help Peruvians, especially the young, find jobs. A couple of examples are *Proyecta tu Futuro* [Project your future] and the multiple job centres across the country; there is indeed an effort at the national level to stimulate the insertion of unemployed and economically inactive Peruvians into the formal job sector. Nevertheless, the main programme in Peru aimed at the development of skills and vocational training is *Jovenes Productivos* [Productive Youth]. It is accompanied by a set of policies, mainly contractual forms to help stimulate the hiring of young Peruvians. The programme is mainly focused on disadvantaged young people, most of whom haven't been able to finish high school and are vulnerable to poverty, marginalisation or criminality; it has already benefited around 90 000 people with a job market insertion rate of 40% and has a growing range of influence across the country, mainly in the urban areas.

The main focus of *Jovenes Productivos* is developing technical skills needed by the productive sector. It is starting to focus more and more on developing a wider range of soft skills to help beneficiaries access a wider range of job opportunities. The system offers diverse courses in different locations, designed with collaboration of the private sector and open for application for anyone interested; it aims to offer a relatively wide range of options so that more people are motivated to join. The courses offered, which last around three months, are expected to have a strong impact on the job prospects of beneficiaries. In the following years, the Ministry of Labour is seeking to expand its capacity and range of programmes, and incorporate more components of cognitive and soft skills.

In terms of entrepreneurship, there is a lack of national programmes, but some initiatives exist at the regional level, notably in Ayacucho and San Martin. There are also incentives to hire young people and provide guidance in private firms through paid internships.

Reference

OECD (2016c), *A Skills Beyond School Review of Peru, OECD Reviews of Vocational Education and Training*, OECD Publishing, Paris, http://dx.doi.org/10.1787/9789264265400-en.

Key indicators: Peru

	Peru		LAC		OECD	
Labour market developments[i] (%)	**2004**	**2014**	**2004**	**2014**	**2004**	**2014**
Unemployment rates - adults (30-64)	3.1	1.4	4.8	3.4	4.6	5.8
Unemployment rates - youth (15-29)	7.9	6.3	12.4	10.3	8.0	12.5
Informality rates - adults (35-64)	77.4	43.0	47.0	38.3		
Informality rates - youth (15-29)	92.4	65.2	62.3	52.3		

	Peru				LAC (17)			
Youth and socio-economic status (%)	**Extreme poor**	**Moderate poor**	**Vulnerable**	**Middle class**	**Extreme poor**	**Moderate poor**	**Vulnerable**	**Middle class**
Youth (15-29)	7.3	9.7	42.6	40.4	15.1	12.4	39.4	33.1

	Peru		LAC		OECD
Activity rates for youth (15-29)[i] (%)	**2004**	**2014**	**2004**	**2014**	**2014**
Student	15.4	18.6	23.0	25.3	13.2
Working student	13.6	16.9	11.3	11.2	35.5
Working	57.3	52.7	43.6	43.1	36.2
NEET	13.8	11.8	22.2	20.3	15.1

	Peru				LAC (17)			
Activity rates for youth (15-29)[i] by socio-economic status (%)	**Extreme poor**	**Moderate poor**	**Vulnerable**	**Middle class**	**Extreme poor**	**Moderate poor**	**Vulnerable**	**Middle class**
Student	11.5	12.5	18.1	21.8	27.0	29.7	30.0	30.7
Working student	25.3	20.8	16.0	15.2	7.8	7.5	8.9	15.0
Working- formal	2.3	9.0	18.2	33.1	4.8	9.6	18.4	28.8
Working- informal	52.0	44.2	33.3	20.4	25.2	22.0	19.1	13.3
NEET	8.7	13.4	14.4	9.5	35.1	31.2	23.7	12.2

Distribution of youth employed[i] (%)	**Peru**	**LAC**	**OECD**
Employee	57.0	70.0	88.0
Employer	1.2	2.2	3.9
Own-account worker	15.8	16.3	5.7
Unpaid family worker	26.0	11.2	24.0

	Peru		LAC		OECD	
Trust in elections[ii] (%)	**Youth (16-29)**	**Adults (30-64)**	**Youth (16-29)**	**Adults (30-64)**	**Youth (15-29)**	**Adults (30-64)**
Share of population that expresses confidence in the transparency of election results	28.9	30.2	36.3	39.3	62.1	63.2
Feeling of safety[ii] (%)						
Share of population that feels safe in their city or area	42.0	45.2	47.0	46.0	70.9	71.3

	Peru		LAC		OECD
Skills[iii] (%)	**Youth (25-29)**	**Adults (30-64)**	**Youth (25-29)**	**Adults (30-64)**	**Adults (25-64)**
Population with complete secondary education	76.1	54.9	55.4	38.6	76.0
Population with complete tertiary education[a]	27.9	21.1	14.6	13.4	34.0

	Peru (2014)	**LAC (18)**	**OECD (33)**
Students in secondary education enrolled in vocational programme[b]	1.4	14.5	26.1

	Peru (2013)	**LAC**	**OECD (2014)**
Public spending in training programmes (% of GDP)[c]	0.01	0.12	0.15

Entrepreneurship[iv] (%)	**Peru**	**LAC**	**OECD**
Necessity as entrepreneurial motivation (share of 18-29 in total early-stage entrepreneurial activity)	23.1	26.2	16.0

Barriers to entrepreneurship index[v]	**Peru**	**LAC**	**OECD**
Complexity of regulatory procedures	0.9	1.2	0.6
Administrative burdens on start-ups	0.8	0.9	0.6
Regulatory protection of incumbents	0.4	0.6	0.4
Total	2.1	2.7	1.7

Table notes: i) Latin America weighted average of LAC-17 countries: Argentina, Bolivia, Brazil, Chile, Colombia, Costa Rica, Dominican Republic, Ecuador, El Salvador, Guatemala, Honduras, Mexico, Nicaragua, Panama, Peru, Paraguay, Uruguay. OECD weighted average for 34 OECD member countries; ii) Latin America unweighted average of LAC-16 countries Argentina, Brazil, Chile, Colombia, Costa Rica, Dominican Republic, Ecuador, El Salvador, Guatemala, Honduras, Mexico, Nicaragua, Panama, Paraguay, Peru, Uruguay, OECD simple average of OECD 35 member countries; iii) Latin America unweighted average of LAC-17 countries: Argentina, Bolivia, Brazil, Chile, Colombia, Costa Rica, Dominican Republic, Ecuador, El Salvador, Guatemala, Honduras, Mexico, Nicaragua, Panama, Peru, Paraguay, Uruguay. OECD unweighted average for 34 OECD member countries; iv) Share of population that see start-up as a necessity (no other options for work) rather than an opportunity. Latin America (10) non-weighted average of Argentina, Brazil, Chile, Colombia, Ecuador, Guatemala, Panama, Mexico, Peru, and Uruguay. OECD (27) non-weighted average of Australia, Belgium, Chile, Estonia, Finland, Germany, Greece, Hungary, Ireland, Israel, Italy, Latvia, Luxembourg, Mexico, Netherlands, Norway, Poland, Portugal, Slovakia, Slovenia, South Korea, Spain, Sweden, Switzerland, United Kingdom and United States; v) The Entrepreneurship Barriers Index is composed of three sub-indices: 1) Complexity of regulatory procedures: measures the licences and permits system, such as the communication and simplification of rules and procedures. 2) Administrative burdens on start-ups: measures the burdens that are face by corporations and sole proprietor firms, and the barriers in services sectors. 3) Regulatory protection of incumbents: measures legal barriers to entry, anti-trust exemptions and barriers in network sectors. The three indicators are based on the 2013 Product Market Regulation questionnaire available at: http://www.oecd.org/eco/reform/PMR-Questionnaire-2013.pdf. The indicator reflects the state of legislation in 2014 for Kenya, Philippines, Rwanda and Uruguay; in 2015 for Bolivia, Ecuador, Guatemala, Panama, Paraguay and Venezuela; in 2013 for all others. Scale 0 to 6 from least to most restrictive. See methodological note for further details.

Table sources: i) SEDLAC (CEDLAS and the World Bank) for Latin American countries and OECD-LFS data for the OECD (2014); ii) OECD calculations based on Gallup Organization (2014), *Gallup World Monitor* (database); iii) (a) SEDLAC (CEDLAS and the World Bank) for Latin American countries (2014); and OECD (2014), *Education at a Glance 2014: OECD Indicators*; (b) UNESCO (2016) and DiNIECE. Ministerio de Educación (2013) for Latin American countries and OECD (2014), *Education at a Glance 2014: OECD Indicators* for the OECD; (c) World Bank LAC Social Protection Database (2015) and OECD/EC Labour Market Programme Database; iv) Global Entrepreneurship Monitor individual data (2015); v) OECD-WBG product market regulation database for all countries except Brazil, Chile, India, Mexico and South Africa, OECD product market regulation database (2014).

Uruguay

Recent trends

Uruguay's economic growth over the past decade was inclusive and led to a significant reduction in poverty and the expansion of shared prosperity. As a percentage of the total population (68% in 2014), Uruguay has now the largest middle class in the region. This positive period of strong growth was also reflected in the labour market. Unemployment almost halved since 2004, according to Socio-Economic Database for Latin America and the Caribbean (SEDLAC) data, reaching 3.7% in 2014, in line with the Latin America and Caribbean (LAC) average and well below the OECD average. The already low level of informality – defined as all employed persons not paying social contributions – dropped to 9% among adults in 2014, the lowest level in the region and far away from the LAC average (38%).

Youth also benefited from the positive labour market climate. At around 14%, however, their unemployment rate remains more than four times the total unemployment rate in Uruguay, and higher than both the LAC average (10%) and OECD average (12%). In Uruguay, around 41% of young people are studying or working students and more than 41% are working. Uruguay continues to be among the LAC countries with the lowest rates of youth neither in employment nor in education nor training (NEETs): around 17% of young people aged 15-29 are NEETs compared with 20% in the LAC region and 15% in the OECD as a whole.

Activity status of youth by single year of age in Uruguay, 2014

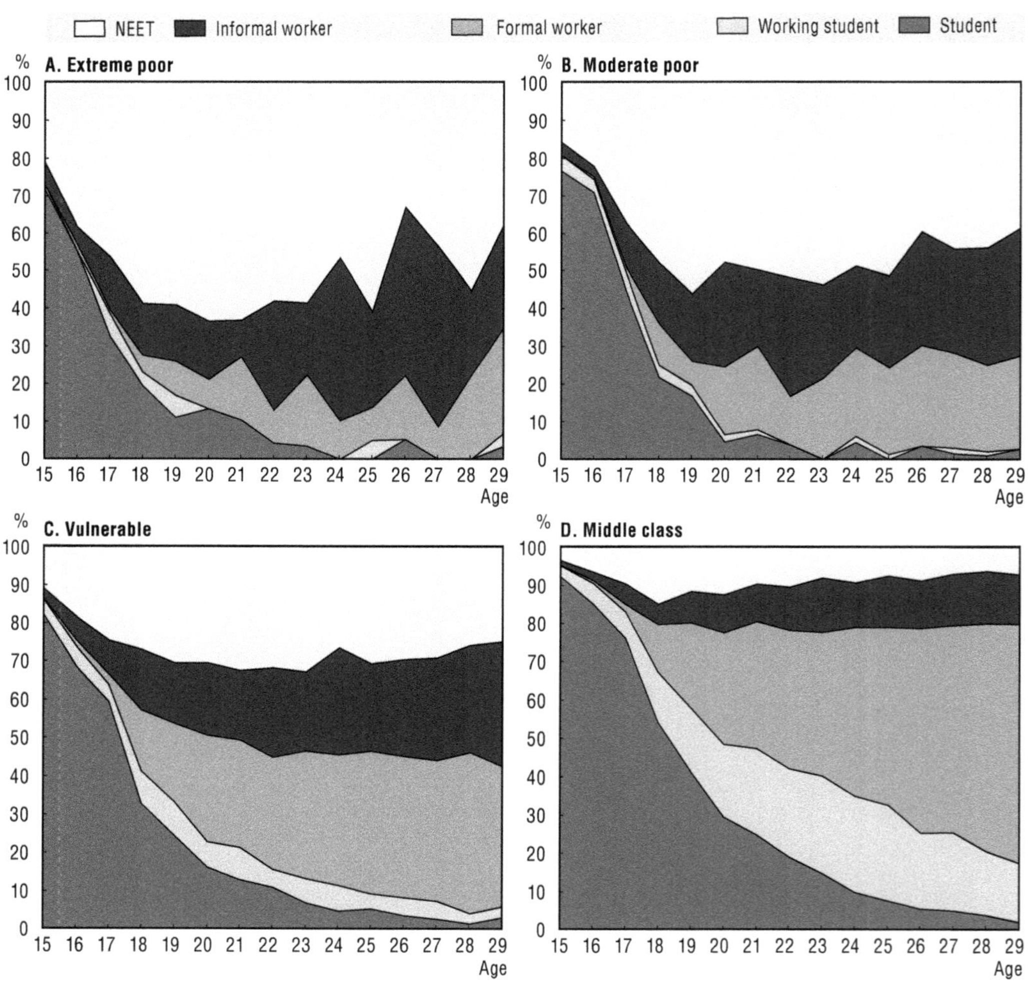

Source: OECD and World Bank tabulations of SEDLAC (CEDLAS and the World Bank).

StatLink http://dx.doi.org/10.1787/888933415488

Young people who are NEETs risk being left permanently behind in the labour market. This risk is especially high for the relatively large share of poor and vulnerable NEETs, who have much higher NEET rates. The poor (extreme and moderate) and vulnerable account for almost 70% of all young NEETS. NEET rates in Uruguay jump to 47% among the extreme poor and to 40% among the moderate poor. This is consistent with other countries in the region (but lower in magnitude). There is a wide gender gap (around 10 percentage points) in NEET rates between young women and men.

Uruguay is also one of the countries in the LAC region with the lowest incidence of youth engaged in informal jobs: 18% of working youth hold an informal job, compared to a LAC average of 52%.

According to Gallup World Monitor survey, the share of the youth population that expresses confidence in the transparency of election results (72%) is lower than that of adults in Uruguay, but significantly higher than the average for the region (36%) and OECD member countries (62%). Moreover, youth safety perception in Uruguay (51%) is higher than that of adults and the regional average for youth (47%).

Despite significant advances over the past decade, educational attainment in Uruguay is still below average for the region: in 2014, the percentage of young people (aged 25-29) having completed tertiary education (40%) was lower than the LAC average (55%) as was the percentage completing tertiary education (11.5% vs. the LAC average of 14.6%). High school dropouts and low completion are at the centre of Uruguay's education challenges: 46% of youth (aged 15-29) have not completed secondary education and are out of school. Recent reforms have made technical and vocational education and training (TVET) more connected to the country's skills demand and attractive to students. As a result, 23% of high school students are enrolled in vocational training programmes, more than in the LAC average (14%) and close to the OECD average (26%).

In terms of entrepreneurship, in Uruguay the majority of self-employed youth are own-account workers rather than employers: 12% of working youth report being own-account workers, while only 1% define themselves as entrepreneurs. Additionally, data from the Global Entrepreneurship Monitor (GEM) shows that in Uruguay, the share of young entrepreneurs (18-29 years old) where necessity is the main entrepreneurial motivation (as percentage of total early-stage entrepreneurial activity), estimated in 17% for 2015, is similar to OECD levels (16%) and below the regional average (26%).

Barriers to entrepreneurship are slightly lower in Uruguay than the LAC average. The most important barriers faced by young entrepreneurs seem to be the complexity of regulatory procedures and administrative burdens on start-ups.

Recent developments in Uruguay's educational and training policies

In Uruguay, secondary education is split between basic and higher education. The basic level (*Ciclo Básico Tecnológico*) works with graduates of primary education, covers all orientations and includes basic vocational training. The higher level consists of diversified and technical careers. Regarding public institutions for vocational training, the Uruguayan University of Labour (Universidad del Trabajo del Uruguay: UTU) plays a major role.

The Superior Technological Institute (Instituto Tecnológico Superior: ITS) was founded in 2005 to organise tertiary education activities, integrating teaching, research and extension, and to train technicians in several production and service areas. There is also the Professional Training Council (Consejo de Capacitación Profesional: COCAP), which has the mandate of enforcing skills and training policies mainly for the industrial sector, but also for the agriculture and services areas.

The National Institution for Employment and Vocational Training (Instituto Nacional de Empleo y Formación Profesional: INEFOP) was created in 2008 as a public-private partnership to carry out vocational training policies aimed at improving opportunities for decent work, mainly for vulnerable groups. An example is the *PROJOVEN* [For Youth] programme, which aims to get young people with difficulties a job and offers them training according to the requirements and the opportunities in productive sectors.

In 2012, the National Directorate of Employment of the Labour and Social Security Ministry (Dirección Nacional de Empleo [DINAE] del Ministerio de Trabajo y Seguridad Social [MTSS]) formulated the programme I Study and I Work (*Yo Estudio y Trabajo*) to strengthen the link between education and the world of work. The programme offers work experience to young people between the ages of 16 and 20 who have never had formal work experience in order to develop competencies. The formal work experience lasts between 9 and 12 months for 20 to 30 hours per week (MTSS 2015).

Recent developments in Uruguay's youth entrepreneurship policies

The newly created National Agency for Economic Development (ANDE) will help implement the entrepreneurship policy in Uruguay, taking care of the different institutions and programmes previously managed by the National Agency of Research and Innovation (ANII) through its *Programa de Apoyo a Futuros Empresarios* (PAFE) [Support of Future Enterpreneurs programme].

Among its initiatives, PAFE has the *Red de Apoyo a Futuros Empresarios* (RAFE) [Future Enterpreneurs Support Net], a network to support entrepreneurs through the entire process of creating and consolidating their new venture. This network aims to develop an entrepreneurial culture and to foster new business ideas. To that end, RAFE finances projects, promotes awareness and holds workshops to develop entrepreneurial skills.

Softlandings Uruguay, a RAFE programme financed by ANII, aims to attract high impact entrepreneurs from around the globe. The programme offers office space to develop new ventures, financing and support in all necessary procedures.

In 2014, the Youth Job Law was approved, which includes youth entrepreneurship as an important pillar. In this line, the *Plan de Acción de Juventudes 2015-25* [Youth Action Plan 2015-25] of the National Institute of Youth (INJU) seeks to monitor compliance of this law. The institute has held several workshops to support youth entrepreneurs and develop an entrepreneurial culture.

Reference

MTSS (Ministerio de Trabajo y Seguridad Social) (2015), *Programa "Yo studio y trabajo" Bases y Condiciones Cuarta Edición* (2015), Unidad de Empleo Juvenil, Dirección Nacional de Empleo, http://www.mtss.gub.uy/c/document_library/get_file?uuid=4b721b02-0d48-45f2-98a8-1f69940f72cc&groupId=11515, (accessed 24 August 2016)

Key indicators: Uruguay

Labour market developments[i] (%)	Uruguay 2004	Uruguay 2014	LAC 2004	LAC 2014	OECD 2004	OECD 2014
Unemployment rates - adults (30-64)	8.0	3.7	4.8	3.4	4.6	5.8
Unemployment rates - youth (15-29)	25.5	14.4	12.4	10.3	8.0	12.5
Informality rates - adults (35-64)	21.0	8.9	47.0	38.3		
Informality rates - youth (15-29)	41.5	18.1	62.3	52.3		

	Uruguay				LAC (17)			
Youth and socio-economic status (%)	Extreme poor	Moderate poor	Vulnerable	Middle class	Extreme poor	Moderate poor	Vulnerable	Middle class
Youth (15-29)	2.2	5.6	33.0	59.3	15.1	12.4	39.4	33.1

Activity rates for youth (15-29)[i] (%)	Uruguay 2004	Uruguay 2014	LAC 2004	LAC 2014	OECD 2014
Student	33.1	28.1	23.0	25.3	13.2
Working student	10.6	13.0	11.3	11.2	35.5
Working	35.8	41.7	43.6	43.1	36.2
NEET	20.5	17.2	22.2	20.3	15.1

	Uruguay				LAC (17)			
Activity rates for youth (15-29)[i] by socio-economic status (%)	Extreme poor	Moderate poor	Vulnerable	Middle class	Extreme poor	Moderate poor	Vulnerable	Middle class
Student	23.4	25.6	28.0	28.3	27.0	29.7	30.0	30.7
Working student	2.1	2.3	5.6	17.9	7.8	7.5	8.9	15.0
Working- formal	8.2	12.9	22.3	34.5	4.8	9.6	18.4	28.8
Working- informal	18.8	18.7	17.6	10.1	25.2	22.0	19.1	13.3
NEET	47.5	40.5	26.5	9.3	35.1	31.2	23.7	12.2

Distribution of youth employed[i] (%)	Uruguay	LAC	OECD
Employee	86.0	70.0	88.0
Employer	1.0	2.2	3.9
Own-account worker	11.7	16.3	5.7
Unpaid family worker	1.3	11.2	24.0

	Uruguay		LAC		OECD	
Trust in elections[ii] (%)	Youth (16-29)	Adults (30-64)	Youth (16-29)	Adults (30-64)	Youth (15-29)	Adults (30-64)
Share of population that expresses confidence in the transparency of election results	71.9	82.4	36.3	39.3	62.1	63.2
Feeling of safety[ii] (%)						
Share of population that feels safe in their city or area	51.1	50.3	47.0	46.0	70.9	71.3

	Uruguay		LAC		OECD
Skills[iii] (%)	Youth (25-29)	Adults (30-64)	Youth (25-29)	Adults (30-64)	Adults (25-64)
Population with complete secondary education	39.9	32.3	55.4	38.6	76.0
Population with complete tertiary education[a]	11.5	13.4	14.6	13.4	34.0

	Uruguay (2013)	LAC (18)	OECD (33)
Students in secondary education enrolled in vocational programme[b]	23.4	14.5	26.1

Entrepreneurship[iv] (%)	Uruguay	LAC	OECD
Necessity as entrepreneurial motivation (share of 18-29 in total early-stage entrepreneurial activity)	17.2	26.2	16.0

Barriers to entrepreneurship index[v]	Uruguay	LAC	OECD
Complexity of regulatory procedures	1.2	1.2	0.6
Administrative burdens on start-ups	0.6	0.9	0.6
Regulatory protection of incumbents	0.6	0.6	0.4
Total	2.3	2.7	1.7

Table notes: i) Latin America weighted average of LAC-17 countries: Argentina, Bolivia, Brazil, Chile, Colombia, Costa Rica, Dominican Republic, Ecuador, El Salvador, Guatemala, Honduras, Mexico, Nicaragua, Panama, Peru, Paraguay, Uruguay. OECD weighted average for 34 OECD member countries; ii) Latin America unweighted average of LAC-16 countries Argentina, Brazil, Chile, Colombia, Costa Rica, Dominican Republic, Ecuador, El Salvador, Guatemala, Honduras, Mexico, Nicaragua, Panama, Paraguay, Peru, Uruguay, OECD simple average of OECD 35 member countries; iii) Latin America unweighted average of LAC-17 countries: Argentina, Bolivia, Brazil, Chile, Colombia, Costa Rica, Dominican Republic, Ecuador, El Salvador, Guatemala, Honduras, Mexico, Nicaragua, Panama, Peru, Paraguay, Uruguay. OECD unweighted average for 34 OECD member countries; iv) Share of population that see start-up as a necessity (no other options for work) rather than an opportunity. Latin America (10) non-weighted average of Argentina, Brazil, Chile, Colombia, Ecuador, Guatemala, Panama, Mexico, Peru, and Uruguay. OECD (27) non-weighted average of Australia, Belgium, Chile, Estonia, Finland, Germany, Greece, Hungary, Ireland, Israel, Italy, Latvia, Luxembourg, Mexico, Netherlands, Norway, Poland, Portugal, Slovakia, Slovenia, South Korea, Spain, Sweden, Switzerland, United Kingdom and United States; v) The Entrepreneurship Barriers Index is composed of three sub-indices: 1) Complexity of regulatory procedures: measures the licences and permits system, so as the communication and simplification of rules and procedures. 2) Administrative burdens on start-ups: measures the burdens that are face by corporations and sole proprietor firms, and the barriers in services sectors. 3) Regulatory protection of incumbents: measures legal barriers to entry, anti-trust exemptions and barriers in network sectors. The three indicators are based on the 2013 Product Market Regulation questionnaire available at: http://www.oecd.org/eco/reform/PMR-Questionnaire-2013.pdf. The indicator reflects the state of legislation in 2014 for Kenya, Philippines, Rwanda and Uruguay; in 2015 for Bolivia, Ecuador, Guatemala, Panama, Paraguay and Venezuela; in 2013 for all others. Scale 0 to 6 from least to most restrictive. See methodological note for further details.
Table sources: i) SEDLAC (CEDLAS and the World Bank) for Latin American countries and OECD-LFS data for the OECD (2014); ii) OECD calculations based on Gallup Organization (2014), *Gallup World Monitor* (database); iii) (a) SEDLAC (CEDLAS and the World Bank) for Latin American countries (2014) and; OECD (2014), *Education at a Glance 2014: OECD Indicators*; (b) UNESCO (2016) and DiNIECE. Ministerio de Educación (2013) for Latin American countries and OECD (2014), *Education at a Glance 2014: OECD Indicators* for the OECD; iv) Global Entrepreneurship Monitor individual data (2015); v) OECD-WBG product market regulation database for all countries except Brazil, Chile, India, Mexico and South Africa, OECD product market regulation database (2014).

Methodological note

Definitions of indicators and variables used

NEETs: are youth (people aged 15-29) not in employment nor in education nor training (i.e. unemployed or inactive).

Classification of socio-economic classes: the encoding used in this report is based on the World Bank classification which defines "Extreme poor" as youth from households with a daily per capita income lower than USD2.5; "Moderate poor" as youth from households with a daily per capita income of USD2.5-USD4; "Vulnerable as youth from to households with a daily per capita income of USD4-USD10; and "Middle class" as youth form households with a daily per capita income higher than USD10, but lower than USD50. Poverty lines and incomes are expressed in 2005 USD PPP per day. PPP = purchasing power parity.

Classification of levels of education: the encoding used in this report is based on the International Standard Classification of Education (ISCED) of UNESCO. ISCED, updated in 2011, is an instrument for compiling statistics on education that distinguishes six levels of education, from pre-primary to tertiary education. The classification for secondary and tertiary education follows the criteria in the table below.

Level	Nomenclature
Secondary education	
Upper-secondary education	ISCED 3
Greater specialisation than lower secondary, with more highly qualified teachers. Students have 9 years of prior learning up to and including the lower-secondary level.	
Tertiary education	
Type-A tertiary education	ISCED 5A
Extensive theoretical basis to provide skills for entry into advance research programmes and professions with high skill requirements. Duration: 3 or 4 years	

Entrepreneurship barriers index: the composed by three sub-indices: i) complexity of Regulatory Procedures that measures the licenses and permits system, so as the communication and simplification of rules and procedures; ii) administrative burdens on start-ups that measures the burdens that are face by corporations and sole proprietor firms, and the barriers in services sectors; and iii) regulatory protection of incumbent that measures legal barriers to entry, anti-trust exemptions and barriers in network sectors The three indicators are based on the 2013 Product Market Regulation questionnaire available at: http://www.oecd.org/eco/reform/PMR-Questionnaire-2013.pdf. The indicator reflects the state of legislation in 2014 for Uruguay; in 2015 for Bolivia, Ecuador, Guatemala, Panama, Paraguay and Venezuela; in 2013 for all others. Scale 0 to 6 from least to most restrictive.

OECD PUBLISHING, 2, rue André-Pascal, 75775 PARIS CEDEX 16
(41 2016 14 1 P) ISBN 978-92-64-26254-6 – 2016

www.ingramcontent.com/pod-product-compliance
Ingram Content Group UK Ltd.
Pitfield, Milton Keynes, MK11 3LW, UK
UKHW051458290926
15471UKWH00008B/1267

9 789264 26254